A SHORT HISTORY OF THE
UNITED STATES

THE MACMILLAN COMPANY
NEW YORK · BOSTON · CHICAGO · DALLAS
ATLANTA · SAN FRANCISCO

MACMILLAN & CO., Limited
LONDON · BOMBAY · CALCUTTA
MELBOURNE

THE MACMILLAN COMPANY
OF CANADA, Limited
TORONTO

A SHORT HISTORY OF
THE UNITED STATES

1492—1929

BY

JOHN SPENCER BASSETT, Ph.D.

PROFESSOR OF AMERICAN HISTORY IN
SMITH COLLEGE

REVISED EDITION
VOLUME II — 1789–1865

New York
THE MACMILLAN COMPANY
1929

COPYRIGHT, 1913, 1921, AND 1929,

BY THE MACMILLAN COMPANY.

Set up and electrotyped. Published September, 1913. Reprinted
October, 1913; February, 1914; January, 1915; August, October,
November, 1916; July, December, 1917; October, December, 1918;
September, November, 1919; June, 1920.
With new chapters, February, April, October, November, 1921;
June, December, 1922; September, 1923; January, November, 1924;
August, December, 1925; October, 1926; December, 1927.
Revised Edition, September, 1929.
Reissue in three volumes, September, 1929.

PRINTED IN THE UNITED STATES OF AMERICA
BY BERWICK & SMITH CO.

PREFACE TO THE FIRST EDITION

In this book I have sought to tell clearly and impartially the story of human achievement in what is now the United States, from the earliest traces of man's existence to the present time. Out of the multitude of facts which may be considered within the domain of American history, those have been recounted which seem best suited to explain the progress of the people as a nation. The influence of physical environment has been discussed in the opening chapter, which also deals with the primitive inhabitants. An attempt has been made to give the colonial period its proper unity and show in what manner the colonies were a part of the general British scheme of imperial government. At the same time one must remember that it is American and not British history which concerns us, and for that reason the narrative must not neglect the individual colonies. From the end of the colonial period the dominant interest is the progress of events which have to do with the common cause of independence, and after that with national development.

Much thought has been given to the proper distribution of emphasis between the various historical factors. Political institutions are the most conscious expression of the national will. They determine the form of the story which the historian has to tell. But social and economic conditions and the actions of leading men give color and contour to the figure and decide whether it be attractive or unattractive, vivid or unimpressive. This volume contains at intervals summaries of the habits and social progress of the people, while throughout it seeks to present the decisions of congress and administrations in the matters which relate to the most important phases of popular welfare. It is believed that, if well done, it thus becomes in the most vital sense a social history. My aim has been to lay the necessary foundation for those who wish to pursue further the subject of American history in whatever phase they may be interested.

In a work like this it is impossible to discuss new historical evidence. I have had to content myself with what has already been done by patient and faithful investigators. I have drawn from the results of their labors freely and gratefully. It has also been necessary to omit many things which I should have desired to include had greater space been allowed by the plan to which the book must conform. It seemed best to deal only with the main currents of history, and to follow these with considerable fullness rather than encumber the narrative with many details. If some of my readers are disappointed

v

through the omission of something they expected to find, I hope they will be consoled by finding that what has been attempted has gained in amplitude of treatment.

The bibliographies at the ends of chapters are intended as an aid to those who wish to read further than this book can carry them. They are classified with respect to subjects, and while they are not critical, no book has been mentioned which does not contain useful information, although some of them must be perused with discrimination. It is suggested that the investigator suppplement the information herein offered by consulting Larned, *The Literature of American History* (1902), Hart, editor, *The American Nation*, 27 vols. (1904–1908), as well as special bibliographies. The books mentioned under the caption, *For Independent Reading*, are popular rather than scientific, but they generally contain reliable information. It is hoped that they may be of value to students who wish to read American history during vacations and to others who read through their own initiative.

Finally, the author's thanks are due to Professor Marshall S. Brown of New York University, who kindly read and criticised the completed manuscript, but who is in no way responsible for the errors herein contained.

J. S. B.

16 Rue Chalgrin, Paris,
1913.

PREFACE TO THE ENLARGED EDITION

The progress of time makes it necessary to add to this book an account of the events that have occurred since the work was published in 1913. At that time a new administration was coming into office: at the present it is going out. To treat in proper perspective a period so close at hand and to interpret rightly its many disputed points may well tax the resources of the wisest historian. I hope for the same consideration from the public in this respect that has been so generously extended to the book in other respects. I have given my serious attention to determining what to omit as comparatively unimportant, and how to combine and emphasize the facts that are presented. If I have made mistakes in doing so, I have at least avoided some I might have made by following another course.

J. S. B.

March 3, 1921.

PREFACE TO THE SECOND REVISED EDITION

Dr. Bassett issued an enlarged edition of this work in 1921, bringing the narrative down to the end of the second administration of Woodrow Wilson. It has now become necessary to add still further pages dealing with the Harding and Coolidge Administrations; and all the material following page 902 has been supplied by Mr. Allan Nevins, who has also added to the bibliographical references earlier in the volume. The new edition is also indebted to Dr. Leo F. Stock for helpful advice given during its preparation.

Of the additional pages it is necessary only to quote what Dr. Bassett himself wrote in 1921: "To treat in proper perspective a period so close at hand and to interpret rightly its many disputed points may well tax the resources of the wisest historian. I hope for the same consideration from the public in this respect that has been so generously extended to the book in other respects."

R. H. B.

May 25, 1929.

CONTENTS

PAGE

CHAPTER I. THE CONTINENT AND ITS EARLY INHABITANTS:

Physical Factors in American History 1
Natural Resources 4
Early Inhabitants 11
The Indians 13
Indian Culture 15

CHAPTER II. THE DISCOVERY AND EXPLORATION OF AMERICA:

Events and Ideas leading to the Discovery 23
The Achievement of Columbus 27
Exploring the Coasts of the New World 31
Exploring the Interior 37

CHAPTER III. THE FIRST ENGLISH SETTLEMENTS IN THE SOUTH:

The Gentlemen Adventurers 41
The Beginning of Virginia 45
Better Times in the Colony 50
The Settlement of Maryland 52

CHAPTER IV. THE SETTLEMENT OF NEW ENGLAND:

The Plymouth Colony 59
The Massachusetts Bay Colony 63
The Settlement of Other New England Colonies 68
New York under the Dutch 72
Early Relations of the Colonies with England 76

CHAPTER V. COLONIAL PROGRESS UNDER THE LATER STUARTS, 1660–1689:

Charles II and the Colonies 80
The Stuart Reaction 88
The Colonies under the Later Stuarts, 1660–1689 92

CHAPTER VI. COLONIAL DEVELOPMENT, 1690–1763:

Development of the Colonial Conflict 99
Typical Colonial Controversies 101
Georgia Founded 109
Growth of New France 111
The French and Indian Wars 115
The Last Conflict between the French and English in North America . 121

PAGE

CHAPTER VII. SOCIAL PROGRESS IN COLONIES:

The Conditions of Settlement 134
Laboring Classes 137
Colonial Industry 140
Trade 142
Race Elements in Colony Planting 145
Religion in the Colonies 148
Education and Culture in the Colonies 153
Local Government in the Colonies 155
Paper Money in the Colonies 157

CHAPTER VIII. THE CAUSES OF THE REVOLUTION:

The Principles at Stake 161
Grenville's Policy 162
Growing Irritation 169
Continental Organization and Attempts at Adjustment 176

CHAPTER IX. THE AMERICAN REVOLUTION:

The Declaration of Independence 186
The Campaign around New York, 1776 188
The Campaigns of 1777, Philadelphia and Saratoga . . . 192
The Alliance with France 198
Minor Events in the North, 1778–1782 200
The War in the West 203
The Navy in the Revolution 204
The Campaign in the South, 1778–1781 206
The Treaty of Peace 214
Civil Progress during the Revolution 217

CHAPTER X. THE FIRST YEARS OF PEACE, 1783–1787

Financial Embarrassments 222
Industry and Trade after the War 225
Forming a New Society 228
The Western Lands 231
Popular Dissatisfaction 235

CHAPTER XI. MAKING THE CONSTITUTION:

The Articles of Confederation 238
Moving toward a Stronger Union 240
The Adoption of the Constitution 247
Nationality and State Integrity in the Constitution . . . 250

CONTENTS

PAGE

CHAPTER XII. WASHINGTON'S PRESIDENCY — A PERIOD OF ORGANIZATION:

The Work of Organization 256
Financial Reorganization 259
Adjusting Foreign Relations 261
The United States and the European War 266
The Whisky Insurrection 267
Political Development under Washington 269

CHAPTER XIII. ADAMS AND THE DOWNFALL OF THE FEDERALISTS:

The Political Character of the Administration 276
The Quarrel with France 278
Overconfidence of the Federalists 283
Overthrow of the Federalists 287

CHAPTER XIV. INTERNAL HISTORY AND FOREIGN AFFAIRS UNDER JEFFERSON AND MADISON:

Republican Reforms 291
The War with Tripoli 295
The Purchase of Louisiana 296
Dissension in the Republican Party 300
The Schemes of Aaron Burr 303
Relations between England and the United States 306
Jefferson's Reply to Europe 309

CHAPTER XV. THE WAR OF 1812:

Origin of the War 313
The Struggle for Canada 321
Operations at Sea 326
The British Campaign on Chesapeake Bay 329
The War on the Gulf Coast 331
New England Discontent 335

CHAPTER XVI. SOCIAL DEVELOPMENT:

Growth of the West and Southwest 341
Industrial Development 345
Slavery made Sectional 350
Religious Development after the Revolution 352
Exploration in the Far West 355
Early Constitutional Interpretation 357

CHAPTER XVII. THE LAST OF THE VIRGINIA PRESIDENTS:

Reforms of 1816–1817 363
Party Cleavage under Monroe 367

CONTENTS

	PAGE
The Acquisition of Florida	368
The Missouri Compromise	371
The Monroe Doctrine	375
The Election of 1824	377
The Presidential Election of 1825	379

CHAPTER XVIII. THE ADMINISTRATION OF JOHN QUINCY ADAMS:

Party Formation under John Quincy Adams	382
The Tariff and the Development of Sectionalism	384
The Election of 1828	388

CHAPTER XIX. PROBLEMS OF JACKSON'S FIRST ADMINISTRATION:

The New President in Charge	392
Internal Improvements Checked	394
Division in the Jacksonian Party	396
The Election of 1832	403

CHAPTER XX. JACKSON'S PRESIDENCY COMPLETED:

The End of Nullification	407
Jackson's "War" against the Bank	411
Foreign Affairs	415
The End of Jackson's Presidency	422

CHAPTER XXI. EARLY PERIOD OF THE SLAVERY CONTROVERSY, 1831–1850:

The Antislavery Agitation	428
Van Buren's Presidency	432
The Administration of Tyler	435
The Maine Boundary and the Webster-Ashburton Treaty	437
The Annexation of Texas and the Occupation of Oregon	438
The Election of 1844	441
Polk's Administration	445
The Slavery Question in a New Form	450
The Compromise of 1850	454

CHAPTER XXII. SOCIAL AND INDUSTRIAL DEVELOPMENT, 1815–1861:

Growth of Population and the Results	461
The Influence of Great Inventions	463
The Indians	465
Social Development in the South	468
The Development of Democracy in State and Nation	472
The Progress of Education	476
Gold in California	480
The Panic of 1857	482

CONTENTS

PAGE

CHAPTER XXIII. EVENTS LEADING TO THE CIVIL WAR, 1850–1860:

Overthrowing the Compromise of 1850 485
The Struggle for Kansas 489
A New Party and the Election of 1856 493
The Dred Scott Decision 497
The Lincoln-Douglas Debates 499
The John Brown Raid 502
The Election of 1860 504

CHAPTER XXIV. THE OUTBREAK OF THE CIVIL WAR:

War or Peace? 511
Lincoln and Secession 514
Preparations for War 516
The Bull Run Campaign 518
Relations with Great Britain 521

CHAPTER XXV. THE WESTERN CAMPAIGNS:

A Bifurcated Invasion 526
Three Preliminary Operations, 1861 526
Grant's Campaign on the Tennessee, 1862 527
Confederate Counter-Movement in Tennessee and Kentucky . . 529
Vicksburg Captured 530
The Campaign for Chattanooga 532
The Campaign against Atlanta 535
Sherman's March through Georgia and the Carolinas . . . 539
The War beyond the Mississippi 541

CHAPTER XXVI. THE WAR IN THE EAST, 1862–1865:

McClellan's Peninsular Campaign 545
Pope and Second Bull Run 550
The Campaign of Antietam 553
The Battle of Fredericksburg. 555
The Battle of Chancellorsville 557
The Gettysburg Campaign 558
From the Wilderness to Petersburg 563
The End of the War 564
Federal Naval Operations 569

CHAPTER XXVII. CIVIL AFFAIRS DURING THE WAR:

Enlisting Troops, North and South 572
Federal Finances 574
The Progress of Emancipation 577
Political Parties during the Civil War 581
The War Powers of the President 585
The Southern Problem and Southern Efforts 586

PAGE

CHAPTER XXVIII. RECONSTRUCTION — THE NATIONAL SIDE:

Two Possible Methods of Reconstruction 594
Lincoln's Plan of Reconstruction 596
Johnson's Plan of Reconstruction 599
Affairs in the South 601
Johnson's Hopes 604
The Fourteenth Amendment 607
The Reconstruction Acts of 1867 609
An Appeal to the Supreme Court 611
The Impeachment of President Johnson 613

CHAPTER XXIX. RECONSTRUCTION — THE SOUTHERN SIDE:

Social Conditions in the South 619
Congressional Reconstruction in Operation 622
The Ku Klux Klan 627
Triumph of the Southern Democrats 630
National Reconstruction under Grant 633
Interpreting the War Amendments 635

CHAPTER XXX. PARTY HISTORY, 1865–1877:

Political Conditions after the War 640
The Election of 1868 641
Foreign Affairs under Johnson 643
Grant's Political Mistakes 644
The Presidential Campaign of 1872 648
Political Decay under Grant 649
The Election of 1876 652

CHAPTER XXXI. ECONOMIC AND DIPLOMATIC HISTORY, 1856–1877:

Financial Reorganization 660
The Legal Tender Decisions 663
Industrial Progress 664
Resumption of Specie Payment 668
Diplomatic Affairs under Grant 669

CHAPTER XXXII. THE DEVELOPMENT OF THE FAR WEST:

The Rocky Mountain Region 676
The Transcontinental Railroads 680
Indian Wars 683
The Sioux War of 1876 687
A New Indian Policy 690

CHAPTER XXXIII. POLITICAL AND FINANCIAL READJUSTMENT, 1877–1881:

Hayes and his Party 693
Course of the Democrats 695

CONTENTS

PAGE

The Bland-Allison Silver Coinage Law 697
Resumption of Specie Payment 699
The Election of 1880 701
Garfield's Short Presidency 703

CHAPTER XXXIV. POLITICAL AND ECONOMIC REFORM, 1881–1897:

Civil Service Reform 707
Ballot Reform . . . . , . . . 711
Tariff Reform 712
The Election of 1884 716
Cleveland and his Party 719
Tariff Reform under Cleveland 721
The Republican Party in a New Stage 723
The McKinley Tariff and the Surplus 724
The Tariff Legislation of 1892–1897 727

CHAPTER XXXV. GREAT INDUSTRIAL COMBINATIONS:

Combinations as Historical Factors 731
Railroad Combinations 732
Trusts 736
Bank Consolidation 740
Combinations of Laborers 741

CHAPTER XXXVI. LAST PHASES OF THE SILVER MOVEMENT:

The Bland Law in Operation 746
The Last Years of Harrison 748
Cleveland and the Panic of 1893 753
Selling Bonds to protect the Surplus 755
The Bryan Campaign for Free Silver, 1896 758

CHAPTER XXXVII. A NEW PHASE OF AMERICAN DIPLOMACY:

Importance of the Pacific 764
The Samoan Incident, 1887–1889 765
The Fur Seal Controversy 767
The Mafia Incident 767
Relations with Chile 768
Hawaiian Annexation 771
Chinese Immigration 774
America and Japan 775
The Venezuela Boundary Dispute 777

PAGE

CHAPTER XXXVIII. THE WAR WITH SPAIN:

Spain and Cuba 782
American Intervention 786
The Work of the Navy 790
Land Operations against Santiago 795
The Destruction of the Spanish Squadron 799
Reflections on the War in Cuba 802
Peace Negotiations 805
Subsequent Relations with Cuba 806

CHAPTER XXXIX. EXPANSION AND ITS PROBLEMS:

The Philippines as an American Colony 809
An American Colonial Policy 813
An Isthmian Canal 814
The Canal at Panama 817
Canal Construction 821
American Diplomacy in the Orient 822
The Alaskan Boundary 825
The New Monroe Doctrine 826

CHAPTER XL. THE ADMINISTRATIONS OF ROOSEVELT AND TAFT:

Roosevelt's Corporation Policy 829
Roosevelt's Second Term 832
Taft's Administration 837
The Presidential Election of 1912 843
Legislative Progress under Taft 849

CHAPTER XLI. POLITICAL MEASURES OF THE WILSON ADMINISTRATION:

A New Administration 853
The Underwood Tariff 856
The Federal Reserve Banking Act 858
Laws Relating to Great Corporations 860
Our Caribbean Policy 863
Dealing with Mexico 867

CHAPTER XLII. THE UNITED STATES AND THE WORLD WAR:

Trying to Preserve Neutrality, 1914–1917 873
The Awakening of the People of the United States . . . 878
At War with Germany — A Year of Preparation 882
The American Expeditionary Forces in France 886
American Troops to the Rescue 888
Operation in the American Sector 891
The United States Navy and the War 896
The Treaty of Versailles 897

CONTENTS

PAGE

The Campaign of 1920 904

CHAPTER XLIII. THE HARDING AND COOLIDGE ADMINISTRATIONS:

Problems of General Demobilization 908
Railway and Shipping Legislation . . ˉ 910
The Return to a High Tariff 912
Farm Depression and Labor Troubles 914
A New Immigration Policy 917
The Washington Disarmament Conference 919
Death of Harding : The Oil Scandals 922
The Election of 1924 925
Financial Relations with Europe 927
Mexican and Central American Affairs 928
The Kellogg Multilateral Pact 930
The Farm Relief Issue 931
National Perplexity with Prohibition 934
The Campaign of 1928 936

INDEX 941

FULL–PAGE MAPS

FACING PAGE

Physical Features of the United States 9
Early Explorations 30
The North during the Revolutionary War 184
The Northwest during the Revolution 202
The Revolutionary War in the South 208
The United States at the Close of the Revolution 216
California and Mexico, 1846 448
The United States during the Civil War 528
Operations in the East 550
The Battlefield of Gettysburg 558
The Transportation Problem of the South 574
The Far West 678
Territorial Development (*double page*) 792
The Panama Canal 820
The Battle Area of France during Four Years of War 886
The Capture of the St. Mihiel Angle 892
The Meuse-Argonne Region 894

MAPS IN THE TEXT

PAGE

Bunker Hill and Boston 181
Campaign around New York 189
Valley Forge, Philadelphia, and Brandywine 193
The Saratoga Campaign 196
The Siege of Yorktown 213
The Canadian Border 322
Washington and Vicinity 329
The Erie Canal 366
The Gulf Region 369
The Vicksburg Campaign 532
Operations around Atlanta 537
The Santiago Campaign 797

A SHORT HISTORY

OF

THE UNITED STATES

CHAPTER XII

WASHINGTON'S PRESIDENCY — A PERIOD OF ORGANIZATION

THE WORK OF ORGANIZATION

JULY 2, 1788, the president of the old congress, in session in New York, rose and announced that nine states having ratified the con-
End of the Old Con-gress. stitution, it was in order to take steps to establish the new government. His hearers agreed with him, and it was resolved that the states should choose presidential elec-
tors on the first Wednesday in January, 1789, who, a month later, should select a president and vice-president; and that a congress elected under the constitution should meet the first Wednesday in March following. After some debate, New York was selected for the place of meeting. This was the last important legislation of the congress which for fourteen years had guided the fortunes of all the states through the dangers of war and the hardly less difficult trials of peace. Would success crown the new system, over whose adoption
An " Ex-periment." there had been so vast an amount of dispute? Some wise ones had serious doubts, and the most hopeful admitted that it was an "experiment," but urged that it be given a fair trial.

For president the unanimous choice was Washington. He was a good general, though not a brilliant one. He was not a good speaker
Washington the First President. and was not versed in the principles of government. But he was honest, fair-minded, dignified, and faithful to the liberty of America. He had the power of commanding obedience, and everybody, federalist and antifederalist, trusted him. With Washington at the helm, faction would be checked and the authority of the union respected. His personal character was worth a great deal to the "experiment." It gave it the confidence of Americans and foreigners. John Adams was elected vice-president.

At the time designated very few members of congress were in New York. The weak-hearted thought this was because nobody cared
Congress Meets. for the new plan, but others showed that it was because the roads were bad. April 6, the senate had a quorum, the electoral votes were counted, and a messenger went to summon the president-elect to the seat of government. April 30, he was in the city and took the oath of office. On his journey to New York he received every mark of affection from the people.

The problems before president and congress were numerous. All that the old confederation could not do had now to be taken up. In the first place, the government was to be organized. The officers of state, great and small, must be appointed; federal courts, high and low, must be created; a revenue law must be devised; the revolutionary debt must be placed on a sound basis; commerce must be regulated; those parts of the treaty of 1783 which were not executed must be carried into effect; our relations with foreign states must be defined in proper treaties; a site for the federal capital must be selected; and many other minor affairs must have attention. They were tasks which demanded the wisdom of the best men in the country, and they engaged the attention of Washington and congress through most of his two administrations. Men approached them with the greater caution, because they felt that all that was done would be taken for precedents in the conduct of the affairs of the future.

Problems of the Day.

The first thing was to raise a revenue. Madison, a member of the house of representatives — generally called "the house" — introduced the subject by moving an import duty of 5 per cent on all articles brought into the country. A Pennsylvania delegate objected. He wished a small tax for revenue, but asked that it be laid so as to protect articles produced in America. The Middle states were then the chief center of American manufactures. After much discussion, the protective principle was adopted, but it was for a long time made incidental to the purpose of getting a revenue.

The Revenue.

Then congress took up the task of creating great administrative departments. In July it created a department of state, in August, a department of war, and in September, a department of the treasury. Over each was to be a head of department, who should ever be nominated by the chief executive and confirmed by the senate. Over the first the president appointed Thomas Jefferson, of Virginia, who had just come back from Paris, where he had been our minister since 1785. Over the third he placed Alexander Hamilton, of New York, then, as later, known for one of the best-informed Americans in questions of finance, a man of fine mind, versed in principles of government, and a leading politician. Over the second he placed Henry Knox, of Massachusetts, a man of no great ability, but popular because he was a revolutionary general and had influence in New England. Congress also created the office of attorney-general, to which Edmund Randolph, of Virginia, was appointed. He was merely law adviser to the administration, had a small salary, and was expected to have outside practice if he wished it. The first three heads of department were brought together to advise the president about problems of administration, and this was the beginning of the cabinet. It was not until 1870 that

The Administrative Departments.

S

the department of justice was formally organized with the attorney-general at the head, but he attended cabinet meetings from the first. Although the laws creating the departments said nothing about the right of removing the heads, it was generally held that it lay with the president, and on this theory later practice has proceeded. It would be unwise to force the president to keep in his cabinet a man who is uncongenial, or who does not have his confidence.

Next came the judiciary. No one objected to a supreme court, but some thought that the state courts should be given jurisdiction over federal cases in the lower stages, with appeal to the higher

Federal Courts Established. court. This did not please the majority of congress, who wished that the government should have a complete court system of its own. It was accordingly decided to create, besides the supreme court, with one chief justice and five associate justices, four circuit and thirteen district courts, whose judges should be appointed by the president and confirmed by the senate. The number of these lower courts has been increased with the growth of the union.

Another duty was to deal with the amendments sent up by the ratifying states. Henry and other prominent antifederalists had

The Amendments. pronounced the plan of ratifying with suggestions of amendments a subterfuge; and for a time it seemed that they were right. Weeks passed and congress took no notice of amendments. Then the complaints at home became so loud that congress dared not delay longer. The suggested amendments were referred to a committee. All that looked toward a modification of the plan of union were ignored, and the twelve which congress sent to the states for adoption were in the nature of a bill of rights. Ten of these were accepted. The antifederalists declared that this confirmed their previous suspicions, and criticized congress roundly. But the subject did not interest the people, and the antifederalist party soon disintegrated; for other measures were coming up to divide the voters into two great parties.

The constitution designed that congress should be entirely independent of the executive. The president could communicate information, but neither he nor his cabinet could speak on the

The Initiative in Congress. floor or vote in its proceedings. Each house was very jealous of interference from that quarter, and he, therefore, has no initiative in legislation. This important function was referred to committees. To them were sent important bills introduced by members. The most powerful standing committee in the house was the committee of ways

Congressional Committees. and means, created in 1795, whose functions were connected with raising and expending revenue. At first the committees were special, but in time standing committees came into general use. In the first congress the committees of each house were elected by the members, but from 1790 to 1911 the speaker of the house, who has been a party man since 1791, appointed the committees in that branch. The senate committees are still elected by the members of the senate.

FINANCIAL REORGANIZATION

The first session of congress lasted until September 29, 1789. One of its last acts was to ask Hamilton, secretary of the treasury, to prepare a report on the state of the finances. He took up the task with accustomed energy, and the result was four reports covering every phase of the matter intrusted to him. The first was submitted January 14, 1790, and dealt with the public debt; the second, submitted December 13, 1790, recommended an excise; the third, December 13, 1790, recommended a national bank; and the fourth, December 5, 1791, argued for the protection of manufactures. The fourth report was not considered when introduced, but the others were enacted into law.

Hamilton's Four Financial Reports.

The debt was then, including arrears of interest, divided as follows: due to foreigners, $11,710,378; to domestic creditors, $42,414,085; and a floating debt of $2,000,000. Hamilton proposed to refund all this at par. Now, the domestic debt had been selling as low as 25 per cent of par, and the first suggestion of paying at par had led the speculators to buy the old certificates wherever found. Should the government enable them to make the handsome profits anticipated now became an urgent question in congress. Hamilton claimed that such a course was necessary to place the public credit on a sound basis; others, mostly men from rural constituencies, urged that the idea was preposterous. They thought he wished to found a party whose center was men of wealth, through whose influence persons dependent on them for financial prosperity should be dominated. It was the first appearance in the new government of party division. Madison supported the latter view and proposed that the debt be paid at par, but that the speculators be given only the ruling price and that the rest up to par be paid to the original holders of the debt. This plan found favor with some members, but the majority thought it impossible to determine who were the original holders, and it was decided to pay the debt as proposed by Hamilton.

Refunding the Continental Debt.

The secretary of the treasury wished also to assume the debt incurred by the states in aid of the revolution. This proposition aroused still greater opposition. Some states had paid much of their revolutionary debt and objected to assuming a part of that of others, as they must do as a part of the union, if the measure carried. But those states which had

Assumption of State Debts.

not settled their debts were in favor of the plan. As leader of the former, now appeared Madison. In 1787 he had been prominent in the party of nationality, but he now argued that the constitution gave congress no power to assume state debts. After weeks of discussion the opponents of assumption had a small majority. But before the vote was finally cast, a compromise was effected, chiefly through the efforts of Hamilton and Jefferson. The Southerners favored locating the capital on the Potomac, but lacked a few votes for that purpose. It was agreed that enough Southern votes should be got for assumption to carry it, if enough Northern votes were secured to get a Southern location of the capital; and on this basis both measures were carried in the spring of 1790. Hamilton and the nationalists were pleased, because they thought assumption would strengthen the national government and invigorate the national credit by removing from the sphere of doubt a large mass of securities which the states, in the existing distress, could not hope to pay for many years. As it turned out, assumption increased the obligations of the United States by $18,271,786.

A Southern Capital.

Refunding, as time showed, was a slow process. In 1795 over a million dollars of the old debt was still unfunded. Including this amount, the total was $77,500,000, of which the foreign debt, $11,710,000, paid interest at 4 per cent, 4½ per cent, and 5 per cent. Of the domestic debt of $65,800,000, about half, 45.4 per cent, paid interest at 6 per cent, while 30.3 per cent paid at 3 per cent, and 24.3 per cent was at 6 per cent with interest payments deferred until 1801.

The Total Debt.

To pay the debt, Hamilton got congress to establish a sinking fund which, it was supposed, would eventually absorb the entire indebtedness. He did not fear a national debt, but said it might even become a national blessing. His adversaries charged that he wished to make it perpetual, like the debt of Great Britain. The majority of the people, like thrifty husbandmen, wished to pay it gradually. But a national debt, by causing the capitalists who held it to look to the government for payment, was a strong bond of union.

Hamilton considered a great national bank, like that of England, a necessity. It would issue large quantities of its notes and thus provide a much-needed and safe currency; it would enable the government to sell its bonds quickly at home and abroad; it would furnish a safe and cheap means of exchange for the people; by establishing branches in the leading cities, it would enable the government to transfer its funds cheaply; and it would furnish a safe place for keeping the public funds. His opponents objected that it would give the bank a monopoly in exchange; that by making its notes receivable for government dues, it would have superior privileges; that it would interfere with the operations of state banks; and that the constitution gave congress

First Bank of the United States.

no power to establish a bank. They stressed the last objection most; and when a bill to create such a bank with a charter for twenty years passed congress, efforts were made to have it vetoed. Washington hesitated, but finally called on his cabinet for advice. Hamilton argued for approval, and Knox supported him. Jefferson took the other side and had the support of Randolph. The president at last decided for Hamilton, on the ground that he would favor the man in whose department, the treasury, the matter lay. The bank began business in 1791 and had a capital stock of $10,000,000, of which the government owned $2,000,000 for which it was to pay in installments. The fact that the government was a large stockholder added to the public confidence in the bank.

The third feature of Hamilton's scheme was an excise, a tax collected on distilled liquors. Congress passed the bill to that effect, and Washington approved it. Hamilton supported it both because it would give a revenue and because, by collecting the tax at the stills, owned chiefly by farmers, the power of the general government would be brought home to the people of every part of the country. Thus, each feature of Hamilton's scheme stood for strong national authority. In opposition to him grew up a party opposed to centralization. The federalists, who supported Hamilton, embraced the large business interests, capitalists, merchants, and manufacturers, together with men who favored a strong government generally. The opposition, led by Jefferson, opposed further concentration and had strong support from the farmers in the South and in the rural parts of the Middle states. Among them were many former antifederalists; but the name was unpopular, because they no longer opposed the constitution. They preferred the name "republican," which gradually came into use.

The Excise Tax.

Hamilton's Nationalism.

Hamilton's financial plans proved very successful. No one could doubt that a country with such immense resources as the United states could pay its obligations, if it wished; and the enactment of the laws he recommended expressed its purpose in the matter. Accordingly, the bonds sold well, the bank he established proved successful, and confidence in the future was high. Bold imagination characterized every scheme he espoused, and in each case he was justified by the result. With the enactment of his suggestions vanished all fears that the nation would be embarrassed by its debts.

Results of Hamilton's Plan.

Adjusting Foreign Relations

Meanwhile, our foreign relations demanded attention. England had not paid for the slaves carried away at the end of the revolution, and she still held five frontier posts extending from Lake Champlain to the north of Lake Superior, all of which was contrary to the treaty.

She justified her failure on the ground that we still impeded the collection of British debts and had not relaxed our regulations against the loyalists. These Western posts were centers of a

The Treaty not Executed. rich Canadian fur trade, to which our own traders wished to get access, and we justly attributed her action to her desire to prolong as much as possible her advantage in that respect. Another complaint was that she would not make a commercial treaty. American traders wished to have her modify her navigation laws so as to allow them to share in the trade with the West Indies. Washington took early notice of the situation, and in 1789 sent Gouverneur Morris to London to see if arrangements could be made. The British ministry was immovable, and Morris, like Adams several years earlier, could think of nothing better than to advise that we draw near to France in commercial affairs, — a threat as impotent now as formerly; for France did not manufacture the merchandise we needed. It was not until the autumn of 1791 that the first British minister to the new government arrived in Philadelphia, the seat of government from 1790 to 1800, but he brought no instructions to make a treaty, and the futile negotiations still went on.

By this time the Indians south of Lake Erie were in a state of ferment. White settlers were appearing north and west of the Ohio, in

St. Clair's Defeat. pursuance of a treaty at Fort Harmar in 1789, which the savages claimed was obtained through fraud. Their fears were stimulated by the Canadian traders, who were alarmed at the prospect of losing a region rich in furs. General St. Clair, governor and military commander in Ohio, asked congress for troops to reduce the Indians to order. Two thousand recruits were sent him, with which he marched from Cincinnati into the forest north of it, where, November 4, 1791, he carelessly allowed himself to be ambushed by the foe. Of the fourteen hundred men on the field, only fifty escaped uninjured, and all the baggage was lost. It was the first battle fought under the new government, and the news of the disaster caused great distress in the East. Washington himself gave St. Clair a severe rebuke and appointed Anthony Wayne, of

Wayne in Command. revolutionary fame, to conduct another expedition against the Indians. October 7, 1793, Wayne marched with 2600 men for the enemy's country. He built Fort Greenville there, and went into winter quarters. In June, 1794, he was joined by 1600 mounted men from Kentucky and began an advance.

The war had now taken on a new phase. From the beginning the

British Complications. Indians received ammunition and guns from the British, and Canadian traders and officials gave them open encouragement. Canada thought England would eventually retain the Western posts, and wished to preserve the Indian tribes intact, both on account of the fur trade and because they would thus have a buffer between their own territory and that of the

United States. In 1793 the hostiles showed a willingness to make peace, but continued the war through the persuasion of the British. In the following February, Dorchester, governor of Canada, made a speech to a number of chiefs, telling them they were wronged by the Americans, and that England and the United States would soon be at war, when the Indians could recover their lands. At the same time British soldiers from Detroit, one of the retained posts, were erecting a fort sixty miles south of that place in territory unquestionably American. All this was known in Philadelphia, and Washington ordered Wayne to carry the intruding fort, if it was in his way. The Indian war, therefore, seemed about to become a war against England.

This eventuality was averted by the rashness of the savages, who chose to risk a battle south of the offending fort. They met Wayne in a body of fallen timber and were repulsed in a sharp encounter. They fell back, but the fort refused to receive **Battle of the** them, and they dispersed into the forest. Wayne sent **Fallen Timber.** out detachments to destroy their fields and villages, but he did not attack the fort. After some time, he received overtures from the hostiles and appointed a council to make a permanent peace in the summer of 1795. The meeting was at Fort Greenville, where a treaty, concluded on August 4, adopted a line from the Ohio to Fort Recovery, thence eastward to the Muskingum, **Treaty of** and thence with that river and the Cuyahoga to Lake **Greenville,** Erie; and the Indians recognized this line as their eastern **1795.** and southern boundary. Thus, most of Ohio was definitely open to white ownership and soon became the scene of active settlement. The war had the good effect of convincing England, and her more confident colonists in Canada, that something must be done to settle the dispute about the Western posts; but it was in another negotiation that the affair was adjusted.

At this time Spain held Louisiana and viewed with alarm the advance of the new republic into the transmontane region. In order to check it she resorted to three intrigues, two with the adventurous settlers themselves and one with the south- **Spain's** western Indians. Holding the mouth of the Mississippi, **Intrigues.** the outlet of the Western trade, she had a powerful argument for the men of Kentucky and Tennessee. In 1785 Spain sent Gardoqui, an able negotiator, to the United States to make a treaty. Three questions came up, the navigation of the Mississippi, recognition of the secret clause of the treaty of peace of 1783, and commercial relations with Spain's American possessions. The men of the seaboard were concerned with the last, those of the West thought most of the first and second. After much discussion, in which the Spaniard asserted that he would never yield on the first and second point, Jay asked permission to make a treaty in which we got concessions only in respect to the third. The Eastern and Middle states seemed complaisant, but those of the South, who had lands on the Mississippi, objected strenuously, and the proposed Jay-Gardoqui treaty of 1786 came to naught.

But the Western settlers were deeply dissatisfied. They took Jay's proposition to mean that the East cared nothing about them. Their **Discontent in the West.** discontent was stimulated by agents whom the Spanish governor at New Orleans sent among them. It was his hope that the Western communities could be induced to revolt and place themselves under Spanish protection. One of his paid agents was James Wilkinson, who distributed Spain's gold among some Kentucky leaders and organized a party who supported the intrigue. The prospect of getting free navigation of the river served, also, as a strong lure to the men of the West. In 1788 the intrigue came to a head in Kentucky, the strongest Western community. But the forces of order were greater than those of revolt, and the Kentuckians rejected Wilkinson's appeals and contented themselves by asking Virginia to consent to the creation of a new state out of her transmontane lands. When the Old Dominion granted this in 1789 much of the discontent subsided, and a still better feeling was engendered when Kentucky was made a state in 1792. In 1790 North **Three New States.** Carolina transferred her Western possessions to the union, but they were not admitted as the state of Tennessee until 1796. In 1791 Vermont had been received as a state, and all this was a pledge that the West should have fair treatment as it grew in population. In this way Spain failed in her scheming to stay the growth of the power of the United States on her borders.

The controversy over the northern boundary of West Florida was not so soon settled. The United States stood firmly for the secret **Florida Boundary.** clause of the treaty, Spain stood against it. She had the advantage of holding Natchez, within the disputed area, and an attempt to oust her by force must lead to war, a thing for which we were not ready. The president and cabinet thought the matter should be deferred without prejudice to our claim; for it could be settled better when our population in that region was strong enough to threaten occupation with decisive effect. But about this time their plan seemed likely to fail by the intrusion of settlements in the disputed region itself. In 1789 Georgia, who claimed **Georgia Land Grants.** that the lands in the disputed region were within her borders, made grants to three great companies, which proposed to plant settlements. One of the companies went so far as to open negotiations with the governor of New Orleans, promising to recognize the authority of Spain if the settlements were not opposed. Such a course must bring us into conflict with Spain, and Washington promptly issued a proclamation warning the people to have nothing to do with it. In consequence, the scheme failed, but the claims of the land companies remained as a source of irritation for many years afterwards.

Spain's third intrigue was destined to come to a fate equally futile, and for this Washington's diplomacy was also responsible. Between Florida and the Tennessee settlements lived the powerful Cherokee, Creek, Chickasaw, and Choctaw tribes, inhabit- **Spain and the Indians.** ing a rich territory and strong enough to muster 10,000 warriors. They were friendly with the Spaniards, who bought their furs and sold them merchandise, and whose trading posts were never followed by farming communities. Alexander McGillivray, a rich and capable half-breed Creek, a tory in the revolution who had suffered at the hands of the whigs and who now hated the Americans, became a Spanish agent to preserve Spain's influence with the Indians. A treaty made in 1784 contained an Indian pledge that no white man should visit the Creeks without a Spanish permit, and efforts were made to get a similar treaty with the three other tribes. About this time Indian attacks began to be made upon the growing settlements in Tennessee, and it was evident that the officials of Florida encouraged the attacks in order to impede settlement in that region.

Thus was created a situation demanding the intervention of the general government. Washington resorted to diplomacy, although the men of the frontier thought that war should have been the instrument. McGillivray was induced to appear at **McGilli-vray's Du-plicity.** New York, where he received $100,000 for the damages sustained during the revolution and was made a United States agent in matters of trade with the rank of brigadier general. In return he promised that the Creeks should be at peace with the United States. The treaty was immediately broken, and his death in 1793 did not improve matters. The Tennesseeans grew restless under their sufferings and wished to retaliate; but the government was carrying on a long-drawn-out negotiation with Spain and ordered that the peace should be observed. For a while **Vengeance** the frontiersmen complied, but at last they were goaded to **of the Ten-nesseeans.** action. In 1793 Sevier, with a band of East Tennesseeans, and in 1794 Robertson, with a party of West Tennesseeans, made raids on the bands of offending Cherokees, burning their villages and killing without mercy. From that time the settlements had peace.

Happily, at this time the negotiations which had gone on haltingly at Madrid since 1791 took a favorable turn. France was at war with Spain, and Genêt, just arrived at Charleston, was or- **Treaty with** ganizing forces to move, regardless of our neutrality, **Spain, 1795.** against Florida and New Orleans. Three expeditions were proposed, one against Florida and two against Louisiana. Spite of Washington's efforts to interfere, preparations went forward rapidly, and only Genêt's recall averted, it seems, serious trouble of this kind. The response of the men of Kentucky, Georgia, and the

Carolinas showed Spain how much unpopularity her policy was developing in our back country, and her tone became more conciliatory. Washington seized the opportunity to quicken the currents of diplomacy, and the result was a treaty arranged by Thomas Pinckney, our minister, with Godoy, a liberal Spaniard, on October 27, 1795. It confirmed the secret clause of the treaty of 1783 relative to the Florida boundary, gave the Americans the right to use the river, and allowed them to deposit in New Orleans products intended for exportation. Kentucky and Tennessee thus got easy access to outside markets, Georgia acquired a better title to the southern half of her Western lands, and the national government closed an annoying dispute with Spain.

THE UNITED STATES AND THE EUROPEAN WAR

In 1793 France beheaded her king, and almost immediately was at war with England and Spain. The year before she had begun a war with Austria and Prussia. The South generally was enthusiastic in her behalf, as well as the farmers and ordinary townsmen of the Middle states. But the trading class everywhere, closely dependent on England, felt otherwise, and they were supported by the rural New Englanders, who, under the influence of the congregational clergy, hated a republic which had enthroned a Goddess of Reason. Washington feared that the ardent French partisans would, by some rash action, bring on war with England, and issued a proclamation of neutrality. Inasmuch as the treaties of 1778 (see page 199) were still in force, the French party took this for British partisanship. The proclamation was roundly denounced in the newspapers of the newly founded republican party and defended in those of the federalists. At this time our politics became divided in accordance with the division in Europe, and from this situation they did not emerge until Napoleon was definitely defeated and France ceased to be at war against the powers around her.

Attitude of Americans.

Neutrality Proclamation.

April 8, 1793, Genêt, first minister from the French republic, arrived at Charleston. The merchants and great planters received him coolly, but the populace were mad with joy. Carried away by his reception, he raised troops for operations against Spain and commissioned privateers against England. Departing for Philadelphia by land, he was received enthusiastically by the farmers of the Carolinas and Virginia and became convinced that the American people were in sympathy with France. Washington received him with reserve, and Genêt grew angry and informed his government that the American people did not approve the neutrality proclamation. He described the president as a weak old man, under British influence. Many of his deeds were as foolish as his words. The republicans gave him encouragement at first, and he

Genêt's Arrival.

formed the intention of getting congress to force Washington to act in behalf of France. Finally, he talked openly about his appeal to the people. The federalists attacked him from the beginning, and they made so much of his ill-advised attitude toward the administration that even the republicans began to forsake him. No calm patriot would tolerate an open attempt by a foreigner to influence the internal policy of the country.

Washington was rarely moved by popular clamor, and he intended to preserve neutrality. The treaties of 1778 provided that the French might bring their prizes into our ports and that enemies of France might not fit out privateers there. Genêt inter- **Interpreting** preted this to mean that French prizes brought in might **the French Treaties.** also be sold, and that France might fit out privateers in American ports. His view was brought before the cabinet, where Hamilton opposed it totally and Jefferson would allow as much of it as would not bring us into war with England. Washington held the balance. He would do all the treaties required; and it was decided that France might fit out privateers in our ports but send them away at once and not use our ports as a base of operation, or send in and sell prizes captured at sea. Genêt complied unwillingly. He had already licensed fourteen privateers which had taken eighty prizes.

A month later, July, 1793, it was known that he was fitting out a prize, *The Little Sarah*, with cannon and was about to send her to sea. When approached, he became angry and talked of appeal- ing to the people; but when he learned that the ship was **Genêt's** about to be seized, he agreed that she would not sail with- **Last Of-** out notice. Ten days later the promise was violated. **fense.** Washington was outraged. "Is the minister of the French republic," he said, "to set the acts of this government at defiance with impunity?" He convened the cabinet, which decided to ask France to recall Genêt. It also determined to exclude French prizes and privateers in the future. The demand caused no dissatisfaction in Paris, where a fresh revolu- tion of party had left the luckless Genêt in danger of his life. In fact, Fauchet, his successor, was instructed to arrest Genêt and send him home for trial. He owed his safety to Washington, who generously refused to allow him to be extradited. He remained in America, mar- ried a daughter of Governor Clinton of New York, and died in that state at an old age.

The Whisky Insurrection

Hamilton's excise law, passed in January, 1791, was very unpopular in the western counties of Pennsylvania and the states southward, a region through which the Scotch-Irish were widely settled. **The Excise** They brought with them the habit of making whisky out **Opposed.** of grain, and by 1791 their stills on every farm furnished so much of the liquor that it superseded the New England rum, which in colonial times was the common tipple throughout the colonies. The tax was not large, but it was resented because it was inquisitorial. The opposition reached actual violence only in Pennsylvania, where four counties had been organized in the valley of the Monongahela, all lying to the south of Pittsburgh. The people there were near enough to the new settlements in the Ohio valley to feel much of that spirit of independence which had caused some men to fear a separation of the West from the East at no distant day.

In 1791 popular meetings began to be held to urge the inhabitants to defy the excise law. The leaders were in a violent mood, and threat-
Violence in Pennsyl-vania. ened to deal with officers collecting the tax. Albert Gallatin, later to have a distinguished career in national politics, lived in the region, attended the meetings, and sought to check the trend to violence. His efforts were futile; for the angry farmers listened more willingly to the harangues of the men of action. They paid no attention to a proclamation of warning which Washington, at Hamilton's suggestion, issued in 1792, and continued to hold meetings, threaten the revenue officers, and cut up the stills of those who obeyed the objectionable law. In 1794 fifty warrants were drawn for persons concerned in these outrages and made returnable to the federal court in Philadelphia.

Trouble arose when they were served. A mob surrounded the house of Neville, an inspector, to make him give up his commission,
The People in Arms. and six men were wounded and one killed by shots fired from his house. The people flew to arms, and Neville fled for his life. The leader of discontent was now Brad-ford, a noisy demagogue, who summoned the counties to send delegates to a general meeting at Parkinson's Ferry in the following August. In the excitement of the time the mail was robbed and the discontented ones assembled in great numbers near Pittsburgh, probably to overawe the small garrison there. But the leaders lost courage and contented themselves with marching through the town as a demonstration of their power.

It was high time for the forces of order to assert themselves, but Governor Mifflin, of Pennsylvania, feared to make himself unpopular
Troops Called Out. with the farmers, and refused to call out the militia. Then Washington decided to interfere. He sent out a proc-lamation against the rioters and called for fifteen thou-sand men from Virginia, Maryland, and Pennsylvania, to march by the first of September. Meanwhile, he sent commissioners to visit the back counties to see if the people could be persuaded to submit to
Insurgents Submissive. the law. They arrived, with two commissioners appointed by Mifflin, while the Parkinson Ferry meeting was in ses-sion. The quick response of the militia was by this time known in the West and caused the people to hesitate. Gallatin took advantage of the lull to urge moderation, and it was decided to

appoint a committee to treat for peace. Bradford raised the cry that the enemy was winning through the use of money. There was much dissension in the back counties themselves, but the onward march of the army gave powerful support to those who wished peace. It was finally decided to send men across the mountains to ask Washington for better terms.

Meanwhile, two divisions of troops were converging on the disaffected region, one by way of Carlisle and Bedford, the other by way of Cumberland and the old Braddock road. They met at Parkinson Ferry on November 8, but no force showed itself against them. At the demand of the military power the people now submitted and took oaths of loyalty; and 2500 troops were left in the country for the winter. Hamilton, who accompanied the army in a civil capacity, secured the arrest of such leaders as did not flee westward, and eighteen of them were sent to Philadelphia for trial. Of these only two were convicted, and they were pardoned by Washington. No further opposition was made to the excise, but it was still denounced by the republicans and was repealed when Jefferson became president. *Collapse of the Insurrection.*

The force called out against the four counties in insurrection was larger than the number of men of military age in their limits. It was larger than most of the revolutionary armies, and larger than any army under Washington before the French alliance. It was only one thousand men smaller than the allied American army which captured Cornwallis with 7000 men at Yorktown. A thousand men could have suppressed the insurrection. In calling for 15,000 Washington followed the suggestion of Hamilton, who wished to demonstrate the power of the government; and in this respect the plan succeeded. But his opponents denounced it as showing the tendency of the federalists toward militarism. Hamilton's general policy of a strong government, which could intimidate the unruly, suited England, which he thought the best-governed country in the world. But it was a mistake in a country in which the unruly all had the ballot, for it tended to make them the political opponents of the party in power. *Significance of the Army.*

Political Development under Washington

Washington was elected president without regard to party. During the revolution all whigs stood together and division in the ranks was deplored. The first cabinet and the first congress were composed of men who had favored the adoption of the constitution; for it was not probable that men should be selected to organize a government which they had not wished to establish. Washington's first appointments in the civil service were generally from the same class. When North Carolina and Rhode *Washington and Party.*

Island gave in their tardy submission to the constitution, he removed the antifederalist revenue officers within their borders and appointed successors who were federalists. Nobody objected, for the antifederalist group had no occasion to continue its existence and immediately disappeared. Washington hoped that his supporters would remain undivided and was distressed when he saw them forming parties.

This process began with the introduction of Hamilton's financial plan, which pleased the property-owning class and the advocates of a strong central government. Hamilton thought wealth **The Federalist Party.** and intelligence would rule, partly because they could act promptly and with bold initiative, and partly because they would ever have great influence over less competent classes. Washington sympathized with this view and supported it when occasion arose throughout his administration. Thus was organized the Hamiltonian party, which took the name federalist because it sought to promote nationality. It was strongest in the trading cities, most of which were north of the Potomac, and among the large planters of the South. It was conservative and mildly aristocratic.

Opposed to these views was Jefferson, who had ever rejected a privileged class and who believed in democracy. He had great organizing ability, but was not a good public speaker. He realized **The Republican Party Forming.** that the middle and lower classes were a vast majority of the voters and might control the government if they could be organized into an effective party. The superior classes had their own organization; he must make one. They had influence over the mass of voters; he must break down that influence. He found many men who disliked Hamilton, never a considerate man to those who differed with him, others who held, as Jefferson, to the democratic theory, others who feared the concentration of national power, and still others who wished to make careers for themselves as leaders of a great party. Jefferson was able to select the best men of these groups, unite them in a common cause, restrain their passions, and furnish them with successful campaign issues. He founded newspapers which, in seeking to destroy the prestige of the federalists with the masses, accused them of many harsh purposes. They even attacked Washington, pronouncing him a monarchist. By these fierce onslaughts, and by taking advantage of every mistake of their adversaries, they slowly increased their power, and in 1800 obtained control of the government. They were known as republicans.

Republican Feeling in the States. There was some discontent in interior New England, but the power of the seaports overwhelmed it, and here the republicans had little hope. Hamilton's enemies in New York, headed by Clinton, came readily into the movement. In Pennsylvania the country people were opposed to the ruling class in Philadelphia and became republicans gladly. In Virginia and North Carolina the great planters lived in the counties along the coast and the small farmers, far more numerous, lived in the uplands and generally followed Jefferson. In Georgia the same thing was true. In South Carolina the planters in the east and the Charleston merchants formed a powerful ruling class, but the men of the interior were republicans. In the new states of Kentucky and Tennessee the frontiersmen were fiercely democratic. Jefferson, therefore, had strong hopes of carrying all the South except Maryland and South Carolina, and had good chances in Pennsylvania and New York. In 1792 these states had a majority of the electoral votes.

Hamilton considered the situation alarming. Washington intended to retire to his estate, and it was likely that the federalists would support John Adams for his successor. Adams was honest and capable, but unpopular out of New England. In this dilemma Hamilton decided that Washington must stand for reëlection. He was met at first with a refusal, but he got others to persuade Washington. Only one man, it was felt, could harmonize the contending parties. So strong was this feeling that even Jefferson joined his voice to the general demand, and in the end Washington consented to run. The republicans did not oppose him, but supported George Clinton for the vice-presidency against Adams. Washington received the votes of all the states, and Clinton those of New York, Virginia, North Carolina, and Georgia, with one from Pennsylvania, a total of 50 to Adams's 77. *Washington Reëlected.*

The hope that Washington would reconcile parties proved futile. In 1793 the European war began, the republicans espoused the cause of republican France, and denounced the neutrality proclamation. For a time this seemed to be an advantage, but the excesses of Genêt reacted against them, and the federalists, most of whom leaned toward England, gained by declaring that their opponents would sacrifice the honor of the country for the sake of the infidel French republic. Indeed, from that time until 1800 the French ministers were in cordial relations with republican leaders and did as much as they dared to secure the defeat of the federalists. Jefferson, now definitely head of the opposition, recognized that he was out of place in the cabinet and withdrew at the close of the year 1793 to give all his efforts to the republican cause. His place was taken by Edmund Randolph, a mild republican, but so strong was the tendency to party government that he retired within a year and was succeeded by Timothy Pickering, an avowed federalist. *The European War.*

The republicans early in 1794 took a bolder attitude. Ceasing to plead for France, they began to demand war against England; and they had cause enough. When the European conflict began, France opened to the world the trade with her West Indian possessions. Too weak at sea to succor them herself, she expected that they would sell their produce, chiefly *Wrongs from England.*

sugar, to the United States and receive American merchandise in exchange. England declared this unlawful, asserting that a trade denied in time of peace could not be opened in time of war. Her men-of-war began to seize American ships bound for the French islands and to treat the captured crews with unusual rigor. The stories of hardship that came back to our shores aroused the deepest horror, and the republicans took advantage of the opportunity to demand retaliation. The first move was made by Madison, in the house of representatives.

Madison's Trade Resolutions. If England, he urged, made restrictions on our trade, we ought to make restrictions of her trade with us. The federalists replied that since seven-eighths of our trade was with England and could not be shifted to another nation, we should injure ourselves more than England by passing the proposed restrictions. It was the same argument which England used against Adams's suggestion of retaliation in 1785. The argument was so good that Madison's resolutions were postponed.

About this time came news that England had ordered the seizure of all neutral ships carrying French goods. In America the excitement was great; for we held that neutral ships made neutral goods. The republicans talked earnestly of war, and congress authorized the erection of fortifications, the enlistment of artillerymen, and the levying of a force of 80,000 militia, to be ready for an emergency. The extreme republicans, led by Dayton, of New Jersey, introduced a resolution in the house to sequester British debts as an offset to the loss from the seizure of American ships. If this were passed, the result would probably be war.

Neutral Ships and Goods.

Washington was alarmed and decided to try to settle the dispute by making a treaty with England. Conservative republicans as well as federalists thought the attempt ought to be made; and in May, 1794, he sent Jay to London with powers to make a treaty which would secure the surrender of the Western posts still in the hands of England, get compensation for the ships recently seized, and effect a commercial treaty which would remove the irritation from further seizures of ships having French goods on board and which would open British West Indian ports to our trade. If these points could be arranged, thought Washington, war would be avoided. When Jay was dispatched, the war feeling cooled and the nation awaited the result.

Jay's Mission.

Jay was a federalist and of an easy temperament. He found the British government determined to maintain their existing navigation laws, and in his desire to make some kind of arrangement accepted terms not allowed in his instructions. The treaty he sent back early in 1795 provided for surrender of the posts by 1796, and admitted us to the trade with the British East Indies, but only put off a settlement for the ships seized by Britain. It contained

Jay's Treaty.

commercial regulations which admitted our ships not larger than 70 tons' burden to British West Indian ports and denied us the right to carry West Indian products, including cotton, to Europe, while British ships were to be unrestricted in our own trade. It also provided that privateers should not be fitted out in our ports by England's enemies, that Americans serving against England should be treated as pirates if captured, and that British trade in America should be on the footing of the most favored nation. These latter provisions were aimed at the French treaties of 1778. The West Indian clause of Jay's treaty were to end two years after the termination of the existing war.

An outburst of indignation greeted its publication in America, the republicans leading the chorus. Even the federalists could support it only faintly, and Washington was much in doubt. But reflection brought soberness. If the treaty were rejected, the nation would almost surely drift into war, for which it was not prepared. This view had weight with the senate, which cut out the features relating to the West India trade and passed the treaty by the necessary two-thirds majority. Washington hesitated to sign it, but finally yielded. He thought that if we could endure for twenty years the inferiority it forced us to accept, we should be strong enough to defy an unjust measure of any power in the world. *Treaty accepted with Amendments.*

An interesting question now arose. The treaty provided for some modifications of the laws and for the appropriation of money to execute it. But this required the consent of congress, and thus the whole matter was debated in both houses in the year 1796. Here conservatism again won, and it was ordered that the treaty be executed. The action in this case became a precedent in making later treaties. The long struggle over the question, culminating in the vehement debate in congress in 1796, served to harden the lines of the two parties, and their strength is seen in the votes; in the senate the resolution to execute the treaty passed without serious opposition, but in the house the vote was 51 to 48, and a resolution declaring it highly objectionable was only defeated by the deciding vote of the speaker. *Execution of the Treaty.*

When this vote was taken, the country was already thinking of a new presidential election. Washington let it be known that he would not be a candidate, and the federalists turned to Adams. He was their strongest available man; but he was tactless, though honest and experienced in public affairs. He was so independent that he would not follow the lead of Hamilton, who had formed a dislike for him, and who now sought to defeat him by an unworthy scheme. He had Thomas Pinckney, of South Carolina, brought forward for vice-president. Both men, he thought, would have equal votes in the choice of electors, but at the last moment he *Election of 1796.*

T

would have some of the electors go for a third candidate instead of voting for Adams, who thus having the second highest vote would be vice-president, while Pinckney, whom Hamilton could probably influence, would be president. The republicans united on Jefferson, their best man. In the final vote some of the electors who were friendly to Adams refused to support Pinckney, lest Hamilton's scheme should succeed; and the result was that 71 men voted for Adams, 68 for Jefferson, 59 for Pinckney, and 78 were divided among ten other candidates. Each elector, it will be remembered, voted for two men. Adams thus became president and Jefferson vice-president. As Adams had only one more vote than a majority of the electors, he was dubbed by his opponents "a president by one vote," an epithet which greatly annoyed his sensitive soul.

Washington, thinking chiefly of his retirement, took little interest in the election. His last care was to prepare his celebrated "Farewell Address," in which he gave much good advice on the prob-

Washington's Retirement. lems of the day. As these problems were necessarily related to the policies over which the parties were divided and as his federalist leaning appeared in his advice, the "Address" was received with coolness by the republicans. He had become very unpopular with that party, and some of its leading men and newspapers rejoiced openly that he was going out of office. As the passions of the moment subsided, he recovered the popularity to which his character entitled him, and the next generation came to look on the "Farewell Address" as a priceless political heritage. Among other things, it counseled his fellow citizens to be loyal to the union, to cultivate harmony at home, and to shun entanglement with European policies. His administration was most important, because his great name had been able to hold in abeyance through the first eight years of the national government the inevitable wrangling of

His Best Service. parties, thereby giving an opportunity to launch the government on a safe and enlightened plan. That critical early period safely past, it was not dangerous for party leaders to battle for their views, a necessary feature of all republican government.

BIBLIOGRAPHICAL NOTE

On Washington's two administrations the most available general secondary works are: Avery, *The United States and its People*, 7 vols. (1904–); Bassett, *The Federalist System* (1906); McMaster, *History*, 7 vols. (1883–); Schouler, *History of the United States*, 6 vols. (1880–1894); Hildreth, *History*, 6 vols. (1849–1852), federalist in sympathy; Hamilton, J. C., *History of the Republic of the United States*, 7 vols. (4th ed., 1879), a biased defense of Hamilton, but it contains valuable letters; Gordy, *History of Political Parties*, 2 vols. (revised ed. 1904), an excellent book on early political parties; Johnston, Alexander, articles on political conditions and institutions in Lalor's *Cyclopædia of Political Science*, republished in Woodburn, *American Political History*, 2 vols. (1905); Gibbs, *The Administrations of Washington and Adams*, 2 vols. (1846), very partisan, but it contains valuable letters; and Stanwood, *History of the Presidency* (1900), an excellent summary of national party divisions.

For original sources see: Peters, ed., *Public Statutes at Large of the United States*, 8 vols. (1845) — treaties, Indian and foreign, are in vols. VII and VIII; *Annals of Congress*, 42 vols. (1834–1856), the early debates, but they are not reported verbatim; Benton, *Abridgment of the Debates in Congress, 1789–1850*, 24 vols. (1857–1863); Maclay, *Journal, 1789–1791* (1900), valuable because the early senate debates are not given in the *Annals; Legislative Journal of the Senate*, 5 vols. (1820–1821); *Executive Journal of the Senate*, 3 vols. (1829); *Journal of the House of Representatives*, 9 vols. (1826); papers relating to the departments — diplomatic, financial, military, and relating to Indians and lands — in *American State Papers*, 38 vols. (1832–1861); and Richardson, *Messages and Papers of the Presidents*, 10 vols. (1897).

For the writings and biographies of Washington, Madison, Hamilton, Jefferson, John Adams, Jay, Patrick Henry, and Gerry see references on page 255. See also: Hamilton, *Writings of Monroe*, 7 vols. (1898–1903); King, *Life and Correspondence of Rufus King*, 6 vols. (1894–1900); Ames, ed., *Works of Fisher Ames*, 2 vols. (1857); Anne C. Morris, *Diary and Letters of Gouverneur Morris*, 2 vols. (1888); Adams, *Writings of Albert Gallatin*, 3 vols. (1879); and Wilkinson, *Memoirs of my Own Times*, 3 vols. (1816), the last mentioned very untrustworthy. See the following biographies also: Brown, *Life of Oliver Ellsworth* (1905); Adams, *Life of Albert Gallatin* (1879); Pickering and Upham, *Life of Timothy Pickering*, 4 vols. (1867–1875); Amory, *Life of James Sullivan*, 2 vols. (1859); and Conway, *Life of Thomas Paine*, 2 vols. (1892).

On the whisky insurrection see: Adams, *Life of Gallatin* (1879); Findley, *History of the Insurrection* (1796), a good contemporary account; H. M. Brackenridge, *History of the Western Insurrection* (1859), written from the standpoint of the participants; and Ward, *The Insurrection of 1794* (Pennsylvania Hist. Soc. *Memoirs*, VI).

On diplomatic affairs see: Trescott, *Diplomatic History of the Administrations of Washington and Adams* (1857), good but rare; Snow, *Treaties and Topics in American Diplomacy* (1894), for students; Lyman, *Diplomacy of the United States, 1789–1826*, 2 vols. (2d ed. 1828); McLaughlin, *Western Posts and British Debts* (Am. Hist. Assoc. *Report*, 1894); Turner, *Correspondence of the French Ministers to the United States, 1791–1797* (Ibid., 1903, II), contains Genêt's correspondence; and Shepherd, *Wilkinson and the Beginnings of the Spanish Conspiracy* (*Am. Hist. Review*, IX, 490).

For Independent Reading

Campbell, *Travels in the Interior Inhabited Parts of North America, 1791–1792* (1793); Griswold, *The Republican Court* (1864); Hamilton, *Life of Alexander Hamilton* (1910); and Woodrow Wilson, *George Washington* (1897).

CHAPTER XIII

ADAMS AND THE DOWNFALL OF THE FEDERALISTS

The Political Character of the Administration

John Adams began his presidency with a divided party. On one side were his own friends, neither numerous nor well organized; on the other were Hamilton and his supporters, probably two-thirds of the federalists and not inclined to submit to the leadership of the other third. Adams retained Washington's cabinet, which supported Hamilton in all party matters, so that the president came at last to realize that he was not head of his own administration. The internal conflict which thus arose weakened the federalist organization and contributed to its overthrow. Adams regretted the situation; for he was peculiarly desirous of having a harmonious administration. When at last he found his cabinet in practical rebellion, he reorganized it, casting out the extremists and calling in moderate federalists, the chief of whom was Marshall of Virginia. But this occurred too late to avert party defeat.

Position of Adams.

Adams's first action as president was an attempt to reunite the two political parties. He had been widely accused of favoring a form of monarchy; but in his inaugural address he sought to overcome this view by announcing his confidence in the constitution. The republicans openly expressed their satisfaction. He also proposed to appoint either Jefferson or Madison minister to France, but the offer was declined by both gentlemen. When the Hamilton faction heard of these negotiations, they objected flatly, and there was no more talk of reconciliation. The negotiations had, no doubt, been encouraged by the wily Jefferson, with the object of widening the breach between the federalist factions.

Attempts to reunite the Parties.

Party rancor now became worse than ever. For Washington even his enemies had a respect which moderated the jibes of the bitterest foe. For Adams there was no such regard. He was pitilessly painted as a monarchist, a tyrant, and a selfish manipulator of patronage. Yet no president strove harder to carry on the government in the spirit of its founders. It was the youth of political discussion in America, and editors and pamphleteers on both sides fought relentlessly for their principles. In France opponents of republicanism had recently gone to the guillotine in shoals; in England defenders of republicanism had been im-

Partisan Abuse.

prisoned or forced to flee the country; it was, probably, as much as could be expected that in our own newly established republic the only violence that occurred was in the exchange of epithets.

It was, also, inevitable that in such a discussion should appear the sharpest division between the British and French sympathizers. Republicans, in defending France, expressed their loyalty to popular government; federalists, in favoring the Brit-ish constitution, expressed their approval of government by the conservative upper classes of society, which implied a distrust of the rule of all the people. To the former the triumph of the Jay treaty seemed to show that British influence was alive in the country; to the latter the ill-concealed attempts of the French ministers in Philadelphia to direct American politics seemed convinc-ing evidence that the court in Paris worked in behalf of the republican party throughout the union.

Foreign Politics Involved.

Unfortunately, the latter contention was true, as events connected with the dismissal of Monroe, late in Washington's second term, made clear. This ardent republican was sent to Paris in 1794 to succeed Gouverneur Morris, whose monarchism made him unacceptable to the French republic. He arrived in August, when no other state, except the small republic of Geneva, had sent a minister to the new government. The Convention then ruled France, and so busy was it with its own struggle for existence that no arrangements had been made to receive foreign ministers. Monroe, not to be thwarted by this fact, made arrangements to be received by the Convention itself. He was accordingly admitted to an open session of that body, where amid the applause of the members he exchanged embraces with the president of the Convention and pre-sented a glowing address, pledging the coöperation in behalf of liberty of the two great republics, the one in the Old, and the other in the New, World. This display of fervor, occasioned protest in England, where Jay was negotiating his treaty; and the federalist administration of Washington sent a reproof to the enthusiastic Monroe.

Monroe's Mission.

Meanwhile, France was concerned at rumors of a treaty of amity between the United States and England, but Monroe, relying on as-surances from superiors, assured her that nothing would be accepted in the proposed agreement prejudicial to the interests of our oldest friend among nations. When the treaty was made, however, it was evident that it did weaken that preferential relation which the treaties of 1778 gave to France (see page 201); and the government in Paris felt that it had been deceived. Monroe himself was deeply chagrined, and neglected to defend the Jay treaty in Paris, as he was instructed to do by Pickering, then secretary of state. More than six months had passed in this way when he learned that the ministry was about to send an envoy to America to make a new treaty. Believing that such an attempt would result in

His Position in Paris.

failure, and peaceful relations would therefore be imperiled, he induced the ministry to delay their project. He was suspected of holding out to them the prospect of a republican victory in the coming presidential elections, then only nine months distant. As the campaign opened, he was known to be sending information to republicans at home, which was used to convince the voters that the federalist administration was about to plunge the nation into war with France.

His Recall. Washington considered this action a breach of trust, and ordered Monroe's immediate recall. The affair caused much comment, the republicans defending and the federalists condemning the dismissed minister. *Aug. 1796   Bassett p 214*

His Revenge. Monroe returned anxious for vindication, and took two ways of getting even. He prepared a long defense and published it in 1797, endeavoring to show that he had been badly treated by Pickering and Hamilton, the chief authors of federalist policy. It was a piece of specious pleading, but it satisfied the republicans and served to bring French affairs sharply to the front in the political arena. His other stroke was at Hamilton particularly. Some years earlier that gentleman was the subject of an investigation to meet the charge of misusing public money while secretary of the treasury. The committee of inquiry, consisting of Monroe and two others, pronounced him innocent, but did not publish the evidence. In fact, Hamilton had proved his innocence only by admitting that the charges grew out of an illicit relation with the wife of the worthless man who preferred the charges, and this evidence the committee agreed to conceal. Soon after Monroe's return it was given to the public in such a distorted form that Hamilton felt **Hamilton's Ignominy.** impelled to confess the whole matter in a published statement. The two other committeemen showed that they had not disclosed the affair, and posterity has concluded that the revelation was made by Monroe. It left a smirch on Hamilton's reputation, which is not removed by the admiration we are compelled to feel for his courageous explanation of it.

Cf Bassett, Federalist System. p 215-17

THE QUARREL WITH FRANCE

When Charles C. Pinckney, who succeeded Monroe at Paris, arrived at his post of duty, he found the government in a resentful mood. He **Pinckney Rejected.** sent his credentials to the Directory, now the head of the government, only to be informed that France would not receive an American minister until her grievances were redressed. A law of the republic, passed when most strangers were held to be spies, forbade foreigners to remain in France without written permission. Pinckney asked for such permission, but received no reply. He disregarded an intimation that a further stay made him liable to arrest, because he wished the responsibility for his departure, if he must go, to rest clearly with the government. After two months of delay he received an official notice that he was liable to arrest, whereupon he asked for his passports and shook the dust of France off his feet in February, 1797. His rude reception was thrown into bolder relief by the evidence of good will which the Directory showered on Monroe, when he took his departure about the same time.

When Pinckney's humiliating treatment was known in America, there was a violent outbreak of feeling, and many expressions of hostility were heard; for the people are ever ready to re- **Clamor for** sent an insult to the national dignity. Among the poli- **Redress.** ticians the extreme federalists wished to suspend relations with France, and if reprisals occurred, which would lead to war, they would be all the better pleased. They were led by Pickering and Wolcott, in the cabinet, and by Harper and William Smith, in congress. The republicans could not defend the action of France, but declared that it only indicated the mismanagement of the federalist party. Between these two views was a middle ground taken by moderate men, who defended the national honor, but were willing to try other diplomatic efforts while preparations for war went on. Of this opinion was President Adams, who in all the clamor of the day did not lose his poise. Hamilton, not willing to sacrifice country to party, took the same ground, although in doing so he failed to act with the faction which generally supported him. The upshot was that Adams nominated Charles C. Pinckney, John Marshall, and Francis Dana commissioners to try to adjust the existing difficulty with France. The republicans supported the nominations which were con- **Commis-** firmed. But Dana refused to serve, and Adams, returning **sioners sent** to a favorite idea, nominated Gerry, a Massachusetts **to France.** republican, in his stead. He thought the presence of a republican on the commission would tend to conciliate the Directory.

Steps were also taken to put the nation in a state of defense. Three years earlier, congress had ordered the construction of six frigates, three of which were actually begun, but were still unfinished through lack of funds. They were now ordered **Prepara-** completed. They were the *United States* and the *Constitu-* **War.** *tion*, of 44 guns each, and the *Constellation*, of 36 guns, the first ships of our navy under the constitution. They were heavily armed for their size, and foreign naval officers predicted they could not be managed safely in battle, — an expectation which later events did not justify. Other measures of defense were a law authorizing the president to call out 80,000 militia when needed and a law to strengthen the fortifications.

By this time serious grounds for trouble had arisen in connection with our trade at sea. When, four years earlier, England began to seize our ships carrying French goods, France retaliated by ordering her

naval officers to seize neutral ships which recognized England's pretensions. If we allowed England's claim that provisions were contraband, contraband they were; and on that ground France would seize
them when they were bound for British ports. Between
French Re- the pretensions of the two great powers it was impossi-
strictions on ble for a nation which had no navy to maintain a posi-
American
Trade. tion of strict neutrality. It was equally difficult for it
to retaliate, unless it was willing to join one of the nations in
war against the other. For such action we were not ready, and the
best we could do was to endure our wrongs and hope to get reparation
for losses after peace returned in Europe. Neither America nor
Europe could foresee that the war then waged was to continue without
considerable interruption until 1815. As time passed, many cases of
seizure occurred, and there was now danger that American shipowners,
already aroused against France, would by some act of reprisal provoke
such severe individual conflicts that it would be impossible longer to
restrain the war feeling on the part of our people. Adams, therefore,
issued an order forbidding merchant ships to go armed, and congress
passed a law prohibiting privateering against a nation with which we
were at peace. By such means it was hoped to preserve peace until
the commissioners to France could make a settlement of the existing
quarrel.

Arrived in Paris, Pinckney, Marshall, and Gerry began to negotiate
in October, 1797. To their surprise they made not a step of progress.
X, Y, and Z. Talleyrand was head of foreign affairs, and the Directory
was corrupt to the core. They had taken an overbearing
attitude toward small European states, each of which had some selfish end to advance, and were collecting bribes from them before they
would allow any arrangements to be made. What they did so freely
with such states, they were now determined to do with the United
States. While our commissioners waited for their business to be taken
up, they were visited by agents, designated in the published reports
of the commissioners as X, Y, and Z, who suggested that progress
would be made if the minister were given $250,000. To this sugges-
tion, several times repeated, the commissioners opposed a steadfast
negative. Then they refused to see the agents, but prepared a statement of the American case and sent it to Talleyrand. His reply, delayed two months, was insulting. He accused the United States of
prolonging the misunderstanding for their own benefit, asked why
three republican commissioners were not sent, and closed by saying
that he would treat with Gerry alone. To this coarse message a dig-
Gerry's nified reply was made, and the commissioners prepared to
Conduct. withdraw. Ere they went, Gerry was invited by Talleyrand to remain and continue communication with the ministry. He hesitated a moment and then accepted, declaring that he
did so only as a private citizen and in the hope that he might be

able to prevent war. His action was ill advised. It produced resentment at home, and Adams summoned him to return instantly.

April 3, 1798, the "X, Y, Z papers," as the correspondence of the commissioners was called, was sent to congress by the president, who declared: "I will never send another minister to France without assurances that he will be received, respected, **An Outburst of Indignation.** and honored as the representative of a free, powerful, and independent nation." The moderate federalists now joined the extremists, and many acts were passed looking to war. By one of them a navy department was created, by another three new frigates and thirty smaller vessels were ordered, by another the navy was authorized to take French ships interfering with our commerce, and by still another the treaties of 1778 were repealed. Another law authorized an army of 10,000 men to serve for three years. All this fell short of a declaration of war, and to that extent the extreme federalists were disappointed. From this time Hamilton was for war.

The few ships in the navy were quickly in West Indian waters, fourteen men-of-war and eight converted merchantmen. There the *Constellation* fell in with *L'Insurgent*, whose commander **Sea Fights.** had seized many of our merchant vessels and was much hated in America. An hour's chase followed, the Frenchman trying to avoid conflict, as he was instructed to do by his superiors. At last he was overhauled, and a spirited action of an hour and a quarter forced him to surrender. As the angry French captain came aboard the *Constellation*, he exclaimed: "Why have you fired on the national flag? Our two nations are at peace." The reply of the American captain, Truxtun, was laconic: "You are my prisoner." The victory aroused great enthusiasm in America. A short time later Truxtun met and fought a drawn battle with the French ship *La Vengeance*, and many other smaller engagements followed. In two years and a half our ships had taken 84 French ships, mostly privateers. The result was a lessening of the number of seizures and added prestige for the navy. This period of retaliation has been called a war with France, but no state of war was recognized by the two governments.

Meanwhile, the organization of the new army was begun. Washington was appointed its commander and accepted, on condition that he should name the chief subordinates. He sent three names to Adams,—Hamilton, Charles C. Pinckney, and **The New Army.** Knox. Confirmed in this order, the first would rank next to Washington. Adams remembered old scores and ordered that they should rank according to their station in the old army,—Knox, Pinckney, and Hamilton. Now the last named was a good military man, and Washington wanted him first among the three. Since the head of the army was too old to take the field, it meant that Hamilton would conduct the field movements. A strong controversy arose between the friends of Knox and Hamilton. Adams decided at first for Knox, but when Washington made a vigorous protest, the president dared not ignore it, and Hamilton received the coveted station. He had retired from civil life, but he loved the soldier's career, and as the federalists meant to make the augmented army a permanent thing, the appointment was very attractive to him. He had much influence with Washington, and used it freely to get that final intervention which forced Adams to change the order of nominations. Adams did not relish the way he was treated; he felt that he was hardly commander-in-chief of the army, as the constitution provided; but he was not willing to withstand the will of Washington.

Hamilton's success did him no good. Recruiting went on so slowly that 1799 was well advanced before a fair beginning was made. By **Recruiting Slow.** this time enthusiasm was waning, and the newly-formed camps became scenes of discontent and disorder. The republicans denounced the whole affair as ill advised. They divined their enemy's purpose to have a permanent establishment, and pointed out the tendency to militarism. This new army became an important argument in the campaign of 1800.

In fact, a little reflection showed that war was unnecessary. France did not wish it, or she would have resented our attacks on her men-of-war. **War Unnecessary.** To have asked our commissioners for a bribe was discreditable to her, but we need not fight on account of it. Many people saw this, Adams among them, and he decided to secure a restoration of harmony, if it could be done with dignity. The proper occasion offered when in October, 1798, Murray, our minister at The Hague, wrote that he was assured from Talleyrand that a minister would now be received. Adams wished to send one, but his cabinet, led by the factious Pickering, opposed. As the winter passed, he realized that the extremists were bent on bringing on war for their own ends, and determined to take affairs into his own hands.

A New Treaty. Without warning, he nominated Murray minister to France, and the senate received the news in disgust. Hamilton, disappointed, declared nothing better could be expected from Adams, and the other extremists raged inwardly. But they could not resist, and accepted the suggestion after substituting three commissioners for the one minister proposed. The result was an acceptable treaty, made in 1800, which settled for a time the chief points of controversy between the two nations. Napoleon was now in control in France. Occupied with vast plans in Europe, he wisely gave up the policy pursued by the directory of nursing American politics in the hope that a republican triumph on this side of the water would promote French interests.

Overconfidence of the Federalists

Adams's attitude toward France has the approval of posterity. Unfortunately, his political principles were as narrow as those of other federalists. Like the rest of his party, he wished to enforce respect for public officials, and he resented the vast amount **Adams's** of abuse which came from the republican editors and **Political** writers. As many of these men were of foreign birth, **Views.** some of them fugitives from their own countries, he felt that they ought to be restrained. Their activity during the year war was imminent with France was the basis of a charge that they were French spies; and on that basis it was easy to conclude they should be sent out of the country. From this conviction proceeded four laws of congress passed with the support of extreme and moderate federalists.

The first related to naturalization. A law of 1795 made five years of residence necessary for naturalization. To most federalists this seemed too short, and many would have withheld the right entirely. But the words of the constitution seemed to imply that **Naturaliza-** naturalization should not be denied, and it was at last **tion Act.** agreed to require fourteen years' residence, with the provision that naturalized persons must have declared their intentions five years before the right could be operative. The law was resented by the republicans, and the provisions of 1795 were restored by a law enacted by them in 1802.

The second law dealt with aliens in times of peace. It gave the president the power to order out of the country any alien whom he thought dangerous to the welfare of the country. If he were not obeyed, he might order the person concerned to **The Alien** be imprisoned for three years, and if such a person should **Laws.** return after going away, imprisonment might be inflicted at the will of the president. This act was to continue two years.

The third act concerned aliens in time of war. They might be ordered out of the country or imprisoned as long as the president chose. The act was limited to the duration of a war. The republicans deplored loudly the fate of the " poor aliens," whose safety was thus put at the disposal of the president. In time of war or an invasion he was to have the power to issue a proclamation declaring what classes of aliens should be allowed to remain in the United States, and the federal courts were to see that it was not defied. Many Frenchmen left the country when the law was about to pass, which is probably all it was expected to accomplish. No attempt was made to apply either alien law to those who remained.

The fourth act dealt with American citizens, who denounced the administration or upheld France. It made it a high misdemeanor "unlawfully to combine" against the legal measures of the government, to impede any officer in the execution of his duty, or to attempt to form any conspiracy, insurrection, or unlawful assembly against the administration. The penalty was to be imprisonment not more than five years and a fine of not more than $5000. It also made it a misdemeanor to issue a false or malicious writing against the president or congress in order to stir up hatred against them. For this offense the defendant, on conviction, was to be fined not more than $2000 and imprisoned not longer than two years. With some difficulty the republicans and moderates introduced into the law a clause allowing the accused to prove the truth of his assertion. The first of these four acts was passed June 18, the last on July 14, 1798.

The Sedition Law.

Many persons were indicted under the sedition act: only ten were brought to trial, and all of these were convicted. The most notable case was that of Dr. Thomas Cooper, then an editor in Pennsylvania. He was arrested for saying that President Adams was incompetent and had, as president, interfered to influence the course of justice. In our day we should hardly notice such a charge, so freely is the conduct of even the highest official held up to ridicule and condemnation. He was tried before Chase, a federal judge, who displayed, as in all such cases, the greatest amount of partisanship. Cooper offered to prove the truth of the charge by summoning Adams and some members of congress as witnesses; but they refused to attend. In default of such evidence he was convicted, fined $400, and sent to prison for six months. Adams was willing to pardon him, but the prisoner refused to petition for pardon unless the president acknowledged wrongdoing in giving out a letter Cooper had written him. The president would make no such acknowledgement, and the sentence was not remitted.

Prosecutions for Sedition.

Every man convicted became a martyr to free speech, in the eyes of the republicans. The issue came up in the election of 1800 and had great weight in convincing the voters that the federalists were drunk with power. All these repressive laws were, in fact, ill-advised. They rested on the theory that the people should not be free to discuss, as they chose, the actions of their rulers. European governments, as Chase pointed out in the case of Dr. Cooper, exercised the right to punish libel; but the European governments were not republican. Punishing a citizen for political utterances is a bad policy in a government resting on popular suffrage.

The republicans believed the alien and sedition acts an invasion of the personal rights which, as they held, were properly within the sphere of action by the states. They also decried the creation of an army under the control of the aggressive Hamilton. It seemed to them that by a system of loose construction the federalists would concentrate the powers of government in the hands of president, congress, and the federal courts, and reduce to a much lower rank the authority of the states, to which the republicans looked as the guarantee of the rights of the individual. The federalists, as in 1787, replied that the rights of the individual would be as safe at the hands of the general government as at the hands of the states. The reply did not satisfy the republicans, who demanded a strict interpretation of the constitution. Some of them despaired of checking the plans of their opponents, and, recurring to an idea entertained by some of the representatives of the large states in the convention of 1787, proposed to Jefferson to begin agitation for the secession of Virginia and North Carolina, in order to establish a great Southern republic into which the power of the trading states of the North would not enter. Such a movement would almost surely have the support of Kentucky and Tennessee; Georgia would probably support it with her control of the great unsettled Gulf region; and it was hardly to be doubted that it would eventually carry with it the state of South Carolina, in which the federalist families of the seacoast held only temporary supremacy. The whole region was more than half of the national domain, giving to the North all the vast unsettled Northwest. It had, however, only 40 per cent of the entire population, and its political strength was still less proportionally through the provision that only three-fifths of its slaves counted in representation.

These suggestions were rejected by Jefferson. We ought not, he said, to become discouraged because of the triumph of opponents, but endeavor to overcome it by political means. Then he unfolded his plan. Believing that all the states had the same interest in protecting their authority, he would unite **Jefferson's Plan.** them in a crusade against national concentration. He secured the coöperation of Madison, and each wrote resolutions condemning the recent enactments of the federalist congress and pointing out in what ways the rights of the states were threatened. Madison's resolutions were adopted by the Virginia assembly. Jefferson's were intended for North Carolina, but the elections of 1798 in that state showed federalist gains in the legislature, and he would not send them thither for adoption. They were placed in the hands of friends in Kentucky, where republicanism was strong, and passed the legislature of that state by a large majority.

The purport of each set of resolutions was the same, although the Kentucky resolutions used language more explicit and emphatic. Both sought to find in the states a power to stay the general government in its assumption that it could interpret the **The Compact Theory.** constitution. Suppose a controversy exists as to whether the union or the state should exercise a certain power, who shall determine it? The federalists asserted that the supreme court had the decision. They stood by the idea that the constitution was made by the people and that the national authority rested on popular con-

Jefferson & Madison — say states must decide question of Constitution.

sent as truly as the state authority. Jefferson and Madison declared
that the states founded the national government by making a compact
whose terms were expressed in the constitution and that it was for
the states, the creators, to determine when the compact was broken.
Both sets of resolutions declared that the alien and sedition acts,
and some other recent legislation of congress, violated the constitution, and called on the states for coöperation in preventing their
execution.

By what means should the state's veto be given? Virginia was dis-
creetly general on the point. If ungranted power was exercised, said
she, the states could and should "interpose for arresting

Means of Correction. the progress of the evil, and for maintaining within their
respective limits the authorities, rights, and liberties ap-
pertaining to them." Interposition by the states might be construed
as calling a convention to amend the constitution, as provided in the
constitution. But Kentucky was more explicit. The states, said
her resolutions, founded the union for specific purposes and gave it
expressed powers, reserving all authority to themselves which they
did not grant to the union; an exercise of ungranted power was illegal;
the union was not a judge of its own powers; and each party to the
compact of the union is a judge of the terms of union, as in all cases
of compact where there is no common judge. In accordance with this
principle they declared the alien and sedition acts and certain other
laws of congress "void and of no force."

In the hot debates of the convention of 1787 nothing was said
directly about the compact theory. Virginia and most of the South
then stood for a national government on a popular basis,

Efficacy of the Compact Theory. evidently thinking their greater size would enable them
to control it. Except for equal representation in the
senate and the tenth amendment reserving to the states
all powers not granted to the national government, there was no
specific limitation of nationality in the constitution. If the convention
had held so important a view, it can hardly be doubted that it would
have defined it. Neither Jefferson nor Madison, in fact, claimed that
words in the constitution, except the tenth amendment, supported the
compact theory. It was a deduction from extra-constitutional sources.
No government with a due respect for its own authority will accept
in practical matters a principle so purely speculative.

Both Jefferson and Madison were experienced politicians. They
did not expect the federal government to accept their view and relinquish its pretended authority. But they believed that

A Political Measure. state resolutions were powerful means of calling attention
to the federalist tendency toward concentration. Although
the two sets of resolutions were sent to the other states in the
union, they did not expect them to be accepted by the federalist
then generally dominant in the Northern legislatures. But they

thought the attention of the voters would be called in the most striking way to an evil they believed to exist with good effect on succeeding elections. Madison asserted in his old age that the Kentucky and Virginia resolutions were planned for political effect. When the republicans came into control of the government two years later, they made no effort to amend the constitution in accordance with the compact theory.

All the states north of the Potomac, through their legislatures, made replies unfavorable to the resolutions, some of them expressed in terms hardly polite. None of the legislatures of states south of Virginia voted on them, probably because **Attitude of Other States.** the republicans thought it wise to let well enough alone. When the Northern replies were received, Kentucky and Virginia passed resolutions reasserting the views in the first sets. In those now announced by Kentucky occurred the sentence: "A nullification, by those sovereignties, of all unauthorized acts done under color of that instrument, is the rightful remedy." This is the only appearance of the word "nullification" in any of the resolutions, but the essential idea is in the first set passed by Kentucky. Thirty years later it came up again in the Nullification **Relation to Nullification.** movement in South Carolina, whose promoters thought that stressing the similarity of their doctrines with those of 1798 would draw Virginia to their side.

OVERTHROW OF THE FEDERALISTS

The congressional elections of 1798 came while the country still looked for war with France, and the results favored the federalists. But that party was still divided into radicals and moderates, **Federalists Divided.** the former led by Pickering with the support of Hamilton, the latter led by Adams with the strong support of Marshall and a group of Southern federalists in the house. When the president threw over the war policy of his party in the spring of 1799 he had the support of the moderates, and the extremists lost a valuable political issue. They expressed their contempt for Adams openly, which only divided his party more than ever. The split became more evident when Adams, in 1800, dismissed Pickering and forced McHenry to withdraw from the cabinet because they refused to carry out his policy with regard to making a treaty with France. He retained Wolcott, equally guilty with the men dismissed, because he did not know the extent of Wolcott's treachery. In Pickering's post he placed Marshall, who was not popular in the North, and the dispossessed faction began to plot to defeat the reëlection of a president who showed them so much hostility. As it was evident that the federalists would take Adams for their candidate in 1800, this dissention augured little for party success.

Meanwhile, the republicans were united for Jefferson. The Virginia and Kentucky resolutions gave them a strong principle on which
Republicans United. to appeal to the voters, and they strengthened their position by criticizing the administration at every possible point. Preparations for war had involved heavy expenses, the national debt had grown during the eleven years of federalist control, and this gave ground for charging the party with extravagance. The evident desire of Hamilton to make the new army permanent induced the charge that he leaned toward militarism. In March, 1800, congress ordered the dismissal of the new army, and this was a blow at the extreme federalists. The assertion of the right to impress
Their Principles. American sailors aroused great feeling against England, which reacted against the party which had usually stood by that country. Beneath all the arguments drawn from these and other sources was the continual assertion that the federalists stood for the rule of a selfish upper class, dominated by the capitalists, while the republicans represented the mass of the people. The assertion was generally true. The federalists had ignored the popular nature of American government, and Jefferson at last had organized the great mass of farmers and working people in a party which would correct recent tendencies toward class domination. It was the first of several great periodic popular upheavals by which the people have shown that they mean the government to rest on the will of all the people.

In this campaign the nominating caucus was fully developed. In 1796 republican and federalist senators and representatives, acting
The Caucus. for their respective parties, held conferences and recommended presidential candidates to the people. But their action was not accepted as binding the party leaders; for although the electors generally favored the caucus candidate for president there was much scattering in the vote for vice-president. Early in 1800 caucuses were again held. Adams was recommended by the federalists, and his friends insisted that the entire party was bound to support him. When Hamilton and his faction showed a contrary purpose they were pronounced party traitors. The republicans had their own internal jealousies. Virginia expected to carry most of the South for Jefferson, but she needed the support of a strong Northern state, for which purpose New York seemed best suited. Clinton, of that state, did not like the Virginia leadership, as was shown in the convention of 1787; but at this time he was held in check in New York by Aaron Burr, able, but distrusted by many men. Burr was willing to make alliance with Virginia, and in 1796 he was supported as the regular candidate for vice-president. But in that year he received only 30 votes to Jefferson's 68, and only one of the thirty was from Virginia. He felt he was badly dealt with, and in 1800 demanded assurances that he would be supported equally with Jefferson. His terms were

accepted by the caucus and by the party; and for many years thereafter the decision of the caucus was considered binding on the party.

In the autumn of 1800 the differences between Adams and Hamilton precipitated a disastrous factional fight.   Adams, frank by nature, expressed himself freely about the opposition of the adverse faction. As several members of the group lived **Hamilton's** in Essex county, Massachusetts, he dubbed them the **Intrigue** "Essex Junto." Hamilton was stung to the quick. He **Adams.** thought his own position in the party threatened, and wrote a pamphlet for secret circulation among the federalists, in which he declared that his friends did not constitute a British faction, as charged by Adams. Had he stopped there the result would not have been bad; but he went on to attack Adams, recognized party leader, and the gleeful approbation of his friends shows that they thought the best part of the affair would be the destruction of the president. The pamphlet fell into the hands of the republicans, who republished it with exaggerations, and thus forced the author to issue an authentic copy.   Then the world believed that Hamilton had violated his party allegiance.   There followed a reaction more damaging to Hamilton personally than to his opponent.   Each man had his followers, and they became so embittered toward one another that party success was impossible.

While the country was still talking about this incident, the election was held.   Adams got all the votes from New England, 39 in number, 10 from New Jersey and Delaware, 7 of Pennsylvania's **The Vote** 15, as well as 5 of Maryland's 10, and 4 of North Carolina's **for Presi** 12 — in all, 65.   One elector in Rhode Island, fearing **dent, 1800.** treachery on the part of the extremists, voted for Adams and Jay, so that Pinckney, running with Adams, had only 64 votes. Jefferson had all the other votes, a total of 73.   Burr, who ran with him, had the same number, and as neither had the highest number of votes cast, there was no election, and the house of representatives must select a president, the delegation of each state having one vote.

The republicans had a majority of the electoral college, and the people had voted with the intention of making Jefferson president and Burr vice-president.   Would the house execute the **Decided in** popular will, or would it act on its own judgment? The **the House,** federalists were of the latter opinion, and made a plan to **1801.** carry their own states for Burr with a hope of bringing him into the presidency while Jefferson got the second place. In a caucus of their party they carried through their plan.   Burr protested against it, but in such weak tones that it was thought that he was privy to the scheme.   It is hardly probable that the federalists would have supported him without some kind of promise in their behalf, though this does not mean that Burr meant to keep such a promise once he was president.   When the house came to act, Jefferson

U

had eight of the sixteen states and Burr had six, two being divided.   Then
Hamilton showed that moral quality which raised him in great crises
above party.   He disliked Jefferson, but believed him better than
Burr, whom he well knew to be faithless to promises.   Through his
efforts the federalist representatives from Vermont, Delaware, and
Maryland were induced to refrain from voting, and on the thirty-sixth
ballot, February 17, 1801, Jefferson received the votes of ten states
and was declared president-elect.   Burr never forgave Hamilton his
part in the election and, although vice-president, was thenceforth an
ill-disposed partner in the republican administration.   This situation,
which caused so much anxiety at the time, was responsible for the
adoption of the twelfth amendment, 1804, by which electors voted
specifically for president and vice-president.

BIBLIOGRAPHICAL NOTE

General secondary works for Adams's administration are the same as those for
the preceding chapter.   The same is true for the original sources and for the writings and biographies of leading men.   On special phases of the administration the
following works are valuable:

The Kentucky and Virginia resolutions: texts are in *American History Leaflets*,
No. 15, and in MacDonald, *Select Documents* (1897); also in Elliot, *Journal and
Debates of the Federal Convention* (1830), IV, App., pp. 357–388, which contains
also the second resolutions with the replies of some of the states; Anderson,
Contemporary Opinion of the Virginia and Kentucky Resolutions (*Am. Hist. Review*,
V, 45, 225), contains a full discussion; Warfield, *The Kentucky Resolutions of
1798* (1887), a narrative history with brief mention of the Virginia resolutions;
Powell, *Nullification and Secession in the United States* (1897), has a chapter on the
resolutions of 1798; Loring, *Nullification, Secession, etc. in the United States* (1893),
combats the theory that the constitution is a growth; and Bassett, *Federalist System*
(1906), chap. XVIII.

On the alien and sedition acts, see accounts in the *Histories* by MacMaster,
Avery, Hildreth, and Schouler; Bassett, *Federalist System* (1906); Rives, *Madison*
(1859–1868); Hunt, *Madison* (1902); Randall, *Jefferson* (1858), partisan; Tucker,
Jefferson (1837), defends Jefferson; Adams, C. F., *John Adams*, 2 vols. (1871),
the federalist side.

On party politics: Gordy, *History of Political Parties*, 2 vols. (ed. 1904), deals
with French situation at length; Stanwood, *History of the Presidency* (1898),
chap. V, a good summary of the elections of 1800 and 1801; Morse, A. D., *Party
Revolution of 1800* (Am. Hist. Assoc. *Report*, 1894); Ibid., *The Politics of John
Adams* (*Am. Hist. Review*, IV); Farrand, *The Judiciary Act of 1801* (Ibid., V);
South Carolina in the Presidential Election of 1800 (Ibid., IV), contains letters from
C. C. Pinckney; also lives and writings of Adams, Jefferson, Hamilton, and
Madison.

On the naval operations of the time: Maclay, *History of the United States Navy*,
3 vols. (rev. ed., 1898–1901); Maclay, *History of American Privateers* (1899);
Spears, *History of Our Navy*, 5 vols. (1897–1898), a popular narrative.

For Independent Reading

Morse, J. T., *Life of John Adams* (1885); Maclay, *History of American Privateers* (1899); Weld, *Travels through the States of North America and Canada*, 2 vols.
(1799), very popular when published; and Dwight, *Travels in New England and
New York*, 4 vols. (1821–1822), an excellent book.

CHAPTER XIV

INTERNAL HISTORY AND FOREIGN AFFAIRS UNDER JEFFERSON AND MADISON

Republican Reforms

From the beginning of his administration Jefferson rejected the ceremonials which his party had denounced, and which the federalists defended on the ground that they created respect for the government. The carriage of state with six horses was discarded, and he rode horseback and unattended through the streets of the capital, like any other well-mounted citizen. The formal weekly receptions became levees to which any citizens who chose might come unannounced. The annual speeches to congress, which reminded the republicans too pointedly of the king's speech to parliament, became written annual messages, reports of the executive on the state of the nation. Federalists ridiculed these changes, but the people were pleased. *Democratic Simplicity.*

The inauguration was equally simple. Jefferson came to Washington as a private citizen, lodged at a tavern, and just before noon on March 4 walked up Capitol Hill, accompanied by a group of friends, to take the oath of office administered by John Marshall, a strong and determined federalist, whom *The In-auguration.* Adams a few weeks earlier had appointed chief justice. His inaugural address has long been considered a great state paper. Good citizens, he said in effect, must recognize the right of the majority to rule, but the majority must not oppress the minority. It was time to lay aside the bitterness of controversy and to remember that political intolerance was as bad as religious intolerance. Differences of opinion are natural, but federalists and republicans are alike Americans and should unite to preserve the union and representative government. He pleaded in noble language for peace, *Conciliation.* coöperation in developing the resources of a great country, and patriotism and good will in realizing the blessings of liberty. These words were calculated to pacify the fears that the republicans would overthrow the foundations of society, so sedulously aroused by the federalists in the late campaign. It was Jefferson's dearest wish to conciliate his enemies, especially those in the North, who had been led to believe him an atheist and something of an anarchist.

He announced his principles in terms his followers never forgot. He wished to see, he said, "a wise and frugal government, which shall restrain men from injuring one another, shall leave them otherwise free to regulate their own pursuits of industry and improvement, and shall not take from the mouth of labor the bread it has earned." He enumerated many means of achieving these ends, among them "equal and exact justice to all men," "honest friendship with all nations, entangling alliance with none," the preservation of the rights of the states as the best guardians of domestic concerns, the support of the union "in its whole constitutional vigor," "the supremacy of the civil over the military authority," the rights of popular election as the only arbiter short of revolution, the sufficiency of a well-established militia, payment of the national debt, and economy in public expenditures. So deeply did these principles sink into the minds of the people at large that no later party or candidate has dared to repudiate them.

Political Principles.

The new cabinet was wisely chosen. Madison became secretary of state, Albert Gallatin, the best financier in the party, became secretary of the treasury, General Dearborn, of Massachusetts, was secretary of war, Levi Lincoln, of the same state, attorney-general, and Robert Smith, of Maryland, secretary of the navy. The postmaster-general, Gideon Granger, of Connecticut, was not then in the cabinet, but the post was important because of the many subordinates. Assigning three of these places to New England shows how much it was desired to conciliate the people of that section. Dearborn and Smith were not strong men, but Jefferson did not propose to make much use of army or navy.

The Cabinet.

In their day of power the federalists were very bitter toward the republicans. They called them "the rabble," filled the offices with their own partisans, appointed only their friends to the federal judgeships, and in February, 1801, created a number of new courts, spending their last moments of power in filling them with their own followers. Their opponents were naturally exasperated, and came into office eager for spoils. Jefferson wisely withstood the demand; for he saw that the thing for his party to do was to dispel the charge that it would overthrow the established order. He refused to remove officials unless it was shown that they were guilty of misconduct or of partisanship. He was thus able to prevent wholesale removals, which disappointed some of his hungry supporters. He refused to deliver commissions for the "midnight appointments," that is, the court officials under the act of February, 1801, which Adams had signed but left undelivered in the executive offices. At his suggestion congress repealed this act in 1802. On the other hand, Jefferson appointed his own followers, saying when as many republicans were in office as federalists he would continue the parity.

Appointments to Office.

Next, he turned to the national debt, which under the federalists had grown from $77,500,000 to $80,000,000. Jefferson was pledged to reduce it and gave Gallatin a free hand. That careful financier examined his resources and concluded that the **Gallatin's Financial Policy.** debt could be paid in sixteen years. The revenue then yielded $10,600,000 a year, of which $4,500,000 went for interest, $5,500,000 for army and navy, and the rest for general expenses. Gallatin proposed to pay $7,300,000 a year for interest and to curtail the debt, and as the ordinary expenses could not well be lessened he would effect most of the saving by reducing the army and navy. At the outset he encountered a difficulty in the loss of $650,000 of the revenue, because the republicans were pledged to abolish internal revenue duties. Thus it happened that he had but $2,650,000 for the support of army, navy, and the civil establishment. This sum he divided with the greatest care. To the army he allowed $930,000, to the navy $670,000, which left $1,050,000 for ordinary expenses. This made it necessary to reduce the army to a mere handful and to tie up in the dockyards most of the ships of the navy. Jefferson was pleased. He did not like a standing army, and considered a navy a useless toy which, as he said, might well be assembled in the eastern branch of the Potomac, where **Jefferson and the Navy.** the ships "would require but one set of plunderers to take care of them." Many congressmen winced under Gallatin's economy; but he was inexorable, Jefferson supported him, and the plan was adopted.

The result justified Gallatin's hopes. At the end of a year the revenue was nearly $3,000,000 more than he had expected, which gave him a comfortable surplus. In 1803 we purchased Louisiana, paying $11,250,000 in bonds and $4,000,000 for claims **Gallatin's Achievement.** (see page 299). Gallatin announced that he could pay the latter out of the surplus and that the new bonds would postpone the payment of the debt only eighteen months. In 1804 congress ordered the construction of a frigate to replace the *Philadelphia*, lost at Tripoli (see page 296), and all eyes turned to Gallatin for the money. He would not take from the funds set aside for the debt, and congress had to lay a special duty, the "Mediterranean Fund." In 1805 the revenues rose to $14,000,000, and in 1806 to $14,500,000, yielding a surplus of $6,000,000. Many congressmen thought the time for economy was now past, but Gallatin and Jefferson urged patience, promising if the policy of economy were followed for two years longer there would be an ample reserve and at least $5,000,000 for such uses as congress might deem fit. 1807 was another fat year, and the surplus was now $7,600,000, and the debt, including the bonds paid for Louisiana, had been reduced from $92,000,000 to $69,500,000. In 1808 the embargo was in force, revenues fell off, and this splendid progress was halted.

Gallatin's financial policy pleased the mass of thrifty people. It was that of the careful husbandman, who, finding himself overwhelmed with debt, sets aside from his annual income a sum neces-

Gallatin and Hamilton Contrasted.

sary to liquidate his obligations within a reasonable time and rigidly reduces expenditures accordingly. It looked to the ultimate extinction of the debt, on the principle that freedom from debt is as good for a nation as for an individual. In contrast with it was the policy of Hamilton, who thought little of paying the debt and much of making the nation strong enough to weather financial storms. He would have a navy to protect commerce, which would increase the revenues, manufactures to build up the industrial efficiency of the country, and a strong capitalist class to promote the development of the nation's resources. He looked farther into the future than Gallatin, but he did not appreciate so well the desires of the average citizen.

Jefferson's first term saw a remarkable and probably an unexpected development of the power of the federal courts. Asserting the right to interpret the constitution, they began to declare null

The Republicans and the Judiciary.

laws both of congress and the state legislatures (see page 357). As the judges were federalists, it seemed that the opposition, ensconced in this seat of power, were defeating the will of the people expressed in the elections. The case seemed more difficult, because the constitution afforded no other way of removing a judge than impeachment, which must be for "treason, bribery, or other high crimes and misdemeanors." But if the senate, as a court of impeachment, chose to consider partisanship in a judge a misdemeanor, no power could gainsay them. So clear was this that the republicans determined to proceed, believing that if they established the principle that the senate could remove the judges, future partisanship in that quarter would be avoided.

The first case was that of Pickering, judge of a district court in New Hampshire, a man whose inebriety had led to insanity. He was impeached and removed from office in 1803, and the people approved, although it seemed singular that insanity was pronounced a misdemeanor by the highest court in the land. Then the republicans turned to Judge Samuel Chase, of the supreme court. He was a violent partisan, as his conduct in the cases under the alien and sedition laws in 1800 showed. He expressed his views openly, and in 1803 declared to a federal grand jury in Baltimore that the republicans threatened the country with mob rule. At this the house impeached him, and the senate sat as a tribunal. John Randolph, an able but erratic Virginian, was chief prosecutor on behalf of the house. He included so many charges besides partisanship that opinion rallied to Chase and the impeachment failed. It was believed that a contrary verdict would have been followed by the impeachment of Marshall. As it was, the republican attack on the courts was checked, and the chief justice remained in a position to exert a powerful influence upon the development of constitutional law.

THE WAR WITH TRIPOLI

For many years Morocco, Algiers, Tunis, and Tripoli laid tribute on trade in the Mediterranean, and the powers of Europe acquiesced. After the revolution our ships began, also, to be seized, and we were forced to buy treaties with handsome presents of arms and money. First and last we paid enough money in this way to build several excellent ships, but for all that the freebooters were not satisfied. In 1801 the pacha of Tripoli cut down the flagstaff of our consulate as a declaration of war, because Tunis received richer presents than Tripoli; and about the same time Algiers showed symptoms of ill will. Jefferson desired peace, because, like Washington in 1795, he felt we were not strong enough to make war on a great power. But this policy did not apply to Tripoli, and early in 1801 he sent Captain Dale with four ships, the *President*, *Philadelphia*, and *Essex*, frigates, and the *Enterprise*, a sloop of war, to teach the Barbary States to respect us.

Dale could not attempt land operations, and when the Tripolitans collected an army and drew their navy up under the guns of their fortifications, he could only establish a blockade and cruise along the coast. Fortune, however, threw in his way an enemy's cruiser, which was quickly taken. Because congress had not declared war, Jefferson had not authorized captures, and the conquered ship, disarmed and dismantled, was allowed to escape to Tripoli, where her crew told such stories of American ferocity that the pacha's soldiers were filled with a respectful terror. In 1802 a second squadron went to the Mediterranean, but did nothing effective. These meager results disappointed the people at home, and the commander, Captain Morris, was dismissed the service. In 1803 a third commander of squadron went out, Captain Preble. With the aid of some small boats borrowed from the king of Sicily, who was also at war with the pacha, he conducted a bombardment of the city of Tripoli, but inflicted little damage. Preble remained in the Mediterranean during the winter, and showed a determination to isolate the enemy completely. In the spring of 1804 he received important coöperation from William Eaton, an eccentric but patriotic American in Egypt, who, without authority from his government, sought Hamet, dispossessed elder brother of the pacha, and set out from Egypt to capture the government of Tripoli by land. The pacha was a usurper and yielded rather than endanger tranquillity at home, although the army of Eaton and Hamet was only 500 men. In 1805, when the eastern half of his kingdom had been won over, he concluded a treaty, retaining his throne, but

Origin of the War.

Naval Operations.

End of the War.

agreeing to remain at peace with the United States in the future without tribute, and to surrender all Americans held in his country. Nothing was done in behalf of Hamet, who was now forced to retire from the positions he had won, but the next year we allowed him a life pension of $200 a month.

The war with Tripoli had a wholesome effect on the other Barbary States, and they were content to remain at peace without further

Results of the War. presents. It also gave the navy exercise in a theater of actual war, and brought it added prestige at home and abroad. It contained incidents of heroism which fired the American imagination. Two of them especially were long remembered. While Preble held Tripoli closely invested from the sea he

Death of Somers. sent Lieutenant Somers among the enemy's ships in the ketch *Intrepid*, loaded with bombs and powder, to explode it in their midst and escape if possible. The American ships waited at a distance for the return of the brave crew. After a time they saw the ketch blow up when in contact with the Tripolitans, but neither Somers nor his men came back. Their fate was not known, but it was believed that he leaped into the magazine with a lighted torch, devoting himself to death to accomplish the object for which he was sent out.

The other adventure was more successful. The *Philadelphia*, pursuing the enemy too eagerly, went aground at the mouth of the harbor of Tripoli, and Bainbridge and his crew were taken.

The Philadelphia. Shortly afterwards the ship was floated by the enemy and taken under the protection of their guns, where she frowned unpleasantly at the Americans in the offing. Stephen Decatur, commanding a ketch, sailed boldly into the harbor, boarded the *Philadelphia*, filled her with combustibles, set her on fire, and escaped in his ketch through a shower of badly aimed shots from land batteries and the ships in the harbor. He was a cool and capable officer, and was promoted for his conduct. In 1815 he returned to the Mediterranean with a formidable squadron and dictated favorable treaties with the Barbary States at the mouth of the cannon.

THE PURCHASE OF LOUISIANA

In 1800 most Americans believed that the settlement of the eastern half of the Mississippi basin would inevitably be followed by the

The Importance of Louisiana. acquisition of the western half. Acute alarm was occasioned in Washington's administration when it was thought England was about to get a foothold in this region; for while no one feared Spain's control of the region in question, England's ownership was another matter. Fortunately, the danger soon passed, but apprehension was again aroused when in the spring of 1801 it began to be reported that Spain had transferred Louisiana to the powerful and aggressive Napoleon, who intended to build up a vast colonial power in its borders. The rumor soon became a certainty, but as months passed and the province remained in the hands of Spain the public mind remained calm. Late in 1802 it was violently agitated when news came that the Spanish governor in New Orleans had withdrawn the right of deposit granted in the treaty of 1795. The public construed this as a change of policy in anticipation of the new régime in Louisiana, and the West was for seizing the mouth of the river before it was too late. Jefferson wisely thought the action of the governor unauthorized, and restrained the popular wrath while he negotiated. **Right of Deposit.** Five months later he was informed by the Spanish minister that the right of deposit would be restored, and this removed the question from the range of possible war and left it freely in the field of diplomacy.

It was the president's plan to impress France with our seriousness in the matter, and to that end he used the strongest language. Let France know, he said, that the nation which held the mouth of the Mississippi was our enemy, and if Napoleon persisted in his purpose we should "marry ourselves to the **Jefferson's Diplomacy.** British fleet and nation," so that England and the United States, coöperating for supremacy at sea, would hold at their mercy the revived French colonial establishment. He let the British minister see what he meant, and at a dinner paid him such marked attention that the French minister made it a subject of comment in his letter to Talleyrand. Generally speaking, Jefferson was pacific, not because of cowardice, as his enemies thought, but because he abhorred war and thought it was usually undertaken through unreasonable impulse. His vigorous attitude toward France shows how positive he could be when he considered a vital issue at stake. Meanwhile, Livingston, our minister in Paris, was instructed to sound Napoleon in regard to the purchase of the Isle of Orleans and West Florida. It is not probable that Jefferson thought the proposition would succeed, but it offered a point of departure in the negotiation.

Unknown to him, events in Paris were shaping themselves more favorably than he dared hope; and to understand them we must go back to the treaty of San Ildefonso, October 1, 1800. By that agreement Napoleon induced Spain to transfer **Treaty of San Ilde-** Louisiana to him in exchange for the Grand Duchy of **fonso.** Tuscany, which, elevated to the kingdom of Etruria, was to be given to the Duke of Parma, son-in-law of the king of Spain, when a general peace was made in Europe. Napoleon promised not to sell the territory thus acquired to any nation but Spain, and it was agreed that later negotiations should be entered into for the cession of West Florida. The treaty was kept secret for the time being, but its essential features were soon known. This vast acquisition of land was to be the basis of a revived colonial empire, which the rising Napoleon thought would increase his popularity with the glory-loving French people.

Before that scheme could be realized the island of Santo Domingo must be conquered.   Here Toussaint L'Ouverture, at the head of an

Toussaint L'Ouverture. army of blacks, was fighting to maintain the power he had founded.   Every step he took in the progress of military despotism seemed but a shadow of the course of a greater despot in France.   The world took notice and smiled, whereat Napoleon, deeply irritated, felt the greater need of suppressing the man who made him ridiculous while he defied French authority.   In February, 1801, Napoleon made the treaty of Lunéville and was at peace with the continent.   England continued the war with little heart, and brought it to an end a year later in the treaty of Amiens. This period of victory offered the triumphant First Consul the opportunity to bring Santo Domingo back to obedience.

January, 1802, arrived in Santo Domingo Leclerc, one of the best French generals, with an army of 10,000, and the war of reconquest

Toussaint Defeated. began.   Toussaint wished to use guerilla methods, but his officers overruled him.   After three months of struggle they began to yield to the blandishments of Leclerc, thinking that it booted little to suffer further in behalf of the black emperor. At last Toussaint himself ventured to surrender, being assured of personal safety.   After six weeks of fancied security he was arrested, sent to France according to the orders of Napoleon, and in less than a year died in a fortress in the Jura Mountains.   Then Napoleon sent an order to restore slavery, his intention from the beginning.   But for that, he might have ruled the island and proceeded with his colonial plans in Louisiana.   As it was, the negro laborers rose to a man.   Toussaint's officers were true to Leclerc, but all the efforts of the combined

French Defeated. white and black forces did not check the onslaughts of the maddened laborers who saw slavery restored in the neighboring island of Guadeloupe.   Then yellow fever appeared. In three months 24,000 men, soldiers and sailors, had died, and Leclerc demanded 17,000 more, with a vast sum of money, before the work of subjugation was done.   He announced that this could only be done by killing over half the lower classes, male and female, above twelve years of age; and he thought that peace once restored, annual revolts might be looked for in the future.   Before such a stupendous undertaking even Napoleon's resolution quailed, and it was decided to abandon the island.

Louisiana Purchased. Louisiana was now useless to Napoleon, and although he had assured Spain he would not sell it, he looked around for a buyer.   April 10, 1803, he told Marbois, head of the treasury, to see if the United States would entertain an offer to buy.   The shrewd Talleyrand, scenting an opportunity for profit, anticipated Marbois, and the following day opened the matter with Livingston, our minister. The two were discussing the purchase of the Isle of Orleans when Talleyrand said, "What would you give for all Louisiana?" The suggestion was unexpected, but Livingston concealed his eagerness, and said that as he expected a special envoy from the United States in two days, he wished the matter to be deferred that long. The envoy was Monroe, whom Jefferson had sent to try to purchase the Isle of Orleans and West Florida. On the thirteenth Marbois and Livingston talked until midnight about the affair, the former inquiring if we would pay 60,000,000 francs in cash and also assume claims of Americans against France worth 20,000,000 francs. Livingston said this was too much, but he felt inwardly that it was a good bargain, and after some haggling the purchase was made on that basis. The treaty was signed on May 2, although it was antedated to April 30. It increased the national domain by 140 per cent.

The transaction pleased Jefferson, but also alarmed him. A strict constructionist, he could find no authority in the constitution for purchasing foreign territory, and he began to prepare an amendment granting congress the right. He seems to **The Treaty Ratified.** have forgotten this when he proposed to buy the Isle of Orleans. An intimation from Paris that Napoleon might change his mind before an amendment could be adopted caused the president to abandon his plan, and the treaty was duly ratified October 21, 1803. December 20, to the gratification of every American in the Mississippi valley, the stars and stripes was hoisted over New Orleans.

Now arose the question of boundaries. According to the treaty we received "the colony or province of Louisiana, with the same extent that it now has in the hands of Spain, and that it had when France possessed it, and such as it should be after the **Louisiana's** treaties subsequently entered into between Spain and **Boundaries.** other states." The words were from the treaty of 1800. Livingston asked Talleyrand what they meant. "I do not know," was the reply, "you must take it as we received it." "But what did you mean to take?" said Livingston, to which the astute Frenchman again said, "I do not know," adding, "You have made a noble bargain for yourselves, and I suppose you will make the most of it." At that time Talleyrand had in his cabinet a copy of the instructions designed for Victor, who was to have been the first French governor of Louisiana, informing him that the boundary on the west was the Rio Grande, and on the east the river Iberville, *i.e.* the eastern border of the Isle of Orleans. This was quite definite, but it was unknown to Jefferson for some time, and meanwhile he adopted a theory worthy of Talleyrand himself.

Before 1762 Louisiana extended to the Perdido, including Mobile, which as the outlet of a river system reaching from Georgia to Mississippi was greatly desired by the United States. Jefferson saw in the

words of the treaty, "that it had when France possessed it," an opportunity to claim this part of what he must have known was undoubtedly West Florida, *i.e.* Spanish territory, and, in
Talleyrand's words, he "made the most of it." He communicated his opinion to congress, which accepted it, and
passed, February, 1804, the Mobile act, erecting the region
in question into a customs district and annexing it to Mississippi territory. Lest this lead to war with Spain, Jefferson tactfully located
the customs house for the new district north of the Florida line. His
plan was to hold the dispute in abeyance until Spain was in a war,
and then seize the desired district. The Southwest, to whom the
Coosa-Alabama line of river communication was of the utmost importance, approved his plan, and thought nothing of the points of national
honor involved. But Jefferson did not trust entirely to the prospect
of war. He would use it, if possible, as a means of forcing Spain to
withdraw, and to that end he hoped to enlist the efforts of Napoleon,
whose influence in Madrid was all but supreme. The French emperor
understood this game and skillfully turned it against the American
president by holding out West Florida when he wished the good will
of Jefferson, and by withdrawing it when his temporary purpose was
accomplished.

How Jefferson Settled It.

DISSENSION IN THE REPUBLICAN PARTY

By the beginning of 1804 Jefferson's popularity was well established.
None of the calamities prophesied by the federalists had followed
his election. On the contrary, the debt was being paid
through Gallatin's wise economy, Louisiana had been
acquired, party rancor was dying, business was prosperous,
and the president manifested a desire to conciliate all sections and
interests. It was also evident that Jefferson directed his party with a
strong hand. He early recognized Burr as a disturbing element and
proceeded to crush him. The character of the New Yorker would
have justified this, to say nothing of his intrigue for the presidency in
1801. Burr was attacked through the New York patronage, which
was sedulously given to Clinton, his bitter enemy. The
vice-president was the least submissive of men, and now
began to lean toward the federalists, and this only increased
the difference between him and his party. Finally, he
fell into the net of Pickering and the extreme New England federalists.
They were so bitter against Jefferson that they planned to carry their
section out of the union before his insidious conciliation should warp
it out of their hands. It was an erratic scheme, and probably would
have been rejected by the people, but the schemers decided to make
the attempt if New York, the great commercial state of the North,
could be induced to join them. To that end they approached Hamil-

Jefferson a Success.

His Attitude toward Burr.

ton, who rejected their proposals. Then they turned to Burr, who was complaisant. They got him accepted as federalist candidate for governor in the spring of 1804, thinking that his own friends and the federalists would elect him. But now **Burr Over-whelmed.** Hamilton exerted himself, and defeated Burr at the polls by disclosing the object for which he had been nominated. This angered the discredited man, and the result was the duel on July 11, 1804, in which Hamilton was killed and Burr's political influence blasted. Jefferson in national affairs and Clinton in state affairs reaped the fruits of that foolish crime.

A more serious party disturbance came through the opposition of John Randolph, a vehement and caustic speaker against whom few members of congress could stand in debate. As chairman of the ways and means committee in the house he was a **John Randolph.** chief exponent of the administration policy. His lofty manner offended many republicans, particularly the men from the North, for whom he openly expressed contempt. His ideas were not always practical, and Jefferson in a quiet way began to oppose the most impossible of them. Randolph then struck back, the occasion being the Yazoo claims, whose origin goes back to Washington's administration.

After the revolution Georgia claimed the lands to the Mississippi by a title formally as good as that by which the other states claimed their Western lands. She also held that the region involved in the secret clause of the treaty of 1782 should come to her **The Yazoo Companies.** because it was originally a part of her domain. The United States might well dispute the latter claim, but left it in abeyance, hoping that all the region would soon be transferred to the federal government. But Georgia wished to realize on the lands, and by several grants sold them to great land companies, known as Yazoo companies. The last of these grants, including the others, was made in 1795 at about a cent and a half an acre. The sale was made by a corrupt legislature, and the next legislature declared it null. Now resulted a pretty piece of confusion, in which the Yazoo lands were claimed by Georgia, the United States, since most of them were in the disputed region, and the grantees, who held that a state could not annul a grant for the corruption of its own agents. Georgia was defiant, and as President Adams did not wish to coerce a state, a compromise was arranged by which Georgia relinquished the lands to the federal government, which undertook to erect them into Mississippi Territory, and to pay damages to Georgia and the companies. Commissions were appointed for the latter **Compromise Proposed.** purpose, and reported among other things that the United States should pay Georgia $1,250,000, and the grantees the proceeds of the sale of 5,000,000 acres of land. In 1803 a bill was before congress to put this compromise into effect.

It was at this point that Randolph opened his attack on the administration. He disliked Madison greatly, thinking him a trimmer. Most of the Yazoo stock was owned by speculators living in the North, and the representatives in congress, from that section, republican and federalist, were anxious to pass the bill. Jefferson favored it, probably because he wished to build up his party in the North. All this aroused the suspicion of Randolph. He made no objection to reimbursing Georgia for her claim, but he denounced the project to pay the companies. His scathing words defeated the bill at that time, but it came up again in 1805, when the speculators employed Granger, postmaster-general, to lobby for the measure. This angered the sharp-tongued Randolph, whose bitter strictures were now thrust at the administration which harbored the lobbyist. The republicans were divided into Yazoo and Anti-Yazoo men, the latter being chiefly Southerners. They were nearly equally divided, and Randolph was able to defeat the bill at this time. Although taken up again from time to time, it was not passed. In 1810, in the case of Fletcher *vs.* Peck, the supreme court held that the Georgia grant of 1795 was a contract, and that the legislature of 1796 could not annul it, and this strengthened the cause of the Yazoo men. In 1814, when Randolph was no longer a member of congress, it was voted to give the company $8,000,000 in settlement of the claims, and with this the matter came to an end.

Randolph and the Yazoo Compromise.

End of the Controversy.

At first Jefferson kept himself clear of the dispute, and he was too strong to be openly attacked. In 1804 he was reëlected president by 162 to 14 electoral votes, getting all the votes of New England but Connecticut's. For the support of New York, Clinton received the vice-presidency. Jefferson, at the height of his glory, announced in 1805 that he would not be a candidate for another term, and it was generally thought he would make Madison his successor. Randolph and his friends began to make plans to support Monroe, who had acted with them. While the breach in the party was thus widened, Jefferson brought before congress a scheme to acquire Florida, which gave Randolph another opportunity to show hostility to the president.

Jefferson Reëlected.

While Jefferson deferred occupation of West Florida to a more favorable time, he renewed diplomatic efforts to get Spain to yield what we wished; but to his overtures the king returned a haughty refusal. In 1805 Talleyrand entered into the affair, communicating an informal suggestion that we trust Napoleon to conduct negotiations for the purchase of all Florida for $7,000,000. He meant that the money sent to Madrid should find its way into the French treasury to pay subsidies which Napoleon exacted from prostrate Spain. The suggestion pleased Jefferson, although he hoped to get the Floridas for

Jefferson's Hope for Acquiring Florida.

less than the price named, and December 5, 1805, he sent a secret message to congress asking for authority to offer $2,000,000. Randolph, chairman of the ways and means committee, was the man to move a grant; but he was obdurate. His influence with the committee was great, and he induced them to report in favor of measures of defense, saying he would never vote a penny to buy territory which we justly owned. The house overrode him, voting after a long debate, 72 to 58, that the money be placed at the president's disposal. But so much time was consumed in discussion that the opportunity was lost. When the suggestion was made, Napoleon needed money. Within four months he won the victories of Ulm and Austerlitz and dictated the treaty of Pressburg, and his coffers were overflowing. He accordingly refused to bring pressure to bear on Spain.

From that time, 1806, Randolph was in open opposition. Now came an unexpected development. His followers would support him when he appeared as a mere critic of one of the administration measures, but when he was an acknowledged insurgent they began to fall away, fearing the power and popularity of Jefferson. **Randolph Shorn of his Strength.** Of the ablest and truest were Nicholson, of Maryland, Macon, of North Carolina, the speaker, and Monroe. Jefferson sought to detach them from their leader, and succeeded with the first by appointing him a federal judge. The second remained unmoved, but the congress elected in 1806 was against Randolph, and Macon was not reëlected speaker. His defeat insured a new chairman of the ways and means committee. Monroe acted with Randolph until the election of 1808 elevated Madison, Jefferson's choice, to the president's chair. In 1809 an arrangement was made, through Jefferson's aid, to make Monroe secretary of state under Madison, an agreement consummated in 1811. Randolph, shorn of his strength, continued to annoy Jefferson. In the house none dared encounter his withering scorn, and he had his way in debate. The president wisely ignored the attacks, although he probably winced in secret under them. The retirement of the annoyer in 1813 to make place for Jefferson's son-in-law, Eppes, only interrupted Randolph's career. He was reëlected in 1814, and with a short interruption served in congress until 1829, an able but eccentric free lance and sometimes a nuisance.

The Schemes of Aaron Burr

When Burr saw his career ended in the East he turned to the West. Had he settled in New Orleans, or some other city in which a duelist was not unpopular, he might have risen to professional and political prominence. But his ambition looked to larger things, and he wished to found a state of his own in the West. **Burr Turns to the West.** For such an adventure he had genius in leadership, but he lacked men and money.   The first he hoped to get in the West and the latter from either England or Spain.

Historians are not agreed on the nature of his plans.   He was indicted for treason in that he attempted to wrench Louisiana from the union and set it up as an independent state.   Most of his contemporaries believed him guilty as charged, and some living historians accept the same view.   According to them he was to collect 1000 men on the Ohio, reach Louisiana about the time the territorial legislature declared the province independent, and with the connivance of General Wilkinson, commanding the union forces there, establish his supremacy.   It is known that he tried to get money for this purpose from the English minister and failed, and that he then tried to get it from Spain, where he also failed.   He promised England to place his new state under English protection, thus opening a vast field for British commerce. He told Spain that his state would present a useful barrier between the United States and Mexico, then in Spanish hands.   It is also known that he was in close conference with Wilkinson, who was capable of any treachery.

Was Burr's Object Louisiana?

The other contention is that his real purpose was to conduct, in coöperation with a band of New Orleans adventureres, a filibustering expedition against Vera Cruz and Mexico City.   He did, unquestionably, tell some of his followers this was his object, and he had maps and other information about Mexico which seemed to substantiate his words.   He revealed this plan to some of the most influential leaders of the West, Andrew Jackson among others, and won their approval; for Spain was much hated in this quarter. To the plainer people of the West he spoke of a colony on the Red river, where he had acquired a large land grant, but this was admittedly a subterfuge.   The real controversy is as to whether his conspiracy was aimed at Louisiana or Mexico.[1]   If it was at the former, Burr lied when he spoke of the latter; if at the latter, he lied when he spoke of the former.   Probably we shall never know in what respect he told the truth.   Wilkinson testified that the conspiracy was against Louisiana; but Wilkinson's word is not ordinarily to be taken.   He was a pensioner of Spain, and was concerned in most of the plans to separate the Mississippi valley from the United States. Wilkinson shared whatever guilt Burr incurred, and he was talking to clear himself; but this was true of some of those who testified that Mexico was the objective.   It must be remembered, also, that it is possible that Burr meant to do both of the things alleged.   It was quite within the power of his audacious imagination to hope to secure Louisiana first and then operate against Vera Cruz.

Or Mexico?

[1] For the view that Louisiana was Burr's objective the best authority is Henry Adams, *History of the United States*, III, chs. 10–14.   For the other view see McCaleb, *The Aaron Burr Conspiracy*.

Be this as it may, Burr gave himself earnestly to his scheme, going hither and thither in the West, collecting boats, supplies, and men at Blennerhassett Island, near Parkersburg, West Virginia. November 15, 1806, was the date set for their departure. **The Scheme Fails.** Rumor was rife all through the West that he would attack New Orleans, and in October, he was indicted for treason in Kentucky. As no positive evidence could be adduced he was acquitted, and continued his preparations. But the indictment checked volunteering, and he could not set out on the appointed day. It was an untoward event; for at New Orleans the situation favored success, if Burr had designs there. The legislature was about to meet, and Wilkinson had taken his army to the Texan frontier, leaving the city unprotected. If the adventurer had appeared with 1000 men, as he promised, the city would have been at his mercy. But the men were wanting, and Wilkinson, able to take care of himself in an emergency, decided to desert a failing cause. He informed Jefferson of a conspiracy to seize Louisiana, but concealed his connection with it. He hastened to the city and noisily gave orders to make the place safe against assault. The president, meanwhile, received Wilkinson's letter. He had heard rumors against Burr before that, but took no action, lest friends of the accused charge him with persecuting a political rival. But now the charges were definite, and he sent a proclamation through the West for the arrest of all conspirators. Burr's friends warned him that it was coming, and hastily gathering all his resources, sixty men and thirteen flatboats, he set off for New Orleans in the last days of the year. He still counted on Wilkinson, but when he learned at Natchez how vain was this reliance he abandoned his followers to their fate, and, disguised, sought to escape through the **Arrest of Burr.** forest to West Florida. At Fort Stoddert, when nearly across the boundary, he was recognized, arrested, and sent to Richmond, Virginia, for trial.

The case aroused wide interest. Chief Justice Marshall presided at the hearing and John Randolph was foreman of the grand jury which presented Burr for trial. Both men were bitter **Burr's Trial.** enemies of Jefferson, and seemed to wish Burr's acquittal. By the constitution, treason is levying war against the government, or giving aid and comfort to the enemy, and two witnesses to the same overt act are necessary for conviction. Marshall ruled that a man must be present when the overt act was committed in order to be guilty of treason within the meaning of the constitution. As Burr was in Kentucky when his followers assembled on the Ohio river, he was not guilty as charged, although it was well known that he planned the whole movement. The ruling was fatal to the prosecution, and Burr was acquitted. Luther Martin, leading lawyer for Burr and long an enemy of Jefferson, outdid himself in making it uncomfortable for the president. One expedient was to summon Jefferson to testify

x

and to bring certain papers with him.   The summons was disregarded on the ground that the president was not to be at the command of the federal courts.   Marshall was a bold judge struggling

Clash between the Executive and the Judiciary.

to establish the independent power of the judiciary, and in this notable case, in which the executive appeared as prosecutor, he went as far as he dared go in his attempt to make the president do the will of the court.   In refusing this subpœna, Jefferson, as Adams in the case of Dr. Cooper, 1800, and other presidents at later times, laid out the line beyond which the court was not to go.

RELATIONS BETWEEN ENGLAND AND THE UNITED STATES

When Burr took up his Western schemes, England and Napoleon were joined in the final struggle to determine the destiny of Europe.

America and the Carrying Trade.

Each striving to cripple the resources of the other came at length to attempts to restrain the trade of neutrals.   As Napoleon after 1806 was dominant on the continent from the Adriatic to the Baltic, the only important neutral was the United States, whose citizens for a time reaped large profits from the sale of American products and by carrying freights between European ports.   American ships were rapidly built, and foreign ships were transferred to American registry, to the discomfiture of British owners, whose own profits were lessened by the high insurance they must pay in the dangerous days of French licensed privateers.   The mobile sailor population of the world was also drawn into the American service, so that not only the British merchant marine but the British naval ships also suffered for lack

Trade Restrictions and Impressments.

of service.   Out of this situation grew regulations to impede the American neutral trade, and a greater activity in impressing sailors on American ships.   The weakness of the American navy, under Jefferson's pacific policy, invited these discriminations.

Impressment rested on inalienable citizenship, held at the time by all the nations of Europe.   America, as a new country, held for transferable citizenship, and the naturalization laws of

Grounds of Impressment.

the United States were framed on that basis.   But in actual practice neither party to the controversy confined itself strictly to the principle at stake.   Sailors on British ships frequently deserted in American ports, took out naturalization papers, and shipped on American vessels without much concealment and with open approval of the American population.   Such duplicity was not to be endured by the mistress of the sea.   British ships-of-war retaliated by boarding American vessels, mustering the crews on deck, and taking off all whom they chose to declare British subjects.   Sometimes they took men who were undoubtedly American born.   Sometimes, also, the men they took had forged papers certifying to American birth. Between these difficulties the ways of Presidents Jefferson and Madison were hard. Impressment was practiced under the federalist presidents, and much negotiation occurred to remedy it, but no results were reached. It recurred with increased energy under Jefferson. Each instance of this wrong announced in the American papers aroused the popular wrath and prepared the way to the war of 1812. When finally the British ships cruised off the American harbors searching all vessels that came out or went in, it was hard for the president to restrain the people from acts which must have led to hostilities.

Less irritating, perhaps, but of greater real hardship, was the increasing number of seizures of ships charged with violating British rules of war. Of these regulations the most noted was the Rule of War of 1756, declaring that a trade not open in peace could not lawfully be opened in time of war. *Case of the Polly.*
The dispute, as we have seen, came up in Washington's administration, but it was not settled. American skippers found a way around it by taking cargoes from the West Indies to their home ports, where the goods became American, and if reëxported to Europe as such were not, as they held, liable to seizure. It was a nice point, but the British courts allowed it, the rule being laid down in the famous case of the *Polly*, 1800, that such goods became American goods and were not liable to capture if they were landed on American docks and paid American duties. For some time after the European war reopened, 1803, this rule favored the Americans. So profitable was the trade that the expense of landing and paying duties was comparatively insignificant. Then came the complaint of British shippers that the Yankees used this as a subterfuge to engross all the trade of the French and Spanish possessions in America. The British government opened certain ports in their American colonies to the goods of enemy nations, with the hope that the trade drawn thither would go thence to England in British ships; but even this did *Case of the Essex.* not break up the objectionable Yankee practice. Then came the decision of the British court in the case of the *Essex*, 1805, in which it was held that a neutral ship pleading the right accorded in the decision of the case of the *Polly* must prove that in landing her cargo in a neutral port it was the intention of the owners to make the cargo neutral goods and not merely to evade the rule of 1756. As this intention must be shown to the satisfaction of the British courts, proving it was difficult. Under the new rule, many ships were seized, and complaints were loud in America. In England the merchants applauded because insurance rates were now raised for their Yankee rivals, and the navy was pleased because officers shared in the prizes seized.

In 1806 died William Pitt, head of the ministry under which this severe policy was conducted. The changes which followed brought

Charles James Fox, long a friend of America, into the foreign office. He assured Monroe, our minister, that he would endeavor to
have the recent restrictions modified, but warned him not
to expect payment for the 500 prizes already taken. Even
this concession was difficult to obtain; for the cabinet
as a whole dared not antagonize the merchants and navy by openly
modifying their rules. Then Fox resorted to a subterfuge, known
as "Fox's Blockade," May 16, 1806. A proclamation declared
blockaded the coast of Europe from Brest to the Elbe, but the naval
officers were instructed to enforce it only from the Seine to Ostend.
Neutral ships, therefore, bound for posts between Brest and the Seine,
and between Ostend and the Elbe, were allowed to go undisturbed,
spite of the rules formerly enforced. It was a clumsy way of doing us
a favor, but it left us the Netherlands with the Rhine valley and the
northwest corner of France; and it might have served until the end
of the war had France acquiesced.

*Fox's Block-
ade, 1806.*

But Napoleon scorned to get his foreign supplies through the connivance of his enemy. Feigning to believe Fox's Blockade effective
for the whole coast line involved, he replied, November 21,
1806, with the Berlin Decree, declaring: 1. Complete blockade for all the possessions of Britain in Europe; 2. All British property, public or private, and any merchandise coming from Britain, whoever owned it, to be prize of war; 3. No ship
coming from Britain or her colonies to be admitted into a port controlled by France, and 4. Confiscation for vessels trying to evade this
blockade by false papers. This outrageous decree, for which Fox's
proclamation was no justification, ignored the doctrine of contraband,
and announced, in effect, that its author was greater than international
law. Moreover, he had not a respectable squadron to enforce it.
Only a few minor class ships-of-war were left to France after the battle
of Trafalgar, 1805, and these, darting out of the protected harbors
at the unprotected merchantmen, besides her privateers, were the
only means of enforcing the blockade against the mistress of the seas.
The only redeeming feature of the decree was that it was not enforced
against the United States for nine months after promulgation.

*The Berlin
Decree,
1806.*

The decree was a challenge to England, and touched her pride.
The reply of the ministry was two Orders in Council, which only increased the distress of the American shippers. The first,
January 7, 1807, forbade neutrals to trade from port to
port of France or her allies. It was a severe blow at our
skippers, who were accustomed to dispose of cargoes in
various markets as prices favored. In April a new election
gave the government a parliamentary majority of two hundred, mostly
country squires chosen on the ground that the church was in danger.
In the tory ministry which now came into power George Canning,
sometimes coarse, sometimes clever, but always patriotic and able,

*First and
Second
Orders in
Council.*

was foreign secretary. November 1, six weeks after Napoleon began to enforce his decree against our shipping, there appeared, in Great Britain, the second Order in Council. It forbade neutral trade with the entire coast of Europe from Trieste to Copenhagen, unless the neutral vessels concerned first entered and cleared from a British port under regulations to be afterwards announced. Canning thought France could not exist without American food products, and he expected by this means to force her to take them by permission of Britain. But Napoleon did not yield readily. December 17 he issued the Milan Decree, ordering the seizure of every neutral ship which allowed herself to be searched by England, or which cleared from an English port. Beyond this was nothing that could distress our commerce. Any ship bound for Europe, except for Sweden, Russia, or the Turkish possessions, was liable to capture by one side or the other. By the end of 1807 our merchant marine, distressed on every side, was threatened with destruction, and loud complaints reached the administration by every ship from abroad.

The Milan Decree, 1807.

JEFFERSON'S REPLY TO EUROPE

Jefferson abhorred war as a means of settling disputes, and thought most questions could be settled by appeal to interest. Neither he nor the majority of his party thought the country able to bear the burden of war. Like Washington, when he accepted the Jay treaty in 1795, they thought it better to bear the insult offered them than appeal to a course which would increase the national debt, involve great expense for a navy, and put in jeopardy the independence of the nation. Neither he nor his party lacked patriotism, but they represented the rural classes and did not feel the attacks on commerce as keenly as the merchants and shipowners, chiefly federalists. All these considerations prompted the adoption of pacific means of defense.

Desire for Peace.

The first was the non-importation act of 1806, passed to force concessions from England. It provided that certain specified goods which could be produced in the United States or in other countries than England should not be imported from the ports of Great Britain after November 25 following. The president did not favor the bill, but accepted it when the republicans made it a party measure. Randolph opposed it, declaring with his peculiar vehemence that we ought either to fight or submit to England. The act was to be followed by negotiations, and Monroe, minister to England, and William Pinkney, now sent thither as his colleague, were authorized to make a treaty which would rectify our wrongs. All this was a reply to the decision in the case of the *Essex*. The act did not go into effect until December 14, 1807.

Non-Importation Act, 1806.

Fox died soon after Monroe and Pinkney began negotiations, and his successor was less friendly. They did the best they could, but got no concessions worthy of the name. The treaty they **Futile** signed in London, December 31, did not give up impress-**Treaty of** ment, but insisted that West India products pay a duty of **Monroe and** **Pinkney.** not less than 2 per cent before they be exported to Europe as American goods, and that European products pay not less than 1 per cent duty in American ports before being exported to the islands. It was to be inoperative unless we bound ourselves not to abide by Napoleon's Berlin Decree. Thus it seemed that England dictated our own taxes and that she was bent on driving us into war with France. Jefferson realized that the treaty would not be ratified, and would not submit it to the senate. He concealed its terms to protect Monroe from the criticisms he believed it would bring down on the negotiators. It showed how futile were the non-importation act and the hopes from negotiation.

Then Jefferson turned to the embargo, in an especial sense his own policy. He would keep American ships from the sea until the time of danger was past, avoid the irritating incidents which were **The Em-** likely to arouse the war spirit in his own people, and force **bargo Act.** England and France to yield in order to get our products. He would thus prove that war is unnecessary and that armies and navies are a useless burden. Congress gave its support, and December 21, 1807, the embargo act was passed. It prohibited the departure for a foreign port of any merchant vessel, except foreign vessels in ballast, and required vessels in the coasting trade to give heavy bonds to land their cargoes in the United States. The president was given discretionary power to modify the operation of the law in specific cases, but its duration was made indefinite. Peaceful coercion was an untried experiment of far-reaching effects, yet it passed the two houses in four days and was a law before the people understood its significance. Congress accepted it on the authority of Jefferson at a time when it seemed that all other measures were futile. If successful, it would be a brilliant climax of a presidential career in which were such achievements as Gallatin's financial policy, the purchase of Louisiana, and the dissipation of partisan bitterness.

The first attempts at enforcement showed that peaceful coercion was impracticable. Shipowners would not give up a trade which be-**Difficulty of** came more profitable as it became more dangerous. They **Enforcing** hurriedly instructed their captains to avoid American ports **the Em-** and to continue in the carrying trade between foreign **bargo.** ports. Those whose ships remained at home in idle-ness complained loudly, and the law was evaded so much that two supplementary acts were soon passed to make it effective (January 8 and March 12). At first the farmers did not feel the embargo as the traders felt it; for the crops were sold when it passed. But by the end of summer it came home to them in lower prices. Products which in 1807 sold unusually high, on account of the war abroad, now sold unusually low because they could not be exported. The federalists made much of this discontent, and their course stimulated it, and thus encouraged evasions of the law. In the autumn two more enforcing acts were passed. Even a rowboat was now subject to the law, and collectors of the ports were given despotic powers over every ship that sailed.

Such was the situation when the election of 1808 occurred. Madison was the administration candidate, C. C. Pinckney had the support of the federalists, and John Randolph was rallying his friends for Monroe. The result was 122 electoral votes for Madison, 47 for Pinckney, and none for Monroe. **Election of 1808.**
George Clinton, who also had 6 votes for president, was elected vicepresident, although he had shown great uneasiness under the Virginia domination. All New England but Vermont was again in the federalist column, and for this change the embargo was responsible. In the house the federalists also gained strength, but their adversaries still held control.

These events, and the increasing defiance of New England, which seemed ready to take arms if the embargo were strictly enforced, shook the determination of the republicans, and sentiment for repeal began to develop in the party. Jefferson observed the trend with great disappointment. He had not lost faith in peaceful coercion as a theory, but he was **Failure of the Embargo.**
forced to see that it could not be enforced unless the majority of the people believed in it, and he was at last brought to sign a bill to supersede the embargo by the non-intercourse law of 1809.
It decreed non-intercourse with England and France, leaving the president to suspend it for whichever of the two nations should first abandon her restrictions. Jefferson signed the bill in much bitterness of spirit, and a few days later **Non-Intercourse Law of 1809.**
retired from office. The new law left open the trade with every nation but England and France, and to these our products went indirectly. For one year this situation continued, the government trying meantime to effect a settlement by negotiations. All was in vain, and May 1, 1810, a third **" Macon's Bill No. 2," 1810.**
act concerning trade, known as "Macon's Bill No. 2," was passed. **It** repealed all restrictions on commerce with the two nations, but authorized the president to reinstate them for one nation when the other repealed its offensive decrees or orders. It was a bid for relaxation, and if accepted by one power was likely to be accepted by the other. The result showed it to be as futile as the preceding measures. Our commerce was caught in a bitter conflict between two great states who would hardly stop cutting one another to pieces to secure the good will of the United States. Jefferson's embargo had important significance in the economic history of the time (see page 349).

BIBLIOGRAPHICAL NOTE

General Works. Besides the *Histories* by McMaster, Hildreth, Schouler, and Avery (see page 274), reference is made especially to Henry Adams, *History of the United States of America during the Administrations of Jefferson and Madison*, 9 vols. (1889–1891), a work unsurpassed for scholarship and clearness, rather extensive for the general reader, but a source of comfort to the student. It has the New England, though not the federalist, point of view, but honesty and good judgment are always evident. Volumes 1–4 deal with the years 1801–1809. A short work of much merit is Channing, *The Jeffersonian System* (1906). Hart, *American History told by Contemporaries*, 4 vols. (1897–1909), is also useful. For sources, see as above. Gallatin's reports are full, and may be found in *The American State Papers, Finance*, I and II. As one proceeds in the story the volumes in the same series on *Public Lands* and *Commerce and Navigation* become additionally important.

For writings and biographies of the prominent men of the time, see above, page 275. Other important biographies are: Dodd, *Life of Nathaniel Macon* (1903); and Battle, ed., *Letters of Nathaniel Macon, John Steele*, and *William Barry Grove* (Univ. of North Carolina *Bulletins*, No. II). On John Randolph two books are available, the first able but hostile, the second favorable but undiscriminating. They are: Adams, H., *John Randolph* (1884), and Garland, *Life of John Randolph* (1850). Adams, H., *Life of Gallatin* (1879), and Stevens, *Albert Gallatin* (1884), present in a convenient form the services of the secretary of the treasury in this period. For extended references on Jefferson see Channing, *The Jeffersonian System*, 274–276.

The Louisiana Purchase. The earliest considerable account is Barbé-Marbois, *Histoire de la Louisiane et de la Cession* (1829, and an English translation in 1830). It was written by one of the negotiators, and defends the sale of the province. The documents on the American side are full and can be found in the *American State Papers, Foreign*, II and *Public Lands*, I. Later American accounts are: the chapters in Henry Adams, *History of the United States*, I and II; Ogg, *The Opening of the Mississippi* (1904); and Gayarré, *History of Louisiana*, 4 vols. (revised edition, 1885).

Burr's Scheme. The usual view that Burr wished to revolutionize Louisiana is best stated by Adams, *History of the United States*, III. The view that Mexico was Burr's objective is defended with ability in McCaleb, *The Aaron Burr Conspiracy* (1903). The important documents are in Robertson, *Report of the Trial of Colonel Aaron Burr*, 2 vols. (1808), *Trial of Colonel Aaron Burr*, 3 vols. (1807–1808); Safford, *The Blennerhassett Papers* (1864), containing Blennerhassett's journal and correspondence with Burr; Wilkinson, *Memoirs of my Own Time*, 3 vols. (1816), presents the author's side, but he is so much distrusted that even his correspondence is not to be accepted.

Relations with England and France. On this subject Adams, *History of the United States*, IV, V, and VI, is very valuable. Many newly unearthed documents, American and foreign, are given at length, and the story is carried forward with spirit and breadth of treatment. The *American State Papers, Foreign*, II, contains valuable documents. Wheaton, *The Life, Writings, and Speeches of William Pinkney* (1826), and Pinkney, *The Life of William Pinkney* (1853), also contain valuable information. For a list of the important pamphlets which the controversy called forth, see Channing, *The Jeffersonian System* (1906), 283–285. Students interested in the subject should examine the writings of Madison, Monroe, Jefferson, and Gallatin (see above, page 255).

For Independent Reading

Maclay, *History of the United States Navy*, 3 vols. (1898); Spears, Story of the *American Merchant Marine* (1900), in which the conditions of the sea-born commerce is well treated. Basil Hall, *Voyages and Travels* (1895), covering the years 1802–1812, valuable for the experiences of British naval ships on the American station. *Memoirs and Letters of Dolly Madison, Wife of James Madison* (1886), interesting for social life in the early days in Washington.

CHAPTER XV

THE WAR OF 1812

ORIGIN OF THE WAR

BOTH England and France seized American ships under the restrictions on commerce just described, but as England had the stronger navy her offenses were more numerous. The losses from this source fell most heavily on the merchants and ship-owners, chiefly federalists and friends of England, who wished for peace with that country. Since Macon's bill No. 2 removed the restrictions on trade, pleasing the maritime class, and as we could not well fight France for doing what her rival did to a much larger extent, the prospect for peace would have been brighter in 1810, if seizures had been the only source of irritation. But another source of resentment was impressments, practiced, it is true, by both nations, but on a much larger scale by England. Here the brunt of wrong fell on the sailor class. As story after story was told of native Americans carried away into the hard service of the British navy, the popular ire rose higher and higher. British ships took sailors from ships in American harbors without regard to the neutrality laws, and lay in wait off the chief ports of the Atlantic coast, searching the vessel that came out. All the old hostility which lingered in American minds from the days of the revolution, or sprang up in connection with Jay's negotiations, now flared up again, and the nation drifted toward war.

War not due to Seizures Alone.

Impressments.

Had England been wise, much of this irritation would have been avoided. It is true she did not wish war with the United States. Engaged in a life and death struggle to stay the advance of Bonaparte in Europe, she had adopted the policy of starving her enemy into subjection. If our merchants tried to evade her regulations, so much the worse for them, and if she seized stringently the sailors she claimed as hers to enable her to man her ships-of-war, so much the worse for the sailors. It was no time, thought Canning, for the niceties of international courtesy. But America did not desire war, and had Canning's position been asserted with more consideration, war would probably have been avoided. As it was, there occurred several harsh incidents, which Jefferson and Madison were willing to overlook, but which goaded the popular mind until they resulted in a wave

England's Attitude.

Irritating Incidents.

313

of hatred which the administration could not resist, until congress at last forced the president to begin the struggle against his best judgment. In this sense George Canning was the chief author of the war of 1812.

The first of these incidents was the *Chesapeake-Leopard* affair, 1807. At that time impressments were very frequent. An English squadron searching for some French ships came into Lynnhaven Bay, near Norfolk, Virginia, and anchored there. Several of their sailors deserted, some of them Americans previously impressed into the British service. At that time the naval ship, *Chesapeake*, was taking on her heavy guns preparatory to her departure for the Mediterranean. It was reported that she had shipped some of the deserting British sailors, and Admiral Berkley, commanding the British ships on the station at Halifax, ordered that she be intercepted at sea and searched. Her captain, Barron, was ordered by the president to take care that no British deserters were in his crew, and thought he had fulfilled his instructions, but one man under an assumed name escaped his notice. Just before he sailed, the British ship, *Leopard*, came to Lynnhaven Bay with Berkley's orders. June 22 she followed the *Chesapeake*, as the latter stood out to sea, came alongside at close range, and signalled that she had dispatches. Barron allowed her to send a boat, and an officer coming on deck handed him Berkley's order with the announcement that if deserters were aboard, they must be handed over. Barron replied that he had none of the kind mentioned. He should have prepared for action, but the letter from the *Leopard* was not explicit, and he did not realize he was about to be attacked. A few minutes after the officer left the *Chesapeake* the British ship came within pistol shot, having the advantage of the wind, fired a shot across the *Chesapeake's* bow, and followed it by a broadside. The two ships were of nearly equal strength, and the British captain did not wish to lose the advantage of beginning his work before his opponent was ready. Barron was entirely unprepared for battle, but hastened his efforts while his helpless vessel sustained for fifteen minutes the enemy's fire. All he could do was unavailing, and he hauled down his colors with three men killed and eighteen wounded. Ere they touched the deck, one of his officers, for the honor of the flag, managed to fire one gun, the only reply the Americans made to the cruel punishment they received. Then the British came aboard, found three Americans who, having been impressed on a British ship had deserted and joined the *Chesapeake*, and the one native British deserter who had enlisted under an assumed name; and these were taken off. The American ship made her way to Norfolk, where her arrival was received with an outburst of rage which spread over the country until the whole nation quivered with excitement comparable to that which ninety-one years later was aroused by the destruction of the *Maine*. Barron was sus-

1. Chesapeake-Leopard Affair, 1807.

pended for five years because he had not been prepared for action, and Jefferson exerted all his art to prevent immediate war.

He recognized the strength of the popular indignation, and for a time showed energy. He promptly issued a proclamation ordering British public ships out of American waters and forbidding American citizens to furnish them supplies. He sent off to London a demand for reparation, for the punishment of Berkley, and for the relinquishment of impressments generally. When Canning received this demand he offered to investigate the incident and do what was just, but he refused to consider the demand that the British government give up impressments. The British press and public, long accustomed to resent the pretensions of the Yankee nation, applauded his position and demanded war, if war was necessary to support England's supremacy at sea. Here was a direct challenge, but Canning thought the president would not accept it. He recalled Berkley, who had acted without orders, but a proclamation was issued warning British seamen who had been "enticed" into foreign service to return to their allegiance, declaring that if taken on board enemy ships they would be treated as traitors, and commanding naval officers to seize them on merchant vessels and to demand them from captains of foreign naval ships. At the same time it was decided to transfer negotiations in regard to the recent affair to Washington, where Erskine was the British minister.

When this was known in America, congress was in session, and the embargo act was soon passed. It showed Jefferson's purpose to negotiate while he employed "peaceful coercion." Four days after it passed George Rose arrived to treat for the settlement of the *Chesapeake* affair. He was instructed to demand the withdrawal of Jefferson's recent proclamation as a condition precedent to negotiations. After some hesitation the president agreed that this should be done and asked Rose to show his instructions. The latter unwillingly complied. He would restore the impressed seamen, he said, if we would disavow Barron for encouraging the desertion of British sailors. This was distinctly what Barron had not done; to concede it would put us in the wrong, and the negotiations came suddenly to an end. Probably Canning had not intended that they should have a more successful course. Rose returned to England, the recent outrage was not redressed, three American-born sailors remained in a British prison, "peaceful coercion" was demonstrating its inadequacy to deal with the situation, and a large portion of the people were coming to the conviction that nothing but war would force the stubborn Canning to a reasonable attitude. But Rose discovered one fact while in America to which he later clung tenaciously. He learned how much opposed to war was the federalist party in New England, and he

Jefferson's Course.

Canning's Attitude.

2. Rose's Mission, 1808.

Rose and Pickering.

made a fast friend of Senator Timothy Pickering, of Massachusetts, who led him to believe that in case of war the states east of the Hudson might be withdrawn from the union and attached to England. Pickering cherished the idea, and his correspondence with Rose in the years immediately following gave prominent Englishmen a mischievous idea of American affairs.

Rose's short course ran through the three first months of 1808. He left British interests in the hands of the regular minister, Erskine, a **3. Erskine's Treaty.** whig, a friend of conciliation, and a man who saw with alarm the rising tide of hostility toward England. Advising Canning that war feeling was increasing, he was in the spring of 1809 instructed to make arrangements for a treaty which would remove all the differences between the two powers. The terms proposed were very hard, but Erskine believed himself justified in modifying them, and concluded a treaty so favorable to America that Canning repudiated it at sight. Before this was known in America many ships loaded with produce set sail for Europe, assured that British restriction would be inoperative when they arrived. Their disappointment was keen, but Canning allowed them to return home without seizure since they sailed under misapprehension.

Erskine was now recalled, and Jackson, a narrow and obstinate Briton, took his place, with the promise that he should retain the post **4. Jackson's Futile Mission.** at least a year. He began by tactlessly telling Madison that Erskine had been overreached by the American government. He was asked to withdraw the expression, and when he refused received a curt notice that no further communications would be held with him. He departed from Washington in high rage, leisurely visiting Baltimore, Philadelphia, New York, and Boston, where the federalists received him with demonstrations of sympathy. According to promise, he was allowed to hold his position until September, 1810. It was evident that England cared little to preserve peace with us, and all the time the popular resentment increased.

At this point the course of our story turns to France. Napoleon's attitude toward the United States was as unfair as England's, but his **The Bayonne and Rambouillet Decree.** power to injure was smaller because of his weakness at sea. He chiefly exercised it in seizing our ships by two notable decrees. Just after he knew of the embargo act, he ordered, in the Bayonne decree, April 17, 1808, the seizure of all ships in French ports flying the American flags. Such vessels, he said, could not be truly American, since the embargo act forbade them to leave their home ports. A great deal of property was thus confiscated, and the American government spent much time trying to get payment for it. March 23, 1810, Napoleon issued the Rambouillet decree, confiscating every ship which had entered a port of France or her dependencies since the preceding May

20. Under it several hundred vessels were taken. The procedure was justified on the ground that the non-intercourse act forbade French ships to come to American ports and authorized their seizure if they violated the act. It was really taken because Napoleon needed money, which he got in large amounts from the sale of the confiscated property.

Before America fully understood this deliberate perfidy, Napoleon was planning another stroke, the object being to lead us to war with England. With Macon's bill No. 2 in mind he caused Madison to be told that the Berlin and Milan decrees would be repealed November 1, 1810, his understanding being that congress had abandoned non-intercourse and would oppose England's restrictions. We had not undertaken to resist England, but only to apply non-intercourse to her commerce. Madison should have remembered this, but he was anxious to open the suspended commerce, and too readily accepted the promises of France. November 2 he gave notice that France had removed her restrictions, and March 2, 1811, congress reimposed non-intercourse on England, as Macon's bill No. 2 contemplated. It was soon evident that Napoleon had hoodwinked our president; for by a system of licenses and a high tariff he made it as hard as ever for the American ships in French harbors. England could see this as well as anybody. She refused to repeal her Orders and complained that we favored France, her enemy. By this time American feeling was so strong against England that our people did not care how she felt. We forgot to blame Napoleon, as we well might have done, and the government had begun to take a stiffer tone toward Great Britain. It was just at this time, April 1, that Monroe, according to the agreement made in 1809, succeeded Smith as secretary of state. He had suffered many indignities while minister in England, and he must have taken keen delight in the rising tide of resistance which he observed in the country and the administration.

Napoleon Hoodwinks Madison.

A clear manifestation of this altered spirit came soon afterwards. In May, 1811, the British frigate *Guerrière* was impressing sailors off Sandy Hook, and the American frigate, *President*, Captain John Rodgers, forty-four guns, was ordered to repair to the post and stop the practice. He sailed promptly, passing the scene of the affair of the *Chesapeake* and *Leopard*, four years unredressed by England, and May 16, off the Virginia coast, encountered a British ship of war headed southward. Hoisting his colors, he gave chase, thinking the *Guerrière* was before him. At sunset he was overhauling the fugitive, who at last came to in the twilight but refused to give her name. Suddenly a shot was fired which struck the *President's* mast. Immediately the American ship began to fire, and after a fifteen-minute battle the stranger ceased to fire and reported herself in distress. Rodgers lay to until morning, when, to his disappointment he learned that he had not attacked the

The President and Little Belt, 1811.

Guerrière, as he supposed, but the *Little Belt*, about half his size. Her captain alleged that the *President* fired first, but the evidence to the contrary was overwhelming. A short time later a new British minister arrived in Washington, announcing that he was instructed to settle the *Chesapeake-Leopard* dispute; but the nation, glowing with enthusiasm for Rodger's action, cared little for the overture. The minister was asked if the trade restrictions would be relaxed, and when he said "No" his work was at an end.

Additional hostility to England was engendered by the outbreak, in 1811, of Indian troubles in Indiana, where the white settlers were

Harrison and the North-western Indians, 1811.
now steadily penetrating. By a treaty of 1809 the Indians of central Indiana ceded a large tract of land on the Wabash. It was the ninth similar step since the treaty of Greenville, 1795. The more patriotic Indians opposed this relinquishment of their ancestral lands, and declared the treaty of 1809 illegal. They found leaders in two brothers, Tecumseh and "The Prophet," men of exceptionable ability, who lived peaceably with an agricultural tribe where Tippecanoe Creek joins the Wabash. They had great influence with the neighboring tribes and united them in a league to oppose further encroachments by the whites. In 1811 Tecumseh went to the South to form a similar league among the Creeks, Cherokees, Choctaws, and Chickasaws.

Battle of Tippecanoe.
Taking advantage of his absence, William Henry Harrison, governor of Indiana Territory, with 800 men, marched into the region recently ceded and came at last to the town on the Tippecanoe. Here he was surprised in the early morning by about 400 Indians, and lost 188 killed and wounded before he beat off the attack. As the foe retreated and left their village to be burned, Harrison was hailed victor throughout the Northwest. The Indians had received arms and ammunition from Canada, and this was taken as an additional wrong from England.

Meanwhile, the popular resentment had expressed itself in the election of 1810, when seventy new members were sent to congress, most

Changed Sentiment in the Election of 1810.
of them replacing advocates of peace. Before this the leaders in congress were men whose experience went back to the time of the revolution. They had seen so many dark days that they feared to hope for bright ones. The new men were young. Their leaders were Clay and Johnson of Kentucky, Porter of New York, Grundy of Tennessee, and Lowndes, Cheves, and Calhoun of South Carolina ; and the average age of the seven was only thirty-four. They had fought for their election

The War Party.
most vigorously, and felt bitterly toward the old Virginia group of leaders, who never quite forgave them their victory. Both factions called themselves republicans, but the newer men rejected many of the more theoretical principles of the old school. They believed that the national honor had been insulted,

and demanded war, their eyes meanwhile being cast at Canada. They began their work by electing Clay speaker and securing the important committees.

Before congress met on November 4 Madison accepted the demands of the war party, and his annual message recounted our wrongs and suggested measures of defense. The old leaders opposed this, but the federalists, thinking to embarrass their ancient enemies, joined the new party in raising an army of 25,000 men and in putting the navy on a war footing. An attempt to raise taxes, however, resulted in failure, and the government was left to support war, if war came, by means of a loan. For that kind of an operation it was seriously handicapped by the refusal of the preceding congress to recharter the United States bank. The many state banks could not make the loan of $11,000,000 now called for. At this time the bonds could not be sold in Europe, and the federalists, who were chiefly the trading class, would not take them because they opposed the war, and when the bids were opened only $6,000,000 had been subscribed. Lack of money was most serious throughout the war about to begin.

Madison Yields to the War Party.

U. S. Bank not Rechartered.

In May, 1812, a republican caucus renominated Madison for the presidency. He had the support of the war party and his small personal following; but the friends of Samuel Smith did not attend the caucus. In New York, where the two Clintons dominated the republicans, much jealousy of the Virginia supremacy appeared, and a movement was rapidly forming for a coalition between the malcontents and the federalists, in opposition to Madison. George Clinton died in April, and Virginia, turning away from the alliance with New York, took Massachusetts for her Northern yoke-fellow, offering the vice-presidency to Elbridge Gerry, who had recently been republican governor of that commonwealth. Clinton's death, however, did not end the plans of the New Yorkers. His nephew, De Witt Clinton, took up his mantle, was nominated for the presidency by the New York legislature, and ran the race with the endorsement of the federalists. When the votes were cast in the following November Madison had 128 of the 217, eight from Vermont and all those from the states south of the Delaware. Had Pennsylvania not given him her twenty-five votes he would have been defeated.

Madison Renominated.

England now saw plainly the drift of the United States toward war. To the American protests was added the fact that the English people were suffering for food products. Wheat sold at nearly four dollars a bushel, and the trade with the continent went on under a system of forged licenses, both British and French, for which honest Englishmen could only blush. Under these conditions there arose a powerful demand that the Orders in

The British Relenting.

Council be repealed, and the ministry were urged to relieve a disastrous situation before an American war should be added to the other burdens. At last they were willing to yield, if the French government would state publicly that its decrees had been repealed. No such statement was expected, but the offer showed that the government was weakening. May 11, 1812, the prime minister, Spencer Percival, who had stood stoutly for the Orders, was assassinated by a fanatic. The friends of America, led by the brilliant Henry Brougham, now

The Orders Repealed, June 23. pressed harder than ever for repeal. Then came news that the United States had declared an embargo for two months as a preliminary step to war. With the nation clamoring for peace, and with Brougham eloquently pleading the cause of the starving people, the new ministry at last gave way, announcing on June 16 that the Orders would be withdrawn, a promise which they redeemed on the 23d.

The British relaxation came suddenly, and the Americans were unprepared for it. The war party was in control in congress, and carried

War Declared, June 18. the president with it. June 1 he sent a war message which occasioned a short and sharp debate, followed on June 18 by a declaration of war for which the vote was 19 to 13 in the senate and 79 to 49 in the house. Had there been a cable the war would probably not have occurred. As it was, there was a feeble attempt to patch up differences when news came from London, but feelings were now too much aroused for such a step, and the project failed. Fourteen of the senators and 62 of the representatives who voted for war lived south of the Delaware. Only 11 of those who voted against it lived in that region, and of these but two were republicans. Thirty-three federalist representa-

Feeling not United. tives issued an address declaring the struggle unjustifiable. Thus the war was sectional, and began with dissension in the nation. The war party thought that harmony would be restored once fighting began, but the event showed how much they were mistaken.

In fact, the country was not ready for war. The president, timid, diplomatic, and unable to control the politicians around him, could not

Weakness of the Administration, Army, and Navy. inspire with energy an administration in which the only first rate man, Gallatin, was harassed out of his peace of mind by enemies in his own party. The army, neglected by the republicans, was without trained officers. The West Point Academy, authorized in 1802, had as yet yielded none of the fruits for which it later was distinguished. Officers who had served in the revolution were now too old for effective duty, and the new political appointees were pompous and inexperienced, and lacked the respect of the privates. The navy, disdained by Jefferson, had only the frigates built by the federalists, and some smaller vessels constructed for use against Tripoli, less than twenty in all. But their officers were excellent, and the sailor population was as good as could be found in the world. The gunboats Jefferson built for harbor defense were not able to take the sea. The treasury was without money, and the country shuddered at the thought of higher taxes. Loans were the only resource, and these were difficult with the moneyed class opposed to war and the money markets of Europe prostrated by the struggle then raging there. The young leaders in the house realized these difficulties, and strove to surmount them. They carried through congress a bill to raise the army, now a little more than six thousand strong, by 25,000 men, and another bill to authorize the president to call out 50,000 militia. They also asked for an addition to the navy of twelve seventy-fours and twenty frigates, but this was refused. When they moved war taxes there was further denial, and they were forced to content themselves with a loan of $11,000,000. All this happened early in 1812. *Efforts of the War Party.*

The war party planned a vigorous campaign in Canada and the occupation of Florida, if Spain, England's ally in Europe, should make war on America. They thought the Canadians would willingly throw off the British yoke in order to unite with the great republic to the southward, and they believed that the war would end quickly and victoriously. They expected the Atlantic ports to be blockaded, and trade to be driven from the sea, but so much had been endured on that score that a little more suffering would hardly make a difference. Kentucky and the Northwest were keen for the Canadian campaign, while Tennessee longed for the signal which would open to them the Coosa-Alabama line of communication, with free exit at Mobile. As it turned out, there was no war with Spain, but Mobile was occupied without resistance. On the other hand, England's plan, more slowly formed, was to beat back the attempt on Canada, to blockade the coast, and crush our ships at sea, and in the latter part of the war to carry offensive operations into the home of the war party, Virginia and Louisiana. Into these four phases, therefore, the actual fighting of the war of 1812 was resolved. *Canada and Florida.* *England's War Plan.*

THE STRUGGLE FOR CANADA

The Canadian defenses were along the lakes, a series of posts from Mackinac to Lake Champlain. It was proposed to break this line at the eastern end, while supporting expeditions carried it at Fort Malden, near Detroit, at Fort Erie, on the Niagara river, and at Kingston. Those places taken, all the columns would concentrate on Montreal. It was thought the campaigns would be accomplished with little or no opposition. Had the commanders been good and the coöperation perfect, such might have been the result. *Canadian Line of Defense.*

The first move was from Detroit, where General Hull commanded with nearly 2500 men. In July he crossed the Detroit river and marched toward Malden. General Brock commanded the British force and made heroic efforts to defend the position. Hull moved slowly, gave him time to concentrate, and then fell back because he dared not attack a force half the size of his own, nearly half of his opponents being Indians. The army was disgusted, their want of confidence in their leader only increased

Hull at Detroit.

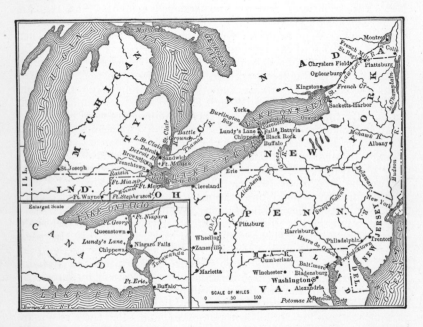

Hull's panic, and when Brock, following the Americans to Detroit, surrounded the place and demanded its surrender, the fort, garrison, and supplies, to his surprise, were handed over without an effort to defend them. Hull pleaded that he was surrounded, his communications cut, and his men likely to be butchered by the hostile Indian if he resisted to the end. His position was indeed perilous, but a braver man would have made some effort to defend himself. A year and a half later he was convicted by a court martial of cowardice and neglect of duty and sentenced to be shot, but the president pardoned him on account of honorable revolutionary services. The loss of Detroit left the frontier open to Indian raids and created disgust for the men directing the war at the time when there ought to have been enthusiasm.

Disgraceful Surrender.

Nor was there more success at other parts of the border. The column sent against Montreal got under way after much delay and in November reached the Canadian line, whereupon the militia refused to leave the country and were marched back by their commander, Dearborn, to winter quarters at Plattsburg. The other column failed also. Assembled on the Niagara to the number of six thousand it essayed to carry the war into Canada under General Stephen Van Rensselaer, a New York politician and an inexperienced general. The regulars under General Smythe refused to coöperate, and Van Rensselaer was driven back from an attack on Queenstown with a loss of 1000. Then Smythe was placed in command. He was as bad a commander as his predecessor, and his attempted invasion in November was repulsed so easily that he was freely accused of cowardice. In these three forward movements the private soldiers showed ability, but their commanders and many of the other officers were evidently unfit for their posts. By the middle of 1813 all these commanders were removed.

Repulse of Second and Third Columns.

After Hull's defeat William H. Harrison, of Tippecanoe fame, was placed over the Western army, which he organized as fast as a poor commissary department permitted. Late in the autumn of 1812 he was in a position to move forward, and marched to attack the British at Malden. He sent General Winchester forward to make preparations at the rapids of the Maumee, fifty miles from Malden. While there, Winchester was called to the help of Frenchtown, on the Raisin river, thirty miles beyond. He hurried forward with 900 men, took the place, but could not fortify it. January 22, 1813, he was attacked and defeated by Proctor commanding more than 1000 whites and Indians. Surrounded in the snow, the Americans were cut down or massacred by the Indians, until the remainder, over 500 in all, were forced to surrender. At night the savages, crazed by liquor, fell on the wounded prisoners, whom Proctor left without guard, and killed them to a man. The act infuriated the men of the frontier, and "Remember the Raisin" became their battle cry for the rest of the war. Harrison was forced to give up his advance, but he did not lose the confidence of the Western people.

Harrison's Campaign in the Northwest.

Throughout the spring and summer of 1813 he made ready for another attack, and in September was before Malden with 4500 men. By this time the Americans had gained control of Lake Erie, and the British, not daring to withstand a siege with no help possible by water, burned Detroit and Malden and retreated. Harrison pursued them on Canadian territory, forced a fight at the river Thames, and won a signal victory. One of the slain was Tecumseh, who from the first had aided the British. It was the first successful battle in the long announced invasion of Canada, and it gave peace to the Northwest.

Detroit Recovered.

Battle of the Thames.

For this valuable result the gunboats on Lake Erie deserve much credit. Hull's surrender showed that we never could retake Detroit
as long as it could be supplied by water. Accordingly
every effort was made to build and buy ships for service
on the lake. By September, 1813, Captain Oliver H.
Perry had six vessels well armed and manned. On the
10th he met and destroyed the British lake fleet, slightly weaker than his own. His dispatch announcing the victory ran: "We have met the enemy and they are ours. Two ships, two brigs, one schooner, and one sloop." The victor became very popular.

Holding Lake Erie and Detroit did not mean the conquest of Canada. Montreal was still to be taken, and for that purpose General
James Wilkinson was called from New Orleans to take
command of the large force at Sackett's Harbor, near
Kingston. He was to march down the St. Lawrence, supported by another army led by General Wade Hampton
by way of Lake Champlain. The only virture in Wil-
kinson's appointment, which was due to his friendship with Armstrong, now secretary of war, was that it made way for Andrew Jackson's command in Louisiana in 1814. Wilkinson was incompetent, and Hampton, who was a good general, coöperated with him reluctantly. Wilkinson moved slowly, as if he did not desire to succeed. Hampton reached an advanced position on the Chateaugay, held it until convinced that the other army would do nothing, and then returned to winter quarters at Plattsburg, on Lake Champlain. Wilkinson, who had fought some skirmishes without success, then fell back to Sackett's Harbor. Hampton, who resented being placed under the incompetent Wilkinson, resigned, and his superior was at length removed from command. Thus ended in failure the second year of fighting on the New York border. The most valuable thing accomplished was that through defeat the army was seasoned to fighting, the old generals had been weeded out, and a number of capable minor officers had been given an opportunity to show their abilities. Of the latter were Major General Jacob Brown, in command of the forces on the Niagara, and Brigadier General Winfield Scott, who served under him, an excellent drill master and a bold fighter.

The year 1814 began gloomily for the Americans. They were discouraged by a war which brought so little success, New England
seemed on the point of withdrawing from the union,
volunteering had nearly ceased in the Atlantic states,
and the treasury was empty. Moreover, Napoleon was
checked in Europe, and England might be expected to
carry on the war with more energy in America. All this sobered the people, and as the months passed men began to forget that it was a republican war and to realize that the life of the nation was at stake.

Perry's Victory on Lake Erie.

Wilkinson's Failure on the St. Lawrence.

Sobering Effect of Defeat.

They were encouraged by news from Brown. All thought of a grand offensive movement into Canada had been given up, but he was not willing to remain idle. Moving about 2500 men into the enemy's territory, he attacked gallantly. Scott, who was selected to lead the advance with 1300 men, met, July 5, Riall with 1500 men and won a signal victory at Chippewa. The Americans showed great efficiency in marksmanship, and lost only 297, while their opponents lost 515. Brown now united with Scott, and they met the main body of the British three weeks later at Lundy's Lane. The action began in the afternoon and lasted five hours, until darkness intervened. Every part of the field was hotly contested, and the Americans gradually pushed the British from their positions. When the fighting ceased they had lost 853 out of 2000 engaged and the enemy had lost 879 out of 3000. So far as actual fighting went, Brown had the better of it, but he considered it advisable to fall back when his opponent received reënforcements. The movement into Canada was abandoned. It had accomplished all that could be expected in showing that American soldiers could win victories when properly led and trained.

Chippewa and Lundy's Lane, 1814.

While this campaign was being fought, Sir George Prevost, commanding in Canada, led a splendid army of 11,000 men along Burgoyne's old route, hoping to pass Lake Champlain and create consternation on the Hudson. Such a campaign, if successful, must have an important influence in New England, where an active group of leaders wished to have those states join Canada in order to be rid of the Virginia predominancy. General Macomb, commanding at Plattsburg, on Lake Champlain, had only 2000 men to meet this invasion, and Prevost felt that he could easily dispose of them. On the lake were two small fleets, the American commander being Captain Thomas McDonough, a young man of thirty, who proved to have remarkable capacity. The fighting strength of the British ships was double that of the Americans. To succeed in his plans Prevost must destroy McDonough, and the two squadrons joined in deadly combat on September 11, while the army before Plattsburg awaited the result. The British expected the victory because their largest ship, a frigate of thirty-seven guns, outclassed our strongest vessel. They concentrated their attack on the *Saratoga*, McDonough's largest ship. After two hours' fighting it was disabled, when the commander, by a daring maneuver, turned it around so that a fresh broadside was brought to bear, with the result that the British frigate struck her colors in half an hour. By that time the whole British squadron was defeated, and Prevost's army retreated to Canada. McDonough's achievement occasioned an outburst of joy throughout the country, and, like Perry's victory on Lake Erie, it rendered safe an important part of the frontier.

McDonough's Victory on Lake Champlain.

For the blundering in this important part of the theater of war the Virginia régime was chiefly responsible. Jefferson's non-resistance policy was more creditable to his heart than to his head. His predecessors filled army and navy with federalist officers and showered contempt upon republicans who might have been appointed. He repaid their scorn with interest, and in army appointments he ignored the federalists and collected as weak a group of incompetents as could be found in any service. Their selection can only be explained on the theory that he believed they would never have anything of importance to do. That the navy did not undergo the same deterioration was due to the fact that its officers were taken from the maritime class, mostly federalists in sympathy, and to the effect of the Tripolitan war in keeping alive the best traditions of the navy. With regard to the army Madison continued the same course as Jefferson. Eustis, secretary of war from March 7, 1809, to December 31, 1812, was a shiftless politician who knew not how to choose the generals or to plan a campaign. His successor, Armstrong, more active than Eustis, muddled things by holding to his friend, the incompetent Wilkinson, and by going to the field himself, where he produced confusion by interfering with plans of better men, until at last, overwhelmed by the loss of the capital, he was forced out of office August 30, 1814. He was succeeded by Monroe, a more practical administrator though not an ideal secretary, who outlasted the war. Hamilton, secretary of the navy from March 7, 1809, to January 13, 1813, was as weak as Eustis and did little to strengthen his department. His successor in office until December 1, 1814, was more active and strengthened the navy by constructing small ships of war to operate against the enemy's commerce. Thus in these two important departments defeat and disaster taught wisdom as truly as in the command of the armies. It required much sad experience to teach the nation the necessity of training in order to conduct such an important affair as a great national struggle.

Why the Army was Weak.

OPERATIONS AT SEA

The war party did not despise the navy, as their project to build seventy-fours and frigates shows; but they could not overcome the prejudices of the regular republicans. In 1807, when Barron's failure to fight the *Leopard* caused great disgust among those who opposed a navy on principle, it was decided to discharge the crews of the leading frigates and to raise the number of gunboats to 257. Congress indorsed the policy. Jefferson preferred gunboats because they confined the navy to harbor defense and were cheap. The federalists jeered at his idea that small craft armed with light guns could keep the enemy's ships out of our ports, and the experience of war showed they were

State of the Navy in 1812.

right. The war party in 1812 had come to realize this, and failing to get the new ships they wished they put the vessels we had in a proper state of service. Eight ships, four of them forty-fours, with an equal number of smaller vessels, was the strength of the navy. Most people thought that to send them against the mistress of the sea was but to throw them away; but many inward-bound merchant ships were on the ocean in need of protection. Five ships, commanded by Rodgers and Decatur, were in New York harbor when the official information of the declaration of war reached that place, and in an hour they were at sea searching for a British convoy known to be on the ocean. They sailed boldly across the Atlantic to the English coast, thence to the Madeiras, and then to Boston without adventure.

The day before Rodgers arrived in Boston came, also, the *Constitution*, Captain Isaac Hull, nephew of the commander at Detroit, with thrilling news of victory. August 19 she met and defeated the British ship *Guerrière*, 38 guns, after a fight of half an hour. The disabled ship could not be taken into port, and was fired and abandoned. She had been **Successful Naval Duels.** very active in impressments, and her destruction occasioned joy from one end of the coast to the other. Then followed a series of naval duels in which the Americans bore themselves with distinction. In October the *Wasp* captured the *Frolic* and started with her for an American port, but both ships were later taken by a larger enemy vessel. Shortly afterwards the *United States* took the *Macedonian* and carried her safely into Newport, while in December the *Constitution* defeated and burned the *Java*, 38 guns. February 24 the *Hornet* sunk the *Peacock* after an action of fifteen minutes. In all these affairs the American ship, except the *Wasp*, was stronger than her opponent; but the accurate fire and good seamanship of the Americans astonished the enemy and brought them to realize that their best efforts were demanded on this side the Atlantic. In America, also, the effect was marked. A wave of enthusiasm for the navy swept the country, and congress voted to build sixteen new ships of war.

June 1, 1813, came a disaster which sadly checked the American ardor. Captain Lawrence, who commanded the *Hornet* against the *Peacock*, was now in charge of the *Chesapeake*, fitting in Boston, with orders to cruise off the mouth of the St. Lawrence in order to intercept supplies for the British in Canada. **Defeat of the *Chesapeake*.** Blockading the harbor was the *Shannon*, Captain Broke, with some smaller ships. He was anxious for a combat with the *Chesapeake*, sent in a challenge, and ordered his companion ship away so as to induce Lawrence to come out. The latter needed little urging. He was rashly brave, and the recent victories had made him overconfident. He had been in command only ten days, his best officers were ill and absent, and his crew were raw and sullen.

The ships were nearly of equal size, but the *Shannon* was manned by a well-drilled crew who adored their commander. Lawrence had not received the Briton's challenge when he learned that only a frigate kept the blockade. He was not averse to action, and the opportunity to get to sea seemed too good to miss; so he boldly sailed out, and at six o'clock the action began at the outer edge of Massachusetts Bay. In sixteen minutes Lawrence was mortally wounded, and his ship had surrendered after a brave battle. The *Chesapeake* was carried to Halifax, where the body of her commander was given honorable burial by the victors. The remains were later reinterred in New York. Lawrence's utterance as he was carried below, "Don't give up the ship," was repeated far and wide, and the people forgot his rashness in admiration of his courage.

The repeal of the Orders in Council by England led her to hope that the war might be avoided, but she would not give up impress-

Naval Success Checked. ments, and the hope of adjustment vanished. It thus happened that it was not until the spring of 1813 that she gave her best strength to the task before her. At this time the blockade was made stringent, commercial ships were vigorously seized, and a strong naval force continued off the coast. Decatur, with the *United States* and *Macedonian*, trying to get to sea by way of Long Island Sound, was forced into New London harbor and bottled up for the rest of the war. In the spring of 1814 he was transferred to the *President*, blockaded at New York. It was not until the following January that he was able to get out in a storm, the blockaders pursuing and forcing him to an unequal fight, in which he surrendered. Similar fates awaited most of the other ships in the navy. The *Adams* was burned in the Penobscot, 1814, to prevent capture by the enemy; the *Argus* was defeated by the *Pelican* off the coast of Wales in 1813; the *Enterprise*, the newly built *Frolic*, and the *Essex* were all taken before the close of the war. The *Constellation* and the *Congress* were also securely blockaded in

Growth of Navy, 1812–1815. American harbors. At the beginning of the war we had ten effective ships and seven smaller vessels ranked as brigs. So fast had the navy grown, spite of losses, that at the close of 1815 it contained seventeen ships, three of them new seventy-fours, nine brigs, thirteen schooners, and three sloops.

War was hardly declared before American privateers were on the seas. Subscription lists posted at the merchants' coffeehouses

American Privateers. invited all adventurous persons to share the expense and profit sure to come through despoiling Great Britain's rich maritime trade. In Massachusetts, New York, and Maryland the response was particularly generous. Three-fourths of the 492 licensed privateers were from these three states. Good sailing and the ability to get out of tight places were necessary qualities of a good privateer. Some of the captains displayed great boldness, attacking British privateers, and even small naval ships, with success. Half of the ships engaged in the field did not come up to these requirements and took no prizes, but those best fitted for the enterprise paid their owners handsome profits, while they enriched our naval history with some of its most thrilling exploits. In the war of 1812, 1344 prizes were thus taken from Great Britain, the last in which the United States have resorted to privateering.

THE BRITISH CAMPAIGN ON CHESAPEAKE BAY

In the summer of 1814, as Prevost prepared his invasion of New York by Lake Champlain, a British fleet under Admiral Cochrane and a army of 4000 men under Major General Ross appeared in the Chesapeake to create a diversion for the benefit of the northern operations. The plan was to take the capital and to seize Baltimore, especially disliked *Object of the Expedition.* for its part in privateering. Ross landed without opposition at Benedict, on the Patuxent, forty miles from Washington, and marched unopposed on the city. News of his movement had reached the president seven weeks earlier, and the militia were frantically called out. They came together slowly, commanded by General Winder, a man of little determination. Falling back before the advancing foe, he at last faced them at Bladensburg, five miles from the capital. His position was good, a hill commanding a bridge across the Patuxent, and he had sufficient artillery. His forces were between six and seven thousand, all raw militia except five hundred marines and sailors under Captain Barney, of the navy. They were just assembled, did not know their officers, and Winder had no influence over them. As the British approached the bridge they received the American artillery fire, but dashed across,

formed, and advanced on the Americans. The militia delivered one or two fires, and fled pell-mell. Barney's men stood their ground,

firing with steadiness until about to be surrounded, when they
fled from a field on which they now had no support. The British
on the evening of the same day, August 24, entered

Washington Taken. Washington, from which president, officials, and many
residents had fled. The capitol, president's house, and
the executive offices were burned by the troops. Ross justified
this piece of vandalism as retaliation for the destruction of the parliament building at Toronto in the preceding year. The

Public Buildings Burned. Americans did not pretend to justify the outrages at
Toronto, but asserted that it was the action of pri-
vates, whereas the torch was applied in Washington at
the direction of the commanding general. As an act of retaliation
Ross's course went far beyond the action alleged as its justification,
and it was committed with such evident relish by him and his officers
that it cannot be defended as soldierly conduct.

While Ross moved against Washington seven small vessels appeared
before Alexandria, levied a contribution, and rejoined the main force
as Ross, his work at Washington done, embarked his

Baltimore Attacked. force and moved on Baltimore. September 11 he landed
at North Point, twelve miles from the city, against which
he advanced on a narrow neck of land between the Patapsco and an
arm of the bay, saying he would winter in the city even if "it rained
militia." Next morning he was mortally wounded in a skirmish,
but his army continued to advance. The people of the city and state
had collected to the number of 14,000, and earthworks were constructed
to protect the place. The harbor was impeded by sunken hulks and
defended by Fort McHenry, well garrisoned by regulars and sailors.
While the army approached by land the navy under command of
Admiral Cochrane began to shell the fort. After several hours' bombardment the admiral reported that he could not advance; and
although the infantry had carried the American first line, they did
not feel like charging the works before them, and it was decided to
withdraw to the ships. The expedition dropped down the bay,
and a month later sailed out the capes to take part in the expedition
against Louisiana.

The attack on Washington showed as clearly as the

The Value of Militia. operations in Canada the weakness of untrained militia.
It is still more evident that the disaster was due chiefly
to the lack of intelligent general officers. But the campaign about to
be conducted around New Orleans revealed the value of militia when
well trained and well led. The destruction of the cap-

Resignation of Armstrong. ital aroused great indignation against the administration,
and Armstrong, secretary of war, resigned. He was chiefly
responsible for the inertness in his department, although
Madison and congress, it must be admitted, had given him slender
resources. Armstrong was succeeded by Monroe, who for nearly a
year was head of the state and war departments.

Meanwhile, British troops had landed at various harbors in Massachusetts and Connecticut, burning such crafts as they found. A more serious demonstration was an expedition against the eastern coast of Maine. The country as far as the Penobscot was seized after little resistance by the natives, with the intention of holding it after peace was made, in order to establish a safe route from Montreal to Halifax. When it was given up in 1815, the inhabitants, it was said, regretted that they did not continue under British sway.

Attacks on Maine and Elsewhere.

THE WAR ON THE GULF COAST

It will be remembered that the war party hoped for an opportunity to acquire Florida. Spain was England's ally, her South and Central American colonies were revolting one after the other, at home she was struggling for existence against Napoleon: what better opportunity could there be, thought the expansionists, to oust her from the part of the coast which destiny evidently meant us to occupy? Madison accepted the idea, and would have carried it out by invading Florida without other pretext than the Louisiana treaty, had not the senate restrained him. Spite of this, two important events happened on the Florida border, one of them resulting in increase of American territory.

The Desire for Florida.

In 1810 the inhabitants of the part of West Florida nearest the Mississippi revolted against Spain, proclaimed themselves a state, seized the post at Baton Rouge, and asked for annexation to the United States. Madison by proclamation ordered the governor of the territory of Lousiana to extend authority over this district without coming into conflict with any Spanish post. He asserted our right to West Florida by the Louisiana treaty and proposed to hold the region in question subject to future agreement with Spain. Thus our authority was extended to the Pearl river, beyond which was Mobile in undisturbed Spanish possession.

Baton Rouge Acquired.

The revolt of the Spanish colonies in South America was suggestive, and a plan was made for a similar movement in East Florida. When it was accomplished, the United States, it seems, was to step in and annex the territory, as at Baton Rouge. In 1811 congress in a secret act authorized the president to take possession of Florida under certain conditions, and Madison appointed two commissioners who repaired to the Georgia frontier. Amelia Island, just within the Florida line, was the scene of much smuggling, which it was desirable to break up. Here occurred a weak attempt at a revolution, and American soldiers occupied the island, but the revolt had so little support from the inhabitants that Madison did not dare carry out the plans made for him. Amelia Island was held, however, until 1813.

Amelia Island.

In the autumn of 1812 Madison called out 2070 west Tennessee militia under Andrew Jackson, to march to Natchez, expecting to use them against Florida. This was merely an execu-

Seizure of Florida Balked by Congress, 1813. tive act, and when congress refused to sanction the proposed expedition Jackson was recalled to Nashville. The west Tennessee militia were eager for war, and had confidence in their leader. Their opportunity came late in 1813, when it was decided to send them as one of three expeditions against the Creek Indians, who were on the warpath in sympathy with the Indians of the Northwest. The Tennesseans were to march into the Creek country from the north, the Georgia militia from the east, and an expedition from New Orleans was to approach through Mobile Bay and the Alabama river.

The most difficult task was Jackson's, but it alone was successful. When the winter closed in he had reached the upper Coosa, after

The Creeks Subdued. winning two victories over his adversaries. Four days of marching and one good victory would have given him complete success, but he could not get supplies, and his men mutinied and were sent home. With only a handful of followers he held what he had gained until new troops were raised, and March 27 completed the subjugation of the Creeks in the victory of Horse Shoe Bend, or Tohopeka. His campaign showed that he had remarkable power of command as well as resourcefulness and energy. In consequence he was made a major general and assigned

Mobile Seized. to the command of the seventh military district. Besides Louisiana, the district included Mobile, which had been annexed without resistance in April, 1813. Now, as in regard to Baton Rouge, Madison acted under his interpretation of the Louisiana treaty.

Jackson's first act in his new capacity was to make the treaty of Fort Jackson, August 9, by which the Creeks gave up their lands in

The Treaty of Fort Jackson. southern and western Alabama. He thus opened a vast region to white settlement, and made safe the Coosa-Alabama line of communication. Next he turned to Mobile. The advance guard of the great expedition against New Orleans had arrived at Pensacola; Jackson seized the town regardless of neutrality obligations, and the British sailed away.

Pensacola Occupied. He was hardly back in Mobile when he learned that New Orleans was threatened by a body of more than 10,000 troops. He hastened to the city, which was nearly undefended, calling the militia from Tennessee, Kentucky, and Georgia as he went. Had Winder, in the preceding summer, shown half Jackson's energy, Ross would not have reached Washington.

December 10, the British fleet anchored in Lake Borgne, and early on the 23d a division of the army was landed eight miles below the city on a strip of land less than a mile wide, between the river and the swamp. Instantly Jackson was in motion, delivering in the evening and early night a sharp battle which drove the enemy to take refuge under the levee until reënforcements came up from the ships. Then Jackson fell back and began to construct breastworks. Pakenham, the British commander, was cautious, and would not move until all his forces were landed, including the artillery. He thus allowed Jackson time to construct formidable defenses, which the royal artillery could not destroy. On January 8, 1815, he threw away his caution and attempted to carry these works. He and his whole army held American militia in contempt, and thought they would break when charged vigorously by British regulars. In the early dawn two red-coated columns rushed on Jackson's lines, one near the river and one near the swamp. They met a withering rifle-fire from which the bravest soldiers must have recoiled. Twice they were rallied and led forward by their best officers, and each time repulsed with great slaughter. Pakenham and General Gibbs were killed, and General Keene severely wounded. The loss in this part of the army was 1971 killed and wounded, and on Jackson's side 13. Meanwhile, Colonel Thornton, with 600 regulars, crossed to the west bank of the river to carry some batteries there, which bore on the ground over which the British must attack on the east side. He met an insufficient force of Louisiana and Kentucky militia, swept it aside, took the batteries, and held the west bank at discretion. Fortunately for the Americans, this movement was delayed until after the attack on their intrenchments on the east bank was repulsed, and by that severe blow the British were so crippled that they relinquished the campaign and withdrew to their fleet.

Arrival of the British at New Orleans.

Battle of New Orleans.

The victory at New Orleans was one of the great events in American history. It not only saved the mouth of the Mississippi from conquest and restored to the people confidence in their ability to win battles, but it gave the Western people, who had won it without much help from the seaboard, the confidence to assert a greater influence in national affairs. To these people, and to many others in all parts of the country, Jackson became the greatest living American. He had, besides his military qualities, political courage and integrity, which sustained him in a long and important career. He was unschooled in the arts of war and statesmanship, but in each field his remarkable natural sense made him essentially efficient. No American has left a stronger mark on our political history.

Significance of the Victory.

Before Jackson's victory was won, peace was made between England and the United States. The Russian Czar, from 1812 an ally of England, sought to end the war, and believed it might be done since the Orders in Council were repealed. He offered each party his services as mediator. Madison accepted, and in the spring of 1813,

Peace Negotiations Begun. Bayard, of Delaware, and Gallatin, set out for St. Petersburg to join John Quincy Adams, our minister there, in a peace commission. The action was hasty; for England had not accepted the mediation. She told the Czar that the question between her and the United States did not admit of mediation. But she did not wish to offend her powerful ally, and expressed a willingness to treat directly with the American commissioners. Such a course would give her a freer hand in the negotiation. After some delay the British ministry repeated the offer to Madison, and congress, accepting it for what it was worth, sent Clay and Jonathan Russell as additional commissioners of peace. England appointed three men of little prominence, Lord Gambier, Henry Goulburn, and Dr. Adams. The Americans took it as a slight that more capable men were not named, but the ministry expected to keep the negotiations well in hand. The commissioners began their labors at Ghent early in August, 1814.

The Americans asked that impressments and the right of search be relinquished. The British replied with such demands that it

Progress at Ghent. seemed they did not desire peace. We were asked, for one thing, to accept an Indian buffer state on our northwest as an offset to our attack on Canada. The war against Napoleon was then believed to be ended, the English people were elated, they had not heard of the better fighting of the Americans on the northern frontier in the third year of the war, and the result was stout demands on their part. The American commissioners reported the demands to Madison, who made them public. An outburst of indignation ensued in nearly every part of the United States. Lord Castlereagh, the prime minister, seeing that the war would go on with more energy than before, concluded to modify his terms. England was exhausted by the long war on the continent and needed peace more than she needed to triumph over America. Castlereagh had begun to see that the continental nations would be secretly against England in adjusting the affairs of Europe, and he did not wish at that time to be embarrassed by a transatlantic war. So it happened that as the American commissioners were about to go home the British abandoned the worst of their conditions. From day to day they gave up still more, with the result that finally a treaty was signed, December 24, in which neither side gained or lost. It provided

A Treaty Signed Dec. 24, 1814. for the cessation of arms, the restoration of conquests, and a commission to settle the long-disputed Canadian boundary. The matters for which we went to war were not mentioned; but as England was to reduce her navy with the coming of peace, the question of impressment was no longer important. February 15, 1815, the treaty was unanimously approved by the senate. For the first time since the constitution was adopted the United States faced the future without anxiety about their foreign relations.

NEW ENGLAND DISCONTENT

New England generally chafed under Southern control. Non-importation, embargo, and non-intercourse affected her business prosperity more than the South's. Moreover, it seemed likely that she, a trading community, would continue to be outclassed by the agricultural section. Every new state admitted to the union added to the strength of the rural classes. New York itself, once fair fighting ground for the commercial class, was becoming a farmer's state through the settlement of her rich western lands. What hope was there that commercial New England should get justice from this powerful aggregation directed by the authors of the existing policies? Probably the majority of New Englanders were not concerned with this question, but it rankled in the breasts of the federalists. Their only hope of return to power was in the defeat of the republicans, which seemed impossible, or in separation from the union. In 1803–1804 Pickering and his friends planned for separation with the support of New York, but they failed through the opposition of Hamilton (see page 300). When war against England threatened, they took up the plan again, this time hoping to join New England with Canada under British protection, thus making a great state in which the New England states would have good opportunity for commercial and political expansion. Not all New Englanders favored this plan, but the radical federalists cherished it and hoped to utilize the popular discontent to carry it through.

Isolation of the Commercial States.

Plans of the Extreme Federalists.

Their attitude was known in England. Did not Pickering keep his friend Rose, minister for the early months of 1808, well informed? And did not Jackson revel in federalist flattery from Baltimore to Boston? In 1809 came John Henry to Boston, an agent of the governor of Canada, seeking to learn just what could be expected in that quarter. His letters were discreet, but they reveal great dissatisfaction on the part of the leading federalists there. In 1812 Foster, the English minister in Washington, was in close coöperation with the federalists, they urging that England should not yield to the administration. If war came, said they, it would be short and disastrous to America, and the administration would be overthrown. And when war was declared, 34 federalists in the house, 19 of them from New England, issued an address declaring the war unjustifiable and defending England's attitude. All this was well considered in London, and as a token of appreciation the ministry in establishing the com-

Efforts to Turn Discontent into Disunion.

mercial blockade exempted the New England ports north of New London. When Madison called on the states for quotas of militia in 1812, Massachusetts and Connecticut refused to raise troops to serve out of the state, but took steps to equip their forces for state defense. There was much unemployed money in the New England banks; probably half the specie in the country was in New England. Yet the war bonds of the government could hardly be sold there, less than $3,000,000 being disposed of, while the Middle states took nearly $35,000,000. With this opposition the president could not deal. He was forced to conduct the war without much aid from the states east of the Hudson.

Early in the war the federalists in Essex county, Massachusetts, issued an address written by Senator Pickering for a convention to consider the situation within the state. There was much animated discussion in other parts of the state, but a number of conservative federalists in Boston, led by Dexter, secretary of war under Adams, checked the movement in that city, and the other towns hesitated also. The movement was revived in the autumn of 1814, when Washington was in ashes and part of Maine, then under Massachusetts authority, was occupied by the British. Governor Strong, much opposed to the war, now called out the militia to repel the invader. He placed it under state officers and asked the secretary of war if the expenses would be paid by the national government. He was told that the secretary had no authority to pay troops not in national service. Then the extremists declared that the state was abandoned in time of need, that the taxes she paid generously were not used for her defense, and that she must look out for her own interests. The governor called a meeting of the legislature, in which the program of the extremists was adopted by 250 to 76 votes in both houses. The majority chose twelve delegates to a convention at Hartford, December 15, to consider the condition of the country. Connecticut approved the movement and appointed seven delegates, while Rhode Island appointed four. The lower house in New Hampshire's legislature approved, but the council was republican and no delegates were named. Nor were any sent from Vermont. It was a rural state and had no sea-going commerce, and it was not so badly alienated.

Hartford Convention Called.

While these things occurred, came the congressional elections of 1814. In New England the federalists gained nine seats, and of the whole forty-one the republicans had only two. But in the entire country the federalist representation shrank from 68 to 65. Thus while the war party gained 12 places outside of New England, it lost within that region. The explanation is that the calamities of 1814 were uniting the people of the Middle and Southern states, and it seems that but for the efforts of the extremists the same results would have occurred in the Northeast.

Senator Pickering, in Washington, observed the meeting of the Hartford convention with delight. He had his following in it, mostly young men, who wished immediate steps taken toward separation. But another spirit prevailed. A group of more conservative men gained the ascendancy and made George Cabot, a timid man, president. Two *The Convention in Session.* delegates appointed by popular meetings in New Hampshire and one chosen by the town of Windham, Vermont, presented themselves and were given seats, making the membership 26. The meetings were secret, and continued until January 5, when an adjournment was ordered to meet in Boston at the call of the president. An address was published in justification of its conduct, filled with ideas taken from Madison's Virginia Resolutions (see page 285), and upholding the opinion that a state should conduct her defense when invaded. Seven suggested amendments to the national constitution were also announced, which, with the report, were submitted to the states represented in the convention. From the people at large and from the legislature they met a warm approval; and Massachusetts and Connecticut sent delegates to lay the demands of New England before the national government. Just at this stage, when disunion seemed inevitable, came news of the treaty signed at Ghent, December 24, and the whole movement collapsed.

Contemporaries freely charged the Hartford convention with promoting disunion, and sometimes it was pronounced traitorous. One of the members, Harrison Gray Otis, to vindicate himself in after years, published the journal of the convention. But it was a mere skeleton of the proceeding, and contained no speeches or other matter to show what the delegates really intended. Theodore Dwight, secretary of the convention, published a history of the convention, but it was in the tone of an advocate, and has not been received as a frank statement. The amendments proposed by the convention demanded concessions which congress and the nation must have denied. They asked for a relinquishment of the compromise of the constitution by which three-fifths of the slaves were counted in representation and in the apportionment of direct taxes, for a two-thirds vote to admit a new state to the union, for a like vote to declare war, or to establish commercial non-intercourse, for the prohibition of officeholding to naturalized citizens, for the ineligibility of a president for two terms, and for the denial of the authority to lay an embargo longer than sixty days. The men who announced this program were experienced political leaders. They must have had some policy in reserve to be adopted if their demands were refused. They doubtless knew they had aroused a great popular impulse which could hardly be turned backward. It is difficult to believe they expected the national government to yield, and failing that, it seems very probable

z

that they meant to carry the movement they had so carefully and ably developed to its logical conclusion, some sort of disunion.

On the other hand, it must be remembered that the union in 1814 was not so sacred a thing as later. Recently entered into on the ground that it was best for the states to act together, it was to most men still a thing of political expediency. The New Englanders were in a position to ask what it was worth to their section. The extreme federalists repudiated the republican doctrines, rejected government by all the people, and Puritan as they were, felt an aversion to a government controlled by men openly charged with skepticism. They thought, also, about their commercial interests and about the possibility of being overwhelmed by new states. From their standpoint it was not unnatural to ask if the union was an advantage to New England. These thoughts were strongest in the minds of the extreme federalists. To them the collapse of their plans with the end of the war must have been a disappointment. But to the mass of New Englanders, moderate federalists as well as republicans, the passing of the crisis was probably a relief. They quickly regained their confidence in the union, and New England discontent immediately disappeared. The federalist party, from its apparent sympathy with the Hartford convention, received a blow from which it did not recover.

One test of the efficiency of a state is its ability to meet a great crisis; for example, its ability to wage war. In this sense the war **The Lesson of the War.** of 1812 gives us an opportunity to see how far we had come in the road of political self-direction since we became an independent power. Badly as the struggle was fought out, it was carried on more successfully than the revolution. Until it began we had not seriously determined whether or not we could make war. We had no army, and a weak navy. We had no corps of trained officers to marshal the citizen soldiers. We had no machinery of credit to enable the government to place its emergency loans, and the sense of nationality was not developed to enable the government to draw the support it ought to have from all sections. The calamities of the first two years of war showed every man these weaknesses, and the lesson was well learned. When war ended, the people were aroused, they had acquired a good military organization, they were determined to have an adequate navy, they had come to see the need of common effort, they were ready for a better financial system, and they were fighting their battles better than before. When the struggle was over, the whole system of inefficiency was a thing of the past. From that time to the present the nation has never gone back to the old state of unpreparedness, the army has been better organized, the navy has been respectable, and the national resources have been held in hand with a reasonable sense of national needs. The war of 1812 was worth all it cost in national humiliation; for it taught the American people to take seriously its function of national defense.

BIBLIOGRAPHICAL NOTE

The general works on the period treated in this chapter are the books by Adams, McMaster, Schouler, Hildreth, and Wilson (see page 312), and Babcock, *Rise of American Nationality* (1906). Adams's treatment (vols. VI–IX) is the fullest, the best presented, and most scholarly, and it contains many extracts from original documents. Most histories of this period show too much sense of humiliation at the conduct of the war. It is perhaps a federalist survival. The war was badly conducted, and the people of the time were chagrined at its failures, but the historian may well suppress his feelings in order to unfold the patent causes of the failure. The only considerable work in this better spirit is Mahan, *Sea Power in its Relations to the War of 1812*, 2 vols. (1905).

The sources, legislative, diplomatic, executive, administrative, and others, are the same as for the preceding chapters (see page 312). Niles, *Weekly Register*, 76 vols. (1811–1849), begins to be valuable for this period. See also, Hart, *American History told by Contemporaries*, vol. III, chap. XIX (1906), and MacDonald, *Select Documents* (1898).

On the British side see Martineau, *History of England*, 4 vols. (American edition, 1864). Volume I deals with the years 1800–1815. The treatment is unsatisfactory, but an adequate history of England for this period remains to be written. Broderick and Fotheringham, *The Political History of England* (Hunt and Poole, editors), vol. XI (1906), treats the period in a condensed and dry manner, six pages being given to the war with the United States. Valuable documents are in Castlereagh, *Correspondence*, vols. VIII–X (1851–1853). See also the two English series, *Parliamentary Debates* (Cobbett) and *Parliamentary Papers*, and *The Annual Register*, 1810–1815. The best Canadian works are: Kingsford, *History of Canada*, 10 vols. (1887–1898), not always reliable for details; and Withrow, *Popular History of the Dominion of Canada* (1899).

Besides the biographies and writings of leading men cited on previous pages (see pages 275, 312) the following are useful: Schurz, *Life of Henry Clay*, 2 vols. (1887); Morse, *Life of John Quincy Adams* (1882); C. F. Adams, editor, *Memoirs of John Quincy Adams*, 12 vols. (1874–1877); *Writings of John Quincy Adams* (Ford, ed., 1913–); and Kennedy, *Memoir of the Life of William Wirt*, 2 vols. (ed. 1860).

Military Operations. On the American side the documents will be found in abundance in the *American State Papers*, *Military Affairs*, vol. I, and *Naval Affairs*, vol. I. Adams, *History of the United States*, vols. VI–IX, contains the best American account. It contains valuable extracts from reports. See also: C. J. Ingersoll, *Second War between the United States and Great Britain*, 4 vols. in two series (1845–1849, 1852), strongly republican; Lossing, *Pictorial Field-Book of the War of 1812* (1868), not always accurate in details; Brackenridge, *History of the Late War between the United States and Great Britain* (1817 and many later editions), a straightforward narrative; Johnson, *History of the War of 1812–1815* (1882), clear and readable; and Soley, *Wars of the United States*, in Winsor, *Narrative and Critical History*, vol. VII, contains good bibliography. The following special works are also useful: McAfee, *History of the Late War in the Western Country* (1816); Dawson, *Civil and Military Services of Major General William Henry Harrison* (1824); Cruikshank, *Documentary History of the Campaigns upon the Niagara Frontier* (1896–1904); Latour, *Historical Memoir of the War in West Florida and Louisiana in 1814–1815* (English translation, 1816); Bassett, *Life of Andrew Jackson*, 2 vols. (1911); and Parton, *Life of Andrew Jackson*, 3 vols. 1860.

British Operations. Treated in James, *Military Occurrences of the Late War*, 2 vols. (1818), — worth reading, though questioned by American writers; Gleig, *Campaigns of the British Army at Washington, Baltimore, and New Orleans* (1821), a good account; Richardson, *War of 1812* (1842, rev. ed. 1902), deals with the Canadian campaigns; and Tupper, *Life and Correspondence of Major General Sir*

Isaac Brock (rev. ed. 1847). For contemporary notice see *The Annual Register,* 1812–1815.

Naval Affairs. The leading American books are: Mahan, *Sea Power in Its Relations to the War of 1812,* 2 vols. (1905), very judicious; Maclay, *History of the United States Navy,* 2 vols. (new ed. 1901–1902), readable and generally trustworthy; Maclay, *History of American Privateers* (1899); Coggeshall, *History of the American Privateers and Letters of Marque during our War with England* (1856). The British accounts are often at variance with the American accounts. See James, *Naval History of Great Britain,* vols. IV–VI (1886), Ibid., *The Chief Naval Occurrences of the Late War* (1817); and Williams, *The Liverpool Privateers* (1897).

On the Treaty of Ghent the documents are to be found in *American State Papers, Foreign,* vol. III; Gallatin, *Writings,* and Adams's *Memoirs* contain valuable information about the negotiations. See also J. Q. Adams, *The Duplicate Letters, the Fisheries, and the Mississippi* (1822), and Ibid., *Writings,* W. C. Ford, ed. (1913–). Hildt, *Early Diplomatic Negotiations of the United States with Russia* (Johns Hopkins, *Studies,* 1906) has an account of the Russian offer of mediation.

New England Discontent. Adams is the best general authority. Other works are: Adams, *Documents Relating to New England Federalism, 1800–1815* (1878); Dwight, *History of the Hartford Convention* (1833); Carey, *The Olive Branch, or Faults on Both Sides* (1814, many times reprinted); and Goodrich, *Recollections of a Life-time,* 2 vols. (1851), contains incidents relating to the Convention.

For Independent Reading

Maclay, *A History of American Privateers* (1899); Hollis, *The Frigate Constitution* (1900); Goodrich, *Recollections of a Lifetime,* 2 vols. (1851); Dwight, *Travels in New England and New York* (1821–1822); Stone, *Life and Times of Sa-go-ye-wa-ha, or Red Jacket* (1841); Brighton, *Admiral Sir P. V. Broke* (1866); and *Memoirs and Letters of Dolly Madison* (1886).

CHAPTER XVI

SOCIAL DEVELOPMENT

GROWTH OF THE WEST AND SOUTHWEST

THE vastness of the natural resources of the continent impressed the colonists from the earliest days, and the success of the revolution strengthened this confidence. Masters of their own future, the men of 1783 eagerly looked forward to an era of rapid empire-building. In imagination they saw the interior of the continent settled by many people and divided into rich and happy states. Already the tide of settlement had passed into Kentucky and Tennessee and was beginning to penetrate the region north of the Ohio and south of Lake Erie. Further south a similar movement was rolling back the forests of western Georgia.

A glance at the early census returns shows how well the hopes of the men of 1783 were realized. In 1790 the West, exclusive of Georgia, had a population of 109,368, in 1815 the same territory contained about 1,600,000 inhabitants; and in these were not included a very numerous migration from the East to western New York. This progress was achieved at the expense of the older states, which increased in the same period from 3,819,846 to about 6,800,000 inhabitants. As all Europe was then at war, emigration to America was inconsiderable, and the rapid gain in Western population came chiefly from the older states. The South contributed its share to Tennessee and Kentucky, and to the region immediately north of the Ohio. New England was not well adapted to agriculture, and stories of the opportunity in the West carried away a constant stream of humanity from her farms and villages. New England saw their departure with chagrin. The census reports indicate how disastrous it was for her. The population of Connecticut, 237,946 in 1790, was only 275,248 in 1820, and the population of Massachusetts, exclusive of Maine, grew from 378,787 to 523,287 within the same period. Albany was the immediate objective of those who migrated, thence they traversed the Mohawk valley to the rich Genesee lands beyond it, and on to the lake, which was reached at Buffalo about 1800. In all western New York were fertile lands to which the incomers were diverted. They soon passed beyond the state's borders, following the shore of the lake into northern Ohio, and thence into the much greater forest still farther

Westward Migration.

Western New York.

west. While many New Englanders settled in the West by other routes, this direct road from Albany to Buffalo, a highway for canal and railroad traffic in our own day, was the route by which most of the New England life went to its new home in the West. Since the

Two Strata of Population in the West. Southerners settled largely in the region just north of the Ohio, it happened that for a long time there existed a clear divergence of ideals between the northern and southern parts of Ohio, Indiana, and Illinois. The advance into Georgia was almost entirely Southern, the immigrants being from Virginia and the Carolinas. They carried slaves with them, and quickly established cotton plantations which became the basis of vast wealth.

The sale of the public lands was closely connected with this progress. As long as the settlers were concerned with the Western lands claimed by New York, Connecticut, Virginia, North Carolina, and Georgia,

The Sale of Public Lands. regulations by congress were of no importance; but beyond these were the rich tracts on the Ohio, for whose disposal a land policy had to be devised. From colonial times a usual method of selling public lands was to grant them to large companies or rich individuals who could afford to open them to settlement and to import European purchasers, if necessary. Such a course was less likely to draw off the population from the older parts of the country; and for that reason it now commended itself to the majority in congress. For this reason large tracts were sold in 1788 to the Ohio Scioto Companies, and Symmes, a private speculator, got another great grant in the same year. These projects were located respectively on the Muskingum, the Scioto, and the Great Miami, all more than a hundred miles beyond the point at which the Ohio crosses the boundary between Pennsylvania and Ohio. The land adjacent to that boundary was to be sold by the government to the settlers directly.

This first plan adopted to sell the latter land, announced in 1785 and slightly modified in 1787, provided that the region between Pennsylvania and the eastern corner of the Ohio Company's

The Township System. lands should be surveyed in townships six miles square, each containing thirty-six sections one mile square, or 640 acres. The smallest amount to be sold to one buyer was to be a section, and sales were to be at auction at the seat of government at not less than one dollar an acre. The sixteenth section of each township was to be reserved for schools. In 1787 Ohio

Settlements North of the Ohio. was organized as a territory, with General St. Clair for governor. When Washington became president, the Ohio Company had planted the settlement of Marietta, and Symmes that of Cincinnati. The Scioto Company was an inflated speculation, and was soon in a collapsed condition. Between the Scioto and the Little Miami in a large tract were the mili-

tary lands reserved by Virginia for her revolutionary soldiers. In
1790 nearly 4300 white inhabitants were in the Northwest Territory, 1300 of them in and around Cincinnati, 1000 at Marietta, and
2000 in the country of the Illinois, at Kaskaskia, and on the Wabash.
Six years later the population of the territory was placed at about 15,000.

The men of the West freely declared that this slow growth was due
to the illiberal policy of land sales. The remedy, they said, was to
make purchases easy to the actual settler. In 1796 they
got a small concession. Lands might now be sold in sec- **Laws of**
tions of 640 acres, at not less than $2 an acre, and land **1796 and**
offices were to be opened at Pittsburg and Cincinnati. **1800.**
As sales did not increase, further relaxation was made in 1800 in a
law for which William Henry Harrison was chiefly responsible. Four
additional land offices were opened in Ohio, tracts as small as 320
acres might be bought, and four years' credit was allowed the purchaser.
The price remained $2 an acre. This law promoted immigration, as
was desired. In 1800 the population of Ohio was 45,365, in 1810 it
was 230,760, and in 1815 it was about 400,000.

Another result was a vast amount of land speculation, by small
owners as well as large, who bought on credit, hoping to sell at a profit
before the last payments were due. The suffering connected with the war of 1812 caused a collapse of this spec- **Further**
ulation, and in 1820 a new law gave up the credit system **Changes.**
and provided that small holdings, not less than 80 acres, should be
sold for cash at not less than $1.25 an acre, which since that time has
been the minimum price at which the public land has
been sold. Offering a small farm cheap for cash made it **Law of 1820.**
possible for any man to acquire a homestead who could pay $100,
and it favored the rapid settlement of the West. Distribution was
made still easier by laws of 1830 and 1841 providing that poor persons
settled on land without title should have a preemptive right to their
holdings. The next and last step in easy distribution was the homestead act of 1862, for the gift of small farms to actual settlers. The
provisions mentioned refer to farming lands : since 1820 timber lands
have brought not less than $2.50, mining lands $5.00, and coal lands
$10.00 an acre. All these prices were minimums. Early in the cen-
tury auctions were continually held. As the lands were opened in
districts and the best offered first, they frequently brought more than
the minimum. This was particularly true of the cotton lands in Alabama and Mississippi.

The Northwest Ordinance, 1787, created the Northwest Territory,
with governor, council, and judges appointed by congress.
When it had 5000 free male adult inhabitants a territorial **Northwest**
legislature was to be organized to make local regulations. **Ordinance,**
1787.
It was later to be divided into not less than three nor
more than five territories, and each, when it contained 60,000

inhabitants, might be admitted to the union as a state. Slavery, ex-cept as punishment for crime, was not to exist in its limits. The first congress under the constitution confirmed the ordinance and in 1790 it was adopted for the territory south of the Ohio, with some modifications, chief of which was that slavery was not forbidden in this region. It is the basis of our territorial system.

In 1800 that part of the Northwest Territory west of a line from the mouth of the Kentucky to Fort Recovery and thence north to Canada was set aside as Indiana Territory. The eastern part retained the old name, and in 1803 Ohio was admitted to the union, congress agreeing to turn over the school lands, one thirty-sixth of the total area, and to pay 3 per cent of the proceeds from land sales in the state to the construction of roads. In 1805 Michigan Territory was organized, and Illinois in 1809. These four states and territories, larger than all the Atlantic states north of the Carolinas, had in 1820 a population of 792,719, and were receiving an enormous tide of immigration. Wisconsin became a territory in 1836. As the settlers advanced the Indians fell back. Defeated by Wayne in 1794 and discouraged by the victory of Harrison at the Thames in 1813, they did not resist the encroachments on their domains. In one treaty after another they sold their possessions and retired westward.

Indiana Territory.

Other Territories.

South of the Ohio the unsettled region was on the Gulf. The compromise of 1798 (see page 301) was followed by the creation of Mississippi Territory, between the Chattahoochee and the Mississippi, bounded on the north by a line from the mouth of the Yazoo to the Chattahoochee. The lands north of this territory were conceded to Georgia. In 1802 a second and more extensive agreement was made, by which Georgia ceded to the United States her lands beyond her present boundary, receiving in return the narrow strip just south of Tennessee, $1,250,000 from the proceeds of land sales, and the promise that the national government would extinguish the Indian titles in Georgia "as early as the same can be peaceably obtained on reasonable terms." All this region was now made Mississippi Territory, and congress promised to admit it as a state when its population was as much as 60,000. Within it were Creek, Chickasaw, and Choctaw Indians, the first in what is now Alabama and western Georgia, the second and third along the Mississippi. Settlement in the South proceeded more slowly than in the North, probably because slavery kept back the poorer whites. In the first and second decades under the constitution Georgia absorbed most of the migration southward, and after 1804 Louisiana received another portion of it. During these decades the intervening region, occupied by Indians, was not reached by settlers. Jackson's victory over the Creeks, 1814, and the treaty which followed, cut a wide zone out of the heart of the Indian country,

Settlement of the Gulf Region.

Mississippi Territory.

approximately three-fourths of the later state of Alabama, and opened it to settlement. The land was very fertile, and sold at auction at high prices on credit. A few years later the price of cotton fell, and there was much suffering among the incautious speculators. But the movement brought in a large number of settlers, and in 1816 Alabama Territory was cut off from Mississippi. The settlement of this region increased the demand for slaves, prices rose, and spite of the law of 1807 against importations a great deal of smuggling followed in the Gulf region. In 1800 Mississippi Territory had 8850 inhabitants, in 1810 it had 40,352, and in 1820 it had 75,448. In 1820 Alabama had a population of 127,901. The former became a state in 1817, the latter in 1819. *Alabama Opened to Settlement.*

Meanwhile, the west bank of the Mississippi was yielding to civilization. In 1805 congress created the Territories of Orleans and Louisiana, respectively, south and north of the thirty-third degree, the seat of power of one being New Orleans and of the other St. Louis. They grew moderately. In 1810 Orleans had 76,556 inhabitants and in 1812 was admitted to the union as Louisiana. At the same time Louisiana Territory changed its name to Missouri. Thus by the end of the period under consideration, 1783–1815, the vast Western region had been staked out for the reception of a great number of inhabitants as far as the western limit of the rich strip bordering the Mississippi, and just beyond Lake Michigan in the extreme Northwest. It was not until near the middle of the century that more westerly limits were staked out. *Louisiana and Missouri.*

INDUSTRIAL DEVELOPMENT

In the West, as in the older states, the chief industry was farming. Raising food for the inhabitants themselves was the first necessity of colonies and frontier settlements. Beyond this they had supplies for the outside world, sending them down rivers to the Atlantic seaboard or to the Gulf port of New Orleans from the Mississippi valley. The acquisition of Louisiana gave a great stimulus to the latter region, because it opened to unquestioned use the great river across which Spain's hand in one way or another was generally placed in restraint of our trade. The years under consideration saw the rapid advance of manufactures in England, which raised the price of English wheat and made it more profitable for Americans to send their grain abroad. Then came the long period of European war, lessening the foreign food supply and drawing on the American market at favorable prices. Spite of restrictions on the carrying trade our exports of food products grew steadily. *Agriculture and the War in Europe.*

But the most advance in American agriculture was in cotton production. The interior parts of the South were not adapted to rice, sugar, or tobacco. Cotton they could raise, but the removal of the seed was slow and expensive. In 1793 Eli Whitney, a native of Massa-

chusetts, a graduate of Yale, and for a time a schoolmaster near
Savannah, invented the cotton gin, next to McCormick's reaper the
most important agricultural machine now in use. It
The Cotton Gin. gave a great impetus to cotton raising. From North
Carolina southward was an immense region, not well suited
to wheat production or grazing, and destined to slow development had
not this invention opened another possibility. As it was, the road to
wealth became suddenly broad and plain. Cotton was worth forty-
five cents a pound in England, and the recent development of spinning
and weaving there had made it possible to supply the world with great
quantities of cloth. In 1791 only 38 bales of cotton, of the modern
standard size, 500 pounds each, were exported from the United States.
In 1809 the whole crop was 218,723 bales, and in 1816 cotton exported
was worth $24,106,000 and was by far our most valuable single export.
At that time the price was twenty-eight cents a pound.

The production of cotton stimulated the spread of slavery in the
interior parts of the South. Vast areas of cheap land awaited cultivation for a crop yielding a ready money return, and the
Cotton and Slavery. only lack was labor. White men might have worked
them, but it was easier and quicker to employ slaves.
Besides, the social system already established in the South looked to
the creation of estates, not to a mass of small farmers; and for the
maintenance of estates a permanent laboring class was necessary. In
a new country, where the free laborer became a landowner with facil-
ity, slave labor was the only certain form of a permanent laboring
class. Thus, the introduction of cotton farming on a large scale, just
when slavery seemed in a way to be extinguished (see page 350), hardened the grasp of the institution on the far South, and checked the
growth of antislavery sentiment, then very strong, in the non-cotton-
raising slave states, Virginia, Maryland, and Delaware.

Before the adoption of the constitution the state of our commerce
was confused, and statistics for it are unsatisfactory. In 1790 the
exports were worth $19,000,000. The war which soon
Commerce. began in Europe stimulated our commerce both by raising
the price of products abroad and by making our merchants the purchasers of the products of the French, Spanish, and Dutch colonies,
products reëxported to Europe at a good profit. This colonial trade
was so profitable that complaint was made that it seriously injured
other industry by drawing to itself all the available capital in the
country. By 1795 our total foreign exports reached $67,000,000, of
which $26,000,000 were reëxported products. The colonial trade was
irregular, but it rose generally, until in 1806 it reached a maximum at
$59,640,000, while the exports of domestic origin were then less than
$49,000,000. After that came restrictive measures at home and
abroad which reduced the total exports to an average of about $33,000,-
000. There was much speculation connected with commerce in its

prosperous years, and the influence was probably bad. Merchants took chances in whatever field seemed to offer opportunity, and expected to recoup themselves by one lucky stroke for the loss through an unlucky one.

This rise in commerce was accompanied by similar progress in navigation. Before the revolution more American ships were engaged in the trade with the West Indies than in that with the British ports in Europe. After the revolution the West Indian trade was lost on account of the navigation laws, which induced congress to establish restrictions of its own. In 1789 and 1790 it enacted discriminating duties in behalf of American ships, and the consequent increase in American tonnage was so rapid that the British shipowners were in consternation. Foreign traders then employed 41.19 per cent of all the tonnage engaged in our trade. It fell slowly, until in 1795 it was only 9.7 per cent; and from that time until the war of 1812 its highest proportion was 17.2 per cent. Meanwhile, our actual tonnage grew, until in 1807 it was eight times as great as in 1789. After that it decreased under the operation of our various restrictive acts, but it recovered after the war, and in 1816 was 77.48 per cent of all the tonnage engaged in our foreign trade. The statistics available show that far the larger part of this tonnage was American built. American Shipping.

The fisheries also demanded governmental assistance. In colonial days they yielded great profits and were encouraged by the mother country as a breeding source of seamen. The treaty of 1783 guaranteed the American fishermen the right to fish on the Banks, and in territorial waters as well, but did not allow them to dry fish on any but unsettled shores. Whatever advantage lay in this was later neutralized by restrictions passed in England forbidding the importation of the product of foreign fisheries and by English bounties to fishermen. Loud complaints now arose from the whale and cod fishers of America. Deprived of their best market, they petitioned congress for aid, and so much was it felt that our own nurseries of the sea should be sustained that one of the first steps taken by congress under the constitution was to allow a drawback on fish exported equal to the duty on the salt used in curing them. In 1792 the law went farther, and awarded a bounty in money to persons engaged in cod fishing. Under its operation the industry revived and became prosperous. The Fisheries.

The embargo, the subsequent restrictions, and the war which followed again checked the fisheries, to the great satisfaction of the Canadians, who resented having to share the inshore fishing with the Americans. In their behalf the British government, in making the treaty of Ghent, sought to withhold the right. It held that the war ended the treaty grants of 1783, and would not yield them again unless we allowed The Fisheries after 1815.

British subjects to navigate the Mississippi. To this Clay, one of the negotiators, objected so stoutly that the treaty as finally made was silent on each question. It was, however, agreed that later negotiations should settle the fisheries question. With the return of peace Americans appeared in their old haunts only to be warned off by armed vessels. They might fish, they were told, on the Banks, but they would not be allowed within territorial waters. Then came negotiations, the upshot of which was provisions in the convention of 1818 that our fishermen might take fish off the Magdalen Islands, in the Gulf of St. Lawrence, and along the most unsettled shores of Newfoundland and Labrador, with the privilege of curing fish and getting certain necessary supplies in uninhabited parts. On this basis the fisheries continued with a restricted prosperity.

The years immediately following the revolution saw a sad disorder in the currency. Exports were relatively small and much of the foreign specie which had come into the country in the channels of trade was drained out to pay balances. Seven states sought to remedy the deficiency by a return to paper money, or state notes, a form of currency forbidden in the constitution soon to be adopted. In 1791 a national bank was created with a capital stock of $10,000,000. Its notes were issued cautiously, and were gladly received everywhere. Its power to present for redemption the notes of state banks enabled it to check overissue by such banks. Thus the paper currency was sound until the charter of the bank expired in 1811. The bank asked for a continuation of its existence, but the republican majority was very hostile, and would not even allow an extension to wind up its affairs. Then a swarm of state banks sprang up, each issuing its notes without restraint. The government was soon at war, and, anxious to get money of any kind, gave its bonds for these insecure overissues, and received them for its dues, with the result that it lost $5,000,000 in the process. In 1811 there were 88 state banks with a total circulation of $22,700,000: in 1816 there were 246, with circulation of $68,000,000. This alarming inflation led to the incorporation of the second United States bank, 1816, and by 1820 the circulation of the state banks had fallen to $40,641,574. In the panic which followed the capture of Washington, 1814, all the banks south of New England suspended specie payment and did not resume until 1817. During the war of 1812 $36,680,000 of treasury notes were issued, nearly half of which was outstanding at the end of 1815.

The last quarter of the eighteenth century brought a great revolution in the world's manufactures. Before that time weaving, spinning, nail-making, and most everything else was done by hand in the homes of cottagers. But beginning with Hargreaves's spinning jenny, 1764, several inventions led to the power loom, by which the textile industry was shifted

The Currency.

Distress in the War of 1812.

New Era in Manufactures.

from the cottages of the operatives to the factory of the great manufacturer. The same thing happened in other lines, and the result was the factory system, with its large outlay of capital and its peculiar relation of employer and employees. This process was first established in England, and it was well developed by 1800.

For a time no response to this English development was seen in American industry. There was from colonial days a good deal of manufacturing of the old kind, ironware, hats, shoes, nails, and farm implements being some of the notable products. **Early Manufactures in America.** The lack of capital, the profits of agriculture, and the ability of British manufacturers to undersell served to delay the introduction of the new system. But spite of the difficulties, some advance was made. In 1793, the year Whitney invented the cotton gin, Samuel Slater, in partnership with Moses Brown, set up at Pawtucket, Rhode Island, the first successful cotton factory in the United States. It was supplied with machinery of the British design, and its example was imitated in many other places, although the enterprises struggled along with many drawbacks.

In 1807 began the restrictions of the importation of British merchandise, lasting in one form or another until the war, which, with the blockade that followed it, effectually shut out foreign goods. Thus for eight years the American manufacturers **Influence of the Embargo and the War.** had the home market to themselves. The result was a marvelous rise in manufacturing. In 1807 the cotton industry employed 8000 spindles, two years later it had 80,000; and similar progress was made in other lines. Among all classes spread an enthusiasm for articles made in America, and politicians wishing to be popular appeared on public occasions in homespun clothes. Since the failure in commerce resulted in much unemployed capital and labor in the seacoast region of New England, it was here that manufactures gained most rapidly. The proverbial Yankee skill with machinery and the hard conditions of farming added to the stimulus. At the close of the war New England supplied a large part of the country's merchandise, and the agricultural South was sending thither $6,000,000 a year to **Effects of Manufacturing on Society.** settle balances for goods purchased at higher prices than it formerly paid abroad. It seemed to the federalists a just retribution that they who forced the war on the country should thus be made to feel one of its burdens. The rise of manufactures created a new class of rich men, less prominent in social and business matters than the old aristocracy of commerce. Between the two classes there followed sharp dissensions, but the manufacturers had greater natural strength than their rivals, and with the aid of a protective tariff gained so rapidly in wealth that ten years after the war they dominated the policy of the government in relation to business.

SLAVERY MADE SECTIONAL

In 1776 slavery existed in all the states. Many of the colonists wished to arrest its spread, but the British merchants protested, and the

The Slave Trade in the Revolutionary Period. king vetoed the restrictive colonial laws. The colonists resented his action, and seized the first opportunity to act for themselves. In the "Association" of 1774 slave importations were forbidden, the first congress after independence reasserted the restriction, and for the rest of the

revolution the trade was checked. After the war commerce generally was controlled by the states, all of which but those in the far South forbade the slave trade. There were vast unsettled regions in the Carolinas and Georgia, and it was thought they must have negroes to develop them. But even here the advocates of restriction won, and by 1798 each of these states had forbidden further importations. The constitution, it will be remembered, declared that congress could not prohibit the trade before 1808.

Meanwhile, a movement for emancipation had swept over the entire North. In this section were few slaves, and the opponents of

Emancipation in the North — under Constitutional Provisions; the institution needed only to organize the non-slaveholders, a large majority, to carry laws for emancipation. Vermont led the way in 1777 by declaring slavery illegal in the bill of rights incorporated in her constitution, and New Hampshire did the same in the constitution of 1784. In each state the few slaveholders could only convert

their slaves into servants for wages or sell them out of the reach of the state's jurisdiction. The Massachusetts constitution of 1780 declared that "all men are born free and equal," and in 1783 the court in a test case held that this annulled a master's right to the labor of his slave. Thus in three states the institution passed quietly out of existence.

In others the cause of freedom encountered greater opposition, but its advocates had recourse to the legislatures. Their request for eman-

by Statute. cipation by state statutes was met with argument that to free the slaves was to confiscate property. After

struggles of varying length, they carried each Northern state but one for gradual emancipation, which meant that slave children born after the enactment of the said statutes should be free on reaching a specified age, usually twenty-five years. The first victory of this kind was in Pennsylvania, chiefly through the efforts of the Quakers; and it came in 1780. Connecticut and Rhode Island followed in 1784, New York in 1799, and New Jersey in 1804. The men of New York were not satisfied with their achievement, and in 1817, when the power of the slaveholders was much weakened, a law was carried for complete emancipation after 1827. Delaware alone of the Northern states retained slavery, and here it was safe until the end of the civil war.

The movement for freedom was felt south of the Mason and Dixon line and was strong in Virginia, where Jefferson, Washington, and many other leading men wished to rid the state of an unprofitable form of labor and of the presence of an alien and undeveloped element of the population. But here was encountered a more serious obstacle than had yet appeared. The small proportion of blacks in the North involved no menace to the civilization there, were they slave or free. But the people of Virginia knew not what to do with a great mass of freed blacks. To leave them masters of their own actions in the white population seemed to invite trouble, and to send them to Africa, which many thought the only proper accompaniment of emancipation, was so expensive that it was out of the question. These objections proved fatal to the efforts of the more far-seeing ones; and thus it happened that two plans for abolishing slavery, one announced in 1779 and the other in 1796, were found impracticable. At this time the invention of the cotton gin had begun to have its effect on slavery, making a great demand for slaves in the states to the southward and raising the prices of them to such a point that masters felt a growing unwillingness to part with such an important source of wealth. Thus the seaboard states settled down to a free and a slave section, a basis of opposition in interest which proved very fruitful of later conflict. West of the mountains the same principle was followed. By the Northwest Ordinance the Ohio divided slavery from freedom between the Mississippi and the Alleghanies. Then came the Missouri Compromise line for the Louisiana purchase; but eventually the matter no longer admitted of compromise.

The Emancipation Movement fails in the South.

From the beginning of the national government the South feared the North would use her position in the union to restrict slavery. There was warm debate when in the first congress petitions for restrictions of the slave trade came from abolitionists. The result was the adoption of a set of resolutions guaranteeing that slavery should be left to the jurisdiction of the states and that the slave trade should be undisturbed before 1808. In 1793 a fugitive slave law was passed. It gave the master the right to recover an absconding slave by proving ownership before a magistrate without jury or ordinary forms of law. The law was hard on the slave, but it was necessary from his owners' standpoint. To provide otherwise would enable the slave to have the trial postponed, at heavy expense to the claimant, who might at last lose the suit through the sympathy of a Northern jury. On the other hand, it left the disposition of the freedom of a human being to the irresponsible decision of the lowest rank of courts, a thing not ordinarily allowed in the pettiest property suits. Later it was charged that unprincipled men, by bribing some magistrates, carried away to slavery negroes who were unquestionably free. The reflec-

Slavery in Congress.

First Fugitive Slave Law, 1793.

tion of the historian on this matter is that slavery at its best was an
unhappy relation, involving hardship in its primary and secondary relations, and supporting itself by destroying the commonest personal rights.

For some years after 1793 the question was not discussed in congress.
The Haytian insurrection of 1791 was accompanied by murder and
outrage, and a spasm of terror shot through the South and
North at the thought of what might happen in our own
land if slaves once began to strike for freedom. By general consent it was thought well to let the subject alone.

Revived Movement for Slaves in the South.

But the approach of 1808, when the foreign slave trade
might be forbidden, reminded the South that it must act at once if
it recruited its slave supply before the doors were closed to importation.
In 1803, therefore, South Carolina repealed her law against the slave
trade. This brought protests from the North, and futile efforts were
made to get congress to lay an importation tax of ten dollars a head on
slaves. In 1806 Jefferson, always an enemy of slavery, took up the
cause, recommending congress to pass a law to prohibit the foreign
slave trade after January 1, 1808.

The suggestion was acceptable to congress, but it was hard to agree
upon details, the greatest difficulty being the disposal of slaves illegally
brought in. To return them to Africa was impossible, the
suggestion that they be liberated in the place of capture
was resented by the Southerners, who would not have
free negroes among them, and the idea that they be sold
by the government was rejected by Northerners, since it made the
federal government party to slave selling and but increased the South's
number of slaves. After much discussion it was decided that such
slaves should be turned over to the state in which they were seized,
to be disposed of as it chose. The captured slave dealer should forfeit
ship and cargo, be fined from one to ten thousand dollars, and be imprisoned from five to ten years. To prevent irregularities, it was also
ordered that in the future the coastwise interstate slave trade
should be limited to vessels of forty or more tons and that the slaves
thus carried should be registered. The act of 1807 was to go into
force with the beginning of the following year. It was frequently
violated. Slave prices now became higher than ever, and
adventurous slavers took cargoes into the isolated bays
and rivers of the unwatched coast, where the planters, ever anxious to
get slaves, were as reticent as the smugglers.

Importations Forbidden.

Smuggling.

Religious Development after the Revolution

The English Church was established by law in Maryland, Virginia,
and North and South Carolina, although it had a real hold on the
people only in Virginia and South Carolina. In Massachusetts,
Connecticut, and New Hampshire the Puritan form of religion was

established by law. Only Pennsylvania, Delaware, and Rhode Island had no state church. But the war brought a spirit of religious liberty, and at its end every establishment except those of New England was swept away. The clergy of the English Church in America, bound by strongest ties to the royal prerogative, had been generally loyal to the crown. **The Fate of the Establishments.** Most of them had left the country with the other tories, and the old church, discredited by its opposition to the revolution, was in a state of disintegration, a condition which afforded excellent opportunity for the dissenting churches to gather up the scattered fragments.

The first to take advantage of the situation were the Methodists, who appeared in the colonies about 1760. Their preaching was popular, and their followers, though formed into "societies," were first considered members of the English Church. **The Methodists.** When that church was prostrate on account of the revolution, the "societies" appealed to Wesley, the father of the Methodist movement, who in 1784 advised them to unite in one body, with superintendents, who later were called bishops, and a system of church government, called "the discipline." The result was the organization of the Methodist Episcopal Church at Baltimore during the Christmas holidays, 1784. The world has rarely seen a more zealous body of leaders than the itinerant preachers who now began to penetrate to the remotest settlements, kindling the imagination of the masses by fervid appeals to the conscience, protraying the effects of irreligion, and exalting the power of the spirit. Their most prominent leader was Francis Asbury, a man of heroic zeal, aptly compared by his followers with that other Francis, who in the thirteenth century filled Europe with the echoes of his good deeds. In New England, where congregationalism was firmly rooted, the results were comparatively small; but in the Middle states and the South, and particularly in the new communities of the West and Southwest, they had wonderful success and made themselves a powerful agency in the lives of the people.

Meanwhile the older non-episcopal churches extended their influence. Most numerous, perhaps, were the Baptists, who were especially strong in the South Atlantic states. In colonial times they were generally Calvinists. Their government was **The Baptists.** congressional and they were not held together in a general organization. But the renewed religious life around them, together with the common impulse toward union which came from the formation of a national government, led to the organization of a general convention in 1814. One of the chief objects of this movement was to promote missions, a thing to which those who held to the older forms objected so strenuously that they gradually withdrew from the convention. The seceders called themselves Primitive Baptists, while the others, a more numerous group, were called Missionary Baptists, in contrast. It was a time of general religious activity, and resulted in renewed prosperity of the Presbyterian, Lutheran, Quaker, and other organizations, and several newer bodies, the results **Other** of separating impulses, now came into existence. The **Churches.** Roman Catholics, at first strong in Maryland, and planted in every large seacoast town, also began to increase in numbers, chiefly through the accession of immigrants, many of whom were from Ireland. In this manner did the leaven of nationality work in the creation of a strong native American movement for the establishment of the American type of religion.

All this had its effect on the English Church in America. Threatened with extermination through the failure of its connection with the Church of England, it began soon after the revolution to **The Prot-** reorganize itself on an American basis. Its first need was **estant Epis-** a national organization, something it could not have in a **copal** system which had for cardinal doctrine the ecclesiastical **Church** **Organized.** supremacy of the English king. All efforts to secure the creation of an American episcopate had failed before the revolution, but peace was hardly made before they were renewed. At last Samuel Seabury, of Connecticut, was in 1784 consecrated bishop of Connecticut by three non-juring bishops in Scotland. Then the British parliament gave way, and by act allowed the archbishops of Canterbury and York to consecrate, in 1786, two American bishops, and three years later these, with Seabury, completed in Philadelphia the organization of the Protestant Episcopal Church in the United States. As the survivor of the English establishment, it had much dignity in the new nation and embraced in its membership a large proportion of the men of influence outside of New England, while the Methodist, Baptist, and Presbyterian churches took place as the great popular religious bodies.

Although Puritanism maintained formal hold on New England, it was internally at the point of disintegration. Of its three factions, these who held to strict Calvinism, and the "Hopkinsans," **The Con-** who were followers of Jonathan Edwards, and promoted **gregation-** missions and revivals, considered themselves more orthodox **alists.** than the third party, who were soon to be called Unitarians. This third group was strong in the Boston churches and among the wealthier class on the seaboard. They opposed revivals and questioned so many of the orthodox principles that men began to ask, "Shall we have the Boston religion, or the Christian religion?" The controversy became warm in 1815 when it was known that leaders of the party corresponded with the English Unitarians. The result was a separation in many of the older churches and the open avowal of Unitarian doctrines. The most eminent leader of the movement was William Ellery Channing, of Boston. In 1825 the American Unitarian Association was founded with general oversight of the movement. In the struggle against the Unitarians the two older factions drew closer together, merged their doctrinal differences in a system which became known as the New England Theology, and established in 1808 Andover Seminary as the nourishing center of the faith. Long before this the New England churches had been called "Congregational," to distinguish them from other churches. The term became of special significance in the West, where the large body of New Englanders, planting their own religion, was thrown into contact with other strong organizations. True to the congregational form of government, they had no general law-making authority, but their great common undertakings, as home and foreign missions, were committed to general boards, which gave cohesion to the common movement.

One other reform needed to be made to modernize the religious life of New England: it must accept disestablishment, already existing in Rhode Island and in the Middle and Southern states. Episcopalians, Baptists, Methodists, and every other independent church, and eventually the Unitarians, demanded a change. Defenders of the "Standing Order," as the old system was called, pronounced the demand irreligious and asserted that the power of truth against the reign of evil would be destroyed if the state, by means of the public taxes, ceased to support an orthodox and fearless clergy. As Jefferson was the leader of disestablishment in the South, his political party, the republicans, became defenders of liberalism in New England. Similarly the Standing Order, that is, the town clergy, were stout federalists. The battle was hard, but the orthodox party was worsted. The first relaxation was a compromise, following a line which had appeared in the colonial struggle between Puritans and Episcopalians. It was provided that members of a dissenting church might be relieved from taxes to support religion if they presented certificates that they supported their own organizations. This did not benefit those who were members of no church, and it was resented by all who believed in the separation of church and state as a principle. So the struggle went on until the liberals triumphed in state after state. Vermont led the way and adopted complete separation in 1807; Connecticut followed in 1818, New Hampshire in 1819, Maine in 1820, the year she secured statehood, and Massachusetts after a long struggle in 1834.

Disestablishment in New England.

EXPLORATION IN THE FAR WEST

Although the Mississippi was our western boundary in 1783, we could not but be interested in the vast region beyond it. Owned by Spain, as it was, its Indians might be a menace in war or a source of profitable trade in peace. For many years our sole information about them came from chance travelers and traders, and Jefferson, soon after he became president projected an expedition which should secure more reliable intelligence and establish, if possible, friendly relations with the Indians of the plains. Congress consenting, Captain Meriwether Lewis and Lieutenant William Clark, with 43 men, soldiers and others, began to ascend the Missouri on a voyage which was to make them famous. By this time Louisiana had been purchased, and their exploration had thus acquired added significance. They went into winter quarters near the present town of Bismarck, North Dakota, where they met a squaw, the "Bird Woman," formerly captured from the mountain tribes, who with her husband agreed to accompany them.

Lewis and Clark Dispatched.

In the spring they proceeded to the mountains, encountering many difficulties of a physical nature. Here the savages avoided them until it was discovered that the chief of the tribe was brother of the "Bird Woman." Guides were now furnished, with whose aid the explorers reached the tributaries of the Columbia. Building canoes in the Indian fashion they embarked, and November 7, 1805, reached the mouth of the river, the Pacific ocean before them. The neighboring tribes were hardly friendly, but the explorers built a fort for the winter, claiming the country in behalf of their government. Next spring they returned with many difficulties to the East, exploring, after they crossed the mountains, the Yellowstone river and other tributaries of the Missouri. They were men of intelligence, and their narrative of travel, though full of the irregular spelling of the day, has come to be considered a classic among American books of exploration. Their discovery furnished the most important basis of our claim to Oregon.

Their Discoveries in Oregon.

Another famous explorer of this period was Lieutenant Zebulon Pike. In 1805 he explored the headwaters of the Mississippi, seeking its source. He encountered many hardships in a winter journey and was forced to accept hospitality from agents of the British Northwest Company, who were illegally trading within our boundaries. The frozen condition of streams rendered his conclusions about the headwaters of the great river unreliable. He was back at St. Louis in April, 1806, and in the following August set out to explore the Arkansas and the Southwest. He reached the Rocky mountains and penetrated them near the peak which bears his name. His object is not definitely known, but it is supposed that he intended to reach the Rio Grande and examine the country east of it, which we claimed under the Louisiana purchase. It was a great task, and he lost his way, suffered much from hunger and cold, and at last fell into the hands of Spanish soldiers, who relieved his wants, conducted him in a roundabout way through Texas, and finally set him at liberty on the Louisiana border. Some of his followers were never heard of after they left him in an independent attempt

Pike's Two Journeys.

to return home. Pike published an interesting and very popular account of his travels. He was a brave man and rapidly rose to distinction in the war of 1812 until he met his death as brigadier general at the capture of York, in 1813. His explorations in the Southwest and those of Lewis and Clark in the Northwest appealed to the American imagination and stimulated powerfully the desire to own and settle the Far West.

EARLY CONSTITUTIONAL INTERPRETATION

The makers of the constitution expressed its meaning as clearly as the limitation of language and the necessity of compromise permitted. But however clear its meaning, it was to be expected that congress, president, and the states themselves would construe their rights under the new instrument, each to its own advantage. The arbiter between such contending interpretations was the supreme court, endowed with the power to pass on cases arising under the constitution. It could thus decide whether or not congress, state, or president improperly read the charter of government, and its decision was final. If a question arose of its own power under the constitution, the court passed on this also. Since final power must rest somewhere, it was, perhaps, best to leave it with a small body of learned and unprejudiced men. But many people of the day did not readily accept this view. The three great spheres of government, they said, should be mutually coördinate, and apparently it was so intended by the fathers. Nothing short of a constitutional amendment could settle the dispute clearly, and in default of that the court asserted final jurisdiction in the matter under consideration. *The Function of the Supreme Court.*

At first the supreme court was not inclined to assert its powers, partly because the judges were naturally cautious and partly because they wished to avoid exciting criticism in the early years of the union. But its attitude changed when, in 1801, John Marshall, of Virginia, became chief justice. This strong-willed and aggressive man, who believed the union ought to have the necessary power to execute its will was the controlling personality on the supreme bench from his appointment until his death in 1835. By his strong mind and character he won to his views the associate justices, even the appointees of the republican presidents, and laid down a large body of precedent on the loose-construction theory of the constitution. "He was born," said Pinkney, of Maryland, "to be chief justice of any country in which he lived." *The Influence of John Marshall.*

His first important decision of this nature was in the case of Marbury *vs.* Madison. February 13, 1801, the federalists, about to relinquish power, created sixteen new federal judges, with the ordinary complement of marshals and clerks of court. The law was denounced as unnecessary and as an attempt to fill the courts with federalists before the republicans took control, and one of the first acts of the new administration was to get the law repealed. The original bill was passed so hurriedly that Adams was not able to appoint and install the new officials ere he gave up his power. When the new secretary of state took office, many of the commissions were found in the office undelivered; and Jefferson, holding that an appointment was not complete until the commission was signed, sealed, and delivered, ordered that the commissions should be withheld. He thought an appointment followed the procedure of a deed. Marbury asked the supreme court to issue a mandamus for the delivery of one of these commissions, and the matter was argued in the supreme court. Marshall, who gave the opinion, held that since the supreme court by the constitution did not have original jurisdiction in such a case, Marbury had no right to bring suit in that tribunal. This ordinarily would have ended the matter, but he went on to say, and it was an *obiter dictum*, that a commission was not analogous to a deed, that Madison had no right to withhold one duly signed, and that Marbury, if he had brought suit in proper form, would be entitled to his office. The republicans denounced this decision as partisan. But it had a still wider significance. Congress had previously passed a law giving the court the right to issue a mandamus, and it was under that act that the suit was brought. In declaring the contrary, therefore, the court had annulled a law of congress, and this is the chief constitutional import of the decision.

Marbury vs. Madison, 1803.

In Fletcher *vs.* Peck the act of a state legislature was in question. The assembly of Georgia had granted certain lands, and afterwards declared the grant null on account of fraud. Peck claimed land under this annulled grant and brought suit in the federal courts, urging that Georgia had violated the clause of the constitution which forbids a state to pass a law "impairing the obligation of a contract." Georgia put herself on her sovereignty and replied that a land grant, made by the state in the disposal of its domain, was not a contract. The court held, Marshall giving the decision, that a grant is a contract and that the attempt of Georgia to repeal the grant was illegal. Here the court declared unconstitutional an act of a state legislature. But now appeared a difficulty which has since then limited the power of the court. Who was to execute the decision of the court against a state? Ordinarily it would be the president, but if he thought it advisable to decline to act, there was no power to compel him. This happened to the decision in Fletcher *vs.* Peck. Georgia thus defied the court, and the only way out of the difficulty was the compromise, made in 1814, in which congress by paying money salved the feelings of the claimants under the Georgia grants.

Fletcher vs. Peck, 1810.

These two decisions, it will be seen, were aimed at two doctrines dear to the heart of the republicans. In the first it was held that the popular will as expressed in a congressional law must be restrained by the constitution: in the second the doctrine of state sovereignty was shorn of some of its power; for Georgia's claim that the people of a state acting through the legislature were sovereign in state affairs was made to yield to the supremacy of the federal constitution. The supreme court, under Marshall's leadership, was intent on establishing this general view, and after the war of 1812 proceeded to do so in several other important cases. Two of them are especially significant, and both were decided in 1819.

Political Aspect of the Decisions.

First came McCulloch *vs.* Maryland, relating to the power of congress under the "implied powers" clause of the constitution, article I, section 8. Much popular opposition existed to the bank of the United States, and several states passed laws to tax its notes, one of them being Maryland. The bank resisted the taxes, and the matter came before the supreme court. Two questions arose: Has congress power to create a bank? and have the states power to tax a bank, if created? Marshall answered the first in the broadest possible manner. The government, he said, has all the power implied in the act of its creation: "Let the end be legitimate, let it be within the scope of the constitution, and all means which are appropriate, which are plainly adapted to that end, which are not prohibited but consistent with the letter and spirit of the constitution, are constitutional." If congress should pass a law which by the constitution it may not pass, the court would declare that law of no effect; but if the court pretended to annul a law of congress made in the field proper to the activity of congress, the court would by that action enter the field of law-making, a thing it had no right to do. As the creation of a bank was not prohibited to congress, and as a bank was a thing useful in the happy and prosperous government of the nation, the court must hold that it was within the power of the national legislature to establish it. As for the second question, the right of a state to tax the bank, that was also opposed; for if a small tax could be laid, a large one could also be laid, and thus the bank, lawful in itself, could be taxed out of existence. "The power to tax," said Marshall in words long remembered, "involves the power to destroy."

McCulloch vs. Maryland, 1819.

The second great case decided in 1819, and nearly as important as the McCulloch case, was Dartmouth College *vs.* Woodward. The New Hampshire legislature, in response to the political feeling of the day, wished to get control of the college and amended its charter with that end in view and against the protest of the college authorities. Suit was brought, and the case went before the supreme court, Webster,

The Dartmouth College Case, 1819.

a Dartmouth alumnus, appearing among the lawyers for the college.
Is a charter granted to a corporation inviolate by the legislature? was
the question. The court held that a charter is a contract and not to
be recalled by the legislature provided the grantee observes the conditions on which it was granted. The decision became a precedent in
all cases arising under acts of incorporation, a large part of modern
law. Under it banks, manufacturing, and many other kinds of cor-
porate companies have insisted that they could not be disturbed in
their business relations. As Marshall laid down the principle, the companies seem to have had absolute immunity from interference, a position quite contrary to modern ideas that corporations should be under
state control. This difficulty has been obviated by several subsequent
decisions by which it is held that a legislature may modify a charter
under the exercise of the police power, under its right to pass laws for
good morals, and on other grounds. These later decisions have
greatly modified the force of Marshall's ruling, but in ordinary cases
that rule still remains the great principle for the government of
corporations. It was, when made, a direct blow at the assumed right
of a state to limit the action of an individual through the exercise of
its sovereign power over him.

These decisions were received with indignation by the ultra republicans. Victorious in the elections, masters of the executive and
legislative parts of government, they writhed to see the ju-
Significance diciary annul the will of the people as expressed in the elec-
of Mar- tions, while in decision after decision it completed a system
shall's De- of centralized power greatly at variance with the principles
cisions. of the party which ruled. But for all their contempt,
Marshall did not quail. Doffing the neutrality of an ideal judge he
boldly set himself the task of shaping the constitution in its most
plastic period. His decisions became precedents in every court in
the land. They gave strength and steadiness to a government, which
by the nature of the case, was in the hands of the least competent
portion of its citizens. They saved popular government from the effects of radicalism while the ideals of conservatism struck root in the
crude but ripening society then spreading itself over the face of a new
continent. No greater deed of firm leadership has been performed in
our country than this persistent assertion of the vital will of the federal
republic.

Another case, Chisholm v. Georgia, decided that a state might be
sued by a citizen of another state. It displeased the states and resulted in the eleventh amendment, 1798. Six years later the twelfth
amendment was in force, providing that electors should vote sep-
arately for president and vice-president.

BIBLIOGRAPHICAL NOTE

On the general social history of the period treated in this chapter the best work is McMaster, *History of the People of the United States*, 7 vols. (1883–1910), containing many chapters of interest; Adams, *History of the United States*, vol. I (1889). chaps. I–IV contain valuable accounts of social and intellectual conditions; See also Bassett, *The Federalist System*, Chaps. X–XIII (1906); Hart, *American History Told by Contemporaries*, III (1906); Simons, *Social Forces in American History*, chaps. VIII–XII (1911); Fess, *Political Theory and Party Organization in the United States*, chaps. I–V (1910); and Griswold, *The Republican Court* (1864). On the public lands see Donaldson, *The Public Domain* (Pub. Land Comssn. *Report*, 1881); and Treat, *The National Land System* (1910).

Many European travelers visited America immediately after the revolution and wrote and published their impressions of the country. A list of them with critical discussions is found in Tuckerman, *America and her Commentators* (1864). The most important works of this nature are: Brissot de Warville, *New Travels* [1788] (1791, 1792), enthusiastically biased in favor of republicanism; Duc de Rochefoucauld-Liancourt, *Travels . . . 1795–1797*, 2 vols. (London ed. 1799), has many facts, but the author did not understand American life; Weld, *Travels . . . 1795–1797*, 2 vol. (1799); Campbell, *Travels in the Interior . . . 1791–1792* (1793), relates to New York, the Northwest, and Canada; Dwight, *Travels in New England and New York* [1796–1815], 4 vols. (1821–1822); Melish, *Travels in the United States, 1806–1807, 1809–1811*, 2 vols. (1812); and Bradbury, *Travels in the Interior . . . 1809, 1810, 1811* (1817). After the return of peace in Europe and America came a revival of interest in immigration, and several foreigners who came to the United States to investigate the conditions here wrote books which were published for the instruction of those who proposed to emigrate. Among them are: Fearon, *Narrative of a Journey, etc.* (1817); Birkbeck, *Notes on a Journey in America* (1818); Ibid., *Letters from Illinois* (1818); and Cobbett, *A Year's Residence in the United States* (1819).

Most of these travelers visited the Northwest and described conditions there in frontier days. A general work of great excellence on the settlement of that region is Matthews, *The Expansion of New England* (1909). See also: Turner, *The Rise of the New West* (1906); Boggess, *The Settlement of Illinois, 1778–1830* (Chicago Hist. Soc. *Collections*, 1908); and Hinsdale, *The Old Northwest*, 2 vols. (1888, 1899). Conditions in the South and Southwest are described in: Phillips, *Georgia and State Rights* (Amer. Hist. Assn. *Report*, 1901, vol. II); Schaper, *Sectionalism and Representation in South Carolina* (Ibid., 1900, vol. I); and Pickett, *History of Alabama*, 2 vols. (1851, 1900).

On far western explorations see Thwaites, *Rocky Mountain Exploration* (1904) for a good summary. Lewis and Clark prepared full notes of their explorations, which were edited by Nicholas Biddle, later president of the second bank of the United States. They appeared as *History of the Expedition under the Command of Captains Lewis and Clark, . . . 1804, 1805, 1806, Prepared for the Press by Paul Allen*, 2 vols. (1814). The best modern edition is edited by Thwaites in eight volumes (1904–1905). It is a verbatim reproduction of all the journals kept by the two leaders and other members of the expedition. Pike wrote an account of his travels, published under the title, *Account of Expeditions to the Sources of the Mississippi. . . . And a Tour through the Interior Parts of New Spain*, 2 vols. (1810).

The history of American industry has not been adequately written. Bassett, *Federalist System* (1906) has a brief chapter on conditions from 1789 to 1801. A longer and more general treatment is in Coman, *Industrial History* (1905, 1910); and Bogart, *Economic History of the United States* (ed. 1907). See also Adams, *History of the United States*, vols. V and VIII (1891) for the influence of manufactures; Seybert, *Statistical Annals . . . 1789–1818* (1818) has many valuable statistics on commerce. See also: Dewey, *Financial History of the United States* (1903); Bishop, *History of American Manufactures*, 3 vols. (1864–1867); Bagnall,

Textile Industries of the United States, vol. I (1893), only one volume appeared; Ibid., *Samuel Slater and the Development of Cotton Manufacture ;* Hammond, *Cotton Industry* (Amer. Econ. Assn. *Publications*, 1897); and Swank, *History of the Manufacture of Iron* (ed. 1892).

On slavery the following are important: Locke, *Anti-Slavery in America . . . 1619–1808* (1901); Du Bois, *Suppression of the Slave Trade* (1896); Ballagh, *Slavery in Virginia* (1902); Brackett, *The Negro in Maryland* (1889); Bassett, *History of Slavery in North Carolina* (Johns Hopkins University *Studies*, 1899); and Hurd, *The Law of Freedom and Bondage*, 2 vols. (1858–1862).

No good general history of religion in the United States has been written from the secular standpoint, and the student must rely chiefly on the histories of the individual churches. Of these, perhaps the most satisfactory is the series known as *The American Church History Series*, edited by Schaff and others. The following volumes are especially valuable: Walker, *The Congregationalists* (1894); Newman, *The Baptists* (1894); Thompson, *The Presbyterians* (1895); Allen, *The Unitarians* (1894); Tiffany, *The Protestant Episcopalians* (1895); and Carroll, *The Religious Forces of the United States* (1893), a general introduction to the series. Other works of importance are: Bacon, *History of American Christianity* (1897); Buckley, *History of Methodism*, 2 vols. (1898); Cross, *The Anglican Episcopate and the American Colonies* (1902); Pond, *Sketches of the Theological History of New England* (1880–); Asbury, *Journals*, 3 vols. (many eds.); and Lauer, *Church and State in New England* (Johns Hopkins University *Studies*, 1892).

On Marshall's great constitutional decisions the best work, perhaps, is Cotton, editor, *Constitutional Decisions of John Marshall*, 2 vols. (1905), the decisions given *in extenso*, accompanied by explanatory remarks by the editor. See also: Thayer, *Cases on Constitutional Law*, 2 vols. (1895); Ibid., *John Marshall* (1901); Magruder, *John Marshall* (ed. 1898); Story, *Life and Letters of Joseph Story*, 2 vols. (1851); Babcock, *Rise of American Nationality*, chap. XVIII (1906); and Elliott, *Biographical Story of the Constitution*, chap. VI (1910).

For Independent Reading

Longstreet, *Georgia Scenes* (1897 and many earlier eds.); Irving, *Captain Bonneville* (1849); Dana, *Two Years before the Mast* (1849); Smedes, *Memorials of a Southern Planter* (1887, 1890); and Chittenden, *The American Fur Trade of the Far West*, 3 vols. (1902).

CHAPTER XVII

THE LAST OF THE VIRGINIA DYNASTY

REFORMS OF 1816–1817

AMERICAN history comes to a new period in 1815. Before that year our chief concern was foreign affairs. This was not through the desire of the men of the day, but partly because the new nation must first of all adjust its relation with other powers, and partly because we could not rid ourselves of a connection with the prolonged commotion in Europe. In 1815 all this was past, and the government could give its attention to domestic affairs. Another change was in leadership. For many years after the revolution the men in power were those who planned and won the struggle for independence. They were anxious for the "experiment" of republican government to succeed, and distrustful of federal centralization. In 1815 a new group was in control. They had grown up during the time when Americans thought more of the glory than of the difficulties of the revolution. They had confidence in the future, they were not afraid that a strong central government would destroy liberty, and they were deeply conscious of the evils of weak government as revealed in the experiences of the recent war. They were boldly American, and took up the task of legislation with firm hands.

A New Period.

Their plan of reform contained four measures: 1. All were agreed that adequate provision should be made for the national defense. The army and the navy, which to the old republicans were useless and dangerous to liberty, were now placed on a respectable peace footing, and the military academy was remodeled on the plans of Washington as a place to train officers for the army.

Proposed Reforms: 1. National Defense.

2. Next the second bank of the United States of America was incorporated, 1816, in order to aid the government in its financial operations and to establish a sound paper currency by creating a check on the overissue of notes by the state banks. Its capital was $35,000,000, one-fifth owned by the government, which appointed one-fifth of the directors, and its charter was to run for twenty years. The privileges were valuable: its notes were receivable for government dues, it kept the deposits of the government without paying interest on them, and it was exempt from taxes. In return, it paid the treasury a bonus of $1,500,000, and

2. The Second Bank.

agreed to transmit public funds without cost.   Five of the members of the committee that reported the bank bill were Southerners, and its chairman was Calhoun.   He was then a young man of great promise, popular because he defended the war, and likely to remain so because he espoused all the features of the national program then before congress.   Many years later his own state, South Carolina, would not support a national policy, and then he became the chief leader of the Southerners.   The bank opened its doors early in January, 1817, and was able to bring the state banks to resume specie payment on February 20.   It served so well to correct the state of the currency that the circulation of the state banks fell from $68,000,000 in 1816 to $40,641,-000 in 1820.   Its headquarters were in Philadelphia, but within a year it had nineteen branches widely distributed.

3. The tariff of 1816.   The curve of tariff rates in the United States has two points of sharp ascension, one beginning in 1812, and the other in 1861.   The first tariff rate was about five per cent, and rose gradually until in 1812 it was twelve and a half per cent.   To raise funds for the war it was now doubled with proviso that it should fall to the former level a year after the return of peace. The war being over, the newly established manufacturers were alarmed lest the reduction of the duties should bring them into dangerous competition with British manufacturers, who had accumulated vast stocks of merchandise produced at cheap rates and selling so low that they could break up the American competitors.   The American manufacturers called on congress for protection.   The commercial interests, who throve on free importation, opposed this request, but the republicans supported it because they wished to make the nation independent of foreign supplies in time of war.   They felt that it was for the national interest to make our own supplies at home.   As the commercial interests had opposed the war and were mostly federalists, they got little favor now.   Thus was passed in 1816 a new tariff bill continuing the war tariff with some modifications.   It was intended as a temporary measure, but when the manufacturers once got a taste of protection they continually asked for more until many thought them insatiable.

The tariff of 1816 was of Southern origin.   The bill was reported by Lowndes, of South Carolina, and supported by Calhoun and Clay. The former war party, thoroughly national, was now transformed into the new republicans, equally national. They represented the agricultural parts of the country, which had no selfish interest in a tariff, but they felt that all might sacrifice something to be independent of European manufacturers.   Later on they concluded that protection had gone too far, and opposed it bitterly.   In this change of attitude the South, as the great non-manufacturing section, was most prominent.

3. The Tariff.

The South and the Tariff of 1816.

4. Another measure which aroused much interest was public aid in constructing roads and canals, known as the policy of internal improvements. The war aroused much interest in the rich lands of the Northwest, and peace was hardly established before a great movement of population, partly from Europe and partly from the East, set toward that region. Two ways of reaching it appeared. One was by water, up the Mississippi from New Orleans, a process which the use of steamboats on the great river from 1811 made easier than before. The other was overland from Philadelphia and the Potomac or through western New York to the lakes. But roads and canals were too expensive for individual effort. Moreover, they were of national benefit, and why, it was asked, should not the federal government aid in their construction? Would they not enhance the value of the public lands, and were they not necessary to move troops to defend the frontier, both important national enterprises? Thus originated the demand for internal improvement, for fifteen years one of the great political questions of the day.

4. Internal Improvements.

Against them two objections were found. Did the constitution give congress power to raise money for such a purpose? They could be justified only under the general welfare clause, and all the old strict construction school came to life to protest against such a wide departure from their tenets. Secondly, they were really local improvements. If the merchants of the East, it was said, wished them as an outlet for their trade, let them pay the bills. Pennsylvania and the adjacent states were chiefly concerned, and they ought to pay the cost of these very expensive works. The second argument appealed very strongly to the more remote states, which had constructed their own works and hoped for little of such aid from the general government.

Objections to Internal Improvements-Policy.

Before 1816, in fact, as early as Jefferson's presidency, appropriations for such a purpose had begun on a small scale. But now the demand was for larger appropriations, and it was likely to grow with time until every community would have its own scheme, pushing it so skillfully by log-rolling in congress that it was impossible to say where the scheming would stop. Most of the representatives from the West and from the Middle states were of the internal improvements group, and several of the leading new republicans gave support.

" Log-Rolling."

Among them the most conspicuous leader was Calhoun, who in December, 1816, as chairman of a committee on internal improvements, introduced a bill to set aside the $1,500,000 bonus from the newly established bank as a perpetual fund for constructing roads and canals. He declared that roads and canals were needed to bind together the East and West and to prevent disunion. Clay also favored the project, and it passed both houses by safe majorities. Madison had declared himself for internal

The Bonus Bill.

improvements, but at last he vetoed the bonus bill because he thought the constitution did not authorize such an expenditure. He was ever a strict constructionist, and the arguments of the opponents of the bill aroused all his fears. In his veto message, however, he suggested that an amendment to the constitution might well be proposed in order to avoid the difficulty he foresaw. In the existing condition of parties such an amendment could not be carried, and for a time the demand for internal improvements at national expense was checked.

Roads and canals continued to be built, some by the general government, and many more by the states. Virginia and South Carolina authorized large undertakings, and at this very time Pennsylvania had spent over $2,000,000 for the same purpose. But the great achievement was in New York. Much earlier than this her statesmen had realized the need of a canal from the Hudson to Lake Erie, Albany to Buffalo, across that depression between the Alleghanies and the Adirondacks which nature had provided as the easiest way of getting from the sea-

Internal Improvements by the States.

board to the lake system in the heart of the continent. Many plans had been made, and something was about to be done when the war began and deferred further effort. In 1816 De Witt Clinton was elected governor of the state. He was strongly in favor of the canal and won the legislature to the undertaking. Ground was broken July 4, 1817, and eight years later the task was completed at a cost of $7,000,000. The Erie canal was 363 miles long, and was the greatest engineering feat in the country up to that time. It lowered freight to the West, brought a rich trade to New York city, and enabled that port to wrest from Philadelphia the distinction of being the metropolis of the New World.

1816 was presidential election year, and Monroe was to have his reward. Many republicans objected to the bargain. Some thought Monroe too theoretical, others distrusted him because he deserted old friends to enter the cabinet, some of the strait Virginia school could not forgive his early support of Randolph, and the Clinton-Smith faction had ends of their own in

Election of 1816.

view. This opposition united on William H. Crawford, of Georgia, a man of real leadership, a student of Gallatin's financial policy, and an astute politician. For a moment it seemed that Crawford would secure the nomination, but when the caucus met means had been found to change the New York members to Monroe, who was chosen by a vote of 65 to 54. Tompkins, of New York, was nominated for vice-president, thus restoring the New York-Virginia alliance which the defection of Clinton in 1812 disrupted. Later in the year Crawford became secretary of the treasury, and whisperers said that it had a bearing on the succession. The federalists nominated Rufus King for president, but in the election he got only 34 votes to Monroe's 183. The Hartford convention and the national program of the new republicans had proved too much for the federalists.

PARTY CLEAVAGE UNDER MONROE

Monroe's best quality was conciliation. By bringing factions together, by calming the feelings of disappointed men, and by avoiding the initiation of positive measures, he held together for eight years a party which had no opposition and which contained many possibilities of disruption. "The tall and eel-like Monroe," as a scoffer called him, who had no cure for social hypochondria and only wished to solve the difficulties he encountered, gave the country eight years of political peace, which is more than one says of any other American president.

James Monroe.

He wished to bring into his cabinet the strongest of the new republicans. John Quincy Adams was recalled from diplomatic service abroad to become secretary of state, an office he filled with distinction; Crawford was retained as secretary of the treasury; Clay was offered the war department, and when he refused it, the office went to Calhoun, while William Wirt, an able lawyer, popular with the old republicans, was made attorney-general. Clay's refusal was the only discordant note. He would have taken first place if it had been offered; but he thought it advisable to decline the third place and remain speaker of the house to become leader of the opposition sure to develop.

His Cabinet.

The opportunity he anticipated came speedily. Since 1810 the Spanish-American colonies had been in revolt. They had overcome the weak Spanish garrisons, but were not able to establish effective governments in the large and sparsely settled areas over which their authority stretched. Much sympathy for them existed in the United States, particularly in the Mississippi valley; and the Gulf ports freely furnished them aid until congress in 1817 passed a more stringent neutrality act. In 1817 the question of recognizing the independence of these colonies was brought up, but the cautious Monroe, rather than offend their

Attitude toward South America.

many sympathizers, sent agents to see if the revolutionists deserved recognition. Clay introduced resolutions to accord recognition and to repeal the recent neutrality act, supporting them in a beautifully ornate speech. The administration men united against him, and his resolutions were overwhelmed in the house. But he had done all he could expect; for he had given fair warning to the country that he was leading an opposition, and henceforth all who had grievances against Monroe gathered under his banner. In the winter of 1818–1819 he repeated his action, when the administration was forced to defend Jackson's invasion of Florida but again the administration cohorts defeated him.

By such means Monroe resisted attacks and came to the election of 1820 without a defeat. There was no thought of denying him the honor of a reëlection, — not even Clay went that far, — and "The Era of Good Feeling." he was chosen without opposition. However, one elector who favored him had the whim to throw away his vote on another man, lest Monroe should share with Washington the honor of a unanimous vote. This period of harmony was called "The Era of Good Feeling." The thought pleased the president, and he tried to promote it by what he called his "amalgamation policy," which was to appoint both federalists and republicans to office. His party friends resented the policy, and he was too wise to insist upon it. Already men were beginning to look to 1824, and although the cabinet was officially harmonious, it contained three men who were keenly planning to contest the prize of the presidency when the time came.

THE ACQUISITION OF FLORIDA

Jefferson was our first president who tried to buy Florida, but he made no progress in his plan. While Napoleon occupied Spain, we received no minister from that country, but diplomatic Negotiations with Spain. relations were resumed with the reëstablishment of the old monarchy, and our minister at Madrid renewed the offer to buy the province. He had a polite refusal, but shortly afterwards a political upheaval in Spain brought a new ministry into power, and the envoy in August, 1817, was surprised to receive an offer to exchange Florida for Louisiana. The proposition was inadmissible, but it indicated that Spain was yielding. Secretary Adams now took the matter into his own hands, carrying it on with success, until in June, 1818, diplomacy was rudely interrupted by news that Jackson had invaded West Florida, seized its fortified posts, and expelled its governor and garrison. The information referred to the Seminole war.

The Seminoles were a Creek tribe, living in Florida. To them in 1814 fled a large number of Creeks, escaping the vengeance of Jackson at Horse-Shoe Bend. When the treaty of Fort Jackson in August of

the same year ceded a great deal of the Creek patrimony to the United
States, these fugitives protested against its legality. The reply was
that they had due notice to attend, and failing to do so
had no right to object. The treaty of Ghent provided **Cause of**
that the United States should give up all the land taken **Seminole**
from Indians at war when the treaty was signed. The **Discontent.**
fugitives were advised by some officious British subjects that this
applied to their land and promised that England would support them

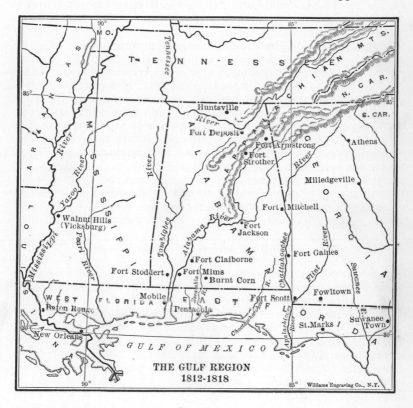

THE GULF REGION
1812-1818

in a demand for its restoration, but the British government repudiated
the promise at sight. The whites held that they were exempt from
the clause in question because the Creek war was terminated by
the treaty of Fort Jackson. They disliked greatly the British subjects
whose assurances had rendered the Seminoles warlike. One of these
persons was Alexander Arbuthnot, a Scotch trader, who wrote the
letters in which the Indians delivered their protests, and the other was

2 B

Captain Ambrister, an army officer who for the love of adventure drilled an Indian company and led it to war. Hostilities began when the savages raided the white settlers on the disputed lands. In November, 1817, the Americans retaliated by burning Fowltown, killing four of its Indian inhabitants, and dispersing the rest, who fled into Florida.

The war department, Calhoun being secretary, now authorized a campaign against the Seminoles, and Jackson, commander of the southern military division, took command. His orders allowed him to follow the enemy into Spanish territory, but forbade him to attack a Spanish post. He considered this limitation unwise, and in a letter to Monroe suggested that he privately be given permission to attack the forts if the Indians took refuge in them. He claimed afterwards that he received the required authority, but Monroe denied that assertion. On it hinged the question of Jackson's responsibility for what was about to happen. He marched straight into Florida, took the forts at St. Marks and Pensacola, sent their garrisons with the governor of West Florida to Havanna, and raised the American flag over the province. At St. Marks he captured Arbuthnot and Ambrister, tried them by court martial, and hanged them forthwith, spite of their British citizenship. Two prominent Indian chiefs, who were also captured, were hanged without the formality of trial.

Invasion of Florida.

These occurrences caused consternation in Washington, where foreign complications were feared. England was at first inclined to protest against the execution of her subjects, but as they were where they had no business to be, the event was allowed to pass. To appease Spain was not so easy. She demanded the surrender of the province and the punishment of Jackson. The first was readily granted, but the action of the general pleased the people, and the administration dared not make him suffer. The secretary of state was, therefore, intrusted with the task of bringing Madrid to reason. In some bold and able dispatches he justified the invasion on the evident ground that Spain had not properly preserved the neutrality of her territory. She had undoubtedly given encouragement, if not aid, to our enemies, and she could not well complain if at last we did what she herself ought to have done. Adams drove this point home with so much energy that Spain accepted the situation, and the waters of diplomacy were at length unruffled. For a time Jackson resented what he took for a reflection on his conduct, but some skillful touches by Monroe brought him to accept in a reasonable spirit the solution of the difficult situation.

Attitude of England and Spain.

At this junction the opposition took up the matter. Resolutions were introduced in each house to investigate the violation of neutrality obligations, Clay taking a prominent part in their defense. Those

before the house occasioned a long debate, at the end of which
Jackson was acquitted of wrongdoing.   The senate referred the
matter to a committee which made an adverse report,
but by this time popular opinion ran so strongly for the   Clay's At-
hero of the invasion that the opposition did not press   tack on
the report to a vote.   The upshot was that Jackson,   Jackson.
already mentioned as a presidential possibility, gained rather than
lost in the public esteem.

Before this phase of the Seminole affair was complete, the negotiations for the purchase of Florida were resumed.   Recent events
served to promote them by showing Spain by what a   Florida
slender hold she possessed the province, and she now came   Purchased.
to a decision to cede.   February 22, 1819, the senate received a treaty to that effect and passed it with little hesitation.   It
provided that we should pay claims against Spain amounting to not
more than $5,000,000, and take all Florida.   It fixed the western
boundary of Louisiana at the Sabine river.   The latter point had
been in dispute since the purchase of Louisiana.   By that bargain our
claim to the Rio Grande was good, but the president thought we
might safely relinquish it in view of the advantage of having an un-
broken coast line from the Atlantic to the Sabine.   Congress took the
same view, but when the Texas boundary question came up more
than twenty years later Monroe received much criticism because he
had thrown away our claim to the rich region between that river and the
Sabine.   The treaty of 1819 was not ratified by Spain until late in
1820.   July 17, 1821, the province was formally handed over to the
United States and Jackson became its first American governor.   It was
made a territory, and in 1845 was admitted into the union as a state.

THE MISSOURI COMPROMISE

In 1812 Missouri became a territory, with a legislature of its own,
and a population of something more than 20,000.   St. Louis, at the
junction of the Missouri and Mississippi, was the center of
activity, its chief industry being the rich fur trade of the   Develop-
Missouri valley.   Three-fourths of its 2500 inhabitants were   ment of
French, proud of their origin and resentful of the aggres-   Missouri
sive Americans who established the laws of the English and   before 1820.
offended the common taste by paving the streets and introducing
rattling, iron-wheeled vehicles.   The clash between the two civilizations was of short duration.   The French were contented with their
state, fond of amusements, in every house a fiddle and on every night
a dance, and they accepted with satisfaction a paternal form of society
which embraced a benevolent ruling class and a large number of care-
free dependents.   The Americans were ambitious, eager for wealth,
forever busy and boastful of their patriotism, and bent on establishing

self-government for the bustling white immigrants who felt their responsibilities as builders of a new commonwealth. The tide of immigration was strong after the war of 1812; for stories of fertile lands in what from its position must certainly be a great state attracted many settlers from the East. They came chiefly from the South, passing through Kentucky and Tennessee in long wagon trains accompanied by their slaves and cattle. By 1820 the population was 66,586. It was the first, and for many years the farthest, advance of the white man's civilization into the great mid-continental plain beyond the Mississippi.

We have seen that by 1800 the states north of Maryland, *i.e.* north of the Mason and Dixon's line, had restricted slavery, and those to the southward continued slave states. By the ordinance of **Division of the West in Respect to Slavery.** 1787 the Ohio was made the dividing line between freedom and slavery for the region beyond the mountains; and thus the country between the Atlantic and the Mississippi was amicably divided between the two great interests. Nothing was done about a similar division when Louisiana was acquired or when territories were first created within its bounds. In the absence of restrictions the slaveholders felt they had equal rights there with other Americans, and they were a large part of the population of Missouri when in March, 1818, congress was asked to make the **Missouri asks for Statehood.** territory a state. No action was taken at that time, although under the rule that a territory could expect statehood when it had 60,000 inhabitants, there should have been no objection to the request. The petition was renewed in the next session, and in February, 1819, the house was considering a state bill when Tallmadge, of New York, offered an amendment to exclude further introduction of slaves into Missouri and gradually to emancipate those already there. After a short and angry debate, the amendment was carried in the house, but lost in the senate.

This discussion lasted but two weeks. It was unexpected, and produced violent commotions. Whenever slavery had been discussed **Significance of the Debate.** before that in congress, hot words had been used; for some of its opponents would denounce it as a crime and some of its defenders would reply bitterly. The quieter men, North and South, had usually agreed to avoid occasions for excitement, and the number of free and slave states was equal. With the admission of Alabama, then imminent, there would be eleven free and eleven slave states. It was to the interest of the new republicans and of every man who had hope of being president in 1824 to keep in abeyance a question which would surely realign political groups and make impossible the enactment of such national measures as tariffs and bills for internal improvements. Jefferson said the debate was "like a fire-bell in the night." The leaders of the party, therefore, regarded with apprehension the hot discussion and the voting of warm resolutions by public meetings and legislatures North and South through the summer of 1819.

The question was intimately related to that sectional jealousy which to this time had not been entirely absent from most of the deliberations of congress. The rule of Virginia was distasteful to New England, and even the New York republicans, though partners in that rule, were restless under it. Tallmadge, who introduced the resolution, was a close friend of Clinton, and Rufus King, leading defender of it, was an old federalist of New York. To the men of the North it seemed that **Sectionalism the Issue: the Northern Side.** Southerners, by extending their peculiar institution into the great Northwest, would establish their power in the Missouri valley and eventually lay hands on all the region west of it. If such a thing was to be prevented, it must be prevented now. If this advance was allowed, there would be a union of the South and the great Northwest, slavery being the common bond which would dominate the future as relentlessly as the Virginia combination ruled the present. Besides this feeling, there was in the North a growing conviction that slavery was a blot on our civilization, and ought to be restricted in area. A small number of Northern people even declared that slavery was a crime and slaveholders criminals. Thus the Southern supremacy in the government was attacked by a powerful combination which threatened to take from it all its support in New York, Pennsylvania, and other Northern states.

Several combined interests existed in the South. Its leaders desired to perpetuate Southern control, in order to ward off unfavorable legislation; they also felt that the growing immigration into the free North would enable that section to people quickly the vast West and establish control in congress. Such a result achieved, it was not doubted that an attempt would be made to amend the constitution with regard to the three-fifths representation of slaves, and perhaps efforts would be made to abolish slavery itself. Besides these considerations, many Southerners were **The Southern Side.** irritated when told that slaveholding was a crime. Their best people owned slaves, and everywhere were seen efforts to make the lot of the blacks as happy as the necessities of bondage permitted. Thus it was that sentiment North and South through the summer of 1819 hardened, and practical leaders became convinced that only a compromise could prevent a general disarrangement of existing party alignments.

January 3, 1820, four weeks after the new congress met, the house passed a bill to admit Maine. Massachusetts, which formerly had authority over Maine, had consented to this action provided congress approved before March 4, 1820. Earlier in the session Alabama was admitted, so that the admission of Maine would give the free states a majority. The **The Missouri Compromise.** situation suggested a compromise, and when the Maine bill reached the senate, it was combined with a bill then before that house to admit Missouri without restriction. This step was approved by the senate by a vote of 23 to 21. Then Thomas, of Illinois, moved to amend by admitting Missouri with slavery and by prohibiting slavery north of 36° 30′, north latitude, in the rest of the Louisiana purchase. Here was the compromise that conservative men wished. It was much like that by which the Northwest was reserved to freedom in 1787 while the Southwest was left to slavery. It would remove the many dangers for persons and measures, and it passed the senate by a vote of 34 to 10. The house had a safe majority for restriction, and was disposed to throw away every thought of other ends to place slavery in a way of extinction, and voted to reject the senate compromise. It seemed that a complete deadlock was reached, when a conference committee was at last appointed. Then came further relenting, until enough members yielded to carry the compromise by a majority of three. Of the 87 who made the minority 33 were from New England, 46 were from the Middle states, and 8 were the solid Northwestern delegation. No Southern or Southwestern representative voted for restriction in Missouri, and 7 New Englanders and 8 Middle states men voted against it. The Missouri Compromise was the work of moderate men, chiefly those who lived in the Middle states and in the northern tier of Southern states. Many years later the South attacked the compromise, and pointed to the fact that it was not accepted by those Southerners who, as it was then put, were true to the rights of the South in 1820.

This debate aroused the Missourians, thoroughly under the control of the slaveholders; and the constitution they framed reflected their determination to hold the state. It guaranteed the existence of slavery in the new state and forbade the immigration of free negroes.

The Missouri Constitution. When in the succeeding autumn it came before congress for approval, it was opposed by the Northern members of the house, who declared that it violated the federal constitution. There was a hot debate over the right of congress to shackle a sovereign state, and the result was deadlock. Clay took a prominent part in the first compromise, and he now came forward with another. He induced the legislature of Missouri, then in session, to agree that the objectionable clause should never be construed to lessen in Missouri the rights of citizens of other states, and with that the constitution was approved.

One other difficulty appeared. Missouri, assuming that statehood was complete, chose presidential electors in 1820 favorable to Monroe, and the returns were sent to the senate. The Southerners **Clay the "Pacificator."** favored their reception on the ground that Missouri became a state by the first compromise act, March, 1820. If this was allowed, the restriction on her constitution was illegal, and the North accordingly insisted that the returns be rejected.

Here was the possibility of an angry dispute, but Clay again smoothed the difficulty, proposing that the result be announced in words like these: If the vote of Missouri be counted, Monroe had 231 votes; if not, he had 228 votes, and in either case he was elected president. For his work in these compromises Clay was called the "Pacificator," a title which pleased his friends. It was considered a great thing to bring jarring factions together and to avert the threatened dangers of disunion.

THE MONROE DOCTRINE

Monroe's unwillingness to recognize the independence of the South American states in 1817 was based on his conviction, shared by Secretary Adams, that the revolutionists had not established a settled government, and on the feeling that rash action in this respect would imperil the plans of purchasing Florida. By 1822 these two reasons were not operative. Florida was secured, and continued successes by the South Americans had made it certain that Spain, unassisted by other European powers, would not be able to reconquer what she had lost. Meanwhile, Clay continued to agitate for recognition, and aroused such enthusiasm that congress early in 1821 resolved that it would support the president whenever he thought fit to extend recognition. Monroe delayed a year and then yielded, notifying congress on March 18, 1822, that he would send ministers to the new states when money was provided for the expenses. Immediate action on the question was retarded by a far more complicated aspect of the matter in the field of general diplomacy.

South America Recognized.

England had watched the South American revolutions with great interest. Having lost the North American colonies as an outlet of trade, she wished new markets in the new republics of the south. All the efforts of the revolutionists had been made with her assistance, sometimes covert, but often open. Her fleet gave important aid on the Pacific, and her citizens sold supplies to the insurrectionary armies. When the European wars were over, the nations of the Old World united in the Holy Alliance to restore the conditions existing before the European upheaval, and began to think of helping Spain to regain her colonies. This would upset the commercial plans of England, and she gave notice that she would not coöperate in the matter. But the other powers were disposed to act of themselves, and England, not wishing to oppose them alone, thought of uniting with the United States to prevent such action. George Canning, the minister whose rude attitude did so much to bring on the war of 1812, was now head of the British foreign office. He turned to Monroe, who was keenly alive to what was going on, and suggested, August 16, 1823, that he unite with England in declaring that Europe should not extend her possessions in the western hemisphere. At that time France was subduing a liberal revolution in

England's Alarms.

Spain, and it was believed that the Spanish monarch, too weak to pay for the service in money, would allow France to indemnify herself by seizing the South American states.

Adams only half approved Canning's suggestion. He did not like, as he said, the idea that his country should "come in as a cock-boat in the wake of the British man-of-war." If we undertook

The Views of Adams. to save the South American states, it was, he thought, more in keeping with our dignity that we act on broad principles announced on our own initiative. The knowledge that England at that time had designs on Cuba and that Russia was seeking to get recognition of a very shadowy claim to the Pacific coast south to the fifty-first degree of latitude convinced him that it was time to take a positive stand. Clay's continual appeals in behalf of a republican system in America with an eye to the recognition of the South American states had prepared the country to support such a policy as the secretary had in mind. It was out of such conditions that the Monroe Doctrine had its origin.

Adams's determination was reached after many months of negotiations. Monroe must have been cognizant of what was done, and he gave it his approval. His cabinet were freely consulted,

Canning's Share. and the members also accepted the ideas of the strong-willed secretary of state, who was at his best in asserting the dignity of his country. And Canning himself could not object; for it was the United States, and not England, which was most concerned in the step about to be taken. His boast some years later that he "called a New World into existence to redress the balance of Old" was not entirely true. His suggestion was doubtless of great importance, and the coöperation of England was essential, but the Monroe Doctrine was an American doctrine and was designed to operate as much against English as continental aggression. He had little confidence in the ability of the United States to enforce their policy to the exclusion of England, and seems to have thought that in future emergencies England would manage to plant herself firmly in South America, a hope which the strong spirit of our government was to make ineffective.

The policy of the United States being formed, it only remained to place it before the world, and the annual message of 1823 was selected as a fitting means. It reached congress December 2 and

The Doctrine Announced. asserted in clear and simple language two interrelated purposes, one referring to the New World and the other to the Old. The language of the message is worthy of perusal by all Americans. "In the wars of the European powers, in matters relating to themselves," it runs, "we have never taken any part, nor does it comport with our policy so to do. It is only when our rights are invaded or seriously menaced that we resent injuries or make preparation for our defense. With the movements in this hemisphere we are of necessity more intimately connected, and by causes which must be obvious to all enlightened and impartial observers. The political system of the allied powers is essentially different in this respect from that of America. . . . We owe it, therefore, to candor and to the amicable relations existing between the United States and those powers to declare that we should consider any attempt on their part to extend their system to any portion of this hemisphere as dangerous to our peace and safety. With the existing colonies or dependencies of any European power we have not interfered, and shall not interfere. But with the Governments who have declared their independence and maintained it, and whose independence we have, on great consideration and on just principles, acknowledged, we could not view any interposition for the purpose of oppressing them, or controlling in any other manner their destiny, by any European power in any other light than as a manifestation of an unfriendly disposition toward the United States."

The Election of 1824

December 3, 1822, an observer in Washington described the political situation there in these words: "While he who now fills the halls of the White House is slowly closing his eyes upon the rich trifles of the world, like an old father he stands surrounded **Division in** by three full-grown sons, each seeking the inheritance **Monroe's Cabinet.** on his departure. John Q., from the favors bestowed by the old man in his lifetime, has been deemed a favorite always: J. C., however, from being possessed of a sanguine temper, sets up also pretensions to the inheritance. William and the old gentleman, you know, it has been reported, are constantly disagreeing in opinion and are hence not quite so friendly as father and son should be; be this as it may, it seems pretty well settled that the Virginia estate, if not already done, will be apportioned to the Latter." These words well describe the opening of the campaign of 1824, but they do not mention two other candidates, Clay and General Jackson.

Of the five aspirants Adams had the support of New England and some strength outside of it in sections where the federalists had been strong. Crawford was the heir of the old organization which directed the Virginia-New York alliance, now sadly **Support of** shorn of its power. Every other candidate made inroads **the Five Candidates.** on it. Calhoun took South Carolina, and Pennsylvania seemed his through his support of internal improvements. Clay had Kentucky and was accorded the new states north of the Ohio with Missouri and Louisiana. Jackson had Tennessee, and was making hard efforts to shame North Carolina out of her old practice of following Virginia blindly. Thus, in getting the old organization, Crawford got little more than his own state, with Virginia, and the support of the

anti-Clintonian faction of New York republicans. In so confused a
state of party no one expected any candidate to have a majority of the
electoral votes, and an election by the house of representatives seemed
likely.

Before the campaign closed, Calhoun was eliminated as a contestant
for first place. He had counted on Pennsylvania because the politicians there were for him. But Jackson, whose candidacy
was announced late, gathered strength with the people
of the state, and the politicians early in 1824 came to
realize that they could not carry Calhoun to victory. They quickly took up Jackson, and Calhoun,
anxiously waiting to hear that this great state had declared for
him, was astonished to learn that it had been swept over to
Jackson. It was fatal to his hopes, but he calmly acquiesced in
a plan to make him vice-president, and in that field he had little
opposition. His decline in position implied the improvement of
Jackson's chances.

Calhoun Takes Second Place.

Crawford was generally esteemed the leading candidate until a
stroke of paralysis laid him low in September, 1823. His friends declared it was slight, his enemies said he was at death's
door. Neither assertion was correct, but he was an in-
valid all through the year 1824, and was, in fact, not physi-
cally strong enough to come back into active national politics. The
organization which had adopted him strove hard to hold its grip on its
following, and was so successful that in the election he had the third
place among the candidates.

Crawford's Illness.

As the organization candidate he would naturally have the strongest
following in the republican caucus, hitherto a strong recommendation.
To overcome this advantage his opponent united to break
down the caucus. This piece of party machinery was un-
democratic, and tended to make the presidency subservient
to a congressional ring. It had been tolerated only because it was
the sole attainable means of securing concentration of purpose in a
largely disorganized party group. To oppose it, nomination by state
legislatures was now resorted to. Various states recommended their
favorites to the people and issued severe criticisms of the caucus
system. So unpopular became the institution that none but the Crawford men would attend, and when in February, 1824, the last republican
caucus that was to meet was called to order, only 66 of the 216 republicans in congress were present. Of these, all but four voted for
Crawford. In the attack on the caucus, the friends of Jackson, who
was hailed as the people's candidate, were most active.

Destroying the Caucus.

The campaign of 1824, like its two predecessors, was conducted on
personal grounds. This does not mean that principles were then unknown, but that on the leading principles under discussion, tariff and
internal improvements, the candidates were practically of the same

opinion. Clay was the peculiar champion of the tariff, but neither of the others opposed it. Calhoun was preëminently for internal improvements, but all the others mildly favored them. Crawford's friends in the South talked about his devotion to the "principles of 1798," the doctrines of strict reconstruction; but national measures were so popular that they dare not press the point. Some Southerners wished to raise the question of Adams's attitude on the Missouri question, but he replied that he was for conciliation. In fact, no one dared bring up this point, since it would injure a Southern candidate in the North as much as a Northern candidate in the South. As the only Northern candidate, Adams got the vote of that large portion of the inhabitants of his section who resented the Virginia domination. He was not personally popular there, spite of his many excellent qualities. *A Personal Campaign.*

No one awaited the election returns more impatiently than Clay. In 1823 he was triumphantly reëlected speaker, and if the election went to the house and he were one of the three highest, his popularity in that body would give him excellent prospects. His fate hung on the action of Louisiana and New York. In the former state he had a majority of the legislature, which chose the electors, but a vote was taken when three of his friends were absent, and the Jackson and Adams men combined and carried the day. In New York the legislature also had the choice, and by skillful manipulation three of the men chosen as Clay men voted at last for his opponents. A loser at these two points, he got only 37 votes, while Crawford got 41, Adams 84, and Jackson 99. His narrow failure to fall among the lucky three was partly atoned for by the knowledge that in the field into which the contest was now committed he would be the arbiter between his rivals. *Clay a Losing Candidate.* *The Result of the Voting.*

THE PRESIDENTIAL ELECTION OF 1825

Both judgment and interest showed Clay the way he should lean. Crawford, incapacitated through health, was out of the question, and the choice was between the other two. Adams was an educated man, Jackson's training was chiefly obtained from frontier conditions. Adams was experienced in public affairs at home and abroad, Jackson was a good fighter and a passable head of a military district, but his temper was violent, he could not make a speech, and in his only administrative office, governorship of Florida, he had, through lack of ordinary tact, allowed affairs to get into a most unnecessary muddle. Between two such men, who could hesitate who had the interest of the country at heart? Moreover, Clay's future interests pointed to Adams, who was really unpopular in the North and would hardly be able to perpetuate his leadership *Clay Turns to Adams.*

more than four years. In the readjustment of parties, which was inevitable, it was more likely that the older states of the North would unite with Clay, popular in the Northwest, than with Jackson, popular in the Southwest. Clay was now the most outspoken champion of the tariff. Was it not more natural for him to expect support in the North, where the manufactures were rapidly increasing, than in the South, where they could not hope to succeed? All these arguments were urged upon him by the friends of Adams, from the time congress met early in December. He seems to have made up his mind from that time, but he said nothing. Meanwhile the friends of Jackson besought him to favor their candidate as a Western man and as the candidate who had the highest number of votes in the recent election. To all their appeals he gave good-humored attention, but was careful to promise nothing.

The number of states was then twenty-four, and the successful candidate must have a majority, or thirteen. Crawford had four states without dispute, Virginia, Georgia, North Carolina, and Delaware, the heart of the old Virginia group. Adams had seven, **The Groups in Congress.** New England and Maryland, the old federalist stronghold. Jackson had Tennessee, Alabama, and Mississippi, representing the new Southwest, South Carolina, a result of his coöperation with Calhoun, and Pennsylvania and New Jersey, which he and Calhoun had wrung from the ancient combination. This group was rather incongruous, and had no other common bond than its opposition to the Virginia school, from which its component parts had formerly received little recognition. Jackson also had Indiana, for local reasons, which gave him a total of seven. Of the other six Clay was able to control four,— Kentucky, Ohio, Missouri, and Louisiana. Illinois, with only one representative, hung for a time in the balance, and then came over to Adams, who, with Clay's four, now had twelve states, and lacked only one of a majority; and that one was New York, whose delegation in the house was badly divided.

Half of New York's delegation were for Adams, the rest for Jackson and Crawford. The leader of the Crawford men was Van Buren, then a senator. He hoped the state's vote would remain **New York Decides the Election.** divided on the first ballot. Thus there would be no choice on that ballot, which would give him opportunity at a later time to cast the New York vote for Adams and secure for himself the honor of president-maker. It was a shrewd scheme, and if successful, would have lessened Clay's prestige. But at the last moment one of Crawford's New York supporters, General Van Rensselaer, changed to Adams, which gave that state to the New Englander and made him president on the first ballot. Much seems to have depended on this action; for if Van Buren could have delivered the Crawford group to Adams, they must have supported his administration for a while, possibly for a long time. As it was, they remained unattached for a year, and then joined the opposition. In 1828 they were, under Van Buren's leadership, an important element of the party which followed Jackson.

BIBLIOGRAPHICAL NOTE

The general works on the period covered in this chapter are the *Histories* by McMaster, Schouler, and Wilson (see page 312); Babcock, *Rise of American Nationality* (1906); Turner, *Rise of the New West* (1906), the chapters on social development are especially good; Burgess, *The Middle Period* (1897), the outline is good; Stanwood, *History of the Presidency* (1898); Hart, *American History told by Contemporaries*, vol. III (1906); and *The Cambridge Modern History*, vol. VII (1903). Perkins, *Historical Sketches of the United States, 1815–1830* (1830), is a reliable contemporary work, but it is scarce. Besides the biographies and writings of Jefferson, Madison, Monroe, and King (see page 275), and those of John Quincy Adams, Clay, and Wirt (see page 312), much assistance can be had from Bassett, *Life of Andrew Jackson*, 2 vols. (1911); Parton, *Life of Andrew Jackson*, 3 vols. (1860); Meigs, *Life of Benton* (1904); Hunt, *Life of Calhoun* (1907); *Works of Calhoun*, 6 vols. (1853–1855); *Letters of Calhoun* (Jameson, ed., 1899); and Shipp, *Life of W. H. Crawford* (1909). The legislative and executive sources are the same as for the preceding chapter. *Niles' Weekly Register* (1811–1849) and *The North American Review* (1815–) are the important periodicals for the period.

The Bank of the United States. Catterall, *The Second Bank of the United States* (1903), contains a good bibliography; Clark and Hall, *Legislative and Documentary History of the Bank of the United States* (1832); Sumner, *History of Banking in all Nations*, 4 vols. (1896), volume I deals with banks in the United States; MacDonald, *Select Documents* (1907), No. 33 presents the charter of the bank.

The Missouri Compromise. Woodburn, *Historical Significance of the Missouri Compromise* (American Hist. Association *Report*, 1893), is the best narrative treatment. The debates are in *Annals of Congress* for 1819, 1820, and 1821. The bill with the important amendments is in MacDonald, *Select Documents* (1907). The background of the incident is in Carr, *Missouri* (1888), but the treatment leaves much to be desired. An interesting view of the life in early Missouri can be had from Flint, *Condensed History and Geography of the Western States*, 2 vols. (1828), and *History and Geography of the Mississippi Valley*, 2 vols. (1832).

The Monroe Doctrine. Reddaway, *The Monroe Doctrine* (1898 and 1906), very good; Ford, *John Quincy Adams, his Connection with the Monroe Doctrine* (Mass. Hist. Soc. *Proceedings*, 1902); Rush, *Memoranda of a Residence at the Court of London from 1819 to 1825* (1845). For the British side see Stapleton, *Political Life of George Canning*, 3 vols. (1831); *Official Correspondence of George Canning*, 2 vols. (1887). For the Spanish American revolt and its relations to the United States see: Paxson, *The Independence of the South American Republics* (1903); Latané, *Diplomatic Relations of the United States and South America* (1900); Callahan, *Cuba and International Relations* (1899). For a less detailed treatment see Hart, *Foundations of American Foreign Policy* (1901); and Moore, *Digest of International Law*, 5 vols. (1906). The Official Correspondence is in *American State Papers, Foreign Affairs*, vol. V. Gilman, *Life of James Monroe* (1883), has a bibliography by J. Franklin Jameson.

For Independent Reading

Mrs. Smith, *The First Forty Years of Washington Society* (1906); Chittenden, *The American Fur Trade of the Far West*, 3 vols. (1902); Drake, *Making of the Great West* (1884); Schurz, *Life of Henry Clay*, 2 vols. (1887); Quincy, *Figures of the Past* (1883); Cobbett, *A Year's Residence in the United States* (1818–1819).

CHAPTER XVIII

THE ADMINISTRATION OF JOHN QUINCY ADAMS

PARTY FORMATION UNDER JOHN QUINCY ADAMS

ADAMS'S first action was to make Clay secretary of state; notice that henceforth the two men would act together. The Jackson-Calhoun group, resenting the coalition which had defeated their leader, began a violent opposition. They voted against the confirmation of Clay, and returned to their homes full of scorn at what they proclaimed a corrupt bargain to obtain the presidency. The mass of people, to whom Jackson was a hero, believed the charge and began to look to the day of vindication. Meanwhile, it was evident that Crawford's health would not be reëstablished, and there was much anxiety about the future conduct of his followers. Van Buren was their leader, and was in close relation with the Virginians and the Georgian, who spoke for the Southern half of the group. Had they divided, he might have gone for Adams, but it was decided that both sections should act together.

Clay and Adams Unite.

Crawford-ites Hold Off.

For leadership the group now looked to Van Buren, and for a year he gave no intimation of what he would do. Then came Adams's first annual message, a strongly national document. It advocated internal improvements and a generally paternal attitude of the government in many measures to promote the common welfare. It was as gall to the old republicans, who, strong in the Virginia faith, had gone with Crawford. Until that time Van Buren had coquetted with the Adams party: if he had continued that course, he would have had no following outside his own state. He now shifted position, and before the winter of 1825–1826 was over was aiding the Jackson men in their onslaught on the president.

Adams's First Annual Message.

Crawford-ites Join Jackson.

Van Buren's accession to the Jackson party was welcome, for dissension was already beginning between the Tennesseeans and the South Carolinians. Calhoun was an experienced public man, Jackson was inexperienced. It angered the followers of the latter to hear it said that Calhoun's wisdom would have to save the party. It seemed to them that the junior partner was seeking to assume the functions of the senior. Now Van Buren was as skillful a leader as Calhoun, and not so self-

Van Buren and Cal-houn.

assertive. From the time he became a Jackson man he was in close association with the peculiarly Jackson group, and thenceforth the party contained a factional conflict which only the necessity of meeting a common danger kept within bounds.

Until 1829 all factions acted together in the bitterest warfare on Adams. He was an honest and able president, but he and his secretary must be broken down. The first occasion was the annual message, in which Adams gave forth his national program. Jefferson had thought the government's functions should be few, and much should be left to individual initiative. Adams frankly announced another policy. Government, he said, should seek to improve the condition of the citizens. Roads and canals should be built, a national university should be founded, scientific discoveries should be promoted, distant seas should be explored, and observatories, "light-houses of the skies," should be established. All this was recommended in an academic sense. There was also high praise for internal improvements and for a nationally organized militia. On these features of the message the opposition fell furiously. Did they not show, it was said, that Adams was mad for concentration? The echoes of the attack were heard in every part of the country, the state rights men leading the van. *Bitter War against Adams.*

Immediately came a specific measure on which the opposition could rally. Bolivar, leader of the South American revolutionists, had conceived a plan for a congress of delegates from the new states north and south of the Isthmus of Panama, and in the spring of 1825 Clay was asked if the United States would accept an invitation to attend. The object of the meeting was not clearly stated, but Clay saw in it an opportunity to extend American influence, and favored an acceptance. Adams was more cautious, and it was decided to ask for more definite information about the objects of the meeting. In the autumn came formal invitations to attend a congress at Panama. They came from Mexico, Guatemala, and Colombia, and named as objects of consideration resistance to the attempts of European powers to interfere in America, the recognition of Hayti, the regulation of the slave trade, and the formation of an American league to offset the continental alliance in the Old World. This announcement seems hardly candid; for the Colombian official press declared that the object of the congress was to form a league to oppose Spain, to liberate Cuba and Porto Rico, and to execute the Monroe Doctrine. Clay's imagination was warm and his diplomacy was aggressive. He welcomed the opportunity to extend the commercial and political interests of his country, and he carried the more cautious Adams with him. Accordingly, a special message went from the president to congress, December 26, announcing the nomination of delegates and asking that appropriations be made to pay their expenses. It disclaimed an intention to incur obligations *The Panama Congress.*

of a belligerent kind or to enter into a league of defense with the states represented at the congress, but it left badly defined the objects proposed for consideration.

Then came an excited debate. The Jackson group questioned the constitutionality of the president's action, said he made too much of Monroe's recently announced Doctrine, and pointed out that dire disaster awaited the slave states if the nation participated in a congress in which sat representatives of the black republic of Hayti and at which plans would be made to free Cuba and Porto Rico from Spain and from the régime of slavery. The last argument was far-fetched, but it appealed to the South. It amounted to saying that if the government gave its countenance to the movement for emancipation in the Spanish American communities, it would thereby weaken the cause of slavery in the South, and that this was an interference with local institutions. Such reasoning could only have been intended to arouse the Southerners against the administration. It had little effect in congress. The senate confirmed the nominations and the house after a hot debate voted the money for expenses. At last the representatives set out for the isthmus, but the debates in congress had so delayed them that it was summer, 1826, before they departed. One of them died on the way, and the other arrived to find that the congress, after a fruitless session, had adjourned, to meet again at Tacubaya. He lingered until the appointed day, but when it arrived internal commotions reigned, and the congress did not assemble.

Attitude of the Jackson Men.

As to political significance the Panama incident was important. It furnished a rallying point for the "friends of Jackson," and their strength is shown by the votes of 24 to 19 in the senate and 134 to 60 in the house. Van Buren is said to have remarked: "If they had only taken the other side and refused the mission, we should have had them." The debate, through the use made by the Jackson men of the slavery argument, tended to bring all the old Virginia following in the South into one alliance with the Tennesseean at the head.

Significance of the Incident.

The Tariff and the Development of Sectionalism

In 1816 the South accepted the protective tariff, but it soon had reason to regret it. The westward migration injured all the old Atlantic states, north and south; but in New England the loss was balanced by the growth of manufactures. In the South was no such compensatory process, and land values fell steadily. The steady fall in the price of cotton through the rapid extension of its area of cultivation in the Gulf region increased the suffering. Then arose a Southern cry that it was all due to the evident inequality of the tariff, which

Effects of the Tariff; North, South, and West.

built up the North at the expense of the parts in which the people had no manufactures, but paid ever higher prices for their supplies. The West was in the same position logically, but it did not feel the burden in the same way. In the first place the continued improvement in transportation tended to lower prices of supplies, while land values naturally rose with the increase of population, and thus the burden was not apparent. Besides this, the prevalent idea in the West was confidence in the future of America. Imagination was keen on the subject, and the people readily adopted the theory of the home market. Let us have manufactures to develop our own cities, which will purchase our own raw product, said Clay, in announcing his famous "American System," and the idea found ready popular response. Add to this the fact that the protectionists wove into their system protective rates for raw wool and hemp, articles produced by the Western farmers, and we shall see why the Western farmers tolerated a system which their Southern brethren thought unjust.

In 1819 occurred a severe panic. A period of prosperity and feverish speculation followed the war of 1812, credit was expanded, and the inevitable collapse came surely. Now arose a cry of hard times. Banks were embarrassed, agricultural products sold at lower prices, labor was unemployed, and manufacturers suffered from competition with foreign goods produced at stagnation prices. Then arose a demand for further tariff legislation, and the result was the tariff bill of 1820. It provided for an increase in most of the schedules, especially in those on woollens, cotton goods, iron, and hemp. It passed the house, but failed in the senate by one vote. In the former body it received all the votes from the Northwest, and all but one from the Middle states. All but five of the votes from the older South were against it and all but four of those from the Southwest, including Kentucky. The parts of New England which represented the older commercial and farming interests were against it, while those which favored the manufacturers were for it. Thus, the agricultural South and Southwest and the commercial and agricultural parts of the Northeast were opposed to protection, and the manufacturing and agricultural Middle states and the Northwest were for it. Defeated by so close a vote, it was inevitable that the measure should come up again.

Several attempts to take up the tariff followed the bill of 1820, but none succeeded until 1824, when an act was carried through the house by a vote of 107 to 105 and through the senate by a vote of 25 to 21. It did not provide as high duties as those of the defeated bill of 1820. By raising the rates on hemp it got the entire vote of Kentucky, and it had the solid support of the Northwest, whose growth in population gave the protectionists a considerable advantage as compared with the former vote. It also raised

Growing Demands of Protectionists.

Tariff Law of 1824.

2 C

the duty on raw wool, which was largely produced in the Northwest. Here again was seen a strong opposition in the South and Southwest, and New England was again divided, Massachusetts, New Hampshire, and Maine casting in opposition 22 of their 25 votes in the house. In these states the commercial interests were in political control, and Webster, voicing their wishes, made an excellent speech against the bill. Every vote of the Northwest and of Kentucky was in the affirmative and every vote of the South and the Southwest, except three from Maryland, one from Virginia, and two from Tennessee, was in the negative. Save for New England, the tariff had become a sectional issue.

The bill of 1824 was a compromise, and the protectionists were resolved to make another effort. In 1827 a woollens bill was introduced, raising the rates on both the manufactured article

Attempted Law of 1827. and the raw product. It passed the house, but was defeated in the senate by the casting vote of Calhoun, the vice-president. But the manufacturers did not lose heart. In the summer of the same year they held at Harrisburg, Pennsylvania, a great convention, at which it was agreed to frame a bill in which all interests were represented and to try to induce congress to pass it. Meanwhile, the press teemed with arguments for and against protection, and feeling became high.

Such was the situation when congress met in December, 1827, the Jackson party in control in the house. Divided nearly equally

Tariff Law of 1828. between friends and opponents of the tariff, they must suffer severely did not some astute politician devise a plan of escape. Keeping their leader in the background, they prepared in committee a bill which should be objectionable to New England but satisfactory to the Middle states. It lowered the rates on the medium priced woollens and raised them on molasses and articles used in ship building, all of which injured New England interests; and if Adams approved, as he must do or lose the support of the Middle states, he would suffer in his own section. It was expected that efforts would be made to amend, and all the Jackson men, Northern and Southern, agreed to reject amendments and force the bill to a vote as it came from committee. They kept their agreement, spite of the bitter jibes of the New Englanders. But at last the unexpected happened: enough New Englanders voted "aye" to pass the bill with the support of the Jackson men of the North and the high tariff men of the North and Northwest. The result left Jackson untouched by unpopularity. His Northern friends could point to their votes to show that they favored the tariff, and his Southern friends could point to their solid vote against it to show that they had fought ably to defeat it. John Randolph pointedly said that the bill "referred to manufactures of no sort or kind, but the manufacture of a President of the United States." But it was an unfair measure, and was popularly called "the tariff of abominations." In the senate the woollen schedule was increased, and this secured better recognition from New England. Webster, now a senator from Massachusetts, voted for the bill, announcing that manufactures had progressed so far in his section that protection was henceforth its chief interest. It was a correct assertion. The long opposition between commerce and manufactures in New England was at an end, and the latter had triumphed. This last stronghold of antitariff sentiment in the North had surrendered. The tariff was now wholly a sectional policy.

This meant that the South had lost. Every one expected that the fight would soon be renewed, and her leaders were actively engaged in formulating an opposition which would stay the victors in what was then considered a selfish and unequal policy. **South Carolina assumes Southern Leadership.** In this process Virginia took an attitude of inactivity. Not herself a cotton-raising state, and lacking very able leaders, she allowed the more positive South Carolinians to take the initiative. From that time the cotton states dominated the Southern policy, and Calhoun, who was soon to be at odds with Jackson, became its spokesman.

The weapon with which South Carolina proposed to secure success was nullification, as the event showed, too extreme a measure to command the support even of the South. Its inception goes back to the Crawford faction in the state, committed to **Origin of Nullification.** state rights and hostile to the national policy of Calhoun. They became outspoken with the enactment of the tariff of 1824 and held many vehement meetings of protest. They gave their cause a constitutional bias, declaring that neither protection nor internal improvements were justified by the fundamental law. Calhoun saw the growing feeling with alarm. He must join, or fight it. He did not hesitate long. By defeating the woollens bill of 1827 he indicated his preference for the support of his own state, while he lost that of the North. In this year appeared "The Crisis," a series of letters by Turnbull, an extreme state rights man, counselling that South Carolina should "resist oppression." He did not say how this should be done, but the inference is that he wished her to use force. In the same spirit were many of his fellow citizens, but they objected to using force. A more pacific way was suggested by Calhoun, who in 1828 wrote a paper which came to be known as "The South Carolina Exposition." It was prepared at the request of the state rights party and was submitted to the legislature as the report of a committee on relations with the federal government. Calhoun's authorship was not revealed at the time, but it was suspected.

"The Exposition" harked back to the Virginia and Kentucky Resolutions, 1798. It declared: (1) that the union was a compact of equal states; (2) that the federal government, created by the states, was their agent to carry out what it had been commissioned to do:

(3) that the constitution was its body of instructions; (4) that the action of the agent was null when it violated the instruction; and (5) that it was for the state to determine when the in-

Theory of Nullification. structions were violated. Applying this doctrine, it was held that the protective tariff was not authorized in the constitution, and that South Carolina, a sovereign state, might lawfully and without incurring any serious penalty resist its execution within her borders. This declaration was not adopted by the legislature, but it was widely published, and found ready acceptance by a people exasperated by the steady increase of a species of taxation which awarded to South Carolina none of its advantages and all of its burdens. To put it into practice was to reduce the national authority to a nullity. Calhoun well knew this, but he thought that the principle once granted, congress would never make laws which would furnish the opportunity to put the theory into force. If it was said that the states could not be trusted to exercise nullification moderately, the reply was that supreme authority was with the state and that it was as reasonable to trust the state to use it moderately as the federal government, which the nationalists wished to make supreme.

Having formulated this doctrine, the South Carolinians rested on their oars, for the necessity for putting it into operation was not immediately apparent. They looked to the approaching

No Intermediate Attempt at Execution. election with much confidence; for was not Jackson, the probable victor, a Southern man and a cotton planter? and was not Calhoun, ranking second in his party, the highest defender of nullification? And if the election were favorable, might not all come right without an open contest?

THE ELECTION OF 1828

In 1825 many men thought that the candidacy of Jackson was a bit of enthusiasm which would subside with his defeat. The union

Jackson as a Leader. of his own and Calhoun's followers with those of Crawford soon showed they were mistaken. It was a strong combination, and kept a united front to its enemy, spite of the slumbering internal feud. Jackson proved a good leader. He was impetuous by temperament, his career was filled with quarrels, and his foes hoped and his friends feared he would commit some deed of anger which would overwhelm him in disgrace. But Jackson in the pursuit of his own affairs and Jackson as a national figure were distinct personalities. Though he chafed inwardly at the attacks showered on him, he was outwardly calm and dignified. In their hope of arousing him, the enemy went so far as to charge that his marriage was contracted at the expense of the happiness of another home. In other times this would have brought from him the fiercest denunciation, but he realized the tactics behind the charge and left the task of dispelling the calumny to his friends. He had married a divorced wife, but was in no sense the cause of her separation from her husband. Thus he came to the end of his campaign without misadventure of the kind expected. To his supporters he was an abused man, a great and good defender of his country, an upright citizen, and the champion of the people against an aristocracy indifferent to the welfare of the people.

Besides his own popularity, the voters were influenced by three kinds of arguments directed to them by the vigorous Jackson leaders: 1. The first was the bargain and corruption cry. No dispassionate man objected to whatever understanding **1. The Cry of Bargain.** may have been made between Adams and Clay in the winter of 1824–1825, but to the people at large it had enough support in fact to make it appear that very wicked things were going on at Washington, where, as they thought, politicians sold the offices for their own advantage. 2. It was urged that the rights of the states were jeopardized by the centralizing policy of a New England president, an argument which appealed strongly to **2. State Rights.** the old Jeffersonian school. To support it was Adams's first annual message, as well as the demand for internal improvements and for a high tariff. Was it not time, said the objectors, to check a process which, if continued, would eventually place the national government in the hands of a selfish majority to tyrannize over the minority?

3. Another plan of attack was to accuse Adams of abusing the patronage. The charge was unfounded, for no president had been less inclined to appoint men for his own advantage. He was rigidly honest, and lost support by refusing to appoint **The Patronage.** men because they worked for his reëlection. One of them expressed his disgust by telling him to his face that he might be right but he would not be reëlected. Yet Adams persisted, even retaining in his confidence McLean, a Calhoun supporter, who as postmaster-general used his large patronage in the interest of the opposition. In truth, the opinion of the country ran strongly for political appointments. Political leaders would not work in the election if they did not have assurance of reward. Edward Everett expressed the feeling of every shrewd observer when he said in 1828: "For an Administration then to bestow its patronage, without distinction of party, is to court its own destruction." Thus, while Adams lost the support of his own friends, he was charged with abusing the patronage, and the country came to believe that the cause of good government demanded that a party be placed in power which, as one Jackson man expressed it, would "cleanse the Augean stables."

Arguments like these pleased the mass of citizens. The government had long been based on the idea that the best men should be chosen to represent the people. The Jackson leaders declared that the representatives had ceased to act as upright agents. They declared that the remedy was to replace the old leaders by others closely responsive to the popular will. So far as they utilized the Crawford and Calhoun organizations they had trained leaders; but here, as in the formation of all new parties, they had many others who had little experience in politics, men of vehement prejudices and radical ideas. Such was the earliest composition of the Jacksonian democracy.

On the other side were ranged the forces of conservatism. The commercial classes, the manufacturers generally in the Middle states, the city people, and the larger landowners, had little sym-**The Adams Party.** pathy with the cause of a Western military hero in whose name class was set against class. With them worked the followers of Clay, strongest in the Northwest, and the Adams men, strongest in New England, whose instincts likewise were for conservative policies. Adams was their logical candidate for the presidency, and Richard Rush, of Pennsylvania, ran with him for the vice-presidency. For the second place the Jackson men supported Calhoun.

As the campaign progressed, it was evident that Jackson's prospects were good. Adams had New England, but hardly anything else. Not even Clay's influence could carry the West for him against **The Election.** such a popular hero as Jackson. The South stood together, and with it went Pennsylvania, destined for many years to be a democratic stronghold. In New York the commercial class favored Adams, but the farmers of the interior, marshaled by the skillful Van Buren, were for Jackson. They were rent in twain, however, by the antimasonic movement, and not even Van Buren could promise a solid Jackson vote from the state. Of its 36 votes, as it fell out, 16 went for Adams and the rest for Jackson. Thus was revived under the leadership of Jackson that old combination of the South and the great Central states under which the Virginia régime was long in power. The total vote was 178 for Jackson and 83 for Adams. The latter got every New England vote but one in Maine, with 6 in Maryland, 8 in New Jersey, 3 in Delaware, and 16 in New York. He had none from the region south of the Potomac and west of the Alleghanies. The result was the defeat of one of the most conscientious of presidents because he could not withstand the tide of popular government then running strong, a movement much like that which carried his father and the federalist party to destruction in 1800.

BIBLIOGRAPHICAL NOTE

The general works and sources continue as for chapter XVII; and the same is true of biographies of leading men, to which add Jervey, *Life of Robert Y. Hayne* (1909). The political history of Adams's administration is treated in Turner, *Rise of the New West* (1906); McMaster, *History of the People of the United States*, vol. V (1900); and Bassett, *Life of Andrew Jackson*, vol. II (1911).

On the growth of the state rights feeling see Hunt, *Life of Calhoun* (1907); Phillips, *Georgia and State Rights* (Am. Hist. Assn. *Report*, 1901, vol. II); Ames, *State*

Documents on Federal Relations, Nos. 3–5 (1900–1905); Houston, *Nullification in South Carolina* (Harvard Hist. *Studies*, 1893); Brown, *The Lower South in American History* (1902), a most suggestive essay; Calhoun, *The South Carolina Exposition* (*Works*, vol. VI, 1854); and Jervey, *Life of Robert Y. Hayne* (1909).

On the tariff a work favorable to the protectionists is Stanwood, *American Tariff Controversies*, 2 vols. (1903); and on the opposite side Taussig, *Tariff History of the United States* (1893, new ed. 1900). The memorials from the manufactures and others are in *American State Papers, Finance*, vols. III–V. See also Niles, *Weekly Register* for the years involved.

For Independent Reading

Morse, *John Quincy Adams* (1882); McMaster, *Daniel Webster* (1902); Bassett, *Life of Andrew Jackson*, 2 vols. (1911); Brown, *The Lower South in American History* (1902); and Shepard, *Van Buren* (1892).

CHAPTER XIX

PROBLEMS OF JACKSON'S FIRST ADMINISTRATION

THE NEW PRESIDENT IN CHARGE

MARCH 4, 1829, Washington was filled with visitors come to see the "people's champion" take the oath of office. They covered the slopes

Inauguration of Jackson. of Capitol Hill from where the peace monument now stands to the crest, where a picket fence inclosed the open square which now separates the capitol from the library of congress. Within this yard another great crowd awaited the inaugural ceremony from the east portico. Just before noon the watchers on the slope saw a knot of gentlemen issue from a hotel on the avenue and move slowly up the hill. In the midst walked Jackson, bareheaded, tall and erect, his white hair conspicuous above the shoulders of his companions. A few minutes later he had entered the building, and in a short time stood before the great crowd in the inclosure and took the oath which John Marshall administered. Then came an inaugural address, safely scanned beforehand by his advisers, lest it say something which would give the carping opposition an opportunity to upbraid him. All went well. The spectacle was so impressive that Francis Scott Key, who stood at a gate of the picket fence, exclaimed: "It is beautiful, it is sublime!" The oath taken, the president mounted his horse and rode to the White House, where a reception was tendered to any one who chose to come.

Now followed a saturnalia. Statesmen and stable-boys, fine ladies and washerwomen, white people and blacks, all pushed into the

The Reception. mansion, grasped the hand of the president, if they could reach him, and rushed upon the waiters serving refreshments. From the rabble he was glad to escape by a side door, but the jostling crowd surged through the rooms, upsetting the trays in the hands of the servants, breaking the dishes, and leaping on the furniture in their eagerness to be served, until at last they were turned aside by some thoughtful person who had tubs of punch carried to the lawns, whither the mob quickly followed. Thus was inaugurated the rule of the democracy.

The Cabinet. The cabinet was already announced. At the head was Van Buren, secretary of state, whom most persons thought an excellent selection. The others were nearly evenly divided between his own followers and the friends of Calhoun. They had all been selected after much conference between the two factions, and it seems that Jackson had been forced to submit to such a choice. The fact shows how far the party had come to be a definite organization, of which the president was only the leader. There was much disappointment, especially among the Virginians, whose state, save for a short time in Madison's presidency, had always had a seat in the cabinet since the beginning of the government. Not another Virginian was to sit there until the ill-starred administration of Tyler, himself a Virginian. The disappointed ones made the best they could of the situation, and some of them were later consoled with high diplomatic appointments.

This cabinet was not to be a body of political advisers. The members who supported Calhoun had not the president's confidence to the same extent as Van Buren, Eaton, and Barry, the inefficient postmaster-general. These men, with W. B. Lewis, F. P. Blair, J. A. Hamilton, A. J. Donelson, and some others, established such superior influence that they were dubbed the "Kitchen Cabinet." They constituted a private cabal in the interest of Van Buren. Flatterers and others who sought favors secured its influence. It was the real council of the anti-Calhoun faction until the reorganization of the cabinet in 1831 enabled the president to have a cabinet in which no Calhounite had place. With that change he consulted his regular advisers more freely, and the "Kitchen Cabinet" lost its importance. The "Kitchen Cabinet."

Among the inauguration visitors were a vast number of office seekers. The impression that Adams officials would be removed was general, and every Jackson man who could do so was present with petitions for reward for party service. Jackson was little inclined to resent the pressure brought to bear upon him. He announced frankly his belief in rotation in office, saying that one honest citizen was as capable as another of serving the public. He believed the campaign charges that the old officials were largely incompetent or touched with partisanship. It must be remembered that the old method of selecting officials was by personal recommendation, that many old men were in office who were no longer able to do the duty assigned to them, which facts gave some basis for the desire to adopt a new system. The treasury, we are told, was popularly called by residents of Washington "the octogenarian department." The removals which followed the inauguration were many more than had occurred before that time, but not so many as were made by later presidents. Most of Jackson's appointees were inexperienced men, many of them were incompetent, and a few proved dishonest. The system he inaugurated had previously grown up in several states, notably in New York. It was characterized by Marcy, of New York, in the phrase, later generally adopted, " To the victors belong the spoils ! " Appointments.

The selection of one member of the cabinet brought out an unexpected protest. Senator John H. Eaton, of Tennessee, a staunch friend of Jackson's, was made secretary of war. January 1, 1829, he was married to Mrs. Timberlake, daughter of a Washington tavern-keeper, who was reported to have had many adventures, a woman whom the society of the city would not receive. Remonstrances were made to Jackson against bringing into his official family one who would undoubtedly be rejected socially. He believed her innocent, and refused to discriminate against her, saying he came to Washington to make a cabinet in the interest of the country and not to please the ladies of the capital. Trouble began immediately, but as official entertainments were not held until society returned to Washington after the summer season was past, an open break was deferred until the fall. Then Jackson gave a dinner, to which all the invited ones came. But their restrained looks showed their feelings toward Mrs. Eaton. When other cabinet officers gave dinners, some members refused to attend. At other places Mrs. Eaton was treated so coolly that before the end of the winter she ceased to accept invitations. Jackson was deeply offended. He took the conduct of society as an affront to himself. He thought a combination was made to discredit his administration.

Mrs. Eaton.

So far, this was only a social affair, but it soon assumed a political aspect. Van Buren was a widower. He had no family to object to Mrs. Eaton, and won the regard of the president by conspicuous attentions to her on every possible occasion. Of those who took the opposite course, Mrs. Calhoun was the leader, and she was supported by the wives of several other cabinet members. Thus Jackson came to associate the vice-president with what he called the conspiracy, and he drew nearer to the friends of Van Buren. He called the protesting cabinet members before him and told them he expected them to induce their wives to treat more courteously the wife of his friend. The only reply they made was that they could not interfere with the social affairs of their families. There was no improvement in the situation of the unhappy woman, and the breach in the administration party grew steadily wider.

Political Significance of the Matter.

INTERNAL IMPROVEMENTS CHECKED

While this affair progressed, Van Buren was able to give his rival another deadly thrust by bringing the president over to the opposition to internal improvements, whose champion Calhoun had long been. The vice-president was the author of the bonus bill, 1817 (see page 365), which Madison vetoed on constitutional grounds. But the friends of improvements persisted, and in 1819 passed resolutions calling on the secretary of war, Calhoun, to report on the roads necessary for

Calhoun and Internal Improvements.

military defense. The secretary complied, but his comprehensive scheme was not acted upon. However, so many appropriations were made for single works that Monroe, himself a strict constructionist, decided to give the country another warning like that of Madison. Accordingly he vetoed, in 1822, a bill to establish toll-gates on, and otherwise to regulate, the Cumberland road, a great national highway designed to run from the Potomac to the capital of Missouri, then the westernmost state. Jackson was at that time in private life, but he wrote to Monroe, congratulating him on the veto. In 1824 a bill was passed directing the secretary of war to have made surveys of such roads and canals as were needed for national development. Next year Calhoun reported a system of roads and canals, the chief features of which were: (1) a canal from the Potomac to the Ohio, to be extended finally to Lake Erie, (2) an inland waterway along the coast from the Potomac to Boston harbor, and (3) a national highway from New Orleans to Washington. Besides these works he pointed out others which ought to be undertaken, some in the South, and some in the West. To the opponents of improvements it seemed a bid for the support of all the parts of the country which would be affected. Nothing was done to carry out this scheme while Adams was president, but it was still in the minds of men at the accession of Jackson. The large group who favored it, strong especially in the Middle and Northwestern states, looked to Calhoun, second in the party and probable successor in 1832, to carry it out. If the weight of Jackson's opposition could be aroused, it would weaken the scheme and at the same time deal a hard blow to the hopes of Calhoun.

Van Buren was the daily companion of the president. He was not a great statesman, but he had tact and common sense, and Jackson, who knew little about practical administration, asked his advice continually. The two men talked freely about the dangers they believed to exist in the growing tendency to get congress to vote money for roads and canals which were purely local, and it was decided that at the first good opportunity a veto should be given which would again call attention to the evils in the practice. Soon afterwards a bill was introduced to authorize the government to take stock in a road from Maysville, Kentucky, to Lexington, in the same state. The road was purely local, and a veto of it could be easily defended. Its passage through the two houses was carefully watched from the White House, and the veto was duly sent May 27, 1830. Many of the president's best friends feared the consequences, saying that it would alienate Pennsylvania and the West. He replied that it was only the contractors and land-boomers, with the politicians who feared them, that opposed the veto, and that the people at large would approve the measure. The news from the people confirmed this foresight. The Maysville veto proved one of the popular measures of Jackson's career. In delivering it he

The Maysville Veto, 1830.

showed one of his most characteristic traits, his ability to divine what the people wished and his willingness to appeal to them over the heads of the politicians.

After rejecting the Maysville bill Jackson objected to many similar measures. He effectively checked appropriations for roads in the states, although many were built in the territories. He did not make the same objection to appropriations for improving rivers and harbors, destined to be for many years the congressman's means of getting benefits for his district. The veto came just when railroads were coming into use, the burden of constructing them was transferred to the states, which made, in the next generation, lavish gifts to such enterprises. The rage for railroad construction at state expense led to much extravagance in the West and was a vital cause of the panic of 1837. After 1850 the Jackson policy was reversed, when great land grants began to be made for the construction of railroads, the most important being the grants in aid of the transcontinental roads during the civil war and immediately afterwards.

Later History of Internal Improvements.

DIVISION IN THE JACKSONIAN PARTY

In 1830 Calhoun was committed to state rights, the program of his friends in South Carolina, and he could not seriously object to the checking of internal improvements. In fact, the South supported the Maysville veto nearly unanimously. It was more concerned in impeding the progress of protection; and the doctrine of nullification, announced for that purpose, was in danger of becoming the general slogan of that section. Many Northern men felt that the doctrine ought to be opposed, and the great Hayne-Webster debate, which occurred at this time, gave them a feeling of relief, since it afforded the greatest champion of the union, Daniel Webster, an opportunity to place before the country the arguments for a stronger federal government.

State Rights and Union Men.

The occasion of this celebrated debate was some resolutions offered December 29, 1829, by Senator Foote, of Connecticut, looking to the restriction of land sales. The Western senators objected immediately, thinking that Foote merely wished to check the drain of Eastern population to the West. Benton, of Missouri, a forceful but bitter debater, took up the cause of the West in one of his characteristic speeches, and much feeling was aroused in the senate. Then the advocates of states rights thought they saw an opportunity to draw the West to their side. They wished to show that it was not strictly constitutional for the federal government to pass laws which bore hardly on any section, and that an attempt to do so was but in keeping with the policy of building up one section at the expense of another, a policy which must lead to hostility of

Foote's Resolution.

section against section with a resulting weakening of the bond of union.

It was impossible to ignore the bearing of this argument on the Southern protest against the protective tariff. It was set forth with much skillfulness by Hayne, of South Carolina, a ready and able debater, the equal, in the opinion of the Southerners, **Webster** of any debater in the senate. Then Webster, senator from **Called** Massachusetts, came to the defense of the North. He **Forth.** denied that his section wished to sacrifice to its own interest any other section, and resented with special force the charge that it was hostile to the West. Hayne had hinted that there was a constitutional way by which a state could undo an unauthorized act of oppression at the hands of the federal congress; and Webster now boldly challenged the theory, his purpose being to force Hayne to a more specific declaration of his meaning. By this time the debate had ceased to be concerned with the sale of Western lands and had become a discussion of the fundamental principles of the constitution. The point at issue was: Can a State legally defy the laws of congress, however much it may think them unwarranted by the constitution?

Hayne could not well avoid Webster's challenge, and to do him justice he had no desire to do so. All the state rights group were with him and waited confidently for his reply. Many times in debate their theory had been appealed to, but never had it been set forth in all its completeness by a master of the art of presentation. Their **Hayne's** expectation was well known in the city and the chamber **Argument.** and galleries were crowded when on January 21, 1830, the Southern champion rose to make his great speech. He was a man of fine appearance and spoke with much grace, although he could utter the sharpest criticisms on an adversary. He was given to making his arguments personal, and resorted to the practice in this speech. In this respect his utterances were neither dignified nor able. But he soon passed on to the constitutional phase, where he spoke with better effect. He accepted the "South Carolina Exposition" of 1828 as sound doctrine, showed that it was in line with the Virginia and Kentucky resolutions of 1798, and affirmed that it was the doctrine that New England espoused when in Madison's administration she found herself, like the South in 1830, suffering from laws enacted by the majority in control of the national government. And then he took up the cause of the South with great earnestness. Is the federal government, he asked, the judge of its own power? To assert the affirmative, whether the power be exercised by congress or by the supreme court, is to make the central government "a government without limitation of powers"! It is to reduce the states to the level of mere corporations. He would speak a word for South Carolina. She was but seeking to preserve herself from measures which had prostrated her industry and would soon impoverish the whole South; she sought to preserve the union of states as it was founded, and to save the states from usurpations which would leave them nothing they could call their own.

Webster's reply was made on the 26th, the senate chamber being crowded to its utmost capacity. Tall, dignified, with a striking leonine face, a rich baritone voice, and a deliberate manner, **Webster's Reply.** he was easily the best orator in the senate. He met the personal thrusts of Hayne with a satirical courtesy which left nothing to be desired by the friends of the speaker, watching anxiously to see if their champion would meet the demands of the occasion. In this respect neither speaker was calm nor properly self-restrained, but even here Webster showed his mental superiority.

It was in his presentation of constitutional argument that we find our chief satisfaction with the Northern champion. Frankly accepting the consolidation theory, he proceeded to combat the **His Constitutional Argument.** doctrine that a state may declare null a law of congress without an appeal to revolution. This doctrine, he said, rested on the false assumption that the federal government was the creature of twenty-four states, each with a will of its own, wills which were apt to be at variance with one another, the exercise of which would reduce the central government to an absurdity. But where lies true sovereignty but in the people for whom both the federal and state governments are agents? Each government derives authority from the same source, each is supreme in its own sphere, and the constitution in all that it pretends to regulate is, by the authority of the sovereign people, the supreme law of the land. So far as the constitution restrains the states, in so far is the authority of the states not supreme. The constitution is a fact. Gentlemen may wish it had been made otherwise than it was made: with that we have nothing to do. It must be obeyed until it is changed. In one state, we may say, the tariff is declared an act of usurpation, in another it is declared constitutional; how shall we reconcile the two points of view if we accept the theory that a state may pass on the matter? If the general government has no power to pass on the contending assertions, is it not "a rope of sand"? It is not claimed that the federal government has unrestricted power. It has all the power given it in the constitution made by the people, all this and no more. Among the specified powers is the creation of a supreme judiciary to pass upon all questions arising under the constitution, and it is to this court and not to any state that we ought to refer the question of the power of congress to make any law it assumes to make. Suppose South Carolina should declare the tariff law null: must her agents not try to enforce the declaration? But the federal government declares it legal, and must its agent not seek to enforce it? What would the result be but civil war? To oppose the execution of the law is treason. Can a state be allowed to commit treason with impunity? If the constitution is imperfect it can be amended by the people who made it, but as long as it is law it should be obeyed.

From this splendid debate each side withdrew with complacent feelings. The Southerners were pleased that their champion had set forth their views of state sovereignty, the Northerners took courage in seeing Webster support the glory and power of the union by such masterly reasoning. But the debate, **Practical Results.** final as it was as a statement of theory, went beyond the practical situation. The country was not yet ready to follow the controversy to the end which Webster so clearly foresaw, to civil war. Each side treasured its own argument in memory for a more strenuous day, while the practical politician took up the tasks actually before him. Of this class were Jackson and Van Buren, generally supposed to lean to state rights, but in their inner hearts willing to see Calhoun and the South Carolinians discredited by the powerful forensics of Webster.

By this time we may freely speak of the South Carolina theory as nullification. Would it be generally adopted in the South? The insistence of its defenders that it was but the doctrine of 1798 shows their anxiety to draw the Virginians to its support. It proved a futile hope; for Virginia, slighted in the make-up of the new administration, would not adopt the leadership of South Carolina. More important was the attitude of Jackson, on whose action the nullifiers waited uneasily. They sup- **Nullification not Checked.** ported him in 1828, their leader, Calhoun, was high in party councils, and they well knew that if the president, a Southerner himself, came over to their side, they would unite the South and be able to force the North into a relinquishment of its high tariff policy. Constitutional arguments are but the theoretical basis of a political movement, and if practical ends could be attained, Webster's reasoning might be ignored.

April 13, 1830, was Jefferson's birthday, generally celebrated by his followers with speeches and toasts. This year the South Carolinians controlled the arrangements of the celebration in Washington and planned to have the speeches express their peculiar views of state rights. The president was invited **Jackson's "Union" Toast.** and was expected to give a toast. He was fully conscious of all that was going on and consulted with Van Buren in regard to his toast. Now at this time Jackson was in sympathy with the Van Buren faction, as were, in fact, all of his "Kitchen Cabinet," and it was decided that he should give such a toast as would show his disapproval of Calhoun's theories. He arose at the feast with this sentiment, "Our federal union, it must be preserved!" The nullifiers could only gasp. Calhoun, who was next called on, tried to retrieve the situation by giving as his toast, "The union, next to our liberty, most dear! May we all remember that it can only be preserved by respecting the rights of the states and distributing equally the benefits and burthen of the union !'' But the words of the president were most significant. They indicated that he would not be brought into the general Southern movement which the nullifiers planned.

In another respect Jackson thwarted the plans of the South Carolinians. In 1802 the United States, approving the cession of Georgia's claim to Alabama and Mississippi, agreed to remove the **Georgia and the Cherokees.** Creek and Cherokee Indians from the limits of Georgia proper "as early as the same can be peaceably obtained on reasonable terms." By several treaties all but 9,000,000 acres of the Indian lands were purchased before 1825 and opened to settlement. But at this time the Indians decided in a council that they would sell no more land. They had their separate form of government, and their land, much of it very fertile, was desired for white settlement. Georgia naturally thought it intolerable that there should be a civil power within her borders which defied her authority, and she called on the federal government to execute the agreement of 1802. Adams hesitated to do anything decisive. Then the state announced that if the Indians were not removed she would exercise her right as a sovereign state, by dividing the Indian lands into counties, opening them to settlement, and establishing a white man's government over them. By the constitution, congress had authority over trade with the Indians and made treaties with them. It was also provided that treaties should be the supreme law of the land. As the Indians pleaded that they were protected by treaties, would not the proposed action of Georgia violate the constitution? The state urged her own sovereignty over the territory within her limits, but the Indians took the matter to the courts. Two important decisions of the federal supreme court were the result. In one, the Cherokee **Status of an Indian Tribe.** Nation *vs.* Georgia, it was held that an Indian tribe, while not an independent nation, was, nevertheless, a state, and under the protection of congress. In the other, Worcester *vs.* Georgia, it was held by the court, Chief Justice Marshall giving the decision, that the attempt of Georgia to extend her jurisdiction over the lands formerly held by the Indians was illegal.

These matters ran past the period to which our story has come, for they extend from the beginning of Jackson's term to 1833; but **Georgia and the South Carolina Controversy.** the sharp controversy they produced was in its critical phase in 1830. They were related to the general attempt of South Carolina to draw all the South to her support because they involved the theory of state sovereignty. If Georgia leant so decidedly on the theory in her Indian controversy, would she not make common cause with her sister state in the fight to lower the tariff? The nullifiers undoubtedly expected as much, but they were disappointed. In the first place the men of Georgia were devoted to Crawford, who was bitterly opposed to Calhoun. They supported Jackson in 1828, but adhered to the Van Buren, rather than the Calhoun, faction. In the second place, Jackson gave them continual support in the Indian matter, informing the Indians soon after his inauguration that there was nothing for them but to submit and remove beyond the Mississippi. As the controversy was still unsettled in 1830 Georgia dared not move against the declared opposition of Jackson, who let it be known to the Georgians that he expected their support in the defense of the cause of union. Thus it happened that South Carolina saw her hopes of uniting all the south in a common cause of nullification fall to the ground; and the turn of events augured no good for the Calhoun faction, whom the Van Buren faction were bent on reducing, with Jackson's help, to a position of inferiority. It was a sad blow to the ambition of the great South Carolinian. Face to face with the loss of his own state in 1828, he had been compelled to turn a somersault from nationalism to a state rights position, and while he was in mid-air the artful Van Buren struck him a blow which made his landing precarious.

In the autumn of 1829, when Jackson was deeply touched by what he considered the combination to discredit Eaton through the exclusion of Mrs. Eaton from society, the "Kitchen Cabinet" revealed to him that Calhoun, formerly secretary of war, **Jackson** wished in 1818 to discipline him for the invasion of Flor- **Turned** ida. Jackson knew that such a purpose was entertained **against** **Calhoun.** in the cabinet at the time, but he supposed that Crawford was its author. Calhoun should have removed this suspicion, but fearing Jackson's wrath, had allowed him to go on thinking that Crawford was the author of the suggestion. When the truth at last came out, Jackson, suspicious and of violent temper, would believe nothing but that the South Carolinian had acted traitorously. He said nothing openly until the Jefferson birthday dinner brought him to the point of declared opposition; for Calhoun had a powerful following, and a false move would cause the public to think that party harmony was jeopardized by personal intrigue. But now Calhoun was identified with disunion and might be attacked with greater safety.

The day after the birthday dinner a friend of Van Buren at the side of the president wrote to Crawford for verification of the story that had been privately revealed. The reply of Crawford, who still hated Calhoun, was all that was expected. Then **An Angry** began a bitter correspondence between president and vice- **Corre-** **spondence.** president, the highest man and next highest in the administration party, in which neither convinced the other of his wrongdoing. It ended with a curt note in which Jackson told his correspondent that future friendship between them was impossible. Van Buren was too shrewd to take open part in the affair. He was careful

2 D

not to talk with Jackson about it, but it is impossible to suppose that he was ignorant of a matter so full of weight for his future. The breach it produced was accentuated by the selection of a new party organ, which up to this time had been the *Daily Telegraph*, edited by Duff Green, a devoted Calhoun man. Frank P. Blair, destined to become one of the most influential party editors of the day, was

The Globe.
brought to Washington, and in December, 1830, he founded the *Globe*, whose influence was soon widespread. Blair was a firm friend of Jackson and gave all his energy to promoting the cause of Van Buren.

Since the president did not publish this correspondence, Calhoun concluded that he feared to do so. Friends, to whom it was freely shown, held the same view and thought that its publica-

Calhoun pronounced Traitor.
tion would crush the crafty New Yorker. Then Calhoun took the initiative, laying his case before the public in a pamphlet which saw the light of day in February, 1831. The *Globe* immediately charged Calhoun with an attempt to sow dissension in the party, the administrative press and politicians, fearing the wrath of Jackson, took up the cry, and by the end of spring Calhoun was fiercely denounced as a party traitor.

By the spring of 1831 the anti-Calhoun men were so strong that they were prepared to thrust their opponents out of the cabinet. But even here the proceedings were marked by consum-

A Purged Cabinet.
mate skill. Fearing that a bald dismissal would plant irreconcilable hatred within the party, it was arranged that Van Buren and Eaton should resign voluntarily. They gave as their reason the desire to relieve Jackson from the embarrassment of their presence, but before resigning they had been promised other positions. Van Buren was to be minister to England, and it was thought that Eaton could be elected senator from Tennessee. When this faction had withdrawn, the president, with every outward appearance of impartiality, called for the withdrawal of the others, so that neither should have the advantage in the cabinet. He thus got rid of the Calhounites, but he did not on that account fail to fill the new cabinet with men opposed to Calhoun. He thus remade the government on a Van Buren basis.

The next feature of the party program was to look out for the nomination for the presidency in 1832. Jackson had formerly declared that he would accept only one term. But his

Jackson Renominated.
friends knew that if he now withdrew, it would be difficult to secure the nomination for Van Buren, openly charged with the intrigue against Calhoun. They had good reason to fear that the South Carolinian, the next most popular democrat to Jackson, would be indorsed by the party. Jackson himself understood the situation, and in the autumn of 1831 let it be known that he would again be a candidate. He planned to have Van Buren remain

in London until the excitement of the recent quarrel subsided, and to return in time to be made candidate in 1836. But in January, 1832, the senate rejected Van Buren's nomination as minister by the casting vote of Calhoun, the vice-president; and such an outburst of feeling came from the Jackson following that it was decided that the only way to vindicate the rejected man was to make him Jackson's running-mate. Thus was taken the last step in the identification of the favored New Yorker with the head of the party. In 1829 the party was threatened with disintegration through the fierce rivalry within it. By the most skillful management, the Calhoun faction had been reduced to a harmless minimum, and led through its own blundering into open revolt at a time when its secession was not a serious danger. At the same time, Jackson had grown in strength with the masses and was at the head of a mighty host which looked to him as the chosen leader against forces of corruption. Jacksonian democracy was completely organized and confident of the future.

THE ELECTION OF 1832

Meanwhile, an opposition was forming under Clay's leadership. All who criticized Jackson's appointments, or rejected his policy of internal improvements, or opposed his attitude toward the bank, — already announced but not pressed to its conclusion (see page 411), — and many others whose chief impulse was dislike for a leader of the Jackson type, all these now came together under the name of national republicans. **The National Republicans.** In calling themselves by this title they seem to have had in mind the division of the party which prevailed in the years immediately after the war of 1812. They also proclaimed themselves faithful tariff men, but on this issue Jackson was not openly against them.

Besides these, a third party was in the field. In 1826 William Morgan, of Batavia, New York, who had published a book purporting to expose the secrets of freemasonry, mysteriously disappeared, and many people believed he had been destroyed by the masons. A frantic movement spread through the adjoining counties for the outlawry of the order, which was denounced as a secret political society. **The Anti-Masonic Party Organized.** The anti-masonic party was thus organized. As Clinton was a mason, it opposed him, and as Jackson was also a mason and had the support of Clinton, it supported Adams in 1828. The party was organized in several other states in this election, and generally opposed Jackson. They were able to hold the balance of power in some states and elected several members of congress.

As the election of 1832 approached, attempts were made to get them to support Clay; but he would not declare for their principles, and they decided to act alone. In September, 1830, they held a national convention in Philadelphia, in which it was decided to organize a national party. This assembly made an appeal to the people and called a convention at Baltimore, September 26, 1831, to select a candidate for the presidency, the first national nominating convention in our history. It met in due time and selected William Wirt, of Virginia, as its candidate for the presidency and Amos Ellmaker, of Pennsylvania, for the vice-presidency. The example of the antimasons was followed by the national republicans, who in December, 1831, assembled in Baltimore and nominated Clay for president, and Sergeant, of Pennsylvania, for vice-president. In the following May a convention of young men who supported Clay met in Washington, accepted the Baltimore nominations, and issued the first "platform" of a political party in America. It indorsed protection and internal improvements, and arraigned Jackson's administration for its policy in appointments to office, and its attitude toward the Indians in Georgia. In May, 1832, the democrats followed the example of their opponents and met in a convention at Baltimore. They nominated Jackson unanimously, and Van Buren by a vote of 208 to 75. This convention ordered that a two-thirds vote should be necessary to a nomination, a rule followed in every succeeding convention of the party.

First National Nominating Convention.

The convention system, thus introduced, has proved a permanent feature of American political life. After the caucus was repudiated in 1824 candidates were nominated by state legislature. In 1828 the candidates were so well designated by the trend of events that this system was satisfactory. It would probably have been satisfactory, so far as Jackson was concerned, in 1832; for his party had no thought of rejecting him as a candidate. Indeed, as the election year approached, he was nominated by many legislatures and local or state conventions. But the other parties were not so fortunate. The antimasons were at sea until the convention assembled, and the national republicans, though united in Clay's favor, needed the effect of a great display of their strength to impress themselves on the minds of voters. In the democratic party a convention was necessary to secure the acceptance of Van Buren, in whose behalf Jackson exerted all his power over his followers. It was, probably, only the fear of offending Jackson which made Van Buren the candidate.

Convention System a Development.

The adoption of nomination by convention shows how democratic parties had now become. The delegates, at first chosen in varying manners, represented the party in the localities from which they came. Their selection was the best utterance of the party's voice then possible. The earliest method was generally to allot to each state as many votes in convention as it had in the electoral college. Later practice has given each state twice as many votes as it has presidential electors.

Democratic Character of the Party.

The campaign which followed these nominations was vehement. The democrats relied on the popular confidence in Jackson. He was, they said, the people's candidate, he would pay the national debt, he would deprive the bank of its privileges, and he protected the treasury from the wiles of the people who wished to have roads and canals at the expense of the national revenues. **The Bank Veto.** Clay's support was of a complex character. In one section he relied on the friendship of the business classes for the bank, in others he appealed to the protectionists, and in still others he talked about the radicalism of Jackson. In July, while the canvass progressed, the president vetoed the bill to recharter the bank. Clay's friends had urged the bill, thinking that a veto would array against Jackson the state of Pennsylvania as well as the powerful financial class. The national republicans received the veto message with undisguised pleasure and pressed the battle more vigorously. They were soon undeceived. The farmers of Pennsylvania cared nothing for the bank, and they rallied to the support of its arch foe in proportion as the capitalists proclaimed their hostility to him. The result of the election was 219 electoral votes for Jackson, 49 for Clay, and 7 for Wirt, while South Carolina, piqued over the treatment of Calhoun, threw away her 11 votes on Floyd of Virginia. **Jackson Elected.** Van Buren carried all of the Jackson votes but the thirty from Pennsylvania, which were given to Wilkins, of that state. Wirt's vote came from Vermont, the only state the antimasons could carry. This poor showing was the death knell of that party. Jackson very naturally took his overwhelming victory as an indorsement of his policies, and prepared to put them into complete execution.

BIBLIOGRAPHICAL NOTE

The period embraced in this chapter is treated in the general *Histories* of Mc-Master, Schouler, and Wilson. The best single volume on the period is Mac-Donald's *Jacksonian Democracy* (1906). With the inauguration of Jackson, Von Holst, *Constitutional History of the United States*, 8 vols. (Mason, trans. 1876–1892), becomes valuable on the constitutional and political side, although it leans strongly toward the party of concentration. An excellent short summary is Wilson, *Division and Reunion* (revised ed., 1909), and nearly as useful is Burgess, *The Middle Period* (1897).

Besides the biographies and writings of Jackson, Calhoun, Clay, Webster, J. Q. Adams, Benton, and Wirt already mentioned (see page 380), the following are valuable: Sumner, *Life of Jackson* (ed. 1897); Shepard, *Life of Martin Van Buren*, (revised. ed., 1899); Stickney, editor, *Autobiography of Amos Kendall* (1872); J. A. Hamilton, *Reminiscences* (1869); Curtis, *Life of James Buchanan*, 2 vols. (1883); *Works of James Buchanan*, 12 vols. (Moore, ed., 1908–1911); Tyler, *Letters and Times of the Tylers*, 3 vols. (1884–1896); Bradley, *Isaac Hill* (1835); Story, *Life and Letters of Joseph Story*, 2 vols. (1851); Hunt, *Life of Edward Livingston* (1864); Hammond, *Life of Silas Wright* (1848); and Jervey, *Robert Y. Hayne* (1909).

The sources are chiefly in the public documents, the most important being: *Executive*, in the series known as *State Papers*, 38 vols., extending to the first years of Van Buren's administration. The most signiñcant for the present chapter are *Finance*, 5 vols., and *Indian Affairs*, 2 vols. See also Richardson, *Messages and Papers of the Presidents, 1789-1902*, 10 vols. (1897-1902). *Legislative*, the debates in the *Register of Debates*, 1825-1837, 29 vols., with valuable appendices containing many reports of committees, etc., and Benton, *Abridgment of Debates*, 16 vols. (1857-1861). *Judiciary*, the reports of the decisions of the supreme court, published in series bearing the names of the reporter until 1882, and from that time they are numbered continuously. Those extending over the years 1828 to 1842 are cited as *Peters*, 16 vols. Bowker, *State Publications*, 2 vols. (1899-1902), is a useful index to published government documents. The laws are in Peters, *Statutes at Large*, 8 vols. (1845-1846), volumes 7 and 8 contain treaties. *Treaties and Conventions* (ed. of 1889) is also very useful. Other important sources are: J. Q. Adams, *Memoirs*, 12 vols. (1874-1877); Ibid., *Writings*, W. C. Ford, ed. (1913-); Benton, *Thirty Years' View*, 2 vols. (1854-1857); Mayo, *Political Sketches* (1839); Wise, *Seven Decades of the Union* (1881); and Niles, *Register*, a weekly newspaper in which appear many documents.

The controversy over the interpretation of the constitution gave rise to many works. The most important on the national side are: Von Holst, *Constitutional History of the United States*, 8 vols. (Mason trans., 1876-1892), is the most comprehensive narrative from the national point of view. Of the same nature is Lodge, *Life of Webster* (1897); and Greeley, *The American Conflict*, 2 vols. (1864-1867). On the state rights side see: Jefferson Davis, *Rise and Fall of the Confederate Government*, 2 vols. (1881); Wise, *Seven Decades of the Union* (1881); and Tucker, *History of the United States*, 4 vols. (1856-1858). For references on nullification see below, page 426.

For Independent Reading

Harvey, *Reminiscences and Anecdotes of Daniel Webster* (1877); Lyman Beecher, *Autobiography*, 2 vols. (1863-1865); Poore, *Perley's Reminiscences*, 2 vols. (1886); Wentworth, *Congressional Reminiscences* (1882); Charles A. Davis, *Letters of Major Jack Downing* (1833), — humorous and widely read by contemporaries, but misleading in regard to Jackson's character; and Sullivan, *Familiar Letters on Public Characters* (1834).

CHAPTER XX

JACKSON'S PRESIDENCY COMPLETED

THE END OF NULLIFICATION

IT was natural for Jackson to think his triumphant reëlection an evidence of popular approval for all his important policies. Thus reassured, and supported by a united party, he could take up the incomplete work of his first administration with **Work to be** the assurance of success. He might secure the removal of **Done.** the Georgia Indians, bring to an end the negotiations with France, and break down the power of the bank of the United States, which he considered a menace to democratic institutions. But the first serious problem after the election was to deal with nullification. It was a problem he did not invite and could not avoid; for the South Carolinians, having lost hope of placing their great leader in the White House, were now determined to put their theory to the ultimate test.

It will be remembered that Calhoun came to open breach with Jackson with the publication of his pamphlet in February, 1831, which he at first hoped would destroy Van Buren and not provoke the opposition of Jackson (see page 401). By **Nullifiers** the middle of May he realized that this expectation was **become Ag-** futile and became the public, as for three years he had been **gressive.** the secret, leader of the nullifiers. July 26 he issued his famous "Address to the People of South Carolina," in which were restated the arguments in the "Exposition" of 1828. It was the avowed platform of his followers, and was widely read, North and South. All through the autumn, winter, and following spring it was widely discussed in South Carolina. The union party there was of respectable size, though not in a majority, and they naturally sought to lessen the weight of his doctrine. In the discussion various **Calhoun's** explanations were given of its meaning, for it was not **Three Great** clear in all its points. At last the nullifiers themselves **Papers on** called on him for a simpler statement, and August 28, **Nullification.** 1832, he published such a summary in what became known as his "Fort Hill Letter," addressed to Governor James Hamilton, Jr. The result of this agitation was that the nullifiers carried the legislature by a large majority.

To this body soon after it met in October came a message from the governor urging that, inasmuch as the federal government was committed to the tariff which was believed to be unconstitutional, it was the duty of the state to look out for the interests of the people. Since the constitution, it said, was authorized by the people of the state, it was for them now to call a convention to inquire if the federal compact had been violated. The legislature accepted the suggestion, and by a large majority called a convention to meet November 19, 1832.

The South Carolina Convention.

No one could doubt what that body would do. By a vote of 136 to 26 it passed on the 24th the South Carolina Ordinance of Nullification, declaring the tariff acts of 1828 and 1832 not binding on the people of the state, forbidding appeals to the federal courts in cases for the enforcement of the said laws, and requiring state officials to take oath to uphold the ordinance. February 1, 1833, was fixed as the day on which nullification should go into effect, and the legislature was directed to pass such laws as should be necessary to put the ordinance into effect.

The Ordinance of Nullification.

November 27 the legislature reassembled. It was foreseen that if a citizen refused to pay duties on goods, the articles in question would be seized by federal officers, and to enable him to recover them the replevin act was now passed. It provided that the owners of goods seized might recover twice their value from the official holding them. As this was a state law, and as the state officials were all nullifiers, it was likely that the replevin act would be executed with liberality toward the persons who refused to pay duties. On the other hand, it seemed certain that the federal government would not tamely give up its power to seize goods for failure to pay duties, and if war came it would come at this point in the controversy. The legislature did not overlook the fact, and it authorized the governor to call out the militia to enforce the laws of the state. There was a great deal of excitement in the state, unionists and nullifiers held nightly meetings, and threats of war and secession were heard on every hand.

The Replevin Act.

While affairs progressed to this state President Jackson kept his eye on the situation. Knowing that the nullifiers only threatened in the hope that they could force congress to modify the tariff, he felt that they would hesitate to go as far as war. But he took occasion in several ways to drop quiet hints that the laws must be obeyed. It was not until the autumn that he came to believe that nullification would actually be attempted. Then he ordered the secretary of the navy to be ready to send a force to Charleston, if necessary. He also directed the commanding officers of the forts in the harbor to be vigilant in detecting resistance, sent a special messenger to report on sentiment in the state, gave constant encouragement to the union party there, and deposited arms in convenient

Jackson's Precautions.

places in North Carolina to be ready for an emergency. Seven revenue cutters and the *Natchez*, a ship of war, appeared in Charleston harbor and cast anchor where they could rake the fashionable "Battery," on which were the residences of the leading citizens. For many weeks the tension was extreme. Nullifiers and unionists, equally desirous of delaying bloodshed, strove to restrain the feelings of their followers, lest some accident should precipitate war before the last efforts for peace were exhausted.

In Washington two groups of men were seeking to meet the situation. One, under the lead of the president, planned to meet force with force and to assert the authority of the government. From this source came Jackson's nullification proclamation, December 10, 1832. It was a firm argument against the theory of nullification, and closed by warning the people of South Carolina against the advocates of nullification. "The laws of the United States must be executed," said Jackson in words like those of Lincoln twenty-nine years later; "I have no discretionary power on the subject; my duty is emphatically pronounced in the constitution. Those who told you that you might peaceably prevent their execution, deceived you; they could not have been deceived themselves. They know that a forcible opposition could alone prevent the execution of the laws, and they know that such opposition must be repelled. Their object is disunion. But be not deceived by names. Disunion by armed force is *treason*." Many of Jackson's followers were state rights men, and they were not pleased with his open espousal of consolidation doctrines. But all the unionists of the country, of whatever party, took fresh courage when they read the proclamation. For once New England and the great cities of the northern coast, following the lead of Webster and John Quincy Adams, were in hearty support of Jackson.

The Nullification Proclamation.

Its Effect.

The second group wished to solve the difficult problem before the nation by enacting a bill for a lower tariff. That done, nullification as a practical measure would vanish. They were lead by the particular friends of Van Buren, who could not hope to have the democratic support in 1836 if the northern and southern portions of the party fell into conflict over state rights. They brought in the Verplanck bill, proposing to lower duties to a basis of 20 per cent in two years, hoping that with the support of the South and as many votes as Van Buren could rally in the North the measure would pass. If the project succeeded, Van Buren would be applauded as "Pacificator." Jackson countenanced the plan, but gave most of his attention to his own plans for preserving the authority of the federal government.

The Verplanck Tariff Bill.

Meanwhile, the attitude of the other Southern states became very important, both to South Carolina and to the president. Georgia wavered for a while, but the fear that she would lose Jackson's sympathy in regard to her Indian question held her in check. If she had gone over to the nullifiers, it is probable that the other Gulf states would have followed her lead. Much anxiety was also felt for Virginia, and the nullifiers tried hard to convince her that they but stood for the Virginia resolutions of 1798. Agents were sent to Richmond to labor with the legislature there. Their best effort could not accomplish their purposes. Although there was strong sentiment in that state for state rights, the most the legislature would do was to send an agent to South Carolina to try to make peace between the state and the federal authorities. North Carolina took an even more conservative stand, declaring that she would defend the cause of union. The nullifiers were thus made to see that if war came, they must proceed alone. But many people feared that if fighting once began, it would be impossible to restrain all the South from rallying to the support of South Carolina in her struggle against the tariff.

What would the South Do?

Jackson was now thoroughly aroused, and thought only of using force. Offers of troop came from many states, and Washington was full of war talk. January 16, 1833, he sent congress a special message on the situation, and on the 21st one of his friends introduced the "force bill," called by the Calhounites the "bloody bill." It gave the president the authority to call out the army and navy to enforce the laws of congress. Jackson used all his influence to have it passed. Calhoun proclaimed it a tyrannical measure, and the states rights men generally considered it an invasion of the rights of the states. This bill and the Verplanck tariff bill were urged contemporaneously, one by the unionists, the other by the democrats generally.

The "Force Bill."

As January neared an end, it became evident that the tariff bill could not pass. In fact, only one man could get enough Northern votes to pass a bill lowering the tariff, and that man was Clay, the father of the "American System." Many people urged him to exert himself for peace and save the union from civil war. For a long time he hesitated, but so much was gained for compromise that on February 1 the leading nullifiers met and decided to suspend the execution of the ordinance of nullification until they could see what congress would do. Then Clay at last yielded. February 12 he introduced in the senate a bill to reduce the tariff gradually during the next ten years, until in 1842 it should be at 20 per cent. The nullifiers and the South supported it, and enough of Clay's friends followed him to make it a law in the last days of the short session. To secure this result Calhoun agreed not to oppose the "force bill," which also became law as the session was about to adjourn. Thus ended the controversy. South Carolina, having secured the reduction of the tariff, repealed her nullification ordinance, and peace returned to the troubled face of national affairs. Clay, and not Van Buren, was hailed "Pacificator!"

Clay's Compromise Tariff.

Jackson's "War" against the Bank

Jackson was pleased to have nullification off the stage, because he thought the time was come to finish his long struggle against the Bank of the United States. Early in his career he concluded that a bank controlled by one group of capitalists was dangerous to the welfare of the country and of doubtful constitutionality. Most of the bank's officers, at its headquarters in Philadelphia, as well as in the branches, were anti-Jackson men, and this gave rise to the charge that the institution worked for Jackson's defeat. The new party believed the allegation, although it was not very clearly proved, and they came into office disposed to use their power against the bank. They at once preferred charges against the Portsmouth, New Hampshire, branch. Nicholas Biddle, president of the "mother bank," as it was called, defended the branch in some warm words which only provoked further the party in power. After a while, he became more moderate, and an investigation showed that the Portsmouth branch was not guilty of the charges made. The incident was later pronounced the origin of the attack on the bank, the argument being that all the opposition that followed was because in this affair the administration was thwarted in a plan to get political control of the bank. The statement is not true. Jackson's attitude dates back at least twelve years, and he had nothing to do with the Portsmouth incident. On the other hand, in the autumn of 1829 Biddle had allowed the Jackson men to get control of several of the Western branches and was trying through friends in Washington to induce the president to agree that a recharter should be granted. Several members of the "Kitchen Cabinet," and the majority of the regular cabinet, favored his scheme, and he was confident of success.

The Beginning.

The Portsmouth, N. H., Incident.

Biddle's First Suggestion of a New Charter.

But Jackson's mind was made up. Rash in the outburst of his feeling, he could be as prudent as any one when policy demanded. He left Biddle in the dark for a month, and gave him a sad disappointment in the first annual message, December 8, 1829. The bank's charter, he said, would expire in 1836, and it was not too soon for congress and the people to begin to consider the wisdom of a recharter. He added that there were grave doubts about the constitutionality of the bank, and that it certainly had failed to establish "a uniform and sound currency." He suggested a bank founded upon the credit and revenues of the government, having in view chiefly the note-issuing and deposit functions. From all that came after, it is clear that he wished to take from private hands the large power and profit the bank then had. Probably he did not realize how severe a shock such a change would give

Jackson Disappoints Biddle.

to business. His party was more prudent, and it shrank from a battle with the powerful bank. On every hand his foes decried the suggestion in the message, and many of his friends held back. But the believers in state rights and the mass of people, whose instincts were against monopoly, were more favorable. In congress two committees reported that the bank was in a good condition, and thus the matter rested for a time.

But in his second annual message, December 6, 1830, Jackson returned to the charge, now unfolding a detailed plan for such a bank as he thought advisable. It was to be connected with the treasury department and managed by public officials. The scheme was at once attacked on the ground that it would vastly increase the patronage of the administration; and the point was a good one; for Jackson's appointments were bad and it did not seem safe to enlarge them in the way he now suggested. Nothing was done in the matter, and congress adjourned in March. The net result accomplished was that the question had been placed fairly before the country and opinion was forming on the inevitable problem, which must be met in one way or another before 1836.

Jackson's Idea of a Bank owned by the Government.

When congress met again, the country was on the eve of a presidential election. Jackson's friends knew they would be embarrassed if the bank were an issue, and he yielded to them so far as merely to restate his position in his message, not asking for positive legislation. Biddle, watching the situation keenly, took this for a sign of weakness. If the attack were made, might it not come better now, when Jackson's cause was before the people, than later, when he was triumphantly reëlected? The national republicans, Clay at their head, thought the bank very popular in the country; they wished to force a new charter through congress, believing that if it were vetoed the president would lose Pennsylvania and other strong commercial states in the East, without which he could not be reëlected. This view appealed strongly to many of Jackson's friends, among them the secretary of the treasury, McLane. During the first weeks of the session there was much conferring in order to prepare a bill which both Biddle and Jackson would accept; but the upshot was that the president would yield nothing, and in January, 1832, Biddle, deciding to proceed without Jackson's approval, formally asked congress for a charter. He was warned that if his bill passed it would be vetoed. Indeed, after all Jackson had said against the bank he could hardly do otherwise. But recharter was pressed, the bank employing an able lobby in its behalf, and Biddle himself, a man of great ability, going to Washington to lead the fight. In July the charter passed by safe majorities and was immediately vetoed. The veto message was a shrewd campaign document. It declared

Biddle Carries a Charter through Congress.

The Veto Sustained.

the bank unconstitutional, pronounced it a monopoly, and appealed to the people's hostility toward great capitalistic institutions. To the friends of the bank these reasons seemed very flimsy; but the veto appealed to the people, and supported by Jackson's prestige it proved unassailable. His election by a vote of 219 to 49 for Clay and 7 for Wirt was received as evidence that the country indorsed the veto.

In the next session of congress nullification and the tariff played a leading part, and the bank question was not brought forward. But Jackson had his plan made, and as soon as the South Carolina crisis was safely passed he began to put it into **Biddle still has Hope.** execution. It was evident that Biddle did not accept the election as a final verdict. To close up the business of the bank in 1836 would mean calling in a great mass of loans and the withdrawal from circulation of much bank money. From both processes business must suffer. Many men foresaw this, foes as well as friends of the bank. Would the country at the last willingly undergo the calamity? Biddle thought that when the crisis came he might be able to carry a charter over a veto; Jackson believed the same, but he put it another way. He said that the bank would wait until **To be** the last and use its power of calling in loans to produce a **checked by** panic and thus wring a charter out of congress in spite of a **the Removal of the** veto. He was thoroughly angry with Biddle, and believed **Deposits.** him capable of any wickedness. He therefore proposed to meet the emergency by breaking the power of the bank in 1833, so that in 1836 it should not be able to produce a panic; and his means of breaking it was to withdraw the public deposits, place them with the leading state banks, and gradually strengthen those institutions, so that in 1836 they would be able to take over the duties of the great institution and lessen the shock of the country from its destruction.

The charter provided that the deposits might be removed by the secretary of the treasury while congress was not in session, provided he gave his reasons for the removal to congress when it assembled. As congress would not meet until December, there was **The Appointment of** ample time for the proposed action; but Secretary McLane **Duane.** was unwilling to order removal, and Jackson, wishing to avoid another explosion in his cabinet, hesitated to dismiss him. After some conference it was agreed to send Livingston, secretary of state, to France as minister, to promote McLane to the vacant place, and to get a new secretary of the treasury. The man hit upon was William J. Duane, son of that former editor of the *Aurora*, who was long the tribune of the people in the important state of Pennsylvania. If the order for removal were given by such a man, it would go far to relieve the act from the expected criticisms of the enemy in the home state of the "mother bank." The offer flattered Duane, who was hitherto little known, and he entered upon his new duties late in May.

But now appeared many difficulties. The new secretary said he was not sure the deposits were in danger, and he was told to take time to consider. At the end of a month he thought the matter

Duane a Disappointment.
could be left until congress met. Then there were many conferences, at the end of which he assured the president that he would examine the question again and would resign if he did not give the desired order. At the middle of September he was again interviewed, and declared finally that he would neither remove the deposits nor resign. Jackson was very angry, and dismissed Duane summarily. The bank men said much about the sacrifice of a faithful secretary, but posterity has little sympathy for him. He must have known for what purpose he was appointed, and he should have refused in advance or withdrawn as soon as he knew the attitude of the president. On the other hand, there is no reason to believe that the deposits in the bank were unsafe, as Jackson claimed.

Roger B. Taney was now appointed secretary of the treasury, and an order issued at once designating certain great state banks at which all government funds should be deposited from October 1, 1833.

Taney and Removal.
July, 1833, the public deposits were $6,512,000, and it would have been disastrous to withdraw so large an amount at once. Jackson, therefore, was satisfied to cease to deposit with the bank and to draw out the money very gradually. January 1, 1836, it still had $627,000 of government funds. Nevertheless, the action of the president caused serious financial distress. The bank must call in loans, and making ready to close its business it could not increase its circulation. The winter, spring, and summer following

The Effect on Business.
removal brought severe business depression to the country. Jackson's friends declared that the distress was artificial, and due to Biddle's malice; and they declared that it was only a speculator's panic and did not injure the mass of merchants and producers. It is hard to say how much truth was in this opinion. Certainly Biddle was in an ugly frame of mind, and did little to soften the blow his adversary had given to business. By refusing to lend money in the darkest days of necessity he brought the country to think the charges against him were true. His own friends began to leave him, and at last he was forced to resume lending. This happened in March, 1834, and by the middle of summer business was returning to normal conditions.

Meanwhile, the matter was in the hands of the politicians. Taney sent to congress, as required by the charter, his reasons for trans-

Jackson Censured.
ferring the deposits. Clay made them the occasion for two resolutions, one of which declared that Jackson acted illegally in regard to the deposits, and the other that Taney's reasons for his action were not sufficient. After an angry debate Clay carried his resolutions through the senate. Jackson made a dignified protest against the resolutions censuring him, and when they passed,

his friend, Benton, of Missouri, gave notice that he would in the future move to expunge them. This he did in successive sessions, until at last there was a majority of democrats in the senate, and January 16, 1837, an order was passed to write across the original entry in the journal the statement that the resolutions of censure were directed to be expunged. Clay in 1834 was also able to get the senate to reject Taney's nomination as secretary of the treasury, but in 1836, through support of Jackson, Taney became chief justice, in succession to John Marshall.

Thus ended in complete triumph Jackson's attack on the bank, the severest political conflict in our national history. It was the occasion of many angry and false charges. The bank was well managed and rendered valuable service to the government **Significance** and people, and the allegations to the contrary were the **of the** outgrowth of ignorance and prejudice. On the other **" Bank** hand, it was a private monopoly, which reaped rich re- **War."** ward for the service it rendered, and it was destroyed because the people, in support of the president, felt that no corporation should have so much advantage. Jackson represented the popular will. He went into the conflict with a divided party, but he fought so wisely and boldly that he united his party and made his word its law. His success was the despair of his enemies.

FOREIGN AFFAIRS

Jackson displayed in foreign affairs the same energy and directness that characterized his conduct of domestic relations. Three important problems of this nature came before him, and they were all disposed of in such a manner as to satisfy the American people and to increase our prestige with other nations. Two of them were old disputes which had dragged on without prospect of fair settlement under his predecessors, and one was a new problem.

The first concerned the trade with the West Indies, before the revolution a source of great prosperity. This branch of our commerce was of great importance to New England and the Middle states, and many efforts to secure it on an equal footing with Eng- **The West** land were made while the federalists controlled the national **India Trade.** government. The same eagerness was not manifested by the republicans under Jefferson and Madison, and the development of manufactures, absorbing much of the business energy of the country, lessened the demand for commerce. But all the time there was a feeling that the lost trade should be recovered if England could be induced to yield it. The matter was under consideration in making the treaty of Ghent, but it offered so much difficulty that it was postponed for a separate convention, which met in 1815, but effected no results. It was taken up again by Secretary Adams in 1818, and was a constant subject of negotiation during his secretaryship, but nothing was accomplished. Indeed, the net result was that each side became irritated, the United States undertook to retaliate, and England became firmer than ever in her refusal. Adams was ever an outspoken man, zealous for national interests, and apt to be assertive in his diplomacy. To force concessions from the self-sufficient and rather overbearing Briton required more tact than he possessed.

The real obstacle to success was the navigation laws. From their enactment it had been the policy of England to consider her colonies the proper field for the profit of her merchants **The Naviga-** and her shipowners. Our ministers might try as they **tion Laws** could to show her the advantage of open trade, but they **Receding.** were not able to convince her. Preferential duties continued to be charged in the West Indies against all comers, and the United States fared as the rest of the world. But just at this time English opinion was changing in regard to the navigation laws. The loss of the American market through the development of manufactures here and the raising of the tariff bars had put the British merchants to thinking. On the other hand, a wide demand for British goods in South America and elsewhere had produced a great wave of prosperity, which tended to make the merchants think their remnant of colonial trade of less importance than their commerce with the outside world. At the same time, a group of liberals under the leadership of Huskisson and Robinson were striving to bring the British public to see that the existing acts did not suit the needs of a nation dependent on happy trade relations with the whole world. In 1825 they induced parliament to make a first step in concession. Foreign nations were now offered in the colonies such commercial **The Conces-** privileges, both as regards tariffs and tonnage duties, **sion of** as they themselves conceded to Great Britain; and **1825.** one year was allowed during which the offer might be accepted. The concession was open to any government, but it most concerned the United States, by their position and industrial enterprise the strongest competitor of the mother country in these colonies. Many nations accepted the offer, but our rising sentiment in favor of protection and a willingness of the opposition to impede any action suggested by the administration prevented concessions by congress within a year. At the end of that time English prosperity had been checked, parliament abandoned its liberal attitude, and although a special American envoy went to England to make a treaty, nothing could be gained in that quarter.

This was the situation when Jackson became president, with the tactful Van Buren secretary of state. To win a victory where others had failed appealed to both men, and McLane, the minister to London, departed in full hope of doing something. He was allowed to write his own instructions, and he incorporated in them the sentiment that our former position was wrong and had been repudiated by the people in a national election. For this Van Buren was severely criticized by his enemies, and it was urged The Negotiation resumed under Jackson. as a main reason for his rejection as minister in 1832. It was certainly not dignified for a secretary in a communication to a foreign power to take cognizance of a domestic party difference.

But the advance pleased Great Britain, and the negotiations then resumed soon led to success. Acting on a hint from McLane, congress gave the president power to remove the discriminating tonnage duties as soon as England did the same. Their Success, 1830. This condition was easily met, and October 5, 1830, Jackson by proclamation opened the trade with the British West Indies. The arrangement did not involve a remission of custom duties, but we could hardly expect another nation to give up her tariff against us as long as we maintained our tariff against her. The best result of the agreement was to remove a source of irritation between the two nations. The democrats declared it a great victory and were disposed to think it might have been secured sooner if Adams had used more tact and patience.

The second diplomatic success concerned claims we had long urged against France for property seized by Napoleon. Other nations had formerly had such claims, but they were paid after the fall of the Corsican. The United States had no The Claims against France. friend at the congress of Vienna and were left to deal with the French government as they could. To their protests the Bourbon kings replied that France could not undertake to pay for all the depredations of Napoleon, the usurper. Our rejoinder that she had already paid for those committed by him against other powers met this position effectively; but the monarchy was continually in need of money, and the claims were left unsettled. Rives, our first minister under Jackson, went out with instructions to press vigorously for settlement. He proceeded so well that in less than a year he got the French ministry to propose to pay a definite sum to cover all losses. Then France advanced a counterclaim for damages alleged under a clause of the Louisiana purchase treaty guaranteeing certain commercial privileges to France. This checked the negotiations until it was finally proposed to offset it by lowering the American duties on certain French wines. Rives now hoped for success, but all came to naught when in July, 1830, the king, Charles X, was driven from his throne and Rives's Treaty, 1831. Louis Philippe took his place. After some delay negotiations were resumed, and July 4, 1831, the persistent and cautious Rives was gratified by signing a treaty by which we were to receive 25,000,000 francs for all our claims, to make the re-

2 E

ductions desired in wine duties, and to pay 1,500,000 francs for claims made by France.   The amount promised was to be handed over in six annual installments, the first to be paid a year after ratification, which, as it turned out, was consummated February 2, 1832.   In this, as in the arrangement with England, we gave up some of our demands, taking what we could get, and removing a long-standing source of ill-feeling between the two powers.

But the matter was not entirely ended; for the French chambers must appropriate the money for actual payment, and as the country's revenues were much embarrassed, the money was not voted. **The Money not Promptly Paid.** The treaty was unpopular in France, spite of the advantage it gave the wine growers; and so it happened that when the first installment was due, no provisions had been made to meet it.   Jackson was himself scrupulously honest in money matters, and considered the course of the French government essentially dishonorable.   He met it in a characteristic manner. He ordered the secretary of the treasury to draw a draft on the French treasury, placed it with the bank of the United States, which sent it to Paris, where it was duly protested.   Then came a sharp conflict with Biddle, already at odds with the administration, who demanded protest charges at the ordinary rate, amounting to nearly $170,000.   The demand from a bank having in hand many millions of the public money was indignantly refused.   Biddle replied by holding back the disputed sum out of the dividends due the government on its stock in the bank.

This controversy diverted attention for only a short time from the issue between the president and France.   Jackson was convinced that nothing but a firm stand would bring the chambers **Stern Measures advocated by Jackson.** to execute the treaty, and in his annual message of 1833 he recommended that congress authorize the seizure of enough French property in our borders to satisfy our claims.   Such a course, if carried out, would mean war. Probably it was only a threat; but the suggestion of it created a storm of indignation in Paris.   The French minister in Washington was recalled, and Livingston, now in Paris, was informed that his passports were at his disposal.   A bill to vote the money was then before the French legislature.   After a long and angry debate it was passed with the proviso that the money should not be paid until **Intercourse Suspended.** Jackson's offending language was explained.   At this Livingston withdrew from his post, leaving the office in the hands of a *chargé d'affaires*, who, when the ministry still further refused to pay, closed his office and withdrew also. This was November 8, 1835, and for a year we had no representative in Paris.

For a while the American public expected war, but time brought reflection.   The point at issue was too trivial to justify hostilities, for it was now only a question of words. Clay, leading as caustic an opposition as that which embarrassed Adams in 1825–1829, carried unanimously through the senate resolutions opposing war. The campaign of 1836 was approaching, and that also tended to moderate the attitude of the administration. **The Affair Adjusted.**

A further step was taken when in the annual message of 1835 the president expressed the hope that France would pay the money and so remove the obstacle to harmony between the two powers. Then England offered her good services to bring the two states together. Her advances were acceptable to both sides, and by the next spring France had declared herself satisfied with the amicable words of the message of 1835 and four of the promised installments were paid. Jackson's course had undoubtedly been abrupt, as was his nature; but it showed Europe that the American government could act energetically, and it thus strengthened our influence in many a court.

The third diplomatic problem arose in connection with Mexico. The region now embraced generally in the states of Texas, New Mexico, Arizona, Utah, Nevada, and California, and a part of Colorado was in 1829 in the hands of the newly created federal republic of Mexico, which ruled its inhabited parts as states and provinces. One of these states was known as Coahuila and Texas, divided into four departments, one of which was Texas. The state had a constitution of its own and exercised its functions under the authority of the federal republic. **Mexico and the Possession of Texas.**

The department of Texas, vast and inviting, lay between the Sabine and Nueces rivers. Under Spanish rule it contained a large number of Indians and about 4000 white men, chiefly in the region of San Antonio. Its fine lands early attracted the adventurous land hunters of the East, and from 1821 to 1827 there was a continuous stream of settlers from the United States. Among them Stephen F. Austin, who led the first colony, was the leading man. In 1832 arrived Samuel Houston, a friend of Jackson, a distinguished soldier in the Creek war, formerly a congressman and governor of Tennessee, who for personal reasons wished to begin life in a new country. These two men played an important rôle in the early history of Anglo-American Texas. **Early History of Texas.**

At first the Mexican authorities encouraged the immigration of men from the East, giving them large grants of land; but the community showed much vigor, and the authorities began to fear a movement for a separate state. It was probably this apprehension that caused them to attach Texas to the distinctly Mexican state of Coahuila, giving it only onesixth of the representation in the state's legislature. But immigration was steady, and the new arrivals numbered 15,000 by 1827 and about 30,000 in 1836. Then came efforts to restrict immigration. In **Mexico fears the Growth of Texas.**

1829 the Mexican president, of his own unauthorized power, issued an order abolishing slavery in the republic. As this institution then existed only among the Anglo-American settlers of Texas, the manifesto was construed as a blow at that community. Austin, however, protested, and was able to secure a second order exempting Texas from the operation of the first order. In 1830 came a Mexican law forbidding further colonization from abroad and prohibiting the subsequent introduction of slaves. The Texans saw in this a deliberate attempt to check their growing power. They were not disposed to abide by its purpose, and colonists and slaves were secretly received in defiance of the weak central authority. From that time the Texans began to dream of revolution with ultimate annexation to the United States.

Meanwhile, the American government made an effort to purchase Texas. Adams authorized our minister to Mexico to open negotiations to that end, but the minister discovered so much sensitiveness on the part of Mexico on the subject that he did not press the matter. The southern republic was in dire straights, one president after another overthrew his predecessor only to be driven out by a more formidable rival, and each had such an insecure hold on power that he dared not risk the displeasure of his country by consenting to a division of the republic's domain. When Jackson became president, he took up the matter, but met the same difficulties. His representative in Mexico, Colonel Anthony Butler, was a shifty adventurer, suspected by the Mexicans, and when he could accomplish nothing by direct diplomacy, he undertook to gain his ends by corrupting some of the men nearest to the Mexican president. His intrigues became known, and the only results were to discredit Butler, who was duly recalled, and to create on the part of the Mexicans a disgust for our diplomacy. It is fair to say that Jackson was not a party to the trickery of his agent.

Futile Attempts to buy Texas.

The story now returns to the Texans, who had come to believe that they could escape the annihilation of their political rights only through a revolution. The outbreak came in 1835, the people rising to a man and driving the Mexican forces beyond the Rio Grande within the space of two and a half months. Then came a convention to form a civil government, while arrangements went on to meet the counterstroke which Mexico was sure to attempt. Never did the American stock fight better than the Texans in the next three months. For a time bravery seemed useless. The Texans were assembled in small bands which fell singly before the army of several thousand with which Santa Anna crossed the Rio Grande to crush the revolution. In the early days of March, 1836, post after post was lost and the revolutionists began to lose heart. But one small band of 183 under W. B Travis gave an evidence of courage and devotion which restored the

The Texan Revolution, 1835-1836.

spirits of the whole community and enabled it to make the united stand which insured final success. They held the old fort of The Alamo, at San Antonio, and refused to retreat, although more than a thousand Mexicans under Santa Anna closed in around them. After a thirteen-day siege all the defenders but six fell at their posts before the place was taken by storm. The remnant of survivors was shot by Santa Anna, spite of the protest of some of his officers. This created great horror among the Texans, and after that their battle cry was "Remember the Alamo!" *The Alamo.*

News that the Texans were struggling for liberty aroused great sympathy in the United States. The Mississippi valley and the Gulf states were most outspoken, but mass meetings and contributions indicated the warm interest of the sea- board region as far north as Boston. Many boatloads of sympathizers sailed from New Orleans for Galveston. In response to protests from Mexico, orders were given to stop all volunteers for Texas, but the intercepted ones declared they were colonists seeking homes in Texas and were allowed to pass freely. Arrived at their destination, they at once joined the ranks of the revolutionists, whose power of resistance thus increased daily. *Sympathy for the Texans.*

After the first disastrous efforts to hold various disconnected positions in the South, the Texan forces were united under General Sam Houston, who, ever falling back, drew Santa Anna far northward. For a time it seemed that all was lost, but Houston only waited his opportunity. April 21 he turned on Santa Anna, who was overconfident and unprepared, and crushed him in the battle of San Jacinto. The Texans charged irresistibly, breaking the enemy's lines, shooting down those who ran, and finally capturing all but fifty of the survivors of the 1600 men who faced them in the beginning of the engagement. Santa Anna himself was taken, and 630 of his followers were slain. Two months later he secured his release by signing treaties in which he and the other Mexican generals in Texas agreed to remove all their troops and to endeavor to secure the independence of the country with the bounds no farther south than the Rio Grande. This agree- ment proved the actual achievement of Texan independence; for although Mexico repudiated it and meant to reinvade the rebellious region, she was so beset by internal struggles that Texas was left undisturbed. *Battle of San Ja- cinto, 1836.*

But the 30,000 inhabitants of the wide area between the Sabine and the Nueces could not support the burden of its defense, and appeals were made to the United States for annexation. Jackson acted cautiously. Texas had made the preserva- tion of slavery one of the grounds of revolution, and if annexed it would be slave territory. The question imme- diately became a sectional one. Calhoun and the South urged that *Shall we Annex Texas?*

this vast region be acquired without delay. John Quincy Adams and Webster both made speeches on the other side. Jackson was bending all his efforts to carry the election of Van Buren and so perpetuate his policy against the bank; and he was unwilling to jeopardize party harmony by introducing the Texan question into the campaign. Then it was urged that we recognize the republic as independent. He disposed of this by sending a special agent to Texas, who reported that the new republic could not sustain itself against its enemies. On this basis Jackson advised congress that recognition should be deferred. But in February, 1837, when it seemed that England was about to grant recognition, he changed his attitude, and resolutions favorable to Texas passed in each house, and the president sent a minister. Annexation, however, must wait until another day.

The Recognition of Texas.

THE END OF JACKSON'S PRESIDENCY

Jackson and his party were now supreme in national politics. A man of little education and not broadly informed in statecraft, he nevertheless was trusted by the people, whose champion he was. He had an average man's view of good government and extraordinary ability to organize and rule a party. The hopes of Clay, Webster, and Calhoun were reduced to nullity by his success. The first and second, each a little suspicious of the other, were holding together the Northern minority, which, dropping the name national republican, now began to be known as the whig party. It embraced avowedly the conservative and property-holding class, and was in plain contrast with the democrats, who declared themselves champions of the people. Many of the older states retained a property qualification for voting and allowed the legislature to select governors and judges. Such practices were approved by the whigs, but the democrats considered them unequal privileges, and demanded a wide popular participation of the people in the government. Rotation in office, strict economy in expenditures, and the least possible federal concentration were also fundamental principles of the democrats. In 1835 the last of the national debt was paid, much to the gratification of Jackson, who, however, warned the country that this ought not to be made the excuse for future extravagance.

Party Divisions.

The National Debt Paid.

Meanwhile, the position of Calhoun was singular. Committed to state rights, and dependent upon South Carolina, he could not find a place in the party of Webster and Clay; nor could he return to the democrats while Jackson's influence predominated. He was a democrat, but he led a small faction at war with Jackson. In 1832 he had hopes of defeating the nomination of Van Buren for vice-president, but failed signally.

Calhoun's Position.

Then he sought to embarrass the administration in its bank and other policies, but he failed in this also. In some minor matters he played a similar rôle with varying results. But his opportunity came with the reviving importance of the slavery issue. By the most vigorous appeals to the South he stimulated sectionalism, made a Southern faction in the democratic party, and laid the train that led to secession. Jackson understood this purpose and foresaw its results long before the country could see them. With characteristic warmth he pronounced Calhoun a traitor, bent on disrupting the democratic party, whose integrity, said Jackson, was the best guaranty against disunion.

While the democrats saw the opposing factions thus arrayed, they had to give strict attention to domestic finances. The twenty-three "pet banks," as they were dubbed, which received the public money after October 1, 1833, were selected with all **The Deposit** possible care, but it was impossible to keep political **Banks.** motives entirely in the background. They were denounced by the whigs as unsafe, and their notes, with which the government paid some of its bills, frequently were less than par. This led to a new act in 1836, imposing stricter conditions for the selection of such banks of deposits, requiring them to furnish security, and to redeem their notes in specie. The payment of the national debt, and the steady increase of the revenues, resulted in a surplus of government funds, and it was so profitable for a bank to have the deposits that pressure was brought on the treasury to include other banks in the list. Thus it happened that in 1836 the number of "pet banks" was 89, with total deposits of nearly $50,000,000.

Along with this development went a wide expansion in the volume of bank notes. Thoughtful people foresaw that in an emergency these notes could not be redeemed in specie, and a demand arose for laws which would force more gold and silver **Attempt to** into circulation. The demand came most loudly from **force Specie** Senator Benton, of Missouri, who for his part in this **into Cir-** movement got the nickname of "Old Bullion." The **culation.** result of the agitation was laws to make foreign gold and silver coins legal tender and a law to change the ratio of gold and silver so as to allow free coinage of the former, which at the old ratio was more valuable than silver. Under the last law $1,500,000 in gold was coined by the mint. Democratic orators provided themselves with green silken mesh purses through which shining yellow coins, popularly called "Benton's mint drops" could be seen, and these were ostentatiously displayed in taverns and on the stump in illustration of the politicians' arguments for what they called the "currency of the constitution." Attempts were made to make bills of less value than five dollars no longer legal tender, in the hope that the vacuum thus created in the currency would force the ingress of specie from abroad. At that time we mined little of either precious metal and were dependent on importations. All these well-meant attempts to establish a hard-money currency accomplished little. Local banks, protected by state law, existed everywhere, and the country was full of their bills. The whigs cast derision on all that was done. They wished to prolong the existing confusion in the hope that it would make necessary the recharter of the bank of the United States, which they asserted was the only way out of the country's financial bewilderment.

Another evil of the day was the accumulation of a government surplus of many millions after the payment of the debt of the nation.

The Problem of Surplus Revenue. It could not be reduced by lowering the tariff, since the compromise tariff of 1833 was to run through ten years, until 1842. No better method of disposing of it was suggested than to deposit it with the states. Jackson in the beginning of his presidency favored the suggestion, but soon changed his mind. He came to believe that the constitution did not authorize such a use of public money. On the other hand, the measure was favored by Clay, who was not embarrassed by similar constitutional views. He thought the principle might be applied to the proceeds of the land sales, since the land belonged to all the states. In 1832 he carried through both houses a bill for such a distribution, but it was given a "pocket veto" by Jackson, who thought a better way would be to sell the lands more cheaply, a plan which pleased the West greatly. In fact, it was a perilous thing to lead the states to look to the federal government as a source of largesses.

But the surplus continued to grow, and in 1835 Clay carried another distribution bill through the senate. So strong was opinion for it that the administration became alarmed and introduced into the house a slightly different bill, which, it was said, would be accepted by Jackson. It was carried through both houses with a rush, and was approved by the president June 23, 1836. It did not give, but loaned, the surplus to the states and provided that all the surplus in the treasury on January 1, 1837, above $5,000,000 should be deposited with the states in four equal quarterly installments according to federal population. The money thus deposited might formally be demanded for repayment at the discretion of congress, but it was understood that no such demand would ever be made. Jackson accepted the bill with great reluctance, and he said plainly it should not be a precedent. He yielded, undoubtedly, because the measure was very popular, and because he feared a veto would imperil the election of Van Buren, whose success he believed of supreme importance. As it turned out, $36,000,000 was on hand to be distributed, and the first and second installments were paid and half of the third; but the panic of 1837 then intervened, and there was no money in the treasury to pay the rest.

The last notable incident of his administration was the specie circular, issued July 11, 1836. The West was carried away with land speculation. Here, too, were a large number of insecure banks, whose notes were being received in pay- **The Specie** ment for lands. It was evident that the bubble must **Circular,** soon burst; for the lands could not go on increasing **1836.** in value, speculators in them would fail, and the banks from which they had borrowed would be embarrassed and cease to pay their notes in specie. The result would be that the government in such a contingency would find its hands full of worthless paper money and the loss would be immense. Jackson, therefore, ordered land offices to take no money but specie. For a time there was a feverish movement of gold and silver to the West, but soon that failed. Then creditors of the Western banks began to demand specie of them. Thus came the panic of 1837. The specie circular did not produce this crisis, as the whigs charged, but it hastened its coming.

While these things happened, the country came to the election of 1836. Jackson was supreme in his party and was able to dominate it, though he did so by the most wanton exercise of his personal will. May 20, 1835, more than a year before **Election of** the election was to come, a convention, half of it office- **1836; The** holders, met in Baltimore and nominated Van Buren **Democrats.** for president and R. M. Johnson, of Kentucky, for vice-president. Outside the convention was much party dissatisfaction with the nomination, but no one dared oppose the will of Jackson. Van Buren, accepting the proffered honor, said he would "tread generally in the footsteps of General Jackson," a sentiment which received much ridicule from his opponents.

The whigs were not strong enough to carry one man through triumphantly, but they hoped to take advantage of the dissatis- faction among their opponents and throw the election **The Whigs.** into the house, where they expected to defeat the demo- cratic candidate. They, therefore, held no convention, united with all the malcontents, and sought to win a total majority for three men. In the Northeast they supported Webster, whom the Massachusetts whigs nominated. In the Northwest they united on General W. H. Harrison, and in the Southwest on Senator White, of Tennessee, nominated by the legislature of his own state. Ohio had her own candidate, Judge John McLean, who was popular with the remnant of the antimasonic party. South Carolina would support none of the candidates; and she was especially opposed to Van Buren, whose intrigue had prostrated her champion, Calhoun.

The result was a surprise to the whigs. Van Buren received 170 elec- toral votes against 124 for all his opponents and was declared elected. Johnson had only 147 against a combined opposition of 147 and was, therefore, not elected.   For the only time in our history the senate was to choose a vice-president, the choice being Johnson by a vote of 33 to 16.   Of the defeated candidates Harrison had 73 votes, White had 26, among them the votes of Tennessee, Webster had the 14 votes of Massachusetts, and the 11 votes of South Carolina were thrown away on Willie P. Mangum, of North Carolina.   As the democrats maintained their control of each branch of congress, Jackson retired from office, assured that the bank would not be rechartered and the great democratic principles for which he had striven would be perpetuated.   He closed his labors with a "Farewell Address," in which he summed up the chief features of his political faith.   He retired to his home at the "Hermitage," near Nashville, saying: "When I review the arduous administration through which I have passed, the formidable opposition, to its very close, of the combined talents, wealth, and power of the whole aristocracy of the United States, aided as it is by the monied monopolies of the whole country with their corrupting influence, with which we had to contend, I am truly thankful to my God for this happy result."

Election Results.

BIBLIOGRAPHICAL NOTE

The general works, biographies, works of leading men, and legislative and executive sources are the same as for the preceding chapter (see page 405).   The special topics treated in this chapter and the leading works on them are as follows:

On Nullification: Houston, *Nullification in South Carolina* (*Harvard Historical Studies,* 1896); Phillips, *Georgia and State Rights* (Am. Hist. Assn. *Reports,* 1901, vol. II); Ames, *State Documents on Federal Relations,* vol. IV (1902); Jervey, *Robert Y. Hayne and His Time* (1909); Stillé, *Life and Services of Joel R. Poinsett* (1888); Powell, *Nullification and Secession* (1897); Bassett, *Life of Andrew Jackson,* vol. II (1911); Sumner, *Life of Andrew Jackson* (ed. of 1897); Calhoun, *Works,* 6 vols. (1853–1855); Jameson, ed., *Correspondence of Calhoun* (Am. Hist. Assn. *Report,* vol. II, 1899).

On Jackson's attack on the bank of the United States: Catterall, *The Second Bank of the United States* (1903); Dewey, *The Second United States Bank* (National Monetary Commission *Report,* 1910); Ibid., *Financial History of the United States* (1903); Sumner, *History of Banking in the United States* (vol. I of *History of Banking in All the Leading Nations,* 1896); White, *Money and Banking* (2d ed., 1902); Bassett, *Life of Andrew Jackson,* vol. II (1911); Sumner, *Andrew Jackson* (revised ed., 1897); Clark and Hall, *Legislative and Documentary History of the Bank of the United States* (1832); Gallatin, *Considerations on the Currency* (1831), and other references in Catterall, *Second Bank,* pages 513–526.

On the tariff controversy see: Taussig, *Tariff History of the United States* (ed. of 1898), opposes protection; Stanwood, *American Tariff Controversies,* 2 vols. (1903), favors protection; Curtiss, *Protection and Prosperity* (1896), favors protection and contains list of tariff measures; Bishop, *History of American Manufactures,* 3 vols. (1867); Michael and Pulsifer, compilers, *Tariff Acts Passed by the Congress of the United States, 1789–1895* (1896).

On foreign affairs see *American State Papers, Foreign* for the important documents; Richardson, *Messages and Papers of the Presidents,* vols. II and III (1902), contains papers on the relations with France; Bassett, *Life of Andrew Jackson,* vol. II (1911), summarizes foreign affairs; Sumner, *Andrew Jackson* (1st ed., 1886), contains summary of relations with Great Britain; and Schuyler, *American Diplomacy* (1886), good for commercial negotiations.

On Texas, its early history and relations with the United States, see Garrison, *Texas, a Contest of Civilizations* (1903), the best short history; Ibid., ed., *Texan Diplomatic Correspondence*, 2 vols. (Am. Hist. Assn. *Reports*, 1907 and 1908); Rather, *The Annexation of Texas* (Texas Hist. Assn. *Quarterly*, 1910); and Reeves, *Diplomacy under Tyler and Polk* (1907).

For Independent Reading

Mrs. Trollope, *Domestic Manners of the Americans* (1832); Dickens, *American Notes* (many editions); Fanny Kemble [Butler], *Journal*, 2 vols. (1832–1833); and Dodd, *Statesmen of the Old South* (1911), treats of Jefferson, Calhoun, and Jefferson Davis.

CHAPTER XXI

EARLY PERIOD OF THE SLAVERY CONTROVERSY, 1831–1850

THE ANTISLAVERY AGITATION

Two phases of antislavery agitation occurred in the United States during the nineteenth century, one pacific and intended to persuade the South that slavery should be given up, the other seeking to induce the North to use her influence in congress to wipe out what was considered a blot on American civilization. Of the first movement Benjamin Lundy, a New Jersey Quaker, was the leading spirit. He was persistent and patient, and wished to secure the coöperation of slaveholders, who generally feared that antislavery agitation would suggest insurrection to the minds of the slaves. He traveled extensively in the South, organized emancipation societies, and published a paper, *The Genius of Universal Emancipation*, as a means of promoting his ideas. He met no opposition from Southerners, but succeeded only in the sections in which there were few slaveholders, and chiefly with his fellow Quakers. His period of activity extended from about 1815 to 1831.

The Two Movements.

Benjamin Lundy.

In 1816, while his movement was still in its hopeful stage, the American Colonization Society was founded. Its first president was Bushrod Washington, a justice of the supreme court, and Clay and many other prominent men gave it support. The object was to promote emancipation by sending the freedmen to Africa; for it was believed that slaveholders would emancipate more readily if the emancipated ones were returned to their original homes. To aid its operations the government in 1822 established the colony of Liberia, on the west coast of Africa, and branch colonization societies north and south collected money to sustain it. By 1830 the society had sent 1162 negroes to Liberia, most of whom fell victims to the pestilential fevers of the place.

American Colonization Society.

At that time it was evident that colonization, like emancipation by persuasion of the masters, was a failure. The truth is that the expansion of cotton farming and the consequent rise of the prices of slaves were increasing the hold of slavery in the South. A new generation of Southerners had grown up since 1800. They had not the zeal for human rights so prevalent in revolutionary days and they were eager to develop their immense regions of fertile lands. To such men the

New Attitude of the South.

428

negro, who accepted bondage easily, seemed happier in slavery than out of it; and so it came about that most conscientious men in the South, while recognizing the harshness of slavery, eventually came to consider it fixed in Southern life. The efforts of Northern men to remove it seemed to them mischievous interference with Southern affairs, a course likely to lead to insurrection and massacre.

The second movement originated in 1831 when William Lloyd Garrison began to publish the *Liberator* in Boston. He was young, poor, and friendless, but a passionate hatred of slavery filled his heart. He had been imprisoned in Baltimore for an article in Lundy's paper, and the remembrance of it whetted his purpose. "I shall contend for the immediate enfranchisement of our slave population," he said; "I will be as harsh as truth and as uncompromising as justice on this subject — I do not wish to think, or speak, or write with moderation — I am in earnest — I will not equivocate — I will not retreat a single inch, and *I will be heard!*" Drawing to himself the more earnest opponents of slavery in New England he was soon a power in the land. Local societies were founded, money was raised by contributions, fairs, and other means, and then he proceeded to unite the local societies into a common organization. In 1832 was formed the New England Antislavery Society, and in 1833 the American Antislavery Society. The object was to oppose slavery in every possible manner. In 1840 there were 2000 local organizations, with a total membership of nearly 200,000. Soon after its origin this phase of the antislavery movement began to be called "abolitionism." *William Lloyd Garrison.*

While Boston remained the center of abolitionism in the East, Oberlin, Ohio, became the center in the West. This village was founded around a coeducational school in 1833. In 1835 it received an accession of three professors and thirty students from Lane Theological Seminary, Cincinnati, all abolitionists who had left Lane Seminary because it frowned on their opinions. Oberlin college was incorporated, and negro students were admitted to its courses. The village became an important point for Western abolitionists. A leading Ohio abolitionist was James G. Birney, who had left Kentucky because he was opposed for teaching the doctrine of freedom. *Oberlin and the Western Abolitionists.*

About this time appeared the "underground railway," conducted by abolitionists to help slaves to escape from the South. "Stations" were formed at regular distances at the homes of trusted persons, called "agents," while other persons, known as "conductors," went South and escorted fugitives secretly from "station" to "station" until safety was reached at last in a free state or in Canada. The persons connected with the "underground railway" were men of great probity in ordinary matters, but they thought it no crime to snatch a slave from bond- *The "Underground Railway."*

age. It is estimated that 2000 slaves a year thus escaped from their masters from 1830 to 1860. By such means as these the abolitionists attracted a great deal of attention, exasperated the Southerners to the point of fury, and called the attention of Northern people to the harshness of slavery. Their efforts at first were denounced by most people in the North, and sometimes their meetings were violently broken up, but opinion there gradually changed, so that the Northerners, by 1850, would do nothing to aid masters in recovering runaway slaves.

Let us look at the other side of the picture. In 1831 the South was probably already more proslavery than in 1800. It received the Garrisonian movement with violent scorn. Many **Effect in the** bitter things were said about those who would recklessly **South.** incite the slaves to murder their masters. The "black terror" was ever the nightmare of the community. In 1831 Nat Turner, a black slave in Southampton county, Virginia, began an insurrection, killing sixty whites before he was captured and hanged. It was believed he had read the literature of the abolitionists. The incident sent a shock of horror throughout the South. Out of the shock came the motions in the Virginia legislature to abolish slavery, and a great debate followed in the succeeding winter. But no one could suggest a satisfactory way of disposing of the freedmen, and all the discussion came to naught. Virginia was not willing to have the negro population freed and left within the state. The upshot was to convince the South that the blacks were a fixed part **The Revised** of its population and that if they remained, they could **Black Code.** be best controlled as slaves. From that time the negro's lot became harder. Laws were passed to forbid his instruction in reading and writing, his free use of the roads, his preaching to his own people, his right to assemble in meetings of any kind where no white man was present, and whatever else might enable him to combine for any action which might lead to freedom. This new "black code" now became common to all the Southern states, and by 1860 the negro was completely cowed. As abolition gained in the North, proslavery gained in the South. In 1800 Southern statesmen and preachers generally considered slavery an evil, though they knew not how to remedy it: in 1860 Southerners of both classes were found who argued that slavery was a blessing to the negro, a benefit to the South, and a beneficent institution whereby peace and happiness was established for society.

This growing division between the sections soon found expression in congress. Southerners were alarmed when abolition **Antislavery** literature began to be sent South, some of it to ne- **and the** groes, and in 1835 a great group of indignant citizens **Mails.** of Charleston, South Carolina, seized and burned a mass of such papers before they were delivered. Appeals were sent to the postmaster-general to refuse the use of the mails for such purposes. He did not think such action legal, and a compromise was reached by which abolition papers were to be accepted by postmasters when offered for mailing, but need not be delivered at the offices to which they were directed. Then Calhoun offered a bill in the senate to forbid sending antislavery literature through the mails to places in which it might not lawfully circulate; but the proposition received an adverse vote. The incident attracted much attention, and that helped the abolitionists in the North.

Much more excitement was aroused a few months later by the attitude of the house of representatives toward antislavery petitions. Many such appeals had come to the house in recent years, and they were beginning to irritate Southern members. Yet the number of petitions did not diminish; **Antislavery Petitions.** for the abolitionists got them signed more with the purpose of giving their efforts a definite form than with the expectation of success in the object asked for. Finally on May 26, 1836, the house resolved that such memorials in the future be tabled without reading or other action on them. John Quincy Adams, now a member of the house, protested against the resolution as unconstitutional, and a violation of the rights of his constituents. The abolitionists could now say the right of petition, the ancient bulwark of liberty, was denied, and more memorials than ever were sent to Washington. Adams took upon himself the task of presenting them. Whenever the regular hour for petitions arrived, he could be seen at his desk in the house, a huge pile of papers before him. As the order of the day was announced, he would rise with words like these: "I hold in my hands a request from citizens of the town of —— praying the abolition of slavery in ——." At this point the hammer of the speaker would fall, and Adams would be declared out of order. Not abashed, he would take another paper from the pile, begin with the same words, only to be cut off in the same manner, proceeding thus until the pile was exhausted. His action made him very unpopular with Southern members, but he became the honored champion of the abolitionists. At last the friends of slavery came to see that the "gag rule" in regard to petitions but strengthened the abolitionists in their **John Quincy Adams.** appeals to the North, and in December, 1844, the offending rule was repealed. In resenting an irritating practice of the abolitionists the Southern members had put themselves in the wrong and given their adversaries a point to support the general argument that slavery tinged with cruelty and despotism whatever it touched.

Van Buren's Presidency

Van Buren became president through the grace of Andrew Jackson. He had all the virtues of mediocrity without the capacity of leadership. He was honest, cool-headed, courteous to his contem-

Character of Van Buren. poraries, and loyal to his cause. He favored economy in expenditures, and although the spoils system throve during his administration, he sought to secure efficient persons for the offices within his gift. He was an intimate friend of the New York literary men of his day, and appointed Paulding, the novelist, secretary of the navy. His weakness was that he had not the capacity of command, and his party, no longer restrained by the strong will of Jackson, fell into confusion and lost the confidence of the country.

The first incident in his administration was the panic of 1837, symptoms of which began to appear before he was inaugurated. The

Panic of 1837; its Cause. cause was overspeculation, chiefly in the newer parts of the country. The past six years had been a period of great confidence everywhere. Railroads were being built, immigrants were buying land at rapid advances, banks were lending money far in excess of their means, cotton rose to sixteen cents a pound in 1835 and fell to ten cents in 1836, "wildcat banks" were incorporated whose chief activity was to issue money to the land speculators, and the whole industrial community lived on the expectation that the morrow would carry the wave of speculation higher than it was to-day. Only a slight shock was needed to hurl the whole structure to the ground.

Two things operating jointly served to furnish this check. The specie circular of 1836 (see page 425) forced land buyers to pay in

The Specie Circular. specie, they asked the Western banks for gold and silver in redemption of notes, and the institutions which had most overissued began to suspend specie payment. The distribution of the surplus (see page 424), beginning in January, 1837, drew money from the deposit banks to transfer it to other

The Distribution of the Surplus. places. This necessitated the calling in of loans, which implied the suspension of industrial development, and the reaction reached the remotest point of the country's business life. Then demoralization quickly arrived. European holders sent back bonds and demanded cash, owners of specie locked it in vaults, importations of goods fell off, and the public revenues ceasing, the government expenses used up the treasury's surplus so that the third installment of the deposits was suspended when only half of it had been distributed.

So acute was the situation that congress was called in extra session in October. Though the government was out of debt, it had no money for its expenses, and since the law required public dues to be paid in specie or in notes of specie-paying banks, there was not enough currency in the treasury to enable it to carry on its business. The first thing, therefore, was to issue temporarily $10,000,000 in treasury notes. Van Buren was urged to repeal the specie circular, but refused steadfastly. The whigs declared that all the trouble came from the destruction of the bank of the United States and hoped to carry a bill for recharter, but congress and president remained firm, and this demand failed. **An Extra Session of Congress.**

Then Van Buren brought forward a plan to have the government take care of the deposits, known later as the sub-treasury bill. Let the government, he said, keep its own money, leaving it with the treasurer, the mints, postmasters, collectors, and other receivers until it was ordered paid out. At once arose a cry that these keepers were not responsible, and that the scheme, if adopted, would dangerously enlarge the patronage. The whigs hoped the distress would make a new bank seem necessary, and voted steadily against the sub-treasury. The democrats were divided; one part, strong in the Eastern cities, opposing the suggestion as unsafe, and the other supporting it. The second faction called itself the antimonopolists, but it was generally known as the "Locofocos," a nickname given by its enemies in New York. In the popular parlance of the day the sub-treasury bill was "the divorce bill," because it sought to "divorce the government from all banks." It failed in the extra session, came up in a simpler form in 1838, but was again lost. It was taken up again and successfully passed and signed July 4, 1840. When finally passed, it created sub-treasuries to keep and pay out the public money at Boston, New York, Philadelphia, St. Louis, and New Orleans, which, with the treasury at Washington left the funds in six important centers of business. It also provided that after the end of June, 1843, only specie should be received for public dues. The whigs fought the bill to the last, for its adoption meant the relinquishment of their hope for a bank; they repealed it in 1841, in the first days of their triumph, but the democrats restored it in 1846, omitting the specie feature. **Sub-treasury Suggested.** **Adopted in 1840.**

Before this law was passed, the presidential campaign of 1840 was being conducted. Van Buren's nomination by his party was easily secured in a convention at Baltimore, May 4, 1840. Several states had named candidates for the vice-presidency, and the convention thought it best to refrain from deciding between them. It was probably expected that the choice would at last fall to the senate. A platform strong in Jacksonian principles was adopted as the ground on which the country should continue to manifest its confidence in the existing administration. **Election of 1840.**

2 F

The whigs approached the election year in high spirits. The long period of financial stringency, the inability of the democrats to unite on a positive remedy, and the many opponents of Van Buren in his party indicated that the democrats would have strong opposition. Clay saw the situation and had high hopes. It seemed that his opportunity was at last at hand. The convention was called at Harrisburg, December 4, 1839. As the time approached, a strong anti-Clay opposition appeared within the party. He was a mason, he had spoken against the abolitionists, and he was already twice defeated for the presidency. These facts, it was urged, made him an unavailable candidate, and Harrison, leading whig candidate in 1836, was pointed out as a stronger man. The opponents of Clay were well led by Thurlow Weed, party manager in the important state of New York. When the convention met, Clay had 102 votes on the first ballot, mostly from the slaveholding states, Harrison had 91, and General Winfield Scott had 57. Scott was a stalking-horse for Clay's enemies, who now began to shift their support to Harrison, with the result that the latter was finally named. Clay, deeply disappointed, burst into a rage when he learned the news. Walking rapidly to and fro, in a group of his friends, he exclaimed, "If there were two Henry Clays, one of them would make the other president!" John Tyler, of Virginia, deeply attached to the defeated leader, was nominated for vice-president. No platform was adopted, for in the groups of men supporting the action of the convention were so many of conflicting views that it was perilous to attempt to devise a body of principles on which they should appeal to the people. The whigs were content to rest their fate on the cry of "Down with Van Buren!"

No one doubted how New England and the bank men outside of it would vote, but it was not certain what the rest of the country would do. Fortunately for the whigs the campaign had "Tippe-canoe and Tyler Too." hardly opened when a lucky accident showed how they could be reached. A disappointed friend of Clay was heard to say that Harrison, whose talents were very limited, if given a pension and a barrel of hard cider would retire to his log cabin and think no more of the presidency. The democrats seized on the remark and dubbed Harrison the "log-cabin candidate." But the blow reacted. The whigs made it a symbol of honor, saying it showed that their candidate was a man of the people, disdained by the aristocrats, whose heads were turned by their long lease of power. At every political meeting of the whigs a log cabin, a jug of cider, and a coon were displayed as tokens of their candidate's love of the people. A popular song lauding him as the "hero of Tippecanoe" also did much to create enthusiasm for his cause. This wave of popular excitement accomplished the object for which it was raised, and in the final test Harrison and Tyler, "Tippecanoe and Tyler too," were chosen by 234 to 60 electoral votes. Van Buren lost his own state and carried only Virginia, South Carolina, Missouri, Alabama, Arkansas, Illinois, and New Hampshire.

This overwhelming victory resulted fatally for the victor. Duly inaugurated in March, 1841, he was at once overwhelmed by a horde of hungry whig office seekers, who dogged his steps, exhausted his strength, and so disturbed his peace of mind that he yielded to an attack of pneumonia one month after he took the oath of office. One of his last acts was to call congress in extra session for May 31, 1841. When it met, Tyler was president.

Death of Harrison.

THE ADMINISTRATION OF TYLER

Tyler now found himself at the head of a party with which he had little political sympathy. He believed in state rights, opposed a bank and a high tariff, and had only left the democratic fold because he resented the towering methods of Jackson. His nomination had been made without the slightest expectation that he would ever be in a position to veto a bill which the whigs had carried through congress.

Tyler's Position.

On the other hand, Clay, the real head of the party, was in no mood to resign his leadership. Harrison, had he lived, would have had a sharp struggle with this imperious man, who was not disposed to bow before so insignificant a figure as Tyler. When, therefore, the extra session began, Clay, a member of the senate, took charge of the situation like a military commander. He offered a resolution specifying what work the extra session should perform, the chief features being: the repeal of the sub-treasury act, the incorporation of a bank, the enactment of a higher tariff law, and the distribution of the proceeds of land sales. Tyler was very cautious, but he was also stubborn, and Clay's dashing assumption of power aroused him. He accepted a bill to abolish the sub-treasury, but sent back with a veto a bill to incorporate a great bank in the District of Columbia with branches in the states. The whigs had a safe majority in each house, but they could not pass a bill over a veto. They were greatly disappointed; for hearing rumors of Tyler's objections they thought they had eliminated from their bill all the features to which he was opposed. Smothering their resentment outwardly, they conferred with the president to know what kind of a bank bill he would approve. What he said became later a matter of dispute, but they hastily prepared a charter for a "Fiscal Corporation," passed it without difficulty, and sent it to the president. Tyler had expressed his opposition to the word "bank," and so the word was not used. The bill was said to have been shown to the president and to have had his approval. Great was the anger of its friends, therefore, when it came back in six days with a veto. Many had expected such action,

Clay's Attitude.

Tyler and the Bank Question.

spite of his previous approval; for the second bill differed from the first in little but the names it gave to bank and branches. Under it the great institution would have been able to do most of the things which Jackson had found so distasteful. Both vetoes showed that Tyler was fundamentally opposed to a bank on constitutional grounds. He had evidently tried hard to reconcile his desire for party harmony with his long-proclaimed principles, but the badly veiled discourtesy of Clay and other leading whigs in setting him aside as leader had wounded his pride and made him feel disposed to show them that he was still president. While the second veto was being prepared, congress passed a bill to distribute among the states the proceeds of land sales. Tyler accepted the bill, but it was repealed in the following year.

The "Fiscal Corporation" was vetoed on September 9, 1841. Two days later all the cabinet but Webster, secretary of state, resigned as a token of their disapproval. They published letters denouncing what they declared Tyler's false conduct, and Clay, wishing to detach as many whigs as possible from the administration, secured a caucus of the leading members of the party which solemnly declared that "all political connection between them and John Tyler was at an end." Webster also gave reasons for his conduct, saying that he did not think it wise to leave the cabinet without giving the president time to select another secretary. Negotiations pending for the determination of the Northeast boundary made it desirable that he should remain in office. He was not on good terms with Clay, and resented the manner in which that leader sought to bend the whigs to his will. Tyler saw in this a good omen. He hoped to build up a party in which the dashing Kentuckian should not be supreme, and immediately filled the cabinet with men who, like himself, had once been Jacksonians, but who had left the democratic fold because they did not like the Jacksonian rule. As a party move, the step was a failure. Even Webster soon came to realize that Tyler was not the man to lead the whigs, and in May, 1843, when the administration was leaning strongly toward the annexation of Texas, he also withdrew from the cabinet.

Tyler repudiated by the Whigs.

The only other distinctly whig measure passed through congress during Tyler's presidency was the tariff of 1842. The term through which the compromise of 1833 was to run was to expire June 30, 1842. Before that date the treasury had a deficit. There was much alarm for the future, and some attempts were made to devise a plan for relief; but the president stood by the compromise of 1833, and it was allowed to run its course. Finally, on August 30, 1842, a bill was passed fixing the duties on most articles at the rates in force in 1832, and the president gave it his approval. It involved the repeal of the distribution act of the previous year, and on that ground received enough democratic votes to pass the senate.

The Tariff of 1842.

THE MAINE BOUNDARY AND THE WEBSTER-ASHBURTON TREATY

When Webster decided to remain in the cabinet in 1841 he had begun important negotiations with England. The treaty of 1783 provided that the Northeast boundary should begin at the mouth of the St. Croix river, follow its course to the source, thence due north to the highlands separating the tributaries of the St. Lawrence from the streams that flowed into the Atlantic, along the said highlands to the source of the Connecticut, thence with that river to the parallel 45° north, and thence due west to the St. Lawrence. The commissioners knew little about the real geography of the Northeast. There were several rivers which the early inhabitants had called the St. Croix, and the British naturally claimed that the westernmost should be taken for the true starting point, while the Americans held for the easternmost. From the source of the stream claimed by the British a northward line reached the eastern end of some hills running westward, which it was claimed were the highlands which ought to be accepted as the boundary. The Americans were sure that the real St. Croix was either the river now known as the St. Johns or a smaller stream called by the Indians the Magaguadavi, about twenty-five miles east of the present St. Croix. A line due north from the source of that stream did not touch the hills just mentioned, but passed on through level country, across the St. Johns, until it reached high ground which paralleled the St. Lawrence, about 140 miles northward, and following these hills southwestwardly this boundary gave to the United States about 12,000 square miles of territory more than that conceded by the British line. This disputed region was drained in part by the Aroostook river, which flows into the St. Johns, and whose valley by 1840 was being settled by inhabitants of Maine. Various attempts to determine the rights of each nation in the matter had been made, but none succeeded. Maine meanwhile exercised jurisdiction over the Aroostook lands, frequently driving out persons cutting timber under Canadian authority. In 1838 the intruders were more numerous than ever, and Governor Fairfield, of Maine, sent 150 men to oust them. The intruders fell back to New Brunswick, gathered reënforcements, and only the exercise of moderation on the part of the governor of New Brunswick prevented bloodshed. Throughout Maine was great indignation, and the president was called on for help. Van Buren advised negotiations, but congress with practical unanimity gave him the authority to call out 50,000 men to defend the rights of the country, if he thought force necessary. Several irritating incidents had recently occurred on the Canadian frontier, and the country was in no friendly mood toward Great Britain. At this time the English and American governments

Nature of the Dispute.

The " Aroostook War."

agreed to desist from further operation on the Aroostook, and Maine, already prepared to enforce her claim by force, was induced to withhold her hand until diplomacy had its opportunity. This period of disturbance was popularly called the "Aroostook war."

Such was the situation when Webster became secretary of state in 1841. He immediately opened negotiations with England, which

The Treaty Concluded. had no other wish than to dispose of the Aroostook incident without injury to her rights. Lord Ashburton, a reasonable and courteous diplomatist, was sent to Washington to have special charge of the British side of the case, and on August 9, 1842, the Webster-Ashburton treaty was signed, disposing of the controversy through a compromise satisfactory to all moderate persons. It adopted a line which gave 7015 square miles of the disputed area, including the Aroostook valley, to the United States. The treaty also pledged the two contracting powers to keep a joint squadron in African waters to suppress the slave trade. Maine and Massachusetts received from the United States money payments for land claims they had in the region awarded to England. A British map not accessible to Webster in 1842 supports the American claim and makes it evident that England gained by the treaty 5000 square miles more than the treaty of 1783 allowed her.

The Annexation of Texas and the Occupation of Oregon

During Van Buren's administration the annexation of Texas was held in abeyance. The South desired it, but the North was sure to

The Situation in Texas. object, and the question was too dangerous to party harmony to be taken up as long as it could be avoided. Texas herself understood the situation, and after 1838 ceased to offer herself where there was no prospect that she would be accepted. Meanwhile, she had many difficulties. Immigration was not very rapid, the struggle for independence over, many of her adventurers returned to the United States, and the expense of keeping an army and navy to repel Mexico but added to her heavy debt. She was in need of foreign assistance, and some of her people were showing a willingness to accept it from any available source.

In 1843 Washington learned that England and France had induced Mexico to make a truce with Texas with a view to a permanent treaty.

The Alleged English Scheme. Our government was surprised that these European nations were taking such active interest in Texan affairs. Then came reports that England was to advance money to free the slaves in Texas, the republic guaranteeing the interest on the loan. Why was Great Britain, it was asked, concerning herself in this quarter? The answer was in order that she might have the trade of Texas and secure a vast source for the supply of cotton she needed for her factories.   Moreover, it was evident that if she got as strong a hold over the country as this plan involved, nothing but a war would shake her off.   The report, although denied by the British government, was credited in the South and by many people in the North, and the impression grew that if we did not wish to see this valuable region slip out of our grasp, we must act at once. The North, however, laughed at the rumors and declared they were manufactured to influence the action of congress.   Later investigations have made it clear that they were well founded, although England's activity had not gone as far by 1843 as the Southerners believed.

Tyler and Upshur, his secretary of state, believed the reports and suggested to the Texans that it would be well to renew offers of annexation.   Samuel Houston, the Texan president, assumed indifference, saying that if negotiations were now reopened *Tyler suggests Annexation.* the newly established friendship of Texas and England would be weakened.   This whetted the desire of Tyler, and he consulted with his friends and satisfied himself that a treaty of annexation could be carried through the senate.   He took a warmer tone with Houston, who at last offered to treat for annexation if the United States would send an army to the frontier to aid the republic in case Mexico attacked while negotiations progressed.   The condition was accepted, but later modified, so that we did not promise to aid the republic until a treaty was accepted.   At this juncture Upshur was killed by the explosion of a cannon on the ship-of-war *Princeton*, and when the negotiations actually began, Calhoun was secretary of state.   They ended in a treaty, signed April 12, 1844, in which Texas was to become an American territory and surrender its public lands, its indebtedness of $10,000,000 being assumed by the United States.

All this was done as quietly as possible, but secrecy could not be maintained when the document came to the senate.   Its publication was not a surprise to the country, but it met none the less a vigorous protest in the North.   The South, it was said, *Treaty Rejected.* had assumed the aggressive and was seeking to acquire an immense region for the extension of the sphere of slavery.   On the other hand, the Southerners replied that they only wished to enlarge the national domain and that the North selfishly sacrificed the glory of the country in order to gratify an unreasonable feeling against the South.   As early as this the two sections had come to the inevitable conflict between slavery and freedom.   The problem now became a very practical one for the politicians.   The presidential campaign was beginning, neither party was willing to assume the responsibility of annexation, and so the treaty, which at first seemed safe, was defeated in the senate.   Calhoun and Tyler had the matter much at heart, and were sorely disappointed at the miscarriage of their plans.

While Texas thus engaged the attention of the South and North, Oregon had become an important matter to the people of the West.

For many years after the explorations of Lewis and Clark little was done to occupy that region. But by 1840 many settlers following the Missouri river had crossed the Rocky mountains to the **The Oregon Question.** fertile valley of the Columbia, where England also had claims to territory. The controversy to which these conflicting claims gave rise was an intricate one. The British claim went back to 1778, when Captain Cook sailed along the **Claims of England, Spain, and Russia.** Pacific coast as far as about 54° north latitude; Spain also had claims in the same region, but relinquished them in the Florida purchase treaty of 1819, by which she gave up to the United States all right she may have had to the coast north of 42° north latitude. Russia, also, had once held that her Alaskan possessions extended south as far as Oregon, but in 1824 Secretary Adams induced her to agree that her authority should not extend south of 54° 40'. Thus in 1824 the region between 42° and 54° 40' was free of Spanish and Russian claims, but there was still the dispute with England. This we tried several times to arrange, but always without success. In 1818 it was decided to leave the country, now definitely known as "Oregon," to the joint use of both powers for ten years; and at the end of that period joint occupancy was renewed indefinitely, either party to terminate it by **Joint Oc-cupancy of Oregon.** giving a year's notice. The Hudson Bay Company, with strong trading interests at Vancouver, was the center of the British influence, and the Americans, missionaries and traders with a few farmers, were settled chiefly on the Columbia. In 1841 they numbered 400. In 1818 England and the United States had agreed that the parallel 49° north should be the common boundary as far as the Rockies, and the United States were now willing to extend it directly to the Pacific, but to this proposition England objected. She wished to have the Columbia for the southern boundary of her Pacific coast possessions. On this basis nothing could be determined, and so the matter was left to drift along until the settlement of Oregon should make it necessary to come to a more definite understanding.

The transference of American life to Texas, creating in Jackson's administration a lively interest in southwestern expansion, could not but awaken a similar feeling in regard to the Far North-**Oregon a Political Issue, 1844.** west. About 1838, therefore, Linn, senator from Missouri, a state whose position gave her great interest in Northwestern expansion, opened a campaign for the erection of forts along the Oregon trail as far as the mouth of the Columbia. Of course, this would violate the existing agreement with England and might lead to war. Another objection was that Oregon was so far away that when settled it would become a colony, a thing for which the constitution made no provision. Linn's efforts met strong opposition in the East and for a while in the South. But in 1843 the

Texan question came up, and Southerners concluded that it could be united with the Oregon question, since both related to expansion. This gave the Northwest more hope. The feeling in that quarter was now intense. Ignoring our former offer to accept the 49th parallel, the West demanded all of Oregon, and the slogan, "Fifty-Four Forty or Fight" was originated to express its position. It was accepted by the democrats, who in the platform of 1844 demanded the "reoccupation" of Oregon and the "reannexation" of Texas.

Meanwhile, the settlers in Oregon were rapidly increasing through immigration, for agitation stimulated interest in the country. So much did the people suffer from lack of a legal government that in 1843 they formed an irregular government of their own to continue until congress made further provisions for them. In May, 1844, a caravan of 1000 persons, with 1967 oxen, horses, and cattle, started from the Kansas river on the journey across the mountains. They were mostly from Missouri. These events of necessity aroused the diplomats and led to a renewal of negotiations. Great Britain opened the question, but offered nothing better than the old terms, which were promptly rejected. Then she suggested arbitration, but this was also refused. At this point the negotiation was suspended, probably to await the result of the election, then near at hand.

Immigration into Oregon.

Renewed Negotiations.

THE ELECTION OF 1844

Early in 1844 Van Buren and Clay were generally considered the inevitable candidates of their respective parties in the coming campaign. The former had much reason to feel satisfied with the outlook, for the congressional elections of 1842 gave the democrats a majority of 70 in the house, and the discouragement of the whigs through the quarrel with Tyler had added greatly to their embarrassment. Across this promising sky fell the cloud of antislavery. The year was hardly begun before each candidate was forced to reply to questions as to his position on the annexation of Texas. The democratic leader replied in a letter which showed that he was at last in the same position that his ancient enemy, Calhoun, was in when the nullifiers forced his hand in 1828. He must oppose annexation and lose the support of the South, or favor it and lose the support of his own section. He chose the former course, hoping, no doubt, that he could so soften the blow as to retain the good will of the South. He believed annexation constitutional, he said, but inexpedient because it would involve a war with Mexico, violate our neutrality obligations, and hold us up to the world as willing to extend our power through a war of conquest; but if Mexico

Van Buren and Texas, 1844.

carried herself toward Texas so as to threaten our interest, the people of the United States could be relied on to unite against her, and in that case he would, if president, submit the matter to the wisdom of congress.

Calhoun must have remembered the days of his own humiliation when he saw this letter. He had spent the past thirteen years in arousing the South on slavery, and the result was now apparent. From every slaveholding state came protests against the man who could temporize in such a situation. Van Buren, said the Southern democrats, could not be trusted; he was intimidated by the Northern antislavery men, and he must not be nominated. From that time his selection, as even his best Southern friends admitted, was impossible. Andrew Jackson, old but keenly watching the political field, could only exclaim: "I would to God I had been at Mr. V. B.'s elbow when he closed his letter, I would have brought to his view *the proper conclusion*. We are all in sackcloth and ashes!"

Van Buren's Failure.

If Clay thought he would profit by his rival's predicament, he was mistaken. He also had written a letter, known as his "Raleigh Letter," from the place in which it was written; and in it he took almost exactly the same ground that Van Buren took. It did not defeat his nomination, for it pleased the North, where his greatest strength lay; but it caused dismay in the South, and so many requests that he soften his expressions came from the whigs there that later in the summer he wrote other letters saying that he had no personal objection to annexation "without dishonor, without war, with the common consent of the union, on just and fair terms." We shall see how this apparent juggling of the question worked his ultimate undoing.

Clay and Texas.

The two leading parties held their conventions in Baltimore in May, 1844. The whigs made their choice harmoniously, naming Clay without a dissenting voice, and Frelinghuysen, for vice-president, on the fourth ballot. The democrats were in sad confusion. A majority of the convention was instructed for Van Buren, but some of the pledged delegates were opposed to him, and the two-thirds rule was used to prevent his nomination. For a time it seemed that the party would be seriously divided. Most of the Northern delegates stood by Van Buren, while the Southerners were divided, some going for Cass, of Michigan, who had strong Western support. As the ballots were taken, Van Buren declined and Cass gained strength, until on the seventh he seemed in a fair way to succeed. He was unpopular with the Old North, and an adjournment was carried until next day in order to stop the trend toward him. During the night much was done to find some man to beat him. James K. Polk, of Tennessee, urged by his friends as a man vouched for by Jackson, was now brought forward. On the first

The Candidates Selected.

ballot taken next morning he had 44 votes, and on the second Van Buren was withdrawn and Polk nominated by a union of North and South which swept away in the enthusiasm with which it was received even the original Cass support.   The nomination for vice-presidency was offered to Wright, of New York, Van Buren's ablest lieutenant, but he declined peremptorily, and it was then given to George M. Dallas, of Pennsylvania.   The platform declared for Texas and Oregon and reaffirmed the party's opposition to a bank and to the distribution of the funds derived from lands.   Polk was not a brilliant man, but he was a steady and industrious politician, and his party put away its dissensions and entered the canvass hopefully.

Two other conventions were held.   One nominated Tyler for president with no other platform than his Texas record.   The other was held by the Liberty party, organized 1840, when it cast 7100 votes for James G. Birney.   He was now renominated, with Morris, of Ohio, the candidate for vice-president. *Tyler, Birney.*

The campaign was full of bitterness and excitement.   Clay traveled widely, making speeches to immense audiences.   The Texas men of the South began to declare for annexation or a dissolution of the union with such fervor that whigs and democrats became alarmed, and hastened to say that no one ought to think of disunion.   In Pennsylvania Polk was openly accused of being a free trader.   In a letter to Kane, of that state, he said he was for a judicious tariff yielding enough revenue for the expenses of government economically administered.   It was a clever statement, pleasing the South, which was alarmed at the turn toward protection manifested in the tariff of 1842.   It also gave the democrats in protectionist Pennsylvania an opportunity to proclaim him a supporter of the tariff of 1842, which was enacted to get money to defray the expenses of government.   They raised the cry, "Polk, Dallas, and the tariff of 1842!" and thereby held the state in its old political faith.   Still more important was the attitude of the antislavery whigs, strong in New York.   Their first inclination was for Clay, but his quibbling over annexation was so evident that several thousand of them voted for Birney, thus reducing Clay's vote until it was below Polk's by 5104.   If he had received New York's 36 electoral votes, he would have been elected.   As it was, he got 105 votes, while Polk got 170.   Polk lost North Carolina, the state of his birth, and Tennessee, the state of his residence.   He carried all the Gulf states, where annexation was strongest, and all of the Northwest, where Oregon was an important issue, while Clay carried all New England, where annexation was opposed, and the Middle and the upper Southern states were divided. *A Suggestion of Disunion.* *The Tariff in Pennsylvania.* *The New York Vote.* *Polk Elected.*

Polk's victory indicated that Texas would be annexed, and Tyler used the last weeks of his administration in securing the prize. He was **Annexation Authorized.** now completely identified with the democrats, having proved his friendship in the summer before the election by withdrawing from the campaign lest the South be divided. When congress met in December he again brought up the Texan question, recommending immediate annexation by a joint resolution. This method, requiring only a majority vote in each house, was preferred to annexation by treaty, which required a two-thirds majority in the senate. The Texas men took up Tyler's suggestion with alacrity. The house passed it by a vote of 120 to 98, and the senate by the close vote of 27 to 25. The democrats generally voted in the affirmative, and a few of the Southern whigs, not willing to go against the strong feeling of their section, took the same position. The resolution, as passed, provided that Texas might become a state when her constitution was accepted by congress, that four additional states might with her own consent be formed out of her territory, that boundary disputes should be settled by future negotiations between the United States and any other foreign power who made objection, that Texas should assume her own debt and surrender her land and water defenses, that the principle of the Missouri compromise should be extended to the Texan territory, and that the president should have authority to complete annexation by negotiating with Mexico or by an agreement with Texas, as he saw fit.

The last clause was to meet the objection of a few senators who insisted that honor demanded that Mexico be conciliated. They **Tyler Anticipates Polk.** asserted that they had assurances that Polk would follow this plan if the resolutions passed, but he later denied that he gave such a promise. In fact, Tyler gave him no option in the matter. Though only seven days of the term remained to him, Tyler hurriedly dispatched a messenger to Texas with an offer of annexation. It arrived none too soon, for Texas was considering a proposition for a joint British and French guarantee of Texan integrity, with further joint mediation with Mexico on the question of boundaries. If Polk had resorted to negotiations, he must have encountered this scheme, and Texas might have been lost. As it was, Tyler's offer, and not England's, was accepted by the Texans, **Texas a State.** and December 29, 1845, a new state was admitted to the union. Mexico, watching the progress of annexation, broke off diplomatic intercourse with the United States as soon as congress passed the joint resolution, and a few months later she declared that the admission of Texas into the union would be equivalent to a declaration of war.

POLK'S ADMINISTRATION

The war with Mexico is the chief event under Polk; but before we begin with it three other measures must be described. The first was a new tariff bill, passed and approved by the president in disregard of the campaign assurances of his friends in Pennsylvania. The tariff of 1842 was about as high as 1. Tariff of 1846. that of 1832, and it pleased the protectionists. It did not suit the democrats, who now controlled all branches of the government. They, therefore, lost no time in passing a new bill, to which has been given the name of Secretary of the Treasury Walker. It became law July 30, 1846, and provided for a reduction to a strictly revenue basis. It was in force until 1857, when there was still further reduction. It did not injure the manufacturing interests of the country, and supplemented by other laws yielded sufficient revenue, even in the period of war which followed its adoption.

The second measure was the settlement of the Oregon boundary. Polk was especially anxious to make the Pacific coast American, and showed firmness in executing the Oregon clause of his party's platform. His first move was to offer to settle, on the old basis, the extension of the parallel 49° to the Pacific. The British minister in Washington refused the offer bluntly without referring it to his government. Polk then asked congress to do three things: (1) give notice to terminate the joint occupation of the disputed region; (2) erect forts there; and (3) extend the laws of the United States over Oregon. Such a course might undoubtedly lead to war, but Polk believed that England would yield when she saw we were in earnest; and the result showed he was right.

But congress was divided. The whigs wished to avoid war, the Northwestern members were firm for all the coast to the parallel 54° 40′, and began to suspect that the South, having got Texas, was willing to sacrifice Oregon, while some of the extreme Southerners did not like the idea of enlarging the area which must eventually be free territory. Congress wrangled until late in April, when it was finally decided to give notice to end joint occupancy. England had watched the proceedings closely. She did not wish war over so trivial a matter, and suggested unofficially that we renew our former offer. Polk thought this beneath the national dignity, and suggested that it was for England to reopen the negotiation. She was clearly in the wrong, and yielded as gracefully as possible. June 6, 1846, she submitted a treaty accepting the 49th parallel, and Polk, first getting the approval of the senate, signed the treaty, which was later formally ratified. The Northwest was deeply disappointed, but the rest of the country were satisfied with the compromise. The Mexican conflict was now beginning, and no one wished two wars at once.

The third matter related to California and New Mexico, a vast and thinly populated possession of Mexico. The Oregon immigrants were already entering California, and Polk believed that San

3. An Offer for California and New Mexico. Francisco harbor was necessary to the development of American power on the coast. Its acquisition, therefore, was a prime consideration in his policy from the time he became president. In September, 1845, spite of the rupture of relations with Mexico, he sent Slidell to Mexico to purchase the country, to settle the Texan boundary, and to adjust a mass of claims of American citizens. Slidell was instructed to assume the Mexican claims and pay $20,000,000 for that part of California from and including San Francisco northward, while he might offer $5,000,-000 more for the part including Monterey. For New Mexico, part of which Texas claimed, he might offer $5,000,000; and he was to endeavor to get Mexico to accept the Rio Grande for her Texas boundary. The affairs of Mexico were in great confusion, she was badly in need of funds, and as she had intimated that she would be willing to settle her relations with the United States, it was believed that Slidell by skillful management could get what we wanted.

The result showed that Polk did not understand the Spanish-American temperament. We were so unpopular with the Mexican people on account of the annexation of Texas that our offer was not even received, and Slidell was forced to return without the slightest success. Then Polk realized that if we got California and New Mexico we must resort to war, and for that contingency he was prepared.

Of the three matters of dispute the boundary question was the occasion of the war. Under Spanish and Mexican control Texas

The Texas Boundary. had never extended south of the Nueces, but the agreement with Santa Anna, 1836, had recognized the Rio Grande as the boundary (see page 421), a concession Mexico promptly repudiated. But the Texans persisted in their claim, and our government now took it up. The disputed region was uninhabited, and it is probable that time and diplomacy would have given it to us without a struggle. Such a course was not to be followed, for Polk had other ends in mind.

Pending the results of Slidell's diplomacy, General Zachary Taylor, with 1500 men, took position at Corpus Christi just south of the mouth

The Beginning of the War. of the Nueces, where he remained until early in 1846. When it was seen that Slidell would accomplish nothing, Taylor was ordered to the Rio Grande, and promptly obeyed. General Ampudia, with a Mexican force, was at Matamoras, on the south bank of the Rio Grande near its mouth. He considered the last move of the American general an act of invasion, and demanded that he fall back to the Nueces. He sent a force across the river, which on April 24 surrounded a reconnoitering party of Americans, killing and capturing them all. To Polk this was an act of invasion, and he advised congress that war had been begun by Mexico and that preparations for meeting it ought to be made. The nation was deeply excited, and congress, accepting the statement of the president, ordered the enlistment of 50,000 soldiers, and appropriated $10,000,000 for war expenses. In this way began the Mexican war, May 12, 1846.

Three chief offensive movements were planned by the Americans. One was intrusted to Taylor, who was to conquer the northern Mexican provinces and distress the enemy until they were willing to sue for peace. When in time this was seen to be insufficient, a second was organized to march from Vera Cruz against the Mexican capital. A third expedition, launched in the beginning of the war, was to invade and take New Mexico and then to proceed to the coast and occupy the weakly defended province of California. The purpose was to occupy the disputed region and hold it by force, to distress Mexico until she sued for peace, and to secure California, which Slidell could not get, as war indemnity. **The Three Phases of the War.**

Taylor moved first. News of hostilities had aroused the whole nation, and May 6, before congress had acted, reënforcements arrived from New Orleans, with which he took the field against the enemy, who had crossed the river. In two sharp engagements, Palo Alto and Resaca de la Palma, he defeated them, forced them to recross the Rio Grande, and then took Matamoras on May 18, Arista, the Mexican general, falling back to Monterey. Taylor now paused until he could make more deliberate plans. August 5 he resumed his advance, and September 20 invested Monterey, a strongly fortified town in which a large body of Mexicans were posted. After three days the enemy were so crippled that they asked for terms. They were allowed to march out with their arms, and Taylor agreed not to continue his march for eight weeks. The armistice displeased the president and was set aside, and Taylor advanced and occupied Saltillo without opposition. December 29 he occupied Victoria, the capital city of the state of Tamaulipas. He now had 10,000 men, and was holding a line 200 miles long. To his surprise and disgust he received an order to send half his force to Vera Cruz to join another army designed to march against the city of Mexico. Like a good soldier he obeyed orders, and began to drill the troops left him, chiefly raw recruits. **Taylor's First Battles.**

Almost immediately he learned that he was in great danger. Santa Anna, the Mexican commander-in-chief, had concentrated 20,000 men and was marching northward to crush him. To fall back to the Rio Grande meant a loss of all the prestige of the campaign, and Taylor decided to fight. He took position at the hacienda Buena Vista, five miles south of Saltillo. **Battle of Buena Vista.**

where he was attacked by the Mexicans on February 23. His army was posted between two mountains, and beat off the first attack with a splendid rifle and artillery fire. Santa Anna then rallied his men, turned Taylor's left, and made a bold dash at his line of retreat. Troops less cool would have been thrown into confusion, but the Americans trusted their commander and stood their ground. The flanking party was driven back to the mountain, and only a ruse of a pretended flag of truce saved them from capture. Santa Anna now made his last effort. Massing his reserves, he fell on Taylor's center, took its batteries, and penetrated the line for a considerable distance. Then Taylor pushed forward a battery commanded by Bragg which opened with grape and canister, while Jefferson Davis's Mississippians and a small band of Indiana troops cut them to pieces on the flank. Repulsed here, the enemy withdrew, leaving their dead and wounded on the field. The battle of Buena Vista, taking comparative numbers into consideration, was the best fought engagement of the war. After it was won Taylor remained undisturbed on the Rio Grande.

The expedition of Scott was undertaken because an army could not reach the enemy's capital from the Rio Grande. It was decided to land at Vera Cruz, take well-fortified defenses, and fight through the intervening region until the objective was reached. Selecting a commander caused much trouble. Taylor was a whig, his victories were fast making him a popular hero, and he was already mentioned as a presidential candidate. Ought a democratic administration to continue to afford him an opportunity to achieve laurels? General Scott, head of the army, was also a whig and open to the same objection. But the democrats had no good general of high rank, although Senator Benton, who had great confidence in himself, was willing to resign his seat and lead the second army of invasion. There was much wrangling over the point, and valuable time was lost, but at last good judgment prevailed, and Polk, putting political considerations aside, intrusted the command to Scott, who on March 9, 1847, began to land at Vera Cruz with more than 12,000 men. Before his operations are described we must follow the fortunes of the third movement, undertaken for the conquest of California.

Its conduct was intrusted to Colonel Stephen W. Kearny, who in June set out with 1800 men from Fort Leavenworth, on the upper Missouri, for Santa Fé. His greatest hardships were those of the march through an arid country, but on August 18 he entered Santa Fé, the Mexican army fleeing before him. Following his instructions, he set up a temporary government under the American flag, and a month later set out for California, going by way of the Gila valley to the Colorado and thence due west to San Diego. He started on this part of his campaign with only 300 men, but meeting Kit Carson with news that California was

Kearny's California Expedition.

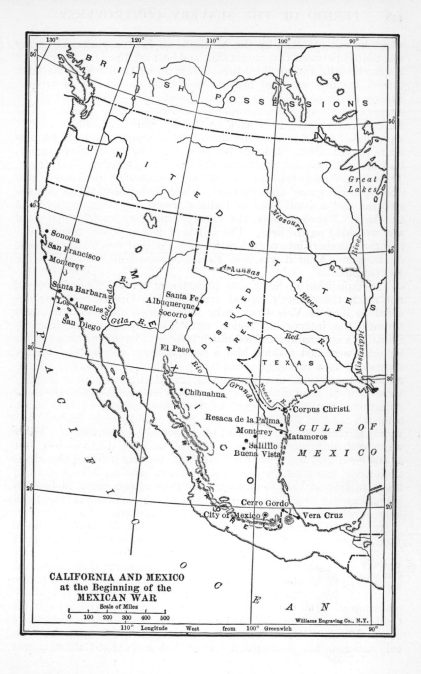

CALIFORNIA AND MEXICO
at the Beginning of the
MEXICAN WAR

Scale of Miles

0   100   200   300   400   500

Williams Engraving Co., N.Y.

already conquered, he sent two-thirds of his detachment back to New Mexico and proceeded with only 100 men.

The events to which Carson referred were strange, and filled with the spirit of adventure. Early in 1846 Commodore Sloat, with a squadron, was off the coast, with instructions to seize the harbors if war began, and the American consul at Monterey was instructed to promote the spirit of independence among the inhabitants. At that time Captain John C. Frémont, prominent as an explorer, was in California, engaged in geographical research, and secretly longing for an opportunity to raise the population, a portion of whom were Americans by birth, against Mexico. The knowledge that war had begun put all these forces into activity. Sloat took the ports of San Francisco and Monterey, and Commodore Stockton, who relieved him, took Los Angeles. Meanwhile, the inhabitants of the province rose against the Mexican garrisons and raised the American flag, Frémont giving such help as his small body of explorers afforded. Thus the whole province fell into American hands, and when Kearny arrived in December, 1846, only the remnants of resistance were to be suppressed. His authority superseded that of Stockton and Frémont, and he was soon at odds with them over the form of government to be established. The latter wished to have a territory with Frémont for governor. But Kearny was ordered to proclaim a provisional civil government with military support, and his compliance with the order was approved by the president.

The Province Seized.

When the news from California arrived in Washington Scott's army was beginning to execute the third important phase of the land operations. March 9 it landed three miles from Vera Cruz and invested the place, while a fleet blockaded the harbor. After five days of heavy bombardment, the town, suffering from hunger and exhaustion, was surrendered. Scott was an excellent general, as his proceedings now showed. Two hundred and fifty miles away was the capital of Mexico, reached by a good road which at eighty miles from the coast crossed a mountain range, the pass of which was guarded by the hill of Cerro Gordo. Here Scott, who advanced rapidly, found the enemy strongly posted on April 17. In a battle which consumed most of two days the army carried the well-fortified hill, drove Santa Anna into disastrous flight, and captured 3000 prisoners and a large quantity of arms and supplies.

Vera Cruz and Cerro Gordo.

Now followed nearly four months of inaction, while futile efforts for peace were made. Early in August the advance was resumed, and on the nineteenth the army had passed around Lake Chalco and faced the enemy at Contreras and Churubusco, two strong places a few miles south of the city. In four days' fighting both positions were taken in the most gallant

The Capital Taken.

2 G

manner. The prize was now all but won, when an armistice was granted and negotiations for peace were again begun. The demands of the Mexicans were impossible, and Scott, convinced that they were only made to gain time, broke off negotiations and took Molino del Rey on September 8. He was now four miles from the city, but before him stood the rock Chapultepec, 150 feet high, crowned with batteries and flanked with outworks, all well manned. On the thirteenth he attacked this place, carrying it after the most desperate resistance and coming at nightfall to the very gates of the city. These he was ready to storm on the following morning when the city officials appeared with a flag of truce and handed over the keys. By this time the army of the defenders had withdrawn to Guadaloupe Hidalgo, and his own troops marched through the gates to the great plaza, where they raised their flag over "the Halls of the Montezumas." With due allowance made for the inferior fighting ability of the Mexicans, it was a splendidly won campaign; and many an officer who served gallantly on one side or the other in the civil war saw here his first active service.

Polk began the war, thinking that Mexico would yield at the show of force, and Trist, chief clerk of the state department, accompanied Scott with the draft of a treaty of peace. This policy **Treaty of** was called "conquering a peace." It was Trist's pres-**Guadaloupe** ence that caused Scott to halt twice in his march on the **Hidalgo.** capital, a course which only made the Mexicans think the Americans timorous. This naturally angered Scott, who saw it interfered with the vigor of his campaign. His protests at last reached Washington, and just as the city of Mexico was entered there arrived orders for Trist to desist and return home. A strong feeling was arising in administration circles to demand all of Mexico. Meanwhile, Trist remained in Mexico, spite of his recall, and February 2, 1848, he signed the treaty of Gaudaloupe Hidalgo, in accordance with the instructions given him nearly a year earlier. It provided that the boundary should follow the Rio Grande to the New Mexican line, thence west to the first branch of the Gila, thence with the river to the Colorado, and from that point with the boundary between upper and lower California to the Pacific. The treaty was not strictly binding, as Trist's authority had expired; but Polk sent it to the senate, where it was accepted, March 10. It gave us New Mexico and California, for which we agreed to pay $15,000,000 and to assume the claims of American citizens against Mexico.

THE SLAVERY QUESTION IN A NEW FORM

Had the spirit of 1820 now prevailed it would have been possible to divide the newly acquired territory between freedom and slavery. Moderate men generally desired such an arrangement, but the most earnest persons on each side of the controversy would not have it. The North generally considered the war an act of Southern aggression and prepared a countermove. In 1846 a bill was before the house to appropriate money to enable the president to make peace, when Wilmot, a Pennsylvania democrat, offered his celebrated proviso that none of the territory acquired in the war should be open to slavery. It passed the house, where the North was in control, and was barely defeated in the senate. It aroused a storm of protest in the South, which believed itself about to be excluded from its fair share in the domain for which it had borne the brunt of war. Spite of the efforts of party leaders, Southern whigs dared not support the measure, and Northern democrats showed a growing unwillingness to oppose it. Sectionalism was rampant, and the union seemed imperiled. But the North did not yield. It had definitely concluded that no more slave states should be admitted to the union. If this plan were followed, the power of the South would soon be broken, and slavery in the South itself would eventually be hampered by irritating and disastrous limitations. The proviso was again before congress in 1847, and again defeated through the opposition of the senate, where the South still maintained its hold.

The Wilmot Proviso.

While the country was awakening to this controversy, the election of 1848 drew near. The whigs nominated General Taylor, staking their all on a military hero. He had no political experience, but the good sense and kindliness which had led his soldiers to call him "Old Rough and Ready" recommended him to popular favor. He was a war hero neglected by the democratic administration, and the people showed their disposition to right his wrongs. He was a Southerner and a slaveholder, which gave him strength in the South, and it was believed his war record would carry him through in the North. For vice-president Millard Filmore, of New York, was named. The whig convention tabled a resolution to adopt the Wilmot proviso.

Election of 1848, — Taylor Nominated.

The democratic party was handicapped by an internal conflict in the important state of New York. One faction was called barnburners. It favored reforms and got its name from a story of a Dutch farmer who burned his barn to destroy the rats in it. Silas Wright was at the head of the group, but he had the support of Van Buren, William Cullen Bryant, editor of the *New York Evening Post*, and many other liberal minded men. The other group, called hunkers, were more practical men, and were supported by the Tammany society. Their leader was William L. Marcy, and they got their name because they were supposed to hunger, or "hunker," for office. The two factions hated one another so much that Polk was bound to have trouble. In the beginning of his administration he offered to take a barnburner into his cabinet, but the men selected declined, and he made Marcy secretary of war. Then

Barnburners and Hunkers.

followed trouble over the patronage, widening the breach until in 1848 nothing could bring the two factions to act together, and the result was two sets of delegates to the national nominating convention, which assembled at Baltimore, May 22, 1848.

Aside from the New York wrangle, the meeting was harmonious. Recognizing the Wilmot proviso as a dangerous subject, the leaders kept it in the background, and a resolution in its behalf was **Cass Nominated.** tabled by a large majority. Several persons were suggested as candidates, but Lewis Cass, of Michigan, led from the first ballot and secured the nomination on the fourth. He had been in Jackson's cabinet, and was a man of ability and a popular leader in the West. With a candidate who pleased the West and a platform which pleased the South success seemed assured. The hope was defeated by the New York factions, each of which had been allowed to cast half of the state's vote. Each refused this settlement, but the hunkers pledged themselves to support Cass, while the other faction protested against the tabling of the Wilmot proviso and repudiated Cass.

Returning from the convention, the barnburners called a state convention at Utica and nominated Van Buren for the presidency on a platform which demanded the adoption of the Wilmot pro- **Free Soil Party Organized.** viso. Then followed a movement to consolidate all who opposed the extension of slavery. In November, 1847, the liberty party had nominated Hale of New Hampshire, while a radical offshoot of that party, the liberty league, in June, 1848, nominated Gerrit Smith. Moreover, many democrats and whigs were disappointed because their respective conventions had avoided the slavery issue. To unite all these elements a convention was called at Buffalo, August 9, which founded the free soil party, two of whose demands were that the territories be devoted to freedom and that the public lands be distributed free to actual settlers. This done, Van Buren was made the free soil candidate for president and Charles Francis Adams, of Massachusetts, the candidate for vice-president. Hale withdrew, and the liberty party and the barnburner organization was merged into the free soil party. In the election which followed the New York situation was the deciding factor. Taylor **The Election Results.** carried the state with 218,000 votes against 120,000 for Van Buren and 114,000 for Cass; and this meant a whig victory. Had the barnburners supported Cass, he would probably have carried the state. He had 127 electoral votes and Taylor had 163.

Although both democrats and whigs avoided in their platforms the question of slavery in the territories, the issue would not down. It was now more urgent than ever, because a government **Oregon made a Territory.** must be established in Oregon and because gold having been discovered in California the country was filling up with an adventurous population. The issue was strongly drawn in May, 1848, when Polk sent congress an urgent request for a territorial government for Oregon. A bill was framed which approved the laws already adopted by the temporary government there. Calhoun objected because, as he said, congress had no power to exclude slavery from any territory. The antislavery men, on the other hand, demanded specific restrictions. There was a long debate, the upshot of which was a compromise bill applying the principles of the Northwest Ordinance to Oregon and creating the territories of California and New Mexico without power to pass on slavery, either for or against it. The house tabled the bill, and finally, after much bitterness, the provisions of the bill in relation to Oregon were passed as a separate act. Thus Oregon became a territory without slavery, but California and New Mexico must wait.

The next session of congress was a short one. The house passed a bill to organize the territory of California without slavery, but the senate refused to concur. Various other propositions on the same subject were made, but none were acceptable. **Futile Session of Congress, 1848-1849.** In this session, as in the former, Polk urged that the whole question be settled by extending the Missouri compromise to the Pacific, and some favored the idea. Probably the South would have accepted it, but the North was aroused and was determined to check the spread of slavery, so that Polk's suggestion was not adopted. While this subject was being discussed, Northern members brought in a bill to forbid the slave trade in the District of Columbia. It passed the house, but was reconsidered and tabled. The Southern members were aroused, and replied by asking for a committee to prepare a more effective fugitive slave law. The request was not granted, but it served to call the attention of the country to a concrete grievance of the South. The Southern congressmen in an address described the growth of discrimination, and soon afterwards the southern legislatures passed resolutions of similar nature. Northern legislatures replied by demanding the exclusion of slavery from the territories.

On March 4, 1849, congress adjourned after three months of bitter debate, in which no progress was made toward removing the sectional differences. Threats of disunion were freely uttered **Threats of Disunion.** by Southerners, and before adjournment they organized a committee which sent forth an address on the position of the South. It reviewed the rise of opposition to slavery, arraigned the aggressive spirit of the North on the question, declared the South was denied a fair share of the territory it had done so much to conquer in the recent war, and called on all Southern people to stand as a unit in resistance of the treatment it received. The address was warmly commended in the slave states by both whigs and democrats. In the North there was also much excitement, and many legislatures there passed resolutions for the prohibition of the slave trade in the District of Columbia.

The Compromise of 1850

When the next congress met, December 3, 1849, affairs were no nearer a settlement. California, tired of awaiting the action of congress, had set up an irregular state government with the **The Longing for Harmony.** tacit approval of President Taylor, and was asking for statehood, while New Mexico suffered many inconveniences through the lack of a regular government. Something must be done, but no one could say what. Behind all was the ominous and growing movement for disunion. Cool-headed men, business interests, and conservatives generally recognized the necessity of compromise; and party managers, alarmed at the way negro slavery interfered with older political alignments, wished to find some road to harmony. The issue was fast destroying the whig party in the South, and it threatened to undermine the democracy in the North.

Three suggestions of compromise came into the minds of the leaders. One was the extension of the Missouri line to the Pacific. We have **Popular Sovereignty.** seen that this was opposed by the antislavery North. The second was to refer the question to the territories. It was first made in 1847, when the Wilmot proviso was being discussed; and Cass in the same year adopted it in a letter to a Tennessee supporter. It meant that congress should do nothing about slavery in a territory, allowing slaveholders and non-slaveholders to settle there as they chose, and that the people of the territory should decide the question for themselves when the territory became a state. This doctrine, so consonant with the theory of state rights, would probably have been accepted by the South in 1848. Brought up later by Douglas, who named it "popular sovereignty," it played an important part in the conflict over Kansas and Nebraska. The suggestion did not please the antislavery men, who meant that slavery must be given no opportunity in the territories.

The third suggestion came from Clay. For nearly eight years he had been in retirement, and was now sent back to the senate because **Clay's Suggestion.** his friends thought he could do something to save the union. At heart he favored the Wilmot proviso, and since California and New Mexico evidently wished to save themselves from slavery, he thought they ought to be gratified. Looking over the field he prepared a plan of compromise which gave something to each side. He thought all moderate men would unite to pass it in order to remove the slavery question definitely from the field of national politics. It appealed to his imagination that "the Great Compromiser," as he was called, who had done good services in the crises of 1820 and 1833 should finish his career with another compromise, greater in its significance than either of the other two.

January 29, 1850, he introduced a series of resolutions providing for: 1. The admission of California as a free state; 2. The creation of the territories of New Mexico and Utah without restric- **His Reso-** tion as to slavery; 3. The assumption of the debt of Texas **lutions.** contracted before annexation and the relinquishment of her claim to a large part of eastern New Mexico; 4. The prohibition of the slave trade in the District of Columbia with the refusal to pro- hibit slavery there without the consent of Maryland; 5. The more effectual return of fugitive slaves to their masters; and 6. The asser- tion that congress could not forbid the interstate slave trade.

A week later Clay made a two days' speech in defense of his reso- lutions. The nation had come to the point of dividing, he said, and it was time for each side to make concessions. The South was defending its interests, the North was contending **Clay's Com-** for a sentiment; and it was easier to relax sentiment than **promise** interest. The first and fourth resolution would favor the **Speech.** North, and on these the South must be content to give way. The others favored the South, and he pleaded that the North would be reasonable and yield on these. His speech was filled with protesta- tions of loyalty to the union of the fathers, a union which he and every other old man present had seen born and develop through the preced- ing sixty years. He spoke with wonderful effect to an audience which filled every available foot of space in the senate chamber.

On March 4 Calhoun tottered into the capitol to speak to the reso- lutions. He had come from a sick-bed, and could only sit and watch the senators while his words were read by a friend. He too was born before the constitution was written, but his **Calhoun's** speech was no plea for concession. He had long been **Speech,—** rallying the South against the growing power of the North, **the** and this last appeal was a message of warning. The union, **South Out-** he said, began with an equal distribution of power between **distanced.** the North and the South, but at the end of sixty years the equilibrium was destroyed. The census about to be taken would show a vast preponderance of population in the North, and this was not due to natural causes, but to three lines of policy followed by the federal government. The first was the Northwest ordinance and the Mis- souri compromise, by which the South was excluded from many of the territories; the second was the protective tariff; and the third was the growth of consolidation by which the power of the federal government had come into the hands of the North. For a long time there was a complete equilibrium in the senate, but of late the char- acter of Delaware was become neutral, giving the North 28 and the South 26 members of the senate. At present there were two Northern territories, Minnesota and Oregon, and no Southern territories, in a formative process. Add to this the proposition of the North for the exclusion of the South from California, New Mexico, and Utah, and the prospect was that there would be five more states added to the power of the North. Could there be any doubt whither this situation would lead?

About 1835, he continued, began the antislavery agitation, proclaiming as its purpose the destruction of slavery, an achievement which would overturn the social system of the South. **The Growth of Disunion.** At first ignored by the two great parties, it had grown until whigs and democrats were afraid to oppose it, and its latest demand was the exclusion of slavery from the territories. Would it ever be weaker than now? Was it not evident that if something were not done to check its progress the South must choose between abolition and secession? The evidences that disunion is growing are seen in the churches. The Methodists and Baptists are already divided on the question of slavery, the bonds of the Presbyterian church have begun to yield, and only the Episcopalians, of the four great Protestant bodies, are not affected by the great dissension. The same tendency is seen in the two great parties. Cord after cord has broken, and if the agitation goes on, not a bond will remain to bind together the two great sections of the country. This is disunion.

Calhoun then came to his remedy for this aggravated situation. He proposed an amendment to the constitution guaranteeing the South an equal position in the territories, a fair execution **Calhoun's Remedy.** of the fugitive slave act, and a cessation of antislavery agitation. Would the North accept this? She would if she loved the union as she professed. It was not a gift in the possession of the South, the weaker section. "If you who represent the stronger portion," he said to the Northern senators, "cannot agree to settle them [the points mentioned] on the broad principles of justice and duty, say so; and let the states we both represent agree to separate and part in peace. If you are unwilling we should part in peace, tell us so, and we shall know what to do, when you reduce the question to submission or resistance. If you remain silent you will compel us to infer by your acts what you intend."

This speech was the last warning of the Southern Nestor, and four weeks later he was dead. There are flaws in the argument, but he stated clearly the situation of the South. It had played **Significance of Calhoun's Speech.** a losing game in the race for progress, it was now face to face with the inevitable, and it must submit to the will of the North and allow slavery to be put in a way to be extinguished, or it must separate from the North and establish a government of its own. Compromise was entirely without Calhoun's ken. He realized that it was only a palliative and pleaded calmly for Northern conciliation in a saddened eloquence which would have been better expended if it had been used to reconcile his own people to the inevitable progress of civilization.

March 7 Webster rose to speak. He too had seen the union pass from its birth through a period of doubt to a splendid maturity. He grew up to manhood when patriotism was a passion, the best efforts of his life had been given to establish the ideals of *Webster's* union, and he was dismayed at the prospect which Calhoun *Speech,* held up so firmly. Moreover, Webster, like many other *March 7.* cooler Northerners, had no enthusiasm for abolition. He did not believe slavery as undesirable as disunion, and he now threw his whole soul into the task of calming the Northern mind, charging the abolitionists with excessive severity, and pleading that the South be not driven into the last ditch. Conservative Northerners approved the speech, but the verdict of the antislavery men was far otherwise. One compared him with Benedict Arnold, another exclaimed: "Webster is a fallen star! Lucifer descending from heaven!" and he was freely charged with bidding for the Southern whig support for the presidency. He undoubtedly had his ambitions, but he would hardly have risked his standing at home if he had not felt that duty impelled him. The avalanche of criticism under which he was buried shows how much the North was aroused against slavery.

Clay's resolutions were debated, with some intermissions, for three months before bills embodying their principles were introduced. One was called "the Omnibus Bill," because it contained his recommendations in regard to California, New Mexico, *The Com-* Utah, and Texas; another prohibited the slave trade *promise* in the District of Columbia, and still another provided a *Adopted.* better fugitive slave law. As the debate proceeded, the "Omnibus Bill" was broken up into three measures, each of which, with the two other propositions, was adopted through the efforts of Clay. Thus the North gained the admission of California as a free state and the prohibition of the slave trade in the national capital. The South had a distinct gain in the new fugitive slave law, which gave to the federal courts the execution of the law, and Texas was relieved of her debt incurred in the struggle to win and maintain her independence. In the creation of New Mexico and Utah as territories the North lost to the extent that the Wilmot proviso was not applied, but the net gain was bound to be hers as one of the territories was north of the Missouri line and the other could not hope soon to be a state.

June 3, while the compromise was being debated, a Southern convention met in Nashville, nine states being represented. The delegates from South Carolina and Mississippi were for extreme measures, but cooler heads restrained them, and the con- *The Nash-* vention contented itself with demanding the extension *ville Con-* of the line 36° 30′ to the Pacific. For all Calhoun's de- *vention.* liberate gloom the Southern people were not yet ready to secede. But the convention had an important influence on the action of congress. The extreme Northerners declared it a mere threat, and believed that

the talk of secession was gasconade. In the light of later events we
know that disunion had taken a strong hold in the South, although it
had not yet been accepted by the great mass of people there.

July 9 President Taylor died. Although not experienced in politics,
he had made a good executive. He had a soldier's love of duty and
a leaning toward the enforcement of authority which

Fillmore President.
reminds one of Jackson. Talk of secession aroused his
opposition, and he was not favorable to compromise. Fillmore, his successor, was conservative by nature and gave active support to Clay's plans. The great compromise having passed, he
sought to enforce it, and wished it to be, as it was intended, a final
settlement of sectional dissensions. His administration was void
of other important events.

July 5, 1850, was ratified the Clayton-Bulwer treaty, referring to
the construction of an Isthmian canal. Hopes of such a waterway
had long been entertained in Central America, but the

Clayton-Bulwer.
interest of the United States in it sprang chiefly from their
acquisition of their Pacific coast. In 1846 a treaty was
made with New Granada, looking to a canal at the Isthmus of Panama.
Soon afterwards a railway was begun at this point, but no canal construction was attempted. At the same time Great Britain was moving
to get possession of the Nicaraguan route. She had acquired the eastern, and was making efforts to get the western, terminus. Nicaragua
feared that these steps would lead to the most serious results, and
sought to play the United States against England. Our general
opposition to an increase of British influence in Central America was
sufficient to arouse interest. American capital was also negotiating
for a canal charter, and in 1849 a treaty was negotiated with Nicaragua, but not ratified, by which we got a concession for a canal and
agreed to guarantee the integrity of Nicaragua. Then followed complications with Great Britain, the result of which, 1850, was the treaty
which bears the names of the American secretary of state and the
British minister in Washington, Clayton and Bulwer. It pledged each
nation to maintain the neutrality of any interoceanic canal which either
should construct at any point in Central America, agreed to admit
other nations to the benefits of the treaty, and promised that neither
power should extend its possessions in that region.

BIBLIOGRAPHICAL NOTE

The best general works are: McMaster, *History of the People of the United
States*, vols. VI and VII (1906, 1910), the fullest and most reliable general treatment;
Schouler, *History of the United States*, vols. IV, V (1891); Von Holst, *Constitutional
and Political History*, 8 vols. (Eng. trans., ed. 1899); Wilson, *History of the American People* (1905); Garrison, *Westward Extension, 1841–1850* (1906), very satisfactory; and Stanwood, *History of the Presidency* (1898).

The leading biographies are: Schurz, *Henry Clay*, 2 vols. (1887); Shepard, *Van
Buren* (1888); McLaughlin, *Cass* (1891); Morse, *John Quincy Adams* (1882);

Lodge, *Webster* (1883); Curtis, *Daniel Webster*, 2 vols. (1870); Meigs, *Life of Benton* (1904); Curtis, *James Buchanan*, 2 vols. (1883); Hunt, *Life of Calhoun* (1907); Hart, *Salmon P. Chase* (1899); Bancroft, *Life of Seward*, 2 vols. (1900); and Dodd, *Statesmen of the Old South* (1911).

For the sources see: *The Congressional Globe*, 108 vols. (1834–1873); Benton, *Abridgment of the Debates*, 16 vols. (1857–1861), extends to 1850; *House Executive Documents, Senate Executive Documents, House Reports*, and *Senate Reports, a Table and Annotated Index* was published in 1902; Richardson, *Messages and Papers of the Presidents*, 10 vols. (1896–1899); MacDonald, *Select Documents, 1776–1861* (1898); Haswell, *Treaties and Conventions* (1889); and Peters, *Statutes at Large*, 8 vols. (1845–1846), continued in *United States Statutes at Large*.

Of the contemporary periodicals the most valuable are: *Niles' National Register* (1811–1849), whig in sympathy, but contains many documents; *The National Intelligencer* (Washington, 1800–1870), whig organ; *The Globe* (Washington, 1830–1845), democratic organ; *The Enquirer* (Richmond, 1804–1877), voiced the old Virginia influence, ably edited by Ritchie; *The Evening Post* (New York, continuous from 1801), supported the barnburners, edited by Wm. Cullen Bryant from 1828 to 1878; *The New York Tribune* (1841–), antislavery, very influential; *The Liberator* (Boston, 1831–1865), extreme antislavery; and *The National Era* (Washington, 1847–1864), antislavery, but moderate.

Many contemporaries left memoirs or narratives. Among them are: John Quincy Adams, *Memoirs*, 12 vols. (1874–1877), very valuable; Benton, *Thirty Years' View*, 2 vols. (1854–1857), to be used with caution: Tyler, *Letters and Times of the Tylers*, 3 vols. (1884–1896); *Polk's Diary*, 4 vols. (1910); Webster, *Works*, 6 vols. (1851), in 7 vols. (1897); Calhoun, *Works*, 6 vols. (1853–1859); Ibid., *Correspondence* (ed. by Jameson, Am. Hist. Assn. *Reports*, II, 1899); Garrison and Garrison, *William Lloyd Garrison*, 4 vols. (1885–1889); Wise, *Seven Decades of the Union* (1881); and Buchanan, *Works of*, 12 vols. (Moore, ed., 1908–1911).

Financial matters are treated in Dewey, *Financial History* (1903); Bolles, *Financial History*, 3 vols. (ed. 1897); Taussig, *Tariff History* (ed. 1898); Stanwood, *Tariff Controversies*, 2 vols. (1903); Kinley, *The Independent Treasury of the United States* (1893); Dunbar, *Laws Relating to Currency, Finance, and Banking* (ed. 1897); Scott, *Repudiation of State Debts* (1893); and Sumner, *History of Banking in the United States* (in *History of Banking in All Nations*, 4 vols. 1896).

The antislavery literature is very abundant, but the following books are sufficient for most students: Hart, *Slavery and Abolition* (1906); the best recent book, impartial and supplied with a good bibliography; Garrison and Garrison, *William Lloyd Garrison*, 4 vols. (1885–1889); Pierce, *Memoir and Letters of Charles Sumner*, 4 vols. (1877–1893); Birney, *James G. Birney and His Times* (1890); and Smith, *The Liberty and Free Soil Parties in the Northwest* (Harvard Studies, 1897).

Texas annexation is well treated in Justin H. Smith, *Annexation of Texas* (1911); Garrison, *Westward Extension* (1906); Ibid., *History of Texas* (1903); Ibid., "The First Stage of the movement for the annexation of Texas," in *Am. Hist. Rev.*, X, 72; Reeves, *Diplomacy under Tyler and Polk* (1907); Adams, *British Interests and Activities in Texas* (1910), should be used in connection with Smith's review, *American Historical Review*, XVI, 151; and *Texas Diplomatic Correspondence*, 3 parts (Am. Hist. Assn. *Reports*, 1908).

On the northeastern and northwestern boundary disputes see: Moore, *Digest of International Arbitrations*, 6 vols. (1895); Ganong, *Boundaries of New Brunswick* (Royal Soc. of Canada *Transactions*, 1901–1902); Mills, *British Diplomacy in Canada* (Royal Colonial Institute's Journal, *United Empire*, 1911); Gallatin, *Right of the United States to the Northeast Boundary* (1840); Greenhow, *History of Oregon and California* (1844); Twiss, *The Oregon Question* (1846); and Bourne, *Legend of Marcus Whitman* (*Essays in Historical Criticism*, 1900, also in *Am. Hist. Rev.*, VI).

On the war with Mexico see: Ripley, *The War with Mexico*, 2 vols. (1849); Wright, *General Scott* (1894); Howard, *General Taylor* (1892); Scott, *Memoirs*,

2 vols. (1864), to be used with discrimination; Livermore, *War with Mexico Reviewed* (1850), on the political side; Bancroft, *History of Mexico*, 6 vols. (1883–1888); Ibid., *History of California*, 7 vols. (1886–1890); and Hittell, *History of California*, 4 vols. (1886–1897).

On the compromise of 1850 see: Rhodes, *History of the United States*, 7 vols. (1892–1906); Greeley, *The American Conflict*, 2 vols. (1868–1870); Schurz, *Henry Clay* (1887); Stephens, *War between the States*, 2 vols. (1868–1870); and Davis, *Rise and Fall of the Confederate Government*, 2 vols. (1881).

On the Isthmian canal see: Keasbey, *The Nicaragua Canal and the Monroe Doctrine* (1896); Huberich, *The Trans-Isthmian Canal* (1904); and Travis, *History of the Clayton-Bulwer Treaty* (Michigan Pol. Sc. Assn. *Publications*, 1900).

For Independent Reading

Davis, *Recollections of Mississippi and Mississippians* (1891); Higginson, *Cheerful Yesterdays* (1898); Wise, *Seven Decades of the Union* (1881); Parkman, *The Oregon Trail* (1892 and other editions); Irving, *Astoria* (many editions); Royce, *History of California* (1886); and Clarke, *Antislavery Days* (1884).

CHAPTER XXII

SOCIAL AND INDUSTRIAL DEVELOPMENT, 1815–1861

GROWTH OF POPULATION AND THE RESULTS

DURING the years 1815–1860 the westward movement of population continued the most noticeable feature of our domestic affairs. In the former year the Atlantic states had about 5,800,000 inhabitants, in 1860 they had 15,895,971, while the region lying westward had increased from 1,500,000 in 1815 to 15,484,350 in 1860. Had the óld feeling of opposition between the East and the West persisted, the latter section would in 1860 have been nearly in the supremacy. That it did not persist was due to two causes. 1. The democratic party, founded as an expression of the will of the rural classes, had a strong hold in all parts of the country. It was a truly national bond. 2. The rise of the slavery question introduced a new kind of sectionalism, the North against the South. By this newer alignment the North was very powerful. Including the free West, it had in 1860 a population of 20,309,960, while the South had 11,133,361.

A New Kind of Sectionalism.

In a new country the birth rate is high, and to this must be attributed the greater part of the rapid growth in numbers. But another important fact was immigration, which increased swiftly after the war of 1812. The growth of manufactures and the development of the West created a great demand for labor, while disturbances and suffering in Europe gave an impetus for emigration to a land where wages were high and homes awaited those who would have them. The records of immigration, kept from 1820, show that from that year to 1860, inclusive, 5,055,938 aliens, including travelers, arrived in the United States, most of them coming from three countries. Ireland, afflicted with famine and many other ills, led with 1,880,943, Germany came next with 1,545,508, and England was third with 744,285. France, Switzerland, and the Netherlands sent considerable numbers; but the nations from which we have lately received most of our immigrants then sent few. For the entire period, only 16,776 came from Italy, Russia, and Poland.

Immigration.

The immigrant avoided the states in which slavery was the prevalent form of labor. He could not compete with it in wages, and it made it difficult for him to become a proprietor of his own enterprises. In 1860 the foreign-born population was 4,136,175, and

461

of this the fifteen slave states had 471,000, more than half of whom
were in the border states of Missouri and Maryland.

Immigrants Avoid the South. It was said at the time that white labor could not thrive in the South. The experience of the last half century shows that the opinion was erroneous. It seems evident that but for the presence of slavery the South would have the share of immigration to which its fertile soil and agreeable climate entitled it.

The immigrant was rarely a pioneer. The hard task of exploring the wilderness and pushing the Indian westward was assumed by the natives, while the less adventurous European was content to arrive when towns were being planted and farming lands were being taken up. Thus, in the seven territories in existence in 1860, with a total population of 220,197, there were only 35,476 foreign-born persons, while in the five states of the old Northwest, with a total population of 6,926,884, there were 1,197,736 foreign-born persons. The rapid growth of manufactures in the East absorbed a large portion of the newcomers. In the six great manufacturing states, New York, Pennsylvania, Massachusetts, New Jersey, Connecticut, and Rhode Island, with a total population in 1860 of 9,324,818, there were 1,930,139 persons of foreign birth. Thus we see that in eleven states, constituting the older agricultural West and the manufacturing East, were concentrated 75.6 per cent of the immigrant population.

Location of the Immigrants.

Most immigrants were good laborers, and a few were able to purchase farms. Some were diseased, and it was known that parishes in Europe had sent their paupers. By 1830 public opinion, which was all for immigration in 1815, began to change, and demands were heard for discrimination among the incoming multitude. The Irish caused special alarm. They were more numerous and clannish, clung to the cities, and soon fell into the hands of designing politicians. As they were generally Catholics, a solid Irish vote caused alarm to those who feared the American doctrine of strict separation of church and state might be weakened. As a result, much was said about denying to the immigrants the right both to vote and hold office, but neither of the great political parties was willing to espouse such a principle.

Opposition to Immigrants' Voting.

Finally the advocates for reform effected a distinct organization, calling themselves Native Americans. They appeared chiefly in the cities, and nominated candidates for city office. In Boston in 1837 a riot grew out of the excited feeling of the "Natives" and the Irish. In the same year the Native American Association was created, demanding of congress the repeal of the naturalization laws. Throughout the succeeding years there was much ferment. City after city fell into the hands of the Native Americans; and in the summer of 1844 there was prolonged rioting in Philadelphia, occasioned by a protest of the Catholics against the use of the

The Native Americans.

Protestant Bible in the public schools. The matter became a campaign issue, the democrats espousing the cause of the naturalized citizens, and denouncing the spirit of persecution. The victory of Polk did not discourage the Native Americans, and in 1847 they held a national convention and indorsed Taylor for president. Violence, which had never been approved by the leaders, was now abandoned, and the organization seemed losing its influence. But the impulse persisted, and in 1850 was founded the Order of the Star Spangled Banner, which proved the germ of the Know Nothing movement (see page 493). Voting by newly arrived immigrants, which was the chief complaint of nativism, has been allowed to this day most liberally by the states, who have jurisdiction of the suffrage.

Vast changes in the national domain occurred between 1815 and 1860. A schoolboy in the former year would learn that Florida was Spanish and that our southwestern border was Texas and New Mexico. Our claim to Oregon was so indefinite that it hardly counted at that time in the popular mind. By 1860 our western boundary was the Pacific, and 444,053 Americans were settled on the coast. Here already were two states — California, admitted in 1850, and Oregon, a state in 1859 — and one territory, Washington, set off in 1853. In 1815 no state but Louisiana existed beyond the Mississippi. We have seen how Missouri was admitted in 1820, balancing the free state of Maine. The process continued steadily as the settlement of the territories proceeded. In 1836 Michigan and Arkansas were admitted, in 1845 Texas and Florida came in, followed by the two free states of Iowa in 1846 and Wisconsin in 1848, and in 1858 Minnesota was admitted. Thus by 1860 a belt of states extended the whole length of the Mississippi on the west. Beyond it to the confines of Washington, Oregon, and California was a great area embracing the territories of Kansas, Nebraska, Utah, and New Mexico, destined within a short time to be divided into several territories. The only part of the national domain not organized into territories in 1860 was the portion of the two Dakotas lying between Minnesota and the Missouri, a region in which the powerful Sioux tribes had their homes.

New States and Territories.

THE INFLUENCE OF GREAT INVENTIONS

In 1815 the United States had already begun to use power machinery in industry. The first effects were seen in New England, every stream of which had water power. Manufactures now took the place of commerce as the chief form of industry, and the seat of wealth was no longer confined to the seaports. The immigrants furnished an operative class and the towns grew rapidly; while the farmers, drawn more and more away to the West, left agriculture in a languishing state.

Manufactures and the Growth of Towns.

In the Middle states towns grew as readily as in New England, but the greater fertility of the soil sustained the prosperity of agriculture, spite of the drain of men to the Western lands.

For all this rich life transportation was an essential. It was needed to carry merchandise to the interior, to bring farm products to the seaboard, and to bind the remote regions to the seacoast. **Navigation and Canals.** Steamboats, canals, and railroads all served this purpose. The first were especially useful on the rivers of the interior. In these initial days of Western development, when every promoter could call up a vision of wealth, the papers were full of schemes to establish navigation companies. Many of the plans proved failures, others had short careers and gave place at last to rail-roads, and some were established successfully.

In 1828 canals were much in vogue in the West and in the seaboard states. New York was reaping great advantages from the Erie canal, then three years completed. Pennsylvania had just **Railroads.** inaugurated a system of roads and canals which would deliver a vast amount of the Western traffic to Philadelphia, and the Potomac people were planning to construct a canal parallel to the river, whence by easy roads they could reach the tributaries of the Ohio. If these routes were opened, Baltimore's thriving trade would be turned aside and her glory would be gone. In desperation she thought of a railroad, and July 4, 1828, the first stroke was made on the Baltimore and Ohio line. The success of the undertaking led to many other similar enterprises, North, South, and West. Sometimes the state built the railroad and operated it, but more frequently it was built by a chartered company and received aid from the state either in bonds given in exchange for stock, or in land donated. By 1840 the railroad had demonstrated its superiority over the canal and was in general use. Most of the roads were short, built to connect important towns or cities, and the era of consolidation did not appear until just before the civil war (see page 733). It was not until 1853 that Chicago had an all-rail line of travel to the seacoast. The development of railroads gave great importance to the great business corporation, whose shares became a medium of investment and speculation. Now arose also the necessity of making laws defining the relation of railroads to the public. They could no longer be looked upon as mere private enterprises, since they were vitally connected with the welfare of the communities through which they ran. Out of this relation arose, chiefly after the civil war, a great conflict between capital and the public.

While railroads largely superseded steamboats on the small streams, they did not soon replace them on the great rivers. On the Mississippi the boats were especially numerous and luxurious. They vied with one another in speed and comfort, and the trip from St. Louis to New Orleans was long remembered by the traveler who took it on one of these fine craft. For many years it was said that a steamboat could never cross the Atlantic because she could not carry the necessary fuel; but the *Savannah* disproved this in 1819, going with auxiliary steam power, and the *Sirius* and *Great Western*, going entirely by steam, in 1838. In 1840 the Cunard line began to operate steam packets regularly between New York and Liverpool. Other steamships were soon crossing the ocean, but for many years the fast and graceful clippers of the day continued to be the favorite means of passing over the Atlantic.

Steamboats on River and Ocean.

Many other inventions of this period contributed to the progress of the country. In 1844 Morse invented the electric telegraph, which he did by combining in a practical way several discoveries of scientists who preceded him. As a means of bringing one part of the country into close business and social relations with another part, it was hardly less important than the railroad. In 1834 McCormick invented the reaper, building, also, on many principles discovered by men who preceded him. It was vastly improved in 1845–1847, and found a ready place in the agricultural life of the country. It revolutionized industry in the West, where the fertile lands were well adapted to wheat-raising. With the reaper to harvest the grain and the railroads to take it to the seaports, the West became in a short time a granary for many parts of Europe. In 1846 Elias Howe patented his sewing machine, after many years of struggle against poverty and illness. It was destined to revolutionize the clothing-making industry and to lighten the labor of housewives in all parts of the world. These important inventions, with many others of less importance, testified to the versatility and strength of the inventive faculty in the United States, and gave the American people a prominent place among the progressive industrial nations. They were accompanied by a quick witted adaptation of the great inventions of other countries, which powerfully stimulated the development of business and general comfort.

The Telegraph, the Reaper, and the Sewing Machine.

The Indians

In 1815 Indian tribes lived east of the Mississippi in the extreme Northwest, in Tennessee and the region south of it, and in Florida, which was still in the hands of Spain. The advance of the whites gradually pushed them back in the lake region, and they gave up their lands in a series of treaties which by 1830 left them only the prairies south of Lake Michigan and the lands between that lake and the Mississippi. In the southern parts lived the Sacs and Foxes, who in 1804 ceded their lands between the Illinois and the Wisconsin, retaining permission to occupy and hunt on them until they were sold to the whites. During the war of 1812

East of the Mississippi.

some of the Sacs crossed the Mississippi, but the remainder continued in the valley of the Rock river. By 1830 the
Black Hawk War. surrounding country was filling with settlers who looked
longingly at the fine Indian lands. Then followed a deed
which, from its frequent recurrence in similar situations, may be pronounced the normal way of beginning an Indian war. Late in the
year, while the men were hunting, white intruders broke up their
village, drove the women and children to the forest, and established
themselves in the fertile corn land at the mouth of Rock river, the site
of the present town of Rock Island. When the hunters returned they
took up arms under the leadership of Black Hawk and retook their
village. Troops were called out, but hostilities seemed avoided when
Black Hawk moved his people across the Mississippi after promising
never to return. In the following year, however, he was back in the
tribal lands, committing depredations against the whites. He was
now pursued by a force of regulars and militia, driven into Wisconsin,
and captured after a severe battle at Bad Axe. The Black Hawk war
was the last Indian struggle on the northwestern frontier until the gold
hunters began to invade the Rocky Mountain region more than thirty
years later.

This affair in Illinois must have been a striking object lesson to the
Georgia Indians, who, as we have seen (page 400), were in the same
year, 1832, at the height of their contention with the state
The Situation of the Georgia Indians. authorities. In 1830, congress, following the suggestion
of the president, offered to give lands beyond the Missis-
sippi to such eastern Indians as would remove thither.
But the Indians refused to move, and appealed to the
supreme court, relying on their treaty rights. The verdict was in their
favor, but through President Jackson's failure to execute it they
profited nothing by it; and Georgia proceeded to establish her civil
authority in the region over which the Indian law had extended. She
also began to sell their hunting lands and threatened to take their
farms and homes. What she did for the Cherokees and Creeks within
her borders, Mississippi was ready to do for the Chickasaws and Choctaws within her limits.

Under such conditions, the Indians could do nothing but yield.
The Creeks sold their lands to the federal government in 1832, the
Chickasaws and Choctaws in 1833, and the Cherokees in
Removal Accomplished. 1835. A few members of the last-named tribe refused to
abide by the sale and were removed by force. For all the
land these Indians sold the federal government promised
liberal annuities, or agreed to sell the relinquished lands and
hold the proceeds in trust for the Indians. It also paid the cost
of removal and donated new lands in the West. In 1834 congress established Indian territory in the fertile valley of the Arkansas. More accurately speaking, it was a series of reservations,

on each of which a nation was placed with the assurance that it would never be moved and that no white man should settle within its border without a license. Each nation was to have its own council and make and execute its own laws; and assistance was given to enable the Indians to contend with the worst difficulties of life in a new environment. There was no regular territorial government, and no hope of statehood was held out. A large part of the Indian territory was left unassigned in order that the Northwestern tribes might be induced to settle on it. As this expectation was not realized, these unsettled lands were many years later opened to settlement by the whites and became organized as Oklahoma territory.

Indian Territory.

In one other quarter occurred trouble with the Indians. In Florida lived the Seminoles. Many fugitive slaves had settled among and intermarried with them, and it was considered desirable to remove this tribe, also, to the West. In 1833 they were induced to make a treaty for that purpose, and the next year an agent was sent to execute it. This aroused the resident fugitive slaves, who foresaw that they would be returned to bondage. They joined with the less submissive Indians and made up a party who defied the government under the lead of Osceola, an able half-breed whose father was a white man named Powell. His wife was the daughter of a negress, an escaped slave, and in 1835 she was seized when on a friendly visit to Fort King. Osceola protested and was arrested. Feigning submission, he was released, only to make secret plans for resistance. In November, 1835, he put himself at the head of the discontented ones, drove the friendly chiefs into the forts of the white men, retired into the swamps, and made himself a source of terror to the settlements. Troops were now hurried to Florida, but Osceola, fighting with great energy and bravery, drove them back to the forts and held at his mercy all the open country south of St. Augustine. Reënforcements were called for, but these had little better success. The years 1836 and 1837 witnessed many encounters in which the Indians, having fought as long as they dared, fled at last to the swamps, into which they could not be followed. In 1837 the Seminoles agreed to go West if allowed to take with them "their negroes, their *bona fide* property." Many of them assembled at Tampa, and transports were ready to take them to New Orleans, when white men appeared to claim the fugitive slaves. Resistance was immediately renewed, and the struggle went on again more bitterly than ever. Later in the year Osceola was seized at a conference under a flag of truce and sent to Fort Moultrie, at Charleston, where he died in January, 1838. In the following December Colonel Zachary Taylor defeated the Indians in an important battle in Okechobee Swamp, but he was not able to follow the survivors into the recesses of the swamp, and so the war dragged on until the last remnant of re-

The Seminole War.

Osceola.

sistance yielded and the Seminoles finally consented to remove in 1842. Even then a few remained in the everglades of southern Florida, where their descendants are still found. Since the surrender of the fugitive slaves was the chief question at stake, this long and expensive struggle aroused strong criticism from the antislavery men of the North, who denounced the affair as a slaveholders' war.

By this time nearly 125,000 Indians had been induced to cross the Mississippi, either to Indian territory or to the unorganized region of the Northwest. Many small bands remained near their old homes, mere fragments of the older tribes and shorn of all power to resist the advance of the white man's civilization. For the western tribes the reservation system was now well developed. It meant that the government would keep the Indians quiet by distributing rations and blankets, establishing agencies for distribution, regulating the traders who came to monopolize the profitable Indian trade, and restricting as much as possible the sale of spirits to the savages. For these purposes the government spent liberally, and as the reservations were remotely located the system offered rare opportunity for fraud through the collusion of traders, agents, and the contractors who furnished supplies. The system, moreover, lessened the Indian's sense of self-dependence, and offered him little inducement to acquire habits of thrift and industry. It tended to pauperize his spirit and to give him a contempt for the white man's ideals. At this time the lavish expenditure of money on Indian education had not begun.

The Reservation System.

SOCIAL DEVELOPMENT IN THE SOUTH

The lands of the South are of three kinds: 1. Mountainous, extending as far southward as northern Georgia, fertile in itself but heavily timbered and inaccessible. The small valleys between the ridges, popularly know as "coves," fell into the hands of poor men who drifted in from the lowland, and the society that resulted was provincial and unenterprising, but essentially bold and self-sufficient. Here and there was a small town, but the country was generally covered with forest broken at intervals by small clearings. Very few of the inhabitants were slaveholders, and in 1860 they were mostly for the union.

1. The Mountain Region.

2. The Piedmont region, adjacent to the mountains and not adapted to cotton cultivation. The inhabitants were generally small farmers and owned few slaves, many of them none at all. The lands along the infrequent rivers were fertile, and supported large plantations stocked by slaves. But most of the people were poor. Some tobacco was raised, but the isolation of the region made it difficult to market the crop. This was a food-producing section, and most of the large planters in it were rich be-

2. The Piedmont Region.

cause their slaves were fruitful. From 1825 to 1860 there was a steady emigration of the small farmers to the new states of the Northwest.

3. The Atlantic and Gulf coast region, together with the level plains on each side of the Mississippi, was the favored part of the South. All this area produced cotton except the parts lying in Maryland, Virginia, and Kentucky. Throughout **3. The** its entire extent were settled the large planters, rich **Coast** through the labor of the slaves and possessed of an influ- **Region.** ence which gave them control in all matters social and political. A few planters owned as many as a thousand slaves, many owned more than two hundred, but far the larger number owned less than one hundred. The richest planters were men of culture, had handsome estates, and had established an aristocracy which was intended to resemble that of the English country gentry; but the smaller planters were hard-working men who superintended their own farms and gave personal care to the welfare of their own slaves. In 1860 there were 384,000 slaveholders in the South. As these were generally heads of families, and as there were 9,000,000 white people, or about 1,750,000 families, it seems safe to say that four-fifths of the heads of families were not slaveholders. But the other fifth were the men of influence, as men of wealth and intelligence are ever the men of influence.

The non-slaveholders were mostly small farmers; and as one of the social classes they were a large part of the population. They were hard-working men, but as the planters bought the best land whenever it was on the market, and as hired **The Non-** labor was scarce, there was little opportunity for them to **Slave-** better their condition. As the schools were very bad they **holders.** could not educate their children beyond the rudiments of reading and writing. To the visitors from other parts of the world they seemed unintelligent and miserable, but they were neither. They were as keen-witted, honest, and courageous a body of yeomanry as lived in their day; and in the civil war they made excellent soldiers. The term "poor whites" has been applied to this class in a peculiar sense. The South had no more shiftless and lazy men than other communities, and the great mass of small landowners ought not to be designated by such a term. The industry and resourcefulness with which these people restored their fortunes when the abolition of slavery had given them opportunity, shows that they were of the genuine American stock, and were sound in mind and morals.

During the period from 1815 to 1860 slavery concentrated itself in the South. Gradual emancipation reduced the bondsmen in New England from 3763 in 1790 until there were **Disappear-** none in 1850. In the Middle States there were 45,210 in **ance of** 1790 and 1816 in 1860. Of the latter number 1798 were **Slavery in** in Delaware, where the number was gradually falling **the North.** from 8887 in 1790. In the Old Northwest, where a few slaves existed before the famous Ordinance of 1787, and where others were brought in as servants bound for life, the number decreased from 1107 in 1820 until there were none in 1850. In the South, however, there was an increase from 648,651 in 1790 to 3,951,944 in 1860; and this latter number was almost evenly divided between the region reported in the census of 1790 and that not reported until after 1790.

Changes in Southern Slave Population. In the South itself the slaves tended to move to the cotton-growing states. In Maryland there was decrease of 16 per cent from 1830 to 1860, in Virginia the increase was only 4 per cent in the same period, and in North Carolina it was 35 per cent. In Georgia and the Gulf states during the same period the increase was 276 per cent. The increase in the Far South was not merely due to cotton, but to the general prosperity of the farmers in those states. There was, also, a steady development in Kentucky and Missouri in the same period, where farming was profitable without cotton, the increase being 36 per cent in the former and 397 per cent in the latter.

Much was said about the cruelty of masters towards slaves. It is hard to separate this question from the feeling engendered by the bitter discussion of the antislavery and the proslavery parties. Slavery is always a hard institution, and the negro, being unenlightened and submissive by nature, invited severe treatment to induce him to labor hard and refrain from evil conduct. Whipping was used freely, because the masters felt it was the punishment most effective with him. Some masters were benevolent, some were severe and careless of the interests of their slaves, but the typical master considered his slave from the standpoint of efficiency, and fed and clothed him, restrained him from the enervating vices, cared for him in sickness, and afforded him religious instruction with the object of making him a sound, moral, and docile laborer. He did not promote his intellectual development or his sense of self-dependence, since such a course would make the slave wish for freedom. The iron law of slavery was that nothing should be afforded the slave which would weaken the hold of slavery as an institution. The antislavery agitation in the North, by arousing the feeling of the masters, led them to revise the slave codes, and laws now appeared on Southern statute books forbidding slaves to be taught to read and write, prohibiting their assemblage without the presence of a white man, establishing patrols to keep them from traveling the roads without written permission, and restricting them in many other ways.

The first three decades of the century constitute the mildest stage of American slavery. At that time the negro had made a real advance in rudimentary civilization over African barbarism, and the harsher reaction of 1830–1860 had not begun. During this intermediate period there were indications that an ameliorating process had begun. The best Southern opinion openly regretted slavery, manumission was encouraged in the press and on the platform, negroes were taught to read the Bible, and a superior class was forming within the race. In most of the Southern states we hear of negro ministers who preached to congregations of whites and blacks, and in one state at least — North Carolina — was a negro schoolmaster who fitted for the university the sons of the leading white people. Whatever hope was in this softening of slavery into a milder form of service was destroyed by the resentment of the whites against Northern interference. There had always been in the South men who believed a rigid regimen of slaves was necessary, but they were overruled by the more benevolent element. Utilizing the popular resentment against the agitation, they now became the majority, overrode the party of milder measures, and so captured the minds of the rising generation that by 1860 there remained hardly anything of the gentler measures but the fact that slaves were members of the white churches and listened to sermons by white ministers.

How Proslavery Grew in the South.

Nothing could better show how slavery divided the country than to observe how it divided the churches. The Methodist church was essentially a popular organization in the South, as in the North. Its polity provided for bishops who went on circuit to hold the church conferences in all parts of the union. Its earliest efforts in the South embraced work for the slaves, and about 1800 a large part of its members were colored. Soon after this a controversy arose between the Northern and Southern wings over the ownership of slaves by ministers. In 1816 it was decided that ministers should not own slaves in any state in which slaves could be legally emancipated. For many years afterwards peace existed in the church, but the rise of the abolition movement was strongly reflected in the Northern portion of the church, which was the larger part. In 1832 Rev. James O. Andrew, of Georgia, was elected a bishop, one of the recommendations being that he was a Southern man who did not own slaves. In January, 1844, he married a woman who owned slaves, and in the following May the general conference of the church resolved that he should "desist from the exercise of his office so long as the impediment remains." The vote was the occasion of a long and warm debate, in which the Southern members freely predicted that it would end in the disruption of the church. It was carried almost entirely on sectional grounds. Immediately the Southerners took steps to form a Southern Methodist church, and a plan looking to amicable division was adopted. In formal resolutions the Southerners declared that if they had submitted to the censure of their bishop, the position of the church in the South would have been damaged; and in other resolutions the Northern members declared that if they had tolerated a bishop tainted with

Slavery Divides the Churches.

slaveholding, the church would have lost strength in the North, all of which shows how deeply this large portion of the population had become divided on the question of slavery.

The division of the Methodists into two bodies attracted the attention of the country. Clay, in deprecating it, said: "I will not say that such a separation would necessarily produce a dissolution of the political union of these states; but the example would be fraught with imminent danger, and, in coöperation with other causes unfortunately existing, its tendency on the stability of the confederacy would be perilous and alarming." The effect was seen immediately in the Baptist churches, which though congregational in polity, were united in a general convention. The board of missions had ruled that slaveholders would not be appointed missionaries, and in 1845 the Southern conventions began to withdraw, setting up in the same year the Southern Baptist convention. The Presbyterian and Protestant Episcopal churches remained undivided. McCormick, the inventor of the reaper, used to say that the Presbyterian church and the democratic party, to both of which he belonged, were "the two hoops which hold the union together." But in May, 1861, the assembly of the former body adopted a resolution offered by Dr. Gardiner Spring, of New York, its most eminent member, pledging the church to support the union, and the result was the Southern presbyteries withdrew their allegiance, and in August, 1861, met and founded the "Presbyterian Church of the Confederate States of America." The Protestant Episcopal church took nearly the same attitude. The Southern dioceses, after some preliminary steps, met in October, 1861, and organized the Protestant Episcopal Church of the Confederate States of America. The Northern branch of the church did not recognize the division, and in its convention during the war continued to call the names of the absent bishops. With the downfall of the confederacy the Southern branch was abandoned and the Southern dioceses were again represented in the conventions of the Protestant Episcopal Church of America. The separate organization of the other churches continued after the war, for the spirit of division had become too deep in them to permit early reunion.

THE DEVELOPMENT OF DEMOCRACY IN STATE AND NATION

All of the thirteen states of revolutionary days incorporated in their constitutions some of the British ideals of colonial days. For example, none of the states provided for absolute manhood suffrage. Four states, New Hampshire, Pennsylvania, Delaware, and South Carolina, were willing to allow the suffrage to all taxpayers; but all the others had some property requirement for voters who chose one or both branches of the assemblies. Some of the states required that the officials should be

Suffrage in the Original States.

property holders, others, distrusting popular elections, provided that governor, chief executive officers, and judges should be chosen by the assemblies. Much as these restrictions may seem out of place, they left the suffrage more liberal in the United States than in most other countries.

Soon after the adoption of the national constitution the spirit of democracy began to make itself felt, and state after state modified some of the restrictive features of its constitution. In this the action of the new states, always more democratic than the old, was very influential. Vermont showed the way by establishing manhood suffrage in her first constitution, and Kentucky soon afterwards did the same. Ohio, admitted in 1803, enfranchised taxpayers, but after her each state adopted manhood suffrage and elected the governor by popular vote. Along with this came demands for reforms in the old states. Delaware, Maryland, and New Jersey had yielded to the reformers by the end of 1810, and other old states were deeply agitated over the matter The reformers were called Jacobins, and much was declaimed about the dangers lurking in wild and demagogic theories. In Connecticut, where the charter of colonial days was now the constitution, the oligarchy was very powerful. Seven men, the majority of the council, had in their hands the control of the state. In 1818, after a long struggle, was adopted a new constitution, far more liberal than the old, although it still lacked something of real democracy and equality.

Extending the Suffrage.

The wave of reform next reached New York, where conditions were astonishingly bad. Only freeholders and renters of tenements could vote, and by this means more than 50,000 leaseholders were excluded from the ballot. A council of appointment, consisting of five members, named more than 15,000 officials in all parts of the state, and had become as flagrant a political machine as ever existed in this land. There was also a council of revision, the governor and supreme judges among its members, which had vetoed so many laws that it had virtually made itself a third house of the assembly. Against this system arose such a clamor that the defenders of the old condition were overwhelmed, and a constitutional convention met in 1821. It quickly swept away the councils of appointment and revision, and a hard fight followed to abolish the last vestige of property qualification. No opposition was made so far as the choice of governor and members of the house went; but the conservatives rallied when it came to choice of senators. Much was said about the sacredness of property, the incompetence of the propertyless class, and the horrors of the French revolution. The best leader on this side was Chancellor Kent, who added to his lawyer's instinct for conservatism a splendid mind and a weighty reputation. Against him the chief leader was Martin Van Buren, just elected a federal senator. His plea for no property qualification was effective.

The Reform in New York.

and thus the reform program, with some finishing strokes in 1826, was completed in New York. In Massachusetts, in 1820, a constitutional convention abolished the property basis for voters but retained it for senators.

In Virginia the privileged class was fortified behind property qualifications and an allotment of legislative seats by which the small slaveholding counties of the East outvoted the large and populous counties of the West. Large numbers of the men of the latter section became so discouraged through the long futile fight for equality that they moved away to the Northwest, where privilege was unknown. At last the eyes of the Easterners were opened, and a convention was called for 1829. The results of its deliberation was an extension of the suffrage, but a moderate property basis was retained. There was, also, a reallotment of seats in the assembly, but it was so made that the slaveholding East retained control. In 1850, however, manhood suffrage was secured. Slavery was a strong support of privilege, and where it existed the march of democracy was slow. In 1835 North Carolina made important amendments to her constitution, one of them being the popular election of the governor, but the property qualification was not touched. In a nine years' struggle, 1848 to 1857, it was, however, carried through, and equal suffrage was established. The property basis was abandoned by Delaware in 1831, by Mississippi in 1832, by Georgia in 1833 and 1835, and by Tennessee in 1834. During this period of constitutional change many other reforms were made by the states, one of the most important being that religious tests for voting or holding office should be given up, and in many states popular election of judges was adopted.

Reform in Virginia.

It has often been said that Jackson established democracy, but it would be more accurate to say that from 1820 there was a great popular movement toward democracy, and that he became its exponent. He did much to guide it, but it existed before he was a presidential candidate, and his successes were based upon its power. He furnished a rallying point for the new movement, and his bold attacks on the older political leaders broke their rule and called into national and state offices men who were in sympathy with the democratic spirit of the day.

Jackson and the Democratic Reform.

The state which held most tenaciously to the old system was Rhode Island. Her constitution was the old colonial charter, liberal in its time, but it limited the franchise to freeholders. The rise of manufactures introduced a large operative class who were not property holders. Then followed a contest to change the old system, but the property owners of the cities in alliance with the landowners of the country were too strong for the operative class. Yet the demand for reform would not down. It found an active and persistent leader in Thomas W. Dorr, who announced that the people had an

The Struggle in Rhode Island — Thomas W. Dorr.

inalienable right to participate in government. The "log-cabin" campaign of 1840, which was a popular movement, stimulated them to most vigorous agitation. Great mass-meetings and parades occurred in Providence, Newport, and elsewhere, and the plainest hints of violence were given. The legislature finally ordered a convention, but it was to be chosen by the existing voters, and the disfranchised party would not accept it. They accordingly called a convention of their own, which prepared a constitution and submitted it to the people. It received 13,944 votes in an election held in the closing days of 1841. This instrument was called the "People's Constitution." The strong following of Dorr now alarmed the old party, who, in the convention ordered by the legislature, prepared a constitution known as the "Freemen's Constitution." When this came before the people it received 8013 affirmative, and 8689 negative, votes, and was declared lost. The most important difference between the two instruments was that the former provided for white manhood suffrage and the latter required one year's residence for landowners, two years for natives who were not landowners, and three years after naturalization for foreign-born citizens.

Since their own constitution had more votes than that of their rivals, the Dorr party now announced that their scheme was law, and ordered an election for governor and legislature. The existing legislature pronounced such a step illegal, the governor issued a proclamation against it, and he called on President Tyler for aid against threatened rebellion. Dorr's Appeal to Force. Tyler replied that he could do nothing until violence had begun. Thus the election was held, Dorr was selected for governor, an assembly was chosen, and May 3, 1842, the People's Government went through the forms of an inauguration. For two weeks Dorr essayed the part of governor, while his assembly made "laws" for the state of Rhode Island. Outside of the state the whigs generally flouted him, but the democrats gave him much support, and great meetings in sympathy with his struggle for liberal suffrage were held in Philadelphia and New York. May 18 came a conflict between Dorr and the rival governor. The latter was about to arm the members of his party when Dorr marched on the arsenal with cannon, but was kept from actual violence because the pieces would not fire. His action frightened away the courage of most of his supporters, who deserted him in shoals, and he fled with a handful of companions to Woonsocket, followed by whig shouts of derision. In the following summer he returned to Rhode Island and fortified himself in the northwestern part of the state. The militia were sent against him, but his followers fled again. Many were arrested, but he escaped. Returning a year later he was arrested, tried for treason, and sentenced to jail for life. He did not serve the term. His followers had made so plain an exhibition of strength that the conservatives relented and called a convention which adopted a liberal constitution, and in 1845 Dorr was set at liberty.   To his efforts, right or wrong, the new constitution was chiefly due.   The victory of democracy in Rhode Island wiped out the last considerable vestige of landed privilege.   Traces did, indeed, remain in a few states, but they were eventually removed from the constitutions, the last of them by the new constitutions established in the South in reconstruction days.

THE PROGRESS OF EDUCATION

While liberal suffrage advanced in the old states, educational reform, equally democratic, was also in full course of development.

Origin of the Educational Movement. Schools were early established in every colony, but usually on a private basis, and frequently under church supervision.   The ability to read the Bible was essential in general religious instruction, and the spread of intelligence was bound up with sound morals, so it was natural that the churches as promoters of moral ideals should have felt themselves responsible for the people's attitude toward education.   But where government was intrusted to the competent, as was the case professedly out of New England, there was little feeling that every man must be educated by the government in order that he might properly exercise his function of citizenship.

It is hard to say whether the educational impulse in early New England was chiefly religious or political.   The two functions were closely related, and we may well say they acted jointly.   Massa-

Schools in Massachusetts. chusetts took the lead, passing in 1647 an act which has been called "the mother of all our school laws."   It ordered each town of fifty families to support an elementary school, and each of a hundred families to support a grammar school under penalty of fine.   The teachers were to be appointed and paid by the people and were to teach all children who came to them.   It was not always enforced, especially as regards grammar schools, but it remained an ideal throughout the colonial period, and in 1789 a comprehensive act was passed, the terms of which show how far public education was developed.   The towns were divided into districts, with a school in each supported by the public; towns of 200 families were to have grammar schools.   Teachers were to be college graduates or to have certificates of attainments from "learned ministers," and the selectmen were to see that the schools were well taught and that the children attended.   This act was in force with little amendment for nearly fifty years.

In 1837 Massachusetts created a state board of education, and Horace Mann was appointed its secretary.   This was one of the remarkable educational reforms in the century.   The old district school no longer served the wants of the community.   Incompetent teachers had been appointed by officials interested in local politics, there were no trained superintendents of teachers, and the amount of money spent on education was proportionally small. Within the past half century the state had grown rich. Horace Mann realized that the old district system was insufficient, and assumed the task of making it modern. He was in **Work of Horace Mann.** office twelve years, and when he retired trained superintendents of schools existed in the towns, appropriations were liberal, normal schools had been established, the school term was lengthened to six months, and many other progressive features were added to the system. He succeeded because of his earnestness and capability. He traveled and spoke much, and wherever he went he left his impress on others. It was largely through his efforts for the schools that a revival of town libraries spread throughout the state. His achievement was truly statesmanlike. He found the school system of Massachusetts large, well meant, and rather formless: he gave it that cohesion and energy which in the political phase of society makes the state a living thing.

The Middle states had many schools from the earliest colonial periods, but the impulse was religious or individual, rarely public. The Dutch made a good beginning in New York, but there was decline of interest with the conquest of the province by the British. It was not until after the revo- **Schools in the Middle States.** lution that the state seems to have realized its duty in public education; and then we find land granted in the western counties and assistance voted to educate poor children in the schools already established in the eastern parts of the state. Throughout the years 1815 and 1860 these states were gradually perfecting school systems, many laws being necessary before a satisfactory result was obtained. It was not until 1849 that the New York system was well established. The same result was achieved for Pennsylvania in a law of 1854; for New Jersey it did not come until 1867, and for Delaware not until 1875.

Efforts to establish public schools were made in the South early in the nineteenth century. They resulted in "free schools," poorly taught for short periods, and designed only for the poor. The children of the well-to-do went to private schools, which were numerous. Among the older Southern states **Public Schools in the South.** the best "free school" system was probably in North Carolina, which was the most democratic of the Southern states. Little more interest was shown in the newer states of the Gulf region. Texas, however, made liberal land grants to her school system, and Tennessee and Florida received lands for the same purpose from the federal government. It was not until after the civil war that the former slave states established an efficient public school system.

While public education thus slowly won its way in the Middle and Southern states, it secured and maintained a more vigorous position in the Middle West.   Three causes are to be noted : 1. The

Public Schools in the West.   generous gifts of land by the national government; 2. The wide diffusion of New Englanders in this region; and 3. The conviction of the Westerners that schools attracted desirable immigrants.   The lands given by the federal authority for education went to the states, which determined their use, some going to the common public schools, some to academies, and some to state universities, which dated from the early days of settlement.   State aid was supplemented by funds derived from local taxes and state laws provided the administrative machinery.

Preceding the rise of the public common school came a movement for academies.   This type of school abounded among the English dissenters of the eighteenth century.   Its curriculum

The Academy.   covered from three to five years, and embraced Latin, Greek, philosophy, with a smattering of Hebrew, science, and sometimes theology.   It fell in readily with the condition of the non-conformists who had no standing in the universities and were not found in the great public schools.   It held a place between preparatory school and university, and was pronounced superficial by those who held to the old classical schools.

It is not strange that this kind of school was easily established in America, where dissenters were in the majority and where the thorough ideals of European instruction had not yet taken deep hold.

The Era of Academies in the United States.   Sometimes an academy grew out of the efforts of a devoted and generous family, as Phillips Academy, at Andover, Massachusetts, founded in 1778.   High-grade academies existed in most of the states and served excellently in preparing boys for college.   But with the beginning of the nineteenth century came an era of rosy dreams of future developments. Most extreme in the West and South, it was nevertheless well defined in the North, and one of its results was an abundant crop of academies. This sporadic growth stood for much real interest, and spite of the failures many useful institutions survived.   In 1850 there were 6085 academies in the United States, and they had 263,096 pupils.

During the years 1820 to 1860 as many as 174 colleges and universities were founded in the United States, 80 of which were in the North Central, and 52 in the Southern, states.   Many of them

Many Colleges Founded.   were founded by churches, and many others represented the ambition of new communities with anticipations of future growth and culture.   The law of the survival of the fittest has brought to an early grave a great number of these institutions, but others have survived and reached positions of wide usefulness.   Not all were wisely founded, but who shall decry the earnest hope that gave them their beginning!

It was in this period that the state university took form.   The older ideal of a college or university in America was a place at which men were fitted for the ministry, law, or another learned pro- **The State** fession.   Its studies were strictly arranged in groups, a **University.** thing long traditional in Europe.   The students were from the upper class of society, and there was generally some kind of ecclesiastical oversight.   Two tendencies, one domestic and one foreign, operated against this idea about 1800.   One was the prevalence of philosophic doubt in the first generation after the revolution.   At the same time the French educational system was reorganized on a rationalistic basis, and the university of Berlin was established under the guidance of Fichte.   Such wonderfully important movements at home and in Europe could not fail to have a corresponding phase in American education.

The process was first seen in the founding of state universities in North Carolina, Tennessee, Georgia, and South Carolina, and in the reorganization of the University of Pennsylvania on a state basis, all of which occurred between 1779 and 1815.   At **Jefferson** this time the movement took a more definite shape at the **and the** hands of Jefferson, equally devoted to democracy and **of Virginia.** liberal thought.   He gave much of his later life to the task of remodeling higher education in Virginia.   He first wished to remake William and Mary College on the secular plan, but failing in that turned to the task of founding a new institution.   In 1818 the legislature approved, and in 1825 the University of Virginia opened its doors.   Jefferson was head of the commission which prepared its plan, head of its first board of visitors, and his colleagues allowed him to have his way in all that pertained to the university.   It began with an elective system, and opened its doors without examinations to all who came, rejecting after trial those who showed themselves unprepared for its classes.   All this was a part of the author's plan for a thoroughly democratic institution.

The influence of the University of Virginia was strong in the newer states of the West and Southwest.   It extended, however, more to the form and democratic spirit of the university than to the method of instruction.   In regard to the latter, the New **Western** England influence has been strong, at least in the West.   **State** The complete separation of the university from church **Universities.** control gave rise to the charge that Jefferson's university was hostile to religion.   A warm controversy sprang up in Virginia, and has appeared in most other states where the state university has been introduced.   As a result, the churches founded institutions of their own for the education of their own youth.   The controversy has not disappeared in many states to this day.

During the period of Western and Southwestern expansion the older institutions of the Northeast developed hardly as much as might have been expected.   Largely devoted to preparing men for the professions, most of their students came from the leisure class in the North and South.   The condition is well shown in the history of Harvard College, the oldest of them all.   In 1836, its two hundredth

Progress in Northeastern Colleges.

anniversary year, there were 233 students in the college proper, and in 1856 there were 382.   But the law and medical schools were well attended, having in the latter year 231 students, with 57 in the Lawrence Scientific School, which was founded in 1848.   The Divinity School had in 1856 only 22 students. It seems unquestionable that the establishment of new colleges and universities during this period operated to lessen the numbers who would otherwise have gone to the older institutions.   The rapid growth of the Eastern seats of learning, with which the present generation is so familiar, came after the civil war.

The spread of intelligence brought about a movement to reform manners.   Attention was especially directed to the misuse of spirituous liquors, which early in the century were generally used

The Temperance Movement.

by all classes.   Total abstinence societies began to be formed about 1824, and in five years more than a thousand had been organized.   Zealous preachers of temperance went into every part of the country, with the result that many people were enlisted in the movement.   In 1830 the temperance organizations began to be known as Washington societies.   After years of agitation the movement began to work for the prohibition of the sale and manufacture of spirituous liquors.   By 1850 several states were in active commotion over the question.   Only one of them, however, carried the demand to success.   Through the leadership of Neal Dow, Maine, by several laws culminating in 1851, committed herself to prohibition.

GOLD IN CALIFORNIA

January 24, 1848, yellow particles were observed in the sand on the exposed bottom of a mill race on the American river.   Workmen

The Discovery.

washed out a portion of the earth and secured three ounces of gold dust, and investigation showed gold along the whole length of the river.   The secret was kept for a few weeks and then spread throughout California.   In May a Mormon walked along the San Francisco streets with a bottle of gold dust in his hand shouting: "Gold! Gold! Gold from the American river!" Previous reports of the discovery had attracted little interest, but the sight of the yellow metal was electrical on the population of the town. At the end of a month hardly an ablebodied man remained there. Ships anchoring in the harbor were left without crews, the two newspapers suspended because typesetters had fled, and the streets were lined with closed shops.

Late in the autumn the news reached the East, where it spread like wildfire. Companies of adventurers were formed, ships were hastily bought, and by the end of the year every important Atlantic seaport had sent out its fleet for the "Land of Gold." When spring came, the western frontier was filled with great caravans waiting for good weather to begin a long and dangerous journey to the same destination. More *The "Rush" to California, 1849.* than 20,000 persons set out by this route with their cattle and provisions, and encountered much hardship before they arrived on the Western coast as winter closed in. How many arrived this year is difficult to say, but in 1850 the population of California was 92,597, which was more than that of either Delaware or Florida. San Francisco became a city of rude huts and tents, filled with speculators and travelers hurrying to the mines. A town meeting fixed the price of gold dust at sixteen dollars an ounce, and it became the money of the coast. Wages became exorbitant, a carpenter getting sixteen, and an unskilled laborer ten, dollars a day. Gamblers and worse men abounded, and violence was frequent. But the majority of the immigrants were average Americans, strong in the instinct of self-government, and the result showed that they were not willing to allow the unruly element to dominate the country. The only authority established by law was military, and it could not be exercised in the many camps and towns that sprang up wherever there was gold. Nor could it well exercise the ordinary functions of courts in the protection of life and property. Appeals for a settled government were sent to congress, but the slavery question arose there, and for a while nothing could be done (see page 453).

The first move for self-government was expressed in miners' committees or mass-meetings, which dealt with disorders and settled disputes. This suggested a wider organization; and in September, 1849, at the call of General Riley, the *de facto* civil governor, a convention assembled at Monterey and made a constitution excluding slavery, establishing laws of property, fixing the bounds of California as at present, and providing a *A Government Established.* full state government. Before the year ended a governor, a legislature, two representatives in congress, and two senators had been duly chosen. The state officers immediately entered on their duties and the legislature took up the task of lawmaking, but the senators and representatives, who repaired to Washington, were kept waiting until the compromise of 1850 was completed; and it was not until September 9 of that year that California at last became a state.

Nor did statehood bring good order at once. So deeply was the old habit of lawlessness implanted that the state officials could not easily secure control of the situation. Robberies, murders, and other outrages abounded, and the people, turning aside from the slow process of law, openly expressed their contempt for lawyers and judges, and

21

frequently took into their own hands the task of repressing crime and disposing of criminals.   The presence of many persons of Spanish-American birth stimulated this spirit of violence.   They were suspected, hated, and mistreated.   Sometimes they deserved nothing good, sometimes they were innocent of evildoing.   Originally the miners were generally men of average peacefulness, but the excitement of the day, the tendency to heavy drinking and quarreling, overcame good impulses, and the years following the settlement of the state were a period of chaos, out of which the best men could see no better road to good order than vigilance committees, which too often expressed the mere rage of the mob.   But as the communities became settled, and as capital became fixed in mining, real estate, and commerce, the conservative element triumphed.   The turbulent class went on to the newer mines in the distant mountains, leaving peace behind them. By 1858 the area of order embraced most of the state.

Lawless-ness Yields Slowly.

Vigilance Committees.

THE PANIC OF 1857

The discovery of gold in California and elsewhere in the West together with the rapid increase of the money supply promoted the spirit of speculation.   Railroads were built through sparsely settled regions from which for a time it was impossible to get enough revenue to pay dividends.   Manufactures were stimulated, and increased their output beyond reasonable demands.   To support this vast volume of business the banks lent freely, straining their own resources to the utmost.   In fact, it was one of those "boom" periods with which our industrial history is filled, the inevitable end of which is reaction.   It was facilitated by the loose state-banking system, under which the banks, eager for profits, assumed impossible burdens in order to lend at high rates to railroads, manufacturers, and speculators of every kind.

A Wave of Prosperity.

In 1857 the bubble could expand no further.   Speculators could not sell their lands and bonds at a profit.   The Western banks from which they had borrowed began to fail, and this communicated the shock to the Eastern banks from which the Western banks had secured funds, and a general panic reigned. Generally speaking, the banks of Baltimore, Philadelphia, and New York closed their doors, and those of New England suspended specie payment.   With a few exceptions, those of the West failed completely. Thousands of depositors were ruined, and legitimate business was at a standstill.   Factories closed, labor was out of employment, the prices of agricultural products dropped, and fourteen railroads failed completely.

The Panic of 1857.

The West suffered most; for at this time the Crimean war was ended, and a large area was thrown open to wheat cultivation, on account of which the price of that commodity fell from $2 to 75 cents a bushel, entailing ruin to producers and all who depended on them. The South, on the other hand, felt the panic less heavily; for its staple, cotton, was still in demand at former prices. The South- **Area of** erners, observing their advantage, felt more confidence **Panic.** than ever in their assertion, "Cotton is King."

So far as the banks were concerned, the spasm was of short duration. By the spring of 1858 most of them had resumed specie payment, and were cautiously lending money to the traders and manufacturers who were still carrying on business. But this **Recovery** year and that which followed were years of "hard times," **from the** and it was not until 1860 that industry was again in a **Panic.** normal condition. This panic, like all the others in our history, was only a readjustment of temporarily inflated business. Beneath its swirling current was the firm surface of immense economic resources.

Probably the most permanent result was the unexpected impulse it gave to protection. Just before the crash the tariff had been lowered because of the unusually large sums derived from the great volume of imports. But with slackening business came a reduction of imports, and with that a deficit in the national treasury. Notes were issued and bonds sold in the hope that the want would be temporary. But through the years of "hard times" importations continued reduced and the minds of men began to turn toward higher duties. Suffering manufacturers seized the moment to ask for greater protection, and the two forces combined to secure the Morrill Tariff, which failed to pass the senate in 1860, but became law early in 1861 after several Southern senators had withdrawn. It restored most of the rates of 1846 and made others higher.

BIBLIOGRAPHICAL NOTE

Few monographic studies have been made in the social development of our country during this period. McMaster, *History of the People of the United States*, vols. IV–VII (1895–1910), contains in several chapters the most valuable general account. See also Schouler, *History of the United States*, 6 vols. (1880–1894); and C. R. Fish, *The Rise of the Common Man* (1928). The first volume of J. F. Rhodes, *History of the United States from the Compromise of 1850*, 8 vols. (1893–1919), contains an account of American society in the fifties; and much material on Western and Southern society is scattered through A. J. Beveridge, *Abraham Lincoln, 1809–1858*, 2 vols. (1928). A thoughtful discussion is Leroy-Beaulieu, *The United States in the Twentieth Century* (trans. by Bruce, 1906).

On the growth and distribution of population one must consult the statistics of the census bureau, but for practical purposes they are well summed up in its bulletin entitled, *A Century of Population Growth* (1909). Immigration in general is discussed by R. Mayo Smith, *Emigration and Immigration* (1890). For the opposition to immigrants see McMaster, *History of the People of the United States*, vol. VII, pages 369–384; Scisco, *Political Nativism in New York* (1901); and Schmeckebier, *The Know-Nothing Party in Maryland* (1898).

On the influence of great inventions see: E. W. Byrn, *The Progress of Invention in the Nineteenth Century* (1900); Doolittle, *Inventions of the Century* (1903); Waldemar Kaempffert, ed., *A Popular History of American Invention*, 2 vols. (1924);

Johnson, *American Railway Transportation* (1903); J. W. Starr, *One Hundred Years of American Railroading* (1928); M. F. Miller, *Evolution of Reaping Machines* (1902); Wells, *Our Merchant Marine* (1890); Bates, *The American Marine* (1897); A. H. Clark, *The Clipper Ship Era* (1912); and J. V. Woodworth, *American Tool-Making* (1911).

Our relations with the Indians have not yet been fully described. A good brief manual is Flora Warren Seymour, *The Story of the Red Man* (1929). The student may well use McMaster's volumes in connection with the official collection called *Indian Affairs, Laws and Treaties*, vol. II (Kappler's ed., 1904). Very valuable is Miss Abel, *Indian Consolidation West of the Mississippi* (Am. Hist. Assn. *Report*, 1906). On the Black Hawk War see T. C. Pease, *The Frontier State* (Centennial Hist. of Illinois, vol. II, 1918); Ford, *History of Illinois* (1854); Thwaites, *Story of the Black Hawk War* (Wis. Hist. Soc. *Collections*, vol. XII); and McCall, *Letters from the Frontier*, (1868) which bears also on the Seminole War. On the war in Florida see Fairbanks, *History of Florida* (new ed., 1898).

Much has been written about the society of the South. Two indispensable books are Ulrich B. Phillips, *American Negro Slavery* (1918), and *Life and Labor in the Old South* (1929). W. E. Dodd, *The Cotton Kingdom* (1919) is an illuminating short volume. The best approach to English travels in the South is through Allan Nevins, *American Social History as Recorded by British Travellers* (1923). The best books of travel by a Northerner are F. L. Olmsted's *A Journey in the Seaboard Slave States* (1856), *A Journey through Texas* (1857), and *A Journey to the Back Country* (1861). Among other volumes are some delightful memoirs: Mrs. Pryor, *Reminiscences of Peace and War* (1904); Mrs. Clayton, *Black and White under the Old Régime* (1899); and Mrs. Smedes, *Memorials of a Southern Planter* (1900). See also Ingle, *Southern Sidelights* (1896); Hammond, *The Cotton Industry* (1897); Brooks, *The Story of Cotton* (1911); and Hurd, *Law of Freedom and Bondage*, 2 vols. (1858–1862), which contains summaries of statutes affecting slaves and free negroes.

On the development of democracy see: Dodd, *Revision and Amendment of State Constitutions* (1910); Borgeaud, *Adoption and Amendment of Constitution* (1895, trans. by Hazen); Lobingur, *The People's Law* (1909); Oberhaltzer, *Referendum in America* (ed. 1911); Poore, *Federal and State Constitutions*, 2 vols. (1877); Thorpe, *American Charters, Constitutions, and Original Laws*, 7 vols. (1909), contains errors and should be used with caution. See also: Mowry, *The Dorr War* (1901); King, *Life of Thomas W. Dorr* (1859); and McMaster, *History of the People of the United States*, vol. V, 373–394.

Educational progress is shown in: Boone, *Education in the United States* (1889); Dexter, *History of Education in the United States* (1904); E. E. Brown, *Making of Our Middle Schools* (1907); Martin, *Evolution of the Massachusetts Public School System* (1894); Weeks, *Beginnings of the Common School System in the South* (U. S. Comsr. Education, *Report*, 1896–1897); H. B. Adams, editor, 33 monographs on history of education in various states, issued as *Circulars of Information* by the Commissioner of Education (1887–1902); H. B. Adams, *Thomas Jefferson and the University of Virginia* (1888); and Hinsdale, *Horace Mann and the Common School Revival* (1898).

On the discovery of gold in California and the conditions which followed see: Hittell, *History of California*, 4 vols. (1886–1897); Bancroft, *History of California*, 7 vols. (1884–1890); Willey, *Thirty Years in California* (1879), good for early social conditions; Shinn, *Mining Camps* (1885), very suggestive; and Letts, *California Illustrated* (1852).

For Independent Reading

Bayard Taylor, *Eldorado* (1850); Mowry, *The Dorr War* (1901): Mrs. Pryor, *Reminiscences of Peace and War* (1904); Mrs. Clayton, *Black and White under the Old Régime* (1899); Hubbard, *Memorials of a Half Century* (1887), deals with experiences in the Old Northwest; *Four American Universities*, by Professor Norton and others (1895), deals with Harvard, Yale, Columbia, and Princeton; and Olmstead, *A Journey in the Seaboard Slave States* (new ed., 1904).

CHAPTER XXIII

EVENTS LEADING TO THE CIVIL WAR, 1850–1860

OVERTHROWING THE COMPROMISE OF 1850

CONSERVATIVE men North and South wished the compromise of 1850 to be final. Politicians, business men, and conservatives generally hoped it would remove the slavery question from politics and introduce an era of harmony. In April, 1852, the house of representatives adopted a resolution to that effect by a vote of 103 to 74, and the democratic convention of the same year enthusiastically resolved to accept the compromise as final and to resist any attempt to renew the slavery agitation. In the whig convention a similar resolution was adopted, with 66 dissenting votes, all of which came from the North, and were from men who supported Scott as party leader. *Finality of the Compromise.*

The democrats had much trouble to name a candidate. For forty-eight ballots fortune leaned in turn to Cass, the defeated candidate of 1848, to Buchanan, of Pennsylvania, to Marcy, of New York, and to Stephen A. Douglas, a brilliant senator from Illinois who had just completed his thirty-ninth year and for whom his admirers predicted the highest honors. On the thirty-fifth ballot Franklin Pierce, of New Hampshire, was brought forward by Virginia as a "dark horse," and on the forty-ninth he received the nomination, William R. King, of Alabama, being named for vice-president. The whigs also had their difficulties, but General Winfield Scott won on the fifty-third ballot, taking the honors from Webster and Fillmore, through a combination of the Southern whigs with the Northern wing of the party under Seward, who led a large group of men opposed to the fugitive slave law, a part of the great compromise. William A. Graham, of North Carolina, was nominated for the vice-presidency. The free soil party nominated John P. Hale, of New Hampshire, and denied the finality of the compromise. *Nominations.*

The only important issue in the campaign that followed was keeping the compromise. Scott was pledged to it, but he was supported by those who would be glad to see it overthrown. Pierce, it was not doubted, was sincerely for it, while Hale repudiated it altogether. The results showed how much it was desired by the people. The democratic candidates received 254 electoral votes, the whigs had 42, carrying Massachusetts, Vermont, Kentucky, and Tennessee, and the free soilers had none. Hale had only half as *The Election.*

485

many votes as Van Buren got in 1848, and this was taken to show that the cause of political abolition was declining.

Pierce took office amid the plaudits of the citizens. He was a handsome man and knew how to conciliate his opponents. Could he not perpetuate the spirit of compromise, if any man could?

Pierce's Cabinet. Yet his cabinet appointments aroused apprehensions. Dix, of New York, who was a free soiler in 1848, was denied a position after it had been offered him, and the reason for the change of intention was his unpopularity with the South. Jefferson Davis, of Mississippi, was made secretary of war, and Caleb Cushing, of Massachusetts, a warm friend of Davis, became attorney-general. Moreover, the inaugural address hinted pretty plainly at the acquisition of Cuba, a thing much desired by the slaveholders. It was not long before whisperers began to say that the administration was under Southern domination.

This seemed ominous for the spirit of compromise, but a still more threatening thing was the hostility of many Northern people to the execution of the fugitive slave law. In the two and a half years since the law passed nearly every fugitive arrested in the North had been taken by a mob from the hands of the federal marshal and spirited away to freedom. In Syracuse, New York, Gerrit Smith and the Rev. Samuel J. May led a mob of respectable men who forcibly rescued a negro, Jerry McHenry, from the hands of an assembled court and smuggled him into Canada; and they were not punished. These affairs, which occurred before the election of 1852, aroused the moderates North and South and went far to secure the large democratic majority of that year. They were, however, not forgotten, and the extremists of both sides predicted freely that the fugitive slave law, which the South considered its only gain in the great compromise, could not be enforced.

But it was slavery in the territories, and not the rendition of fugitives, that kindled anew the slumbering fires of strife. The unorganized Nebraska country west of Missouri and Iowa became important as soon as the Oregon question came up; and the migration to California and the plans proposed for a railroad to the Pacific gave it added interest. Attempts to have it made a territory had been defeated by the slavery men, because under the Missouri compromise it would be free. The Missourians themselves, though much desiring that the territory be erected, would not demand it as a home of freedom. Senator Atchison, leading the slavery party in that state, declared that he would "see Nebraska sunk in hell before he would vote for it as a free soil territory"; and he helped defeat a Nebraska bill in 1853. In the summer of that year his seat in the senate was being contested, and his opponents boldly charged him with neglecting the interests of Missouri. To make Nebraska slave, it was said, he was sacrificing the opportunity to have St. Louis the terminus of the Pacific railroad and excluding Missourians from the rich lands to the west. It was a hard blow, and he met it by a change of front. He would never see Nebraska free soil, he now said, but he would vote to make it a territory on condition that the people who settled there could decide for themselves the question of slavery or freedom. This, it was pointed out, was what had been done for Utah and New Mexico in 1850. The discussion in Missouri was warm throughout the summer of 1853, and just before congress met in December, it was taken up by the democratic papers of the East. The antislavery men could hardly believe what they read when they saw a prediction that a bill would be introduced in congress to create Nebraska territory under the plan just described. They did not take the prophecy seriously, and pointed out that the proposed step repealed the compromise of 1820 and overthrew the harmony established in 1850.

Events showed they were mistaken. In December, 1853, an Iowa senator introduced a bill to create Nebraska territory. It went to the committee on territories, S. A. Douglas, chairman. January 5 it came from committee, Atchison's slavery proposition engrafted on it. The change was made with the consent of Douglas, whose motive is a matter of dispute. *The Kansas-Nebraska Act, 1854.*

He favored a new territory in the region through which the proposed Pacific road would run, and he may have adopted Atchison's idea because he saw it was the only way to get the support of the Southerners. On the other hand, he wished to be president, and as his opponents charged, he may have merely sought Southern support to that end. He was a self-made man, with some crudeness of manner, spite of his great forensic ability, and more than once had been made to realize that he was not popular with the Southern members. He now showed them how much he could serve them. Holding together in a solid phalanx all who wished the railroad built, those who desired the territory for its own sake, those faithful friends who wished to see him advanced to the presidency, and above all the willing Southerners, he forced his bill through both houses and made it a law. Before it passed it underwent an important amendment. Two territories, instead of one, were now provided for, it being a return to the old parallelism by which was preserved the balance of free and slave states. Kansas, the more southern of the two, it was expected, would be settled by slaveholders, and Nebraska by non-slaveholders. A clause in the bill when finally passed specifically repealed the Missouri compromise.

Douglas expected a hard fight from the antislavery men, but he had arguments to meet them. The bill, he said, was the only practicable way to get the territory created, and the North need not be alarmed, since slavery could not live in the region concerned. If one spoke of violation of the compromise of 1850 the reply was that the bill did not violate, but only confirmed, the *Its Significance.*

compromise; for did it not apply to Kansas and Nebraska exactly the principle applied to Utah and New Mexico? For all this, it was as plain as a barn door that the bill was a defeat for the antislavery party, that it opened to slavery territory which the compromise of 1820 dedicated to freedom, and that the proslavery party won a victory which would give slavery its share in the unsettled Northwest, unless natural conditions proved too hard for it. Though Douglas carried his measure through congress, a great wave of protest was aroused out of congress, and from 1854 all thought of the finality of the compromise of 1850 was abandoned.

Douglas called his doctrine "popular sovereignty," since it announced the right of the people in the territory to settle the vexed question for themselves. His enemies with a tinge of contempt called it "squatter sovereignty," a term which immediately had an extensive use. The most striking early effect of his move was that some Northern democrats would not vote for his bill, or support him afterwards. They held together, and were known as "Anti-Nebraska" democrats.

"Popular Sovereignty."

It is evident that a new spirit ruled in the country in 1854. Four years earlier the old men, led by Clay and Webster, loving the union and lamenting the tendency of the young men toward radicalism, united and carried a compromise over the heads of the radicals. In 1852 died both Clay and Webster — Calhoun had died in 1850. Thus in 1854 the militant younger men were in control on each side. The most conspicuous Northern leaders were: Seward, of New York, an able politician and a man of influence because he could carry the most important state in the union; Chase and Wade, of Ohio, both strong debaters; and Sumner, of Massachusetts, who was a fervid orator and a biting foe to the slave power. In the South Jefferson Davis, of Mississippi, a cool-headed and logical debater, was most eminent, and by his followers was pronounced the heir of Calhoun's leadership. He was a member of Pierce's cabinet, but returned to the senate in 1857. Toombs, of Georgia, warm and audacious in manner, but conservative in ideas, was an able second to Davis. Neither of these men in 1854 would advocate secession, but they were ready to accept it if necessary to save the South from an antislavery majority in the North. Another group of Southerners, the most prominent of whom were Yancey, of Alabama, and Rhett, of South Carolina, were avowed secessionists. Among Northern democrats the leaders were Douglas, now bitterly disliked because of the Kansas-Nebraska act, and Buchanan, of Pennsylvania, an old man trained under the Jackson régime, whose best asset was that he was minister to England in 1854, and so was not forced to vote for or against Douglas's celebrated bill.

New Men in Control, North and South.

The Kansas-Nebraska bill opened a new strife between these two contending sides, which by regular steps led straight to the civil war. The chief events in this progress are the following: 1. The struggle to settle Kansas; 2. The organization of the republican party; 3. The Dred Scott decision; 4. The Lincoln-Douglas debates of 1858; 5. The John Brown raid; and 6. The election of Lincoln in 1860. It is now necessary to take up these events in order.

Consequences of the Kansas-Nebraska Act.

THE STRUGGLE FOR KANSAS

At first most people expected Kansas to become the home of slavery, and Missourians began to move into its fertile valleys as soon as it was a territory. The antislavery men were not willing that this should be accomplished without opposition. Eli Thayer, of Massachusetts, organized the "Emigrant Aid Society" to assist New Englanders to settle in the territory. When its protegés began to arrive, an angry cry arose from the settlers from Missouri. The wealthy North, it was said, was pouring in colonists to organize the country so as to exclude slavery, and appeals were made for Southerners to help settle Kansas. The response was ready in Missouri, and on election day, 1855, more than 5000 men rode from that state and cast votes in the choice of members of the first territorial legislature. Governor Reeder, of Kansas, appointed by Pierce, who was known to favor the Southerners, did not approve the proceedings, but he did nothing to check them. The result was that the new legislature met, declared some of the delegates chosen from the districts of the New Englanders illegally elected, and made a code of laws in support of slave property. This they did on the theory that popular sovereignty meant that slavery should not be discriminated against until the territory itself determined whether or not it should be established.

Northern and Southern Immigrants.

The First Legislature.

By this time immigration from New England was large, and the free state party felt strong enough to defy their antagonists. They found a leader in Dr. Charles Robinson, who had lived in California long enough to know how to deal with the chaos now in Kansas. All the Missourians had done was pronounced illegal, and plans were made to organize an irregular government, adopt a constitution, and ask for admission to the union. Thus assembled the Topeka convention, chosen entirely by the party of freedom. The other side pronounced it extra-legal, gave it no countenance, and declared their sheriff and legislature the only legal authority in the territory under the governor, who was appointed by Pierce and in sympathy with the slavery men. Fortunately, the two parties had settled in different districts, and each legislature, though claiming jurisdiction over all Kansas, was content to exercise authority

Two Governments Appeal.

merely over its own district. The Missourians, in their hasty entrance to the territory, took the rich lands along the Missouri on whose banks they planted the towns of Atchison, Leavenworth, and Kickapoo. But the New Englanders, with a better sense of future development, settled along the Kansas river, and thus their towns, Lawrence, Topeka, Lecompton, and Ossawatomie, penetrated nearly a hundred miles into the territory.

Early in 1856 the Kansas situation was before congress. Both contending governments were tainted with illegality, and if the federal government had carried out the true spirit of Douglas's popular sovereignty theory, both would have been overthrown, and new elections held. Unhappily, the country was deeply aroused and divided in sentiment, and both the president and congress were no more disposed to act calmly than the Kansas settlers. Pierce, a democrat, naturally followed his party, the larger part of which were Southerners. He issued a proclamation against lawless men in Kansas, and authorized the governor, now Shannon, to use federal troops if necessary.

Attitude of the East.

To preserve order in Kansas was only a temporary remedy for the chaos there. A more permanent remedy was suggested by Pierce in a recommendation that it be admitted to the union as soon as sufficiently populous; and in March, 1856, Douglas, in the senate, introduced a bill to authorize the Kansas legislature to call a convention to prepare a constitution for admission to the union when the population of the territory should be 93,420. Such a convention would undoubtedly be under the influence of the Missourians, and the proposition was bitterly opposed by the opposite side, who demanded that Kansas be admitted under the Topeka constitution. Then came one of the most exciting debates in the history of congress. Douglas and many Southerners spoke on one side, Seward, Collamer, Hale, and Sumner on the other. The speech of Sumner was very bitter. He was a man of the highest purposes and the deepest feelings; he hated slavery, and thought its supporters entitled to no consideration. He was now highly wrought up by recent events, and prepared a speech on "The Crime against Kansas," into which he put as much denunciation as his intense soul could utter. He himself called his speech "the most thorough philippic ever uttered in a legislative body." Into it he brought some biting personalities, attacking especially Douglas and Senator Butler, of South Carolina. The former replied in words equally biting, but the latter was avenged by his nephew, Brooks, who represented a South Carolina district. Two days after the speech was made Sumner was leaning over his desk writing, the senate having adjourned. Brooks approached, uttered a few words of reproach, and fell to beating Sumner over head and shoulders until bystanders interfered. The

Statehood as a Remedy for the Confusion.

Warm Kansas Debate.

Sumner Assaulted.

attack left the senator with injuries from which he did not recover before 1860.

When Sumner finished his extraordinary speech, Cass, the Nestor of the senate, broke the painful silence of that body by saying: "I have listened with equal regret and surprise to the speech of the honorable senator from Massachusetts. Such a Effects of speech, the most un-American and unpatriotic that ever the Incident. grated on the ears of the members of this high body, I hope never to hear again here or elsewhere." These words might have represented the judgment of posterity concerning Sumner's utterances, had not Brooks's violent retaliation taken off their edge. In the days when one gentleman caned another, he sought to overwhelm him by the indignity rather than by the severity of the affair; but Brooks attacked most savagely, breaking his cane and finishing the chastisement with the butt. His achievement found many defenders in the South, and he might have finished his days, had he so wished, in belaboring abolitionists with the many canes he received from admiring Southerners. In the North his deed and the approval of it in the South elicited the deepest horror. It did more to arouse the average man against the South than any speech Sumner ever made. Meanwhile, all this trouble accomplished nothing for Kansas. Congress could not agree on a plan, and the territory continued to be the prey of faction.

These struggles came to a head in Kansas the day before Sumner was injured. A proslavery grand jury had indicted several of the antislavery leaders, and a posse under a federal marshal marched to Lawrence and made the arrests. They de- Violence at stroyed, on the ground it was a nuisance, a large stone hotel Lawrence. built there, probably with the purpose of having it serve as a fort in case of need. The posse contained many lawless men under slight restraint, and there was much drinking and plundering. The newspaper offices were looted, stores were sacked, and the house of the governor under the Topeka constitution was destroyed. While Brooks's violence filled every mind, news of this occurrence reached the East and but added to the excitement.

To one free-state Kansan it seemed to call for vengeance. John Brown, of Ossawatomie, hated slavery to the verge of insanity, and he believed himself ordained by providence to redress the wrong of his party, five of whom had been slain. With John seven followers he entered the settlements of the slavery Brown's Re- party on Pottawatamie Creek, took five men from three taliation. homes, and left their bodies by the roadside lifeless and mutilated. "God is my judge," exclaimed he, "the people of Kansas will yet justify my course." Approve it they could not, but it was the signal for the outbreak of a guerrilla struggle in which nearly two hundred lives were sacrificed. This state of affairs was largely due to the lax rule of Governor Shannon, who gave ill disguised sympathy to the slave party. Its effect on the presidential canvass then in progress in the states was so great that Pierce was forced to send another governor. Geary, who arrived on the scene September 9, won the respect of both sides and eventually restored order. He resigned March 4, 1857, feeling that he was not supported by the president.

Buchanan, who became president on the same day, was anxious to have affairs settled in the territory. His party's platform had declared for a just application of popular sovereignty in Kansas, and he wished to redeem the pledge. After much persuasion he induced Robert J. Walker, a Mississippi democrat and a man of ability and fairness, to accept the governorship. During the past two years many Northern men had moved to the scene of conflict, and Walker realized that they were by far the majority of the population. He gave up hope of saving Kansas for slavery, and tried to save it for his party. Elections to a constitutional convention were announced, and he urged all free state people to vote in them, promising that the constitution to be prepared should be submitted to the people for approval. The appeal was futile. Of the 18,000 voters thought to be in the territory only 2200 took part in the election, most of them proslavery. Had his advice been taken, much trouble would have been avoided.

Governor Walker's Attempt to Restore Order.

When the Southern politicians in Washington learned that their friends controlled the convention, which met at Lecompton in September, 1857, they acted quickly. Agents went to Kansas, and a scheme was arranged by which the minority might control. The constitution as a whole was not to be submitted to the people, but only the clause in reference to slavery. The vote was to be "the constitution with slavery" or "the constitution without slavery." If the latter prevailed, the slaves already in Kansas, not more than 200, would not be liberated. The vote on the constitution was to be taken by officers appointed directly by the convention. These unusual details suggested dark designs, and Walker denounced them openly and set out for Washington to protest to the president himself. He found that Buchanan was committed to the Southerners.

The Lecompton Constitution.

The country was beginning to forget Kansas, but this turn of affairs caused it to remember. Most of all, Douglas was alarmed and outraged. He had risked much of his own popularity for the South, and he could not but feel that he was betrayed. Telling the president plainly that he should oppose the scheme, he went into the senate to make a bold speech against the constitution made at Lecompton. "If Kansas wants a slave-state constitution," he said, "she has a right to it; if she wants a free-state constitution, she has a right to it. It is none of my business which way the slavery clause is decided. I care not whether it is voted up or down." He got little for his trouble; the South turned against him,

Opposed by Douglas.

and the republicans could only see that he was seeking to secure in 1858 his reëlection to the senate. His action defeated the bill to admit Kansas with the Lecompton constitution; for though it passed the senate the Douglas democrats in the house cast the deciding votes against it. But the English bill, a faint-hearted compromise, was finally passed. It offered Kansas a gift of land if it became a state, ordered an impartial election on the question of receiving the gift, and authorized the president to admit the state by proc- lamation if the vote was in the affirmative. The Kansas **The English** free-state party considered the bill a proffered bribe and **Bill.** rejected it by a vote of 11,300 to 1788. From this time, August, 1858, the struggle in Kansas dropped into the background, the territorial government was in authority, and it was not until 1861, after some of the Southern states had seceded, that difficulties disappeared with the acquisition of statehood.

Douglas, like many other politicians, cared little for either slavery or abolition, but wished to remove from the political field an annoying question, and he thought his popular sovereignty theory would accomplish his aim. He believed that other North- **Position of** erners like himself, with the help of the South, could keep **the South.** the question in the background, spite of the antislavery Northerners, whom he rightly believed in the minority. But the South would not play his game. It believed itself entitled to Kansas, and was angered when the North tried to fill the territory with settlers. It met this move, which it believed perfidious, with fraud and violence, which deepened at each step. It was too unfair a proceeding to be permitted by the nation, and was not in keeping with the former conduct of its authors. It was the last desperate hope to preserve the equilibrium of states, and its failure left Southerners the choice between submission to the limitation of the slave power and withdrawal from the union.

PARTY AND THE ELECTION OF 1856

The whig party suffered much by the compromise of 1850. If it repudiated the agreement, its southern wing would be wrecked; to accept it sacrificed the good will of many earnest anti- slavery whigs. It was freely said that the party would **Death Blow** never win another victory. Although it had a strong **of Whig** position in Massachusetts, New York, and other states, **Party.** and managed to preserve its national organization, its fate was sealed.

For a time it was thought it would yield place to the know-nothing party. This was a secret political organization with the same principles as those of the Native Americans. When **Know-** one of its members was asked any question about it he was **Nothing** instructed to give a formal answer, "I don't know," and **Party.** from this came the name. As the Irish Catholics were usually democrats, the organization naturally drew largely from the whigs, and as it had the open denunciation of Douglas and other leading democrats it felt drawn to those who opposed the Kansas-Nebraska bill. By judicious combination and much work it polled in 1854 one-fourth of the entire vote of New York, two-fifths of that of Pennsylvania, and nearly two-thirds of that of Massachusetts. In the last-named state it elected the governor and other general officers and controlled the legislature. This silent machine, without canvassers or other outward evidence of activity, but sweeping so much before it, struck terror to the old party leaders. Late in 1854 it decided to require all its members to take oath to support the union, and the decision drew many anti-Nebraska men to its ranks, as well as a large number of union men in the South, mostly old whigs. In the spring of 1855 it carried Connecticut, New Hampshire, and Rhode Island, and freely boasted it had 1,000,000 enrolled voters. It now abandoned secrecy, hitherto its greatest weakness. The light of day showed that it was chiefly the old whig party under another name, and from that moment disappeared all hope of building up out of it a great union party. In 1856 it lost its antislavery wing when it refused to demand the restoration of the Missouri compromise. In this year its candidate, Fillmore, carried only one state, Maryland.

Its Failure.

Meanwhile, the republican party had been organized on the basis of open opposition to slavery extension. While congress debated the Kansas-Nebraska bill, 1854, many mass meetings were held to protest against the measure, and one of them at Ripon, Wisconsin, March 20, went beyond the others by recommending a new party to fight slavery extension. July 6 a convention of all who would coöperate to resist "the encroachments of slavery" met at Jackson, Michigan, nominated a state ticket, and called on the other free states to do the same. The sources of its strength, and the proportion of its distribution, are shown in the fact that three of the nominees were former free soil men, five old whigs, and two anti-Nebraska democrats. Wisconsin followed Michigan's example, while Vermont, Indiana, and Ohio nominated anti-Nebraska tickets. The movement prevailed in Ohio by a majority of 75,000. It was, however, forestalled in the great Eastern states by the rise of know-nothingism. But the check was temporary, and in 1855 its eastward march was resumed.

Republican Party Founded.

Whig leaders in the East watched the rise of the republican party with keen interest, and this was especially true of Seward, leading whig and opponent of slavery extension in congress. His own party was disintegrating: should he follow the exodus and unite with the republicans to build up a great sectional organization? His answer was most important; for he controlled, with the aid of his astute friend, Thurlow Weed, the action of his

Seward and New York.

party in the most important state in the union. He hesitated for months, but by the autumn of 1855 his mind was made up. Plans were made to unite the whigs and republicans, and each party met in convention at Syracuse in September. To one of his friends who asked which convention an opponent of slavery ought to attend, Seward replied that it made little difference; for although the delegates would go in through two doors they would come out at one. The whigs had hardly assembled before they resolved to join the republican party, and the leaders, followed by all but a small remnant, marched to the republican convention and took seats in good fellowship. In Massachusetts similar results were secured by means less spectacular. Slavery had already divided the whig party in this state, its opponents being called "Conscience Whigs," and the conservatives "Cotton Whigs," and the former now generally became republicans. By the end of 1855 the republican party was established throughout the free states.

Massa-
chusetts.

In the South a like movement toward sectionalism was in progress. Here the whole Kansas incident was considered an act of bad faith toward the South, and the whigs could not defend their Northern brethren from the charge of participating in it. So rapidly did the party fall away that its leaders became utterly discouraged, and the most ambitious of them went over to the democrats, henceforth the Southern sectional party.

Decline of
Whig Party
in the South.

Two republican conventions were held in 1856. One was at Pittsburg, February 22, to organize the party nationally. It was cheered by the news that the seceding know-nothings would join them. After adopting a platform demanding the exclusion of slavery from the territories and the admission of Kansas to the union it called a nominating convention in Philadelphia for June 17. Pending that date there was much discussion of candidates. At first most republicans looked to Seward, the ablest politician in the party; but as the spring advanced they began to think that the signs of the time pointed to a victory if the right man were nominated. Then arose a feeling against Seward. He had made many enemies, particularly among the know-nothings, and it was generally said that a man who could win should be taken. The argument prevailed, and John C. Frémont, prominent because of his career in California in 1846, was nominated. Seward, who did not believe the party could win at that time, was content to wait for future honors.

Frémont
Nominated.

The democratic convention met at Cincinnati June 2. Since the Kansas policy was to be the chief issue it was to be expected that Pierce or Douglas would be nominated. But so great was Northern resentment of that policy that the delegates dared not name a man prominently responsible for it. Thus they took Buchanan, who had been minister to England and was not

Buchanan
Nominated.

connected with anything that had been done in America during the past three years.   He was acceptable to the South, which he had never opposed, and he appealed to Northern conservatives of all parties, who thought the republican position on slavery a kind of radicalism. The whigs held a convention and indorsed Fillmore, whom the regular know-nothings had previously nominated.

The chief issue of the campaign was Kansas, "Bleeding Kansas," as the republicans called it.   It was an unwelcome issue to the democrats **Campaign of 1856.** in the North, who tried to supplant it by the question of union.   Did any one think the South, said they, would submit to be ruled by a president and congress elected entirely by the free states?   Toombs, speaking for his section, said that the election of Frémont would be the end of the union.   In fact, Frémont and "black republicanism" were so hateful to the South that it was hardly safe for a man to espouse them.   A professor in the university of North Carolina who said he would vote for this ticket if it were offered him was set upon by the press, and when he wrote a moderate article in reply, the trustees of the university asked him to resign his professorship.   For the South there was but one ticket, and it was in the North the battle was to be fought.   Conservative whigs in this section realized that the real contest was between Buchanan and Frémont, and many of them preferred the former.   The republicans, on the other hand, had with them the majority of the ministers, college professors, and literary men of the North.   The religious press worked for them.   It was a moral issue, and appealed strongly to the young men.   As the campaign progressed it became evident that Pennsylvania was the most critical state.   All eyes centered on it, and the democrats gave a cry of joy when in a state election in October they carried it by less than 3000 votes.   This presaged success in the national election in November ; and the hope was realized when counting the returns of that day's battle gave Buchanan 174 electoral votes, Frémont 114, and Fillmore 8.   It was a narrow escape for the democrats, for in most of their northern states the majorities were small. The republicans had done exceedingly well for a party which had never before taken part in a national campaign.   The historian cannot but reflect that the Kansas-Nebraska bill which Atchison forced on Douglas in 1854 and which Douglas carried through congress by his brilliant leadership was become a most expensive experiment for the slaveholding power.

In this campaign an important part was played by Mrs. Harriet Beecher Stowe's novel, "Uncle Tom's Cabin," published in book form in **"Uncle Tom's Cabin."** 1852, as a protest against the execution of the fugitive slave law.   It had an immense circulation, and was translated into many languages.   It was a most earnest protest of a sensitive soul against slavery, and it was difficult for one to read it without feeling an impulse to do something to destroy the

system. The Southern people resented its pictures of slavery and
slaveholders. In fact, the condition was not as bad as it was portrayed,
but it was bad enough to cry for reform.

The Dred Scott Decision

From the time the Wilmot proviso was before the public suggestions
of the power of the supreme court to pass upon the status of slavery in
the territories were heard. When by the compromise of 1850
New Mexico and Utah were created as territories without   Appeal to
restriction as to slavery, it was understood that if a question   the Supreme
arose in connection with slavery in their borders it was to   Court.
be referred to this tribunal. In every debate over Kansas the constitutionality of the Missouri compromise was freely challenged by the
South. The logical tendency was to bring the dispute sooner or later
before the highest court in the land. This tribunal had declared
against many laws : Why should it not relieve the intensity of feeling
in the country and decide once for all the controversy which threatened the existence of the union? Beyond this was another question :
Would its decision be accepted as final by the losing side ?

Dred Scott was the slave of an army surgeon residing in Missouri
who took the slave into Illinois and Minnesota, and returned after
more than two years' residence in free territory. Shortly   Dred Scott.
afterwards the master died, and Dred sued for his freedom.
The case first came up in Missouri courts, which had jurisdiction ; but
while it was in progress he was sold to a citizen of New York, who hired
him out in Missouri. He then brought suit in the federal courts. He
claimed to be a citizen of Missouri, and on that ground contended that
his case came within federal jurisdiction, since the federal courts may
try cases between citizens of different states. He also claimed that
when his master took him voluntarily into the land of freedom the
shackles of slavery fell off, and that his return to a slave state could
not be construed as reënslavement. He insisted that the Missouri
compromise, a federal law, protected him in this contention. The
two points before the courts, therefore, were: was Dred Scott a citizen
of Missouri, and did the Missouri compromise protect him? The
defense denied the first contention, and asserted the compromise was
unconstitutional.

The case was first argued in the supreme court early in 1856. Seven
of the justices were democrats, and of these five were Southerners.
One was a republican, and another, Curtis, was a whig.   The Dred
At first the case attracted little attention outside of the   Scott Case.
court, but after a while it became known that it involved
the Missouri compromise, and the public, especially the Southerners,
began to take notice. In view of this the court had it reargued in
December, 1856, every point being taken up most carefully. Even

2 K

then the court hesitated.   Should it merely settle the status of Dred Scott and his family, or should it by passing on the two fundamental points raised exert its power in the very center of the great sectional controversy?   To do the former would avoid the unpleasant task of making an enemy of either Northern or Southern faction; but it would also lay the court open to the charge of cowardice.   "What," it would be asked, "was a court for but to settle disputed constitutional points?"   Some pressure was brought on the court by outsiders to get them to take up a broad attitude, chiefly by the Southerners, who felt that the majority of the justices leaned their way.   They succeeded, and March 6, 1857, when the decision was announced, was an important day in the great antislavery struggle.   It showed that the court was on the Southern side.

Each member of the court read an opinion, all of the Southern justices and one Northerner, Grier, a democrat, agreeing materially. The opinion of Chief Justice Taney was taken as that of the majority.   It dealt with two important points: was a negro a citizen of the United States? and was the Missouri compromise law constitutional?   In regard to the former, Taney asserted that federal and state citizenship were not identical, that Scott's citizenship was to be determined by the law in force in the state of his residence, and that since Missouri did not recognize him as a citizen he could not be considered a citizen of the United States.   As to the rights of the citizens of one state resident in another, Taney held that such rights were only maintained during temporary residence, and that the constitution did not intend to take away in this respect the right of a state to decide so vital a point as what classes of persons should be admitted to state citizenship.   As to the Missouri compromise, the court felt impelled to pass on its constitutionality; for if it were valid, Dred Scott became free by his residence in Minnesota, and if he was free there it was assuming a great deal to say that his undisputed return to Missouri would bring reënslavement.   Taney accepted the Southern view on this point.   The claim that congress could legislate for the territories was disposed of by holding that the words were restricted to the territory actually owned by the federal government in 1787, and not to the Louisiana purchase.   The constitution, he further held, recognized the existence of property in slaves, it gave no part of the government the right to destroy such property, and an act of congress claiming to exercise such a right was unwarranted.

Taney's Opinion.

Judge Curtis, supported by McLean, the republican justice, took the contrary view in a well written opinion.   Free negroes, he said, were citizens of North Carolina and several Northern states in 1789, and voted there, and he held that any citizen of a state is a citizen of the United States, and was such in 1789. If this was true, Taney's first point, relating to citizenship, was demolished.   As to his second point, Curtis was equally successful.

Curtis's Opinion.

Congress, he pointed out, was given power "to make all needful rules and regulations concerning the territory of the United States." Taney held that this did not apply to territory acquired after the constitution was adopted, but Curtis disputed the point with a great deal of strength of argument. If congress had such power, it might forbid the entrance of slaves into a territory, and in doing so it did not violate the clause which forbade it to deprive a citizen of property without due process of law.

It was the fate of these two lines of reasoning that one enunciated the view for which one side had long contended, and the other that for which the other side had been equally earnest. One was supported by the justices who favored the democratic party, and the other by those who leaned toward the other parties. Perhaps it was impossible that honorable judges should have been uninfluenced by the storm of discussion amid which they had lived during the past decade. The democrats, North and South, exulted that they had the majority of the court with them and flouted the opinion of Curtis. The opponents of slavery in the North found Curtis entirely convincing, and denounced the majority of the court as subservient to the slave power. The upshot was that the attempt of the court to intervene in the great sectional conflict was a total failure. We may consider it a certainty that when the court gives an opinion adverse to the previously formed view of a majority of the American people, its decision will be futile and its influence will be lessened. The status of slavery in the territories was, in fact, no longer a judicial matter. It had become a political issue, and it was not wise for the court to undertake to settle it.

Futility of a Judicial Decision.

The administration party was not surprised by the outburst of indignation which met the Dred Scott decision, but they thought it would soon blow over. There followed, however, the attempt to admit Kansas with the Lecompton constitution (see page 492), and this added to rather than lessened the excitement. Meanwhile there came the midsummer panic of 1857, which occasioned great distress in the business world. The democratic secretary of the treasury, Howell Cobb, of Georgia, showed little ability to retrieve the treasury from its consequent embarrassments; and when the manufacturers of the North asked for higher tariff rates to protect their prostrate businesss, the Southern senators objected. The result was, therefore, a diminished respect of the powerful business element for the party in power.

Democrats Lose Strength.

THE LINCOLN-DOUGLAS DEBATES

Early in 1858 the worst of the panic was over, the Lecompton scheme was defeated, and there was a breathing spell in which the politicians had time to think of the presidential election of 1860. To the shrewdest men it seemed that fortune favored Douglas. Much of the enthusiasm of 1856 had subsided. The Kansas-Nebraska law did not seem quite so bad now that it was evident that popular sovereignty did not mean the establishment of slavery in a territory. Douglas's opposition to the Lecompton constitution had brought him the good will of many conservative republicans, who could not fail to acknowledge his genius, and it was even whispered in some quarters that Northern democrats and republicans might unite to make him president. Douglas could not have had expectations of this nature, but he took no pains to check them on the part of others. Two years of peace, it was believed, would go far to remove the sectional strife, and if Douglas could be supported in 1860 by the South, the Northern democrats, and the conservative republicans, what might he not expect to do? True, he was unpopular in the South, where his Lecompton votes were pronounced acts of treachery, but he was a most facile man, and no one who knew him doubted that he would find means of restoring himself to Southern favor before the critical time arrived. We are now to see how his prospects were blighted by Abraham Lincoln.

Douglas's Position Early in 1858.

Douglas's term in the senate expired in 1859, and his party in state convention in 1858 nominated him to succeed himself. The republicans named Lincoln as his opponent, and a series of joint debates was arranged between the two candidates. No other public discussion in our history has been more important. It not only sealed the political fate of one presidential candidate, and established another in the road to the presidency, but it educated the North to the true nature of the problem before it and convinced the South that secession was the only way to escape the ultimate extinction of slavery.

The Debates Arranged.

In the beginning of his campaign Lincoln attacked boldly. The time had come, he thought, to announce frankly that the war on slavery was uncompromising, and he did it, in accepting his party's nomination, in simple words which will never fade from our history. "'A house divided against itself cannot stand,'" he said; "I believe this government cannot endure permanently half slave and half free. I do not expect the union to be dissolved — I do not expect the house to fall — but I do expect it will cease to be divided. It will become all one thing or all the other. Either the opponents of slavery will arrest the further spread of it, and place it where the public mind shall rest in the belief that it is in the course of ultimate extinction, or its advocates will push it forward till it shall become alike lawful in all the states, old as well as new — North as well as South." Hitherto republican campaigners were content to attack the slave power for its aggression in Kansas, and they feared to lay the axe to the root,

The "House-Divided" Speech.

ıest conservatives, whigs and democrats, be driven off. They trembled when Lincoln assumed a bolder front, and one of them was heard to call his "house-divided" announcement "a fool utterance." But Lincoln was in earnest, and he could not bring out the best in him unless he spoke in all sincerity. Douglas in the course of the debates made much of this advanced utterance, pronouncing it the froth of abolition ravings; but his opponent stood by it manfully, explaining it in a spirit of far-sighted statesmanship which convinced more men than it repelled. It was probably the most convincing point of his argument.

Lincoln saw in the joint debate an opportunity to make Douglas unacceptable to the South, and for that purpose asked him this question in the discussion at Freeport, "Can the people of a United States territory, in any lawful way, against **How** the wish of any citizen of the United States, exclude **Lincoln** slavery from its limits prior to the formation of a state **Douglas.** constitution?" The reply of Douglas became known as his Freeport doctrine. Slavery, he said, could not exist in a territory without local police regulations to protect it, and these could only be made by the local legislature, which would oppose slavery if the people who elected the legistators were opposed to it. "Hence, no matter what the decision of the supreme court may be on that abstract question, still the right of the people to make a slave territory or a free territory is perfect and complete under the Nebraska bill." This utterance saved its author in his senatorial contest. When Lincoln was urged to drive him from this position, he refused, saying he was looking for higher game than the senatorship. He foresaw better than the other republicans that it would kill Douglas in the South; for it was the negation of all the slaveholders saw in the Dred Scott decision. The Freeport doctrine was known and discussed far and wide. It was read most attentively by the men of the South. From this time, Judge Douglas, try as you may, you will never again induce the Southern friends of slavery to think you their safe champion and defender!

And yet we must not too easily blame Douglas. He was in the difficult position of Calhoun in 1828 and Van Buren in 1844; he must give up the support of his own state or that of the section opposite to his own. He chose, as they, to preserve the **Douglas's** good will of his state, realizing that here was his first **Dilemma.** element of safety. He was one of the ablest Americans then living, and he loved the union. He sought to preserve it by saving the great democratic party as the last and strongest national bond then in existence. He won his senatorship, but all he hoped for in behalf of union was lost.

Lincoln also showed himself a great American. Was it not great to defeat the great Douglas? His powerful logic, which forced the issue down to the narrow point of slavery or no slavery in the territories, and his courage and sincerity, which cast aside the last remnant of temporizing and made it clear that the contest waged was nothing less than a war to put slavery in a way of ultimate extinction,—these were his weapons. No man before that day, or afterwards, wielded them more brilliantly. He had the advantage of his opponent in this, that he appealed to a more populous and homogeneous section, the rich and prosperous North. It was a North ready to be convinced that slavery should be reduced to a minority power, and his splendid strokes convinced it.

Lincoln's Service.

The congressional elections of 1858 showed how fast the tide ran for the republicans. Two years earlier the elections resulted in a house containing 131 democrats, 92 republicans, and 14 know-nothings. In 1858 they gave 109 republicans, 86 democrats, 13 anti-Lecompton democrats, and 22 know-nothings. In the senate the democrats still held a majority, having in the congress then chosen 38 members to 25 republicans and 2 know-nothings. But they had lost one senator, and it was evident that the trend of events would soon array against them every free state senator. As the short session of 1858-1859 ran by with no other achievement than angry debate over a democratic proposition to buy Cuba, the Southerners came to realize how completely they were defeated, and even their conservative leaders began to say in sober earnest that the election of a "black republican" president would justify secession.

Republicans Gain the House.

THE JOHN BROWN RAID

Before the succeeding congress assembled came the attempt of John Brown at Harper's Ferry. The farther we get away from the excitement of 1859 the more we are disposed to consider this extraordinary man the victim of mental delusions. He hated slavery fervently, and despised those who talked of constitutional methods. "Without the shedding of blood, there is no remission of sin," he said time and again to those who discussed the subject with him. In the confusion of the day no steps were taken against him for killing five men in Kansas in 1856, and early in 1858 we find him in New York secretly planning another bloody deed. He attended an antislavery convention in Boston as a spectator, and turned away, saying: "These men are all talk; what we need is action — action!" Assembling some of the prominent leaders, he unfolded his own scheme. It was to collect a band of devoted armed followers, seize and fortify a position in the mountains of Virginia or Maryland, and from it make raids into the farming communities to liberate slaves. As he succeeded, he said, friends from the North would join him, his power

His Idea of the Contest against Slavery.

His Plan.

would grow, and soon he would make slavery insecure throughout Virginia. This was nothing less than to raise insurrection, but Brown and the academic leaders of abolitionism were so carried away by the wrongs done to enslaved negroes that they considered it only just retaliation; and money was promised to enable him to launch his enterprise. News of the project came to Seward and Senator Wilson, of Massachusetts, and they forbade Brown to use the arms which had been collected to defend the free state men in Kansas. By this time suspicions were generally aroused, and to allay them he went to Kansas, where his name was a terror to the proslavery men. After lying idle a short time he made a raid into Missouri, rescued eleven slaves, and escaped with them through Kansas, Nebraska, Iowa, Illinois, and Michigan to the soil of Canada. The country was aroused, and the incident served to draw attention from Brown's projected operations in Virginia.

In the spring of 1859 he was back in New England, soliciting funds. Some of the most prominent abolitionists would have nothing to do with him, but others gave money, something more than $4500 first and last, and June 30 he arrived at Harper's Ferry, Virginia, thirty miles south of the Pennsylvania line. Leasing a farm, he spent the next ten weeks in carting arms from Chambersburg, Pennsylvania, and in collecting the twenty-one followers with whom he proposed to put his dangerous scheme into execution. October 16, with eighteen of these men, he seized the United States arsenal in Harper's Ferry, captured thirty or more of the citizens, whom he held as prisoners, cut the telegraph wires, and for twenty four hours held his own against the citizens and near-by militia companies which hurried to the scene. It was not until dawn of the 18th that he was captured by a detachment of marines commanded by Colonel Robert E. Lee, assisted by Lieutenant J. E. B. Stuart. John Brown himself, with four of his men were taken prisoners, seven escaped, and ten were slain, two of them being sons of the leader. The prisoners were sent to the county jail at Charlestown to await trial. A grand jury on October 25 found true bills, and after a fair trial Brown was sentenced to hang on December 2.

Seizes Harper's Ferry.

Had John Brown been killed in the eventful night when he was taken prisoner, the raid would have gone down to history as a foolish deed prompted by an unbalanced mind. But the firm and calm bearing he displayed at his trial and during the month between conviction and execution touched the hearts of even his jailers. In the North he became a martyr to the antislavery party. On his trial and afterwards he declared that he came merely to rescue slaves, and the abolitionists could see no harm in such a purpose. As a matter of fact, he came with a thousand pikes to place in the hands of slaves and a large number of rifles and revolvers. It was not strictly true that he did merely what conductors

Bearing as a Prisoner.

of the Underground Railway did. But the antislavery portion of the North, in the excitement of the moment, did not stop to inquire into niceties. To them a man of firm heart had risked life to overthrow slavery and was now facing a hangman's death without a tremor.

December 2, 1859, the verdict of the court was executed, the prisoner dying with fortitude. As the death group marched to the gallows **Executed.** it was surrounded by a strong body of militia, and fifteen hundred troops formed a hollow square around the scaffold. Many hints had been given that Brown's Northern friends had planned a rescue, and this display of force was precautionary. It elicited much derision at the time, but later researches have shown that some of the abolitionists were eager to attempt a rescue and were deterred only by their inability to raise the necessary funds.

The influence of the incident in the North is hard to estimate. It undoubtedly aroused the antislavery party to a high pitch. John Brown died for his conviction, and he did it willingly and **Significance** with dignity. But Northern conservatives did not change **of John** their views because of the rash attempt of an enthusiast **Brown.** who did not hesitate to take the sword to redress what he believed the wrongs of the negroes. It was to them a sufficient evidence of the impracticability of the scheme that it found no response among the slaves of Harper's Ferry and the surrounding region. The effects on the South, however, were very definite. Up to this time the ideas of the secessionists had not been taken very seriously by the southern voters. Much had been said about the intention of the abolitionists to come into the South, set the slaves against their masters, and forcibly overthrow the institution which was at the bottom of society; but the union leaders there had always met it successfully by saying this was but the imagining of men unnecessarily alarmed. Here, however, was a concrete instance which the secessionists declared proved all they had predicted; and the enthusiasm shown in the North for John Brown seemed to the masses to confirm all that was said. Harper's Ferry gave a strong blow to union sentiment in the South.

THE ELECTION OF 1860

We are now arrived at the culmination of the harsh struggle which followed the passage of the Kansas-Nebraska act. The disorders in Kansas, the Dred Scott decision, and the John Brown **Election of** raid divided the people of the North and South beyond **Speaker,** possible conciliation. The prelude of the great struggle **1859.** came when the house elected in 1858 met in December, 1859, and sought to choose a speaker. John Sherman, of Ohio, had most of the republican votes, but lacked several of an election. A Missouri member introduced a resolution that no man should be speaker who had indorsed Helper's "Impending Crisis of the South."

This book, by one from the small farmer class in North Carolina, was a severe indictment of salvery from the standpoint of the non-slave-holders of the South and called on them to support the republican party in order to liberate themselves from the leadership of the slaveholders. Its language was bitter, but its doctrine might well cause to tremble the men who held the upper hand in the slave states; for it was as plain as day that if the non-slave-holding Southerners were organized against slavery its doom was written. In 1859 the book was brought out as a campaign document with a recommendation by prominent republicans, among them Sherman and Grow, both candidates for speaker. The resolutions against "The Impending Crisis" precipitated a bitter discussion of the whole slavery situation, threats of secession were freely made, and more than once members were at the point of personal violence on the floor of the house. It was not until February 1 that the contest ended with the election of Pennington, a conservative republican of New Jersey. In these strenuous days the Southern members freely said that the election in the coming autumn of a "Black Republican" president would bring dissolution of the union, and the violent state of feeling in the South indicated that the utterance was not an idle threat. Such was the spirit in which the country came to the election of 1860.

Helper's Book.

When this incident occurred the selection of delegates to the national nominating conventions was imminent. Douglas was now at the head of the Northern democracy. His opposition to the aggressive program of the republicans won for him the hatred of the antislavery men. It pleased the democrats in the free states and it was thought it would win the votes of many old whigs, supporters of Fillmore in 1856. But Douglas would not go as far as most Southerners wished. Their views were expressed in a series of resolutions introduced into the senate by Jefferson Davis, February 2, 1860, demanding that congress guarantee slave property in the territories. As the day approached for the meeting of the convention it became clear that these resolutions were the Southern ultimatum, made as much to force the Northern democrats to show their position as to consolidate the South in support of secession, if secession should be deemed necessary. Douglas parried the thrust, and was told pointedly that he could not get the Southern vote unless he accepted the ultimatum. He dared not yield, for no Northern state would tolerate forcing slavery into a territory against the wishes of the inhabitants.

Douglas and the Southerners.

The convention met at Charleston, South Carolina, April 23. The extreme Southerners, "fire-eaters" they were called by their opponents, held a caucus and indorsed the Davis resolutions, while the Northern delegates decided to stand by Douglas. The platform committee reported in favor of the former. It was composed of one member from each state, and was

The Factions at Charleston.

thus in Southern control. A minority report held to the Douglas position and accepted the Dred Scott decision. Yancey, the most polished orator among the Southerners, spoke for his section. Reviewing the origin and progress of the great controversy, he came at last to describe the crisis before the country. Slavery, he said, was right: its existence was bound up with the prosperity of the South: and yet with the growth of the great Northwest the South had become a minority and was threatened with ruin through the pro-

Yancey's Speech. posed action of the republicans. The democrats of the North had not met the issue squarely. Accepting the proposition of the abolitionists that slavery was wrong, they had sought to palliate: they had asked the North to withhold their hands against the South because the wrong was not of Northern doing. This attitude Yancey regretted. Had the Northern democrats frankly declared that slavery was not a wrong, the abolitionists would long ago have been silenced, and harmony would now reign in the country.

Yancey's speech was not a new note in the South. Many times he had said the same thing, only to have it rejected as the counsel of an extremist. But in 1860 the Southern temper had

The Convention Disrupted. changed. His bold words now received the tumultuous approval of his section, and the Northern democrats were made to see how grave was the situation. Pugh, of Ohio, a friend of Douglas, spoke in their behalf. He thanked God, he said, that a brave man had at last spoken and the full demands of slaveholders were made known; but the ultimatum was an impossibility, and he declared with the utmost plainness that it would not be accepted. Next, the convention took up the platform. By a vote of 165 to 138 the Douglas position was adopted, the first time in years that the plea of the South on this question had been ignored in a democratic convention. Then rose the chairman of the Alabama delegation with a serious and fixed countenance. According to the instruction of the party in his state, he said, Alabama must withdraw from the convention. As he and his colleagues walked out they were followed by the delegates from seven other States, — South Carolina, Mississippi, Louisiana, Florida, Texas, Arkansas, and Georgia. North Carolina, Virginia, Tennessee, Kentucky, and Maryland were less radical than the Gulf states, and remained with the convention, although their delegates sympathized in the main with those who withdrew.

After balloting three days the diminished Charleston convention could not get a two-thirds majority for any candidate, and adjourned, to meet again in Baltimore, June 18. When it reassembled

Two Tickets. it nominated Douglas for president and Herschel V. Johnson, of Georgia, for vice-president. The seceders at Charleston effected an organization, adopted the Southern platform, and adjourned to meet in Richmond, Virginia, on June 10. On that day they again adjourned, this time to Baltimore, June 28, where they finally named J. C. Breckenridge, of Kentucky, for president and Joseph Lane, of Oregon, for vice-president. Thus came to inglorious failure the attempt, inaugurated by Clay in 1850 and renewed and fought for by Douglas from 1854 to 1860, to remove slavery from national politics.

Let us now turn to the republicans. After the defeat of Frémont in 1856 Seward was generally accepted as the leader of his party, and few doubted that he would be its candidate for president in 1860. Opposition existed at isolated points, but it was expected that he would be able to overcome it. The most

Seward's Position.

patent danger was in New York, where Horace Greeley, editor of the New York *Tribune*, was at the head of a devoted band of abolitionists who considered him untrustworthy. Shrewd observers thought Greeley's chief grievance was that he was not consulted in the affairs of the party, and they were not surprised when in the spring of 1859 Seward dined with him at the Astor House, and the papers announced that a reconciliation had taken place. Simon Cameron, who controlled the party in Pennsylvania, was also in opposition, but Seward made a trip to Philadelphia, and the report went out that he had conciliated Cameron also. Seward himself thought he had now arranged things to his satisfaction, and seized the opportunity to make a journey to the Holy Land. While he was gone occurred the John Brown raid and the subsequent wrangle over the election of speaker; and on every hand Seward was proclaimed as the man who had planted the seed from which came the plant of insurrection. L. Q. C. Lamar expressed the Southern view in addressing the republicans of the house in these words: "I was on the floor of the senate when your great leader, William H. Seward, announced that startling program of antislavery sentiment and action against the South, . . . and, Sir, in his exultation he exclaimed — for I heard him myself — that he hoped to see the day when there would not be the footprint of a single slave upon this continent. And when he uttered this atrocious sentiment, his form seemed to dilate, his pale, thin face, furrowed by the lines of thought and evil passion, kindled with malignant triumph, and his eye glowed and glared upon Southern senators as though the fires of hell were burning in his heart!" In the midst of this commotion Seward returned. In 1850, in opposing Clay's compromise, he had declared that "a higher law" than the constitution demanded the extinction of slavery; and in 1858 he had said in a speech long remembered that the North was engaged in an "irrepressible conflict" which must make the nation all slave or all free. These two utterances made him seem to the South the very head of all their woes, and he sought to lessen their fears and reassure moderate Northerners in a mild speech which he delivered February 29. The compromising disposition it betokened was to reappear many times in his career.

There were several other candidates, Abraham Lincoln, whom the Illinois convention indorsed on May 9, 1860, Bates, of Missouri, Cameron, of Pennsylvania, no longer in accord with Seward, and seeking his own advantage in the prospect of making a combination with another candidate, and three Ohioans, Wade, Chase, and McLean, no one of whom was likely to be selected. Seward was believed to be stronger than any of these men, but all of them opposed him strongly and were willing to combine to defeat his nomination. Lincoln, whom events were soon to make so famous, had, before the convention met on May 16, the support of Indiana, Illinois, and Iowa, and a few other delegates, but he was little known east of the Alleghanies. *Harper's Weekly* was the only New York journal which considered him a possibility, and it placed his name last in a list of eleven.

Other Candidates.

Making a platform occupied the first and second days of the convention, and nominations were set for the third. Early indications pointed to Seward's success, and his opponents made preparations for a rapid concentration on Lincoln, whom they found to be the most feasible candidate. Cabinet positions seem to have been promised to the other candidates in order to secure this coöperation, although Lincoln, who was not present, knew nothing of the offers. On the first ballot the vote was $123\frac{1}{2}$ for Seward, 102 for Lincoln, $50\frac{1}{2}$ for Cameron, 49 for Chase, 48 for Bates, and 42 for other men. Two hundred and thirty-three were necessary for a choice. On the second ballot Lincoln gained 79 and Seward 11. On the third, the Illinois candidate received $235\frac{1}{2}$, and was nominated. Seward was defeated partly because it was thought unadvisable to nominate a man who had so many enemies, and partly because of the personal hostility of men who disliked him. Greeley, whose reconciliation was short-lived, was present, and worked hard against him. When Lincoln made up his cabinet in the succeeding March, four of the six members were men who had been candidates before the Chicago convention. Hannibal Hamlin, of Maine, was nominated for the vice-presidency.

Lincoln Nominated.

May 9 all that was left of the whig and know-nothing parties assembled in convention and nominated John Bell, of Tennessee, for president and Edward Everett, of Massachusetts, for vice-president. They called themselves the constitutional union party, and appealed to those who decried party rancor and sectionalism to help them save the country.

Bell and Everett.

No one thought either Douglas, Breckinridge, or Bell could carry the country. The best their followers could hope for was to throw the election into the house. Everywhere they attacked the republicans and declared that Lincoln's election meant the disruption of the union. This argument the republicans derided. It was, said Lowell, "the old Mumbo-Jumbo" con-

Lincoln Elected.

jured up to frighten old women and stock speculators. Seward, who canvassed actively in behalf of his successful rival, said: "I do not doubt but that these Southern statesmen and politicians think they are going to dissolve the union, but I think they are going to do no such thing." This assurance, reiterated in many forms, allayed the fears of the mass of voters in the free states, so that they were nowise prepared for the events the succeeding winter witnessed. In October Pennsylvania and Indiana elected republican governors, premonitions of the result in November, when Lincoln came triumphantly through with every elector from the free states except three of New Jersey's seven. He had in all 180 votes to 72 for Breckinridge, 39 for Bell, and 12 for Douglas. The popular vote was Lincoln 1,857,610, Douglas 1,291,574, Breckinridge 850,082, and Bell 646,124. Lincoln, therefore, received 930,170 votes less than his combined opponents. In each house of congress, also, the republicans were in a minority against the combined opposition.

BIBLIOGRAPHICAL NOTE

The most satisfactory general work on the period embraced in this chapter is Rhodes, *History of the United States from the Compromise of 1850*, vols. I and II (1892). Two excellent books are : Smith, *Parties and Slavery* (1906), and Chadwick, *Causes of the Civil War* (1906), both in Hart, editor, *The American Nation*. They contain good bibliographies. Von Holst, *Constitutional History of the United States*, 8 vols. (trans. 1899), should not be neglected. It shows much research and keen analysis, but is unsympathetic. Schouler, *History of the United States*, 6 vols. (1880–1894), is readable and accurate. Fite, *The Presidential Campaign of 1860* (1911), is very complete, and Brown, *The Lower South* (1902), is very suggestive. Burgess, *The Middle Period* (1897), and *The Civil War and Reconstruction*, 2 vols. (1901), are valuable, but replete with detail.

Among the newer biographies of Lincoln several are of peculiar value. They are : Albert J. Beveridge, *Abraham Lincoln 1809–1858*, 2 vols. (1928) ; Lord Charnwood, *Abraham Lincoln* (1917) ; N. W. Stephenson, *Lincoln* (1922) ; and Carl Sandburg, *Abraham Lincoln, The Prairie Years*, 2 vols. (1927).

The biographies and works of leading men are : Nicolay and Hay, *Abraham Lincoln, a History*, 10 vols. (1890) ; Ibid., *Complete Works of Lincoln*, 2 vols. (1904) ; Tarbell, *Life of Abraham Lincoln*, 2 vols. (ed. 1900) ; Bancroft, *Life of Seward*, 2 vols. (1900) ; Baker, editor, *Works of William H. Seward*, 5 vols. (1853–1884) ; Moore, editor, *Works of James Buchanan*, 12 vols. (1908–1911) ; Pierce, *Memoir of Charles Sumner*, 4 vols. (1877) ; *Works of Charles Sumner*, 15 vols. (1870–1883) ; Edward Everett, *Orations and Speeches*, 4 vols. (1853–1868) ; Johnson, *Stephen A. Douglas* (1908) ; Hart, *Salmon Portland Chase* (1899) ; Villard, *John Brown, a Biography* (1910) ; Sanborn, *Life of John Brown* (1891) ; Dodd, *Jefferson Davis* (1907) ; Du Boise, *Life and Times of Yancey* (1892) ; Johnston and Brown, *Life of A. H. Stephens* (1878) ; Trent, *William Gilmore Simms* (1892) ; and Curtis, *James Buchanan*, 2 vols. (1883). For other biographies see Smith, *Parties and Slavery*, pp. 309–314, and Chadwick, *Causes of the Civil War*, pp. 347–351.

The original sources are to be found chiefly in public documents, of which the most important are : *The Congressional Globe, House and Senate Journals, Executive and Miscellaneous Documents*, and *Reports of Committees*. The laws are to be found in *The Statutes at Large of the United States*, and much valuable information is in Richardson, *Messages and Papers of the Presidents*, 10 vols. (1897–1899).

On Kansas and the matter pertaining to it, see : Ray, *Repeal of the Missouri Compromise* (1909), gives prominence to Atchison's influence in the matter ;

Dixon, *True History of the Missouri Compromise*, 1899, accepts Douglas's arguments, but shows that he was not the author of the Dixon amendment; Charles Robinson, *The Kansas Conflict* (1892, 1898), by a leading actor on the free state side; Blackmar, *Life of Charles Robinson* (1902), sane and reliable; Spring, *Kansas* (1885), fair to both sides, written by a participant; Ibid., *Career of a Kansas Politician* (*Am. Hist. Review*, 1898); Fleming, *The Buford Expedition to Kansas* (Ibid., 1900); Villard, *John Brown, a Biography* (1910). See also the "Howard Report," 34 Cong. 1st ses. Rept. No. 200. The attempt to adopt the Lecompton Constitution occasioned an investigation by a house committee. Its report (H. Ex. Docs., 36 Cong. 1st ses. No. 648, the "Covode Report") brought out much evidence of misdoing, presented in a very partisan manner.

For party history see: Theodore C. Smith, *The Liberty and Free Soil Parties in the Northwest* (1897); Curtis, *The Republican Party*, 2 vols. (1904); Fite, *Presidential Election of 1860* (1911); Macy, *Political Parties, 1846–1860* (1900); Ibid., *Party Organization and Party Machinery* (1904). Rhodes, *History of the United States*, 7 vols. (1892–1906), contains much party history carefully prepared from original sources. See also the biographies of leading men, especially Lincoln, Douglas, Buchanan, Jefferson Davis, and Seward.

On the Dred Scott decision see: *U. S. Supreme Court Reports* 19 Howard, (1857), the official decision; it was widely reprinted at the time; Hurd, *Law of Freedom and Bondage*, 2 vols. (1858–1862), reviews with much learning the legal status of slavery; Tyler, *Memoir of Taney* (revised ed., 1872); Biddle, *Constitutional Development as Influenced by Taney* (in Rogers, *Constitutional History as Seen in the Development of Law*, 1889); Curtis, *Constitutional History of the United States*, 2 vols. (1896); and Corwin, *The Dred Scott Decision in the Light of Contemporary Legal Doctrines* (*Am. Hist. Review*, 1911).

On the John Brown Raid much has been written, but most of it is partisan. A full bibliography is in Villard, *John Brown, A Biography* (1910), the best of Brown's biographies. See also *The Report of the Senate Committee to Investigate the Late Invasion* (the "Mason Report"), 36 Cong. 1st ses. Rept. Com. No. 278.

For Independent Reading

Forney, *Anecdotes of Public Men*, 2 vols. (1873, 1881); Trent, *Southern Statesmen of the Old Régime* (1897); James Freeman Clarke, *Antislavery Days* (1883); Davis, *Recollections of Mississippi and Mississippians* (1889); Conway, *Autobiography*, 2 vols. (1904); Abbott, *Henry Ward Beecher* (1903); Morse, *Abraham Lincoln*, 2 vols. (1893); Tarbell, *Life of Lincoln*, 2 vols. (ed. 1900).

CHAPTER XXIV

THE OUTBREAK OF THE CIVIL WAR

WAR OR PEACE?

ALTHOUGH the Gulf states furnished the ablest leaders of the South in the critical situation of 1860, South Carolina, the home of Calhoun and nullification, was fully abreast with the secession movement. In this respect she was ahead of Virginia, **South Carolina Secedes.** which was not a cotton state, and whose ancient Southern leadership was now little more than a name. The Carolina legislature still elected presidential electors, and was in session when the telegraph flashed the news that Lincoln was to be president. It immediately called a convention to consider the state's relation to the union. Thus it happened that a convention at Columbia on December 20, 1860, declared in solemn manner the dissolution of "the union now subsisting between South Carolina and the other states, under the name of the 'United States of America.'"

Now appeared in all other Southern states two parties, secessionists, mainly Breckenridge democrats, and union men. The former were the stronger in the Gulf states, where the rank prosperity of the preceding half century had produced a vehement **The Gulf States Follow.** and overconfident civilization. In these states the union had not the same force as in the northern tier of Southern states, and it was natural that the first victories of secession should be won here. The arguments that prevailed were the evident danger to slavery from a republican administration and the assertion that the South could make better terms out of the union than in it. It cannot be doubted, however, that most of the secessionists hoped for a permanent separation, thinking this the only safe way of preserving Southern institutions. By February 4 secession was declared in six states, South Carolina, Georgia, Alabama, Mississippi, Louisiana, and Florida, and on that day a convention at Montgomery, Alabama, established a provisional constitution for "The Confederate States of America," chose Jefferson Davis its president and **The " Confederate States of America."** Alexander H. Stephens its vice-president, and invited the other slave states to join it. Texas at this time had submitted secession to the people, who ratified it on the 23d. With these seven states in repudiation of the union the movement for secession halted for a time.

Meanwhile, all eyes turned to President Buchanan, a state rights man, a democrat, and long in declared sympathy with the South.

Buchanan's Attitude. Three members of his cabinet, Cass, Black, and Holt, urged him to send troops to hold the forts in the South. Three others, Cobb, Thompson, and Floyd, all Southerners, believed in secession as a right and exercised a strong influence over the president. They told him, and it was probably true, that to reënforce the Southern forts would alarm the South and drive the other Southern states into secession. For a time they had their way, with the result that Cass resigned from the cabinet. The president's annual message showed that he was at heart with the Southerners. It argued against the right of secession, declared that he would act strictly on the defensive, and made it clear that the aggression of the South would not be disturbed as long as the existing administration was in office. At the same time the New York *Tribune*, and abolitionists generally, were asserting plainly that the North could not conquer the South and that the South, if it so wished, should be allowed to "depart in peace." From this situation the secessionists took much comfort. It seemed that the stars were for them.

These bright hopes dissolved at last before the problem of the disposal of the eight forts in the seceding states. Six of them were without garrisons, and were easily occupied by the secessionists.

Forts in the South. The other two were Pickens, at Pensacola, and Sumter, at Charleston. In Sumter was Major Anderson with 84 men all told, and he showed such a spirited desire to protect the place that the sympathy of the North was aroused for the first time in many weeks of irresolution and delay. South Carolina, however, was arming her citizens, and during the rest of Buchanan's administration each side lay on its arms, neither wishing to strike the blow which would precipitate war.

One half-hearted attempt was made to reënforce Major Anderson. January 5, 1861, the *Star of the West*, a merchant vessel, sailed

The Star of the West. from New York with supplies and 204 men and officers for Sumter. Although efforts at secrecy were made, her departure was known at once in Charleston, and she was received on her arrival with a fire by the confederate batteries at the harbor entrance. Anderson could have silenced the batteries from Sumter, but he had not been informed of her departure, and hesitated to open fire. The result was that after coming within a mile and a half of the fort without receiving aid from that quarter she turned back to New York. This effort having failed, the policy of inaction went on until the coming of the new administration. Meanwhile, Fort Pickens, with a garrison of 48 men, remained in federal hands.

The anxiety to avoid an overt act of force was largely due to a desire that a compromise should be prepared by which the South would consent to abide in the union. This hope was reflected in congress, which created a senate committee to report a plan of compromise. Five of the thirteen members were republicans, two were from the cotton states, three were from border slave states, and three were Northern democrats. They were among the best men in public life, were desirous of peace, and showed their seriousness by agreeing in the beginning that they would accept no scheme which a majority of the republican members would not support. Many resolutions were referred to them, the most notable being a set known as "the Crittenden Compromise." It suggested a constitutional amendment excluding slavery from all territory north of the parallel 36° 30′, and establishing it with federal protection in all territory south of that line. Against this proposition the republicans were a unit. It was their principle, and they said so frankly, to agree to nothing which would admit slavery into another territory. For this reason the proposition failed. The senators from the cotton states voted against it as a matter of form, but it is known they would have accepted it if their republican colleagues had done the same. Other suggestions of compromise were made, but none came as near acceptance as Crittenden's. Here, as in the preceding political campaign, the antislavery and the proslavery forces had come to the irreconcilable stage of the "irrepressible conflict," and the committee of thirteen could only report on December 28 its inability to come to an agreement. We shall see later what part Lincoln took in bringing the republican committeemen to their determination to yield nothing.

Efforts to preserve Peace.

But Crittenden did not despair. He was the successor of Clay, as a Kentucky senator, and he worked hard for compromise. January 3, 1861, he asked the senate to order the sense of the people to be taken on the resolutions which had been rejected in committee, and Douglas supported him in a masterly speech. Could the vote have been taken, many republicans would undoubtedly have voted for it. All the Northern democrats and the Bell and Everett men would have gone the same way, so that it would have carried the North. In all the slave states which had not seceded the result must have been the same; and before this overwhelming approval the republicans in congress must have given way. But the proposal never came to a vote in the senate. The republican senators delayed its consideration so long that the cotton states seceded, and then it was not thought worth while to press the matter further. That the compromise, if adopted, would have brought harmony temporarily seems true, but it is doubtful if it would have solved the problem permanently. Lincoln opposed it on the ground that it would have been followed by attempts on the part of the South to acquire territory in Cuba and Mexico, and that the old threats of disunion would have recurred if the North had objected to such expansion of the proslavery interest.

Crittenden would Appeal to the People.

2 L

One other effort at compromise was to be made. February 4, at the call of Virginia, delegates from 22 states assembled in Washington to hold a peace convention. Ex-president Tyler, a Virginia delegate, presided, and the debates were secret. Threshing over the old straw, they at last advised a constitutional amendment somewhat less favorable to the South than Crittenden's. It was opposed by Virginia and other Southern states. As no one thought it would either satisfy the slave states still in the union or conciliate those which had seceded, the recommendations came to inglorious defeat in the senate. Thus ended the period of hesitation and doubt between the election and the inauguration of Lincoln. Buchanan, indecisive by nature, brought up to believe in the theory of state rights, bound to the South by long years of political and personal association, and unwilling to shoulder the responsibilities of a situation which his enemies had created, came at last to the end of his term without an actual resort to force. His successor, whose election had precipitated the crisis, must decide what the future would bring forth.

The Peace Convention.

LINCOLN AND SECESSION

The actuality of secession alarmed the business interests and conservative men of the North; and many republicans, who flouted the threat of secession in the preceding November, now felt they had gone too far. Such persons turned to Seward, whom they considered the real republican leader. They thought Lincoln inexperienced, and were pleased when it was said that Seward would be secretary of state. Thus, powerful influences worked to make the senator from New York think that he alone could save the country. He was not an idealist, and he seems to have concluded that he must invent some plan by which the South would be conciliated and the seceding states brought back.

Seward's Position.

But Lincoln had a firm conviction about the situation. He would not accept the Crittenden compromise or retreat from any position occupied during the campaign. To do so, he said, would be an abandonment of principle, would not satisfy the slave power, and would destroy the republican party. He gave no intimation of yielding on the main question, the exclusion of slavery in the territories; but he said clearly that he would not interfere with it in the states in which it existed. This did not satisfy the proslavery men. They believed that once the free states gained ascendency in the senate progressive restrictions of slavery would follow. They knew, also, that at no moment could secession be so well carried in the South as at the present, when the popular terror at a republican administration was greater than it would ever be again. If a Southern confederacy was to be attempted, now was the best time to launch it.

Lincoln's Firmness.

All the country, North as well as South, awaited anxiously the advent of March 4. Would the inaugural address announce conciliation or would it defy secession? To those who heard it delivered it seemed to do neither. It began with an assurance that slavery in the South was safe, and that fugitive slaves ought to be restored to their masters, and it asserted that the union was perpetual and secession impossible. There was, also, much benevolent argument against the wisdom of secession. Lincoln's strongest trait, perhaps, was his loving-kindness, and he seems to have meant to envelop his opponents in it so that he might win back to the union all who were not past the reach of reason. As to the forts and customhouses he said they must be held by the government, but he promised he would not needlessly irritate the Southern people by sending strangers into their communities to fill the various federal offices. This tone of remonstrance and evident reluctance to use force was interpreted by the secessionist as a sign of weakness.

The Inaugural Address.

March 5 Lincoln was shown a letter from Major Anderson, in Fort Sumter, saying that his provisions would be exhausted in a few weeks and that the confederate works around Sumter were so strong that 20,000 men would be required to maintain the post. Two of the cabinet wished to hold and strengthen the place, Blair unconditionally and Chase if it could be done without civil war. The others were for withdrawal, Seward taking the lead. He would avoid war, leave the seceding states to think over their position, and use the slave states still in the union as an influence to bring the wanderers back. Lincoln withheld his decision, but sent confidential messengers to South Carolina, who reported that there was no union sentiment in the state worth speaking about. Anderson himself favored evacuation, and General Scott, head of the army, held the same view.

Fort Sumter.

Meanwhile, three agents of the confederate government were in Washington to negotiate for the recognition of independence, the surrender of the forts, and an adjustment of monetary losses to the federal government through the surrender of federal property in the South. Opinions were exchanged between them and Seward, who saw them at least once. With his policy of conciliation in view he suggested they delay an attack on Sumter, and they agreed on condition that the existing status in Charleston be not disturbed. They were not officially received, but on being assured through a third party that Sumter would be evacuated, they decided to remain in Washington. Their withdrawal would have been followed by an attack on Sumter. They waited until the end of March, and when at that time they saw no evidences of evacuation, they began to be uneasy. Rumors reached them of an expedition to succor the forts. To their remonstrances Seward said, through an

Confederate Agents in Washington.

intermediary, "Faith as to Sumter fully kept; wait and see." Next day, April 8, ships for the relief of Sumter began their journey from New York and the confederate commissioners broke off their negotiations.

Seward had not intentionally deceived the confederates. All he did was in pursuance of his policy of delay. His assurances as to Sumter were given on his own responsibility. They failed be-

Lincoln Overrules Seward. cause at this time Lincoln had come to a decision that the authority of the union must be asserted at all hazards. It was he who gave the order to succor the fort, overriding Seward's scheming and teaching him and the country that Lincoln was a real president. Had the secretary had his way a shifty policy would have been followed, the confederacy would have been established, probably beyond the possibility of overthrow, and the union sentiment of the North would have been so dissipated that war would have become an impossibility. In this sense the civil war was Lincoln's war, and the preservation of the union was Lincoln's act.

When the confederate president knew that provisions were coming to Sumter he held a long and anxious cabinet meeting. To fire on Sumter would precipitate war and unite the North in defense of union. The cooler advisers felt that the hope of secession lay in avoiding war. Lincoln said he would only land supplies and not men if the fort was not attacked. The more hot-headed advisers thought that the possession of a federal fort in the limits of the newly established confederacy was not to be tolerated. This view prevailed, and the order was

The Attack on Sumter. given to reduce the works. More than 5000 troops lay in the strong batteries around the place waiting for the order to fire. Anderson offered to surrender in three days if not provisioned or overruled by his government. From the confederate standpoint the offer should have been accepted, but rash counsels prevailed, and just before dawn on April 12 a solitary mortar gave the signal for the attack. The bombardment which followed lasted 34 hours, at the end of which time Anderson surrendered and marched out with the honors of war. Not a man on either side was killed, but the fort was badly wrecked from a fire which destroyed the barracks and exploded some of the magazines. The confederates expressed their admiration for the heroic defenders in loud cheers; and Anderson saluted his flag with fifty guns before he transferred his men to the relief ships which had arrived during the bombardment but were unable to reach Sumter. About this time Fort Pickens was reënforced, and it was held throughout the war.

PREPARATIONS FOR WAR

Firing on the flag dispelled the last doubts of the North. Stephen A. Douglas issued an appeal for his friends to rally to the defense of

the union. Bell and Everett whigs were equally loyal, and within a month the whole North was holding mass meetings in which thousands of speakers aroused the men to take up arms. April 15 Lincoln called for 75,000 volunteers, and three weeks later for 42,000 more. He also ordered the enlistment of 23,000 additional regulars and the increase of the navy by 18,000 men.
To these demands the response was more than adequate, and by July 1, he had an available force of 310,000. April 19 he declared the southern ports blockaded. The ships of the navy were widely dispersed by direction of Buchanan's secretary of the navy, but orders were sent to hasten their return, and every effort was made to purchase and arm other ships to make the blockade effective. In this way, though with much confusion, the machinery of government was set going by the master hand in the great process of war.

Lincoln's Call to Arms.

The Blockade.

In the South, meanwhile, was a similar state of activity. President Jefferson Davis was a West Point graduate; he had rendered distinguished service in the Mexican war, and no one doubted his energy and earnestness. He called for 100,000 volunteers, and hastened the preparations for war. The attack on Sumter showed the slave states still in the union that they must fight for or against the confederacy, and four of them quickly joined the seven which had already seceded. They were: Arkansas, May 4; Virginia, May 17; North Carolina, May 20; and Tennessee, June 24. Strong Southern feeling existed in Maryland, Kentucky, and Missouri, and for a long time they hung in the balance, while Lincoln used his utmost tact to save them for the union. If the war were fought to destroy slavery, they would go with the South, but if slavery were not threatened, they would not secede. Lincoln was very tactful by nature, and succeeded in calming the apprehensions of the border state slaveholders. Time worked in his behalf; for as the seriousness of the struggle became apparent, secession became less popular in these states. Thus the crisis passed peaceably in Kentucky and Maryland. But Missouri was temporarily in convulsions. Jackson, the secessionist governor, refused to furnish troops at the call of the president and made preparations to carry the state over to the side of the South. Friends of the union, however, led by F. P. Blair, Jr., raised four regiments, which were accepted by the federal authorities and placed under the command of General Lyon. Then followed four months of commotion, during which the people flocked to Lyon's standard and enabled him to seize the city of St. Louis and call a state convention which declared against secession and deposed the governor. Thus the danger passed in the third of the border states; but from each many volunteers joined the confederate armies. At Gettysburg an important part of the field was contested between two bodies of Maryland troops, one in blue and the other in gray.

Arming in the South.

The Border States.

Missouri.

Let us consider for a moment the relative strength of the two sides in the war about to begin. In population the North was greatly superior. Her 22,000,000 inhabitants confronted 9,000,000 in the South, 3,500,000 of whom were blacks. But the blacks were a factor in the war, although they did not count man for man with the whites. They remained on the farms and produced the supplies for the army. Counting two of them as worth one white man in their contribution to the struggle, the numerical force of the North was to that of the South as twenty-two to seven. The South realized this inferiority in population, but expected to overcome it by what she considered the superior fighting ability of her soldiers. An arithmetic published in the South during the war stated the problems in terms like these: "If one confederate soldier can whip seven federal soldiers, how many federal soldiers can nine confederate soldiers whip?"

Relative Strength of North and South.

In the beginning of the war the Southerners seemed to fight better than their opponents. They were used to outdoor life, they were fighting on their own soil, resisting what they considered an "invasion," and they were well acquainted with the country in which they operated. Moreover, they drew the minor officers from the planter class, men accustomed to command and trained to exercise influence over their poorer neighbors, who now made up the privates. Thus the Southern volunteers took up the soldier's life more readily than their opponents, and the Southern army was more quickly drilled into veterans. The union troops awoke slowly to their task; it took a long time to develop efficient lower officers, but at last all was achieved, and then it was not possible to discover any notable difference in the fighting ability of the two armies, the capacity of the generals and the numbers being equal.

Relative Fighting Ability.

In material resources the North had a great advantage. Her people had all the facilities for manufacturing arms, ammunition, comfortable clothing, and the other necessary supplies. Besides this, the markets of the world remained open to her during the struggle. The South had no manufactures and very few trained mechanics, her supplies were cut off by the blockade, and, spite of strenuous efforts to make what was needed, her troops suffered greatly through lack of clothing, medicines, and the munitions of war. In the beginning she derived much benefit from arms taken in the forts she seized, and in Harper's Ferry; but this, as Rhodes points out, only gave her about the part of the national supply of arms which she felt rightfully belonged to her as a part of the old government.

Material Resources.

THE BULL RUN CAMPAIGN

July 4 Congress met in extra session. Lincoln reported what had been done to meet the emergency and asked for approval. The response was all he desired. He was authorized to raise the army to 500,000 men, to borrow $200,000,000, and to issue $50,000,000 in treasury notes. The tariff was raised as much as it was thought the industry of the country would stand, and other taxes were levied. Four months earlier the country seemed to prefer disunion to war, but through the tactful measures of the president all doubts were now dispelled, and a war policy was approved in the house with only five dissenting votes. *The Extra Session of Congress, July 4.*

By this time 30,000 men under General McDowell were assembled south of Alexandria, while 22,000 more under General Patterson were at Martinsburg, in the northern end of the Shenandoah valley. Opposing each force was a confederate army. One of 23,000 under Beauregard was at Manassas, and another of 9000 under Joseph E. Johnston was at Winchester, in the valley. *An Advance on Richmond.* The whole North rang with a demand for an advance on Richmond, since the secession of Virginia the confederate capital, and Lincoln ordered McDowell to make such a movement. He also ordered Patterson to keep Johnston engaged so that the troops of the latter should not join Beauregard at the critical moment. July 18 the armies of McDowell and Beauregard came into proximity with one another some miles northwest of Manassas. The confederates were drawn up behind Bull Run, their left holding the stone bridge by which the road from Alexandria crossed the stream and their right extending toward Manassas. Beauregard appealed to his government for reënforcements, and Johnston was ordered to join him. Obeying instantly, he moved toward Patterson to deceive him, which proved an easy task; for that officer most unaccountably moved his whole army northward until it was 22 miles from Winchester. *Position of the Confederates.* Johnston then turned backward, and at noon, July 20, joined Beauregard with 6000 men, leaving most of the rest of his army, 2300, to approach as fast as they could.

Meanwhile, McDowell made an excellent plan of battle. All his force was in position on July 20, and the attack was fixed for the next morning. While the main army rested on Bull Run in readiness to cross, Hunter's division was ordered up the stream to turn the enemy's left. The movement was executed very successfully. *McDowell's Excellent Attack.* At ten o'clock, while Beauregard expected an advance across the stream, Hunter's regiments suddenly struck his right, forced it back with hard fighting until the fords and the stone bridge were uncovered, and by noon the whole union army, pouring across the stream, threw itself on the confederates, who by much exertion were brought into line to hold a small plateau just east of the bridge, known as the Henry plateau. At this point the battle raged fiercely. Thomas J. Jackson, commanding a confederate brigade, held it so firmly that General Bee, another confederate, exclaimed: "Look at Jackson *Defence of the Henry Plateau.*

There he stands like a stone wall!" and thus originated the name "Stonewall Jackson." But Jackson's firmness was overcome; his men were driven from the plateau by the federals, whom McDowell brought up with great rapidity. The confederates rallied and retook the place, but were themselves driven off by their opponents. At three o'clock it seemed they would not return, and McDowell believed the field was his. At this moment Kirby Smith with a large force of fresh confederate troops arrived, joined their repulsed brethren, and reopened the battle. It was the remnant of Johnston's valley army, 2300 strong, who had hastened to the field, guided by the firing of cannon. Through the tired union ranks, exhausted by five hours of fighting on a hot summer day, ran the murmur, "Johnston's army has come," and panic was created. Seasoned troops would have held the ground or retreated in order. The new levies under McDowell did neither. They quickly fell back to the stone bridge — crossed it, and at nightfall were retreating in a confused mass to Washington. No efforts of the officers could stay them, and before morning the routed army was, as McDowell said, "a confused mob, utterly demoralized." The battle was well planned and well fought until three o'clock, but the untrained soldiers could not stand the shock of a repulse. Their terror was unfounded; for the confederates, themselves exhausted and off their guard, did not pursue. Had they followed promptly, they might have occupied the capital with little resistance. The union loss was 1584 killed and wounded and 1312 captured; the confederates lost 1982 killed, wounded, and missing. The defeat at Bull Run nerved the North to renewed efforts; it gave the South greater confidence in ultimate success. Both sides realized the need of long and patient drill in order to make soldiers out of the volunteers.

Arrival of Kirby Smith.

" A Confused Mob."

Results.

Meantime important developments occurred in the western counties of Virginia. The people of this region were generally non-slaveholders. For a long time they had been at odds with the people east of the mountains, claiming that the latter, led by the slaveholders, ruled the state, built railroads, and filled the offices in the interest of the East. The Westerners opposed secession and began to denounce it in mass meetings as soon as the convention at Richmond declared for the confederacy. Soon after hostilities began, they were in arms for the union, and, joining with a federal army under McClellan, drove out in a series of small battles the forces which the confederates sent to hold this region. Then was carried through a movement for a new state. The federal constitution provides that a state shall not be divided without its consent, and with this in view a convention at Wheeling, May 13, representing 26 counties, declared that by secession all the Virginia officials had forfeited their offices; and it called on the people to select a convention to

The Western Counties of Virginia.

reëstablish a lawful government. The result was that June 11, 1861, delegates from 40 counties met in convention, took the oath of loyalty to the union, declared themselves the convention of "re- stored Virginia," and having purged the state of treason ordered an election of a governor and other officials over all Virginia. Accordingly, F. H. Peirpoint was chosen governor, and a newly elected legislature filled the places vacant by the withdrawal of the recent senators. The appointees were given seats in the senate.

"Restored Virginia."

August 6 the convention reassembled to take up the question of a new state. It was ordered that a popular vote be taken on the sub- ject, with the result that the proposition prevailed by a vote of 18,408 to 781. Then a constitution was framed for the proposed "State of West Virginia," the 39 west- ern counties. It said nothing about slavery, but in the election the people expressed in an unofficial vote an overwhelming opinion against the institution, and thenceforth they were assured of the support of congress. The next thing was to get the consent of Virginia. To that end Peirpoint's "restored" legislature met, and went through the form of sanctioning the division of the "Old Dominion." Then the appli- cation went to congress, which duly declared that Virginia having consented to the act of division, the state of West Virginia was ad- mitted to the union. The act of admission was approved by Lincoln, December 31, 1861. The proceedings were most irregular, but it was a time when the rules of peace were not strictly considered. The people of Virginia have ever considered the rending of their common- wealth an unconstitutional and malevolent action.

New State Movement.

By cutting off from his government the western counties, Peirpoint's "restored" Virginia was limited to the counties around Alexandria, Fortress Monroe, and Norfolk — places all held by union arms. Over these he kept up the formality of an adminis- tration until the end of the war, living safely within the union lines at Alexandria. His "state" was a farce, but Lincoln wished it kept alive in the hope that it would furnish the nucleus for reconstructing Virginia when her resistance should have been overcome (see page 601).

The Alexan- drian Gov- ernment.

RELATIONS WITH GREAT BRITAIN

From the beginning Europe took much interest in the war. As England was most intimately related with the contestants, France and other European powers let it be known they would follow her lead. Her ruling classes, chiefly the landed gentry, merchants, and manufacturers, felt much friend- liness for the South, some of them because the South was supposed to be aristocratic, and others because the South, having no factories of her own, was expected to purchase freely of England. The confederates

Feeling for the South.

understood this feeling and hoped for much from it. They, also, thought that since the English cotton factories depended on them for raw material, English ships would come to America, break the Southern blockade, and establish an outlet for the great Southern staple as well as an inlet for the supplies which were so much needed. To prevent this became the chief item of the foreign policy of Lincoln's government; and for this purpose he discovered a most excellent agent in

Charles Francis Adams.

Charles Francis Adams, son of John Quincy Adams, whom he sent to London as minister. Adams was persistent and fearless, and spite of the evident unfriendliness of Palmerston, the prime minister, and Earl Russell, the foreign secretary, he succeeded in preventing by his vigilant protest many acts of assistance to the South. He found his chief support in the fact that the confederacy fought to preserve slavery. John Bright, Richard Cobden, and W. E. Forster, champions of any reform that

Feeling for the North.

made for social betterment, worked mightily to arouse the middle classes in favor of the union. Their influence was great, and the ministers did not dare antagonize this sentiment in order to open a market for the merchants and manufacturers. Three incidents arose over which the two nations nearly came to a rupture of friendship.

1. The recognition of the confederacy as a belligerent. As soon as the government was organized at Montgomery, confederate agents in

Status of Belligerency allowed to Confederates.

London began to ask for the recognition of confederate independence. The request was not granted, but the queen issued, May 13, 1861, a proclamation of neutrality in which each side was given the rights of belligerency within British jurisdiction. Adams landed in England the day the proclamation was issued, and the action of the ministry was considered discourteously precipitate. It also violated Lincoln's theory that the confederacy had not the status of a power, but represented only a group of insurgents. The confederates too were disappointed; but consoled themselves with the reflection that belligerency gave their privateers a standing in foreign ports, and they hoped that future successes would compel the recognition of independence.

2. For a time the union papers were full of recrimination for England, and November 8, 1861, the feeling burst forth when the American

The *Trent* Affair.

ship, *San Jacinto*, Captain Wilkes, seized Mason and Slidell on the British mailship, *Trent*. These two confederates were bound for Europe, one to represent his government at London and the other at Paris. They had escaped through the blockade to Havana and there taken the British steamer, *Trent*, for Southampton. The seizure was on the high seas, and was by force. News of it put the North into a delirium of joy, Wilkes was hero wherever he went, and congress and the secretary of the navy extended him their thanks. Lincoln and only one member of the cabinet, Postmaster-general Blair, regretted the occurrence. They foresaw that Great Britain would demand a disclaimer, and believed that in the excited state of the public mind war might occur. They promptly informed England that Wilkes had acted without instructions, and awaited her further procedure.

In all Britain was great indignation, for the flag had been violated at sea. A large fleet was assembled, and 8000 troops were sent to Canada, embarking, it is said, to the tune, "I wish I were in Dixie." The government prepared an offensive demand for the surrender of the confederates. The Prince Consort, then suffering from a fatal illness, saw the dispatch, and suggested softer expressions, by which it was possible for the American government to accept the demands, Mason and Slidell were released, but no apology was made. In a long reply Seward stated the American position. **Mason and Slidell Surrender.** Had Wilkes seized the *Trent* and sent her before an admiralty court he would have been within his right. As it was, he had exercised the right of search, something the American government had ever opposed. Thus ended the *Trent* affair at the very close of 1861.

3. The other irritating incident was fitting out cruisers for the confederacy, certainly a violation of the neutrality England had so hurriedly announced. In March, 1862, the *Florida*, built at Liverpool, was allowed to depart for Nassau, in the Bahamas, where she was libeled for violation of neutrality. **The Confederate Ships, *Florida*.** But a court ordered her release, and she sailed on a career of destruction as a confederate ship.

Meanwhile, a more powerful ship was being built at the same place — evidently for the same purpose. June 23 our minister, Adams, asked for an inquiry to see if she ought to be held. A superficial investigation was made by the Liverpool authorities, who were in sympathy with the South and who re- **The *Alabama*.** ported that no evidence was found that the ship was destined for that country. Still Adams persisted, securing undoubted evidence, which was referred to Sir John Harding, Queen's Advocate. Harding was on the verge of a mental collapse, and the papers lay unopened by him for five days before they came to other hands, and were so reported that the order to detain the ship was given on July 29. But the step was too long deferred; for on the same morning the steamer got out to sea for a trial trip and did not come back. She went to the Azores, where she took on her armor and a confederate crew and began her momentous career as the commerce destroyer, *Alabama*. Ten years later an arbitration court at Geneva declared that England had not used due diligence in enforcing neutrality in regard to these two ships. Early in 1863 it became known that three other powerful ships were under construction at Liverpool, but the government prevented their departure. The *Florida* and the *Alabama*, with some smaller ships, constituted the confederate navy. They were not able to meet the ships of the union, and contented themselves with destroying unarmed merchantmen, of which during the course of the war they took 285, at a total loss of about $15,000,000.

These three incidents, so full of possible misfortune for those who struggled to preserve the union, thus ended favorably to the North.

The South found herself disappointed in her hope of foreign
The Results favor the North.   aid, and the war settled down to a long-drawn out assault of one section against the other. The point on which the decision of England and France turned was slavery. Spite of all that the Southerners said, the real question was the perpetuity of slavery, and the world abroad was not prepared to support the side which upheld it.

BIBLIOGRAPHICAL NOTE

The general works are : Rhodes, *History of the United States*, 7 vols. (1892–1907) ; Schouler, *The United States under the Constitution*, 6 vols. (1880–1897) ; Chadwick, *Causes of the Civil War* (1906) ; Hosmer, *The Appeal to Arms* (1907) ; von Holst, *Constitutional History of the United States*, 8 vols. (ed. 1899) ; Greeley, *The American Conflict*, 2 vols. (1864), valuable for extracts from documents ; Draper, *History of the Civil War*, 3 vols. (1871) ; Ropes, *Story of the Civil War*, 2 vols. (1899), unfinished but continued by Livermore, two vols., announced in 1913 ; and Reed, *Brother's War* (1905), a recent Southern book.

For works and biographies of leading men see : Nicolay and Hay, *Abraham Lincoln, a History*, 10 vols. (1890) ; Ibid., edr., *Complete Works of Lincoln*, 2 vols. (1904) ; Baker, edr., *Seward Works*, 5 vols. (1853–1884) ; *Autobiography of Seward* (1877) ; Bancroft, *Life of Seward*, 2 vols. (1900) ; *Mr. Buchanan's Administration on the Eve of the Rebellion* (1866), Buchanan's own defense ; Moore, edr., *Works of James Buchanan*, 12 vols. (1908–1911) ; Curtis, *James Buchanan*, 2 vols. (1883) ; Coleman, *Life of John J. Crittenden*, 2 vols. (1871) ; Welles, edr., *Diary of Gideon Welles*, 3 vols. (1911) ; John Sherman, *Recollections of Forty Years*, 2 vols. (1895) ; Julian, *Political Recollections* (1884) ; McClure, *Lincoln and Men of War Times* (ed. 1894) ; Black, edr., *Essays and Speeches of J. S. Black, with a Biographical Sketch* (1885) ; Alfriend, *Life of Jefferson Davis* (1868) ; Johnston and Browne, *Alexander H. Stephens* (1878) ; Avary, edr., *Autobiography of Alexander H. Stephens* (1910) ; Pendleton, *Alexander H. Stephens* (1907) ; Wise, *Seven Decades of the Union* (1881) ; Trescott, *Negotiations between South Carolina and President Buchanan* (*Am. Hist. Review*, 1908) ; and Hart, *Salmon Portland Chase* (1899).

On this brief period the important public documents are in : Richardson, *Messages and Papers of the Presidents*, 10 vols. (1896–1897) ; *The Congressional Globe*, for the debates ; *War of the Rebellion, Official Records*, very full for military affairs North and South ; *Official Records of the Union and Confederate Navies ;* and Poore, *Descriptive Catalogue of Government Publications, 1774–1881* (1885). Of great value are the newspapers and periodicals of the times, especially the *Tribune*, *Evening Post*, and *Times*, of New York, the Boston *Advertiser*, the Springfield *Republican*, the Albany *Evening Journal*, the Chicago *Tribune*, the Philadelphia *North American*, the Richmond *Enquirer*, the Charleston *Mercury*, and the Washington *Union*.

On the struggle in the border states see : Harding, *Missouri Party Struggles* (*Am. Hist. Assn. Reports*, 1890) ; Snead, *Fight for Missouri* (1886) ; Woodward, *Nathaniel Lyon* (1862) ; Brown, *Baltimore and April 19, 1861* (1887) ; and McCarthy, *Lincoln's Plan of Reconstruction* (1901), for the creation of West Virginia. Many books of personal observations have appeared, among them the following of much value: Russell, *My Diary North and South* (1862), by an intelligent correspondent of the London *Times;* Jones, *A Rebel War Clerk's Diary*, 2 vols. (1866); Gurowski, *Diary from March 4, 1861, to November 12, 1862* (1862); and Pike, *First Blows of the Civil War* (1879).

On the fall of Fort Sumter see: Crawford, *Genesis of the Civil War* (1887); Doubleday, *Reminiscences of Forts Sumter and Moultrie* (1876); and Roman, *Military Operations of General Beauregard*, 2 vols. (1884).

Books in sympathy with the South are: Jefferson Davis, *Rise and Fall of the Confederate Government*, 2 vols. (1881); Stephens, *War between the States*, 2 vols. (1867); Curry, *The Southern States in Relation to the United States* (1894); Fowler, *Sectional Controversy* (1865); Du Bose, *Life of W. L. Yancey* (1896); and Wise, *Life of Henry A. Wise* (1899).

For Independent Reading

Russell, *My Diary North and South* (1862); Reuben Davis, *Recollections of Mississippi and Mississippians* (1900); Wilmer, *Recent Past from a Southern Standpoint* (1900); Clayton, *White and Black under the Old Régime* (1899); Morse, *Life of Lincoln*, 2 vols. (1893); Riddle, *Recollections of War Times* (1895); and Forney, *Anecdotes of Public Men* (1873).

CHAPTER XXV

THE WESTERN CAMPAIGNS

A Bifurcated Invasion

THE task of the North was to enter Southern territory, suppress resistance, and restore the authority of the union: that of the confederacy was to resist conquest. The Northern invasion was a bifurcated movement, one part operating on the east and the other on the west of the Appalachian mountains. It was hoped that each would roll back the confederate resistance and, by uniting below the southern end of the mountain system, give the finishing stroke to the confederacy somewhere in northern Georgia. As it fell out, the union advance was checked by Lee's army in the East, but it was steadily successful in the West. The Mississippi river and all of Tennessee were gradually secured, and by the middle of 1864 northern Georgia was occupied by a strong and victorious army. The western division had done its allotted task, and now turned northward to help the Eastern troops complete the capture of Richmond. The present chapter will describe as a whole the Western movements and the succeeding chapter will deal with the operations in the East.

THREE PRELIMINARY OPERATIONS, 1861

The conquest of the West began properly in 1862, but in 1861 there were three important preliminary episodes: 1. While the people of western Virginia were busy creating a new state a union army under General McClellan drove back the confederate forces which came from the east to maintain the Virginia authority. In several sharp engagements McClellan's fame was established, and he was called to Washington to command a greater army. In the western counties he was succeeded by Rosecrans, who had Robert E. Lee for an opponent. Lee's force was inadequate, and was forced over the mountains, and it was not until he had won his brilliant victories in the campaign around Richmond in the following year that the Southern people forgot his present ill fortune. 2. The success of the unionists in preventing secession in Missouri (see page 517) was followed by a determined confederate effort to retake the state by arms. At first it seemed successful, and the federal General Lyon was killed. But he was avenged by General

1. West Virginia.

2. Missouri.

Pope, who with a strong force drove the confederate army out of Missouri. Late in 1861 Halleck was given command on both sides of the Mississippi, with headquarters at St. Louis. He well understood the art of war, but proved slow in execution. Under him, however, served several brilliant generals, and affairs in his department progressed favorably. 3. The confederates wished to make the Ohio river their line of defense, although they had not **3. Holding the Ohio.** troops enough to hold Kentucky. But in September, 1861, General Grant, then acting under Frémont, defeated this plan by seizing Paducah and Cairo. The result was that the enemy established his lines from the Mississippi at Island No. 10, New Madrid, and Columbus, thence eastward to Forts Henry on the Tennessee and Donelson on the Cumberland, and after that at Bowling Green, Kentucky, a place nearly due north of Nashville, with which it was connected by sixty miles of railroad. To the eastward a small force occupied central and eastern Kentucky, where union sentiment was strong; but a federal force drove it back in January 1862. By these three preliminary movements the border states of Missouri and Kentucky, which Lincoln's tact had kept from secession, and the new state of West Virginia, were saved from the confederate arms. From that time the fiercest field of western operations was Tennessee.

GRANT'S CAMPAIGN ON THE TENNESSEE, 1862

Late in January Grant formed a plan to cut the confederate line at Forts Henry and Donelson, only eleven miles apart. Receiving permission from Halleck he moved up the Tennessee with 17,000 men and seven gunboats. The confederates did not **Fort Henry Captured.** allow themselves to be surrounded, and surrendered the place after most of its defenders had withdrawn to Fort Donelson (February 6), which Grant lost no time in attacking. He sent his gunboats back to the Ohio and up the Cumberland, while he marched overland to Donelson. Here the first attack of the boats was repulsed, and they retired for repairs. Then Grant threw his force around the fort on the land side and was in a position to starve or storm it. For such a fate the occupants would not wait. At dawn on February 15 they attacked and drove back the union right, so that for a few hours the road was open. Grant was four miles away, and rode hurriedly to the danger point. Learning that the knapsacks of the **Surrender of Fort Donelson.** captured confederates were filled with food, he divined that an escape was intended, and ordered an assault along all his line. It was delivered with great spirit, the confederate defenses were penetrated, and retreat was made impossible. During the night the generals in the fort, Floyd, Pillow, and Buckner, decided that surrender was necessary. Floyd had been Buchanan's secretary of war, and feared to be taken prisoner. He handed over the command

and escaped across the river in a skiff under cover of darkness.   Two small steamboats arrived at dawn, and on them Pillow and some troops escaped.   A body of cavalry under Forrest, who was soon to be a noted leader of light-horse troops, escaped along the river bank.   The rest of the confederates, nearly 15,000, were surrendered by Buckner.   In this action the union army numbered 27,000.

The situation in Tennessee now shifted rapidly.   Albert Sidney Johnston, in chief command of the confederates, hurriedly withdrew the force from Bowling Green to Nashville, and Buell, who had been watching it, followed leisurely.   If he and Grant united their armies, the story of Fort Donelson would be repeated at the state capital.   Johnston was too wise to be caught in a trap, and continued to retreat, spite of the censure of the Southern press.   He finally halted at Corinth, Mississippi, important because it commanded the railroad from Chattanooga to Memphis. While he collected supplies and reënforcements his opponents leisurely overran western Tennessee.

Johnston Falls back to Corinth.

March 17 Grant, following the Tennessee river, arrived at Savannah with 45,000 men.   Buell, with 35,000, was approaching from the northeast, and the plan was that the two forces should unite and crush Johnston, who had only 40,000.   Grant thought his opponents could not take the offensive, and carelessly placed five divisions at Pittsburg Landing, on the west side of the river, twenty-three miles from Corinth, holding Lew Wallace's division at Crump's Landing, five miles north of that point.   He failed to intrench, though ordered to do so by Halleck, and had his headquarters at Savannah, eight miles north of his main force and on the opposite side of the river.   He was daily expecting Buell, who, in fact, reached Savannah April 5, where he was allowed to halt.

Grant's Confident Approach.

Johnston was an able general, and was anxious to fight before Buell came up.   Moving out of Corinth, he fell on the union force in the early morning of April 6.   Grant heard the firing, and hastened to the scene by boat.   To his surprise, he found a heavy battle in progress, and his men fighting for their lives.   He ordered Wallace and Buell to come up, and calmly watched the fray.   Throughout the whole day the fighting continued, the federals being driven back, and Shiloh Church, the key of the field, was taken by Johnston, who, fighting with great courage, was struck in the leg as he led a regiment into a hazardous charge.   He had previously ordered his surgeon to attend to the wounded elsewhere, and bled to death before aid could be found.   His death discouraged his men, who, however, at nightfall held the ground the union force occupied in the morning and had forced their foe to take protection under the fire of the union gunboats.   In the night Grant received 20,000 fresh troops from Wallace and Buell, and next morning renewed

The Battle of Shiloh.

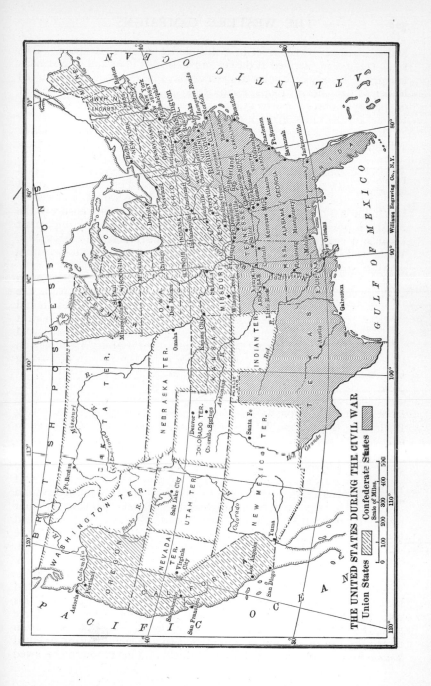

THE UNITED STATES DURING THE CIVIL WAR

Union States ▢ Confederate States ▨

Scale of Miles.

0 100 200 300 400 500

Williams Engraving Co., N.Y.

the battle. After eight hours of fighting on this day, the confederates withdrew to Corinth. The total union loss was 13,000 killed, wounded, and captured. The total confederate loss was 10,700. **The Result.** Johnston fought to crush his opponent and to drive him from his advanced position in the heart of the confederate southwest, and since that object was not achieved, the battle of Shiloh, as it is called, was a confederate defeat. Halleck now came to Pittsburg Landing in person, and after raising the army to 100,000 men, moved cautiously on Corinth. When he was ready to besiege it, the confederates withdrew and allowed him to have it without endangering their safety.

The campaign on the Tennessee river left exposed the confederate posts on the upper Mississippi. Columbus was abandoned, New Madrid and Island No. 10 were invested and taken by Pope in March and April with more than 7000 prisoners. **Success on** Gunboats then passed down the river, and June 5 and 6, **the Missis-** a week after Corinth was taken, Fort Pillow and Memphis **sippi.** were in union hands. Meanwhile, a naval expedition under Farragut, aided by Porter, had appeared in the lower Mississippi. After futilely bombarding the forts on the river for five days, Farragut with great daring ran past them safely, and April 25 New Orleans fell into his hands, receiving a garrison of 2500 men under Benjamin F. Butler. The forts then surrendered to Porter.

CONFEDERATE COUNTER-MOVEMENT IN TENNESSEE AND KENTUCKY

After the capture of Corinth, Halleck remained inactive, while the confederates recruited their armies and prepared another movement. They placed Bragg, with 35,000 men, in Chattanooga, the key of southeastern Tennessee, and Buell was ordered **Bragg's** to operate against him. This union general collected his **March on** force at Murfreesboro, 35 miles southeast of Nashville, **Louisville.** protecting the latter place from Bragg. Before he could move farther Bragg left Chattanooga, August 28, and dividing his army turned Buell's left and marched into Kentucky. Lexington was seized, and Louisville and Cincinnati were in a paroxysm of terror lest they should be taken before succor arrived. Buell meantime gave up all thought of Chattanooga, and hurried back to Louisville. Bragg was ahead of him, and probably could have taken the city, but he became discouraged when the Kentuckians did not join him, as he expected, and allowed his opponent to reach the goal. Buell thus recruited his force to 58,000 and turned backward to face his foe. **Battle of** Seven days later, October 8, the two armies fought at **Perryville.** Perryville, 65 miles southeast of Louisville. Neither side was entirely concentrated, but after fighting until dark Bragg withdrew his force and reached Chattanooga safely. At Perryville he lost

2 M

3400 men, and his opponent 4200.   Buell was ordered to follow Bragg
and hold east Tennessee, but he thought he could not support his
men so far from his base and took position at Nashville.   For doing
so he was removed from command and Rosecrans took his place.

The new general was ordered "to take and hold east Tennessee,"
but like Buell he refused to attempt it.   He remained in Nashville
for weeks, and Bragg quietly came back to Murfrees-
Battle of boro, where he intrenched.   Finally, on December 26,
Stone's 1862, Rosecrans moved on his opponent, and on the 31st
River, or a great battle was fought at Stone's river, three miles
Murfrees- from Murfreesboro, by which name the action is some-
boro. times known.   Each general proposed to attack the
other's right; but Bragg moved at dawn, while the union attack was
ordered for 7 A.M.   The confederate onset led by Hardee drove back
the union right, which was only saved by the immovable center under
Thomas.   After a hard day's fight darkness closed the struggle.
Rosecrans seemed beaten, but would not retreat.   January 2, Bragg
renewed the attack, but was beaten off and retired to Chattanooga.
The casualties were a union loss of 13,000 out of a total force of
43,000, and a confederate loss of 10,000 out of 38,000.   The southerners
carried off 28 captured guns and claimed the victory; but they had
failed to drive away Rosecrans and to rescue Tennessee from union
control.   The net result of the war in the West for 1862 was that all
of Kentucky and western and central Tennessee as well as a large
part of the Mississippi river were wrenched from the confederacy.

VICKSBURG CAPTURED

After losing Memphis and New Orleans the confederates fortified
Vicksburg most carefully; for it was the one strong position left them
on the river.   If it were taken, the trans-Mississippi region
Importance would be cut off, the importation of light supplies through
of Vicksburg. Mexico would be made difficult, and a fertile source of
food for the armies would be lost.   For the same reasons that the
South wished to hold it the North wished to take it.

In the summer of 1862 Halleck was called to Washington to aid
the president in the chief command of the army, and Grant was
left in command of the great army at Corinth.   For weeks he remained
inactive, and the confederates, taking heart, tried to retake Corinth,
but were easily beaten off.   For this delay he was bitterly criticized
by the press.   His incaution at Shiloh was recalled, and rumor ran
that all his dilatoriness was due to the intemperate use of liquor.
But Lincoln stood faithfully by Grant.

This confidence was justified by a double expedition against Vicksburg, which got under way late in 1862.   Sherman with 30,000 men
and a fleet of gunboats was sent down the river from Memphis,

while Grant, with the same number, started forward along the railroad for Jackson, Mississippi, whence he would approach Vicksburg from the east.   The advance of the land column was soon checked when the confederates cut its communications at **First Attempt to take Vicksburg.** Holly Springs.   Sherman's force reached Vicksburg and attempted to land on the high ground north of the town. Here the Yazoo bottoms must be crossed in the face of a destructive fire, and Sherman withdrew after satisfying himself that Vicksburg could not be taken from the north.

Then Grant determined to land south of it and approach by the high ground between the river and Jackson.   His first idea was to cut a canal through a bend of the river on the west bank in order to take his supply ships past the confederate **Second Expedition.** batteries.   After weeks of digging, a March freshet destroyed the canal, and Grant determined to run the batteries.   It seemed a hazardous thing, but was made by the supply boats in the night and with slight loss.   The army marched down the west bank and was set across the river by the boats several miles below Vicksburg, and April 30, 1863, Grand Gulf was captured.   The confederates had not supposed a federal army would begin its operations in this quarter, and the place was weakly defended.

Two hundred miles south of Vicksburg was Port Gibson, above which the union gunboats could not go.   Banks had been ordered to take the place and open the way for a fleet supporting Grant's army; but his advance was delayed and Grant **Grant's Brilliant Strategy.** learned that he could expect no aid from the southward at the same time that he heard that confederate troops were concentrating on Jackson, Mississippi.   His position was uncomfortable.   If Pemberton's 40,000 men in Vicksburg were joined by the 15,000 J. E. Johnston was leading up by way of Jackson, the 43,000 men at Grand Gulf would fare badly.   In the face of this difficulty, Grant's action was admirable.   Abandoning his base, he quickly seized Jackson before Johnston could reach it, thus placing all his force between the divided enemy.   Pemberton was a cautious general, and remained a few days in his stronghold, although ordered out by Johnston.   Then he changed his mind, and moved out with about 30,000 men.   Johnston had turned northward, hoping to get into Vicksburg.   Pemberton should have gone in the same direction to meet him, but with a strange fatality he turned southward to cut Grant's communications with Grand Gulf.   He soon learned that the union commander had abandoned his base and was living on the country.   Then he tried to get back to the North, but Grant was in between. Johnston realized that he could not unite with Pemberton, and was forced to leave the latter to his fate.   Then **Pemberton Besieged.** Pemberton stood still for battle, first at Champion Hill and then at the crossing of the Big Black river.   In each action he was defeated, and May 18 he retired within his intrenchments at Vicksburg.   Grant followed and established his lines of siege from the high banks of the Yazoo to the Mississippi below Vicksburg.   He thus came again into communication with the union fleet, and supplies were now landed and reënforcements were sent from the North, so that he soon had 75,000 men, enough to finish Pemberton and beat off any army which could be sent to raise the siege.

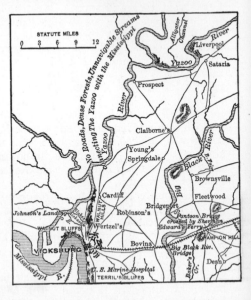

The confederates returned to Vicksburg much discouraged, but they repelled

Vicksburg Taken.

firmly two assaults on their position.   Then the problem became one of starving out the defenders.   While the siege cannon and mortars played continually, and the sappers and miners brought Grant's lines ever nearer to those of the confederates, the work of King Hunger went on.   The confederate authorities needed every available man to hold back Rosecrans at Chattanooga, and reluctantly left Vicksburg to its fate. In June the rations began to fail.   On the 28th the soldiers were on the point of widespread desertion and themselves suggested surrender.   July 3 Pemberton asked for an interview with Grant, and next morning the articles of surrender were signed.   The confederates were liberated on parole, 29,491 in all.   They gave up 170 cannon and 50,000 small arms.   This event, coming the day after the battle of Gettysburg, made the national holiday a day of rejoicing.   It was followed by the fall of Port Hudson, and union gunboats now held the entire course of the great river.   These operations placed Grant beyond the cavil of his critics, and the nation generally recognized in him its greatest general.

The Mississippi Opened.

The Campaign for Chattanooga

While Grant moved against Vicksburg, Rosecrans with an army of 70,000 remained in Nashville, his eye on Bragg, who was charged with the defense of Chattanooga. Unwilling to begin one important campaign while another was in progress, he remained inactive until Grant's success was assured. Meanwhile, Bragg advanced to Shelbyville. But late in June Rosecrans took the field, **Advance of Rosecrans.** and flanking cleverly forced him back into Chattanooga without a battle. The place was very strong. It lies on the east bank of the Tennessee, a bold stream, and is surrounded by mountain ridges. To the south the country is quite rough. It is more practicable to the north, and Bragg thought his opponent would approach from that direction. The idea seemed supported by the fact that Burnside had just moved with a strong column from Kentucky into East Tennessee, and was at Knoxville in a position to move southward in coöperation with the expected flanking movement across the river. As Burnside did not move at once, Bragg concluded an attack was not imminent. He thus allowed himself to be surprised in another quarter.

Rosecrans determined to approach by the south. It was a hazardous movement, but it was unexpected by Bragg, and it threatened the communications with Atlanta. The union commander did not know the country beyond the river, and was **Bragg's Lost Opportunity.** floundering about for more than a week in the disconnected valleys, his right and left wings sometimes nearly three days march from his center. Had Bragg been alert, he must now have beaten his opponent in detail. But he dallied too long, and when on September 18 he offered battle at Chickamauga Creek, twelve miles south of Chattanooga, Rosecrans was concentrated before him. It was a period of inactivity in the Virginia campaigning, both sides resting after Gettysburg; and Longstreet had been sent to aid Bragg, who was also reënforced by Buckner's army, which Burnside had driven southward from Kentucky. The confederates were thus in superior numbers, having about 66,000 to their opponents 58,000. In making the detour to reach their opponents they had so moved that Rosecrans was between them and Chattanooga.

Behind the union position was Rossville Gap, penetrated by the road into Chattanooga. Bragg wished to seize this pass and isolate his opponents. Withholding his own left, he struck hard against the federal left, where Thomas commanded. **Battle of Chickamauga.** This brave commander stood firm, but the rest of the line was weakened to send him reënforcements. At noon, September 20, by mistake, a division was moved from the union center. Longstreet, just opposite and waiting the word to charge, saw the movement and sent eight brigades through the breach. They crushed the union center, threw the left into confusion, and threatened Thomas on the right. Both parts of the line retreated in great disorder. Rosecrans tried in vain to rally his men but could only follow them through Rossville Gap into Chattanooga. He thought the day lost, and sent orders to Thomas to protect the rear as well as he could. But Thomas was not beaten. Surrounded on three sides, he repelled charge after charge until night came, and then withdrew to the Gap, where he took a strong position and held Bragg in check until ordered to join the rest of the army in Chattanooga. This important engagement was fought on September 19 and 20. It resulted in the loss of 19,500 killed, wounded, and captured on the confederate side, and 16,000 on the union side. Thomas's heroic fight saved the union army from a complete rout and won for him the title of "The Rock of Chickamauga."

After the battle of the 20th the federal forces kept within Chattanooga, Bragg following and fortifying himself on Missionary Ridge and Lookout Mountain, east and south of the town. As **Rosecrans Besieged.** Lookout Mountain commanded the railroad, Rosecrans could not bring his supplies by railroad farther than Bridgeport, whence they must be carried by wagons over wretched roads around the great bend of the river, a distance of sixty miles. A month later the army faced starvation or retreat. Lincoln was alarmed and took vigorous steps. Sixteen thousand men under Hooker were sent from Virginia, and Sherman with many more was ordered up from Vicksburg. Thomas was placed in command of the army, succeeding Rosecrans, whom the situation seemed to demoralize; and Grant was put in command of all the West but New Orleans, and **Arrival of Grant.** ordered to Chattanooga. October 23 he arrived and immediately took steps to open the railroad between Bridgeport and the army. Throwing Hooker across the river, the road from Bridgeport was seized in a safe place four miles from Chattanooga. A new road was then constructed by Brown's Ferry, which was operated without molestation, and the danger of starvation was averted.

The next task was to drive Bragg away from the height above the town, and Grant decided to make the attempt as soon as Sherman arrived. The confederate line extended from the northern end of Missionary Ridge along the crest to Rossville Gap, thence across the valley of Chattanooga river to Lookout Mountain. Bragg thought it very strong, and not anticipating an early attack weakened it by withdrawing Longstreet from its center to strike Burnside at Knoxville. He thought Longstreet would return before his services were needed at Chattanooga. He underestimated the energy of Grant, and Longstreet was far away when on November 24, Sherman having arrived, the battle began.

Grant's plan was to turn the confederate right on the extremity of Missionary Ridge, and for this purpose he selected Sherman. **Lookout Mountain.** While this movement was being made he proposed to keep the enemy in position with a strong feint by Thomas in the center and Hooker on the union right. November 24, Sherman crossed the Tennessee in the early dawn, and drove the confederates some distance along the top of the ridge they defended. At the same time Thomas approached nearer to the base of the Ridge at the center, and Hooker, starting to skirt Lookout Mountain, changed his course, carried its steep slope, and finally placed the union flag on the top of the tall peak which adorns its crest. This spectacular achievement, though not very difficult, greatly heartened the soldiers. On the morning of the 25th the confederates were still in strong position on Missionary Ridge, and Sherman took up again the work of clearing it by hard fightng. To aid him, Grant directed Thomas to advance and take the works on the lower slopes. The order was executed, but the soldiers found themselves exposed to a hot fire from the crest of the Ridge. Without orders, and even against orders, they started for the top, 400 feet above them. Grant, watching the battle, exclaimed, "By whose orders is this?" "By their own, I fancy," replied Thomas at his elbow. But the line went steadily forward. At the crest was a brief struggle and then victory. Thirty guns were taken, and Bragg hastily withdrew to Ringgold. The confederate loss in killed, wounded, and captured was 6500, and that of the federals, 5500. Hooker's engagement high up on Lookout was called "the Battle above the Clouds."

Meanwhile, Longstreet had begun operations against Burnside at Knoxville. To his surprise he found the inhabitants loyal to the union. He made no headway, and after the battle of Chattanooga returned to Virginia. Thus all Tennessee was safely restored to the union, and a victorious army held the key to Atlanta and the Georgia uplands.

THE CAMPAIGN AGAINST ATLANTA

After Chattanooga, both armies were exhausted and went into winter quarters, the confederates at Dalton, Georgia, and the federals in the city they had taken. Bragg was removed from command. He had been severely criticized in the South, and only Jefferson Davis's warm friendship had kept him so long in a position he clearly was not able to fill. *Bragg Replaced by Johnston.* His successor, Joseph E. Johnston, was able and vigilant in defense, but he was curt to his superiors, and early in the war aroused the ill-will of Davis. Grant once said he feared Johnston more than any other general he faced. The confederate general began his campaign of 1864 with 53,000 men, but was soon reënforced until he had 75,000. The hope of the southwest was in the defense of Atlanta.

February 29, 1864, congress revived the rank of lieutenant general, and the position was given to Grant, who thus became commander under Lincoln of all the union troops in the field. He immediately assumed the direction of operations in Virginia. The force in Chattanooga, 90,000 strong, thus went to Sherman. Under him served Thomas, commanding Rosecrans's old army, McPherson with the troops which Sherman had brought from Vicksburg, and

Sherman and his Army.

Schofield with the forces which formerly operated at Knoxville. The material in each army was excellent. Political appointees had been weeded out, tried officers of all ranks had come into responsible position, and the soldiers, seasoned by two years of hard fighting, were veterans of the best quality. The hilly country over which they must operate abounded in good defensive positions, which Johnston knew how to utilize.

Its Task.

The critical feature was the railroad from Chattanooga to Atlanta — serving as a means of communication for each army. As Johnston fell back he destroyed it, but Sherman had efficient engineers who repaired bridges and tracks so rapidly that the confederate rear guard usually could hear the whistle of the locomotive which accompanied the federal advance.

It was Sherman's habit to take the initiative, and early in May he appeared before Dalton. Finding the confederates strongly placed,

Progress by Flanking Movements.

he moved around their left and threatened so much the railroad at Resaca that they hastily fell back to that position, while he gained twelve of the 120 miles between Dalton and Atlanta. Again Johnston offered battle in strong intrenchments, but Sherman was too wise to accept it. He waited a few days, and once more flanked by the left, only to be again confronted by Johnston in a strong position. This kind of campaign continued until, at the end of June, Johnston was strongly fortified at Kenesaw Mountain, 25 miles from Atlanta. At this point Sherman abandoned caution and determined to accept battle. Selecting what he thought the weakest point in Johnston's line he delivered a power-

Kenesaw Mountain.

ful assault with the hope of breaking through. But confederates held firm, and the attack was repelled with a loss of 3000 federals and only 800 confederates. Thomas, whose steadiness frequently tempered the impetuosity of Sherman, was asked if he thought the assault should be repeated. He replied that "one or two more such assaults would use up this army"; and he added that he did not favor "butting against breastworks twelve feet thick and strongly abatised." His advice was taken, another flank movement was made, and Sherman on July 9 reached the north bank of the Chattahoochee, his opponent retiring in good

On the Chattahoochee.

order to the south bank. At this place the union troops were within six miles of Atlanta. During this campaign of two months, although no great battle had been fought, there had been continuous skirmishing and two or three sharp affairs, with the result that the union loss was 16,800 and that of the confederates 14,500.

In falling back on Atlanta, Johnston merely did as Lee was then doing before Grant from the Wilderness to Cold Harbor. If he fought less, it was because Sherman advanced more cautiously than Grant. But Southern opinion was not equally considerate of the two leaders, and Johnston was severely criticized. July 17 he was replaced by General J. B. Hood, a man who would fight. Sherman crossed the Chattahoochee, the **Hood in Command.** same day, and rejoiced when he knew he had a new opponent. He believed there would be fighting, and thought his numerical superiority would give him the victory. Within eleven days Hood fought and lost three battles, — Peach Tree Creek, July 20; Atlanta, July 22; and Ezra Church, July 28. His total loss was 10,841 and Sherman's was 9719. But for all this, Atlanta was not taken. Then Sherman

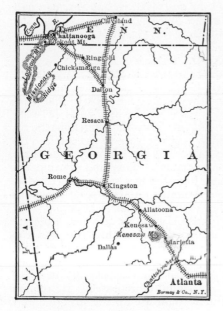

threw his columns out to the west and south, enveloping the city and threatening its communications with the South and East. This movement required a month, during which the North began to despair of his success. It was, said the doubtful ones, but a repetition of Grant's costly campaign, and after it a siege, the result of which no one could foretell. But Hood did not allow himself to be besieged. September 2 he evacuated Atlanta, and next day it was occupied by the **Atlanta Captured September 3, 1864.** union forces. The news occasioned great joy in the North, for it was the first decided success of a year of hard fighting and heavy sacrifice. By the very exultation of his friends, Sherman could see how necessary it was that he should retain what he had captured.

But his situation was not altogether safe: he was in the midst of a hostile country, and his line of communication was a single railroad held by strong garrisons, but liable to be cut by a large and efficient column. Hood realized this situation and tried to utilize it. He first moved westward and fell on Allatoona, a railroad station 45 miles north of Atlanta. **Hood Threatens Sherman's Base.** It was firmly held, and the attack was beaten off. Had it succeeded, Sherman must have recovered Allatoona or suffered serious consequences. Then Hood made a detour still farther westward, going as far as Decatur, Alabama, on the Tennessee river. The place was 110 miles south of Nashville, with which it was connected by rail. Here he halted, hoping that the union leader would become frightened and hasten back to Nashville.

But Sherman was not alarmed. Thomas was sent to Nashville with the veterans who had served under Buell and Rosecrans, and

The Task of Thomas. reënforcements were hurried to him from various quarters until he had nearly 60,000 men, quite enough to beat off the attack of Hood, who had only 54,000. As long as Hood was near the Chattanooga railroad, Sherman followed him; but when the confederate commander's plan was revealed by his crossing of the Tennessee, October 20, Sherman ceased to follow and concentrated at Atlanta a well-seasoned army of 60,000 men. He had for weeks been asking his superiors for permission to strike for the seacoast, and Grant now reluctantly consented. Nothing could show better the exhaustion of the South than the possibility that its

Sherman's Bold Plan. opponents could divide their western army into two columns, each of which was larger than the total force the confederacy could muster in that region. Sherman had before him no opposition worthy of the name, and he felt confident that Thomas could deal with any force Hood could gather.

Let us first follow the movements of Hood. He was a good fighter, but he had lost Atlanta, and his soldiers, regretting the removal of

Battle of Franklin, November 30. Johnston, were not in good spirits. Delayed for three weeks in southern Tennessee to collect supplies he could not move until November 21, which gave his opponents time to prepare for him. Across his path was Schofield with 29,000 men, instructed to retard his advance and fall back. The confederate commander should have surrounded this force, but, although he sought it most vigorously, he lost his opportunity through the carelessness of a subordinate. Schofield was hard pressed when he arrived, November 30, at Franklin, on the Harpeth river, to find the bridge partly wrecked and his trains in great danger. He intrenched hastily, and while the bridge was being repaired Hood arrived and assaulted with great ardor. Each side fought most desperately from four o'clock in the afternoon until dark, but the union line held firm, and by morning Schofield was across the river and proceeded unmolested to Nashville, 20 miles away. He had lost 2326 men, while his opponents, who fought recklessly and without cover of breastworks, lost 6000. Hood followed more leisurely, and took position on the hills south of the city, his army reduced by fighting and marching to 23,207. It was the last hope of the confederacy in Tennessee, and its chances seemed slender in the presence of the union force of more than 50,000.

Thomas was deliberate by nature and would not fight until ready. As he remained inactive day after day the country, and even Lincoln himself, became impatient, lest Hood should escape. But Grant, who once said that if Thomas came to a furrow he would stop to intrench, showed most concern. All his telegrams did not bring on a battle, and December 9 he ordered Thomas to hand over the command to Schofield, but on consideration the order was suspended. At last Thomas was ready, and December 15 he moved on the enemy, driving him back about four miles by hard fighting. The battle was renewed on the 16th, the confederates standing at bay for a life and death struggle. All their valor was unavailing. Surrounded and broken, they had no chance, and at last fled southward in whatever formation they could maintain. December 27, when they crossed the Tennessee river, they numbered less than 15,000 infantrymen. Many had been killed, many others were captured, and some had gone home under the impression that the war was over. Nine thousand of the survivors were later sent to North Carolina under Joseph E. Johnston to oppose Sherman. But from this time the task of the western army was accomplished. Mobile and a few posts held out, but nowhere could the Northern arms be resisted between the Ohio and the Gulf.

The Battle of Nashville.

SHERMAN'S MARCH THROUGH GEORGIA AND THE CAROLINAS

November 15 Sherman began from Atlanta his celebrated march to the sea, burning before he started the machine shops in Atlanta and destroying the railroad to Chattanooga. The telegraph wires were cut, and for nearly a month his government only knew of his movements from the newspapers of the confederacy. His army marched along parallel roads covering a zone sixty miles wide. It had supplies for twenty-five days and was ordered to "forage liberally." In describing his purpose before he set out Sherman himself said he would "make Georgia howl." In his report of his movements he said: "I estimate the damage done to the state of Georgia and its military resources at $100,000,000 at least $20,000,000 of which has inured to our advantage and the remainder is simply waste and destruction." The misery thus inflicted on the non-combatants was as great as it was unnecessary. December 10 he was before Savannah, having accomplished his progress of 360 miles without serious opposition. Hardee, who was holding the town with 15,000 men, would not allow himself to be besieged and withdrew on December 20.

From Atlanta to Savannah.

The military results of Sherman's bold step were very important. It encouraged the North and discouraged the South, showing both sides plainly that the war was near an end. It cut off supplies from Richmond and reduced the area of the confederacy to the Carolinas and a part of Virginia. But all these results might have been secured without the wanton destruction that

Results.

was inflicted on the country. The people of Georgia and South
Carolina were to remain Americans, and good policy, as well as humane
warfare, demanded that they should not be so dealt with that the
national flag should be remembered as a symbol of calamity.

Sherman remained in Savannah from December 20 until February 1,
and then started northward, his march impeded by storms and
wretched roads.   No opposition could be made by Hardee,
and pillaging was more severe than in Georgia.   South
Carolina's initiative in secession made her especially disliked by the federal army, officers and privates, and there
was slight effort to restrain them.   "The whole army," wrote Sherman to Halleck, "is burning with an insatiable desire to wreak vengeance upon South Carolina. I almost tremble at her fate but feel
that she deserves all that seems in store for her." He gave orders
against plundering private dwellings, but they were not well enforced.

From Savannah to Columbia.

Reaching Columbia, the capital, he found in the streets
the smouldering remains of cotton. The soldiers of the
advance guard obtained liquor, broke from the control of
their officers, and during the entire night the streets were a scene of
riot. Bands carrying torches marched through the streets firing the
houses. In the morning a town which had sheltered 8000 inhabitants
was in ruins. A heated controversy arose over the question, "Who
fired Columbia?" One side claimed the fire started from the cotton
fired by the retreating confederates, and it is possible some buildings
might have been thus destroyed; for a strong wind sprang up in the
evening and fanned the smouldering cotton into flame. But it seems
undoubted that most of the damage was the result of the action of
the uncontrolled soldiery, many of whose officers appear to have been
little inclined to restrain them. It was the culmination of that bitter
feeling which the entire army had shown up to this point, and which
a more magnanimous commander would have restrained in the beginning. To the people of the North the devastation of this army
was very pleasing. Even Phillips Brooks exclaimed: "Hurrah for
Columbia! Isn't Sherman a gem?"

Columbia Burned.

The occupation of Columbia forced Hardee to evacuate Charleston.
He hastened to North Carolina in order to place his army before that
of the conqueror. March 11, Sherman reached Fayetteville, where he destroyed an arsenal, but spared the town.
In fact, he made efforts to limit the pillaging in this state,
and the inhabitants, although sorely distressed by soldiers
and "bummers," fared better than those of South Carolina and Georgia.
By this time Joseph E. Johnston had been placed in command of the
confederate troops in the Carolinas. Gathering all the soldiers he
could he stood before Sherman on March 16 at Averasborough, thirty
miles north of Fayetteville. Beaten back, he made another stand
three days later at Bentonville, but the result was the same, although

Sherman in North Carolina.

for a few hours it seemed that he might throw into confusion the union left, which marched incautiously. Proceeding thence Sherman came, March 23, to Goldsboro, 160 miles south of Richmond, against which Grant was about to complete his operations. Two days earlier Schofield had arrived at Goldsboro with 20,000 men, coming by way of Wilmington, which had been taken in January, and Newbern, which had been in union hands since 1862. But Sherman was not needed before Richmond. After a two weeks' halt at Goldsboro he learned that Lee was retreating toward the mountains and turned westward in order to intercept him. Before him Johnston slowly withdrew to Raleigh and then to Greensboro, where, as we shall see, he at last gave up the contest in April.

Halt at Goldsboro.

Thus ended in triumph the work of the Western army. Some of its contests were drawn battles, but none resulted in retrograde movements. From Forts Henry and Donelson to Shiloh and thence to Corinth, in withstanding Bragg at Perryville and Murfreesboro, in the operations against Vicksburg, Chickamauga, Chattanooga, and Atlanta, in all these important movements there was steady and hardwon success. How well the confederates used their inferior resources is shown in the long series of losses they inflicted on the victors. They were exhausted, and collapsed utterly before the vast power that was brought against them.

THE WAR BEYOND THE MISSISSIPPI

While Grant, Sherman, and their assistants made the grand three years' movement through Kentucky, Tennessee, and Georgia to the sea, severe campaigning occurred west of the Mississippi. Texas saw but little fighting, attempts of the confederates to secure New Mexico came to naught, and western Louisiana was too much isolated by the fall of New Orleans in May, 1862, to become a scene of serious opposition to the union cause. But in Missouri and Arkansas the case was otherwise. When the union men in the former of these two states flocked to Lyon's standard and enabled him to save St. Louis to the union, the secessionists assembled under General Sterling Price, disputing all that Lyon did and precipitating a state of civil war.

Missouri and Arkansas.

Both leaders showed resourcefulness, but Lyon had the initial advantage. He moved rapidly, and at Booneville, on June 17, dispersed the confederate force. It soon reassembled in larger numbers, and at Carthage beat off an attack by Sigel, one of Lyon's lieutenants. Price was now reënforced by troops from Arkansas, so that his army was 10,000 strong. His opponent had only 6000, but risked battle at Wilson's Creek, August 10, 1861. The result was union defeat, Lyon being killed. His army was forced back into northern Missouri, and

Confederates Expelled from Missouri.

there came a pause while both sides recruited. Frémont, who now commanded the union forces in Missouri, soon had 40,000 men, but as he was about to attack he was removed, and Hunter, his successor, gave up the plan of offensive movements. Soon Hunter was removed, and Halleck, who succeeded him, sent forward a force under Curtis, before whom Price retired into Arkansas. Van Dorn was now placed in command on the confederate side and met Curtis in a decisive battle at Pea Ridge, Arkansas, March 7 and 8, 1862. Although the confederates brought 16,200 men against 10,500, they were beaten, and withdrew from the field. The confederates in Tennessee were now hard pressed and the force under Van Dorn was so weakened that Arkansas was at the mercy of Curtis, who gradually extended his area of authority until at the end of 1862 most of the state was in union hands. Schofield superseded him in 1863, but although he had 50,000 men he could not complete the task assigned him.

The center of confederate power here was the Red River valley, which the confederates held with 25,000 men under Kirby Smith and "Dick" Taylor, his lieutenant. Along the river were great stores of cotton which the federals wished to seize. In 1863 Banks at New Orleans was ordered to move on this region, but he refused because of the low stage of water in the river. Early next year he got under way, with a land force of 27,000 men and a fleet of gunboats under Commodore Porter. His objective was Shreveport, at which place he was to be met by 15,000 men from Arkansas. His progress was slow, the country being very difficult. At Sabine Cross Roads, April 8, when in two days' march of Shreveport, he was repulsed by Taylor and was glad to escape with a loss of several of his gunboats. The net result of the expedition was to deprive Sherman of a valuable body of troops for the operations against Johnston between Chattanooga and Atlanta. Kirby Smith continued to hold the country around Shreveport until the end of the war. He surrendered at Baton Rouge, May 26, 1865, his force being 17,686.

The Red River Expedition.

One other western campaign remains to be noticed. In September, 1864, General Price marched into Missouri from Arkansas with 15,000 men. The war had reached such a stage in the West that large movements were not to be undertaken by the confederates, but they had enough troops to made destructive raids, like those of Forrest and Morgan on the east bank of the Mississippi. Price's objective was St. Louis, which he approached rapidly. Finding its defenses too strong to carry he turned off to Jefferson City. By this time the union forces in the state were concentrating rapidly. Price must fight them at several places, and moved so swiftly and fought so vigorously that he was not surrounded. But he failed to inflict serious injury on his opponents and was glad to escape to Arkansas after four weeks of

Price's Raid into Missouri, 1864.

campaigning. He carried with him most of the guerrillas, who had infested the state up to that time, and thenceforth Missouri was free from confederate troops.

BIBLIOGRAPHICAL NOTE

The general history of the war is ably treated in Rhodes, *History of the United States*, 7 vols. (1892–1907); and in his shorter *History of the Civil War* (1917). Among other volumes see: J. K. Hosmer, *The Appeal to Arms*, and *The Outcome of the Civil War* (1907); William Wood, *Captains of the Civil War* (1921); and Walter Geer, *Campaigns of the Civil War* (1926). Much material of value will be found in Edward Channing, *History of the United States*, VI (1925). A pictorial history is offered in Wood and Gabriel, *In Defence of Liberty* (The Pageant of America, Vol. VII; 1928). See also Schouler, *History of the United States*, 6 vols. (1880–1897); Wilson, *History of the American People*, 5 vols. (1902); Burgess, *The Civil War and the Constitution*, 2 vols. (1901); and Greeley, *The American Conflict*, 2 vols. (1864).

Among recent works of value may be named Sir Frederick Maurice, *Robert E. Lee, the Soldier* (1925); Louis A. Coolidge, *Ulysses S. Grant* (1917); E. C. Smith, *The Borderland in the Civil War* (1927), Gamaliel Bradford, *Union Portraits* (1916) and *Confederate Portraits* (1917); and Joseph Hergesheimer, *Swords and Roses* (1929).

Of the many military histories, see: Dodge, *Bird's-Eye View of the Civil War* (1897), very useful in connection with a larger work; Ropes, *Story of the Civil War*, 2 vols. (1894–1898), unfinished at the death of the author but continued by Livermore, two volumes of whose work are promised for 1913; Count of Paris, *The Civil War in America*, 4 vols. (trans., 1875–1888); *The Campaigns of the Civil War*, 13 vols. (1881–1890), mostly by generals who participated, important but not impartial; Fletcher, *The Civil War in America*, 3 vols. (1865); Wood and Edmonds, *The Civil War in the United States* (1895); and Henderson, *The Science of War* (1905), by an excellent English authority, five chapters relate to our civil war. Fox, *Regimental Losses* (1889), and Livermore, *Numbers and Losses* (1901), are also valuable. The Southern side is presented in: Evans, edr., *Confederate History*, 12 vols. (1899), a coöperative history by states; Pollard, *The Lost Cause* (1867); and Wood, *The Confederate Handbook* (1900).

The leading biographies and memoirs on the Northern side are: Nicolay and Hay, *Abraham Lincoln, a History*, 10 vols. (1890), a storehouse of information but always commendatory of Lincoln; Cox, *Military Reminiscences*, 2 vols. (1900), a good book; Grant, *Personal Memoirs*, 2 vols. (1895); Badeau, *Military History of Grant*, 3 vols. (1868–1881); W. T. Sherman, *Memoirs*, 2 vols. (1886); Sheridan, *Personal Memoirs*, 2 vols. (1902); Schofield, *Forty-six Years in the Army* (1897); Schurz, *Reminiscences*, 3 vols. (1907–1909); Woodward, *Nathaniel Lyon* (1862); Coppee, *George H. Thomas* (1893); and Lew Wallace, *An Autobiography*, 2 vols. (1906). All of these relate to men who served in the West. On the Southern side see: Joseph E. Johnston, *Narrative of Military Operations* (1874); Johnston, *Life of Albert Sydney Johnston* (1879); Hood, *Advance and Retreat* (1880); Polk, *Leonidas Polk*, 2 vols. (1893); Taylor, *Destruction and Reconstruction* (1879); Wheeler, *Wheeler and His Cavalry* (1899); Lee, *Memoirs of General Pendleton* (1893); Wyeth, *N. B. Forrest* (1899); and Roman, *Pierre G. T. Beauregard*, 2 vols. (1884). In this connection one must mention *Battles and Leaders of the Civil War*, 4 vols. (1888), reminiscences of participants, interesting and valuable.

The sources are embraced in several collections published by the national and state governments. Of these the greatest is *The War of the Rebellion, a Compilation of the Records of the Union and Confederate Armies*, 69 vols. in 128 books, with an atlas. It contains the reports of officers in both armies with other matter relating to military operations. A companion work is *Official Records of the Union and Confederate Navies*, 22 vols. (1894–1908). An important source of information is the *Reports of the Joint Committee on the Conduct of the War*, 8 vols. (*passim*).   Most of the states, North and South, have published regimental histories and muster rolls.   Moore, *Rebellion Record*, 13 vols. (1861–1868), is a compilation of contemporary utterances, an interesting mine of personal incidents, war poetry, speeches, etc.   *Appleton's Annual Cyclopedia* (beginning in 1861) is also important.   See *Photographic History of the War*, 10 vols. (1911), for photographs.

On army experiences, see: Boynton, *Sherman's Historical Raid* (1875); McClure, *Lincoln and Men of War Time* (1892); Hosmer, *The Thinking Bayonet* (1865); Browne, *Four Years in Secessia* (1865), by a war correspondent; Boynton, *Chattanooga and Chickamauga* (1891); Nichols, *The March to the Sea* (1865); McCarthy, *Detailed Minutiæ of a Soldier's Life* (1882); Goss, *Recollections of a Private* (1890); and Wilkeson, *Recollections of a Private Soldier* (1887).   On the Southern side: Jones, *A Rebel War Clerk's Diary*, 2 vols. (1866); Gilmour, *Four Years in the Saddle* (1866); Smedes, *A Southern Planter* (1899); Wilson, *Life in the Confederacy* (1885); Hague, *A Blockaded Family* (1888); and Headley, *Confederate Operations in Canada and New York* (1906).   The use of negroes as soldiers is described in Williams, *History of Negro Troops* (1888).

For Independent Reading

Chestnut, *Diary from Dixie* (1905); Gay, *Life in Dixie during the War* (1892); Hague, *A Blockaded Family* (1888); Smedes, *A Southern Planter* (1899); Morse, *Life of Lincoln*, 2 vols. (1893); Tarbell, *Life of Lincoln*, 2 vols. (ed. 1900); Trent, *Life of Lee* (1899); and Dana, *Life of Grant* (1868).   For those who have much interest in military history the memoirs of Grant, Cox, and Joseph G. Johnston will be interesting.   Rhodes's *History* is probably the most interesting story of the war.

CHAPTER XXVI

THE WAR IN THE EAST, 1862–1865

McClellan's Peninsular Campaign

THE most striking feature of the story of the union armies in the East is the efforts to find a successful general. From the beginning of the war until March, 1864, six commanders were tried without success. Then the task was given to Grant, whose successes at Vicksburg and Chattanooga indicated that he was the long-sought leader. Under his direction the struggle was conducted to its close. The confederates, however, were as fortunate in this respect as the federals were unfortunate. Their first leader, Joseph E. Johnston, was an excellent commander; and when he was incapacitated, his successor was Robert E. Lee, the equal of any American soldier.

The Commanders.

The first of the union commanders was McDowell, who fought a well-planned battle at Bull Run and lost it because of no fault of his own. But failure damaged his prestige with the army, and he was followed, July 27, 1861, by McClellan, fresh from victories in West Virginia (see page 526). McClellan was a man of good address, and soon had the devotion of his soldiers. His unusual ability as an organizer quickly improved the efficiency of the army. But he displayed some unfortunate personal qualities. He overestimated the strength of his opponents; he was sensitive of interference by others; he quarreled with General Winfield Scott, until October 31, 1861, the commander of the army, and McClellan's superior; and he openly criticized the war department for political appointments. On the other hand, it must be remembered that McClellan was a good general, and his irritation at the meddlesomeness of the politicians was natural. In politics he was a democrat, and the open hostility of Stanton, the secretary of war, was supposed to arise from an unwillingness to enhance the popularity of one who might in the future be a formidable presidential candidate. The McClellan controversy is still a matter of dispute.

McClellan.

By the end of October, 138,000 men were under arms near Washington, and public opinion demanded an advance, but McClellan was not ready. October 21, at Ball's Bluff, 2000 men, who had been incautiously thrown across the Potomac, were surrounded and half of them lost. One of the slain was Colonel Baker, of California, an officer of much promise, whose death

His Tardiness.

2 N

was deeply regretted. The blow caused profound sorrow in the North, but McClellan did nothing to retrieve it. The weather was fine through November and most of December, but still he kept his camp. Then he fell ill of typhoid fever and was prostrate until the middle of January. Finally Lincoln, who was generally patient with McClellan, issued an order for an advance by all the armies, East and West, on February 22. The order was impracticable and was ignored.

But McClellan's plan was made. He proposed to take the army to Fortress Monroe, and from that point to reach Richmond up the "Peninsula," between the James and York rivers. By McClellan's Plan. this plan he would have support from the navy and maintain his communications by water. To the objection that he would thus leave Washington exposed, he replied that Washington was safe as long as his army kept the confederates busy near their own capital. Lincoln did not wholly approve the plan, but consented to it on condition that enough troops be left at Washington to secure it from danger. After McClellan was well on his way, he learned that McDowell with 40,000 men, on whom he had counted, was to be retained on the Potomac. He complained bitterly, but Lincoln held that the retention of McDowell was in keeping with his agreement.

Early in April McClellan had 100,000 men at Fortress Monroe and began to advance cautiously. The confederates made a show of opposition at Yorktown, stretching a thin line across His Advance to the Chicka- hominy. the Peninsula, at that place thirteen miles wide. It could have been carried easily, but McClellan thought it required siege operations. He brought up his heavy guns, constructed intrenchments, and after a month's delay was ready to open fire when the enemy quietly left their position. At Williamsburg they fought a rear-guard action in which they lost 1570 men to their opponents' 1866. But they still retreated, and were closely followed. The fleet with the supply ships passing up the York seized White House Landing, twenty miles from Richmond, and made it a base of supplies for the army, which was thrown out to the Chicka- hominy, ten miles from the city. This was the situation on May 16.

The federal advance into the interior made Norfolk unsafe for the confederates, and they evacuated it, destroying the ram *Virginia* James River Opened. (*Merrimac*), which they could not remove. This left the federal fleet without opposition in these waters, and it ascended the James to Drury's Bluff, six miles from Richmond. Here it encountered strong batteries, beyond which it did not go. A coöperating land force could have taken this position, but McClellan was on the York, which allowed him to keep his army between the confederates and Washington.

Meanwhile, the confederates clung to Richmond, and Lincoln, losing his fears for Washington's safety, ordered McDowell to Fredericksburg, and thence to the aid of McClellan. Six days later, May 24, the order was reversed on account of unexpected developments in the Shenandoah valley. This region furnishes a safe approach to Harper's Ferry, sixty miles from the capital and seventy-five from Baltimore. Stonewall Jackson was in its lower part with 17,000 men, watched by Banks with 19,000 near Strasburg, and Frémont, with 15,000 in the mountains to the westward — all within easy distance. Besides these, there were 7000 men at Harper's Ferry. Milroy, under Frémont, stood with 3500 men at McDowell, 25 miles west of Staunton, so that if Jackson advanced on Banks, Milroy might close in on his rear. *Jackson's Diversion in the Valley.*

The approach of McClellan to Richmond made it advisable for Jackson to create a diversion, so as to draw off McDowell, and he began a brilliant campaign which well illustrates what an inferior force, when well handled, may do in conflict with a divided opposition. First he fell unexpectedly on Milroy and defeated him, and pursuing him northward threw Frémont into such terror that he was not a factor in the situation for several days. Then returning to the valley, he moved swiftly on Banks at Strasburg, whose force had just been weakened by sending 10,000 men under Shields to help McDowell in his movement to the aid of McClellan. Jackson was nearly on Banks before his approach was known. The latter was too weak to fight, and hastened northward, the confederates in hot pursuit. At Winchester, May 25, they overtook Banks, charged him at dawn, and sent his force beaten and demoralized toward the Potomac, which the fugitives crossed the next day, Jackson stopping at Harper's Ferry. This unexpected movement created consternation in Washington, which, the authorities thought, was Jackson's objective. It was on this account that McDowell was ordered to turn away from Fredericksburg. Lincoln hoped to throw him into the valley south of Jackson's position, to bring Frémont from the west into the same position, and thus surround and capture Jackson. Orders to this effect were given; but Jackson knew his danger and began a retreat as rapid as his advance. He barely slipped into Strasburg before Shields and Frémont reached them from opposite directions, and, when they tried to follow him down the valley, hurled them back in two sharp battles. In a month's campaign he had captured many prisoners and vast supply trains, which he safely sent off from Port Republic, and he had drawn McDowell so far westward that he was worth nothing to McClellan, who must fight Johnston unaided. *Plan to Trap Jackson.*

But McClellan was not in danger. He had nearly 120,000 men, and his pickets were in sight of Richmond, within which Johnston could muster but 63,000. The union army was in five corps, two of which under Keyes and Heintzelman were south of the Chickahominy, then swollen by rains, and the others under Porter, Sumner, and Franklin were north of it to protect the railroad to White

House Landing and to touch hands with McDowell, who was expected up to May 24. Johnston saw his opportunity and fell on the two isolated corps of Keyes and Heintzelman on May 31 at Seven Pines, or Fair Oaks. He fought hard and drove back his opponents, but they were not crushed, and late in the day Sumner crossed the river and saved the battle ere dark. Next day other troops were thrown over, and the united army drove back the confederates to their position in the beginning of the action. At sunset on the 31st, Johnston was severely wounded, and June 1 Robert E. Lee succeeded him. Two roads ran from this region into the city, and across them he began to throw up breastworks, behind which his army was placed. Rain for two weeks made the ground impossible for artillery, and Lee was thus able to finish his defenses before they could be assailed.

The Battle of Seven Pines, May 31.

Lee in Command.

McClellan has been criticized for not assaulting, but he had another plan of battle. He was strong in artillery and proposed to plant it advantageously and force the confederate lines by approaching in siege fashion, — a slow but sure method for a superior force. Davis and Lee both admitted that it would be successful. Not daring to await such an attack, they planned a movement around the federal right. Jackson, still in the Shenandoah valley, was to elude McDowell, and march to the north of McClellan's lines, while Lee, coming out of his intrenchments, would join Jackson at the right moment, cut McClellan's communications, and surround and capture him, or send him in confusion back to the York river. The danger in this was that Jackson's coöperation might be ill-timed or that McClellan might penetrate Lee's lines when they were weakened and occupy Richmond. Lee knew both his lieutenant and his foe. He did not believe the former would fail him, nor that the latter had enough enterprise to strike for Richmond at the critical moment. In both conclusions his judgment proved good.

Siege Approaches Planned.

Confederate Plan of Attack.

Jackson cleverly got out of the valley and, marching with that rapidity which won for his men the name of "foot cavalry," was north of Richmond on June 26. Here Porter's corps, about 25,000 strong, protected the federal right at Mechanicsville, the only federal troops north of the Chickahominy. At this moment Lee ordered out A. P. Hill's, Longstreet's, and D. H. Hill's divisions to unite with Jackson and crush Porter. The former moved at the appointed hour and fought a vigorous battle at Mechanicsville, June 26; but Jackson was half a day late and Hill's attack was beaten back. In the night the four confederate lieutenants united their forces and faced Porter with 55,000 men. The latter was badly placed, and by the orders of his superior fell back to Gaines's

Mechanicsville, June 26.

Gaines's Mill, June 27.

Mill, where he received and checked the first confederate charge about noon of the 27th. All through the afternoon he fought desperately, but at sunset his lines were broken by a general assault and his defeated corps, numbering with reënforcements 31,000, was forced off the field and sought safety south of the river. During this day McClellan had over 60,000 men south of the river, between Lee and Richmond, in which were only 25,000 defenders. He might well have overcome this force and taken the city, but his overcautious mind thought at least 100,000 confederates were in Richmond, and he thought this was proved by the fact that Lee did not hesitate to leave the place for operations against Porter. *McClellan's Lost Opportunity.*

The capture of the north bank of the Chickahominy placed Lee across the communications of the federal army. He believed the federals would either fight their way back or retreat down the peninsula to Fortress Monroe. On the morning of the 28th clouds of dust to the east seemed to show they had taken the latter course, and he made arrangements to follow. It was not until next morning that he learned he was mistaken. McClellan had determined to shift his base to the James and was rapidly executing that movement, much benefited by the twenty-four hours' start Lee unwittingly gave him. He was followed with haste on the 29th, but held his own in a hard fight at Savage's Station, and again on the 30th in a still harder encounter at Frayser's Farm, or Glendale. July 1 he was on the bank of the James, marching southeastward to Harrison's Landing, where the anchorage was good. He took a strong position at Malvern Hill, overlooking the river, and for a moment the confederates hesitated to attack. But Lee believed he had defeated most of the federal army at Gaines's Mill, and thought his opponents so demoralized that they could not make a successful resistance. He ordered the assault, and his forces were received with well-directed artillery and infantry fire and defeated with heavy loss. It is conceded that the battle of Malvern Hill was an error on the part of the confederate commander, due to his underestimation of the strength and condition of the federals. *His Change of Base. Savage's Station and Frayser's Farm, June 29 and 30. Malvern Hill, July 1.*

The Seven Days' Battles, June 26 to July 1, comprised five engagements in which McClellan lost 15,849 and Lee 20,135. The result was a union defeat in the sense that Richmond was not taken. But McClellan at Harrison's Landing was only twenty miles from Richmond, and had a safe base of operations. His army, though exhausted and dispirited, was not demoralized, and might have taken the offensive again after a short period of rest. He himself had no thought of giving up and called for reënforcements. But the confidence of the government in the general was undermined. *Results.*

reënforcements were not sent, and after ten days of hesitation it was determined to recall him to Washington and move his army to northern Virginia. The controversy that arose over his treatment is historic. Personally he was arrogant, and his letters to Lincoln were full of bitter reproaches. The president's replies are always in the kindest terms, and it cannot be doubted that he supported his unpopular general as long as the country at large would have it. But spite of his faults, McClellan was a safe campaigner of the deliberate kind, and if he had been given his way, he would probably have hung on at Richmond until he stormed it into surrender. It is in his favor that the city finally fell before a nine months' siege in which Grant approached from practically the same quarter that McClellan selected in the beginning of the war.

The McClellan Controversy.

POPE AND SECOND BULL RUN

July 11, ten days after Malvern Hill, Halleck was recalled from St. Louis and made commander of all the union armies with headquarters in Washington. For the success in the West his subordinates were chiefly responsible, but this was not as clear then as later. He became, in fact, military associate with the president and the secretary of war, who, since January, 1862, was the strong-willed Stanton. The armies of Frémont, Banks, and McDowell were consolidated, in all 43,000 men, and Pope, victor at Island No. 10, was placed in command. He was an aggressive general, but incautious. He issued a proclamation to his new army containing these words, and others of similar import: "I have come to you from the West, where we have always seen the backs of our enemies; from an army whose business it has been to seek the adversary and to beat him when he was found. . . . I presume that I have been called here to pursue the same system." This overconfident spirit offended the officers and privates, who were sensitive about their recent defeats. In an unlucky moment he said, by common report, that his headquarters would be in the saddle, a phrase which set his soldiers laughing at his expense. Early in July he mobilized his army in front of Washington and turned its face southward along the line of railroad that ran to Manassas, arriving undisturbed at Culpeper. He was much under the influence of Stanton and other radical politicians whose interference frequently created difficulties for Lincoln and the generals.

Halleck and Pope.

At Culpeper, Pope threatened Gordonsville, where the railroad from the north crosses another from Staunton going eastward. To protect it Lee sent forward Jackson with nearly 24,000 men, who reached Gordonsville and turned northward, while Banks, followed at an interval by Sigel with Frémont's old army, was hurrying

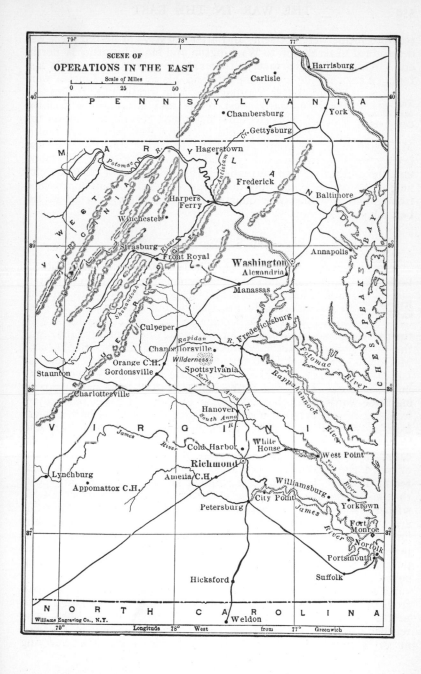

SCENE OF
OPERATIONS IN THE EAST

Scale of Miles

0   25   50

Williams Engraving Co., N.Y.

Longitude   78°   West   from   77°   Greenwich

southward.   August 8, Jackson struck Banks, whose force was only 8000, at Cedar Mountain.   The federal troops remembered the valley campaign and fought desperately, but they were outnum- bered two to one and were forced back on Sigel late in the   **Jackson** afternoon.   Then Jackson halted for the arrival of Lee,   **Meets** who, at last satisfied that McClellan's army was withdraw-   **Banks at** ing from Harrison's Landing, was moving rapidly on Gor-   **Mountain.** donsville.   McClellan's men were then marching overland to Yorktown and Fortress Monroe to embark for Acquia Creek, on the Potomac, whence they would undoubtedly be sent to strengthen Pope; but as this movement would require two weeks Lee hoped by a quick concentration to crush Pope before reënforcements reached Cul- peper.   But Pope displayed unexpected caution.   From a captured dis- patch he learned Lee's plan and fell back behind the Rappahannock and was 35 miles from Acquia Creek, where troops were already land- ing.   There was much confusion in high circles in Washington, but Pope was ordered to hold the Rappahannock at every hazard, and it was believed that a forward movement would follow a federal con- centration.

All this came to naught through a brilliant movement, probably conceived by Stonewall Jackson.   It was, in brief, to send Jackson with 25,000 men well around Pope's right to cut the rail-   **Confederate** road by which the union supplies came up.   Pope, it   **Plan of** might be expected, would fall back and fight Jackson,   **Attack.** who must manage to beat him off for a short time, while Lee, making a still wider detour to the west, would come up as Pope fought, take position by Jackson's side, and complete the work of federal demoralization.   It was a hazardous measure, but Lee felt he could risk something in the presence of a general so unwary as Pope.   The result showed that his confidence was well founded.   In fact, the plan worked better than was anticipated; for Jackson was able to elude his enemy until Lee was actually at hand.

The start was made August 25, and twenty-five miles were covered that day in safety.   Pope heard that a large body of troops was march- ing on his right and should have occupied the passes in that direction, but he thought the confederate army was moving   **Jackson** into the Shenandoah valley by Front Royal, and neglected   **Reaches** to protect his rear.   Eight miles north of the Rappahan-   **Pope's Rear.** nock a range of hills, the Bull Run mountains, runs away north- ward, broken sixteen miles west of Manassas by Thoroughfare Gap. Passing beyond these hills, which screened his movements, Jackson halted before the Gap on the night of the 26th, and next morning passed through it, moving rapidly eastward.   In the late afternoon he reached Bristoe Station, cut the telegraph lines, broke the rail- road track, and sending a portion of his force to Manassas destroyed a vast depot of federal supplies after appropriating all his troops could consume or carry with them. In this process he spent all of the 27th, throwing out detachments north and south to save his main force from surprise.

About 8 o'clock on the 26th, Pope learned the confederates were in his rear. He did not think they were divided, but thought they could not have gone further than Warrenton and that the demonstration at Bristoe was only a feint. He gave orders, therefore, to concentrate at Warrenton, where he expected to offer battle. But riding to Bristoe late in the day he discovered that Jackson was resting at Manassas and gave sharp orders for a concentration at that point. McDowell had divined the true situation and occupied the approaches to Thoroughfare Gap, by which Lee must come up. If he had held them, the force at Manassas must have been isolated and badly handled. But he obeyed orders, and on the 28th withdrew just as Longstreet, commanding the other half of Lee's army, approached it from the west. He moved toward Manassas, where Pope arrived at noon of the same day. To the surprise of Pope his prey had gone in the night. No one knew just where, but it was said he went to the northeast. Pope supposed the confederates were trying to reach Alexandria and gave orders to move northward. Jackson's departure to the northeast was only a feint. He soon doubled back toward Thoroughfare Gap and took a strong position on the heights of Groveton, two miles west of the old Bull Run battlefield. He concealed his force as well as he could through the night and next forenoon, August 29, and awaited news from Longstreet. On the same morning the supporting column cleared the Gap, and Jackson, hearing the good news, revealed his position and opened fire on union columns moving along the roads toward the north. Longstreet, hearing the guns, hurried his steps, and arriving at noon found his friend warmly engaged, the union brigades coming up rapidly and forming line of battle as they arrived. Longstreet placed himself on Jackson's right, before which Porter's corps had taken position. Pope was determined to fight a battle, and ordered Porter to turn Jackson's right; but Porter, finding masses of infantry before him, refused to sacrifice his men, and reported the situation. Pope paid no attention to this information, for he still thought Longstreet beyond the Bull Run mountains. He therefore assaulted Jackson's center, and renewed his orders to Porter to turn the confederate left. Again Porter refused to attack, action for which he was cashiered and removed from command, only to be completely exonerated by congress after many years of discussion. At nightfall the confederates were still in position, the union assaults in the center had been beaten off, and Pope's army was dispirited.

But the general, who six weeks earlier had talked so confidently of victory, could not make up his mind to fall back as he should have

Pope's Hasty Retrograde Movement.

Jackson Opens Battle.

done. He remained in his tracks, and on the morning of the 30th resumed the battle. Moving Porter from the left he sent him against Lee's center. This gallant officer, stung by criticisms of the previous day, now showed the greatest bravery; but his best efforts were in vain. Then Lee took the offensive, charging the federals persistently, forcing them back to the Henry House, on the battlefield of the preceding year — where by a desperate stand the confederates were held at bay until the demoralized federals had crossed Bull Run and blown up the famous old bridge behind them. The army marched on toward Washington, Lee sent Jackson in a pursuit which ended on September 1, when the pursuers were barely defeated at Chantilly, where gallant Phil Kearny lost his life. In this campaign Pope lost 14,000 out of 80,000 men and Lee lost 9000 out of 54,000.

Second Battle of Manassas.

Thus ended Pope's campaign. In the flood of unpopularity which came upon him the country forgot his good qualities. He was as hard a fighter as Hood, who impetuously wore himself out fighting Sherman and Thomas. But, like Hood, he was arrayed against very able generals. He was deceived by Jackson's remarkably rapid march and by Lee's audacious tactics. He lost his self-control when he found himself cut off from his base and gave orders in utter distraction; but when once the enemy's position was revealed he turned and fought bravely. It is due him, also, to say that he was much hampered by his superiors. Halleck assumed to direct his movements, kept him in ignorance of the plans of campaign being made in Washington, and left him ignorant of the movements of reënforcement which had been promised. But the disaster at second Bull Run destroyed Pope's influence over his army, and his removal became a necessity.

Pope as a Commander.

The Campaign of Antietam

Lee was not strong enough to besiege Washington, and foresaw that to wait at Manassas would invite a federal countermove, before which he must fall back with a loss of prestige. He concluded to proceed at once into Maryland, hoping the people there would join his army in numbers. His plan was to march to Hagerstown, where he would force a battle with the union army, and beating it to threaten Harrisburg and probably Baltimore. As it was just at this time that Kirby Smith and Bragg were operating successfully in Kentucky (see page 529) it was hoped that such an impression might be made on European opinion that recognition of the confederacy would follow. September 4, less than a week after Pope's crushing defeat, his advance under Jackson crossed the Potomac twenty-five miles above Washington, and by the 7th the rest of his army was in Maryland. Reënforced by the

Lee Invades Maryland.

troops he had left in Richmond he had hardly 60,000 men. September 6, Jackson reached Frederick, where the now repudiated Barbara-Frietchie incident was said to have occurred. To his surprise the farmers drove off their cattle and would not sell their grain. Then Lee decided to open a line of supplies through the Shenandoah valley, at the entrance of which was Harper's Ferry with a garrison of 12,500 men. To remove this obstacle he sent Jackson on the 10th, with orders to complete his task and rejoin his commander as quickly as possible. To divide his army thus in the presence of the enemy was ordinarily bad generalship; but he knew his opponents were slow and he believed no harmful results would follow. Jackson's march was swift, as usual, and on the 14th he occupied the hills which encircle the place, and the garrison, with many valuable stores, was surrendered without a battle.

Harper's Ferry Captured.

But let us return to the army of Pope, marching on September 5 hopelessly back to Washington. Near the city the vanguard was met by McClellan with orders to take command. In a moment the spirit of the soldiers changed, and shouts of joy welcomed him as he rode past the regiments. Pope was assigned to other duties in Washington. The same day orders were given to enter Maryland and follow Lee, but it was not until the 10th that McClellan had reorganized the army, and the 12th before he reached Frederick, through which the confederates had passed a few days earlier. Here he was handed, at 6 p.m. on the 13th, an order from Lee to D. H. Hill, recently found by a private, which revealed the plans of the confederate commander. It showed him that his opponent's army was divided, and he decided to place himself between its two parts. Twelve miles west of him were the South mountains, with two gaps in them, beyond which the roads connecting the two confederate forces were no more than eight miles away. Had he marched in the night he might have occupied these passes, but he waited until daylight, and when he reached them found they were held by the confederates. By hard fighting the gaps were both carried on the 14th, but the loss was severe. By this time Lee had learned the fate of the lost order and was falling back from Hagerstown. He stopped at Sharpsburg, threw up intrenchments in a strong position with Antietam creek on his front, and waited Jackson, who on the morning of the 15th received the surrender of Harper's Ferry and immediately set out to rejoin Lee, fifteen miles away. From Lee's position to the South mountains was only nine miles, and McClellan easily covered them by noon of the 15th. If he had fought in the afternoon he would have had half the confederate force at his mercy; but he chose to wait while his army recuperated. Next morning Jackson's men were coming up rapidly, but the last divisions did not

McClellan in Command.

His Slow Approach to Lee.

arrive until the following morning, the 17th. Yet McClellan was idle on the 16th. Nothing could better show how little he was capable of seizing upon a favorable situation.

There was skirmishing late on the 16th, but it was not until dawn of the 17th that the battle was opened. Three corps, Hooker's, Mansfield's, and Sumner's, had approached Lee's left on the 16th, showing him where to expect attack. He drew back his lines and strengthened the point threatened. In the early morning Hooker came up most vigorously. As he struggled for the high ground in front of him, Mansfield came up and joined in the battle. But the latter officer was killed, Hooker was severely wounded, and soon afterwards their corps fell back out of the deadly fire. Then Sumner advanced on the same position unsupported. He received the concentrated fire of Lee's left wing, and was so cut up that he had to withdraw with severe loss. Thus by one o'clock the fighting on Lee's left ended in a repulse. It was immediately renewed on his right, where Burnside's men pressed against lines which had been weakened to meet the charge on the left. They carried the battle before them and seemed about to seize the high ground which commanded this part of the field when A. P. Hill's division of Jackson's corps rushed up, completing an eighteen-mile march from Harper's Ferry. Without orders from Lee they fell on the advancing union line and drove it back with bloody effect to its original position. Then night came, and the battle of Antietam was over. Lee's army of 60,000 had repelled the attack with a loss of 11,000 killed and wounded. McClellan with 87,000 lost 12,400.

Battle of Antietam, September 17, 1862.

Next morning each army was in position, but McClellan did not renew the battle. Lee's advance into Maryland was checked, and nothing was left but to recross the Potomac, which was only two miles behind his position. This he did on the 19th without interference from his unaggressive adversary. September 17 was the bloodiest single day in the war. The union soldiers fought splendidly, and justified the confidence of their commander. The nation received the news with joy; for although the confederacy was not destroyed, the union army's prestige was reëstablished and the North was relieved from invasion. McClellan's failure to impede the confederate retreat again brought his serious failing into prominence, and for this he was removed, the command going, November 5, to Burnside.

Results of the Battle.

THE BATTLE OF FREDERICKSBURG

Burnside did not wish to lead the army, but the appointment came as an order, and he obeyed it. The whole situation demanded a move on Richmond. Indeed, it was for not moving that McClellan was displaced. Two railroads ran from the Potomac southward; one from

Washington by way of Manassas, through a rolling country in which the rivers are narrow, the other from Acquia Creek through Fredericksburg to Richmond, crossing rivers comparatively

Burnside in Command. broad. Along the former both McDowell in 1861 and Pope in 1862 had operated. If the country was more practicable than that to the eastward, it gave a longer approach to Rich-
mond. Burnside, weighing all advantages and disadvantages, concluded to move by Acquia Creek and Fredericksburg, and

His Plan of Advance. Lincoln, after some hesitation, accepted the plan. Lee was then at Culpeper with Longstreet, and Jackson was far away in the valley. Burnside ordered pontoons, and eluding Lee moved quickly to the Rappahannock opposite Fredericksburg, hoping to cross the river and hold the heights south of it before Lee could arrive. But his pontoons were not ready promptly, and when they arrived Longstreet held the southern heights and Jackson was coming up rapidly. Burnside had 113,000 and Lee, with Jackson at hand, had 78,000 men.

The ground adjoining the river on the south is a plain from a mile to a mile and a half wide, covered by Burnside's guns on the north
bank. Behind it rise hills, on the crest of which Lee took

Battle of Fredericks-burg, De-cember 13, 1862. position. His left was held by Longstreet and his right by Jackson, who arrived there on the 12th and was not well intrenched on the day of the battle. Burnside divided his force into three grand divisions under Hooker,
Franklin, and Sumner. The first remained in reserve on the north bank, but the second and third he threw across the river on the 12th, where they remained safely on the plain. Franklin con-
fronted Jackson, and Sumner, protected by the streets of Fredericks-
burg, was before Longstreet. Burnside by this time showed that the problem on his mind overwhelmed him. He displayed little decision, and his lieutenants were full of misgivings. Early on the 13th Franklin received an order which might mean to carry the works before him or to make a reconnaissance in force. The former was Burn-
side's intention, but Franklin in some doubt sent forward Meade's

On the Union Right. division, and some time later supported it with Gibbons's division. The former went forward with great courage, found a weak point, and penetrated Jackson's line, but he was not well supported, and was driven back with heavy loss by the confederate commander. With this, fighting ceased on this wing.

On the Union Left, Marye's Heights. In the town Sumner had been held in restraint, but now came on to assault Longstreet. It was a murderous task; for here the confederate position was exceedingly strong. Its center was Marye's Heights, well defended at the top by artillery and at the bottom by an infantry line behind a stone wall. Across the plain by which it was reached was an old canal, which would impede a charge, and the whole plain was so well covered that a confederate engineer remarked that it would be impossible for a chicken to live on it, once the confederate guns opened fire. Sumner's brigades, however, were thrown six times across this deadly spot, each time recoiling with enormous loss. Hooker, who had come over the river, rode hastily back to Burnside, on the north bank, to urge that the assault cease, but the general would not relent until 8000 of his men lay on the fatal slopes. The total loss in that day's fighting was 12,653 federals and 5377 confederates. December 15, under cover of night and a violent storm, the union army withdrew to the north bank. Grief and despair reigned in army and nation. Burnside himself was crushed, some of his highest officers were at open feud **Hooker in Command.** with him, and he asked for their dismissal or the acceptance of his own resignation. January 26 he was removed, and the command went to Hooker, chief of Burnside's critics.

THE BATTLE OF CHANCELLORSVILLE

Hooker was a good fighter, and the soldiers liked him. His appointment to command them restored the broken spirits of the men, and by April they were anxious to meet their foes. Recruiting had brought the numbers up to 130,000, while Lee in Fredericksburg had only 60,000. April 27, Hooker **Hooker's Excellent Initiative.** broke up his camp opposite Lee, sending three corps thirty miles up the river. Here they crossed and turning eastward on its right bank approached Chancellorsville, nine miles from Fredericksburg. On the 30th another corps crossed the river and joined the other three, so that Hooker by clever marching was in good position beyond the river with 40,000 men and on Lee's left flank. While this was going on, Sedgwick with 20,000 men had crossed the Rappahannock south of Lee's position and threatened his rear. May 1, Hooker moved a short distance toward the enemy, but when he suddenly met them coming toward him, eager for battle, his confidence forsook him, and he fell back to Chancellorsville against the advice of his generals. Here he selected a position **Abandons the Offensive.** with his back to the river, near a ford, and awaited attack. Since he far outnumbered Lee, it would have been better to have made the attack. Part of his line lay in the "Wilderness," a region covered with small trees and chaparral and difficult for marching troops. His officers and soldiers were disgusted that he so quickly relinquished a **Battle of Chancellorsville, May 2, 3, and 4, 1863.** promising offensive and accepted a careful defensive. May 2, Lee was before him ready to attack, spite of his numerical inferiority. Jackson is said to have suggested the plan of battle which was adopted. While the confederate line made feint after feint along the union front, he made a detour of fifteen miles, until at five o'clock in the afternoon he fell unexpectedly on Hooker's extreme right, routing Howard's corps and badly demoralizing the corps next to it.   Then darkness closed down, and it seemed that the coming of dawn would witness a renewed and successful fight by the terrible Jackson.   But his end was at hand.   In the twilight he rode past his own sentinels to reconnoiter in the enemy's rear.   Half an hour later a group of horsemen galloped back on the sentinels and received a volley, after which a voice out of the dark called: "Boys, don't fire again: you have hit General Jackson!"   They carried him through lines of his own awe-stricken men to a hospital, and May 10 he died.   Had he been at Gettysburg, as Lee truly said, the story of the battle would have been different.

Death of Jackson.

May 3 the battle was renewed, and by 10 o'clock the field belonged to the confederates.   Hooker, dazed by the effects of a cannon ball, which struck a column against which he leaned, drew back toward the river.   Sedgwick now approached behind Lee, after driving off Early with 9000 men, whom Lee left at Fredericksburg.   Lee believed Hooker was past active resistance, and turned his back on him to crush Sedgwick.   He found him on the river's edge, five miles from the camp of his superior commander, and pressed him so disastrously on the 4th that Sedgwick crossed to the north bank during the night.   Then Lee turned again on Hooker's 80,000, who stood not to fight, although they would have done it with a better general, but withdrew to the north bank by the morning of the 6th.   Through three days of fighting at Chancellorsville the losses were 17,287 on the union side and 12,463 on the confederate side.   It was the last great confederate victory.

The Victory Completed.

The Gettysburg Campaign

Lee's motives in invading the North were three: 1. He wished to transfer the war to enemy's territory.   2. It was becoming evident that Vicksburg would fall, and he wished to counteract its effect by a victory of his own equally decisive, *i.e.* by taking Harrisburg, Philadelphia, Baltimore, or even Washington.   3. He knew the North was tiring of the war, that the terms of enlistment of her soldiers were expiring, and he thought a great defeat now would tend to make her accept peace on the basis of Southern independence.   Calling to him Longstreet's corps, which was not in the battle of Chancellorsville, he had nearly 80,000 men, while his antagonist could hardly muster more until the new levies could be assembled.   The rest of his army was in two corps: Jackson's old corps, now commanded by Ewell, and another commanded by A. P. Hill.   To Ewell was given the van, and he

Lee's Motives.

His Plan.

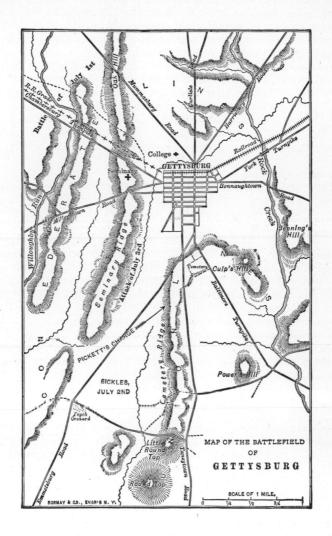

MAP OF THE BATTLEFIELD
OF
GETTYSBURG

SCALE OF 1 MILE.

0   1/4   1/2   3/4

BORMAY & CO., ENGR'S N. Y.

started June 1ɔ for the Shenandoah valley, which he easily cleared of union troops. June 15 he began to cross the Potomac, whence he moved to Hagerstown, Maryland. A few days' march behind him went Hill, and after him Longstreet, so that by June 26 the three corps were across the Potomac. So well did Lee's cavalry screen his movements that these initial stages of his campaign were accomplished without revealing his intentions to Hooker. But in the last days of June its leader, Jeb Stuart, made one of his daring raids, passing between Washington and the federal army **The Confederate Cavalry.** into Pennsylvania. He reached York after Early had left it, went on to Carlisle, to find Ewell was not there, and only arrived at Gettysburg on July 2, his horses so exhausted that they were not fit for service. At Hanover, on his march, Stuart had a sharp battle with the federal horse, an arm which Hooker had brought to a high state of efficiency. His absence from Lee's immediate front gave the federal commander an opportunity to observe the confederate movements, and the result was a more rapid union concentration than Lee had expected.

Meanwhile, Ewell marched rapidly toward Harrisburg. June 27, he reached Carlisle and sent Early's division eastward to York, which was forced to pay a contribution. Early tried to seize the Columbia bridge over the Susquehanna, so as to ap- **Ewell's Advance on Harrisburg.** proach the state capital from the east; but a retreating militia regiment had the forethought to burn the bridge, and this point marked the limit of Early's eastern advance. At the same time Ewell, halting at Carlisle, prepared to attack Harrisburg with his main force. His cavalry, in fact, reached the Susquehanna opposite the town, but on June 29, Lee, who with Longstreet and Hill had reached Chambersburg, ordered him back with all his corps, and the Pennsylvania capital was no longer in danger.

Lee's order to Ewell was due to an unexpectedly rapid concentration of the union army. Hooker, who was at cross purposes with Halleck, was forced to remain in Virginia as long as Lee was there. When at last he crossed the Potomac to **Meade in Command.** Frederick, he had been so hampered by his superiors that the union columns were widely separated. In despair of getting them together, he proposed to resign. The offer was accepted, and thus it happened that on June 27 General Meade was placed in command. He was an able general, of the McClellan school, and he could get on with Halleck. He hastened northward to place himself between Lee and Baltimore, entering Pennsylvania June 30. Lee was at Chambersburg when he learned he was being **Concentrating on Gettysburg.** pursued, Hill and Longstreet with him. The former he sent to Gettysburg at once, and ordered the latter to follow, while Ewell was directed to move from his advanced position to the same place. This convinced Meade, then at Taneytown,

Maryland, that Lee sought a battle, and he selected the ground he would take at Pipe Creek, just south of the Maryland line — about 13 miles from Gettysburg. To delay Lee, he sent Reynolds forward to Gettysburg with three corps, expecting they would fall back as they were pressed. Ahead of them marched Buford's cavalry, which arrived at Gettysburg June 30, in the night.

Three roads from the south and southeast converge on Gettysburg, from Emmitsburg, Taneytown, and Baltimore. Along them on the morning of July 1 marched the union troops from **The Battlefield.** six to thirty miles away. Of the several roads on the west and north, one leads from Chambersburg, and along it were marching Hill and Longstreet, while another approaches from Carlisle, and along it came Ewell. Just south of the town in the sharp angle between the Emmitsburg and Taneytown roads is a hill on whose top was the town cemetery. The ground rises to it gently, and from its southern edge a ridge runs away for a mile or more, beyond which is a small hill, Little Round Top, and a much larger one, Round Top. East of the cemetery is a slight depression, beyond which is another elevation, Culp's Hill. Taken as a whole it offers an ideal battlefield for an army fighting on the defensive. Its gentle slope gives good play for artillery. Stone walls and bowlders on its crest furnish cover for the infantry, its outward curve makes its interior lines short and easy, and the hills at either extremity protect it against flanking movements.

Past this strong position rode Buford when he entered the town, Reynolds's infantry a few miles behind him. He well knew the confederates were approaching, and early in the morning **The Battle Opened, July 1.** moved out on the roads by which they marched. Across the Chambersburg pike, three-quarters of a mile from Gettysburg, he posted his men on a wooded height known as Seminary Ridge. At nine o'clock Hill's van came in sight, halted, formed a line of battle, and opened fire. Every moment the line grew stronger, and about eleven Buford was about to be driven back when Reynolds's force arrived and the fight continued, brigades on each side being thrown into the battle line as fast as they arrived. Just before noon Reynolds was killed. His men were discouraged, but held their position until 3 o'clock, when Ewell's corps was coming up from the north. They formed on Hill's left and enveloped the union right so that it fell back, lest it be surrounded. Hill now advanced and held Seminary Ridge, while Ewell pushed his line through Gettysburg to the town's southern limits, five hundred **Ewell's Lost Opportunity.** yards from the cemetery on the hill. This quiet spot was the scene of much confusion as the union columns reached it. Cannon were not in position for defense, and the men were too tired to make a spirited stand. If Ewell had advanced with his relatively fresh troops, he must have carried the hill and forced the union troops to concentrate at Pipe's Creek. But Ewell let the opportunity go, and Hancock, who had just arrived to take Reynolds's place, recognizing the strength of the position, intrenched as rapidly as possible, placed his guns in position, and sent messengers urging Meade to bring up all the troops. By dark they were arriving rapidly, and at one o'clock in the morning Meade arrived and confirmed Hancock's decision to fight at Gettysburg. By dawn Cemetery Ridge was well defended.

By this time Lee's army was at Gettysburg, or in easy distance. Hill lay on Seminary Ridge, stretching away to the southward. Ewell was on Hill's left, his own left going as far east as Culp's Hill, and Longstreet, who at nightfall of the 1st was on the Chambersburg Pike in Hill's rear, was ordered to move at dawn as quietly as possible to Hill's right and **Longstreet's Attack, July 2.** seize Little Round Top, from which batteries, as Lee saw, could sweep the whole union line. Had the order been given to a Stonewall Jackson, it would probably have been executed; but Longstreet did not favor forcing the battle and wished to flank Meade out of his strong position. He did not get his force into position until the afternoon, and when he charged against the hill it had been occupied by a federal force, and the assault was driven back. But just north of the hill Longstreet encountered Sickles's corps, thrown out beyond the ridge, and against it he delivered a severe battle. Meade sent division after division to stem the tide, and by six o'clock the attack here was repelled, although Sickles, severely wounded, was driven back to the top of the ridge. During the afternoon, but later, Ewell made an attack on Meade's right. At Culp's Hill he **Ewell's Attack, July 2.** carried all before him, and when his advance was stopped by darkness, his troops were within dangerous proximity to the union rear. That night Meade held a council of war. He had been pushed back on both wings, and the losses were heavy; but it was decided to stand another day and fight the battle to a finish. To Gibbon, commanding the union center, Meade remarked: "Your turn will come to-morrow. To-day he has struck the flanks. Next, it will be the center."

July 3, the attack came, most dramatically. Early in the morning there was severe fighting around Culp's Hill, but the federal lines held. The rest of the forenoon the two lines lay quietly on their arms, a mile or more apart. At 1 o'clock came the sharp **The Attack on the Center, July 3.** crack of two rifled cannon, the signal for a cannonade from the confederate guns: 80 union cannon, all that would bear on the scene, opened in reply, and for an hour and a half the heavens reverberated in a mighty symphony. At 2.30 P.M. the federals ceased firing, because their ammunition was running low. Their adversaries then slackened fire, and the word was passed to the infantry to charge the union center where Hancock

2 O

commanded. Pickett's division, numbering 5400, stood in front of Cemetery Ridge, a mile away, with orders to penetrate the opposing line, supported by 10,000 men from Hill's corps. Stuart's cavalry was made ready to follow and cut up the federals when they should be pressed back. Longstreet was Pickett's superior. He said that no 15,000 men could take the position, but his orders were explicit, and he directed the advance. The charging column started as steadily as on parade. For a quarter of a mile it was protected by a little swale; but as it reached the crest the union guns reopened with deadly effect. At 600 yards came canister, making great gaps in the advancing column, which did not waver. At closer range the guns were silent, and thick ranks of infantry, hitherto lying down behind the batteries, rose, advanced before the guns, and poured a withering fire into the fast diminishing column. But its approach was not halted until it struck the union infantry, carried them back beyond their own guns, where a new line met and checked it. For a brief space, some said twenty minutes, but no man could count the minutes in such a time, it held its advance; but Hancock, still fighting though severely wounded, threw out regiments to take it in flank, and the assailants were either shot, captured, or driven back across the deadly plain by which they approached. Hancock said: "I have never seen a more formidable attack." Lee's army was badly shattered, and he prepared to receive the countercharge he thought **Lee Returns to Virginia.** would surely come. But Meade's plans were defensive, and the confederates were allowed to remain undisturbed in their lines. All night and all the next day they remained in camp, and on July 5 they withdrew to the south, Meade making no serious effort to strike them ere they crossed the Potomac on July 13. The losses in the three days' fight, killed, wounded, and captured, were 23,003 federals and 20,451 confederates.

The battle of Gettysburg was a very hazardous undertaking from Lee's standpoint. With an army of 70,000 he invaded enemy's territory and fought an aggressive engagement against an **Lee's Generalship.** intrenched and well-placed army of 93,500. His attack could only be justified on the ground that his opponents were much worse fighters than his own men. Ordinarily he was cautious, but he had beaten his opponents so often that he had come to underestimate them. Pope's, Burnside's, and Hooker's campaigns failed because of bad generalship, not because of an incapable soldiery. Lee assumed in his invasion that the leadership of Hooker would continue. In Meade a better type of commander opposed him, and at a time when the confederate general undertook a more serious task than ever before. Meade was not a brilliant general, but he showed no serious faults at Gettysburg, and he had in his great battle the confidence of his army, officers and privates, as well as the entire support of the war department, advantages not enjoyed by either Pope, Burnside, or Hooker.

FROM THE WILDERNESS TO PETERSBURG

After Gettysburg, the two armies remained inactive in Virginia. There was some maneuvering by which Lee managed to keep Meade in northern Virginia, but neither general risked a battle during the autumn. It was in this autumn that Bragg was being forced out of Chattanooga by Rosecrans and Grant, an operation which demanded the best efforts of each government. In March, 1864, Grant, as we have seen (page 535), was made lieutenant general and took command of all the union armies. Meade was left in actual command of his army, but Grant joined it and directed its movements. During the winter it lay north of the Rapidan on the railroad that ran through Manassas, Lee's army just south of the same river. Grant had 122,000 men well drilled and amply equipped; his adversary had about half as many, and they lacked many of the necessities of war.

Grant's Preparations.

May 3, Grant moved forward by his left, crossing the Rapidan into the dense thicket known as the Wilderness. Lee was very vigilant, and May 5 confronted the federals in this tangle of undergrowth, whose roads he knew well. Grant's plan was to go ahead by sheer hard fighting, and he threw his men on Lee's lines without hesitation. In such a place his superiority in artillery was of little use, and the two days' fighting was a severe contest of infantry against infantry (May 5 and 6). The result was a check for each army; for, the battle ended, each force stood in its tracks. Grant had thought Lee would fall back. Disappointed in this, he determined to flank still further to the enemy's right, and May 8 reached Spottsylvania Court House, twelve miles to the southeast. His movement was observed by Lee, whom he found across the road well intrenched. Should it be an attack or a flanking movement? Grant chose the former. Time after time he assaulted or skirmished, thinking to break the lines by sheer weight of superior numbers. At every point he was repulsed. May 12, the fighting and losses were heaviest; for on this day the union loss was 8500. At last the commander gave up his attempt to break through, and flanked again by the left. From May 5 to 21, his total loss was 34,000. It was at Spottsylvania that he wrote the dispatch in which he said: "I propose to fight it out on this line, if it takes all summer."

The Wilderness, May 5 and 6.

Spottsylvania Court House, May 8–21.

May 23, Grant reached the North Anna, only to find Lee on its south bank so well fortified that even Grant did not assail. The result was another flank march to the east, Lee always anticipating the maneuver. By this means the two armies reached by May 28 the ground McClellan occupied in May, 1862. June 2, after heavy skirmishing, they faced one another at Cold Harbor, six miles from the fortifications of

Cold Harbor, June 3, 1864.

Richmond. Grant wished to crush the confederate army before it entered these defenses, and gave orders for an attack all along the line. It was delivered at dawn, June 3, in a grand assault by 80,000 men. Officers and privates were confident it would fail, but they did not flinch. No troops could withstand the heavy fire they encountered, and in twenty-two minutes the assault failed with a loss of 7000. Hancock's corps alone lost 3000. The space between the lines was covered with the dead and wounded, but Grant would not ask for a truce to remove them, and for four days they were neglected. The confederate loss was about 600. For his indifference to human life at Cold Harbor, Grant was severely criticized. He himself later declared the assault an error. The result convinced him that Lee was not to be crushed in battle, and he moved for the James river in order to lay siege to Richmond. From the Rapidan to the James his total loss was 54,929. Lee lost about 19,000.

THE END OF THE WAR

June 14, Grant crossed the James at City Point. At Bermuda Hundred, five miles to the west, Butler with a strong force lay inactive. Two months earlier he had moved up the James, with First Attempts against Petersburg. 30,000 men, to take Petersburg, commanding Richmond from the south. But so soon as he left his base at City Point, Beauregard, commanding the confederates, had threatened his communications, beaten off his assault on the Richmond defenses at Drury's Bluff, and "bottled him up." To him came Grant on June 14 with orders to attack Petersburg at once. Butler did not move promptly, and next day Smith, leading Grant's advance corps, was ordered to take the city, then very weakly defended. He advanced, took the outworks, but halted. Had he gone forward that night, he might have succeeded. But next day troops were sent to oppose him, and all hope of surprising Petersburg was lost. June 18, Lee, at last convinced that his enemy was south of the river, moved his army to Petersburg. The Siege. Grant wasted 10,000 lives in trying to carry it by assault, and then settled down to siege operations. July 30 a great mine was sprung under the confederate works, and for a moment an open road existed into the rear of their position; but here also was mismanagement. The troops "The Crater." which ought to have poured through hesitated — probably through fault of their division commander, and the confederates, rallying, were able to drive back with great slaughter the assaulting column. This bloody affair of "the Crater" cost Grant 4000 lives without any compensating advantage.

These misfortunes created great distress throughout the North. Grant, it was whispered, was drinking again, and all his costly sacrifice of men, at this time 75,000 since he crossed the Rapidan, had not given him the confederate capital. But his work was not lost. Lee had been greatly weakened, and his exhausted government was not able to send him reënforcements. Through- **Depression and Hope in the North.** out the autumn and winter the union army worked stead- ily with pick and spade, and every week it became more and more evident that ultimate success was certain. July 1, while the siege progressed, Lee sent Early with 17,000 men to drive the federal forces from the Shenandoah valley and to threaten Washington. The confederates moved rapidly, driving Sigel's weak opposition before them. They crossed the Potomac and turned east- ward. At the Monocacy Lew Wallace delayed them a day with a weak force, but they put him to flight, and July 11, in the afternoon, were at the doors of the national capital. Had Early continued his advance the place might have been taken, but he delayed until morn- ing and was repulsed by troops which had arrived during the night from Grant's army. Early then fell back, and by good management escaped his pursuers to Strasburg, Virginia. Four days later he again moved north, defeating a union force at Kernstown and sending a column into Pennsylvania, where Chambersburg was burned because it did not pay a contribution. This action was not justifiable.

To drive Early from the Valley, Grant now sent Sheridan with 40,000 infantry and 15,000 cavalry. Lee also sent reënforcements before which Sheridan retired to the Potomac. But Lee was in dire need at Petersburg, and withdrew the succor **Sheridan Devastates the Valley.** he had sent. Sheridan then assumed the offensive with twice his opponents' strength. In two battles — Win- chester, September 19, and Fisher's Hill, September 22 — he drove his opponent far southward with severe loss on both sides. Then Sheridan, with Grant's permission, adopted a policy of devastation. Barns, mills, and even residences were burned, grain, cattle, horse, and agri- cultural implements were taken or destroyed, and the rich valley was left so denuded of supplies that, as Sheridan said, "a crow flying over the country would need to carry his rations." It was the very frenzy of war, and was defended on the ground that it made it impossible for a confederate army in the future to operate by this way against Washington.

In the South a sharp cry for vengeance arose, and Lee again sent reënforcements to Early, who took the offensive. Following the fed- erals, he came upon them at Cedar Creek, October 19, when their commander was absent. The attack at dawn on front **Battle of Cedar Creek.** and flank was a surprise, and seemed a complete success. Only the sixth corps stood firm, but it fell back four miles trying to rally the fugitives as it went. Had Early concentrated his force on this splendid body, he might have had complete success. Sheridan slept the preceding night at Winchester, twenty miles from his army. Riding leisurely southward in the morning he learned of the situation at front and rode rapidly to the scene. At noon he was at the head of the sixth corps, had rallied the fugitives, and was marching confidently against Early, who believed himself the victor. Though taken unawares, the confederates fought courageously, but were swept off the field by the superior numbers of the union forces. At nightfall they were in flight before Sheridan's cavalry, and they were never again a menace to Washington.

The first weeks of 1865 saw the confederacy in imminent danger of collapse. Hood was crushed in Tennessee, Early was driven from the Valley, federal cavalry rode at will throughout all of

Hampton Roads Conference, February 3, 1865.

Virginia north of the James, and Sherman marched without opposition through the Carolinas. Lee's army in Richmond, poorly fed and clothed, was no more than 50,000 men, and Johnston, who sought to check Sherman, had only 37,000. Southern defeat was so clearly inevitable that it was believed the confederate government must accept peace if it was offered. Under these conditions private individuals secured a meeting of commissioners on each side at Hampton Roads, February 3, 1865. Lincoln attended on the part of the North. He offered to end the war if the South would accept emancipation and submit to the authority of the union. He also promised to ask congress to pay the slaveholders for the slaves, but he frankly said he could not promise that congress would accept the suggestion.

The negotiation failed because Jefferson Davis insisted that the independence of the South should be the basis of any agreement. Had he been less blindly persistent, an armistice might have been arranged, during which Lincoln could have brought congress to some form of compromise by which much of the turmoil of reconstruction days would have been avoided.

As spring approached, Grant before Petersburg threw his left out to reach the Petersburg and Lynchburg railroad, one of the two lines by

Richmond Taken.

which supplies were carried into Richmond. To oppose him, Lee must extend his own line, which by reason of his inferior numbers became very thin. April 1, Sheridan was sent against the extreme confederate right at Five Forks and won a success. It was nine at night when Grant heard the result, and he immediately ordered an assault at dawn along his entire front. This also resulted favorably, the confederate works being penetrated at two points. April 3, he proposed to press his advantage and throw his left still farther around Petersburg. Threatened thus with a complete envelopment, Lee decided to evacuate Petersburg during the night and concentrate his troops, scattered around Richmond, on the southwest of the city, so as to escape along the line of railroad to Danville. To this end he gave Davis notice at 10.40 A.M., on the

2d, in order that the confederate officials might escape from the doomed city. April 3, his army was marching along four roads which converged at Amelia Court House on the Danville railroad, thirty-five miles from Richmond. He hoped in this way to join Johnston, who, then near Raleigh, North Carolina, was ordered to Greensboro, fifty miles south of Danville.

Grant sent troops to hold the evacuated city, but lost not a moment in jubilation. His object was to bag the quarry before a junction with the North Carolina force could be effected. He marched by every road available, often fighting when Lee threw out a force to protect the confederate rear. In the morning of **Lee Overtaken.** the 4th, Lee reached Amelia Court House, where he expected supplies. None were at hand, and he lost a precious day collecting them. On the 5th, Sheridan with the cavalry seized the railroad to Danville, which caused the confederates to turn towards Lynchburg. On short rations, dispirited, and sick, they were deserting in squads. Sheridan followed rapidly, and during the evening of April 8 got in front of Lee at Appomattox Court House. At the same time, a large body of infantry under Ord, by marching throughout the night, also got around and took position behind Sheridan. Next morning, the 9th, Lee ordered his weary troops to disperse the cavalry and march toward Lynchburg. As they moved out Sheridan drew off his troopers and revealed Ord's solid formation, an obstacle the confederates could not overcome. It was the end of the chase.

Lee now raised a white flag and met Grant at the McLean house in Appomattox village. He wore a handsome gray uniform and a splendid sword, and was in striking contrast with the victor, who was dressed in "a rough traveling suit" with the straps **The Surrender, April 9, 1865.** of a lieutenant general. After some friendly conversation Lee inquired on what terms surrender would be received. Then Grant wrote out the conditions, which were accepted. Officers and men were to be paroled and not to fight again until exchanged, in consideration of which they were not to be disturbed by the federal government so long as they observed the law. Officers were to retain their side arms, their horses, when they owned them, and their private baggage. Lee, after a moment's hesitation, said that many of his cavalrymen and artillerists owned their horses, and Grant agreed that they might keep them "for the spring plowing." By these terms Lee did not have to surrender his sword, a generous courtesy on Grant's part which endeared him to Southern people. A touching farewell of Lee to his own soldiers, reduced by his march and desertion to 26,765, completed the tragic event. The broken host in gray returned to their homes, and their commander rode back to Richmond. Grant's soldiers marched back to the James river, and the northern part of the nation broke into pæans of joy that the bitter struggle was over.

Lincoln was at City Point when Richmond was evacuated.   On the 9th he returned to Washington, deeply concerned with the work of restoration.   To one who said that Jefferson Davis must be hanged, he replied, "Judge not, that ye be not judged."   On the 14th he met his cabinet and discussed a policy of reconstruction.   "I hope there will be no persecution," he said, "no bloody work after the war is over.   No one need expect me to take any part in hanging or killing those men, even the worst of them. . . .   We must extinguish our resentments if we expect harmony and union."   That evening he attended the theater with his family.   While the play progressed, John Wilkes Booth, an actor who foolishly thought he was redressing the wrongs of the South, gained access to the president's box, fatally wounded him with a pistol shot, and escaped with a broken leg, by leaping to the stage, whence he passed to the street and rode rapidly away into Maryland.   He managed to escape to Virginia, where he was tracked to his lair and shot at bay in a burning barn.   One of his accomplices wounded Seward seriously in his house.   Four conspirators were hanged, including Mrs. Surratt, who was probably innocent, and several others were imprisoned.

Lincoln Assassinated, April 14, 1865.

Lincoln lived until 7.22 A.M. on the 15th.   His death was a poignant blow to the nation.   In the darkest hours of the war he had never wavered in hope and effort; in a thousand trying events he had shown good sense and persistent good will; in many a personal attack he had borne himself with patience and self-forgetful fortitude; and in every phase of the war he had been the chief support of union.   He was great in all the great phases of public leadership, but greatest of all in that overspreading consciousness that all the people, white men and black men, Northern men and Southern men, were within the bounds of his responsibility and protection.

Lincoln's Greatness.

When Lee surrendered, Sherman was at Goldsboro, North Carolina, and Johnston was near Raleigh, fifty miles to the west.   Hearing that Lee marched for Danville, the latter had turned toward Greensboro, where he stood when he heard the news from Appomattox.   To him came Jefferson Davis, fleeing southward.   The confederate president wished the general to march to the mountains and carry on the war.   Johnston objected, saying the soldiers desired peace, and it was agreed that he should ask for terms of surrender.   April 17 and 18 he met Sherman at Durham, North Carolina, where an armistice was agreed to pending the reference of certain terms of peace to the president.   These terms embraced the recognition by the president of the governments of the states then in condition of resistance, the reëstablishment of the federal courts in the South, and the parole of officers and privates of all the confederate armies still in existence.   Sherman consented to these terms because

Surrender of Johnston.

he thought it would be difficult to bag Johnston and because his army did not relish another campaign in the region through which it had recently fought. But he had exceeded his instructions, and his terms were disapproved by the government in Washington because they dealt with civil affairs. Then Johnston accepted the terms offered Lee by Grant, April 26, and disbanded his army, numbering 37,047. May 4, General Taylor surrendered all the troops in Alabama and Mississippi, and May 26, Kirby Smith surrendered his department west of the Mississippi river. The total **Resistance Abandoned.** number of confederates who thus laid down their arms, in these momentous two months, was 174,223. May 10, Jefferson Davis was captured in southern Georgia and sent prisoner to Fortress Monroe. Alexander Stephens and other high confederate officers were also made prisoners; but all were eventually released.

FEDERAL NAVAL OPERATIONS

The work of the navy during the civil war resolved itself into three spheres of activity: (1) the blockade, (2) coöperation with the army in land operations on the coast, and on the rivers, and (3) chasing down and destroying the small number of commerce destroyers the confederacy was able to place on the sea.

The blockade was proclaimed April 19, 1861, and a dozen ships were at once sent to the most important harbors in the South. By purchasing merchant ships, and even tugs, and building new ships, this number grew steadily until three hundred **The Blockade.** were on the blockading line at the end of the war. They were divided into four squadrons, the North Atlantic, from Fortress Monroe to Cape Fear; the South Atlantic, including the coasts of South Carolina, Georgia, and Eastern Florida; the East Gulf, including the coasts of Western Florida, Alabama, Mississippi, and a part of Louisiana; and the West Gulf, from the mouth of the Mississippi to the Rio Grande. Life on the blockaders was monotonous. There were days and nights of watching, the ships lying a few miles off the harbor during the day and closing in to anchor during the night, like sentinels on each side of the harbor's entrance. Occasionally, usually in the night, a luckless blockade runner was seized as she tried to dart through the opening. Sometimes she stole through so cautiously as to elude the blockaders, and sometimes she was forced on the shallows and burned by her crew in order to avoid capture. The blockaders did not dare follow her under the guns of the confederate forts which usually commanded the interior channels.

Early in 1862 the South undertook to break the blockade by constructing heavy ironclads. The first undertaken was named the *Virginia*, though history remembers her as the *Merrimac*, the name she bore as a merchantman before the war began. Her super-

structure was removed and a roof of railroad rails took its place
with heavy guns beneath the roof.   March 8, 1862, this dangerous
craft steamed out of Norfolk harbor and destroyed three
federal frigates off Newport News.   Next day she reap-
peared to complete her work of ruin.   She encountered a
strange-looking ironclad craft, a hulk level with the water and
supporting a revolving turret within which were powerful
guns.   It was the *Monitor*, designed by Ericsson and appropriately
described as "a raft with a cheese-box on it."   A fierce encounter
followed, at the end of which the Southern ship retired in a damaged
condition.   She did not resume the attempt to raise the blockade.
The conflict proved the efficiency of ironclad ships and opened a new
era in naval construction.   The American government built many
monitors before the war ended.

The Monitor and Merrimac.

The most important movements of the navy in coöperation with
the army against harbors and on the rivers were as follows: 1. The
attack on Roanoke Island, August 29, 1861.   The navy
seized Hatteras and Ocracoke inlets, in North Carolina,
giving the North command of the entrance to Pamplico
and Albemarle sounds.   In the following January an
expedition under General Burnside took Roanoke island, lying
between these sounds, and afterwards Newbern and Plymouth
on the mainland were occupied.   The first intention was by this
approach to move into the interior of North Carolina and cut off
supplies for Richmond, but on consideration the project was given
up as impossible.   The expedition was serviceable because it effectually blockaded this part of the coast.

In Eastern North Carolina.

2. Operations against Charleston, November 7, 1861.   Port Royal,
South Carolina, was taken, giving the South Atlantic squadron an
excellent base.   Immediately afterwards the sea islands
were seized.   From Port Royal in the following April,
an expedition took Fort Pulaski, commanding the mouth
of the Savannah river.   As the smaller harbors fell easy
prey, it happened that by midsummer of 1862 all the Atlantic coast
was under federal control, except Wilmington, N. C., and Charleston.
Against the latter a strong fleet of newly constructed monitors was
sent in April, 1863.   It sailed boldly into the harbor, but retired with
much loss from the fire of Forts Sumter and Moultrie with the aid of
other shore batteries.   In July the attack was renewed, an army now
landing and moving against the defenses on Morris Island, south of
the harbor, while the fleet at close range attacked the works on the
island.   Before the line of advance was Battery Wagner — often called
"Fort Wagner," a work strongly placed and well defended.   Two
unsuccessful assaults were made on it, in the second of which fell
Colonel Robert G. Shaw at the head of his negro regiment.   After
a seven days' bombardment from the fleet, Fort Sumter was in ruins,
although a small infantry force remained in it until the evacuation of

In South Carolina Waters.

Charleston, February 17, 1865. By regular approaches Battery Wagner was at last taken and Morris Island was in federal hands; a useless achievement, for the harbor was supposed to be mined and no further attempt was made against the place for a year and a half.

Besides the capture of New Orleans, 1862, the most notable naval achievement in the gulf region was seizing Mobile bay in 1864. The place was an important outlet for blockade runners and was well defended by Fort Morgan and several vessels, among them the powerful ram, *Tennessee*. August 5, Farragut, with eighteen ships, four of them monitors, ran past the fort and batteries and engaged the fleet within the bay. The *Tennessee* became the target of the union fleet. Ship after ship struck her armored sides, desirous of sinking her. She withstood their blows, but having a weak engine, could not be brought effectively against her opponents. Finally her steering gear was disabled and she surrendered. The rest of the confederate ships retired or were destroyed, and the fort capitulated when 5000 troops had been landed. The city of Mobile was not taken until the following spring.

BIBLIOGRAPHICAL NOTE

For the Eastern campaigns the same general works and sources are available as for the Western operations (see p. 543). Of a more specific nature are the following: *McClellan's Own Story* (1887), contains many letters; Swinton, *Campaigns of the Army of the Potomac* (1882); Grant, *Personal Memoirs*, 2 vols. (1895); Sheridan, *Personal Memoirs*, 2 vols. (1902); Walker, *W. S. Hancock* (1894); Poore, *Ambrose E. Burnside* (1882); Butler, *Butler's Book*, 2 vols. (1892); Cox, *Military Reminiscences*, 2 vols. (1900); Bache, *George Gordon Meade* (1897); Haupt, *Reminiscences* (1901); Long, *Robert Edward Lee* (1886); Longstreet, *From Manassas to Appomattox* (1903); J. E. Johnston, *Narrative of Military Operations* (1874); Hood, *Advance and Retreat* (1880); McClellan, *J. E. B. Stuart* (1885); Henderson, *Stonewall Jackson*, 2 vols. (1900); and Alexander, *Military Memoirs*, (1907).

On army experiences, besides the authorities mentioned on page 543, see: Noyes, *The Bivouac and the Battlefield* (1863); Townsend, *Campaigns of a Non-Combatant* (1866); Eggleston, *A Rebel's Recollection* (1905); Maury, *Recollections of a Virginian* (1894); McGuire, *Diary of a Southern Refugee* (1865); Sorrel, *Recollections of a Confederate Staff-Officer* (1905); Stiles, *Four Years under Marse Robert* (1903); and Taylor, *Four Years with Lee* (1878).

On naval history of the civil war see first of all: *Official Records of the Union and Confederate Navies*, 22 vols. (1894–1908). See also Maclay, *History of the United States Navy*, 3 vols. (ed. 1898–1901); Scharf, *History of the Confederate States Navy* (1894); Porter, *Naval History of the Civil War* (1886); Semmes, *Service Afloat* (1887), relates to the *Alabama;* Wilson, *Iron-Clads in Action* (1897); Bennett, *The Monitor and the Navy under Steam* (1900); Wilkinson, *Narrative of a Blockade Runner* (1877); and Mahan, *Farragut* (1892).

For Independent Reading

Rhodes, *History of the United States*, vols. III–V (1900–1906), the best general history of the war, and it is readable. Other suggested works are: Porter, *Campaigning with Grant* (1897); Walker, *W. S. Hancock* (1894); Eggleston, *A Rebel's Recollections* (1905); Dana, *Recollections of the Civil War* (1898); Wise, *The End of an Era* (1899); Schaff, *The Sunset of the Confederacy* (1912); Bradford, *Lee the American* (1912); Stiles, *Four Years under Marse Robert* (1903); and Bennett, *The Monitor and the Navy under Steam* (1900).

CHAPTER XXVII

CIVIL AFFAIRS DURING THE WAR

ENLISTING TROOPS, NORTH AND SOUTH

THE first soldiers enlisted on each side were volunteers, furnished by the states in response to calls made by the respective presidents.

Creating Armies. They came freely in a period of great enthusiasm, and were of the best quality. But ardor eventually cools, and by the end of 1862 volunteering in the North was nearly at an end. In the South it ceased to be considerable at an earlier date. By this time the federal congress realized how serious a struggle was being waged, and used its power to enforce military service. The result was a law ordering a draft of all men liable for military duty. Enrollment districts were created, and drafts were held by officers duly appointed. A man drafted might furnish a substitute or be exempt on payment of $300.

The act was attacked by the democrats as unconstitutional, and it undoubtedly contravened the principles of state rights to which they were bred. Although it was generally enforced, the

Draft Riots in New York. criticism of the democrats found much support with the people who were unable to secure substitutes or purchase exemption. In New York the Eastside population broke into riots. The people were largely foreign-born, and recognized an ancient grievance in forced military service. On the second day of the draft, July 13, 1863, they broke up the drawings and, joined by habitual thieves, looted stores until they ruled in the city from Union Square to Central Park. Negroes were beaten and hanged to lamp posts, well-to-do citizens were robbed, and the police were powerless. The city had been stripped of soldiers to oppose Lee at Gettysburg, but at last on July 14 an armed force of more than 3000 policemen, marines, and citizens were able to check the depredations. Next day troops began to arrive, and by the 16th the mob was under control, after 1000 persons had been killed or wounded and private property worth $1,500,000 had been destroyed. Investigation showed that the allotments of the democratic enrollment districts were excessive, and when the error was corrected the draft proceeded quietly. News that the chief Northern city was resisting the draft gave the confederates a passing hope that the North would not support the war.

After July, 1863, the people accepted the draft as a military necessity, but it was very unpopular. Out of 470,942 persons drawn in two drafts in 1864, July 18 and December 19, those failing to report were 94,636. To stimulate enlistment, large bounties were offered, not only by the federal government, but by the state and county authorities. In New York City in 1864 these aggregated $677. The regular pay of a private was $16 a month. Two evils now appeared, "bounty-jumping" and the activities of substitute brokers. The latter fixed the scale of payments for substitutes, and often were able to prevent the acceptance of a man as a substitute who did not have their services. They were in close association with "bounty-jumpers," men who deserted as soon as the bounty was received and enlisted elsewhere under other names. A case was discovered in which a man had "jumped" the bounty thirty-two times. Serious charges were made in many places involving the integrity of officers and physicians who conducted enlistments. The system was undoubtedly badly administered; but there was little disposition to look closely into it as long as it furnished men for the defense of union. The early enlistments were the pick of Northern manhood, and to the last there was excellent material in the new men; but as the months passed, the proportion of newly arrived foreigners and shirkers increased. This gave rise to the charge that the armies were recruited from European mercenaries. When the war ended there were 1,052,038 men in the army.

" Bounty-Jumping."

In 1863, after the emancipation policy was adopted, negro troops began to be enlisted. Among the prisoners captured in New Orleans, May, 1862, was a colored regiment organized by the confederates. This was an example which the antislavery element of the republican party in the North thought worthy of imitation. Lincoln, with the opinion of the border states in mind, opposed such a step; but the confiscation act of the summer of 1862 gave him authority to use such troops for the defense of the union. In the final emancipation proclamation he announced that negro volunteers would be accepted. The first regiment of them was the 54th Massachusetts, led by Colonel Robert Gould Shaw, socially and intellectually eminent in Boston. Many persons had predicted that negroes would not fight, but the result proved the contrary. Though generally used for garrison duty, they exhibited marked courage in some severe emergencies. At Fort Wagner Shaw's regiment charged most bravely and suffered severe loss. Grant, and many others in a position to know, declared that the negro troops fought well. At the end of the war 183,000 had been enlisted.

Negro Troops.

The confederate congress enacted May 1, 1863, that white officers commanding negro soldiers should when captured be treated as

persons inciting blacks to insurrection, but there is no evidence
that the threat was carried into execution.   Negro soldiers when
captured were sometimes killed by their captors, but
Negro Soldiers as War Prisoners. such cases as occurred were due to the feelings of the
privates and not by order of the confederate authorities.
The most notable case was at the capture of Fort Pillow
by Forrest, April 12, 1864; but investigation showed this
was without orders of Forrest, who offered to receive the negroes
as prisoners of war when he demanded the surrender of the fort.   His
demand was refused, and as no flag of surrender was raised, his storm-
ing party slew its defenders, white and black, who fought desperately,
until Forrest himself arrived on the scene and stopped the slaughter.
When negro prisoners were identified as escaped slaves they were
returned to their masters. The confederacy was unwilling to exchange
negro prisoners, and on that ground all exchanges stopped for a while;
but from this attitude the confederates retreated early in 1864, only
proposing to retain those who were known to be fugitive slaves.   At
this time Grant was determined to send no prisoners back to swell the
ranks of the Southern armies, and no exchanges of any kind occurred
until January, 1865, when the confederacy was in its last gasps.

FEDERAL FINANCES

Providing funds for war expenses was a mammoth task. When
congress met in extra session, July 4, 1861, the national debt was
considered large at $76,000,000. The people, therefore,
Measures of 1861. were startled when they knew that the legislature had
authorized a loan of $250,000,000 in bonds and interest-
bearing notes. Additional taxes were laid by which it was expected
that a total revenue of $75,000,000 would be raised. Two features
of the plan were a tax of three per cent on incomes over $800, and a
direct tax. It was believed that these taxes were as heavy as the
country would stand. The execution of the financial laws fell on Chase,
who proved himself an able secretary of the treasury.

But expenses were enormous, and when congress met again, December 2, there was a deficit of $143,000,000. The war had sorely dis-
tressed business, bonds were selling slowly, specie had
The Legal Tender Act of February 25, 1862. been drawn out of the country, and December 30 the
banks suspended specie payment, compelling the govern-
ment to follow their example. Something must be done
quickly or the war could not go on. The result was the
law generally known as the Legal Tender Act of February 25, 1862,
providing for: 1. The issue of $100,000,000 in treasury notes, which,
as well as the $50,000,000 authorized in July, 1861, were to be legal
tender for all dues but imports and interest on the public debt; and
2. An additional loan of $500,000,000 in six per cent 5–20 bonds,

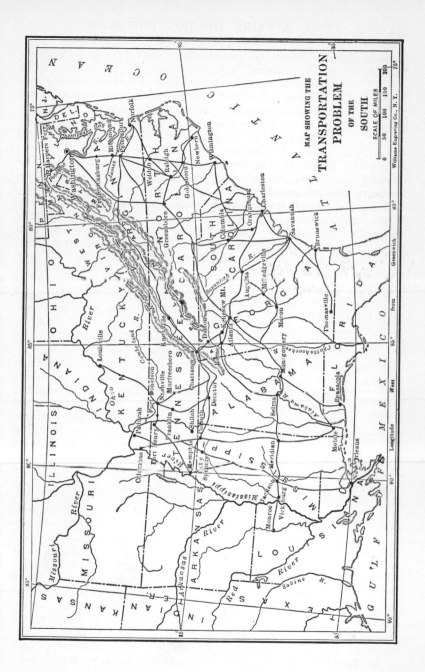

MAP SHOWING THE
TRANSPORTATION
PROBLEM
OF THE
SOUTH

SCALE OF MILES

Williams Engraving Co., N. Y.

interest payable in coin. There was much opposition to the legal tender feature of the bill, and Secretary Chase hesitated long before accepting it. It was passed because it was pronounced absolutely necessary in the crisis at hand. At the same time another bill was carried through congress to raise import duties and lay other taxes. It was so comprehensive that it has been called "an act which taxed everything." A proposition to create a national banking system was deferred to another date. By the measures here adopted it was expected that the funds would be obtained to defray the war expenses for a year. The expenditures were then $2,000,000 a day.

At the beginning of 1863 the treasury was again empty, and clamor arose for more legal tender. Congress yielded to the extent of authorizing $100,000,000, a measure which Lincoln regretfully approved. It also authorized a loan of $900,000,000. **The National Banking Act, 1863.** February 25 it took a more important step in passing a national banking act, by which it was designed to charter banks under national authority with the privilege of issuing money secured by national bonds. The act as passed proved inadequate, and was amended from time to time. The plan which resulted may be summarized as follows: 1. The comptroller of the currency, an official now first provided for, should supervise this system. 2. Each bank before beginning business must deposit national bonds equal to one-third of its paid-in capital, but the interest on these bonds was to go to the bank depositing them. 3. It would receive from the comptroller bank notes in amount equal to ninety per cent of the market value of the deposited bonds, and when signed by the officers of the bank these notes were to be receivable for all dues to the United States except imports. 4. The capital stock of a national bank was not to be less than $50,000. 5. A national bank must keep a cash reserve equal to 15 per cent of its circulation, but one-half of this might be left with certain specified central banks, whose reserves, it was ordered, must be 25 per cent of the circulation, and 6. Shareholders were made responsible for the debts of the bank above their stock held to an amount equal to the par value of their stock. In 1865 an act was passed to tax at 10 per cent, after July 1, 1866, the circulation of state banks. This law impelled state banks to change to national banks, with the result that 1634 of the latter existed on July 1, 1866. The national banks made a market for government bonds, and drove out of circulation the currency of the state banks.

Spite of the measures of 1863 the revenues proved insufficient, and in 1864 import duties, excise, and most internal taxes were raised as high as the country would stand. An additional **State of the Currency.** loan of $400,000,000 was authorized, and authority was given to extend the amount of legal tender to $450,-000,000. As a matter of fact, it reached during the year the sum of $431,000,000, and went only a million higher in the following year.

The increase of national bank notes served partly to satisfy the demand for treasury notes. The legal tender notes, popularly called "greenbacks" ceased to circulate at par with specie as soon as they were issued. Gold rose until, June 30, 1864, it sold for 250, and when Early was before Washington, July 11, it reached 285, the highest price during the war. As prices of commodities were expressed in legal tender they rose proportionally with gold. Throughout the summer of 1864 a paper dollar was worth about forty cents in gold. One result was to drive fractional specie out of circulation. "Shinplasters," small private notes from 5 to 50 cents in value, took its place, but these were eventually forbidden, and for a time postage stamps were used. Their disadvantage was soon evident, and the government issued fractional paper currency on its own account.

Early in the war the national bonds ceased to sell, although the interest was 7.3 per cent. The plan of sale was to award the bonds at a fixed rate to associated bankers in installments **Bonds at** of about $50,000,000, the banks selling at home and **Popular** abroad at what profit they could make. In 1863 Secre-**Subscrip-** tary Chase adopted a new method. Selecting a great bank-**tion.** ing firm as his agent, Jay Cooke and Company, he offered the bonds to the public in popular denominations. It was an appeal to the patriotism of the nation, and was fully justified by the results.

Two confiscation acts were passed by congress, partly to get revenue and partly to punish the confederates. The first, August 6, 1861, authorized the confiscation of property used in **Two Con-** aid of the confederacy, and the liberation of slaves em-**fiscation** ployed on fortifications or in other warlike labor. The **Acts.** second, July 17, 1862, was more drastic. It fixed death as the punishment for treason, but allowed the courts to substitute fine and imprisonment, and it decreed that the slaves of all who supported the Southern cause should be free. It further provided for the confiscation of the property of six classes of persons who supported the confederacy, including the higher officials, who were believed to be especially responsible for the war. Another provision was to authorize the enlistment of negroes in the union armies. This second act was urged especially by the radical opponents of slavery, and Lincoln would not sign it until congress adopted explanatory resolutions, one of which provided that it was not to be used to extend the taint of treason to the issue of confederates. So far as its confiscatory features were concerned, it was very sparingly used during the war, partly because Lincoln opposed severe measures, and partly because the jurisdiction of federal courts did not in reality extend to the vast majority of the Southerners, who were within the confederate lines. At the end of the war, when federal courts were reëstablished in the South, a policy of conciliation prevailed, and confiscation was not put into operation.

THE PROGRESS OF EMANCIPATION

Early in the war the extreme republicans began to urge that measures be taken to destroy slavery. The large majority of voters in the border states, as well as many persons in the free states, opposed this policy, and Lincoln discountenanced it because he felt that the only means of success was to make the war solely for the preservation of the union. *Demands of the Radicals.* His influence prevailed, and the day after Bull Run, congress passed, with only nine dissenting votes in the two houses, resolutions declaring that the North did not mean to interfere with slavery, but only sought to perpetuate the union. From this position president and congress, under pressure of public opinion, were to recede in a little more than twelve months.

When Virginia seceded, May 23, General Butler commanded at Fortress Monroe. To him came many fugitive slaves, whose owners demanded their surrender. The request was refused by Butler on the ground that having worked on confederate fortifications they were "contraband of war." *"Contrabands."* His position was not legal, but he was supported by Northern opinion, and the government did not overrule him. The first confiscation act, August 6, 1861, gave freedom to slaves working on confederate fortifications and engaged in military operations, but it did not mention ordinary fugitives, who came to Butler in great numbers. The secretary of war was asked to define the status of the second class. He replied that they should be received into the service of the United States and employed as seemed best, and added that when the war was over congress would, no doubt, "provide a just compensation to loyal masters." Butler was also ordered to refrain from interference with the slaves of peaceful citizens and not to encourage them to leave their masters. Nor should he prevent their voluntary return unless the public good seemed to demand it. Such instructions left wide discretion to the generals commanding in regions which could be reached by fugitives. Some of them were less inclined to antislavery views than Butler, and surrendered fugitives freely. Others gave little help to such masters as came to look for their runaway slaves.

Of those who were most hostile to slavery was General Frémont, presidential candidate in 1856. He was popular with the extreme republicans, through whose influence he was called home from Europe to command the army in Missouri. Arriving at New York early in July, 1861, he loitered three weeks in the East, conferring with political friends before he repaired to St. Louis, where he was greatly needed. His incompetence was soon evident from the manner in which he yielded himself to a group of contractors who surrounded and flat-

2 P

tered him for their selfish ends. Soon followed military reverses, and public opinion rose high against him. To regain his popularity he issued his remarkable order of August 30, 1861, directing the confiscation of the property of all who had taken arms against the union, offering freedom to their slaves, and creating a "bureau of abolition" to supervise the execution of the order. His action aroused enthusiasm among the radical opponents of slavery, but alarmed the unionists of Kentucky, then trembling in the balance. Lincoln first knew of the order from the newspapers, and suggested to the author that it be modified. The advice was rejected with scant courtesy, and Lincoln coolly directed that the order be modified in conformity with the first confiscation act. After some further manifestations of his incompetence, Frémont was removed, and General Hunter succeeded to the command. The affair aroused the anger of the radicals, who sharply criticized the president for his part in it.

Yet Lincoln wished to abolish slavery if it could be done in a proper way, and was already moving for emancipation with compensation in the slave states still loyal. In March, 1862, he sug-

Emancipation with Compensation.

gested such action to congress, and thought an average of $400 might be given for each slave in Maryland, Kentucky, Missouri, Delaware, and the District of Columbia, incurring a total expense of $173,000,000, which was less than the cost of the war for 87 days. The suggestion pleased neither congress nor the people of the states concerned, and no action was taken on it. But April 16 a bill was passed for the emancipation with compensation of the slaves in the District of Columbia.

The second confiscation act, July 17, 1862, gave freedom to the slaves of persons resisting the union, forbade their surrender, and authorized their "colonization" on the abandoned lands

Second Confiscation Act and the Slaves.

of the confederates. As the law would not be obeyed in the seceding states, little more was expected from it than that it might serve to free fugitives who reached the union lines. Lincoln, and many others, considered it of doubtful constitutionality, and he gave it a mild interpretation. For this, also, he received the censure of the radicals.

May 9, 1862, General Hunter, commanding the recovered territory around Beaufort, South Carolina, issued an order declaring free all the slaves in South Carolina, Georgia, and Florida.

Hunter's Order.

He acted on his own authority, but had the approval of Chase and the other radicals. Lincoln reversed the order at once. But he sought to break the blow by calling on the loyal slave states to accept gradual emancipation with compen-

Compensation Abandoned.

sation. In reply, the congressmen from the border states signed an address suggesting that congress should act first in the matter. July 14 the president laid the matter before congress, which did nothing. By this he was convinced that nothing was to be hoped from emancipation through compensation, and he turned to other means.

July 22 he read to his cabinet a tentative emancipation proclamation to apply to the seceding states, justifying his proposed action on the ground of military necessity. Blair alone of the cabinet objected, as he thought the proclamation would endanger the autumn elections. Seward suggested that the announcement ought to wait until the army won a victory, otherwise the proclamation would be construed as "the government stretching forth its hands to Ethiopia," a confession of weakness. This view prevailed, and the matter was laid aside for a favorable opportunity. *The Tentative Emancipation Proclamation.*

The action of the cabinet was secret, and the radical opponents of slavery, ignorant of what was going on, continued their strictures on the president. August 20, Horace Greeley, editor of the New York *Tribune*, summed up this view in an editorial entitled, "The Prayer of Twenty Millions." He reproached the president for being influenced by "certain fossil politicians" from the border states, for repudiating Frémont's and Hunter's orders and enforcing an order of Halleck to exclude fugitive slaves from the union camps, and for failing to execute the provisions of the second confiscation act touching slavery. Although this "Prayer" was addressed to Lincoln, he saw it first in the newspapers. He wrote and published in the same medium a reply which could not fail to crush his critics in the minds of the impartial people of the country. "As to the policy," he said, "I 'seem to be pursuing,' as you say, I have not meant to leave anyone in doubt. I would save the Union. I would save it the shortest way under the Constitution. The sooner the national authority can be restored, the nearer the Union will be 'the Union as it was.' If there be those who would not save the Union unless they could at the same time save slavery, I do not agree with them. If there be those who would not save the Union unless they could at the same time destroy slavery, I do not agree with them. My paramount object in this struggle is to save the Union, and is not either to save or destroy slavery. If I could save the Union without freeing any slave, I would do it; and if I could save it by freeing all the slaves, I would do it; and if I could save it by freeing some and leaving others alone, I would also do that. What I do about slavery and the colored race, I do because I believe it helps to save the Union; and what I forbear, I forbear because I do not believe it would help to save the Union. I shall do less whenever I believe what I am doing hurts the cause, and I shall do more whenever I shall believe doing more will help the cause. I shall try to correct errors when shown to be errors, and I shall adopt new views so fast as they shall appear to be true views." This letter was widely read and had a great influence on public opinion. *Greeley's "Prayer." Lincoln's Reply.*

September 17 Lee's invasion of Maryland was checked at Antietam, and Lincoln on the 23d issued the celebrated preliminary emancipation proclamation. It announced that the slaves
would be declared free in all states resisting the union on
January 1, 1863. It also spoke of compensation for the
slaves of loyal states. It was a warning to the South, but
it only elicited jeers from that section, and January 1 a final proclamation appeared declaring slavery abolished by military authority
in all the South except Tennessee and the parts of Louisiana and
Virginia then held by union arms. The proclamation satisfied for a
time the radicals of the North and strengthened the cause of the
union in Europe, by showing that the war was fought to put an end
to slavery. Even the border states could not complain, for they were
not affected, and it was evident that ample time had been given the
secessionists to escape emancipation by submitting to the union.
The proclamation had no basis in the law of civil affairs, as Lincoln
well knew, but he believed it was within his authority as commander-
in-chief of the army and navy.

The Emanci-
pation Proc-
lamation.

In the annual message, December 1, 1863, Lincoln returned to
the subject of compensated emancipation for the border states, and
a bill of that nature to apply to Missouri passed the house
and had a conditional approval in the senate. But it
was opposed by the democrats, mostly border state men,
who thought the South would not be conquered, and, as
some republicans gave it a very lukewarm support, the
measure finally failed in the short session. When congress met
again, the cause of the North was more promising on the battlefield, and congress was less inclined to concede anything to slaveholders.
They were now concerned with an amendment abolishing slavery
outright.

Compen-
sated Eman-
cipation
again
Suggested.

Reflection showed that Lincoln's proclamation was of doubtful
constitutionality. Moreover, it abolished slavery at best in only
about half of the territory in which the institution existed,
and it did not prevent the future reëstablishment of bondage by a state. To meet these difficulties, a thirteenth
amendment was introduced in congress, March 28, 1864. It passed
the senate, but failed to get the necessary two-thirds majority in the
house. January 31, 1865, it came up again in the house and passed
by the necessary majority. With its ratification by three-fourths of
the states, it became a part of the organic law of the land, December
18, 1865. Before it was ratified, slavery had been abolished by state
amendment in Arkansas, January, 1864; Louisiana, September, 1864;
Maryland, October, 1864; Tennessee, February, 1865; and Missouri,
June, 1865. February 5, 1865, after the thirteenth amendment had
passed, Lincoln submitted to his cabinet the draft of a message proposing to pay to the slave states $400,000,000 in bonds on considera-

Thirteenth
Amendment.

tion that the war cease by April 1. The cabinet thought such a measure could not pass congress, and the matter was dropped. Thus did Lincoln, whose sympathy for the South never failed, make his last effort to save for the slaveholders some portion of their property which the progress of the age was going to take away.

POLITICAL PARTIES DURING THE CIVIL WAR

During the war the Northern voters became divided into four classes. 1. The regular republicans. They followed Lincoln in a mild opposition to slavery, and put the preservation of the union above all else. 2. The radical republicans, **Four Groups.** also strong unionists, but in favor of an extreme anti-slavery policy, and disposed to deal harshly with the South after the war ended. 3. The war democrats, protesting their faith in democratic principles, but opposed to secession, and loyal to the union at the polls and on the battlefield. They were not well organized as a group, but in some cases were of great importance because they coöperated with the Lincoln republicans in important local elections. 4. The regular democrats, outwardly professing devotion to the union, but criticizing the conduct of the war and undermining as much as they could the national support of it. Many of the leaders of this group were party men who wished to keep their organization intact, and whose most evident means of reaching their end was to criticize the party in power in whatever way offered. The first, second, and third groups usually acted together on the all-important issue of the war; the fourth, always a minority in congress, made vigorous attacks on their opponents, but were unable to modify the course of events. To many people their efforts seemed little less than treason to the union.

The first notable political contest after 1860 was in 1862. It was a year of military reverses. McClellan did not take Richmond, and Pope was beaten in Virginia. Grant's campaign from Fort Henry to Corinth was a steady success, and Lee was **The War Policy** forced back from Maryland after Antietam, but after each **Criticized.** campaign came a period of inactivity. The war was begun to crush the confederacy, and the people were discouraged because this object seemed indefinitely distant. And so the democrats — calling themselves conservatives — pronounced the war a costly failure. The emancipation proclamation they also criticized. It was arraigned as a violation of the constitution and as evidence that the war was not waged to preserve the union but to destroy slavery. Out of these two lines of argument was evolved the battle cry: The constitution as it is and the union as it was!

Other arguments were found which did good service. Military

arrests began to be made as soon as the war began: they became more numerous when campaign speakers fell to discussing the war in candid terms. Stanton, who generally ordered the arrests, was charged with doing so in order to suppress political dis-
Elections of 1862. cussion. In Ohio several men highly esteemed were thus thrown into prison, and the political effect was great. The vast expenditures for military supplies led to jobbery and corruption on a large scale, as investigation committees in Washington clearly showed, and out of this the democrats made capital. Moreover, there was a natural reaction from the buoyant war feeling of 1861. The result was seen in the elections of 1862. New York, Pennsylvania, New Jersey, Ohio, Illinois, Indiana, and Wisconsin chose anti-administration state officials, and the house of representatives, which in 1861 had 42 democrats against 106 republicans and 28 union men, had, two years later, 75 democrats against 102 republicans and 9 "border state men." Since the democrats were opposed to the existing method of conducting the war, this meant that their policy had gained materially in the house of representatives.

Within Lincoln's own party there was abundant trouble. The radicals thought him unequal to the presidency. Men of dignity themselves, they could not tolerate his lack of formality,
Attack on Lincoln. carelessness in dress, and lack of method in business. They thought him under the influence of Seward, who was avowedly a conservative. Finally a caucus of republican senators in December, 1862, resolved that the president ought to dismiss those members of the cabinet who interfered with the successful conduct of the war. The blow was aimed at Seward, who offered his resignation forthwith. In a joint meeting of the rest of the cabinet and a committee of the senators, Lincoln cleverly forced Chase, who was probably at the bottom of the discontent, to resign also. That done, he refused to accept either resignation, and was able to continue with a two-sided administration. Chase and the radicals were forced to abate their opposition, but events showed that it was not extinguished.

Meanwhile, "Copperheads" appeared. The epithet was applied by their enemies to all democrats; but it should properly be given only to those extreme opponents of the war who went so far as
Copperheads. to seem by their agitation to give aid to the South. The name came from the habit of wearing as a badge a button cut out of a copper cent, on which was the head of the Goddess of Liberty. The movement began late in 1862. It was accompanied with violent speech-making, and one of its most active leaders was Clement L. Vallandigham, of Ohio, bold of speech and sharp of tongue.

Arguments were not wanting to reach men bred in the school of state rights. Congress had passed laws giving the president control over the sword and purse of the nation; slavery was annulled by a mere word; and hundreds of persons were in prison without civil trial through military arrest, charged with no other offense than words spoken against the government. The war was a republican war; it would not have begun but for the election of Lincoln, and it was now carried on, said the agitators, to preserve the political power of the republicans. In the winter of 1862–63, Napoleon III offered to mediate between the North and the South. Lincoln's refusal to accept the offer was declared evidence that the war was fought to subjugate a portion of the American people.

Arguments of Copperheads.

After his defeat at Fredericksburg, Burnside became commander of the department of the Ohio, where copperheads were most outspoken. With a soldier's impatience of defiance, he issued an order, April 13, 1863, in which he said, "the habit of declaring sympathy for the enemy will not be allowed. . . ." Vallandigham was then a candidate for the nomination for governor of Ohio, and was making caustic speeches against the republicans. He considered Burnside's order a challenge, and accepted it. May 1 he made one of his customary speeches, although he knew he was watched. Four days later he was arrested and sent before a military commission which acted without forms of law. He was pronounced guilty of "declaring disloyal sentiments" in order to weaken the power of the government against its enemies, and the sentence was confinement until the end of the war. Approved by Burnside, it went at length to Lincoln, who commuted the penalty to banishment to the confederacy. The prisoner was sent through the union lines in Virginia, and reached Richmond. He was received coldly by Jefferson Davis, and escaping through the blockade, arrived safely in Canada, from which secure retreat he directed his campaign in Ohio. Now a martyr in the eyes of his friends, he was nominated for governor, and the immense public meetings which the democrats held seemed to indicate certain triumph at the polls. The union party was alarmed, and nominated Brough, a war democrat, to oppose him. The election came in October, with the result that Brough was chosen governor with a majority of 101,099. Probably the victories at Gettysburg and Vicksburg, by showing that the war was not a failure, were the chief cause of the unionist success. At the same time, other states were carried by the friends of Lincoln with large majorities, among them New York, Pennsylvania, and Illinois. These favorable results encouraged the republicans, and the support of the war did not weaken.

Arrest of Vallandigham.

This difficulty was hardly passed before the radicals began to show that they wished to defeat the nomination of Lincoln for president in 1864. They united on Chase who, spite of the fact that he was in the cabinet, showed that he desired the proffered honor. They formed a committee with Senator Pomeroy, of Kansas, for chairman, and early in 1864 it sent out a circular in behalf of Chase. February 25, however, Chase's hopes fell when Ohio, his own state, declared for Lincoln. He withdrew his countenance of the movement, but the radicals continued their opposition, their candidate now being Frémont.

The Pomeroy Circular, 1864.

The convention of the national union, or the republican party, met June 7. Four days earlier, Grant's bloody campaign against Lee came to a halt in the costly sacrifice of life at Cold Harbor, and Richmond was still in confederate hands. At the same time, Sherman, after many days of skirmishing and one fierce battle at Kenesaw Mountain, was still outside of Atlanta. To the North, it was the same old story of slaughter, expense, and defeat; and the democratic press denounced bitterly a president whose policy resulted only in such losses. But the convention was true to Lincoln and nominated him unanimously. For vice-president, it named Andrew Johnson, military governor of Tennessee. Lincoln is said to have been responsible for the choice. There was a strong feeling that a Southern man should be on the ticket, in order to give it a non-sectional character. Lincoln, in his characteristic way, said his own nomination came because the convention thought "it was not best to swap horses while crossing the river." Now followed weeks of utter gloom in the North. Unless the confederacy could be crushed before the election, said Greeley, the union party would be defeated. Prominent men declared that Lincoln ought to withdraw, or be set aside for a stronger candidate. The president himself thought his reëlection doubtful, and wrote a memorandum for his own use to the effect that if defeated he would coöperate with his successor-elect to "save the union between the election and the inauguration, as he will have secured his election on such grounds that he cannot possibly save it afterwards."

Lincoln Renominated.

The successor he had in mind was General McClellan, whom the democrats nominated at Chicago in August. He was the strongest candidate they could have selected, and he would surely be popular with the soldiers and the masses of the people. The platform demanded the cessation of bloodshed and the calling of a convention to restore peace "on the basis of the federal union of the states." The stoutest hearted unionists feared the result of a political campaign on this issue. Their apprehensions were relieved when, on September 3, Sherman entered Atlanta, and thus proved that, in one of its most important movements, the war was not a failure. It was an argument the democrats could not answer; and cheered by it the union men took up the campaign with such spirit that Lincoln, in November, was successful by 212 electoral votes to McClellan's 21.

Election of 1864.

It is a noteworthy thing that in the remarkable days of the civil war the man elected president in 1864 by a vote so sweeping was, at the same time, at variance with a majority of each house of congress on the most important civil question then before the public, *i.e.* the reconstruction of the Southern states. Throughout this last winter of war the two factions subordinated their quarrel to the task of conquering the South; but no one doubted that, this accomplished, a great struggle would occur between the president and the radicals to determine who should dominate in reconstruction. From this conflict Lincoln was saved by Booth's wicked deed.

Lincoln and Congress.

The War Powers of the President

The constitution provides that congress shall have power to declare war and suppress insurrections. The war of 1812 began with a declaration by congress. The Mexican war began with a declaration by Polk that Mexico had begun war by sending troops into the territory of the United States. To many people it seemed at the time a dangerous thing to allow the president to determine, when another nation had begun war, since to do so was tantamount to giving him the power to declare war. In 1861 the situation was even more urgent. That congress, called to meet in July, would recognize the existence of insurrection, was not doubted. To meet the active war measures of the confederacy, prompt action on the part of the union was necessary. Should Lincoln wait for the authority of acts of congress? He was too practical a man for such a course, and boldly decided to assume that he had necessary powers, and trust that congress would by its approval legalize what he had done. He accordingly called for troops, organized armies, and proclaimed a blockade of Southern ports. In doing so he established a precedent for similar situations, if such should arise in the future.

The Right to Declare War.

A more doubtful matter was connected with the suspension of the writ of *habeas corpus*. On this subject the constitution only says, "The writ of *habeas corpus* shall not be suspended, unless when in cases of rebellion or invasion the public safety may require it." But the constitution did not say whether the president or congress should suspend the writ. Here again the necessity for immediate action was apparent. Maryland was full of Southern sentiment, the legislature was called to meet to consider the situation, and it was believed that a majority of its members would favor secession. If the state joined the confederacy, Washington would be isolated and the cause of union would be severely injured. Lincoln again assumed responsibility. He ordered the military authorities to arrest the members of the legis-

Suspending the Writ of Habeas Corpus.

lature who seemed to be plotting treason, and to hold them prisoners without benefit of *habeas corpus*. From their prisons they
appealed to Taney, chief justice, who readily decided that they had
committed no crime against the civil law. But they were not released,
and there was no power in the courts to force the executive to adopt
Taney's construction of the constitution. This action also became
a precedent under which, we may believe, it will be held that in a
future emergency the president may suspend the writ if he thinks the
public safety demands it. In this, as in all other cases, he is subject
to impeachment for exercising his power without a due sense of
responsibility. As Professor Dunning well says, it made the president a temporary dictator.

Military arrests, however, were not confined to Maryland. In
all parts of the North men were imprisoned on the charge of aiding
the South. September 24, 1862, Lincoln issued a procla-
Many Military Arrests. mation for the arrest of persons discouraging enlistment
or resisting the draft. They were to be tried by military
courts, and to prevent the interference of civil officers they
were to be denied the privileges of *habeas corpus*. This step was
defended on the ground of military necessity. It placed for the time
being the life and liberty of citizens in the hands of the president
to an extent that was never contemplated in the much decried alien
and sedition laws of 1798. Under it, numerous arrests were made, and
the victims were frequently kept in duress without trial. So great
was the popular disapproval that congress, March 3, 1863, attempted
to regulate the matter. It gave the president the authority to suspend the writ, ordered that persons then in prison should be discharged
unless they were indicted by a grand jury, and that in
Habeas Corpus Act of 1863. the future no arrested one should be held longer than
twenty days unless so indicted. The natural consequence
was to take such cases out of the hands of the military
courts and leave them with the federal courts. Spite of this act
military arrests of civilians continued to the end of the war, though
not in as large numbers as formerly. The civil courts were not able
to assert their authority against commanders of the army and were
forced to submit. It was not until 1866 that they found an opportunity to declare themselves in the decision of the case *ex parte Milligan* (see page 612). Although the supreme court here asserted the
supremacy of the civil arm in districts not immediately subject to military authority, it is difficult to see how its contention could be enforced
if the country should again have to encounter a situation like that of the
civil war.

THE SOUTHERN PROBLEM AND SOUTHERN EFFORTS

It is regrettable that this work is not large enough to embrace a de-
scription of the civil war from the southern side. Nothing in American

history is finer than the ability and devotion with which the confederacy, once it was organized, met its difficulties and utilized its scant resources to beat off the armies that were thrown upon it. Here it is only possible to mention the most prominent facts and to show how they affected the struggle.

The confederate constitution was the old constitution modified to remedy what the South thought were bad interpretations of the old instrument. Internal improvements and protective tariffs **Confederate** were forbidden, slavery was guaranteed in territories, a **Constitution.** confederate official serving solely within a state might be impeached by a two-thirds vote of each house of the legislature within that state, and a two-thirds vote of each house was made necessary for admitting a new state into the confederacy, the vote in the senate being by states. In these particulars, each of which suggests old points of dispute, it was attempted to guard the rights of the state against the central authority. Several other features are noteworthy. In order to make it easy to modify the constitution in keeping with the changing needs of the country, a new convention must be called when demanded by three states. Another feature took from the state the right to enfranchise foreigners who had not been naturalized, and still another made the president's term of office six years with ineligibility for reëlection. Cabinet members were to appear and speak in congress on matters pertaining to their departments, but they could not vote; and no money was to be appropriated without a two-thirds vote except the sums specified in annual estimates by the departments. Several of these latter features had no reference to the sectional controversy, but were considered improvements warranted by experience.

The Montgomery government was provisional and was to exist for one year only. By autumn the permanent constitution was adopted, and elections were held for presidential electors and members of congress. In the former Jefferson Davis was elected president for six years, and February 22, 1862, he was inaugurated in a downpour of rain which caused the superstitious to tremble for the fate of the new government. In fact, trouble soon appeared. Davis was a man of strong will and little tact. He was a West Point graduate, and took effective control of the war policy. He dominated a cabinet and congress hardly equal to the great work thrown upon them. His plan to withhold cotton from Europe in the first year of the war, when the blockade was not very efficient, was condemned by many planters. His military appointments were supposed to be due to favoritism; it was said that he showed too strong a preference for Virginians, and some of the states claimed that he overrode states' rights in executing the conscription laws and the laws to impress horses and supplies for the army. Before the end of the war the discontented class was large, and one heard in many quarters that it was "a rich man's war and a poor man's fight." But in most respects Davis had his way; and it is doubtful if any other Southerner then in public life could have filled his difficult position so well. The chief objection to him as president is that he was too stout-hearted, and that he allowed the war to continue too long after it was an evident failure. In the light of later events it would have been better if in the autumn of 1864 he had relaxed his stubborn purpose to resist until death, sacrificing his own ideas for what he should have known was the interest of his people.

As the hope of success retreated, a peace party began to appear, most of its members being those who had clung longest to the union in 1861. Davis and the whole confederate government opposed it strongly, the writ of *habeas corpus* was suspended, and every effort was made to keep alive the loyalty of all the people. In North Carolina and Georgia the peace movement was strongest, and even Stephens, the vice-president, was known to look upon it with favor. The elections of 1864 were awaited as a test of the matter, but they resulted in victory for the friends of resistance, and the two states held on to the cause, though it was evidently desperate.

The Peace Movement.

Turning from internal affairs in the South, let us consider foreign relations. Although selling bonds and buying supplies and ships concerned confederate agents in Europe, they gave most attention to efforts to secure the recognition of their government. The decision of England in May, 1861, to give the South only the status of belligerency was disappointing, but hopes ran strong that confederate military success would be followed by recognition. Time showed that this was a vain expectation. The campaigns of Bull Run, the Peninsula, and second Manassas were confederate victories, and though Antietam was a practical reverse, Fredericksburg was a decisive victory, and spite of them no signs of recognition appeared. In fact, England steadily refused to recognize the confederate representative, Mason, and he reported that regard for the dignity of his government demand that he be recalled. He was, however, instructed to remain at his post in the hope that he might influence public opinion. He spent money freely for newspaper articles, and a newspaper was established in London presenting to the British public facts and arguments favorable to the South. By this time England was trying hard to produce cotton in her colonies and succeeding, although the quality of the cotton thus secured was below that produced in the South. The British people were strongly opposed to slavery, and Adams, the American minister, lost no opportunity to show them to what extent the cause of the South was connected with the prolongation of the institution. It is not too much to say that slavery alone stood in the way of European recognition of the confederacy. After the battle of Gettysburg and the fall of Vicksburg, recognition became impossible, and Mason withdrew from London to Paris, remaining in Europe until the end of the war, with little to do.

Confederate Foreign Affairs.

Meanwhile, it seemed for a time that better success would come from negotiations with France. Napoleon III wished to revive the French colonial empire, and Mexico seemed to offer a favorable field of action. In order to collect some debts which this improvident country had failed to pay, a joint French, British, and Spanish expedition occupied it in 1861–1862. Mexico now came to terms in regard to the debts, and England and Spain withdrew. But the French troops remained, and Napoleon, by taking sides with one of the two political factions then in the country, soon made himself lord of the country. Setting aside all pretext, he boldly began to inaugurate his colonial scheme. He expected no embarrassment on account of our Monroe doctrine; for the United States government had its hands full at home. On the contrary, he was disposed to make a friend of the confederacy. He caused the confederates to believe that early recognition was inevitable, and said he only awaited England's initiative. Early in 1862 he said he was ready to open the blockade of New Orleans, but the place was taken by Farragut, and the plan became impossible. Late in the same year he suggested joint intervention by himself, England, and Spain, with an armistice of six months to arrange for a permanent peace. The proposition was rejected by England and brought forth a firm protest from the United States, with the result that it accomplished nothing for the confederacy. But France did not cease to countenance the confederacy. Napoleon even sanctioned the building of heavy corvettes of the *Alabama* type provided they could go to sea without their destinations becoming known. Work on the ships was begun, but the American minister learned of it and protested to the emperor, who forthwith revoked the permission he had given. The ships, six in all, were completed, but Gettysburg had then been fought, and it was impossible to get permission for their departure unless they were sold to a neutral power of recognized standing. One of them was sold fictitiously to Denmark, got to sea, where her name was changed to the *Stonewall*, but it was not done until January, 1865, and although the vessel reached Havana, it was too late to be of service to the confederacy. The action of France in refusing permission for the ships to depart came just at the time the British authorities took similar action in regard to the confederate rams built in English waters (see page 523), and the fate of the much desired confederate navy was thus sealed. Cut off from activity on the sea, the confederacy could not raise the blockade, and the war was left to be fought out on land. Of the ships which the South managed to get armed and on the sea, the most notable were the *Alabama, Florida, Sumter, Shenandoah, Tallahassee,* and *Georgia.*

The Southern army was first raised by volunteering, as in the North; but although enthusiasm was abundant in 1861, it soon was inadequate for the demands of the hour, and in April, 1862, a conscription

France in Mexico.

France and the Confederacy.

act was passed, making all males between the ages of 18 and 35 liable to military duty. Five months later the limits were made 18 and 45, and before the end of the war boys as young as 16 years were made liable to service. The confederate historians place the aggregate number of troops in their armies at 600,000 to 700,000. The northern authorities contend that this is too small, and think about 1,000,000 the right number. Unfortunately, the confederate records were lost, and the dispute cannot be decided. The white population of the confederacy was only 5,500,000, which, by the accepted method of estimating the available military class as one-fifth of the population, would give 1,100,000 of military age. It is hardly to be expected that nearly all of these were drawn into the army. In the North the men of military age were about 4,400,000, of which about 2,500,000 went into the army.

The conscription laws of the South produced the same evils as in the North. Substitutes were allowed, and substitute brokers appeared. The men thus furnished were considered inefficient soldiers, and deserted freely. Men of this class, as well as those who evaded service, frequently fled to the woods and became the scourge of peaceful communities. In the last months of the war there was much complaint on this score. As the Southern armies were reduced in numbers, surgeons went everywhere, examining the men not in the armies, and taking all who could be of any use as soldiers. In this way the confederate government brought out a very large proportion of the men capable of fighting in its behalf. By Christmas, 1864, it was estimated by the authorities that there were 100,000 deserters in the South.

The financial resources of the confederacy were also severely taxed. The strictness of the blockade reduced import duties to an inconsiderable basis, and the chief source of funds was loans and internal taxes. The former consisted of bonds and treasury notes, issued both by states and the confederacy. Specie was chiefly sent abroad to pay for public supplies, and the rapidly depreciating paper money sank in value until it was only received at enormous reduction. Even towns, counties, insurance companies, and mining companies issued their promises to pay. Before the end of the war the notes of the confederacy alone were more than $1,000,000,000. Produce loans were resorted to, *i.e.* bonds were given in exchange for cotton, tobacco, and turpentine, which might be sent abroad on blockade runners, or which, stored against the day of victory, might serve as security for loans floated in Europe. Finally, a tithe of agricultural products was required for the support of the armies. The slaves, although not used as soldiers, furnished by their labor the food which supported the armies. When the confederacy collapsed the South contained enough food supplies to support the struggle for a much longer period.

Before the war the South had very few manufactures, and though strenuous efforts were now made to repair the deficiency, the lack of machinery and trained operatives presented insurmountable difficulties. Shoes, clothing, paper, hats, and a thousand other articles were very hard to obtain. The blockade **Manufactures.** kept out foreign supplies, and the small amount that got through on the swift blockade runners sold at exorbitant prices. Coffee and tea became almost unknown, and many substitutes were invented. For sugar, sorghum was used. Medicines were also obtained with difficulty, especially quinine, which was much needed on account of the prevalent malaria. Spite of such privations the spirits of the people were good; for there was always confidence that victory would soon come and that the rigorous blockade would be raised.

Railroads could not be repaired, and were not able to carry supplies from the rich fields of the Gulf states to the army in Virginia. Manufactured articles such as there were could not be distributed to the people on the farms. Machine shops, **Railroads.** which might have worked for the repair of railroads, ran to their full capacity on material of war. In despair the government offered aid to the railroads, but there were not in the South the necessary iron mills to produce the means of keeping up or extending railroad service. There were rich beds of iron ore in the South, but in the devotion of the people to agriculture they had been unworked, and it was impossible to develop them under pressure of war.

Before 1861 a favorite secession argument was "Cotton is King!" and it did much for the cause of secession. In substance it was that Europe and the manufacturing North were so dependent on Southern cotton that war was very improbable, and if it **The Part Played by Cotton.** did come, so much suffering would occur in England that she would interfere to end the struggle. It is true that the business interests of the North deprecated war, but they were swept away by the rising of patriotic fervor which followed the attack on Sumter, and from that time this part of the cotton kingdom paid no attention to the "King." In England there was much suffering, the small supply of cotton that went out through the blockade counting for nothing in the situation. But the people of England disliked slavery too much to take its part, and endured financial loss until slavery could be wiped out of its last important stronghold. Under these conditions, cotton, which early in 1861 brought 14 cents a pound in Liverpool, sold at the end of the war for 50 cents in the same place. Great quantities of it accumulated in the South, spite of the efforts of the confederate congress to induce the planters to raise food products only. In 1861 appeals were made to the planters by the government to burn their cotton lest it be sent abroad and relieve the scarcity, and 1,000,000 bales are said to have been thus destroyed. When New Orleans fell, the federal authorities offered to allow cotton from the interior to pass out, but very little appeared for that purpose. By the end of 1862 the confederate authorities changed their opinion and sought to send cotton out through the blockade in order to get supplies. But at this time the blockade was too rigid to allow a considerable exportation. Trade between the lines was ordinarily forbidden, but when west Tennessee was occupied a demoralizing trade sprang up which the strictest orders did not prevent. Cotton was given in exchange for salt, clothing, and even military supplies, and there were many complaints that officers of the posts shared the profits. General Butler, who commanded at New Orleans from May to December, 1862, and at Norfolk in 1864, was generally believed to have reaped handsome reward by conniving at a trade in which cotton exchanged for salt and other supplies at 15 cents a pound sold in the North for 60 cents.

One of the most exciting phases of the war in the South was blockade running. The low price of cotton within the confederacy, and the high price without, made it a practice as profitable as adventurous. A ship which could make two or three trips successfully netted a handsome return to her owners if she were captured afterwards. For the service, vessels of great speed were used. They were low, rakish-looking craft, painted as nearly the color of the water as possible, and were usually manned by foreigners, who, if captured, were not prisoners of war. Coming back, they managed to reach the bar of the home port at high tide on a dark night and tried to steal unobserved between the sentinel ships that guarded the entrance. If discovered, they tried to dart between the blockaders, and sometimes succeeded by reason of their speed. Blockade runners were usually required to carry a portion of their incoming cargoes for the account of the confederate government. Nassau and Havana were the favorite ports to which they ran, and Wilmington, North Carolina, and Charleston the best ports from which to escape. The former is protected by shoals stretching far out to sea, which made the work of the blockaders difficult. It remained open until Fort Fisher, which guarded the entrance, was taken, January 16, 1865.

Blockade Running.

BIBLIOGRAPHICAL NOTE

For civil affairs during the war, the same general works are suggested as for military affairs (see page 543). But the same cannot be said in regard to sources. In this respect one must rely on: *The Congressional Globe*, for debates in congress; *The Statutes at Large*, for laws passed; and the *Executive Documents* for reports of committees or of high officials. Especially important are the reports of the Joint Committee on the Conduct of the War, in 8 vols. The United States government has published the journals of the confederate congress, and Richardson, *Messages and Papers of the Confederacy*, 2 vols. (1905), contains some of the documents to which the title directs attention. *The Confederate Statutes at Large*, published contemporaneously at Richmond, contains all the confederate laws but those of the last days of the government. See also: Moore, *Rebellion Records*, 12 vols. (1861–1868), much information culled from newspapers, pamphlets, and public speeches; and

Appleton's Annual Cyclopedia. Of the newspapers of the times the following are important: The *Tribune, Herald, Times,* and *Evening Post,* of New York; the *Journal* and *Advertiser* of Boston; the *Times* and *Tribune,* of Chicago; the *Republican,* of Springfield, Mass.; the *Democrat,* of La Crosse, Wisconsin; the *Examiner, Whig,* and *Dispatch,* of Richmond; the *Mercury,* of Charleston; and the *Picayune,* of New Orleans.

The memoirs and lives of the prominent politicians of the period yield much important information. The most important are: Nicolay and Hay, *Abraham Lincoln, a History,* 10 vols. (1890), very important; Bancroft, *Life of William H. Seward,* 2 vols. (1900), a scholarly work; John Sherman, *Recollections of Forty Years* (1895); Adams, *Charles Francis Adams* (1900); Pierce, *Charles Sumner,* 4 vols. (1877–1893); Greeley, *Recollections of a Busy Life* (1868); Julian, *Recollections of War Times* (1884); Gorham, *Edwin M. Stanton,* 2 vols. (1899); McCall, *Thaddeus Stevens* (1899); Blaine, *Twenty Years in Congress,* 2 vols. (1884); Hart, *Salmon P. Chase* (1899); Coleman, *John J. Crittenden* (1871); McClure, *Lincoln and Men of War Times* (1892); McCulloch, *Men and Measures* (1900); Fessenden, *Life of W. P. Fessenden,* 2 vols. (1907); Mrs. Davis, *Jefferson Davis* (1890); Dodd, *Life of Jefferson Davis* (1907); Cleveland, *Alexander H. Stephens* (1866); Stovall, *Robert Toombs* (1892); Du Bose, *Life of William L. Yancey* (1892); Capers, *Life and Times of C. G. Memminger* (1893); and Woodburn, *Thaddeus Stevens* (1913).

On the meaning of the constitution as regards the issues brought up by the war see: Parker, *Constitutional Law with Reference to the Present Condition of the United States* (1862), refers especially to military arrests; Alexander Johnston, *American Political History, 1763–1876,* 2 vols. (1905), collected from Labor's *Cyclopedia* by Professor Woodburn; Dunning, *Essays on the Civil War and Reconstruction* (ed. 1904); Whiting, *War Powers of the Government* (1864); Von Holst, *Constitutional History of the United States,* 8 vols. trans. (1876–1892); Wilson, *Political Measures of the United States Congress* (1866); and Binney, *Privileges of a Writ of Habeas Corpus* (1865). On the southern side, see Davis, *Rise and Fall of the Confederate Government,* 2 vols. (1881); Stephens, *Constitutional View of the War between the States,* 2 vols. (1868–1870); and Curry, *Civil History of the Confederate Government* (1901).

On the support of the war see: Dewey, *Financial History of the United States* (1903); Knox, *American Notes* (1899); Stillé, *How a Free People Conduct a Long War* (1863); Stanwood, *American Tariff Controversies,* 2 vols. (1903); Sumner, *American Currency* (1874); Oberholtzer, *Jay Cooke,* 2 vols. (1907); Schwab, *Confederate States of America, Financial and Industrial* (1901); and Fleming, *Reconstruction in Alabama* (1905). On numbers and losses: Livermore, *Numbers and Losses of the Civil War* (1901); Fox, *Regimental Losses in the Civil War* (1889); and Wood, *The Confederate Handbook* (1900).

On diplomatic relations: Moore, *Digest of International Law,* 8 vols. (1906); Wharton, *Digest of International Law of the United States* (1886); Adams, *Charles Francis Adams* (1900); Bancroft, *William H. Seward,* 2 vols. (1900); Bigelow, *France and the Confederate Navy* (1888); Bulloch, *Secret Service of the Confederate States,* 2 vols. (1884); Callahan, *Diplomatic History of the Southern Confederacy* (1901); and Bonham, *British Consuls in the Confederacy* (Columbia *Studies,* 1911).

For Independent Reading

Tarbell, *Life of Lincoln,* 2 vols. (ed. 1900); McClure, *Lincoln and Men of War Times* (1892); Adams, *Charles Francis Adams* (1900); Hart, *Salmon P. Chase* (1899); Riddle, *Recollections of War Times* (1895); Dodd, *Life of Jefferson Davis* (1907); Russell, *My Diary North and South* (1862); and R. E. Lee, Jr., *Recollections and Letters of R. E. Lee* (1904).

INDEX

"A. B. C. Powers," 870.

Abercrombie, expedition against Canada, 126.

Abolition. *See* antislavery.

Academies, for educational use, 478.

Acadia, settled, 112.

Acadians, removal of, 124.

Adams, the, 328.

Adams, Charles Francis, nominated for vice-president, 452; minister to England, 522; and the Geneva arbitration, 673.

Adams, John, defends soldiers, 172; and the declaration of independence, 187; peace commissioner, 214; first minister to England, 226; opposed to Cincinnati, 229; vice-president, 256; reëlected vice-president, 271; Hamilton's opposition to, 273; elected president, 273; presidency of, 276–290; relation to his party, 276; desires to conciliate republicans, 276; and French quarrel, 278, 282; political views, 283; and Dr. Cooper, 284; reorganizes cabinet, 287; opposed by Hamilton, 273, 276, 282, 287, 288, 289; defeated, 288–290.

Adams, John Quincy, commissioner at Ghent, 334; opposed to Hartford Convention, 336; secretary of state, 367; share in the Monroe Doctrine, 375; candidate for presidency, 376, 377, 378, 379; elected, 379–380; bargain charged, 379, 389; parties forming under, 382–384; message, 382; war on, 383; Panama congress, 383; and the patronage, 389; his support in 1828, 390; supports Jackson in nullification, 409; on West India trade, 416; opposes annexation of Texas, 422; and antislavery petition, 431.

Adams, Samuel, colonial leader, 170; and "Boston Massacre," 172; and committees of correspondence, 174; opposed to Cincinnati, 229; on ratification, 248.

Adamson, W. C., and the control of trusts, 861.

Adjusted compensation, 913.

Africa, western coast explored, 25.

Agrarian bitterness, 934; revolt, 915.

Agriculture, in early Virginia, 50; in the early Carolinas, 83; in colonial period, 140; state of, 1800–1815, 345; progress after civil war, 665.

Agricultural bloc, 914, 915; depression, 931.

Aguinaldo, leads revolts against Spain, 809; Dewey aids, 809; captured, 810.

Airplanes, production of, 883, 884.

Aix-la-Chapelle, treaty of, 120.

Alabama, territory created, 345; population, 1820, 345; a state, 373; ratification of her constitution, 624; readmitted, 624; republicans overthrown, 632.

Alabama, the confederate ship, 523.

Alabama Claims, the, under A. Johnson, 670; Sumner's statement of, 671; arbitration of, 672–674.

Alabama-Mobile river system, 3.

Alaska, purchase of, 643; boundary controversy, 825; and Cunningham syndicate, 838; civil government in, 851.

Albany, Congress at, 1690, 116; 1754, 122.

Albemarle, settlements in, 82.

Aldrich, N. W., and tariff of 1883, 715; and Payne-Aldrich bill, 837; report on currency, 850.

Aldrich Commission, report of, 856, 859.

Algiers, at war, 295, 296.

Algonkins, the, 18; and the French, 113.

Alien Laws, passed, 283; Jefferson's way of meeting, 285.

Allen, Ethan, exploits of, 182.

Altgeld, Governor, pardons convicted anarchists, 743; and Pullman strike, 743.

Alverstone, Lord, 825.

Amadas, Philip, discovers Roanoke Island, 42.

Amador, Dr., 819.

Ambrister, Captain, executed by Jackson, 369.

Amelia Island, occupied, 331.

Amendments, suggested by the ratifying states, 248; method of making, 253; ten amendments, 258; eleventh and twelfth, 360; suggested by Hartford convention, 337; thirteenth, 580, 590; fourteenth, 607–609; rejected by South, 608, 619; accepted under congressional reconstruction, 610; war, interpreted, 635–638; for income tax, 838; for popular election of senators, 851; eighteenth, 904, 934; nineteenth, 905.

America, named, 33.

American Colonization Society, 428.

American Expeditionary Forces, crossing the Atlantic, 886–888; two phases of their campaign in France, 888; actual fighting in France, 888–895; placed at Foch's disposal, 889; corps organized, 891; St. Mihiel Campaign, 892; Meuse-Argonne, 893; in Italy, 895; in Russia, 895; in Siberia, 895.

American Federation of Labor assails strike injunction, 910.

American Tobacco Company, dissolution suit, 840, 842.

Ames, Oakes, 650.

Amherst, Jeffrey, at capture of Louisburg, 125; at capture of Montreal, 128.

Amnesty, proclamation of 1863, 596; Johnson's, 600; act of 1872, 634; act for general, 634.

Anarchists, Chicago, 742.

Anderson, Major, in Fort Sumter, 512, 515; surrenders, 516.

Andover Seminary, founded, 355.

André, John, concerned with Arnold, 202.

Andrew, Rev. J. O., and slavery issue, 471.

Andros, Edmund, governor of New England, 94; strong measures, 95; overthrown, 96; and slavery controversy, 902.

Anglican church, in New England, 148; in Virginia, 151; in Maryland and the Carolinas, 151; in other colonies, 152; the Bishop of London, 152; proposed American bishop, 164; as an establishment, 352; reorganized, 354.

Annapolis Convention, 241.

Antietam, battle of, 555.

Antifederalists oppose ratification, 247–249; on the first amendments, 258; disappearance of, 269.

Antimasonic party, organized, 403; opposed Clinton, 403.

Anti-Saloon League, 904.

Antislavery, early period of movement, 428–431.

Apaches, 685.

Appalachian Mountains, influence of, 1, 2.

Appointments to office, 292, 393.

Arabic, destruction of the, 877.

Arapahoes at war, 684, 686.

Arbitration treaties, rejected by Senate, 833.

Arbuthnot, hanged by Jackson, 369.

Archbald, Judge, 843.

Area of United States, 1.

Argentina, and "A. B. C." Commission, 870.

Argonne Forest, 893.

Argus, the, 328.

Aristocracy, suspected, 218, 228, 229, 230.

Arizona, mining in, 678; a territory, 679, 680; a state, 680, 851.

Arkansas, a state, 463; war in, 541; reconstructed under Lincoln, 597; readmitted, 624; republicans overthrown, 632.

"Armed Neutrality," league of, 206.

Armistice, with Germany, 899.

Armstrong, John, Secretary of War, 326, 330.

Army, a British, in the colonies, 164; pay in arrears, 223; plot of officers, 224; seize Philadelphia, 224; half-pay to officers, 229; Cincinnati, 229; in whisky insurrection, 268, 269; to serve against France, 279, 281; condition of in 1812, 320, 326; value of militia, 330; after war of 1812, 363; in civil war, 517, 572–574; organization in 1898, 795; and the captured Spaniards, 802; disease at Santiago, 803; wounded recover, 803; state of, 1914, 878; the Hay Bill, 878, 882; supplies for, 883; aviation, 883, 884; emergency officers, 883; rifles for, 883; and machine guns, 884; transported to France, 886–888; Pershing in command, 887; training in France, 887; size of a division, 888; in actual combat in France, 888–895; forces organized into corps and army, 891, 892.

Army, confederate, raising, 572, 590; bounties, 573, 590; negro troops, 573; numbers, 590.

Army, union, organizing, 572; "bounty jumping," 573; negro troops in, 573; numbers, 590.

Arnold, Benedict, in Canada, 184, 194; against St. Leger, 196; his treason, 201; in Virginia, 211; in Connecticut, 212.

"Aroostook War," the, 437.

Arthur, Chester A., nominated for vice-presidency, 702; removed from collectorship, 702, 708; becomes president, 705; and civil service reform, 709; and nomination in 1884, 716.

Articles of Confederation, committee to prepare, 187; adopted 1781, 217, 238; analysis of, 238–240; weakness of, 222; attempts to amend, 225, 240.

Asbury, Francis, 353.

Ashburton, Lord, in Washington, 438.

Assembly, the colonial development of, 100; in New York, 103.

"Assiento," 120.

"Association," the, 179.

Association of Nations, 906.

Asylum, the Right of, in Chile, 770.

Atchison, and the Kansas-Nebraska act, 486.

Atlanta, captured, 537.

Austria, surrender of, 898.

Autocracy in Germany overthrown, 899.

Bacon, Nathaniel, opposes Governor Berkeley, 90; his death, 91.

Bacon's Rebellion, 90.

Bad Axe, battle of, 466.

Baker, Colonel, at Ball's Bluff, 545.

Balboa, discovers the Pacific, 37.

Baldwin, decisive vote in Constitutional Convention, 245.

Ballinger-Pinchot controversy, 838.

Ballot Reform, 711–712.

Ball's Bluff, battle of, 545.

Balmeceda, 768, 769.

Baltimore, attacked by British, 330.

Baltimore, the, sailors of, attacked, 771; at Manila, 791.

Baltimore, Lord. See Calvert.

Baltimore and Ohio Railroad, early history, 464; development of, 733, 734.

Bank of North America, 228.

Bank of the United States, first, created, 260; and the currency, 348; McCulloch v. Maryland, 359; second, chartered, 363; service of, 364; Jackson's "war" on, 411–415; charter vetoed, 412; deposits removed, 413; protest charges, 418; lingering hope of recharter, 432; attempted recharter under Tyler, 435.

Banks, combinations of, 740.

Banks, Deposit, 423.

Banks, General, attacked by Jackson, 547; at Cedar Mountain, 551.

Banks, National, created, 575.

Banks, National System, insufficiency of, 858. See Federal Reserve Bank.

Baptists, in the Colonies, 148, 151; early history, 353; Primitive and Missionary, 353; divided by slavery, 456, 472.

Barbary States. See Tripoli.

Barlowe, Arthur, discovers Roanoke Island, 42.

Barnburners, 451; at convention of 1848, 452; secede, 452.

Barré, Col. Isaac, 166.

Barron, Captain, 314.

Baton Rouge, acquired, 331.

Baum, defeated at Bennington, 195.

Bayard, J. A., commissioner at Ghent, 334.

Bayard, T. F., secretary of state, 719; and Samoa, 765.

Bayonne Decree, 316.

Beaumarchais, 198.

Beauregard, General, at Bull Run, 519; against Butler, 564.

Behaim, Martin, 26.

Belknap, Secretary, and Indian frauds, 652.

Bell, John, nominated by whigs, 508; vote of, 509.

Belligerency, recognition of, 522.

Bellomont, Governor, and salary controversy, 101.

Bennington, battle of, 195.

Benton, Thomas H., and censure resolutions, 415; specie currency favored, 423.

Berkeley, Admiral, 314.

Berkeley, Sir William, governor of Virginia, 51; his policy in Virginia, 89; opposed by Bacon, 90; return to England, 91; and the Anglican Church, 151.

Berlin Decree, 308.

Bernard, Governor, of Massachusetts, 171.

Bernstorff, Ambassador, 877; receives passports, 881.

Biddle, Nicholas, asks for new charter, 411; Jackson and, 411; carries charter in congress, 412; continues to hope, 413; and the panic, 414.

Bienville, 115.

Bifurcated Invasion of the South, 526.

Big Black river, battle of, 531.

Big Four, the, 901.

Big Horn, Little, battle of, 688.

Bigot, hampers Montcalm, 127; punished, 127.

"Bird Woman," guides Lewis and Clark, 356.

Birney, J. G., in Ohio, 429; candidate for presidency, 1844, 443.

Black Code, revised, 430; ante bellum, 602; post bellum, 602; effects of, 602.

"Black Friday," 647.

Black Hawk, war of, 466.

Black Hills, gold found in, 679; Indians driven out, 687.

Bladensburg, battle of, 329.

Blaine, J. G., raises Southern issue, 653; secretary of state, 703, 723; nominated 1884, 716; the "Mulligan Letters," 717; and reciprocity, 725; and nomination of 1892, 749; and fur seal controversy, 767; and Mafia incident, 768; and Isthmian Canal, 818.

Blair, F. P., in "Kitchen Cabinet," 393; founds the Globe, 402.

Blair, F. P., Jr., in Missouri, 517; nominated for vice-presidency, 642.

Blair, Rev. James, commissary, 152; founder of William and Mary College, 154.

Blanco, General, command in Cuba, 787; and Cervera, 799.

Bland, R. P., champion of Silver, 699; candidate for nomination, 1896, 760.

Bland-Allison law, 699.

"Blanket Injunctions," 744.

Bliss, General Tasker H., delegate to Peace Conference, 900.

Block, Adrian, explorations of, 72.

Blockade, established, 517; keeping the, 569; running the, 592; in world war, 875.

"Blocks of five," 722.

Blount, J. H., in Hawaii, 773.

Blue, Victor, back of Santiago, 795.

Bœuf, Fort de, 122.

Bonds, in civil war, 574, 576.

Bon Homme Richard, 205.

Bonus Bill, for internal improvements, 365.

Boone, Daniel, 233.

Border States, saved for the union, 517.

Boscawen, failure on the St. Lawrence, 121.

Boston, settled, 64; population, 142; culture of, 155; troops sent to, 171; "Boston Massacre," 172; "Tea Party," 176; port closed, 176; blockaded, 177; siege of, 180–182; evacuated, 182.

Boundaries, 1783, 215.

Boutwell, G. S., secretary of the treasury, 644; financial policy, 662.

Bowdoin, Governor, and Shays's Rebellion, 236.

Boxer Revolt, 823.

Braddock, effect of his defeat, 106; expedition of, 123.

Bradford, William, elected governor, 61.

Bradley, J. P., his appointment as judge, 664.

Bragg, General, in Kentucky, 529; at Perryville, 529; at Stone's river, 530; at Chickamauga, 533; at Chattanooga, 535; removed from command, 535.

Brandywine, battle of, 19.

Brant, Joesph, 203.

Bray, Rev. Thomas, 152.

Brazil, coast discovered, 32; skirted by Cabral, 34; and "A. B. C." Commission, 870.

Breckenridge, J. C., nominated for presidency, 506; his vote, 509.

Brewster, William, at Scrooby, 59; goes to America, 60.

Briand's proposal, 930.

Brock, General, against Hull, **322.**

Broke, Captain, 327.

Brooklyn, battle of, 189.

Brooklyn, the, 800, 801.

Brown, B. Gratz, governor of Missouri, 64; nominated for vice-presidency, 648.

Brown, General Jacob, 324; at Chippewa, 325; at Lundy's Lane, 325.

Brown, John, retaliates on his opponents, 491; his raid, 502–504; his object, 502; his death, 503; significance of, 503.

Brown, Moses, and Cotton Mills, 349.

Brown University, founded, 154.

Brough, governor of Ohio, 583.

Brougham, Henry, 320.

Bryan, W. J., speech in Chicago convention, 759; nominated, 760; his campaign, 761; defeated, 762; not crushed, 762; candidate in 1900, 827; and the convention of 1904, 832; nominated in 1908, 835; influence in democratic nomination, 845, 846–847; secretary of state, 854.

Bryant, William Cullen, and the Barnburners, 451; an independent, 694; civil service reformer, 707.

Buchanan, James, and nomination of 1852, 485; nominated in 1856, 495; elected, 496; attitude in crisis, 512.

Buckner, General, at Fort Donelson, 527.

Budget Bureau, 911.

Buell, General, coöperates with Grant, 528; against Bragg, 529; removed from command, 530.

Buena Vista, battle of, 447.

Buffalo, city of, 341.

Buford, Colonel, at Waxhaw, 207.

Buford's cavalry, at Gettysburg, 560.

Bulgaria, forced to yield, 898.

Bull, papal, dividing the new world, 29.

"Bull Moose" party 845; organized, 847.

Bull Run, campaign of, 518–520; second battle of, 550–553; Lee's plan of attack, 551; its execution, 551–553.

Bunau-Varilla, 818.

Bunker Hill, battle of, 181.

Burchard, Rev. S. D., incautious utterance, 719.

Bureau of Prohibition created, 935.

Burgoyne, General, expedition against New York, 193–198; and Carleton, 195.

Burke Act, concerning Indians, 690.

Burleson, Albert S., postmaster-general, 854.

Burlingame, Treaty, the, 774.

Burnside, General, in East Tennessee, 533; in command in Virginia, 555; the Fredericksburg campaign, 555–557; in North Carolina, 570; military arrests, 583.

Burr, Aaron, elected vice-president, 288, 289, 290; plots with Pickering, 300; kills Hamilton, 301; scheme of, 303–306; trial of, 305.

Burr, G. L., and Venezuelan boundary, 780.

Bute, Lord, colonial policy of, 161.

Butler, B. F., on the James, 564; "Contrabands," 577; charged with cotton sales,
592; prosecutes Johnson, 615; succeeds
Stevens, 633; relations with Grant, 633,
645; and the Sanborn contracts, 651;
Greenback candidate, 698; and civil service reform, 708.
Butler, Colonel John, 203.
Byrd, Col. William, culture of, 155.

Cabinet, constitutional basis of, 252; Wilson's, 854.
Cabot, George, at Hartford convention, 337.
Cabot, John, explorations of, 35.
Cabot, Sebastian, fame of, 35.
Cabral, voyage to Brazil, 34.
Calaveras skull, the, 11.
Calhoun, J. C., elected to congress, 318;
and the second bank, 364; on the tariff,
364; on internal improvements, 365;
secretary of war, 367, 369; candidate for
presidency, 377, 378; elected vice-president, 377; position in Jackson's party, 382;
opposition of Van Buren, 382; supports
nullification, 387; reëlected vice-president,
390; influence in the cabinet, 392; affected Eaton affair, 394; struck through
internal improvements, 394; report on
public improvements, 395; and state
rights, 396; and Jackson's "union" toast,
399; breach with Jackson, 401–402; three
papers on nullification, 407; becomes
Southern champion, 422; secretary of state,
439; Texas annexation, 439, 444; and Van
Buren's letter, 442; on slavery in Oregon,
453; compromise speech, 1850, 455;
death of, 488.
California, purchase desired by Polk, 446;
occupied by American forces, 448; not
made a territory, 452, 453; admitted to
Union, 455, 457; gold discovered, 480;
settlement of, 481; government of, 481;
and Chinese, 774; and Japanese, 776.
Calvert, Cecilius, his policy, 53, 57; checks
the Jesuits, 55; his proprietary rights, 57.
Calvert, George, Maryland granted to, 52.
Calvert, Leonard, governor of Maryland,
53, 54–56.
Cambrai, German drive at, 888.
Cambridge Agreement, 63.
Camden, battle of, 207; burned, 211.
Campos, in Cuba, 784, 786.
Canada, ceded to England, 129; the cession
criticized, 130, 161, 170; and Quebec Act,
177; invaded by Americans, 183, 194;
capture expected, 321; struggle for, 321–
326; line of defense, 321; reciprocity
with, 841, 842. See New France.

Canals, where located, 3; the Erie, 4; use
of, 464. See Internal improvements.
Canning, George, and the Orders in Council,
308; his irritating attitude, 313; on
Chesapeake-Leopard affair, 315; and the
Monroe Doctrine, 375.
Cannon, Speaker, power reduced, 838.
Cantigny, battle of, 889.
Caperton, Admiral W. B., 896.
Capital, the national, located on the Po-
tomac, 260.
Capital, financial, growth after civil war, 665.
Capper-Volstead Act, 914.
Caribbean Policy, 863–867.
Carleton, General, and the Indians, 685.
Carleton, Sir Guy, against Arnold, 184, 194,
195; retained in Canada, 195.
Carlisle, J. G., secretary of the treasury,
753; maintaining parity, 754; bonds for
gold, 754.
Carolina, created, 81, 82; early history, 82–
83; fundamental constitutions, 82; two
divisions, 82; misrule of proprietors, 106;
sale to crown, 107.
Caroline, Fort, 111.
Carpet-baggers, 621.
Carranza, Venustiano, opposes Huerta, 868;
becomes president of Mexico, 870.
Carrizal, fight at, 871.
Carthage, battle of, 541.
Cartier, Jacques, explorations of, 36, 112.
Carver, John, governor of Plymouth, 61.
Cass, Lewis, nominated for presidency,
452; defeated, 452; in 1852, 485; leaves
cabinet, 512.
Catherine of Aragon, and Columbus, 28, 31.
Caucus, nominating, origin, 288; destroyed,
378.
Cedar Creek, battle of, 565.
Cedar Mountain, battle of, 551.
Central American peace league, 866.
Cerro Gordo, battle of, 449.
Cervera, departs from Cape Verde Islands,
790; reaches Santiago, 793; search for,
793; in Santiago, 799; destruction of his
fleet, 800–801.
Chamberlain, D. H., in South Carolina
politics, 655, 657, 694.
Chambersburg, burned by Early, 565.
Champion Hill, battle of, 531.
Champlain, founds Quebec, 112; attacks the
Iroquois, 112.
Champlain, Lake, battle of, 325.
Chancellorsville, battle of, 557–559.
Channing, Rev. William E., founds Ameri-
can Unitarianism, 355.
Chantilly, battle of, 553.
Chapultepec, taken, 450.

"Charlefort," 111.

Charles I, and the colonies, 77.

Charles II, and the colonies, 80.

Charleston, settled, 83; and tea duty, 175; attacked by the British, 183; taken by the British, 207; British driven into, 211; evacuated, 214; democratic convention at, 505; evacuated by Hardee, 540; naval operations against, 570.

Chase, Samuel, at trial of Dr. Cooper, 284; impeachment of, 294.

Chase, S. P., and opponents of Lincoln, 582, 584; presides over impeachment, 615–617; and democratic nomination, 642; and legal tender cases, 664.

Château-Thierry, fighting around, 889, 890, 891.

Chattahoochee, Sherman crosses, 537.

Chattanooga, campaign for, 532–535; battle of, 535.

Cherokees, 18; relations with the English, 121; war against the Americans, 130; at war, 1776, 203; and Spain, 265; punished by Tennesseeans, 265; removal of, 400, 466; in the West, 466.

Cherry Valley, raided, 203.

Chesapeake, the, defeated by the *Shannon*, 327.

Chesapeake Bay, campaign in, 329–330.

Chesapeake-Leopard, incident, 314; settled by the *President*, 318.

Cheves, Langdon, elected to Congress, 318.

Chew house, the, 194.

Cheyennes, war with southern, 684, 686; war with northern, 685, 687, 688.

Chicago, desires transcontinental railroad, 681; a railroad center, 733, 734; strike of 1886, 742.

Chickamauga, battle of, 533; Park, 795.

Chickasaws, removal of, 400, 466.

Chile, revolution against Balmeceda, 768; Eagan's sympathy, 769; the *Itata*, 769; right of asylum, 770; the *Baltimore*, sailors of, attacked, 770; and "A. B. C." Commission, 870.

China, American relations with, 822; Boxer revolt, 823; legations surrounded, 823; army of relief, 823; "open door" in, 920, 921.

Chinese Immigration, 774.

Chippewa, battle of, 325.

Chivington's Massacre, 684.

Choctaws, removal of, 400, 466.

Choiseul, criticism of England's policy, 130.

Churubusco, 449.

Cibola, 39.

Cienfuegos, Schley at, 793, 794.

Cincinnati, society of, 229; city founded, 342.

Citizenship, National, defined by the courts, 635–638.

Civil Rights Bill, of 1866, 606; of 1875, 634; interpreted by courts, 637.

Civil Service Reform, Grant and, 646; origin of reform, 707; Summer and, 707; Jenckes and, 707; first commission, 708; Pendleton act, 709; execution of, 709–711; under Cleveland, 709, 720.

Claiborne, William, claims Kent Island, 55.

Clark, Champ, candidate for nomination, 845.

Clark, George Rogers, 203.

Clark, William, explorations of, 356.

Clay, Henry, elected to Congress, 318; commissioner at Ghent, 334; on tariff, 364; on internal improvements, 365; heads opposition, 367; on South America, 367; attacks Jackson, 370; on the Missouri compromise, 374; candidate for presidency, 1824, 377, 378, 379; makes Adams president, 379; bargain charged, 382; united with Adams, 382; and Panama congress, 383; and the tariff, 385; nominated, 1832, 404; defeated, 405; his compromise tariff, 410; for the bank, 412, 414, 415; censure of Jackson, 414; on surplus, 424; loses nomination, 434; opposed to Tyler, 435; on Texan annexation, 442; and compromise of 1850, 454–457; death of, 488.

Clayton, H. D., and the control of trusts, 861.

Clayton Anti-Trust Act, 862.

Clayton-Bulwer Treaty, made, 458; and a canal, 815; annulled, 817.

Cleveland, Grover, and the civil service, 709, 711, 720; governor of New York, 716; nominated for presidency, 716; elected, 719; as president, 719; cabinet, 719; and opponents, 720; and tariff reform, 721; renominated, 722; on pensions, 726; reëlected, 728; on Wilson-Gorman bill, 729; on silver, 1892, 750; opposition of West and South, 751; nominated, 1892, 751; elected, 752; second cabinet, 753; and the Sherman silver law, 755; protecting the reserve, 755–757; repudiated by his party, 758; Hawaiian policy, 773; and Venezuelan dispute, 778–781; and Cuba, 785, 786.

"Cliff Dwellers," the, 12.

Climate, variations of, 1.

Clinton, De Witt, and election of 1812, 319; and Erie canal, 366.

Clinton, General, demonstration against

Albany, 197; relieves Howe, 200; in the South, 207; aids Cornwallis, 212.

Clinton, George, on ratification, 249; a republican, 270; and vice-presidency, 271; in the election of 1800, 288; Jefferson favors, 300, 301; elected vice-president, 302; death of, 319.

Coal, deposits of, 8–10; anthracite, 9; distribution, 9.

Coal lands, conservation of, 850.

Coal strike, anthracite, 830; of 1922, 916.

Cobb, Howell, 499.

Cochrane, Admiral, 330.

Cod fisheries, 5.

Colbert and New France, 115.

Cold Harbor, battle of, 563.

Colfax, Schuyler, vice-president, 642; and the Credit Mobilier, 650.

Coligny, plants colony in Florida, 111.

Colleges, progress of, 478–479; relation to churches, 478, 479.

Colombia, and an isthmian canal, 814; treaty with, 814; Hay-Herran convention, 818; and Panama revolution, 819.

Colon, the, 800, 801.

Colonial government, struggle for assembly, in New York, 103; colonial treasurer, 104; the New England town, 134, 156; the Southern County, 135, 155; local, 155–158; mixed form of, 156.

Colonial policy, 813–814.

Colonial system, characteristics of, 99–101.

Colonies, British supervision, depends on king, 76; Land's commission, 77; Warwick's commission, 77; Lords of trade, 77; effects of Puritan Revolution, 77; Navigation Laws, 78.

Colorado, explorations of, 39.

Colorado, settled, 677; state and territory, 678, 680.

Columbia, S. C., burned, 540.

Columbia University, founded, 154.

Columbus, Christopher, early life, 27; and Toscanelli, 27; seeking aid, 28; sets sail, 28; land discovered, 29; discoveries, 29, 30, 31; honored in Spain, 29, 31; death of, 31.

Columbus, N. M., raided by Villa, 870.

Comanches, 685.

Combinations, industrial, 731–744; principles of, 731; early, 731; advantages claimed for, 732; in railroads, 732–735; in manufactures, 736–740; in banking, 740–741; in labor, 740–744.

Commerce. *See* trade.

Commerce Court, 839, 843.

Committees of Congress, 258.

Committees of correspondence appointed, 174.

"Common Sense," Paine's, 186.

Compact theory, in 1798, 285.

Compensation, adjusted, 913.

Competition, conditions of, 731.

Compromise of 1850, desire for harmony, 454; Clay's proposals, 455; debated, 455–457; adopted, 457; finality of, 485.

Concord, battle of, 180.

Confederacy, the, arming for war, 517; problems, 586; constitution, 587; its president, 587; peace movement in, 588; foreign affairs, 588; and France, 589; navy of, 589; finances of, 590; manufactures in, 591; railroads in, 591; cotton, 591.

"Confederate States of America," organized, 511.

Confiscation acts, first, 576; second, 576, 578.

Congregationalists, 354.

Congress, flees from Philadelphia, 225; composition of, 250.

Congress, the, 328.

Congress, authority of, 359; approves Lincoln, 519; supports war, 519; majorities in 1913, 853; committees, 853. *See* Continental Congress.

Conkling, Roscoe, and renomination of Grant, 652, 702; quarrel with Blaine, 694, 703; and Garfield, 703; resigns senatorship, 704; on civil service reform, 708.

Connecticut, river towns founded, 69; Lord Saye and Sele, 69; Saybrook settled, 69; New Haven settled, 69; New Haven and Connecticut merged, 69; government of New Haven, 69; Pequot War, 70; and New England Confederation, 71; New charter, 80; and the Dominion of New England, 94; resists stamp act, 168; ratifies the constitution, 247; population, 341; constitutional revision in, 473.

Conservation, 849.

Consolidation, national, checked by courts, 636.

Constellation, the, 279, 328; defeats *l'Insurgente*, 281.

Constitution, federal, prepared, 242–247; adopted, 247–250; analysis of, 250–254; interpretation of, 285–287; interpreted by Marshall, 357; and dependencies, 813.

Constitution, the, constructed, 279; takes the *Guerrière*, 327; takes the *Java*, 327.

Constitutions, state, reform of, 472–476.

Continental Congress, called, 178; two sides in, 178; significance of, 179; second congress, 181; authority of, 217; inefficiency, 217; end of, 256.

Continuous voyage, right of, in world war, 875.

"Contrabands," 577; in world war, 875.

Contreras, taken by Scott, 449.

Contributions, political, from corporations, 834; law on, 839, 851.

Convention, constitutional, advantage of, 241; suggested, 241; elected, 242; meets, 242; proceedings, 242–247.

Convention, nominating, origin of, 404.

Convoy service, 897.

Cooley, T. M., on execution of the interstate commerce act, 735.

Coolidge, Calvin, nominated for vice-presidency, 903, 905; elected, 1904; attitude towards League of Nations, 919; succeeds Harding, 922; reëlected, 925; continues old policies, 926; the Debt Settlements under, 927; vetoes McNary-Haugen Bill, 933; declines renomination, 936.

Cooper, Peter, nominated by Greenback party, 697.

Cooper, Dr. Thomas, trial of, 284.

Copperheads, 582.

Corinth, Johnston at, 528; taken by Halleck, 529.

Corn, Indian, significance of, 8; a staple, 8.

Cornbury, Lord, governor of New York, 103.

Cornwallis, Lord, in New Jersey, 191; in command in the South, 207; at Camden, 207; at Charlotte, 208; pursues Greene, 209; in North Carolina, 209; at battle of Guilford Courthouse, 210; in Wilmington, 210; enters Virginia, 211; surrenders, 313.

Corporation tax, 838.

Corte-Real, Gaspar, 34.

Cortez, Hernando, in Mexico, 37.

Cosa, Juan de la, 38.

Costa Rica and Central American peace league, 866.

Cotton, a staple crop, 8; gin invented, 345; and slavery, 346; area of, 346; production and price, 346.

Cotton, Rev. John, against Roger Williams, 66; against Mrs. Hutchinson, 67; against Quakers, 67.

Council of National Defense, work of, 885.

Council of Ten, 901.

County, the, planted, 135; government, 155; in New York, 156.

Courts, federal, the system, 252; established, 257; jurisdiction defined, 357–360.

Covenant of the League of Nations, 901–903.

"Covington Bill," 861.

Cowpens, battle of, 208.

Cox, J. D., secretary of interior, 644; resignation of, 645.

Cox, James M., nominated for presidency, 903.

"Crater, the," at Petersburg, 564.

Crawford, W. H., and the presidency, 1816, 367; in the cabinet, 367; candidate in 1824, 377, 378, 379, 380; support goes to Jackson, 382.

Crazy Horse, in Sioux War, 687, 688.

Credit Banks, intermediate, 915.

Credit Mobilier, the, 649.

Creeks, the, 18; and the English, 121; relations with the United States, 265; Creeks subdued by Jackson, 332; at treaty of Fort Jackson, 332; relation with Seminoles, 368; removal of, 400, 407, 466.

"Crime against Kansas, The," Sumner's speech, 490.

"Crisis, The," Turnbull's, 387.

Crittenden, Senator, efforts to avoid war, 513.

Crittenden Compromise, 512.

Cromwell, Oliver, and the colonies, 77, 80.

Crook, General, against the Sioux, 687–689; and Dull Knife's band, 689.

Crops, staple, 8.

Crown Point, taken by the British, 127; taken by Ethan Allen, 182.

Crozat, has monopoly in Louisiana, 115.

Cuba, discovered, 29; settled, 31; two parties in, 782; ten years' war, 782; reforms promised, 784–785; revolt of 1895, 785; methods of the Cubans, 785; American intervention, 786–790; reforms offered by Sagasta, 787; and Spanish war debt, 805; condition since the war, 806–807; Platt amendment, 807; reoccupation, 807; our relations with, 864.

Culpeper, Pope at, 550.

Culpeper, Lord, governor of Virginia, 92.

Cumberland road bill, vetoed by Monroe, 395.

Currency, early, 348; in the civil war, 575; "elasticity" of, 857. See Finance.

Curtis, B. R., opinion in Dred Scott case, 498; defends Johnson, 615.

Curtis, G. W., and civil service reform, 646, 707, 708; as an independent, 693, 718.

Custer, General, and the Indians, 686; death of, 688.

Cutler, Manasseh, and Ohio Company, 232.

Daiquiri, landing at, 796.

Dakota, early history, 679; a territory, 679; a state, 680, 748; gold in, 679, 687; Sioux at war, 685, 687–689.

Dale, Captain, in Tripolitan war, 295.

Dale, Sir Thomas, in Virginia, 49.

Dallas, George M., vice-president, 441.

Daniels, Josephus, secretary of the navy, 854.

Danish West Indies. *See* Virgin Islands.

Dartiguenave, President, of Haiti, 865.

Dartmouth College, founded, 154.

Dartmouth College *v.* Woodward, 359.

Daugherty, Attorney-General, misconduct of, 924; dismissed, 925.

Davenport, Rev. John, 69.

Davie, William R., partisan leader, 207.

Davis, J. C. Bancroft, 673.

Davis, Jefferson, at Buena Vista, 448; secretary of war, 486; Southern leader, 488; resolutions in the senate, 505; president of the confederacy, 511; friendship for Bragg, 535; leaves Richmond, 567; proposes to continue resistance, 568; as confederate president, 587; imprisoned, 641; death, 641.

Dawes, Charles G., director of budget, 908.

Dawes Act, concerning Indians, 690.

Dawes plan, 927.

Deane, Silas, in Paris, 198.

Dearborn, in Jefferson's Cabinet, 292; in war of 1812, 323.

Debt, Revolutionary. *See* Finances.

Debt Settlement, under Coolidge, 927.

Debts, British, in treaty of 1783, 216; not paid, 227, 261.

Decatur, 327; burns the *Philadelphia*, 296; in the Mediterranean, 296.

Declaration of London of 1909 in world war, 874.

Declaratory Act, 168.

Deerfield, attacked, 118.

Defense, national, state of, 878; Council of National, 885.

Delaware, settled by Sweden, 75; conquered by Stuyvesant, 75; acquired by Penn, 86; boundary controversy, 87, 88; government, 87; relation to Pennsylvania, 104; ratifies constitution, 247.

De Lesseps, Ferdinand, in the United States, 816.

De Lima *v.* Bidwell, 814.

De Lome, letter published, 787.

Democracy, development of, 1815–1861, 472–476; thought to be at stake in world war, 878.

Democratic party, in the civil war, 581; in elections of 1862, 582; copperheads, 582, 583; in the South after the war, 621; condition of, after the war, 640; in 1868, 642; in 1872, 648; in 1876, 652–657; gain house of representatives, 651; investigating election of 1876, 695; efforts to repeal election laws, 696, 697; in elections of 1878, 697; its progress before 1884, 719;

split in, 653, 702, 716, 720; Western and Southern wings, in 1892, 751; convention of 1896, 758–760; carries house in 1910, 840.

De Monts, plants colony, 112.

Denby, Secretary, resignation of, 925.

Denmark, sells Virgin Islands, 866.

Departments of state created, 257; of the navy, created, 281.

Dependencies, government of, 813, 814.

Depew, C. M., 834.

Dernburg, Bernhard, 783.

Destroyers, the United States, at Queenstown, 896.

Detroit, held against Pontiac, 131; in the revolution, 204; position of, 321; Hull at, 322; recovered, 323.

Deux-Ponts, Colonel, 213.

Dewey, George, ordered to Manila, 791; Battle of Manila Bay, 791; a rear admiral, 791; on Schley-Sampson controversy, 804.

Dexter, and Hartford Convention, 336.

Diaz, Bartholomew, 26.

Diaz, Porfirio, his treatment of foreigners in Mexico, 867; overthrow of, 868.

d'Iberville, settle Louisiana, 115.

Dickinson, John, "Farmer's Letters," 170; and the articles of confederation, 238.

Diedrich, Admiral von, at Manila, 792.

Dingley Tariff Act, 729.

Diplomacy, a new school of, 762.

Diplomatic History of the United States, beginning of, 119; treaty of Paris, 129.

Discourse on Western Planting, 44.

Discovery of America, by the Norse, 23; by Zeno brothers, 23; bearing of oriental trade on, 24; relation to spread of knowledge, 25, 26.

District of Columbia, located, 260; slave-trade abolished, 455, 457.

Division, size of a, 888; naming the, 888.

Doheny, E. L., and the Oil Scandals, 923.

Donelson, Fort, captured, 527.

Dongan, Governor, and the Iroquois, 114.

Dorchester, speech to Indians, 263.

Dorr, Thomas W., struggle for constitutional reform, 474; takes up arms, 475.

Douglas, Stephen A., at nominating convention of 1852, 485; and the Kansas-Nebraska Act, 487; opposes Lecompton Constitution, 492, 493; in debate with Lincoln, 499–503; destroyed by Lincoln, 501; Freeport doctrine, 501; opposition of South to, 505; at Charleston convention, 505; nominated for presidency, 506; supports the war, 516.

Dow, Neal, 480.

Downes v. Bidwell, 814.
Draft, in use, 572; riots, 572.
Drainage systems, 2.
Drake, Sir Francis, 41; at Roanoke Island, 42.
Dred Scott Decision, 497–499; its futility, 499; in Charleston convention, 505.
Drift man, 12.
Drummond, William, execution of, 91.
Drury's Bluff, battle of, 564.
Duane, W. J., secretary of the treasury, 413.
Dudley, and vote purchasing, 722.
Dudley, Joseph, governor of Massachusetts, 95, 102; sentences Leisler, 103.
"Duke's Laws," the, in New York, 83, 157.
Dull Knife's Band, fate of, 689.
"Dunmore's War," 203.
Duquesne, Fort, taken by Forbes, 125; called Fort Pitt, 126.
Dutch, stock in middle colonies, 145.
Duxbury, 62.
Dwight, Theodore, in Hartford convention, 337.
Dyer, Mrs., execution of, 68.

Eagan, in Chile, 769, 771.
Early, General, in Pennsylvania, 559; at Gettysburg, 559; his raid toward Washington, 565; at Cedar Creek, 565.
East India Company, and tea, 175.
Eastward Ho, 44.
Eaton, Dorman B., and civil service reform, 708, 709.
Eaton, John H., in Jackson's cabinet, 392; affairs of his wife, 394; resigns from the cabinet, 402.
Eaton, Mrs. Jackson and, 394, 401.
Eaton, Theophilus, 69.
Eaton, William, 295.
Edmunds, Senator, reform candidate in 1880, 702; and in 1884, 716, 718.
Education, in the colonies, 153–155; colleges, 153–154; the churches and, 154; the college curriculum, 155; middle schools, 155; colonial culture, 155; progress of, until 1861, 476–480; public school system, developed, 476–478; the academy, 478; colleges, 478–480.
Edwards, Rev. Jonathan, 150, 354.
Eighty-Ninth Division, at St. Mihiel, 892.
Eighty-Second Division, at St. Mihiel, 892.
El Caney, attacked, 797, 798.
Elections, when held and how, 251.
Elections, presidential, 1789, 256; 1792, 271; 1796, 273; 1800, 288–290; 1804, 302; 1808, 311; 1812, 319; 1816, 366; 1820, 368; 1824, 379–380; 1828, 390; 1832,

403–405; 1836, 425; 1840, 433–435; 1844, 441–443; 1848, 451–452; 1852, 485; 1856, 496; 1860, 506–509; 1864, 584; 1868, 641–643; 1872, 649; 1876, 652–657; 1880, 702; 1884, 719; 1888, 723; 1892, 752; 1896, 762; 1900, 827; 1904, 832; 1908, 836; 1912, 848; 1916, 879; 1920, 903; 1924, 925; 1928, 939.
Electoral Commission of 1877, 656.
Ellsworth, Oliver, in constitutional convention, 245.
Elkton, 194.
Emancipation, during civil war, 577–581; "contrabands," 577; with compensation, 578, 580; in confiscation acts, 578; proclamation of, 579, 580; thirteenth amendment, 580.
Embargo Act, passed, 310; enforcement of, 310; repealed, 311; effects of, 311.
Emergency Fleet Corporation, 885.
Employees, non-agricultural, 741.
Endicott, John, settles Salem, 63.
Enforcement bill, of 1870, 633; of 1871, 634; of 1874, 634.
Enfranchisement of women, 904, 905.
England, explorations of, 35; refuses commercial treaty, 262; at war with France, 266; neutrality proclamation, 266; influence in American politics, 271, 276; attitude toward neutral trade, 272, 279; restricts American trade, 306–309; impressment, 306; relenting, 319; war plan, 321; and New England discontent, 335; and the fisheries, 347; execution of Arbuthnot and Ambrister, 369; relations with, during the civil war, 521–524; favors the South, 521; grants confederate belligerency, 522; and the Trent affair, 522; confederate cruisers, 523; and Alabama claims, 670, 674; in Samoa, 765; our Samoan relations with, 765–766; and fur seal controversy, 767; and the American war with Spain, 790; and Hay-Pauncefote treaty, 817; rule of, on blockades and contraband in world war, 874; and blockade, 875; and continuous voyage, 875; and submarine warfare, 875; loans to, by the United States, 886; sustains German drives in 1918, 888.
English bill, the, 493.
English stock, distributed, 145.
Enterprise, the, 295, 328.
Eric the Red, 23.
Erie, Fort, 321.
Erie, Lake, battle of, 323, 324.
Erie Railroad, development of, 733.
Erskine, treaty of, 316.
Esch-Cummins Act, 909, 910.

Established Church. *See* Anglican Church.

Estaing, Count d', at Newport, 200; at Savannah, 207.

Essex, the, 295, 328; the case of, 307.

Essex county, 336.

"Essex Junto," 288.

European War. *See* World War.

Eustis, secretary of war, 326.

Eutaw Springs, battle of, 211.

Evans, R. D., at Santiago, 800, 801, 802.

Evarts, William M., defends Johnson, 615, 616, secretary of state, 694; refuses to attend White House dinners, 703.

Everett, Edward, on the patronage, 389.

Ewell, General, in Pennsylvania, 558, 559, 560, 561.

Explorations, on the coast, 31–38.

Explorations of the interior, 37–39.

Ezra Church, battle of, 537.

Fairbanks, C. W., elected vice-president, 832.

Fairfield, Governor, 437.

Falaba, the, sunk by Germany, 876, 877.

Fall, Secretary, and the Oil leases, 923, 924.

Fallen Timber, battle of the, 263.

Falmouth burned, 186.

Farragut, Admiral, at New Orleans, 529; takes Mobile Bay, 571.

Far West, exploration of, 355–357.

Farm-Bloc defeated, 933.

Farm Bureau federation, 915.

Farm depression, 914.

Farm relief issue, 931; measures, 914, 938.

Fava, Baron, withdrawn, 768.

"Federalist," the, authorship of, 247.

Federalists, favor ratification, 247–249; after ratification, 269; strong policy of, 283–285; overthrow of, 287–290; divided, 287; defeated, 288; against war of 1812, 320; and the war of 1812, 335–337.

Federal Budget system, 911.

Federal Reserve Bank, 858–860; the Aldrich report, 859; the Glass Bill, 859; act for, passed, 860; its provisions, 860.

Federal Trade Commission, created by congress, 861.

Ferguson, Major, in North Carolina, 208; at King's Mountain, 208.

Fifth Division, at St. Mihiel, 892.

Filipinos, army in the field, 809; revolt of, 810; revolt subdued, 810; native political party, 812.

Filled Milk Act, 915.

Filmore, Millard, vice-president, 451, 452; president, 458.

Finances, revolutionary debt, 222; continental money, 223; attempts to confer taxing power on congress, 225; first revenue bill of federal congress, 257; reorganization under Hamilton, 259–261; refunding the revolutionary debt, 259; assumption of state debts, 259; Bank established, 260; excise tax, 261; policy of Gallatin, 293; and war of 1812, 319, 320, 321, 336, 348; currency, 1783–1815, 348; in the war of 1812, 348; national debt paid, 422; deposit banks, 423; specie currency favored, 423; surplus revenue, 424; specie circular, 425; subtreasury, 433; in civil war, 519, 574–576; bonds issued, 574, 576; legal tender act, 574; national banks, 575; currency issued, 575; confiscation acts, 576; confederate, 590; Pendelton's ideas, 642; at the end of the civil war, 660; refunding, 661; war taxes reduced, 661, 663; legal tender reduced, 661; resumption of specie payment, 668; inflation demanded in the West, 697; Greenback party, 697; free coinage, 698; Bland-Allison law, 699; resumption achieved, 699–700; tariff reform, 712–715; war taxes, 713; the surplus, 714, 724; McKinley Act, 724–726, 727; Bland law in operation, 746; Silver notes, 746; shrinkage of bank notes, 746; sentiment for silver, 747; Sherman silver law, 747; Windom secretary of treasury, 747; attack on the reserve, 753, 755; repeal of Sherman silver law, 754–755; reserve diminished, 755; "endless chain," the, 755–757; Morgan-Belmont agreement, 756; confidence restored, 757; a corporation tax, 838; currency reform, 850; Aldrich-Vreeland act, 850; Aldrich currency report, 850; Federal Reserve Bank, 858 860.

First Quota Act, 918.

Fiscal readjustment, 911.

First Division, arrival in France, 886; goes into line of defenses, 888; battle of Cantigny, 889; in the operations of July 18, 1918, 891; at St. Mihiel, 892; before Sedan, 894.

"Fiscal Corporation," 435.

Fish, Hamilton, secretary of state, 644; and Santo Domingo annexation, 671; the treaty of Washington, 672; the *Alabama* arbitration, 673; and the *Virginius*, 783.

Fisheries, 4–6; colonial, 141; whaling, 142; and treaty of 1783, 215; condition of, 1783–1815, 347.

Fisher's Hill, battle of, 565.

Fisk, James, scheme to corner gold, 646.

"Five Brothers," the, 861.

Fletcher, Governor, in New York, 103.

Fletcher v. Peck, 302, 358.

Florida, the French in, 111; attacked by South Carolina, 119; West, claimed by Jefferson, 300; Jefferson's plan to acquire, 302; conquest expected in 1812, 321, 331; plans to seize, 332; negotiation to purchase, 368–370; acquired, 370; a state, 463; Seminoles under Osceola, 467; readmitted, 624; republicans overthrown, 632; disputed returns in 1876, 655, 657; surrendered to democrats, 657.

Florida, the confederate ship, 523.

Floyd, General, at Fort Donelson, 527.

Foch, Marshal, in supreme command, 889.

Food products, 7.

Food, government control of, 885.

Foote's Resolutions, 396.

Foraker Act, 814.

Forbes, General, expedition against Fort Duquesene, 125.

"Force Bill," 410.

Fordney bonus bill, 913.

Fordney-McCumbert Act, 912, 918; tariff, 912.

Forest, General, and negro prisoners, 574.

Forests, 6.

Forts, Southern, status of, 512; negotiations attempted, 515; Sumter attacked, 516.

Forts, Western, not surrendered, 262; in the Jay treaty, 272.

Four-Power treaty, 921.

Forty-Second Division, goes into line of defenses, 888; in Marne salient, 891; at St. Mihiel, 892; before Sedan, 893.

Foster, British minister, 335.

"Fourteen-Diamond Ring" Case, the, 814.

"Fourteen Points," President Wilson's, 898; accepted by Germany and the *Entente* allies, 899.

Fourth Division, in Marne salient, 891; at St. Mihiel, 892.

Fowltown, attacked, 369.

Fox, Charles James, 308.

Fox's Blockade, 308.

France, explorations of, 35; colony of, in Florida, 111; a colonizing nation, 111, 115, 129; immigrants from, 145; treaties of alliance and commerce, 1778, 198–200; volunteers, 198; sends d'Estaing, 200; army at Yorktown, 212; relations with, 1793, 266; neutrality proclamation, 266; Genêt in America, 266; interpreting the treaties, 267; in American politics, 271, 276; attitude toward neutral trade, 271, 279; and Monroe's mission, 277; refuses to receive Pinckney, 278; seizes American ships, 279; feeling against, 279; warships

attacked, 281; three commissioners sent, 279; X, Y, Z papers, 280; treaty of 1800, 282; settles claims, 417–419; seizing American ships, 313, 316; in Mexico, 589, 643; and confederate arms, 589; Seward and Mexico, 643. *See* Napoleon.

Franklin, battle of, 538.

Franklin, Benjamin, and Pennsylvania militia, 105; at Albany congress, 1754, 123; supports acquisition of Canada, 130, 161; and Philadelphia culture, 155; on stamp act, 168; and "common sense," 186; and declaration of independence, 187; in Paris, 198; peace commissioner, 214; opposed to Cincinnati, 229; in Constitutional Convention, 242, 245.

Franklin, General, at Fredericksburg, 556.

"Franklin, State of," 234.

Frayser's Farm, battle of, 549.

Frederick, the Great, on Washington, 192.

Fredericksburg, battle of, 555–557.

Free coinage. *See* Silver.

Freedman, attitude in 1865, 601, 603; "forty acres and a mule," 603; receive the franchise, 607, 609–611; as citizens, 620; republicans, 622; on the juries, 637.

Freedmen's Bureau, created, 603; bill of 1866, 605.

Freeman's Farm, battles of, 197.

Free Soil Party, organized, 452; in 1852, 485.

Frémont, J. C., in California, 449; nominated for presidency, 495; in Missouri, 542, 577; emancipation order, 578.

French, activity in Ohio valley, 121; in the English colonies, 145.

French and Indian wars, 115–130; influence of, 100.

Frenchtown, 323.

Friar lands, 812.

Frolic, the, 327, 328.

Frontenac, services to New France, 115, 116; control of the lakes, 116; and the Iroquois, 117.

Frontenac, Fort, destroyed, 125, 126.

Frontier, advance in colonial times, 2, 100.

Frontiersmen, American-born, 148.

Fuel, government control of, 885.

Fugitive Slave Law, 351; a new, 455, 457; not enforced, 486.

Fur seal controversy, 767.

Fur trade, 4.

Gage, General, commander-in-chief, 171; in Boston, 178, 180; attempts to seize supplies, 180; Bunker Hill, 181.

Gaines's Mill, battle of, 548.

Gallatin, Albert, and whisky insurrection,

Hartford Convention, 336.
Harvard College, founded, 153; curriculum, 153.
Harvard University, development of, 480.
Havana, taken by the British, 129.
Haverhill, taken by French and Indians, 117.
Hawaii, early history, 771; work of missionaries, 772; treaty with, 772; revolution of 1893, 772; annexation refused, 772, 773; annexation accomplished, 773; present status, 774.
Hawkins, Captain John, and the slave trade, 41.
Hay, John, treaty with England, 817; convention with Herran, 818; treaty with Panama, 820; and China, 822–824.
Hay Bill, the, 878.
Hayes, R. B., nominated, 653; disputed returns, 654; declared elected, 657; attitude toward South, 658, 693, 694–695; cabinet, 694; a divided party, 695; as president, 703; and civil service reform, 708; and an isthmian canal, 816.
Hayes, Mrs., in the White House, 703.
Haymarket anarchists, 742.
Hayne, R. Y., in debate with Webster, 396–398.
Hayne-Webster debate, 396–398.
Hay-Pauncefote treaty, 817.
Hayti, discovered, 29; settled, 30, 31.
Hearst, W. R., 835.
Heath, Sir Robert, 52.
Helper, H. R., his "impending Crisis," 504.
Hendricks, Thomas A., nominated for vicepresidency, 653, 716.
Henry, Fort, captured, 527.
Henry, John, 335.
Henry, Patrick, resolutions on stamp act, 166; committee of correspondence, 174; and George Rogers Clark, 203; opposes ratification, 249; on amendments, 257.
Hepburn rate-bill, 833.
Hepburn v. Griswold, 663.
Herkimer, General, 196.
Highlanders, settled in the colonies, 147.
High Tariff, arguments on, 912; measures, 912; return to, 912.
Hill, A. P., at Mechanicsville, 548; in Gettysburg campaign, 558, 559, 560.
Hill, D. B., opposed to Cleveland, 720; governor of New York, 720; waives opposition to Cleveland, 722; and the Cleveland vote, 723; candidate for nomination, 750; speech at Chicago convention, 759.
Hill, D. H., at Mechanicsville, 548; lost dispatch to, 554.
Hillsborough, Lord, secretary of the colonies, 171.

Hoar, E. R., attorney-general, 644; dismissed, 645.
Hobson, R. P., at Santiago, 794.
Hohenzollerns, overthrown, 899.
Hojeda, 31, 32, 36.
Holden, W. W., Governor, 600; appeals to martial law, 631; impeached, 632.
Holland. See Dutch.
Honduras and Central American peace league, 866.
Hood, General, succeeds Johnston, 537; fights around Atlanta, 537; threatens Sherman's base, 537; movement against Nashville, 538; beaten, 539.
Hooker, General, in Tennessee, 534; at Lookout Mountain, 534; at Fredericksburg, 557; in command, 557; Chancellorsville, 557–558.
Hooker, Rev. Thomas, 69.
Hoover, Herbert, food administrator, 885, 905; secretary of commerce, 908; plan of farm relief, 938; nominated to presidency, 937; elected, 939; calls special session, 939; makes "good will" tour, 939.
Hornet, the, sinks the Peacock, 327.
Horse Shoe Bend, battle of, 332.
"Hortalez et Cie," 198.
House, Col. E. M., delegate to the Peace Conference, 900.
Houston, David F., secretary of agriculture, 854.
Houston, Sam, in Texas, 421.
Howard, General, at Chancellorsville, 558.
Howe, Elias, 465.
Howe, General George, death of, 126.
Howe, General William, at Bunker Hill, 181; succeeds Gage, 182; operations at New York, 188–191; Philadelphia campaign, 194–195; superseded, 200; battle of Monmouth, 200; not in coöperation with Burgoyne, 193, 195; expedition against Philadelphia, 193–194.
Howe, Lord, off New York, 188; meets d'Estaing, 201.
"Hubbell, My dear," 704.
Hudson, Henry, explorations of, 72.
Hudson Bay Company, founded, 119.
Hudson River, desired by France, 116.
Huerta, General, usurps power in Mexico, 868; and the death of Madero, 868; excluded from office, 870.
Hughes, Charles E., candidate for the presidency, 879; investigates airplane construction, 884; suggests amendments to the League covenant, 901; secretary of state, 908.
Huguenots, in South Carolina, 83; settled in colonies, 145.

Hull, Captain Isaac, 327.

Hull, General, at Detroit, 322.

Humphreys, Governor, removed from office, 623.

Hunkers, 451; at convention of 1848, 452.

Hurons, and the French, 113.

Hutchinson, Mrs. Anne, her heresy, 66; trial, 67; banished, 67; death, 67.

Hutchinson, Chief Justice, 167.

Hyde, Edward. *See* Lord Cornbury.

Idaho, territory and state, 678, 680, 748.

Illinois, territory created, 344; county of, 204; Black Hawk war, 466.

Immigration, 1815–1861, 461–462; distribution of, 462; and politics, 462; growth after civil war, 665; Chinese, 774; Japanese, 776; drastic restrictions on, 917; new policy, 917, 918; Act of 1924, 918; Japanese, 918.

Impeachment of Johnson, collecting evidence, 613; the trial, 615–617.

Impressment of seamen, 306; a cause of war, 313; *Chesapeake-Leopard* affair, 314; negotiations concerning, 315; not settled at Ghent, 334.

Income tax, amendment suggested, 838; adopted, 838; 1913, 857.

Independence, two groups of opinion, 186, 187; states recommend, 187; declaration of, 187.

Independents, the, as a political force, 693; relation to civil service reform, 707–708; in campaign of 1884, 718.

Indians, hold back the frontier, 2; and early man, 12; classification of, 13–15; Algonquian family, 13; Iroquoian family, 14; Muskhogean family, 14; Siouan family, 14; Caddoan family, 14; Shoshonean family, 14; Shahaptian family, 14; Salishan family, 14; Athapascan family, 14; Eskimauan family, 14; Pacific coast tribes, 15; culture of, 15–21; government, 15–17; the clan, 15; the sachem, 16; the chief, 16; the council, 16; the brotherhood, 17; names, 17; wars, 17; leading tribes, 18; wars against whites, 18; character, 19; mind, 19; religion, 19; mythology, 20; houses, 20; pueblos, 20; and civilization, 21; present state, 21; called such by Columbus, 29; enslaved, 30; harsh treatment by Spaniards, 30; of Virginia, 47, 48; wars in Virginia, 51; relations with Plymouth colony, 61; Pequot war, 70; war against New Netherland, 73; King Philip's war, 92; raids on New England, 116, 117;

118; relations with English, 121; Southern friendship sought by France and England, 121; trade with Southern, 121; Cherokees at war, 1759, 130; treaty at Fort Niagara, 132; war in Ohio, 262; treaty of Greenville, 263; depredations in the South, 265; punished by Tennesseeans, 265; plans of Tecumseh, 318; the Southern, 318; Creeks subdued, 332; Northwestern pressed back, 344; Seminole war, 368; in Georgia, 400; status of a tribe, 400; process of removal, 465–468; Black Hawk war, 466; reservation system, 468; of the Far West, 683–689; arrival of white men, 683; game destroyed, 683; far western tribes, 683; wars of, 684–689; commission of 1867–1868, 685; Sioux commission, 688; treaties not to be made with, 690; Dawes act, 690; Burke act, 690; late policy, 690, 691.

Indiana, territory created, 344.

Indiana, the, 800, 801.

Indian territory, conditions of, 467.

Indigo, a staple crop, 8.

Industrial combinations. *See* Combinations.

Industry, after the revolution, 225; after civil war, 664–666.

Inhabitants, early, 11–13.

Injunctions, use against strikers, 744.

"Insular Cases," 814.

Insurance, life, investigating the companies, 833.

Insurgents, the, origin of, 837; victory over Cannon, 838; in campaign of 1912, 843; found the progressive party, 847.

Intermediate credit banks, 915.

Intercourse with Germany broken, 881.

Internal improvements, policy of, 365; bonus bill vetoed, 365; by the states, 366; checked by Jackson, 304–396; Cumberland road bill, 395; Calhoun's report on, 395; later history of, 396.

Interstate commerce act, 735; powers of commission increased, 833, 839.

Iowa, a state, 463.

Iowa, the, 800, 801.

Iron, deposits, 8, 10; early manufacture of, 10.

Iroquois, 18; attitude toward French, 112; power of, 113; relations with the English, 114; Frontenac and, 117, 118; recognized as British subjects, 119; and the Albany congress, 122.

Irrigation, 849.

Island No. 10, 529.

Isthmian canal, and Clayton-Bulwer treaty, 458.

Isthmian canal project, early history of,

814–817; French canal, 815–816; Hayes's idea, 816; Nicaraguan, 817; Panama, 817–818, 821–822.

Italy, and Mafia incident, 767; United States troops in, 895.

Itata, the, 769.

Jackson, Andrew, and Burr, 304; to serve against Florida, 332; conquers the Creeks, 332; at Pensacola, 332; New Orleans campaign, 332–334; enters Florida, 369; attacked by Clay, 370; candidate for presidency, 1824, 377, 378, 379–380; his party in 1825–1829, 382; attack on Adams, 384; as party leader, 388; party demands, 389; elected, 390; inaugurated, 392; his cabinet, 392; checks internal improvements, 394–396; "Union" toast, 399; attitude toward Georgia, 400; open breach with Calhoun, 401; cabinet reorganized, 402; renominated, 402, 404; elected, 405; denounces nullification, 408; and the "force bill," 410; "war" against the bank, 411–415; idea of a bank, 412; resolutions of censure, 415; and West India Trade, 415–417; the French claims, 417–419; and the surplus, 424; on Van Buren's Texas letter, 442; Georgia Indians removed, 466; relation to democratic reform, 474.

Jackson, F. J., minister from England, 316, 335.

Jackson, Fort, treaty of, 332.

Jackson, Stonewall, at Bull Run, 519; diversion in the valley, 547; at Cedar Mountain, 551; takes Harper's Ferry, 554; at Antietam, 555; at Fredericksburg, 556; at Chancellorsville, 557; death of, 558.

Jackson, Mississippi, captured by Grant, 531.

James I, and the colonies, 76.

Jameson, J. Franklin, and Venezuelan boundary, 780.

James River, opened by the federals, 546; McClellan reaches, 549.

Jamestown, settled, 47; early history, 47–50; natural beauty, 47; disease at, 47; starvation, 48; land distributed, 49.

Japan, relations with, 775–777; war with Russia, 824; at treaty of Portsmouth, 824.

Japanese immigration, 918.

Jay, John, peace commissioner, 214; and the "Federalist," 247; on ratification, 249; negotiates treaty, 272.

Jay Cooke and Co., failure of, 666.

Jefferson, Thomas, 174; and the declaration of independence, 187; and Northwest, 232; secretary of state, 257; and assumption, 260; against the bank, 261; forms republican party, 270; leaves cabinet, 271; elected vice-president, 274; and election of 1796, 274; declines French ministry, 276; reply to alien and sedition laws, 285; elected president, 288–290; views of, 291–292; inaugurated, 291–292; cabinet, 292; appointments, 292; and the federal courts, 294; and Louisiana purchase, 296–299; popularity of, 300; and Burr, 300; and Randolph, 301; reëlected, 302; and trade restrictions, 307–311; and Monroe treaty 310; and embargo act, 310–311; on the *Chesapeake-Leopard* affair, 315; failure of his gunboats, 326.

Jefferson and the state university, 479.

Jenckes, Thomas, and civil service reform, 707.

Jenkins, Governor, removed, 623.

Jesuits, in Canada, 113.

Jews, in the colonies, 147.

Johnson, Andrew, nominated for vice-presidency, 584, 599; as president, 599; his plan of reconstruction, 599–601; relations with his cabinet, 600; amnesty of, 600; popularity in 1865, 604; projected party, 604; vetoes freedmen's bureau bill, 605; popularity wanes, 605; vetoes civil rights bill, 606; enforces congressional reconstruction, 611; "swinging-around-the-circle," 611; impeachment of, 613–617; acquittal, 616–617; and negro suffrage, 622.

Johnson, Hiram, nominated for vice-presidency, 847.

Johnson, Reverdy, 670.

Johnson, R. M., 318; elected vice-president, 425.

Johnson, Sir William, 124.

Johnson-Clarendon convention, 670.

Johnston, A. S., defense of Nashville, 528; falls back to Corinth, 528; attacks at Shiloh, 528; killed, 528.

Johnston, Joseph E., at Bull Run, 519; against Grant at Vicksburg, 531; succeeds Bragg, 535; operations against Sherman, 535–537; removed, 537; restored to command, 539; before Sherman in North Carolina, 540, 541; defending Richmond, 545; wounded at Seven Pines, 548; surrenders to Sherman, 568.

Joliet, reaches the Mississippi, 114.

Jones, John Paul, 205.

Jones, Willie, and John Paul Jones, 205.

Jones-Stalker Act, 936.

Jury, the negro on, 637.

Kalakaua, king of Hawaii, 772.
Kalb, arrival in America, 198; killed at Camden, 208.
Kansas, struggle for, 489–493; two streams of settlers, 483; two governments, 483–490; statehood suggested, 490; Kansas debate, 490; violence in, 491; failure of Governor Walker, 492; Lecompton constitution, 492; the English bill, 493; admitted to the union, 493.
Kansas-Nebraska act, origin of, 486; passed, 487; significance, 487; consequences, 489.
Kaskaskia, 343; taken by Clark, 204.
Kearny, General, expedition to California, 448.
Kearney, Phil, killed in battle, 553.
Kellogg Multilateral pact, 930.
Kennebec, colony on, 46.
Kennesaw Mountain, battle of, 536.
Kent, General, at Santiago, 796, 797, 798.
Kent's Island, 55.
Kentucky, Indians attack, 203; aid given against Ferguson, 208; settled, 232, 233; a state, 264; threatened rebellion of, 264; and parties, 271; struggle for union in, 517; defense of, 527; Bragg in, 529.
Kentucky resolutions, 285–287.
Key West, American fleet at, 793.
Kidnapping, 137.
Kieft, William, governor of New Amsterdam, 73.
King, W. R., elected vice-president, 485.
King George's War, 120.
King's Mountain, battle of, 208.
King William's War, 116.
"Kitchen Cabinet," 393.
Knight, Admiral A. M., 896.
Knights of Labor, early history, 741; violent element, 742; and St. Louis strike, 742; and Chicago strike, 742; decline of, 743.
"Know Ye" resolutions, 236.
Know-Nothing party, origin, 493; failure of, 494.
Knox, Henry, secretary of war, 257; supports Hamilton, 261; and new army, 281.
Knox, Senator, 903; resolution of, 903, 908.
Kriemhilde Stellung, 893, 894.
Ku Klux act, of 1871, 629, 634.
Ku Klux Klan, history of, 627–630; methods, 628; organization, 628; congress interferes, 629; achievement of, 629; connected with politics, 630; in North Carolina, 631, 917, 926.

Labor, white servants, 137; redemptioners, 146; department of, 851.
Labor troubles, 914.

Ladrone Islands, 805, 806.
Lafayette, Marquis, volunteers, 198; at Monmouth, 200; in Virginia, 211.
La Folette, Senator, presidential candidate, 843; his filibuster against arming of merchantmen, 881; nominated to presidency, 926.
Lake George, battle of, 124.
Lamar, L. Q. C., on Seward, 507; in Cleveland's cabinet, 720.
Land, bottom, 2, 7; distributed in Plymouth, 61; distribution of, in Virginia, 49; return from, in early Virginia, 50; patroons in New Netherland, 73; distribution of, 134; taking it up, 136; Western, 231–234; surrendered by states, 231; sale of, 232, 342, 343; military grants, 342; great companies, 342; Southwestern, 345.
Lane, Franklin K., secretary of the interior, 854.
Lane, Ralph, and Roanoke Island, 42.
Lansing skulls, 12.
La Salle, explores the Mississippi, 114.
Las Guasimas, 796.
Latin Americans, political ideals of, 863.
Laudonnière, leads colony to Florida, 111.
Laurens, Henry, peace commissioner, 214.
Lawrence, Captain, 327.
Lawrence, Kansas, attacked, 491.
Lawton, General, at Santiago, 796, 797, 798; carries El Caney, 798.
League of Nations, adopted by Peace Conference, 901; the covenant of, 901; debated by the senate, 901; Article X, 903; in the campaign of 1920, 903; first meeting of, 903; divided opinions on, 905; Harding unfavorable to, 909, 918, 919; Coolidge's attitude towards, 919.
Lecompton constitution, the, 492; Douglas opposes, 492; defeated, 493.
Lee, Arthur, in Paris, 198.
Lee, Fort, 188, 191.
Lee, General Charles, in New York campaign, 191; his character, 197; at Monmouth, 200; dismissed, 200; on Gates, 207.
Lee, R. E., repulsed in West Virginia, 526; as commander, 545; takes command, 548; defeats McClellan, 548–549; moves against Pope, 551–553; the Antietam campaign, 553–555; at Fredericksburg, 555–557; at Chancellorsville, 557–558; invasion of Pennsylvania, 558; in Gettysburg campaign, 558–562; his generalship, 562; at the Wilderness, 563; at Spottsylvania, 563; at Cold Harbor, 563; evacuates Richmond, 566; surrenders, 567; captures John Brown, 503.

Lee, R. H., resolutions in continental congress, 187; on ratification, 249.

Lee, the, 182.

Legal tender, retiring the notes, 662; decisions on, 663–664; redemption of, 668; more demanded, 668; resumption act, 669.

Legal tender act, 574.

Leif Ericsson, 23.

Leisler, Jacob, initiates revolution, 96; defeat of, 102.

Leopard, attacks the *Chesapeake,* 314.

Lepe, Diego de, 32.

Lévis, attacks Quebec, 128.

Lewis, Meriwether, explorations, 356.

Lewis, W. B., in "Kitchen Cabinet," 393.

Lewis and Clark, explorations, 355.

Lexington, battle of, 180.

Liberal republicans, origin of, 648; nominate Greeley, 648.

Liliuokalani, Queen, 772, 773.

Linares, General, defender of Santiago, 796, 797; errors of, 802.

Lincoln, Abraham, in debate with Douglas, 499–503; "House divided" speech, 500; destroying Douglas, 501; nominated for presidency, 508; elected, 509; attitude toward secession, 514; first inaugural, 515; calls for volunteers, 517; and McClellan, 545, 546, 549; and emancipation, 577–581; at Hampton Roads, 566; assassinated, 568; his greatness, 568; war policy criticized, 581, 582; his renomination opposed, 583; renominated, 584; reëlected, 584; military law, 585, 586; plan of reconstruction, 596–599; amnesty proclamation, 596; and the Wade-Davis bill, 597; and negro suffrage, 597, 622.

Lincoln-Douglas debates, 499–502; effect of, 502.

Lincoln, General, at Charleston, 207; receives Cornwallis's sword, 213; and Shays's Rebellion, 236.

Lind, John, in Mexico, 869.

Liquor smuggling, 935.

Little Big Horn, battle of, 688.

Little Sarah, the, 267.

Livingston, Edward, minister to Paris, 418.

Livingston, Robert R., 187; on ratification, 249; and Louisiana purchase, 297–299.

Lobby, President Wilson's charges against it, 857.

"Locofocos," 433.

Lodge, H. C., in campaign of 1884, 716.

Logan, General J. A., nominated for vice-presidency, 716.

Logan, James A., culture of, 155.

London Company, created, 45, 46; reformed, 50; services to Virginia, 51; and Maryland settlement, 52; and Pilgrims, 52, 59.

Longstreet, General, at Chickamauga, 533; at Knoxville, 535; at second Bull Run, 552; at Fredericksburg, 556; in Gettysburg campaign, 559, 560, 561.

Lookout Mountain, capture of, 534.

Lords of Trade, 77.

Lorimer, Senator, investigation, 842.

Loudon, Fort, captured, 130.

Louisburg, taken by colonials, 120; futile expedition against, 125; taken, 125, 126.

Louisiana, early history, 115; purchase of, 296–299; boundaries of, 299; and Burr's scheme, 304; territory of, 345; territory of Orleans, 345; admitted to union, 345; population of, 1810, 345; reconstructed under Lincoln, 596; readmitted, 624; republicans overthrown, 633; disputed returns in 1876, 655, 657; surrendered to democrats, 657.

Louis XIV, and New France, 115.

Lowndes, William, elected to congress, 318; on the tariff, 364.

Lumber industry, 6.

Lundy, Benjamin, work of, 428.

Lundy's Lane, battle of, 325.

Lusitania, the loss of, 873, 876.

Lutheran Church, 354.

Lyon, General, and Missouri secessionists, 517, 526; death of, 526; defense of Missouri, 541.

Lyttleton, Governor, and Cherokee war, 130.

McAdoo, William G., secretary of the treasury, 854, 855; director-general of transportation, 885.

McCardle, *ex parte,* case of, 613.

McClellan, General, in West Virginia, 520, 526; in command in Virginia, 545; tardiness, 545; in the Peninsula campaign, 546–550; controversy over, 550; in the Antietam campaign, 554; nominated for presidency, 584.

McCormick reaper, invented, 465.

McCulloch, Hugh, as financier, 660; his refunding plans, 661.

McCulloch *v.* Maryland, case of, 359.

MacDonald, Donald, 183.

MacDonough, Captain, victory on Lake Champlain, 325.

McDowell, General, in Bull Run campaign, 519; and McClellan, 546, 547; at second Bull Run, 554.

Macedonian, the, 327, 328.

Machine guns, supplies of, 884; value of, in covering a retreat, 891.

McGillivray, Alexander, 265.

McHenry, Fort, defended against British, 330.

McHenry, James, dismissed from the cabinet, 287.

McKinley, William Jr., and the civil service, 711; and the tariff, 715; as leader, 723; his tariff bill, 724–726; effect of, 727; nominated, 1896, 760; campaign of, 761; elected, 762; attitude toward Spain, 787, 789; and the *Maine*, 788; demands armistice in Cuba, 789; suggests war, 789; responsible for Manila, 792; and Schley-Sampson controversy, 804; and acquisition of the Philippines, 805; reëlected, 827; death of, 827; later policy of, 829.

McKinley tariff and Sherman silver law, 747.

McLane, Lewis, and the bank, 412, 413; and West Indian trade, 417.

McLean, J. J., for president, 425; in Dred Scott case, 498.

McNary-Haugen bill, 916, 932, 934; vetoed by Coolidge, 933; not acceptable to Hoover, 938.

Macomb, General, 325.

Macon, Nathaniel, speaker, 303; "Macon's Bill No. 2," 311, 313.

"Macon's Bill No. 2," 311, 313, 317.

McReynolds, James C., attorney-general, 854.

Madison, on Potomac smugglers, 241; "Notes" on constitutional debates, 242; author of Virginia plan, 243; and the "Federalist," 247; supports ratification, 249; and first revenue bill, 257; position on refunding, 259; retaliatory resolutions, 272; declines French ministry, 276; and Virginia Resolutions, 285–287; secretary of state, 292; disliked by Randolph, 302; elected president, 311; hoodwinked by Napoleon, 317; favors war party, 319; renominated, 319; reëlected, 319.

Madero, Francisco, becomes president of Mexico, 868; overthrown by Huerta, 868.

Mafia Incident, 767.

Magellan, voyage of, 33.

Mails, use for antislavery literature, 430.

Maine, early settlements in, 62, 70; hold of British in, 331; a state, 373; boundary dispute, 437–438; prohibition in, 480.

Maine, the, destroyed at Havana, 787, 788.

Malden, Fort, 321; Hull before, 322; evacuated, 323.

Malvern Hill, battle of, 549.

Manassas, battle of, 552.

Mangum, W. P., 426.

Manhattan Island. *See* New York.

Manila, battle of, 791; holding the bay, 792; Aguinaldo at, 809; capture of, 792, 809.

Manley, John, 182.

Manufactures, colonial, 140; British restrictions on, 141; new era of, 348; early, 349; effect of embargo, 349; effect on society, 349; demand a tariff, 364, 384–386; growth of, 463; combination in 736–740.

Maps of America, early, 36.

Marbois, and Louisiana purchase, 299.

Marbury *v.* Madison, case of, 357.

Marco Polo, 26.

Marcy, W. L., a Hunker, 451.

Maria Teresa, the, 800, 801.

Marietta, settled, 342.

Marines, United States, arrival in France, 886; near Château-Thierry, 889, 890.

Marion, partisan leader, 207; under Greene, 210.

Marne salient, United States troops in, 889–891.

Marquette, Father, reaches the Mississippi, 114.

Marshall, John, on ratification, 249; commissioner to France, 279; secretary of state, 276, 287; Chief Justice, 291; at Burr's trial, 305; influence on the constitution, 357–360.

Marshall, Thomas R., nominated for vice-president, 847.

Martin, Luther, 242, 245.

Martinique, not ceded in 1763, 129.

Marye's Heights, 556.

Maryland, early history, 52–57; government of, 53, 54; religious toleration, 53; first colony, 53, 54; the assembly, 54; manors in, 55; Jesuits in, 55; struggle for Kent's Island, 55; and Virginia politics, 56; civil war in, 57; toleration act of 1649, 57; battle of Providence, 57; and the restoration, 80; reactionary government under Charles Calvert, 88; revolution, 89, 97; trade, 142; religion in, 151; and western lands, 232; confers with Virginia on trade, 241; struggle for union in, 517; Lee invades, 553–555; military arrests in, 585.

Mason, Captain John, 62, 70.

Mason, George, on ratification, 249.

Mason and Slidell, seized on the *Trent*, 522.

Massachusetts, early settlements in, 62, 63.

Massachusetts, and New England confederation, 71; during the restoration period, 80; charter annulled, 93; and the Dominion of New England, 94; rule of Andros, 93-95; overthrow of Andros, 96; new charter, 97; salary controversy, 101; and paper money, 158; resists stamp act, 167; resists quartering troops, 169; in the revolutionary quarrel, 170; parliament censures, 171; troops sent, 171; committees appointed, 174; charter changed by parliament, 176; general sympathy for, 177; Shays's Rebellion, 236; ratifies the constitution, 248; public schools in, 476; work of Horace Mann, 477; cedes Maine, 373.

Massachusetts, the, 800, 801.

Massachusetts Bay, colony of, charter, 63; population, 64; early government, 64; the franchise, 65; suspected by the king, 66. *See* Massachusetts.

Massasoit, 61.

Matamoras, taken by Taylor, 447.

Mather, Rev. Cotton, and witchcraft, 149.

Mather, Rev. Increase, and witches, 149.

Maximilian of Baden, Prince, German Chancellor, 898, 899.

Mayflower, voyage of, 60.

"Mayflower Compact," the, 61.

Mayo, Admiral, at Tampico, 869; in world war, 896.

Maysville veto, 395.

Meade, General, in command, 559; in Gettysburg campaign, 559-562.

"Meat Trust," 839.

Mechanicsville, battle of, 548.

Mecklenburg county, resolves of, 180.

"Mediterranean Fund," 293.

Mellon, Andrew W., secretary of treasury, 908.

Mellon-Andrews Act of 1925, 935.

Menendez, Pedro, 111.

Merchant-Marine Act of 1920, 910.

Merchantmen, arming of, 881.

Merrimac, the, 569; sunk at Santiago, 794.

Merritt, Wesley, at Manila, 792, 810.

Methodist Church, founded in America, 353; divided by slavery, 456, 471.

Meuse-Argonne Campaign, 893.

Mexican Congress, 929.

Mexico, conquest of, 37; and Burr's scheme, 304; early relations with Texas, 419; refuses to sell Texas, 420; refuses to sell California, 446; war with, 446-450; city of, taken, 450; treaty with, 450; French in, 589, 643; relations with, under Wilson, 867-871; treatment of foreigners under Diaz, 867; Madero and Huerta, 868; Tampico incident, 869; Vera Cruz

seized, 869; negotiations of "A. B. C. Powers," 870; Pershing in, 870; results of Wilson's policy in, 871; friction with, 928.

Michigan, territory created, 344; a state, 463.

Mifflin, Governor, and whisky insurrection, 268.

Milan Decree, 309.

Miles, N. A., and Jefferson Davis, 64; takes Porto Rico, 801.

Military government established in the South, 609-611, 622-625; supreme court on, 612, 613; reëstablished in the South, 622-625.

Military law, in civil war, 581, 585, 586.

Milligan, *ex parte*, case of, 612.

"Millionaire's panic," 739.

Mineral oils, 10.

Minerals, 8-11.

Mines, submarine, 897.

Mining, in the Far West, 677-680; conditions, 678; laws, 678.

Minnesota, a state, 463.

Minuit, Peter, governor of New Amsterdam, 72; in Delaware, 75.

Missionary Ridge, battle of, 535.

Mississippi, territory created, 344; population, 1820, 345; new Black Code in, 602; Governor Humphreys removed, 623; readmitted, 625; republicans overthrown, 632; the "Mississippi plan," 632.

Mississippi river, as a means of transportation, 2; explored by French, 114; opened north and south, 529; opened at Vicksburg, 532.

Mississippi v. Johnson, case of, 612.

Missouri, territory created, 345; development of, 371; asks for statehood, 371; compromise, 373; constitution of, 374; interest in Nebraska, 486; attempt to settle Kansas, 489; struggle for union in, 517, 526, 541-542.

Missouri Compromise, adopted, 371-374.

Mobile, desire to annex, 321; occupied, 332.

Mobile Act, 300.

Mobile Bay, defenses taken, 571.

Mohawk river and transportation system, 3.

Mohawks, 113.

"Molasses Act," 144; renewed, 163.

Molino del Rey, battle at, 450.

Monck's Corners, 211.

Money, continental, 223; paper, after the revolution, 236. *See* Paper money.

Monhegan, 61.

Monitor, contest with the *Virginia*, 546, 570.

Monmouth, battle of, 200.
Monocacy, battle of, 565.
Monroe, James, mission to France, 1794, 277; his blow at Hamilton, 278; and the purchase of Louisiana, 299; and Randolph, 302, 303; makes treaty, 310; secretary of state, 317, 330; elected president, 366; cabinet, 367; and Spanish-American states, 367; and parties, 368; reëlected, 368; and internal improvements, 395.
Monroe Doctrine, origin of, 374; England's relation to, 375; Adams's part, 375; Russia's relation to, 375; announced, 377; new meaning in Venezuelan incident, 778–781; and the Venezuelan incident, 778–779, 780–781, 826; Roosevelt on, 827; and our Caribbean policy, 863.
Montana, settled, 678; a territory and state, 678, 680, 748.
Montcalm, Marquis de, takes Fort William Henry, 125; impeded in Canada, 126; defense of Quebec, 127; death, 127.
Monterey, taken by Taylor, 447.
Monterey, the, at Manila, 792.
Montgomery, Colonel, against the Cherokees, 130.
Montgomery, Richard, in Canada, 184.
Montgomery, Ala., confederacy organized at, 511.
Montreal, site discovered, 36; attempt to take, 116; taken by British, 128; position of, 321; expedition against, 322.
Moravians, settlements of, 147.
Morgan, General, at Cowpens, 208; pursued by Tarleton, 209; retreat of, 209.
Morgan, J. P., system of banks, 740; and bond sales under Cleveland, 756–757.
Morgan, William, against masonry, 403.
Morgan, Fort, taken, 571.
Morris, Gouverneur, and union, 223; minister to England, 262; minister to France, 277.
Morris, Robert, superintendent of finances, 228.
Morris, Captain, in Tripolitan war, 295.
Morrow, Dwight W., Ambassador to Mexico, 929.
Morse, invents telegraph, 465.
Morton, L. P., vice-president, 722.
Morton, O. P., influence at Washington, 633; and renomination of Grant, 653.
Motley, J. L., recall of, 645.
Moultrie, Col., defends Charleston, 183.
"Mound Builders," the, 12.
Mounds, 12.
"Mulligan Letters," 717.
Munitions, sale of, to belligerents, 874.

Murfreesboro, Buel, at, 529; battle of, 530.
Murray, suggests treaty with France, 282.

Napoleon, and Louisiana, 297; and Florida, 302; restrictions on American trade, 307–309; hoodwinks Madison, 316.
Narvaez, explorations of, 38.
Nashville Convention, 457.
Nashville, battle of, 539.
Nast, Thomas, in campaign of 1872, 649.
National Debt reduced, 911.
National Guard, 878, 883; naming the divisions of, 888.
National Monetary Commission. See Aldrich Commission.
National republicans, 403.
National silver party, 761.
Native American movement, 462.
Naturalization, law of 1795, 283; law of 1798, 283; law of 1802, 283.
Natural resources, 4–11; preservation of, 849–850.
Nature, influence of, 1.
Naval limitations, 920; programme, 919.
Navigation Acts, ordinance of 1651, 78; later acts, 81; in practice, 143; evaded, 144; to be enforced, 163; and the revolution, 163; and Massachusetts, 170; bearing on post-revolutionary trade, 226; receding, 416.
Navy, in the revolution, 204–206; against France, 279, 281; seize French ships, 281; department of, created, 281; Jefferson, and, 293; in war with Tripoli, 295; war party favors, 319; condition of in 1812, 320, 326; naval warfare, 326–329; new ships, 327, 328; after war of 1812, 363; federal, in the civil war, 569–571; at New Orleans, 529; liberal appropriations under Harrison, 727; state of, 1915, 879; in world war, 896; the destroyers at Queenstown, 896; convoying service, 897; squadron in the Allied Grand Fleet, 897; submarine mine barrage in North Sea, 897.
Nebraska, demand for a territory of, 486.
Necessity, Fort, 122.
Neesima, J. H., work in Japan, 775.
Negroes. See Freedmen, 601.
Negro troops, 573; as prisoners, 573–574.
Neutrality, proclamation, 266; efforts to preserve, 873–877; the president's proclamations, 873; violated by Germany, 873.
Nevada, settled, 677; state and territory, 677, 680.
New Amsterdam. See New York.
Newburg address, the, 223.

New England, council of, 61, 62; and New Hampshire, 70; the town, 134; life in, 137; trade in, 142, 163; religion in, 148, 150; education, 153; local government in, 156; privateers, 205; British sympathy in, 331, 335-338; ignored by agricultural states, 335; hopes from Canada, 335; migration westward, 341; rise of manufactures, 349; disestablishment in, 335; and the tariff, 385, 386-387.

New England confederation, origin of, 71; constitution of, 71; decay of, 71.

New France, condition of, 1628, 112; explored, 111; settled, 112; Jesuits in, 113; and Indian trade, 121; in the Ohio valley, 121.

New Haven, settled, 69; government of, 69; united with New Haven, 80.

New Hampshire, early history, 62, 70; falls to Massachusetts, 70; and the Dominion of New England, 94; and the revolution, 97; ratifies the constitution, 248.

New Jersey, created, 81, 85; East and West Jersey, 85; granted to Duke of York, 85; Quaker control, 85; and the Dominion of New England, 94; and the revolution, 97; campaign in, 191; tories in, 191; recovered, 192; ratifies the constitution, 247.

New London, taken by Arnold, 212.

New Mexico, attempt of Polk to purchase, 446; occupied by Kearney, 448; not made a territory, 453; made a territory, 455, 457; mining in, 678; territory and state, 680; statehood granted, 851.

New Netherland. See New York.

New Orleans, campaign of, 332-334; capture of, 529; Mafia riots at, 767.

Newport, Captain Christopher, in Virginia, 46, 48.

Newport, held by British, 192; siege of, 200.

Newspaper ownership, 842.

New York, explored and settled by Dutch, 72; patroon system, 73; disorders in, 73; Indian wars, 73; government, 74; English settlers on Long Island, 75; acquired by the English, 75; government, 83; conquered by Dutch, 84; struggle for an assembly, 84; and the Dominion of New England, 94; Leisler revolution, 96, 102; governor's salary, 102; contest for assembly, 103; money votes in, 103, 104; religion in, 152; mixed form of local government, 156; "Duke's Law," 157; stamp act congress, 167; resents quartering troops, 169; assembly suspended, 170; operations around, 188-191; attitude in constitutional convention, 244; ratifies the constitution, 249; and parties, 270; settlement of western, 341; constitutional reform in, 473; public schools in, 477.

New York, the, 800, 801.

New York Central system, development of, 733, 734.

Niagara, Fort, expedition against, 124; captured, 126; Indian treaty at, 132.

Nicaragua, canal through, 815, 816, 817; and Central American peace league, 866; United States protectorate over, 867; re-occupation of, 929.

Nicholson, Sir Francis, governor of New York, 95, 96.

Nicolls, Col. Richard, governor of New York, 75; takes New Amsterdam, 76; approves the "Duke's Laws," 83.

Nine-Power treaty, 921.

Nineteenth Division at St. Mihiel, 892.

Ninety-six, 210, 211.

Nomination, presidential, by convention, 404; significance of, 404. See Caucus.

Non-importation, 1765, 167; revived, 170; employed in 1774, 179; act of 1806, 309.

Non-slaveholders, 469.

Norfolk, burned, 186.

Norsemen, discoveries by, 234.

North and South, relative strength of, 518.

North, Lord, colonial policy of, 171; duty on tea, 173; offers compromise, 1778, 199; resigns, 214.

North Carolina, discovered by Spaniards, 31; colony at Roanoke Island, 42; settlement of, 82; name, 82, 83; evolution of, 106; Cary rebellion, 107; Indian wars, 107; sale to crown, 107; quitrents, 107; controversy over county representation, 135; trade, 143; race elements in, 146, 147; religion in, 151; resists stamp act, 168; Mecklenburg resolves, 180; loyalists in, 182; regulators, 183; battle of Moore's Creek, 183; authorizes independence, 186; against nullification, 410; Cornwallis in, 208-210; American retreat in, 209; ratifies the constitution, 249; and parties, 271; constitutional reform in, 474; "free schools" in, 477; federal operations in, 570; reconstructed by Johnson, 600; readmitted, 624; Holden and martial law, 631; republicans overthrown, 632.

North Dakota, a state, 748.

Northeast boundary adjusted, 437.

Northwest, conquered by Clark, 204.

Northwest Ordinance, the first, 232; the second, 233, 343.

Nova Scotia, ceded to England, 129.

Novus Mundus, 32.

Nullification, and the Virginia-Kentucky resolutions, 285–287; origin of, 385; Calhoun's "Exposition," 387; the theory, 388; and Hayne-Webster debate, 399; Georgia rejects, 400; attempt to execute, 407–410; ordinance of, 408; replevin act, 408; Jackson's proclamation, 409; suspended, 410; compromise tariff, 410.

Oberlin College, antislavery center, 429.

Ocean currents, influence of, 2.

Officers in the army, 883.

Oglethorpe, James, founds Georgia, 109; governor, 109–110.

Ohio, French posts in, taken, 125; settlement of, 232; territory of, 233; Indians at war, 262; lands opened to settlers, 263; settlement of, 342; territory organized, 342; population of, 343; admitted to union, 344.

Ohio Company, 232, 342.

"Ohio Idea," the, 642.

Ohio valley, French in, 121, 122.

Oil scandals, 922, 923, 924.

Okechobee Swamp, battle of, 467.

Oklahoma, 467.

"Old Hickory Division." *See* Thirtieth Division.

Olney, secretary, his Venezuelan dispatch, 778.

Olympia, the, at Manila, 791.

Omnibus Bill, 457.

Opechancanough, 52.

"Open door" in China, 920, 921.

Oquendo, the, 800, 801.

Orangeburg, 211.

Orders in Council, 308; repeal of, 319–320.

Oregon, explored by Lewis and Clark, 356; condition of, 1841, 440; joint occupancy, 440; a political issue, 440; immigration to, 441; adjustment of the question, 445; made a territory, 452; becomes a state, 463; disputed election returns of 1876, 655, 657; vote of in 1876, 696.

Oregon, the, around Cape Horn, 794; at Santiago, 800, 801.

Orient, American diplomacy in, 822–824.

Orinoco river, discovered, 30.

Oriskany, battle of, 196.

Osceola, 466.

Oswald, British peace commissioner, 214.

Otis, Harrison Gray, at Hartford convention, 337.

Otis, James, on American rights, 165; and stamp act, 167; elected speaker, 169; wounded, 172.

"Outlaw" shopmen's strike, 910.

Outrages, Southern, 606; effects of, 606, 625.

Pacific, diplomacy of the, 764; importance of, 764.

Pacific Coast, harbors on, 3; Indians of, 15.

Pacific Ocean, discovered, 37.

Pacific railroad, and the Kansas-Nebraska act, 486.

Pacific treaties, 920.

Pact of Paris, 931.

Paine, Thomas, "Common Sense," 186.

Pakenham, General, at New Orleans, 333.

Palo Alto, battle of, 447.

Panama, route adopted, 818; revolution in, 818–820; republic of, 820; canal treaty, 820; sanitation in, 821.

Panama congress, 383.

Panic of 1837, 432.

Panic of 1857, 482; political effect of, 499.

Panic of 1873, 666, 667.

Panic of 1893, 729, 739, 753.

Panic of 1903, 739, 831.

Paper money, in the colonies, 157; after the revolution, 236; in Rhode Island, 236; and the Shays's Rebellion, 236.

Paris, treaty of, 129.

Parker, Alton B., nominated for presidency, 832; at Baltimore convention, 846.

Parson's cause, 166.

Parties, Washington and, 269.

Patronage, influence of, 1828, 389; under Jackson, 393. *See* Civil Service Reform, and Appointments to Office.

Patroon system, 73.

Patterson, plan of, in constitutional convention, 244.

Pawtucket, 349.

Payne-Aldrich bill, 837; political effects of, 837–838.

Peace, efforts to preserve, Crittenden compromise, 513; senate peace committee, 513; peace congress, 514.

Peace movement, confederate, 588.

Peach Tree Creek, battle of, 537.

Peacock, the, 327.

Pea Ridge, battle of, 542.

Peace Conference. *See* Versailles, the Treaty of.

Peace suggestions, December 15, 1917, 897; Wilson's "Fourteen Points," 988.

Peirpoint, F. H., government at Alexandria, 520, 596, 601.

Pelican the, Drake's ship, 41.

Pell's Point, 190.

Pemberton, General, defense of Vicksburg, 531; surrenders, 532.

Pendleton, G. H., financial ideas, 642; and nomination of 1868, 642.

Pendleton act, 709.

Peninsular campaign, 545.

Penn, family, late history of, 106.

Penn, John, 106.

Penn, William, interested in West Jersey, 85; charter for Pennsylvania, 85; as a colonizer, 85–88; colony lost and restored, 88; grants "charter of privileges," 104.

Pennsylvania, charter, 85; settled, 86; government, 86, 87; Indians conciliated, 86; Penn in the colony, 86, 87; boundary controversy, 87, 97; political changes in, 104; new charter, 104; a militia organized, 105; Germans in, 146; Scotch-Irish in, 147; religion in, 152; university of, 154; education in, 154, 477; ratifies constitution, 247; the whisky insurrection, 267–269; parties in, 270; public schools in, 477.

Pennsylvania railroad, development of, 733, 734.

Pensacola, occupied, 332, 369.

Pensions, policy of, 726; Tanner and, 749; law of 1912, 851.

People's party, organized, 752.

Peppcrell, William, takes Louisburg, 120.

Pequots, war with, 70.

Perry, Oliver H., victory on Lake Erie, 324.

Perryville, battle of, 529.

Pershing, General John J., 887; operations in Mexico, 870; places his army at disposal of Foch, 889; organizes an army, 891.

Petersburg, siege of, 564, 566.

Petitions, antislavery, 431.

Philadelphia, founded, 86; population, 142; culture of, 155; and tea duty, 175; occupied by the British, 194, 199; evacuated, 200; congress forced to flee, 224; seat of government at, 262.

Philadelphia, the, loss of, 293, 295, 296.

Philip, King, war against whites, 92.

Philippines, acquired by treaty of peace, 805, 806; under Spanish authority, 809; revolt of Aguinaldo, 809; government established, 810–812; assembly of, 812; population of, 811; tariff relations, 812; friar lands, 812. *See* Filipinos.

Phillips, Captain, 802.

Phillips, Wendell, Johnson's charges against, 605.

Phips, Governor, salary controversy, 101; fails against Quebec, 117.

Pickens, at Cowpens, 209; partisan leader, 207.

Pickens, Fort, relief of, 512.

Pickering, Judge, impeached, 294.

Pickering, Timothy, secretary of state, 271; and Monroe's mission, 277, 278; desires French war, 279; dismissed, 287; plots with Burr, 300; and Rose, 315; and New England discontent, 335–337.

Pickett's charge, 561–562.

Piedmont region of the South, 468.

Piegans, massacre of, 686.

Pierce, Franklin, elected president, 485; attitude toward Kansas, 490.

Pike, Zebulon, explorations of, 356.

Pike's Peak, named, 356.

Pilgrims, origin of, 59; in Leyden, 59; depart for America, 60.

Pillow, Fort, taken, 574; negro prisoners at, 574.

Pinchot, Gifford, controversy with Ballinger, 838.

Pinckney, C. C., plan in constitutional convention, 243; mission to France, 278–280; command in new army, 281.

Pinckney, Thomas, Hamilton's plan to elect, 273.

Pinckney, William, in England, 309; makes treaty, 310.

Pinzon, Vicente Yañez, 32.

Pitt, Fort, held against the Indians, 131.

Pitt, William, and the Seven Years' War, 124, 125, 129, 130; on stamp act, 168; illness, 169; pleads for colonies, 176.

Pitt, William, the younger, and American trade, 307.

Pittsburg, importance of, 3, 4; Fort Duquesne established, 122; efforts of English to take, 122–123.

Plain, the interior, 1.

Platt, T. C., resigns senatorship, 704; returns to senate, 704; for Blaine in 1884, 716; as leader, 723.

Platt amendment, the, 807; spirit of it applied to Caribbean states, 864; to Nicaragua, 867.

Plymouth, early history, 60–63; settlement of, 60; early suffering in, 60; government of, 61, 62; relation with Indians, 61; common stock, 61; religion of, 61; colony of, 60–63; charter and grant, 59, 61; conditions of settlement, 60, 61; expansion, 62; government, 61, 62; reorganized, 62.

Plymouth Colony and New England Confederation, 71; and the Dominion of New England, 94; joined with Massachusetts, 97.

Plymouth Company, created, 45, 46.

Pocahontas, 52.

Poland committee, the, 649.

Polk, James K., nominated, 442; elected, 443; his presidency, 445–452; and Oregon, 445; negotiations with Mexico, 446; war with Mexico, 446–450.

Polly, the, case of, 307.

Pomeroy Circular, 584.

Ponce de Leon, 38.

Pontiac, at war with the whites, 131.

Pope, General, commands in Virginia, 550; defeated at second Bull Run, 551–553; as a commander, 553.

Popular sovereignty, defined, 454; in 1854, 486, 488; in Lincoln-Douglas debate, 501.

Population, Virginia in 1616, 50; 1624, 51; Maryland in 1660, 58; Plymouth Colony, 62; Massachusetts, 64; Philadelphia, 86; of all the colonies, 1690, 100; in 1760, 101; of South Carolina, 108; of North Carolina, 108; of New France, 113; colonial in 1760, 136; slaves in 1769, 139; Boston, 142; Philadelphia, 142; New York, 142; Charleston, 142; Baltimore, 142; growth, 1790–1815, 341; of Ohio, 343; of the Northwest, 1820, 344; of Alabama and Mississippi, 1820, 345; of North and South, 1860, 461, 518; immigrants, 1860, 461; of slaves, 470; of Philippine Islands, 811.

Porter, FitzJohn, at second Bull Run, 552.

Porto Rico, taken by Americans, 801; and the Spanish treaty, 805, 806; civil government in, 814.

Port Royal, Acadia, captured, 117; taken by English, 118.

Port Royal, S. C., seized, 570.

Portsmouth, N. H., branch bank at, 411; treaty of, 824.

Portugal, African, explorations of, 25; American explorations, 34.

Postal Savings Banks, 839.

Potomac, smuggling on the, 241.

Potter, Bishop, on political ideals, 723.

Powderly, T. V., 741.

Powhatan, 48, 52.

Prairies, the soil, 7.

Preble, Captain, in Tripolitan war, 295.

Presbyterian Church, 354; divided by slavery, 472.

Presbyterians, in the colonies, 148; in Virginia, 151.

Presidency and a prime minister, 856.

President, constitutional status, 251, 258; war powers of, 585–586.

President, the, 295, 328; and Little Belt, 317.

"Prester John," 25.

Prevost in the South, 207.

Price, Sterling, in Missouri, 541, 542; in Arkansas, 541, 542.

Prices and panic of 1873, 667.

Prince Henry the Navigator, 25.

Princeton, battle of, 192.

Princeton College, founded, 154.

Privateers, in the revolution, 204; in the war of 1812, 328.

Progressive party, founded, 847, 926.

Prohibition, 904; difficulties, 934; Bureau of, created, 935; enforcement of, strengthened, 935; violations, 936.

Prophet, the, 318.

Proprietary colony, the, described, 81.

Protestant Episcopal Church, organized, 354; of the confederacy, 472.

Pueblo Indians, 13.

Pujo Committee, 741, 851.

Pulaski, arrival in America, 198.

Pullman strike, 743.

Pure food law, 833.

Puritanism, origin and belief, 63; apology for, 65; attitude toward Roger Williams, 65; weakening, 148.

Puritan Revolution and the Colonies, 77.

Putnam, Israel, at battle of Brooklyn, 189.

Quakers, 353; in Massachusetts, 67, 68; attitude toward oaths, 105; toward military service, 105; in North Carolina, 107; in Virginia, 151.

Quay, M. S., as a leader, 723.

Quebec, site discovered, 36; founded, 112; attempt to take, 1690, 116; Sir Hovenden Walker's failure against, 118; taken by Wolfe, 127; held by Murray, 128; besieged by Montgomery and Arnold, 183.

"Quebec Act," 177.

Queen Anne's war, 118–119.

Queenstown, attacked, 323.

Quesada, Cuban leader, 782, 784.

Race, elements in colonies, 145–148.

Radicals, principles of, 597; Wade-Davis bill, 598; Stanton and, 600; efforts against Johnson, 605; and civil rights bill, 606; and fourteenth amendment, 607; in control of congress, 608; and tenure-of-office act, 611.

Railroads, early development, 464; construction after the war, 665; transcontinental, 680; Union Pacific, 680; Central Pacific, 680; Northern Pacific, 681; Atlantic and Pacific, 681; Santa Fe, 682; Southern Pacific, 682; Great Northern, 682; Constructing the Pacific roads,

682; land grants abused, 682; combinations of, 732–735; in England, 732; combining lines, 733; attempts at coöperation, 734; "Granger laws," 734; railroads and interstate commerce act, 735; as a political issue, 735; the Wabash case, 735; Hepburn rate bill, 833; Rayburn Bill to regulate securities of, 862; under government operation, 885.

Railway and shipping legislation, 910.

Railways restored, 909.

"Rainbow Division." See Forty-Second Division.

Rainfall, 2.

Raisin, the, the massacre at, 323.

"Raleigh, Citie of," 43.

Raleigh, Sir Walter, and colonization, 42–44.

Rall, Colonel, 192.

Rambouillet Decree, 316.

Randall, S. J., and the tariff, 714, 715, 721.

Randolph, Edmund, in constitutional convention, 243; attorney-general, 257; supports Jefferson, 261; secretary of state, 271.

Randolph, Edward, and navigation acts, 93; hostile to the charters, 93, 94; influence on the new charter, 97.

Randolph, John, at impeachment of Chase, 294; opposed to Jefferson, 301; opposed to Yazoo men, 301, 302; shorn of his strength, 302, 303; supports Monroe, 302.

Rawdon, Lord, at Camden, 207; at Hobkirk's Hill, 210; in Charleston, 211.

Rayburn Bill, 862.

Reciprocity, Blaine secures, 725; McKinley on, 829; Canadian, 841, 842.

Reconstruction, question comes up in congress, 585; two kinds, 594; theories of status, 595; Lincoln's plan, 596–599; Wade-Davis bill, 597–598; attitude of South, 1865, 601, 602, 619; committee on, 605; freedmen's bureau bill, 605; civil rights bill, 606; the radical program, 609–611; acts of 1867, 609–611 acts enforced in the South, 622–625.

Redemptioners, 146.

Red river expedition, 542.

Redfield, William C., secretary of commerce, 854.

Reed, Thomas B., on the tariff of 1883, 715; as leader, 723; speaker, 724; breaks down obstruction, 724.

Registration, Southern, 623.

Regulators, in North Carolina, 183.

Reid, Whitelaw, nominated for vice-presidency, 749.

Religion, in Virginia, 46; in Maryland, 53; Maryland Toleration Act, 57; and the franchise in Massachusetts, 65; persecutions in Massachusetts, 65–68; persecution in New Netherland, 74; in the colonies, 148–152; work of the churches, 148; in New England, 148; Witchcraft, 149; "Halfway Covenant," 150; the "Great Awakening," 150; freedom in Rhode Island, 151; Anglican Church, in New England, 148; in the South, 151; British Toleration Act, 152; treatment of Catholics, 152; "Saybrook Platform," 153; churches and education, 154; established churches, 352; Methodists, 353; Baptists, 353; other churches, 354; Protestant Episcopal Church, 354; Congregationalists, 354; Unitarian movement, 355; disestablishment in New England, 355.

Republicanism, inherent, 218, 228.

Republican party, relations with Genêt, 266; formation of, 270; in election of 1800, 288–290; principles, 288, 291–292; dissensions in, 300–303.

Republican party, the second, origin, 494; Seward joins, 494; in Massachusetts, 495; Frémont nominated, 495; gain in 1858, 502; successful in 1860, 508; in the civil war, 581; in 1862, 582; moderate party of Johnson, 604; organized in the South, 621–622; loses the South, 630–633; in Georgia, 631; in North Carolina, 631; in Virginia, Tennessee, and Texas, 632; in Alabama, Arkansas, and Mississippi, 632; loses the South, in South Carolina, Florida, and Louisiana, 633; repressive policy under Grant, 633–634; situation of, after the war, 640; in the elections of 1866, 640.

Resaca de la Palma, battle of, 447.

Resumption of specie payment, act for, 669; achievement of, 699.

Revere, Paul, 180.

Revolution, colonial assemblies and parties, 100, 101; causes of, 161; principles underlying, 161; Bute's policy, 161; King's veto and, 162; navigation acts and, 163; Grenville's policy, 162–164; growing irritation, 169–170; Townshend Acts, 169–170; causes summarized, 173; attitude of three groups, 174; first continental congress, 186–188; declaration of independence, 186–188; indifference of people, 192; army of the patriots, 193; French alliance, 198; compromise offered, 199; war ended, 213; treaty of peace, 214–216.

Reynolds, General, at Gettysburg, 560; death of, 560.

Rheims, German attempt to surround in 1918, 891.

Rhode Island, founded, 66, 68; charter, 68; settled, 68; and New England confederation, 71; new charter, 80; and the Dominion of New England, 94; and the revolution of 1688, 97; religious freedom in, 151; and paper money, 158; paper-money commotions, 236; "Know Ye" men, 236; ratifies the constitution, 249; constitutional reform in, 474–476.

Riall, General, death of, 325.

Ribaut, explores Florida, 111.

Rice, a staple crop, 8; trade in, 142, 143.

Richmond, capitol of confederacy, 519; advance on, 519; captured, 566.

Rifles, supply of, for army, 883.

Right of deposit, at New Orleans, 297.

Rivers, as means of transportation, 3. *See* Transportation.

Roads, colonial, 134. *See* Internal Improvements.

Roanoke Island, settlement on, 42; significance of, 43; taken by Burnside, 570.

Robertson, James, settles in Tennessee, 234.

Robinson, Dr. Charles, in Kansas, 489.

Robinson, Rev. John, at Scrooby, 59; at Leyden, 59, 60.

Rochambeau, against Cornwallis, 212.

Rockefeller, John D., and the organization of the oil trust, 736–739; group of banks, 740.

Rockingham, ministry of, 169, 214.

Rocky Mountains, influence of, 1.

Rodgers, Captain John, 317, 327.

Rodman, Admiral Hugh, 897.

Roman Catholics, early settlers in Maryland, 54; Jesuits in Maryland, 55; treatment of, 152, 354.

Roosevelt, Franklin D., nominated for vice-presidency, 903.

Roosevelt, Theodore, as civil service commissioner, 710; in campaign of 1884, 718; and Rough Riders, 795; and the Panama revolution, 819; elected vice-president, 827; and McKinley, 829; first message, 829; his policy on trusts, 830; appeals to the people, 830; and the coal strike, 830; control of corporations, 831; elected president, 832; relations with the senate, 833; public opinion for, 834; return from Africa, 840; in New York politics, 840; becomes candidate in 1912, 843–844; at Chicago convention, 845; nominated by the progressive party, 847; shot by fanatic, 848; defeated, 848; his relation

to Wilson's policies, 854; his expansion of the Monroe Doctrine, 863; and Santo Domingo, 865; and Panama, 866; efforts to establish peace in Central America, 866; proposed division to be raised by, 886.

Root, Elihu, suggests amendments to League covenant, 901.

Rose, George, mission to America, 315, 335.

Rosecrans, General, at battle of Stone's river, 530; campaign around Chattanooga, 532–534; at battle of Chickamauga, 533; removed from command, 534.

Ross, General, attacks Washington, 329; attacks Baltimore, 330.

Rough Riders, 795; at Santiago, 796, 798.

"Round Robin," at Santiago, 803.

Rule of war of 1756, 307.

Rum, manufacture of, 141.

"Rum, Romanism, and Rebellion," 719.

Rush, Richard, supported for vice-president, 390.

Russell, Jonathan, commissioner at Ghent, 334.

Russian Revolution, effect on our relation to the war, 882.

Russia, efforts of Czar to make peace, 333–334; and the Monroe Doctrine, 375; sells Alaska, 643; United States troops in, 895.

Ryswick, treaty of, 117.

Sabine Cross Roads, 542.

Sacs and Foxes, driven westward, 465.

Sagasta, offers reform in Cuba, 787; yields on armistice, 789.

St. Augustine, founded, 111.

St. Clair, defeat of, 262; governor of Ohio, 342.

St. Lawrence river, as a means of transportation, 2; explored by Cartier, 36.

St. Leger, General, 193; defeated, 196.

St. Louis, founded, 115; desires transcontinental railroad, 681.

St. Louis strike, 1886, 742.

St. Marks, attacked by Jackson, 369.

St. Mary's, Maryland, settled, 54.

St. Mihiel, capture of, 892.

St. Thomas, Island of, 866.

Salary Grab act, 650.

Salvador and Central American peace league, 866.

Salem, settled, 63; witchcraft trials, 149.

Salisbury, Lord, on Venezuela, 779.

Samoa, value of, 765; conflicting interests in, 765; storm in, 766; divided, 766.

Sampson, W. T., off north shore of Cuba,

793; at battle of Santiago, 801; and controversy with Schley, 804.

Sanborn Contracts, the, 651.

Sandys, Sir Edwin, and Virginia, 50, 51.

San Jacinto, battle of, 421.

San Juan Hill, 796, 797; carried, 798.

Santa Anna, opposed to Texas, 421.

Santiago, Cervera at, 793; blockaded, 794, 795; army at, 796–799; defenses of, 794; battle of, 797; surrender of, 799.

Santo Domingo, Napoleon's attempt to conquer, 298; annexation of, 645; treaty for annexation, 671; and foreign debts, 827; financial protectorate over, 864.

Saratoga, surrender at, 197; convention at, repudiated, 197.

Savage's Station, battle of, 549.

Savannah, taken by British, 207; taken from the British, 211; entered by Sherman, 539.

Saybrook, settled, 69.

Saybrook platform, 153.

Scalawags, 621.

Schenectady, taken by French, 116.

Schley, W. S., on south shore of Cuba, 793, 794; at battle of Santiago, 801; controversy, 804.

Schofield, General, at battle of Franklin, 538; reënforces Sherman at Goldsboro, 541; secretary of war, 616.

Schomburgk line, 777.

Schools, public, growth of, 476–478; in New England, 476; work of Horace Mann, 477; in Middle States, 477; in the South, 477; in the West, 478.

Schurman, President, in the Philippines, 810.

Schurz, Carl, liberal attitude toward South, 633; an independent, 693; and civil service reform, 707; in campaign of 1884, 718; as leader, 723.

Schuyler, Fort, siege of, 196.

Schuyler, General, against Burgoyne, 196.

Scioto Company, 342.

Scituate, 62.

Scotch-Irish, settled in the colonies, 147.

Scott, Thomas A., as a railroad builder, 733.

Scott, Winfield, at Chippewa, 325; at Lundy's Lane, 325; Mexican campaign, 448–450; nominated for presidency, 485.

Scrooby, 59.

Seabury, Rev. Samuel, made bishop, 353.

Secession, suggested in 1798, 285; and Hartford Convention, 336; threaten in 1849, 453; Nashville Convention, 457; Davis resolutions, 1860, 505; Yancey's Charleston speech, 506; South Carolina Acts, 511; other states, 511, 517.

Second Division, arrives in France, 886; goes into line of defenses, 888; at Château-Thierry, 889–891; in operations of July 18, 1918, 891; at St. Mihiel, 892.

Sedgwick, General, at Chancellorsville, 557, 558.

Sedition Law, passed, 284; execution of, 284; Jefferson's way of meeting, 285.

Seminary Ridge, 560.

Seminole war, 368–369; under Jackson, 467–468.

Senate, opposed to Roosevelt, 833; popular disapproval of, 834.

Senators, popular election of, 851.

Serapis, 205.

Servants, indented, demand for, 137; kidnapping, 137; voluntary servants, 138; convicts, 138; vagabonds, 138; condition of, 138.

Seven Pines, battle of, 548.

"Seven Sisters," the, 855.

Seven years' war, 124–130.

Sevier, John, 234.

Seward, W. H., Northern leader, 488; joins the republicans, 494; and republican nomination, 495, 507; Lamar on, 507; not nominated, 508; and peace with the South, 514; and the confederate agents, 515; Lincoln overrules, 516; wounded, 568, 600; and reconstruction, 600; forces French out of Mexico, 643; and purchase of Alaska, 643.

Sewing machine, invented, 465.

Seymour, Horatio, nominated, 1868, 642.

Shafter, General, at Santiago, 796; his plan of battle, 797; as a commander, 804.

Shannon, the, 327.

Shaw, Robert G., killed, 570, 573.

Shays's rebellion, 236.

Shelburne, ministry of, 214.

Shenandoah valley, Jackson in, 547; Early in, 565; Sheridan in, 565.

Sheridan, General, in the valley campaign, 565–566; as military governor, 623; and the Indians, 686, 687.

Sherman, J. S., nominated for vice-president, 835.

Sherman, John, as financier, 662; secretary of the treasury, 694; on Hayes's Southern policy, 695; achieves resumption, 699; candidate for nomination, 1884, 716; as leader, 723.

Sherman, Roger, 187.

Sherman, W. T., first move against Vicksburg, 530; at Chattanooga, 534, 535; advance toward Atlanta, 535–539; takes Atlanta, 537; march to the sea, 538, 539; march on Savannah, 539; devastation unnecessary, 539–540; in the Carolinas, 540; halt at Goldsboro, 541; comes to aid of Grant, 548; receives Johnston's surrender, 568.

Sherman anti-trust law, 740.

Sherman silver law, passed, 747; in operation, 754; repealed, 755; the West aroused, 755.

Shiloh, battle of, 528.

Shipping, condition of, 1783–1815, 347; history of, during world war, 885; legislation, 910; Board, 1920, 911.

Shirley, Governor, and Louisburg, 120; expedition against Fort Niagara, 124; and removal of Acadians, 124.

Siberia, United States troops in, 895.

Siboney, landing at, 796.

Sigsbee, Captain, on *Maine* disaster, 788.

Silver, deposits of, 11; free, origin of movement, 698; the Bland-Allison bill, 699; use of small silver notes, 746; silver forced out, 746; silver sentiment, 747; Sherman silver law, 747, 754; Cleveland on, 750; maintaining parity, 754, 755–757; Sherman law repealed, 755; "endless chain," the, 755–756; organize in West and South, 758; control democratic convention, 758; issue in 1896, 762.

Silver mining, 677–678.

Sims, Admiral W. S., 896.

Sinclair, and Oil Scandals, 924.

Sinking fund, established, 260.

Sioux wars, 1866–1868, 685, 687–689; commission to Sioux, 688.

Sitting Bull, in the Sioux war, 687–689.

Slater, Samuel, and cotton mills, 349.

Slaughter-house cases, 636.

Slavery, Indian, 30; in first Northwestern ordinance, 232; in second ordinance, 233; excluded from the Northwest, 344; relation to cotton, 346; abolished in the North, 350; emancipation in the South, 351; method of abolishing, 350; early congressional position, 351; first fugitive slave law, 351; restricted in the West, 351; revived importations, 352; law of 1807, 352; smuggling, 352; and the West, 371; fixed in South, 428; effect of agitation on South, 430; revised black code, 430; new fugitive slave law, 455, 457; as a Southern institution, 468–470; disappearance in the North, 469; numbers of slaves, 470; treatment of slaves, 470; growth of pro-slavery, 471; divides the churches, 471–472; fugitive slaves not returned, 486; the Kansas-Nebraska act, 486–488; new leaders, 488; attitude of

pro-slavery men, 493, 505, 506. *See* Emancipation.

Slaves, in the Carolinas, 108; excluded from Georgia, 110; condition in colonies, 138–140; introduced, 138; Spanish type of slavery, 139; colonial slave code, 139; trade in, 144; carried away by British, 216; three fifths in apportionment, 246; importation before 1808, 246; fugitives, as "contrabands," 577. *See* Slavery.

Slave-trade, 144; beginning of, 41.

"Sleepy Hollow," 202.

Slidell, Mexican mission, 446; seized on the *Trent*, 522.

Sloat, Commodore, in California, 449.

Sloughter, Henry, governor of New York, 103.

Smith, Governor, nominated, 937.

Smith, Captain John, sails for Virginia, 46; services, 48; relations with the Indians, 48, 52.

Smith, Kirby, at Bull Run, 520; in Arkansas, 542; surrenders, 569.

Smith, Robert, secretary of navy, 292.

Smuggling, 144; liquor, 935.

Smythe, General, 323.

"Snap Convention," in New York, 750.

Social classes, 135, 136–137.

Social conditions, in Virginia, 49.

Soils, character of, 6; in New England, 6; in the South, 7; in the West, 7.

Soldier's bonus, 913.

Somers, Lieutenant, at Tripoli, 296.

Sons of Liberty, formed, 166; decline, 169.

Soto, Hernando de, 38.

South, the, county in, 135; life in, 137; trade in, 142; religion, 151; her interests in the constitutional convention, 246; retains slavery, 350–351; social classes in, 468; slaveholders in 1860, 469; non-slaveholders, 469; growth of pro-slavery, 471; *see* Slavery; public schools in, 477; position on Kansas, 1856, 493; effect of John Brown on, 504; attitude on reconstruction, 1865, 601, 619; accepts emancipation, 601, 619; economic ruin, 619; social reversal, 620; in despair, 620; parties forming, 620–621; "Conservative" party, 621; a republican party forms, 621, 622; congressional reconstruction in operation, 622–625; was it lawless? 623; registration of voters, 623; military governors, 623; registration under reconstruction acts, 623; constitutional conventions, 624; constitutions ratified, 624; why radical reconstruction failed, 626; Ku Klux Klan, 627–630; influence in congress, 1913, 853.

South American states, recognition of, 367, 374.

Southampton, Earl of, and Virginia, 51.

South Carolina, misrule in, 106; Indian war, 107; overthrow of proprietors, 108; beats off attack by Spain, 119; trade, 142, 143; religion in, 151; and stamp act, 168; attack of British at Charleston, 183; overrun by British, 207; aid given at King's Mountain, 208; ratifies the constitution, 248; and nullification, 387, 396, 399; not supported by Georgia, 400; federal operations in, 570; readmitted, 624; republicans overthrown, 633; disputed returns in 1876, 655, 657; surrendered to democrats, 657.

South Dakota, a state, 748.

Southern rams, 569.

South Improvement Co., 736.

Southwest, the, growth of, 341, 344.

Soviets, non-recognition of, 909.

Spain, explorations of, in the interior, 37–39; as a colonizing nation, 39; in the seven years' war, 128; aids the American revolution, 198, 199; refuses aid to America, 214; and treaty of 1783, 214; intrigues in Southwest, 263; secret boundary clause, 215, 264; and Southern Indians, 265; treaty of 1795, 265; and the purchase of Louisiana, 299, 300; and Burr, 304; and war of 1812, 321, 331; negotiations for Florida, 368; and American neutrality, in Cuba, 782, 785; the *Virginius*, 783; and neglected Cuban reforms, 784; Cleveland's attitude, 785, 786; Sagasta's reforms, 787; the *Maine*, 787, 788; Cuban armistice demanded, 789; war declared on, 789; peace with, 805–806; and Cuban debt, 805.

Spanish war, 782–807.

Speaker, power under Reed, 724; power reduced, 838; election of 1859, 504.

Specie circular, issued, 425; and panic of 1837, 432.

Sphericity of the earth, belief in, 26.

Spoils system, 393.

Spottsylvania, battle of, 563.

Spring, Dr. Gardiner, 412.

Springfield, settled, 69.

Squanto, 61.

Squatter sovereignty. *See* Popular Sovereignty.

"Stalwarts," 695.

Stamp act, proposed, 164; passed, 166; effects in America, 166; Patrick Henry's resolutions, 166; congress at New York, 167; repealed, 168; effect of repeal, 168.

Stanbery, Henry, opinion of, on Johnson's powers, 612; defends Johnson, 615.

Standard Oil Company, history of, 736–739; fined by courts, 836; suit to dissolve, 840, 842.

Standish, Miles, 61.

Stanton, in Johnson's cabinet, 601; favors the radicals, 601; and tenure-of-office act, 611; suspended, 614; removed, 614; resigns, 617.

Stanwix, Fort. *See* Fort Schuyler.

Star of the West, 512.

Star route frauds, 704.

Stark, John, battle of Bennington, 195.

State governments; formed by advice of congress, 187, 235; varying features, 217; suffrage, 217; sovereignty in, 218; two schools of citizens, 219; powers under the articles, 239; reform of, 472–476.

State rights, and nullification, 387–388; in 1828, 389; party formed, 396.

States, sovereignty of, 218; loyalty to, 230; large and small, controversy between, 243–245; limited by constitution, 253; authority limited by Marshall, 358–360; Southern, *status* of in reconstruction, 595; reconstructed under Johnson, 600, 601.

State universities, development of, 479.

Steamboats on the interior rivers, 464; cross the Atlantic, 464.

Stephens, A. H., confederate vice-president, 511.

Stephens, U. S., founds Knights of Labor, 741.

Steuben, Baron von, his services, 198.

Stevens, Thaddeus, leader of radicals, 604; power in congress, 604, 607, 608; prosecutes Johnson, 615; death of, 625.

Stewart, A. T., nominated secretary of the treasury, 644.

Stillwater. *See* Freeman's Farm.

Stinson, H. L., candidate for governorship, 840; mission to Nicaragua, 930.

Stone's river, battle of, 530.

Stonewall, the confederate ram, 589.

Stony Point, 201.

Strasburg, Va., Jackson at, 547.

Strong, Caleb, at Hartford convention, 336.

Strong, William, appointment as judge, 664.

Stuart, J. E. B., at capture of John Brown, 503; as cavalry leader, 559.

Stuyvesant, Peter, as governor, 74; religious persecutions, 74; takes Swedish settlements, 75; loses New Amsterdam, 75.

Submarines, the use of, in war, 875; ruthless warfare of, adopted by Germany, 881.

Suffrage, in early state governments, 217, 228; grows liberal, 472–474; negro, in fourteenth amendment, 607; in the reconstruction acts, 609–611; Lincoln on, 597, 622; Johnson, 622; in Southern constitutions, 624.

Sugar, and Wilson-Gorman bill, 728.

Sullivan, General, at Newport, 201.

Sumner, Charles, speech on Kansas, 490; attacked by Brooks, 490; a radical, 605; and fourteenth amendment, 607, 608; and civil rights act, 1875, 634; death of, 1874, 635; Lamar on, 635; Grant's quarrel with, 645; states case against England, 671; and civil service reform, 707.

Sumner, General, at Fredericksburg, 556.

Sumter, Fort, relief of, 512, 515; attacked, 516.

Sumter, partisan leader, 207; under Greene, 210.

Supplies for the army, 883; services of supply, 887.

Supreme Court, the, functions of, 252, 357–360; in reconstruction days, 611; interprets war amendments, 635–638.

Surplus, the, 714; lowered by hard times, 715; revived, 715; removed through expenditure, 725.

Surplus revenue, distribution, 424; effects of distribution, 432.

Surplus shipping, problem of, 911.

Sussex, destruction of the, 877.

Sutro tunnel, 677.

Sweden, settlements in America, 75.

Swiss, settlers, 146, 147.

Symmes, land grant of, 342.

Syracuse, convention at, 1855, 495.

Taft, W. H., in the Philippines, 811, 812; restoring order in Cuba, 807; nominated for presidency, 835; elected, 836; administration of, 837–843; and Payne-Aldrich tariff, 837; Ballinger, 838; and Canadian reciprocity, 841; candidate for renomination, 843–844; republican nominee, 845; elected, 848; legislation under, 849–850; suggests amendments to the League covenant, 901; made chief justice, 908.

Talleyrand, and American claims, 280; accepts treaty, 282; and Louisiana, 297–299; and Florida, 302.

Tammany, and Tilden, 653, 702; and Cleveland, 716, 720.

Tampico, landing party arrested at, 869.

Taney, R. B., secretary of the treasury, 414; removes deposits, 414; Chief Justice, 415; decision in Dred Scott case, 498.

Tanner, "Corporal," and pensions, 726, 749.

Tariff, bill of 1816, 364; growing demand for, 384–386; bill of 1820, 385; bill of 1824, 385; bill of 1828, 386; a sectional question, 384–385; South Carolina and, 387–388; Verplanck bill, 409; compromise bill, 1833, 410; of 1842, 436; campaign issue, 1844, 443; of 1846, 445; Morrill act, 483; in McCulloch's time, 661; Wool and Woolens act, 661, 713; tariff of 1870, 663, 713; two methods of reform, 712; tariff of 1872, 713; tariff of 1875, 713; commission of 1882, 714; tariff of 1883, 715; Morrison bill, 715; reform under Cleveland, 721; Mills bill, 721; issue in 1888, 721–722; McKinley bill, 724–726; Wilson bill, 728; Wilson-Gorman bill, 729; Dingley bill, 729; the McKinley and Sherman silver law, 747; an issue in 1896, 762; with Philippines, 812; and the dependencies, 813, 814; McKinley's later policy on, 829; Payne-Aldrich, 837; Canadian reciprocity, 841; democratic bills of 1911, 841; democratic bills of 1912, 842; the Underwood, 856–858; the lobby investigated, 857.

Tariff Commission of 1913, 857.

Tarleton, in the South, 207; at Cowpens, 208; in Virginia, 211.

Tax revision, 911.

Taxation, power of congress over, 359.

Taxes, external and internal, 165, 170.

Taylor, "Dick," commands in Arkansas, 542; surrenders, 569.

Taylor, Zachary, campaign on the Rio Grande, 446–448; nominated for presidency, 451; elected, 452; death of, 458; against the Seminoles, 467.

Tea, duty on, 173; sent to America, 175; action of colonies, 175; "Tea party," 176.

Teapot Dome, 924.

Tecumseh, his ambition, 318; slain at battle of the Thames, 323.

Telegraph invented, 465.

Teller, Senator, and silver, 755; leaves republican party, 761.

Temperance movement, 480.

Tennessee, settled, 232, 234; a state, 264; reconstructed under Lincoln, 597; readmitted, 609; republicans overthrown, 632.

Tennessee, the, 571.

Tenure-of-office act, passed, 611; tested by Johnson, 614.

Territories, government of, 233.

Terry, General, against the Sioux, 687.

Texas, explored by Pike, 356; early history, 419; not to be purchased, 420; revolution in, 420; annexation, 421, 438, 440,

444; opposition of Adams, 421; recognition extended, 422; England's alleged scheme, 438; a state in the union, 444; disputed boundary, 446; boundaries fixed, 450; debt assumed, 455, 457; readmitted, 625; republicans overthrown, 632.

Texas, the, 800, 801, 802.

Thames, battle of, 323.

Thanksgiving Day, 62.

Third Division, arrives near Château-Thierry, 889.

Thirtieth Division, 892; carries the St. Quentin tunnel, 894; at Brancourt, 895; at the Selle River, 895.

Thirty-Second Division, in Marne salient, 891.

Thomas, General, succeeds Rosecrans, 534; in battle of Missionary Ridge, 535; defense of Nashville, 538.

Thomas, Lorenzo, secretary of war, 614.

Thornton, Colonel, at New Orleans, 333.

Thoroughfare Gap, 551, 552.

Thrasher, Leon, 876.

Ticonderoga, attacked unsuccessfully, 126; taken, 127; taken by Ethan Allen, 182; not taken by Carleton, 195; taken by Burgoyne, 195.

Tilden, S. J., governor of New York, 651; nominated for presidency, 653; disputed returns, 654; loses the election, 657; and the independents, 694; in the investigation of the election, 696; not nominated in 1880, 702.

Tillman, B. R., speech in Chicago convention, 1896, 759; and the South and West, 759, 762.

Tobacco, a staple crop, 8; in Virginia, 50; at the restoration, 80, 81; decline of price, 89.

Tohopeka, battle of, 332.

Tompkins, D. D., vice-president, 367.

Tonti, 114.

Topeka constitution, 489, 490.

Tories, as a class, 174, 193; in North Carolina, 182, 208; in Philadelphia, 199; at King's Mountain, 208; compensation to, 216, 227; why disliked, 230; hardships of, 231; in New York, 231; compensation not made, 262.

Toscanelli, letter of, 28.

Toussaint Louverture, 298.

Towns, planted, 134; government, 156; in New York, 156; development of, 463.

Townshend, colonial policy of, 169; his acts, 169, 173; death, 171; repeal of Townshend acts, 173.

Townships, established, 233, 342.

Trade, colonial, 142–145; state of, 1783–1789, 226; England refuses to open, 226; congress to have control, 246; England refuses concessions, 262; restrictions on neutral, 272; and the Jay treaty, 272; the carrying, under Jefferson, 306; British restrictions on, 306–309; condition of, 1783–1815, 346; West India, 415–417. *See* Navigation Acts.

Transportation, rivers and lakes, 2.

Treason, defined, 253.

Treasurer, in New York, 104.

Treaty, with France, 198; with England, 214–216; with Spain, 1795, 265; Jay's, 272–273; with France, 1800, 282; San Ildefonso, 297; Louisiana purchase, 298; of Monroe and Pinckney, 310; Erskine's, 316; of Fort Jackson, 332, 368; of Ghent, 334, 368; with France, 417; Webster-Ashburton, 437; Guadaloupe Hidalgo, 450; Clayton-Bulwer, 458; of Washington, 672; of Fort Laramie, 684; with Hawaii, 772, 774; Burlingame, 774; with Japan, 776; of Paris, 1898, 805; Hay-Pauncefote, 817; Hay-Herran (convention), 818; Hay-Bunau-Varilla, 820; of Portsmouth, 824.

Treaty of 1783, execution delayed, 261, 272, 273.

Trent, the, affair of, 522; negotiations about, 523.

Trenton, battle of, 192.

Tripoli, war with, 295.

Trist, N. P., and treaty with Mexico, 450.

"Truly Loyal," the, 621.

Trumbull, Lyman, leader of moderates, 605; vote on Johnson impeachment, 617; attitude toward South, 633.

Trusts, causes producing, 736; the Standard Oil Co., 736–739; and stock speculation, 739; opposition to, 739; anti-trust law, 740; a "money trust," 740; laws relating to, in Wilson's administration, 860–863; Clayton Anti-Trust Act, 862.

Truxtun, Captain, 281.

Tryon, at New York, 188; raid in Connecticut, 201.

Tunis, at war, 295, 296.

Turnbull, author of "The Crisis," 387.

Turner, Nat, 430.

Twenty-Second joint rule, 598; rescinded, 656.

Twenty-Seventh Division, 892; at the St. Quentin tunnel, 894; at the Selle River, 895.

Twenty-Sixth Division, goes into line of defenses, 888; in operations of July 18, 1918, 891; at St. Mihiel, 892.

Twiller, Wouter van, governor of New Amsterdam, 73.

Tyler, John, nominated, 434; presidency of, 435–436; repudiated by whigs, 436; and Texas annexation, 438–440, 444; favors Polk, 443; presides over peace congress, 514.

"Uncle Tom's Cabin," influence of, 496.
Underground railway, 429.
Underhill, Captain John, fights for the Dutch in New Netherland, 73.
Underwood, Oscar, party leader in the house, 841; candidate for nomination, 845, 846; tariff, 856, 912.
Unemployment Conference, 911.
Union, suggested at Albany Congress, 123; party in favor of, 222; Morris and Hamilton, 223; Washington on, 224, 240; growing sentiment for, 240; Madison for, 240; cause of, in Hayne-Webster debate, 396; Jackson for, 399.
Union League, in the South, 627.
Union Pacific Railroad, and Crédit Mobilier, 649.
Union party, 581, 584.
Unions, in the United States, 741–744; Knights of Labor, 741; American Federation of Labor, 743.
United States, the, constructed, 279; takes the Macedonian, 327, 328.
Unity, influence of territorial, 1.
Upshur, and Texas, 439.
Utah, made a territory, 455, 457; settlement of, 679; a territory, 680; a state, 680, 748; and polygamy, 748.
Utrecht, treaty of, 119.

Vaca, Cabeça de, 38, 39.
Vallandigham, C. L., violent speeches of, 582; arrest and trial of, 583.
Valley Forge, army at, 199.
Van Buren, Martin, and the election of 1824, 380; turns to Jackson, 382; opposition to Calhoun, 382; secretary of state, 392; influence in cabinet, 393; influence on Jackson, 394; and internal improvements, 394; benefits by Jackson-Calhoun split, 401, 402; minister to England, 402; nominated vice-president, 403; elected, 405; on West India trade, 416; elected president, 425; character of, 432; his presidency, 432–435; and the Texan question, 441; a Barnburner, 451; nominated by free soil party, 452.
Vanderbilt, Cornelius, as a railroad builder, 733; and coöperation, 734.

Vandreuil, governor of New France, 118; governor of Canada, 126.
Vane, Sir Harry, in Boston, 66.
Van Rensselaer, General Stephen, 323; votes for Adams, 380.
Venezuela, boundary dispute, 777–781; origin of dispute, 777; Cleveland's demands on England, 779; commission appointed, 780; adjusted, 780; effects, 780; debts to other powers, 826; Germany and, 826.
Vera Cruz, taken by Scott, 449; seized by the United States, 869.
Vergennes, friendly to America, 198; and the treaty of peace, 214–215.
Vermont, a state, 264.
Verrazano, Giovanni da, explorations of, 35.
Versailles, the Treaty of, 897–904; delegates of the United States, 900; in process of making, 901, 902; before the States senate, 902; ratified by Germany and allied powers, 903.
Vespucci, with Hojeda, 31; his pretended discoveries, 32.
Veteran's Bureau Scandal, 923.
Vicksburg, significance of, 530, 532; first attempt to take, 531; second attempt, 531–532.
Villa, Francisco, bandit leader, 868; raids Columbus, New Mexico, 870; raids Glen Springs, Texas, 871.
Vincennes, taken by Clark, 204.
Vinland, 23.
Virgin Islands, purchase of, 866.
Virginia, named, 42; English opinion of, 44; government of, 45; reforms of 1609, 49; intrigues, 49; self-government, 50; charter annulled, 50; royal governors of, 51; divided, 52; and the restoration, 80; Berkeley's despotism, 89; economic condition, 89; Bacon's Rebellion, 90; during the last years of the Stuarts, 92; trade, 142; religion in, 151; the university at Henrico, 153; William and Mary College, 154; and paper money, 158; Patrick Henry's resolutions, 166; revolutionary committees in, 174; declares independence, 187; and conquest of the Northwest, 203; Cornwallis enters, 211; confers with Maryland on trade, 241; plan in constitutional convention, 243; ratifies the constitution, 248; parties in, 270; political leadership, 270; supports Crawford, 377, 378, 379; waning influence, 378, 393; attitude toward nullification, 410; slavery debates, 1831, 430; constitutional reform in, 474; the university of, 479; readmitted, 625; republicans overthrown, 632.

"Virginia, Restored," 521.
Virginia, the, 569.
Virginia City, founded, 677.
Virginia Dare, 43.
Virginia resolutions, 285–287.
Virginius, the, 783.
Vixen, the, 800.
Vizcaya, the, 800, 801.
Volstead Act, 904, 934.

Wade-Davis bill, 597.
Wagner, Battery, attacked, 570, 573.
Waldseemüller, Martin, 33, 36.
Walker, Robert J., his tariff bill, 445; as governor of Kansas, 492.
Walker, Sir Hovenden, 118.
Wanamaker, John, postmaster-general, 723.
War, right to declare, 585.
War of 1812, rise of spirit of resistance, 318; Madison favors, 319; preparations for, 319; war declared, 320; opposed in New England, 335; finances of, 336; effects of defeat, 324, 336; lessons of, 338.
Warfare, lessons of, in battle of Santiago, 803.
Washington, a territory, 463; a state, 748.
Washington, Fort, 188, 191.
Washington, George, journey to the Ohio, 122; expedition to forks of the Ohio, 122; defeated, 122; with Braddock, 123; commander-in-chief, 182; operations around New York, 188–191; New Jersey campaign, 191; Philadelphia campaign, 194; at Monmouth, 200; deceives Clinton, 212; in Yorktown campaign, 212; and kingship, 218; on stronger government, 224; opposes army plot, 224; presides over constitutional convention, 242; elected president, 256; on the bank, 261; and Genêt, 266; and whisky insurrection, 268; attitude toward parties, 269; reëlected, 271; Farewell Address, 274; command of new army, 281.
Washington, Lawrence, gets Ohio lands, 121.
Washington, taken by British, 329; treaty of, 672.
Washington Conference, 1924, 920, 921.
Washington Disarmament Conference, 919.
"Washita, battle of the," 686.
Wasp, the, takes the *Frolic*, 327.
Watauga, Indians attack, 203; sends aid to King's Mountain, 208; settled, 234.
Watercourses. *See* Transportation.
Water-power, distribution of, 11.
Watertown, and taxation, 64.
Waxhaw, battle of, 207.
Wayne, Anthony, at Stony Point, 201; subdues the Ohio Indians, 262.

Weaver, J. B., nominated for presidency, 702, 752; and people's party, 752; vote of, 753.
Webster, Daniel, supports the tariff, 387; debate with Hayne, 396–398; supports Jackson on nullification, 409; opposes annexation of Texas, 422; supported by whigs, 425; remains in Tyler's cabinet, 436; and the treaty with England, 437; on Missouri compromise, 457; death of, 488.
Webster, Peletiah, on a stronger government, 240.
Weed, Thurlow, defeat of Clay, 434; joins the republicans, 494.
Wells, David A., as financier, 660.
Welsh, settled in the colonies, 147.
West, Far, physical characteristics, 676; arrival of miners, 677.
West, settlement of, 232–235; discontent in, 264; and Burr, 304; and war of 1812, 321; at the battle of New Orleans, 333; growth of, 341–344; New England and Southern streams of migration, 342; drawn to support the North, 461; public schools in, 478; state universities in, 479; and the panic of 1857, 482.
West India Company, Dutch, possession of New Netherland, 72.
West Indies, trade with secured, 415.
West Point, Arnold at, 201; military academy, 320; after war of 1812, 363.
West Virginia, formed, 520; defense of, 520, 526.
Wethersfield, settled by Dutch, 69; arrival of the English, 69.
Weyler, in Cuba, 786, 787.
Weymouth, George, aids colonization, 45.
Whale fisheries, 5, 142.
Wheat, a staple crop, 8; area of, increased, 665; prices, 667; crop of 1879, 700.
Wheeler, Burton K., nominated to vice-presidency, 926.
Wheeler, Joseph, at Santiago, 796, 797, 798, 799.
Wheeler, W. A., vice-president, 653.
Whig party, destroyed, 493, 495; "Conscience" and "Cotton" whigs, 495.
Whisky, manufacture of, 267.
Whisky insurrection, 267–269.
Whisky ring, the, 651.
White, Henry, delegate to Peace Conference, 900.
White, Hugh L., for president, 1836, 425.
Whitefield, Rev. George, and the "Great Awakening," 150.
White Plains, battle of, 190.
"White slave" act, 851.

Whitney, Eli, 345.

Wilderness, battle of, 563.

Wilhelm II, Kaiser, abdicates, 899.

Wilkes, Captain, seizes Mason and Slidell, 522.

Wilkinson, James, in Spanish employ, 264; corruption of, 264, 304; relations with Burr, 304, 305; expedition on the St. Lawrence, 324.

William Henry, Fort, taken by Montcalm, 125.

Williams, Rev. John, captured by French and Indians, 118.

Williams, Roger, driven from Massachusetts, 65; gets charter for Rhode Island, 68.

Willing, Thomas, 228.

Wilmington, Cornwallis, in 211; evacuated, 213.

Wilmot Proviso, proposed, 451; in nominating conventions, 451, 452; Clay's attitude, 454.

Wilson, Captain H. B., 896.

Wilson, Henry, vice-president, 649.

Wilson, James, in constitutional convention, 242, 244, 245.

Wilson, William B., secretary of labor, 854.

Wilson, Woodrow, candidate for nomination, 845, 846, 847; elected president, 848; leadership of his party, 854; his cabinet, 854; his New Jersey reforms, 855; inaugurated president, 855; addresses congress in person, 856; arraigns the tariff lobby, 857; his trust policy, 860–863; his domestic reform measures, 863; his Caribbean policy, 863–867; his dealings with Mexico, 867–871; refuses to recognize Huerta, 868; sends Lind to Mexico, 869; and Tampico incident, 869; and the "A. B. C. Powers," 870; orders Pershing to pursue Villa into Mexico, 870; his purpose with regard to Huerta, 871; proclamation of neutrality, 873; on submarine warfare, 876; notes on the Lusitania, 876; efforts to strengthen national defenses, 878; reëlected, 879; peace appeal of, 1916, 880; breaks intercourse with Germany, 881; demands war with Germany, 882; appoints Hughes to investigate airplane production, 884; appoints Hoover and Garfield, 885; halts project of a Roosevelt division, 886; selects Pershing for commander, 887; his "Fourteen Points," 898; gets Germany to accept the armistice, 899; delegate to Peace Conference, 900; his leadership, 900; his appeal to voters in 1918, 900; in the "Big Four," 901; striving for a League of Nations, 901; opposition to, 903; physical collapse, 902, 904; vetoes Knox resolution, 903; issues call for first meeting of League of Nations, 903; vetoes Volstead Act, 904; physical collapse, 904; upholds woman's suffrage, 905; death, 919.

Wilson committee, the, 649.

Wilson-Gorman tariff, 728, 729; effect of, 729, 756.

Wilson's Creek, battle of, 541.

Winchester, General, 323.

Winchester, taken by Jackson, 547; Early defeated at, 565.

Winder, General, at Bladensburg, 329.

Windom, William, secretary of the treasury, 723; ideas of free silver, 747.

Windsor, Connecticut, settled, 69.

Wingfield, Edward Maria, and the Virginia colony, 46, 47, 48.

Winthrop, John, relation to Puritan migration, 63; elected governor, 64; deals with Watertown, 64; presides over trial of Mrs. Hutchinson, 67; death of, 67.

Winthrop, John, Jr., settles Saybrook, 69.

Wirt, William, attorney-general, 367; nominated by anti-masons, 404; vote of, 405.

Wisconsin, a territory, 344; a state, 463; Black Hawk war, 466.

Witches, punished, 149.

Wolcott, Oliver, 279, 287.

Wolfe, General, at capture of Louisburg, 125; against Quebec, 127; death, 127.

Woman's Suffrage, 904, 905.

Women, enfranchisement of, 904, 905.

Wood, Leonard, commands Rough Riders, 795, 905.

Worcester, Dean C., in the Philippines, 810.

World war, the United States and, 873–904; the United States enters it, 882; form of assistance to be given, 882; the part taken by the United States in, 895.

World war Foreign Debt Commission, 927.

World Court, 921.

Wounded, recovery of the, at Santiago, 803.

Wright, Silas, a Barnburner, 451.

Wyoming, territory, 678; state, 680, 748.

Wyoming valley, raided, 203.

X Y Z papers, 280.

"Yankee Division." See Twenty-Sixth Division.

Yates, notes, 243.

Yazoo claims, 301, 302.

Zeno brothers, 23.